Maryland

Leonard M. Adkins

The Countryman Press ✳ Woodstock, Vermont

SECOND EDITION

DEDICATION

For Ann and Denny Messick. Thank you for your friendship—and for Laurie.
—L. M. A.

We welcome your comments and suggestions. Please contact Explorer's Guide Editor, The Countryman Press, P.O. Box 748, Woodstock, VT 05091, or e-mail countrymanpress@wwnorton.com.

Second Edition

ISBN 13: 978-0-88150-669-3
ISBN 10: 0-88150-669-9
ISSN: 1542-1163

Maps by Moore Creative Design, © The Countryman Press
Cover and interior design by Bodenweber Design
Text composition by PerfecType, Nashville, TN
Front cover photograph © Robertstock.com
Back cover photographs © Leonard M. Adkins
Interior photographs by Leonard M. Adkins

Published by The Countryman Press, P.O. Box 748, Woodstock, Vermont 05091

Distributed by W. W. Norton & Company, 500 Fifth Avenue, New York, NY 10110

Printed in the United States of America

10 9 8 7 6 5 4 3 2 1

There is no frigate like a book to take us lands away.

—Emily Dickinson

Also by Leonard M. Adkins

50 Hikes in Maryland: Walks, Hikes, and Backpacks from the Allegheny Plateau to the Atlantic Ocean

50 Hikes in Northern Virginia: Walks, Hikes, and Backpacks from the Allegheny Mountains to the Chesapeake Bay

50 Hikes in Southern Virginia: From the Cumberland Gap to the Atlantic Ocean

50 Hikes in West Virginia: From the Allegheny Mountains to the Ohio River

Walking the Blue Ridge: A Guide to the Trails of the Blue Ridge Parkway

Wildflowers of the Blue Ridge and Great Smoky Mountains (Joe Cook, photographer)

Wildflowers of the Appalachian Trail (Joe and Monica Cook, photographers)

The Appalachian Trail: A Visitor's Companion

Best of the Appalachian Trail: Day Hikes (with Victoria and Frank Logue)

Best of the Appalachian Trail: Overnight Hikes (with Victoria and Frank Logue)

Adventure Guide to Virginia

The Caribbean: A Walking and Hiking Guide

Seashore State Park: A Walking Guide

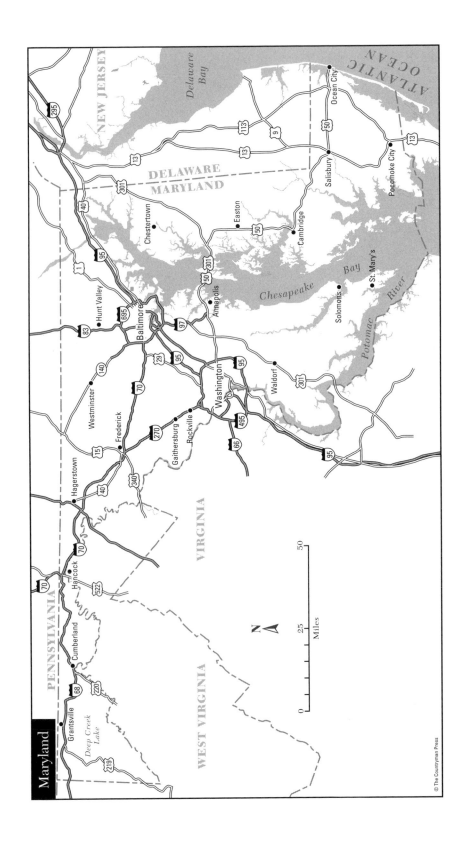

Maryland

© The Countryman Press

EXPLORE WITH US!

Welcome to the second edition of *Maryland: An Explorer's Guide*, the state's most comprehensive travel companion. All attractions, inns, and restaurants are chosen on the basis of merit, not paid advertising. The organization of the book is simple, but the following points will help to get you started on your way.

WHAT'S WHERE

In the beginning of the book is an alphabetical listing with thumbnail sketches of special highlights, important information, and advice on everything from where to obtain the best homemade ice cream to what to do if you get stung by a jellyfish.

LODGING

Lodging establishments mentioned in this book are selected on the basis of merit; no innkeeper or business owner was charged for inclusion. When making reservations, which almost all B&Bs require, ask about the policy on children, pets, smoking, and acceptance of credit cards. Many B&Bs do not accept children under 12, and some places have a minimum-stay policy, especially on weekends, holidays, and during special events.

Rates: The rates are for two people to stay in one room for one night and are weekend rates during what the establishment considers its high season. Weekday and off-season rates may be lower. However, please do not hold me or the respective innkeepers responsible for the rates listed as this book went to press. Changes are inevitable. State, local, and room taxes (which can be well above 10 percent) have not been included.

RESTAURANTS

Please note the distinction between *Dining Out* and *Eating Out*. By their nature, restaurants in the *Eating Out* section are less expensive and more casual. Many restaurants change their menus often; the specific dishes mentioned in this book may not be available when you dine. They are cited to give you a general idea of the cuisine offered. Like the lodging rates quoted in this book, menu prices were current when it went to press. However, as we all know, prices never go down; be prepared for them to have risen somewhat.

KEY TO SYMBOLS

☙ **Special value**. The special-value symbol appears next to lodgings and restaurants that offer a quality not often found at the price charged.

🐾 **Pets**. The pet symbol appears next to places, activities, and lodgings that accept pets. Almost all lodging accommodations require that you inform them of a pet when you make a reservation, and often request an additional fee.

✎ **Child-friendly**. The crayon symbol appears next to places or activities that accept and/or appeal to young children, or have a children's menu.

♿ **Handicapped access**. The wheelchair symbol appears next to lodgings, restaurants, and attractions that are partially or completely handicapped-accessible.

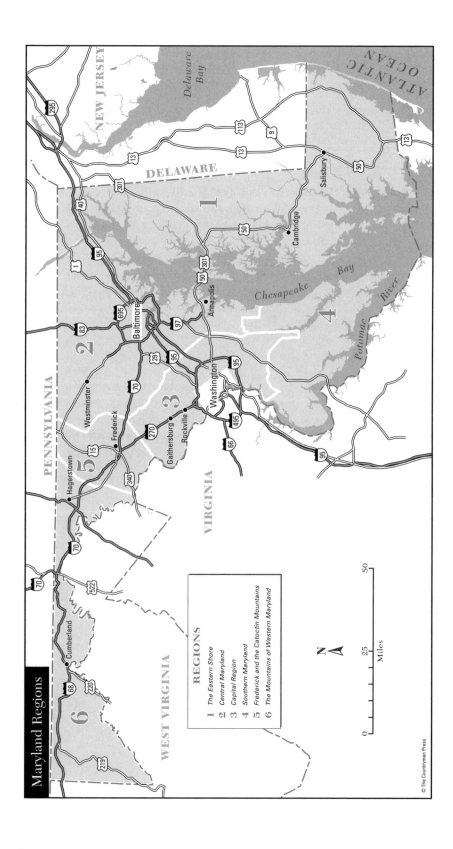

Maryland Regions

REGIONS
1 The Eastern Shore
2 Central Maryland
3 Capital Region
4 Southern Maryland
5 Frederick and the Catoctin Mountains
6 The Mountains of Western Maryland

© The Countryman Press

CONTENTS

11 ACKNOWLEDGMENTS

13 INTRODUCTION

16 WHAT'S WHERE IN MARYLAND

1 The Eastern Shore

39 MARYLAND'S SEABOARD—Ocean City, Assateague Island, and Berlin

66 TANGIER SOUND AREA—Crisfield and Princess Anne

76 SMITH ISLAND

79 SALISBURY

91 CAMBRIDGE AND VICINITY

103 ST. MICHAELS, EASTON, AND OXFORD

121 AROUND THE BAY BRIDGE AND KENT ISLAND

133 CHESTERTOWN AND ROCK HALL

147 AT THE HEAD OF THE BAY—Chesapeake City, Elkton, and North East

2 Central Maryland

165 HARFORD COUNTY—Havre de Grace, Aberdeen, and Bel Air

181 NORTH OF BALTIMORE—Owings Mills, Hunt Valley, Westminster, and Taneytown

201 BALTIMORE

231 WEST OF BALTIMORE—Ellicott City and Columbia

245 ANNAPOLIS AND VICINITY

3 Capital Region

275 LAUREL, COLLEGE PARK, BOWIE, AND UPPER MARLBORO

291 SILVER SPRING, BETHESDA, ROCKVILLE, AND GAITHERSBURG

4 Southern Maryland

315 ALONG THE CHESAPEAKE SHORE—Chesapeake Beach, North Beach, Prince Frederick, and Solomons

333 AT THE MOUTH OF THE POTOMAC—St. Mary's City and Leonardtown

349 ALONG THE POTOMAC SHORE—La Plata, Port Tobacco, and Waldorf

5 Frederick and the Catoctin Mountains Area

363 FREDERICK AND THE CATOCTIN MOUNTAINS AREA

Continued on next page

6 The Mountains of Western Maryland

391 THE GREAT VALLEY AND BLUE RIDGE REGION—Hagerstown, Antietam, and Hancock

413 THE ALLEGHENY PLATEAU—Rocky Gap, Cumberland, and Frostburg

435 AROUND DEEP CREEK LAKE—Grantsville, McHenry, Thayersville, and Oakland

457 INDEX

ACKNOWLEDGMENTS

I relied upon hundreds of people to help me along the way, to make arrangements, point me in the right direction, and introduce me to other people, places, and activities I would have overlooked. Without your unselfish aid, this book would never have been completed. May it reflect the confidence you had in me:

Barbara J. Beverungen and Heather Johnson, Carroll County Office of Tourism; Deb Clatterbuck, Garrett County Chamber of Commerce; Lisa Challenger and Debbie Keitt, Worcester County Tourism; Martha Clements, Town of Ocean City Department of Tourism; Mary G. Galloway, Dorchester County Department of Tourism; Sheila Crites, Allegany County Convention and Visitors Bureau; Norma Dobrowolski and staff, Ocean City Convention and Visitors Bureau; Debbi Dodson, Barbara A. Reisert, and Gayle V. Keen, Talbot County Office of Tourism; Dianne Gleissner, St. Mary's County Division of Tourism; Kelly Groff, Conference and Visitors Bureau of Montgomery County; Julie Horner, Beth Somers, and staff, Somerset County Tourism; Deborah Ing and Rachelina Bonacci, Howard County Tourism Council; Sandy Maruchi-Turner and Bob White, Cecil County Tourism; Diane Molner and Susan Hanna, Discover Harford County Tourism Council; Larry Noto, Baltimore Area Convention and Visitors Bureau; Terry B. Nyquist and Sandy Fulton, Wicomico County Convention and Visitors Bureau; Craig Peddicord and Marge Saunders, Baltimore County Conference and Visitors Bureau; Beth Finneyfrock Rhoades, Tourism Council of Frederick County; Joanne Roland, Charles County Visitors Bureau; Herman E. Schieke Jr., Calvert County, Maryland Department of Economic Development; Kim Shirer, Allegheny County Department of Tourism; Barbara Siegert and Terry M. Miles, Queen Anne's County Department of Business and Tourism; Carl Smith Jr., Prince Georges County, Maryland, Conference and Visitors Bureau; Bernadette Van Pelt, Kent County Office of Tourism; Anedra T. Wiseman, Susan Steckman, and Clare Vanderbeek, Annapolis and Anne Arundel County Conference and Visitors Bureau; and Gigi Yelton and Thomas Riford, Hagerstown/Washington County Convention and Visitors Bureau. Every entry in this book represents hours that someone was willing to take out of a busy schedule to assist me. To those many hundreds more who can't be named here, thank you.

12

ACKNOWLEDGMENTS

Connie Yingling, Maryland Office of Tourism Development—was I ever lucky that you stepped in to help. Dr. Stephen Lewis, Caroline Charonko, Terry Gumming, and Susie Surfas—life goes on, thanks to you. Nancy Adkins, Kathleen, John, Tim, and Jay Yelenic—thank you for understanding why my visits became so infrequent. Laurie—thank you for sharing Maryland with me, and me with Maryland. Life with you is all it should be.

INTRODUCTION

I started the introduction to my book *50 Hikes in Maryland* (Countryman Press) with the tourism-bureau-inspired slogan, "So many things to do. So close together." I stand by that phrase to introduce you to this second edition of *Maryland: An Explorer's Guide*. From the waves of the Atlantic Ocean rolling onto the sands of the Eastern Shore, to the heights of the Allegheny Plateau shadowed by a setting sun in western Maryland, all areas of the state are within a few hours' drive of one another.

As you head to the beach in Ocean City, you could stop to take a fishing trip on the Chesapeake Bay, visit a maritime museum (or two, or three, or more) to learn how people make a living from those waters, watch migrating waterfowl fly overhead by the thousands, kayak a tidal stream, and still have time for an evening ride on a 1902 carousel and a fresh seafood dinner.

In Baltimore, you can take in the exhibits at the city's world-renowned art museums, watch dolphins at play in the aquarium, stand upon the parapets that gave birth to America's national anthem, dine on Spanish food in a jacket and tie, and finish the day munching a freshly made cannoli as you stroll the alleyways of Little Italy.

Within a 30-minute drive of this cosmopolitan atmosphere, you could be bicycling a 20-mile rail-trail through rural countryside, swimming in the Chesapeake Bay, or betting on a horse at Pimlico, home of the Triple Crown's Preakness Stake.

Half a day's drive to western Maryland can introduce you to the 184.5-mile C&O Canal, Civil War battlefields at Monocacy and Antietam, one of the state's finest fine-arts museums, and the opportunity to go underground. You could learn of the upheaval of the land when Africa collided with North America ages ago, enjoy a historic steam-train ride through the forested mountains, go downhill skiing, and exhilarate in whitewater rafting.

To facilitate your explorations, this guide, the most comprehensive of its kind, has been divided into broad geographic regions. Individual chapters then cover areas that can easily be explored from their listed overnight accommodations.

Each chapter begins with an overview of the area, taking in its geographic features, historic aspects, and attraction highlights. There are listings on how to obtain further information, how to get to the area and get around once there, and places to obtain emergency help should the need arise.

Following those are the *To See* and *To Do* sections, which provide you with enough information to decide if a particular museum, historic home or site, family attraction, guided tour, golf course, hiking trail, lake, or other place or activity should fit into your travel plans.

I then give descriptions of places to stay, including B&Bs, inns, resorts, cottages, vacation rentals, and a few motels and hotels. Having stayed in them, or at least visited, I have based my descriptions on firsthand experiences and a propensity to snoop into hidden areas and out-of-the-way places. I try to be as honest as possible in my appraisals. What I saw and experienced is what I wrote about.

The same is true for the dining options provided. I gained quite a few pounds sampling the fare of the upscale restaurants (*Dining Out*) and that of the everyday places (*Eating Out*), in addition to bakeries, candy shops, ice cream parlors, and coffeehouses.

Listings of entertainment venues, outstanding businesses worthy of some of your shopping time, and special events that take place annually round out each chapter.

Within all of these hundreds of listings and descriptions you will find very few negative remarks (and those are usually small comments about something trifling). The reason is that I visited and dined in a few places that I simply did not include in the guide. If I was uncomfortable in a place or found it lacking in cleanliness, I felt that other lone travelers, couples, or families would, too. If a meal was not worth the calories consumed, or the atmosphere made for an unpleasant dining experience, the restaurant was not included. This does not mean that an inn had to be palatial or a restaurant serve five-star cuisine. It just means that you should get a good and fair experience for the money you spend.

I became acquainted with Maryland on an intimate basis when I first hiked the Appalachian Trail as I followed the state's 40 miles of the pathway along the crest of South Mountain. I came to appreciate more of what the state has to offer after I married Laurie, who was born and raised in Annapolis. Journeys to visit her relatives introduced me to the places important to her childhood, while further explorations enabled both of us to discover boundless hiking, biking, canoeing, and other outdoor adventures.

History permeates the air over this land. The first settlement in the New World dedicated to true religious tolerance was established here in 1634. George Washington and many other movers and shakers of the American Revolution traveled throughout, fighting and preaching for the cause. Four of the state's citizens signed the Declaration of Independence, and when the new country needed a place for its capital, Maryland graciously donated the land on which Washington, DC, is built.

As a border state, Maryland was the site of some of the most bitter fighting during the Civil War. The Battle of Antietam was the single bloodiest day in American war history, while the fight along the Monocacy River is credited with having saved Washington, DC, from Confederate invasion.

I had fun doing the field research for this book. I had already experienced many wonderful adventures in Maryland, but the need for current, firsthand knowledge of the state set me off on new explorations. From fly-fishing in a western Maryland creek to touring the hallowed halls of the capitol building in Annapolis, I had the perfect excuse to go to new places and engage in activities I had always wanted to explore but had lacked the time. A walk along the C&O Canal, an afternoon nap upon the Ocean City beach, and a visit to the Calvert Marine Museum in Solomons returned me to places I had long yearned to see again. In addition, since the human body demands fuel and rest, I became privileged to sample the sumptuous offerings of some of the world's most innovative chefs, and engage in friendly and intriguing conversations with the guests and hosts of the state's excessively relaxing and historically rich B&Bs.

George Washington traveled often throughout Maryland and really did sleep here—in many places, in fact. You should, too. Happy exploring.

WHAT'S WHERE IN MARYLAND

AREA CODES More than five areas codes exist in Maryland, with new ones to be added in the future. You must dial the area code on all phone calls, including those made locally. This means that every call is at least a 10-digit proposition.

ADMISSION FEES Admission fees of less than $10 per person are simply listed as "small admission fee." The actual cost is provided if higher. Please keep in mind that, as this book went to press, the rates quoted were accurate but are always subject to change.

AIR SERVICE The state is serviced primarily by three airports clustered around the Baltimore–Washington, DC, area. **Baltimore/Washington International Airport** (1-800-I-FLY-BWI) is located between Baltimore and Annapolis. **Ronald Reagan Washington National Airport** (703-417-8000) is in Virginia across the Potomac River from the District of Columbia. **Dulles International Airport** (703-572-2700), in northern Virginia, may be a bit farther away but often has lower airfares. All three have airline companies with connections around the world.

Philadelphia International Airport (215-937-5400) may be a good choice for those traveling to central Maryland or the northern part of the Eastern Shore, while **Pittsburgh International Airport** (412-472-3525) may be best for those wanting to explore western Maryland.

Smaller, regional airports have commuter connections and are noted in their respective chapters.

AMTRAK Despite its many troubles through the years, Amtrak (1-800-USA-RAIL; www.amtrak.com) service for Maryland is quite extensive. It can get you close to the northern part of the Eastern Shore by dropping you off in Aberdeen, or take you deep into western Maryland at Cumberland. There is, of course, service to Baltimore; Washington, DC; and several towns close to the two big cities.

ANTIQUES New Market has so many antiques shops that it has dubbed itself "the Antiques Capital of Maryland." Other areas with heavy concentrations of dealers include Havre de Grace; Kensington; Historic Savage Mill in Savage; Fell's Point, Federal Hill; and Antique Row in Baltimore. Head to the Eastern Shore to find shops filled with nautical items of yesteryear.

The **Antiques Dealers Association of Maryland** (410-269-1440; www.antiquesinmd.com), 17 Conduit St., Annapolis, 21401, publishes a pamphlet describing more than 50 of its members. A calendar of shows is included.

APPALACHIAN TRAIL The Appalachian Trail follows the crest of the Appalachian Mountains for more than 2,000 miles from Georgia to Maine. Forty miles of the pathway are in Maryland, entering at the C&O Canal across the Potomac River from Harpers Ferry, West Virginia. After following the canal eastward for a few miles, it climbs Weverton Cliffs for a spectacular view of the confluence of the Shenandoah and Potomac Rivers. Staying along the crest of South Mountain, the trail passes by several places of historical interest and one viewpoint after another. It leaves the state at the Mason-Dixon Line near Pen-Mar.

The **Appalachian Trail Conservancy** (304-535-6331; www .appalachiantrail.org), P.O. Box 807, Harpers Ferry, WV 25425, is the source for the *Appalachian Trail Guide to Maryland and Northern Virginia*; *The Appalachian Trail: A Visitor's Companion*; *Wildflowers of the Appalachian Trail*; and other publications and information.

AQUARIUMS You could spend hours, even days, experiencing everything the multilevel, multibuilding **National Aquarium** in Baltimore has to offer. Smaller, but still engaging, are the aquariums in the **Ocean City Life Saving Museum** and at the **Calvert Marine Museum** in Solomons.

ART GALLERIES Baltimore is the state's epicenter of art with the world-class **Baltimore Museum of Art** and **Walters Art Museum**. The eccentric exhibits in the **American Visionary Art Museum** enhance the reputation. The **Annapolis Marine Art Gallery** displays only works of living artists who portray life in and around the water. The architecture of the **Washington County Museum of Fine Arts** in Hagerstown is almost as impressive as its extensive collection of Old Masters and American works.

Smaller in size, but still impressive, are **Strathmore Hall** in North Bethesda, **Gudelsky Gallery** in Silver Spring, and **African Art Museum of Maryland** in Columbia. **Mattawoman Creek Art Center** near Marbury is in one of the most peaceful settings you will find, while the presentation of artwork in the commercial **Ocean Gallery World Center** in Ocean City fits in with the chaos and activity of its boardwalk location.

Many artist-owned galleries have become destinations unto themselves. Places such as **Troika Gallery** in Easton and **Lilyfield Gallery** in Cambridge contain the works of some of the state's best creators. Most colleges

and universities also have a gallery or two, and do not overlook the *Crafts* section in each chapter.

The Web site www.delmarweb .com/maryland/artgallery.html has an extensive list (but no descriptions) of galleries throughout the state.

ARTS COUNCILS Every county has an arts council that is funded, at least in part, by the **Maryland State Arts Council** (www.msac.org). As individual organizations, they vary greatly in how large they are and what they do. Most do sponsor classes in various media, theatrical and musical productions, and festivals. All of them have a gallery where the works of their members are displayed in changing exhibits. Several of the largest and most active are: **Academy Art Museum** in Easton; **Carroll County Arts Council Gallery** inside a refurbished 1928 art deco movie house; and **Washington County Arts Council** in Hagerstown.

The **Elkton Arts Center** in Elkton is a real standout. The **Garrett County Arts Council** has the only fine-arts gallery in its region.

BALLOONING Hot-air balloon rides are available from **Fantasy Flights** (301-417-0000; www.airtravel.com/ fantasy) in Gaithersburg and **Friendship Hot Air Balloon Company** (410-442-5566) in West Friendship.

BEACHES **Ocean City** is, of course, the beach that comes to mind when you think of Maryland. And well it should. With its thousands of motel rooms, attractions by the score, and 10 miles of sand, it is the quintessential East Coast resort town. Just south of it is **Assateague Island** and 30 miles of beach with far fewer people (and

amenities). If you are looking for even fewer people, know that hardly anyone ever takes advantage of the small public beach in **Public Landing**.

The beach on **Janes Island** in the Chesapeake Bay offers great seclusion, as it can only be reached by boat. Other beaches along the bay are easier to get to. **Betterton Beach** is the only one that has been completely free of sea nettles (jellyfish) for decades. **Sandy Point** near Annapolis is considered by many to be one of the bay's finest. **Chesapeake Beach** and neighboring **North Beach** were resort destinations in the early 1900s and are still nice, but now quieter, places. You have to take a hike to reach their beaches, but you can search for fossils once you are upon the sands of **Calvert Cliffs State Park** and **Flag Ponds Nature Park** near Lusby, and **Purse State Park** close to Marbury.

Many state parks have beaches along their lakes, and other small public beaches are mentioned throughout this book.

BED & BREAKFASTS I don't list every one that is in operation, but I have stayed in close to 100 B&Bs in Maryland, and visited and inspected scores more. My selection ranges from modest homes to palatial mansions, and includes working farms, waterfront cottages, historic town houses in busy downtown areas, rustic lodges in isolated woodlands, and more.

Each B&B is different, and it is this diversity that makes each place a new experience. As opposed to staying in a hotel or motel, a visit at a B&B is a much more personal way to get to know the locals and the area in which they live. Although you can make reservations by other means, I like making mine over the phone, as it gives me a chance to chat with the host and establish a relationship before I arrive.

Rates were current when this book went to press, but as in all things monetary, they will probably be a bit higher by the time you visit. Be aware that a number of B&Bs do not accept credit cards or children.

BICYCLING The relatively flat terrain of the eastern portion of Maryland has always made it popular with bicyclists, and the activity's growth in recent years has made the state even more biker-friendly. The "Maryland Bicycle Map" provides information on more than 50 places to road and/or mountain bike, describing several major long-distance trails and even bike-friendly ferry and transportation systems. The pamphlet *Bicycling in Maryland* contains additional biking and contact information. Both are available from the **Department of Transportation** (1-800-252-8776). Local tourism offices usually have detailed information about their respective areas.

The 184.5-mile C&O Canal is probably the most popular biking route, but do not overlook the Northern Central Railroad Trail, Baltimore and Annapolis Trail, Capital Crescent Trail, Rock Creek Trail, Western Maryland Rail Trail, and ViewTrail 100 Bike Trail. Also, many of Maryland's Scenic Byways (see *Scenic Drives*) are great road-riding journeys. *25 Bicycle Tours in Maryland*, by Anne H. Oman, details additional road trips, while *Mountain Bike America: Washington–Baltimore*, by Martin Fernandez and Scott Adams, is for those looking for the thrill of the singletrack.

Adrenaline High (410-749-2886; www.adrenalinehigh.com) puts together customized bicycle tours in and around Somerset County on the Eastern Shore. **High Mountain Sports** (301-387-4199; www.high mountainsports.com) will take you on guided mountain bike explorations of the forests around **Deep Creek Lake** in western Maryland.

BIRDING **Waterfowl** migrating through Maryland during spring and fall may be observed by the hundreds of thousands on the Eastern Shore in places such as **Blackwater National Wildlife Refuge**, **Eastern Neck National Wildlife Refuge**, and **Deal Island Wildlife Management Area**. *Birdwatcher's Guide to Delmarva* provides details on these and other Eastern Shore sites. **Sandy Point State Park** and **Point Lookout State Park** are a couple of hot spots on the Chesapeake Bay's western shore.

In addition to waterfowl, wide varieties of birds are often seen in **Merkle Wildlife Sanctuary**, **Greenwell State Park**, and **Patuxent Research Refuge**. **Clyburn Arboretum** is a favored Baltimore-area birding site, while a number of state-rare breeding species have been observed in **Finzel Swamp** and **Cranesville Swamp** in western Maryland. Rock outcrops along the route of the **Appalachian Trail** on South Mountain are the places to be for the **fall hawk migration**.

The Audubon Society leads bird walks at **Pickering Creek** and **Woodend**. The Wildfowl Trust of North America sponsors a number of walks each year in the **Chesapeake Bay Environmental Center**.

As stands to reason, the Baltimore oriole is the state bird.

BOATING AND SAILING EXCURSIONS To explore Maryland without taking a boating excursion of some kind or another is to miss an essential element of the state. Many of the outings are narrated (and are the ones I think you gain the most from), and you can go onto the water in everything from sailboats to working fishing boats to boats built solely to thrill with speed. The Eastern Shore towns of Ocean City, Cambridge, Hurlock, St. Michaels, Stevensville, Grasonville, Rock Hall, Solomons, and Tilghman Island all offer excursions. Two boats I especially enjoyed were the *Nathan of Dorchester* in Dorchester and the *Lady Patty* in Tilghman Island. Look to the harbors of Havre de Grace, Baltimore, and Annapolis for trips originating on the Chesapeake Bay's western shore.

A boating excursion of a different kind is the 1-hour round-trip ride on the mule-powered *Canal Clipper* on the C&O Canal at Great Falls.

BOATBUILDING **Chesapeake Wooden Boat Builders School** (410-939-4800) in Havre de Grace has classes

on antique canoe repair and restoration, model-ship building, and basic wooden-boat building.

BOAT RAMPS, PUBLIC The map "A Fisherman's Guide to Maryland Piers and Ramps" is available from the **Fisheries Service** (1-800-688-FINS) and highlights more than 240 public water-access areas throughout the state. *The Chesapeake Bay, Susquehanna River and Tidal Tributaries Public Access Guide* provides even greater detail to those particular areas and can be obtained from the **Chesapeake Bay Program** (1-800-662-CRIS; www.chesapeakebay.net).

BOOKS It is always a good idea to read a few books to help you gain a greater awareness, enjoyment, and understanding of your surroundings.

Maryland: A Middle Temperament, 1634–1980, by Brugger, Requardt, and Cottom, is an in-depth survey of the state's history. *Maryland: A New Guide to the Old Line State* by Brugger and Papenfuse covers the state's history by leading you on different driving tours; it would make a good companion to this book. It can be a little heavy on the technical aspects, but Edwin Danson's *Drawing the Line: How Mason and Dixon Surveyed the Most Famous Border in America* chronicles the task of delineating Maryland from Pennsylvania. *Maryland in the Civil War: A House Divided,* by Robert I. Cottom Jr. and Mary Ellen Haward, may be the best way to learn about the state's role during the war without having to read multiple volumes. *Home on the Canal* by Elizabeth Kytle is interesting for its historical information, but even more so when it provides firsthand accounts of those who lived and worked on the C&O Canal.

James Michener wrote what may be the best-selling Maryland novel of all time, *Chesapeake,* which describes life around the bay through the eyes of the early settlers and on up to those inhabiting the land in later years. William Martin's novel of intrigue and romance, *Annapolis,* uses the city as a background.

Tom Horton lived and worked among the local people so that he could write his intimate portrait, *An Island Out of Time: A Memoir of Smith Island in the Chesapeake. Chesapeake Almanac: Following the Bay Through the Seasons* is a collection of newspaper columns by John Page William Jr. that takes you through a year's worth of natural world events around the bay. *Chesapeake Bay: Nature of an Estuary,* by Christopher P. White, is another good book about the environment of the bay.

Baseball fans will enjoy Lois P. Nicholson's *From Maryland to Cooperstown: Seven Maryland Natives in Baseball's Hall of Fame.* In *Discovering Maryland Wineries,* Kevin M. Atticks describes not only the wineries and the wines but also the people behind them.

Maryland author Nora Roberts has sold more than 145 million copies of women's novels, a number of them set in Maryland, while mystery writer Martha Grimes turns out one book after another, some of which also feature locations in the state. The comments of the great Baltimore newspaper writer H. L. Mencken have been gathered into several volumes and should be looked over for their caustic wit and ironic observations.

If planning outdoor activities, I recommend you consult my guidebook *50 Hikes in Maryland* (Countryman Press Guides), as well as *Hikes in Western Maryland* by the Potomac Appalachian Trail Club; *Birdwatcher's Guide to Delmarva;* and *Finding Wildflowers in the Washington, DC/Baltimore Area. Hiking, Biking, and Canoeing in Maryland,* by Bryan MacKay, focuses on outings appropriate for families with children.

BUS SERVICE Carolina Trailways (410-289-9307) services the Eastern Shore towns of Ocean City, Princess Anne, Cambridge, Easton, and Salisbury. **Greyhound** (1-800-229-9424) stops in Salisbury, Stevensville, and Elkton.

Trailways (703-691-3052) and Greyhound both have terminals in Baltimore. Greyhound also serves Aberdeen, Annapolis, Cumberland,

Elkton, Frederick, Grantsville, Hagerstown, and Waldorf.

CAMPING **Reservations** for campsites and cabins in state parks can be made by calling 1-888-432-CAMP or online at www.reservations.dnr.state .md.us. A few are open year-round, but most of the parks' campgrounds are open from early spring to late fall. Backcountry camping is permitted in many state forests, but information (and payment of a fee) must be obtained from each state forest office.

More than 30 campsites, with chemical toilets and drinking water (in-season), are strung along the **C&O Canal National Historical Park**. Only two, Antietam Creek and Fifteen Mile Creek, charge a fee; all others are free, and all are operated on a first-come, first-served basis. Contact 301-739-4200; www.nps.gov/ choh for more information. Reservations can be made for camping in **Assateague Island National Seashore** and **Greenbelt Park** by contacting 1-800-436-2267 or www .reservations.nps.gov. Call 301-663-9388 for camping reservations in **Catoctin Mountain Park**.

The largest percentage of commercial campgrounds listed in this book have hookups and other facilities for those traveling and camping with trailers or RVs.

CHESAPEAKE BAY If there is any one thing that defines Maryland, especially its eastern portion, it is water—and the Chesapeake Bay is the state's most immense body of water. As America's largest bay, it is the catch basin for a far-reaching drainage system that covers 64,000 square miles. Snowmelt that begins its downstream journey near Cooperstown, New York, meets

and mingles in the bay with rainwater that fell on the higher elevations of the Allegheny Mountains on the western Maryland–West Virginia border. The bay is considered an estuary—a body of water in which tidal movements bring salt water upstream, where it comes in contact with the fresh water being carried toward the ocean by river currents.

There are many other estuaries throughout the world, such as Puget Sound in Washington, Cook Inlet in Alaska, and the fjords of Norway, but none of them is nearly as productive as the Chesapeake Bay. Well over 100 million pounds of seafood are harvested from the bay most years, including 50 percent of America's supply of **blue crabs** and a large percentage of its **oysters**. A number of conditions combine to make the bay this productive. Probably the two most important factors are the large amounts of fresh water coming into the bay and the vast acreages of marshlands surrounding it, which produce an abundance of detritus and other nutrients. These wetlands are home to numerous shorebirds and are also major resting areas on the **Great Atlantic Flyway** for migratory waterfowl.

The **Chesapeake Bay Gateways Network** is a system of parks, refuges, historic towns, and museums (most of which are described in this book), each of which tells a part of the bay's natural history and impact on Maryland's way of life. The brochure is available from the **Maryland Office of Tourism Development** (see *Information*); you can also consult www.baygateways.net.

CHESAPEAKE & OHIO (C&O) CANAL
The 184.5-mile C&O Canal, running from Georgetown to Cumberland, has excellent opportunities for hiking, biking, canoeing, camping, horseback riding, insights into history, and more for the entire family. I have included information on these activities in the appropriate chapters. Please consult the **C&O Canal National Historical Park** sidebar on page 295 to learn more about the colorful history of this national treasure and how you can best explore it.

CHILDREN, ESPECIALLY FOR The
crayon symbol ✍ identifies activities and places of special interest to children and families.

CIVIL WAR As a border state, Maryland was a hotbed of activity during the Civil War. **Antietam National Battlefield** at Sharpsburg and **Monocacy National Battlefield** near Frederick preserve the sites of two of the war's most important battles. In Cambridge, the **Harriet Tubman Museum** sponsors guided tours that reveal the story of Ms. Tubman, who led more than 300 slaves to freedom along the Underground Railroad.
   Baltimore Civil War Museum tells of the city's part during the war and in the Underground Railroad.

The **National Museum of Civil War Medicine** in Frederick vividly portrays medicine's role. Other sites, battles, and museums of Civil War significance are detailed in their respective sections of each chapter.
   A brochure detailing a statewide **Civil War Driving Trail** and other information about Maryland's role in the conflict can be obtained from the **Maryland Office of Tourism Development** (see *Information*).

COVERED BRIDGES Spanning a waterway within the Fair Hill Natural Resources Management Area is the **Big Elk Creek Covered Bridge**. About 3 miles north of North East on MD 272 is the **Gilpin Falls Covered Bridge**, the longest covered bridge still standing in the state. The circa-1865 **Jericho Covered Bridge** is near Kingsville. **Utica Covered Bridge**, **Loy's Station Covered Bridge**, and **Roddy Road Covered Bridge** are all north of Frederick.

CRABS Blue crabs can be found from North America's Cape Cod to South America's Uruguay, and even in Egypt's Nile River. It is in the Chesapeake Bay, however, that they reach their greatest numbers, and Maryland

crabs have the reputation of being the finest. The harvest fluctuates from year to year—and has been on a downward trend for a while—yet thousands of pounds are still caught and eaten each year. Crab houses serve up bushels of heavily spiced steamed crabs, and soft-shell crabs are considered a real delicacy, while the state's succulent **crabcakes** are known far and wide. I find it amusing that, as you travel around the state, you will find almost every restaurant that serves seafood has "the region's best crabcakes," "the Eastern Shore's best crabcakes," "the best crabcakes in Maryland," or even "the world's best crabcakes."

One of the most fun activities a visitor to the Chesapeake Bay can do is to go **crabbing** by becoming what the local folks call a "chicken necker." This is done by attaching a chicken neck (or any other bony piece of meat) to a string and casting it a few feet out into the water. Gradually pull the string in when you feel a tug on it. With luck, a crab will be hanging tenaciously on to the bait and you can slip a net under it before you lift it out of the water. Be careful of the claws when you turn the net over to gently shake the crab out! No license is required for recreational crabbing (if you take less than two dozen hard-shell crabs), but I suggest you follow what is the law for commercial crabbing and not keep a crab that is less than 5 inches from shell point to shell point.

The interesting lives of blue crabs are described in superbly entertaining and nontechnical detail in William Warner's Pulitzer Prize–winning *Beautiful Swimmers: Watermen, Crabs, and the Chesapeake Bay.* "Beautiful swimmers" is the English

translation of the blue crab's genus/species name, *Callinectes sapidus.*

DECOY CARVING AND WILDLIFE ART
Steve and Lem Ward are generally acknowledged as being the ones who elevated decoy carving into an art form. Their workshop in Crisfield has been preserved, while the **Ward Museum of Wildlife Art** in Salisbury exhibits their work and chronicles the history of decoy carving. Other significant decoy displays are in the **Upper Bay Museum** in North East and the **Havre de Grace Decoy Museum**. The **Ward World Championship Wildfowl Carving Competition**, held each spring in Ocean City, is the world's largest carving competition.

DELMARVA The word *Delmarva* refers to the entire Eastern Shore peninsula, which is composed of portions of Delaware, Maryland, and Virginia.

EMERGENCIES Hospitals with emergency rooms are noted near the beginning of each chapter. A few urgent care facilities that can handle minor emergencies are also listed. Dialing **911** anywhere in the state will connect you to an emergency service. For highway accidents or assistance, the **state police** can be reached at 410-653-4200, on **CB Channel 9**, or **Cellular #77**.

EVENTS County fairs, arts and crafts demonstrations, fishing tournaments, skill competitions, historic reenactments, music concerts, crab festivals: Some kind of distinctive event or celebration takes places almost every day of the year. Leading annual events are noted in the *Special Events* section at the end of each chapter. *Maryland Celebrates*, available from the **Maryland Office of Tourism Development** (see *Information*), describes hundreds of events that will take place within the calendar year; a number of them are onetime occurrences.

FACTORY OUTLETS There are a number of modern, mall-type outlets, and they are noted in their respective chapters under *Selective Shopping*. There are also several true factory outlets where you purchase the product where it was produced. In Salisbury, you can watch the craftsmen at work in **Salisbury Pewter**. Cumberland's **Biederlack of America** is a major manufacturer of rugs and throws.

FARMER'S MARKETS Farmer's markets can be found in every region of the state and are listed in the *Selective Shopping* section of each chapter. I love going to them, but be aware that the locations and operating days and times of farmer's markets have been known to change frequently.

FERRIES Relics of the past, only a few ferries remain in Maryland. Their historic aspect and the scenic beauty of the waterways they cross make using one as much of a fun excursion as a utilitarian necessity. The **Whitehaven Ferry** is connected to a fixed line and crosses the Wicomico River about 18 miles west of Salisbury. The **Upper Ferry** crosses the Wicomico River less than 10 miles west of Salisbury. The **Oxford–Bellevue Ferry** enables a circular driving tour of Easton, Oxford, and St. Michaels by making a crossing on the Tred Avon River. **White's Ferry**, the only remaining ferry across the Potomac River, permits you come into Maryland near Poolesville from US 15 just north of Leesburg, Virginia.

Much larger, the **Cape May, New Jersey–Lewes, Delaware, Ferry** can save you hours and many miles of driving if you are arriving on the Eastern Shore from New Jersey.

FISHING The **Department of Natural Resources/Fisheries Service** (1-800-688-FINS) can supply the information you need about regulations and licenses, and has free publications geared toward tidal, freshwater, trout, fly-, and other types of fishing.

Within the *Fishing* section of the chapters are places to fish on your own, or companies and individuals who provide guided trips. The Web site for the **Maryland Charter Boat Association** (www.marylandcharter boats.com) contains the largest list of charter-boat captains on the Chesapeake Bay, while local tourism offices (see *Guidance* in each chapter) maintain lists of reliable captains and fishing guides.

GOLF The courses listed under the *To Do* section in each chapter are public courses that do not require payment of a membership fee. The *Maryland Golf Guide*, available from the **Maryland Office of Tourism Development** (see *Information*), outlines public, semiprivate, and private courses.

HANDICAPPED ACCESS The wheelchair symbol ♿ appears next to lodgings, restaurants, and attractions that are partially or completely handicapped-accessible.

HIGHWAY TRAVEL The speed limit on interstates is 65 miles per hour unless otherwise noted. Driver and passengers are required to wear safety belts, and children under the age of 4 or those weighing less than 40 pounds must be in approved child-safety seats. Driving lights must be on whenever you are using windshield wipers. You may make a right turn at a red signal light after coming to a complete stop unless posted signs prohibit doing so.

Call the **State Highway Administration's Construction Hotline** (410-545-0300; 1-800-323-6742) Mon.–Fri. 8–4:30 to obtain the latest information on construction projects

that may impact your travel plans. The commission's Web site (www .marylandroads.com) provides up-to-date road conditions during inclement weather and a wealth of road-travel information.

The official state highway map can be obtained from the **Maryland Office of Tourism Development** (see *Information*). Available at bookshops and many convenience stores, the *Maryland and Delaware Atlas and Gazetteer* (published by DeLorme) is an invaluable navigation tool.

HIKING I have included the state's best hiking excursions under the *Hiking* section of each chapter; look at the *Bicycling, Birding, Parks, Gardens,* and *Nature Preserves* sections for additional opportunities to walk outdoors.

Recommended resources include *Walks and Rambles on the Delmarva Peninsula,* by Jay Abercrombie; *Country Walks Near Washington,* by Alan Fisher; and *Country Walks Near Baltimore,* by Alan Hall Fisher. One of my own books, *50 Hikes in Maryland* (Countryman Press Guides), covers the entire state with outings ranging from easy, 1-hour jaunts to multiday backpacking treks.

HORSEBACK RIDING Places to ride your own horse and businesses offering guided rides are listed under the *To Do* section of a chapter; additional places to ride can often be found by looking in the *Bicycling*, *Hiking*, and *Parks* sections of a chapter. **The Equiery** (1-800-244-9580) publishes a directory to rental stables and guided trail rides in the state.

HUNTING A comprehensive booklet, *Hunting and Trapping in Maryland*, can be obtained from the **Department of Natural Resources** (410-260-8540; www.dnr.state.md.us).

If you like the outdoors but are not a hunter, be aware that hunting is permitted in wildlife management areas, state forests, and some state parks. Although the law is under pressure to change, Sunday hunting was still prohibited as this book went to press.

ICE CREAM, HOMEMADE When I started adding them up, I was amazed at just how many places produce homemade ice cream; no wonder I put on a few pounds researching this book. **Dumser's Drive-In** at Ocean City serves it within a few hours of making it. **Canal Creamery** is on the waterfront in Chesapeake City. **Gourmet by the Bay** in St. Michaels sells its frozen treats in pints only. There is often a line waiting get into Havre de Grace's **Bomboy's Homemade Ice Cream**. **Hoffman's** in Westminster has been using the same recipes since it opened in 1947. **Mother's Federal Hill Grille** and **Maggie Moo's** are located in Baltimore, while **Simple Pleasures Ice Café** can be found in Bowie. **Baugher's** in Westminster and **Queen City Creamery and Deli** in Cumberland serve their ice creams within a restaurant setting, while the peach ice cream at **Kent Fort Farm** in Stevensville is available only during the August Peach Festival.

The crème de la crème is **Lakeside Creamery** at Deep Creek Lake. The owner is such a master at his craft that people travel from foreign lands just to take his classes on producing homemade ice cream.

INFORMATION Regional information sources are described under the *Guidance* section near the beginning of each chapter. The **Maryland Office of Tourism Development** (410-767-3400; 1-800-634-7386; www.mdisfun.org), 217 E. Redwood St., Baltimore, 21202, publishes *Destination Maryland*, an annual guide to many attractions, outdoor opportunities, and lodging facilities throughout the state. The office can also be the source for numerous brochures on specialized topics such as golfing, biking, antiques, canoeing, fishing, and more.

INSECTS Warm weather brings no-see-ums, gnats, fleas, sand fleas, deerflies, mosquitoes, ticks, and more.

Although the mountains have their fair share, the lowlands, marshes, and beaches of the eastern part of the state, especially southern Maryland and the Eastern Shore, can be nearly swarming with them at times. Bring lots of repellent on any outing from late spring through midfall. (And remember that one of the pleasures of travel during the colder months of the year is the absence of insects.)

KAYAKING AND CANOEING The kayaking and canoeing are soft and easy along the streams and creeks of the Eastern Shore and southern Maryland, while winds across the Chesapeake Bay can test the mettle of an experienced kayaker. The rushing waters of western Maryland can require such technical skill that they have been used for national and international competitions and by athletes training for the Olympics.

Included in the *Kayaking and Canoeing* section of the various chapters are guided trips by outfitters as well as places to paddle on your own. Also consult the *Boat Rentals* and *Parks* sections. The books *Maryland and Delaware Canoe Trails,* by Edward Gertler, and *Exploring the Chesapeake in Small Boats,* by John Page Williams and William S. Portlock, can provide additional information.

LIGHTHOUSES Lighthouses have helped provide safe passage for commercial and recreational boats navigating the Chesapeake Bay and other state waters for well over 100 years. Of the 44 once in Maryland, only 25 remain, and most are no longer in service. **Hooper Straight Lighthouse** in St. Michaels and **Drum Point** in Solomons have been moved to museums, and are two of the most

visited. **Cove Point**, the oldest continuously used lighthouse in the state, is at the mouth of the Patuxent River north of Solomons.

Concord Point is along a waterside walkway in Havre de Grace, while **Turkey Point** is reached by a 1-mile hike in Elk Neck State Park. **Sevenfoot Knoll**, now in Baltimore's Inner Harbor, was moved from its original location at nearby Pier 5. **Piney Point** has an adjacent museum, while **Point Lookout** is open to the public only once a year; both are at the tip of southern Maryland where the Potomac River meets the bay.

MARITIME MUSEUMS The **Chesapeake Bay Maritime Museum** in St. Michaels is the state's largest and one of the finest on the East Coast. The **Calvert Marine Museum** in Solomons is another standout. At the head of the bay is the **Havre de Grace Maritime Museum**, while Cambridge on the Eastern Shore has the **Richardson Maritime Museum** and **Brannock Maritime Museum**. **Annapolis Maritime Museum** tells the history of its Eastport neighborhood. **Baltimore Maritime Museum** has no real walls, as it consists of three ships docked about a block from one another.

MOTELS AND HOTELS For the most part, chain motels and hotels have not been listed because information about them is easily obtained from many sources and because their architecture and amenities tend to have a cookie-cutter sameness. Those that are included are in areas where lodging options are few, are in a desirable location, or are outstanding places to stay.

THE NATIONAL ROAD In 1775, British forces under General Edward Braddock, accompanied by a young George Washington, widened a Native American trail through Turners Gap to facilitate their march westward, where they were ambushed (and Braddock killed) by French and Indian troops in Pennsylvania. With funds provided by the state in 1806, the route was improved, extended from Baltimore to Cumberland, and named the **National Pike**. At the same time, the U.S. Congress also authorized federal funds for another road, this one to begin in Cumberland and head westward. Eventually the two roads came to be known as the National Road. As one of the major thoroughfares of the day, it was traveled by such luminaries as Abraham Lincoln, Daniel Webster, Henry Clay, and Presidents Jackson, William Henry Harrison, Polk, Taylor, and Van Buren.

US 40 in Maryland follows the route of what was once the National Road and was named an **All American Road** in 2002. As you explore Maryland, take a break from the interstate to travel the roadway and discover historic sites you would otherwise pass by.

NATURE TOURISM The **Department of Natural Resources** has embarked upon what I think is one of the most exciting and farsighted ventures to come along in years. By using state employees, contracts with private outfitters, and some volunteers, the Nature Tourism program offers recreational and educational opportunities for adults and children of all skill and fitness levels to experience the outdoors. Hiking, biking, rock climbing, caving, horseback riding, kayaking, canoeing, rafting, fishing, birdwatching, camping, and day camps are just a few of the many organized and guided activities the program has offered—usually at a fairly low cost. New ones are being added all the time. The great thing is that the department has hired Nature Tourism employees for each region of the state, so someone is out there on the local level arranging all these activities. Contact 1-800-830-3974 or www.dnr.state.md.us/outdooradventures for detailed information.

OLD LINE STATE One of Maryland's nicknames is the Old Line State. It does not refer to the Mason-Dixon Line as many people believe but goes back to the Revolutionary War. Maryland's Governor Smallwood had led a group of state volunteers to help George Washington in New York. The Marylanders held their line of defense against the British long enough to permit Washington's troops to escape and regroup to fight another day. He was so impressed that Washington ever after referred to Maryland as the "Old Line State."

PARKS, NATIONAL Assateague Island National Seashore shares the barrier island with Maryland's Assateague State Park and Virginia's Chincoteague National Wildlife Refuge. Undeveloped, except for a couple of campgrounds and a few visitors centers, the island offers close to 30 miles of unbroken sandy beaches on which to beachcomb, swim, sunbathe, or surf fish. A hike of 25 miles can be accomplished by making use of designated campsites (and carrying plenty of water!). Greenbelt Park, close to Washington, DC, has a campground and a trail system within a forest bordered by four-lane highways. Catoctin Mountain Park, north of Frederick, is home to the U.S. presidential retreat, Camp David, and miles of pathways leading to spectacular viewpoints.

Other components of the U.S. National Park Service are Antietam National Battlefield, C&O Canal National Historical Park, Fort Washington, Glen Echo Park, Oxon Hill Farm, Piscataway Park, and a number of historic buildings and structures, such as the Thomas Stone National Historic Site near Port Tobacco.

PARKS AND FORESTS, STATE With more than 280,000 acres of land, there is a state park or forest within a 40-minute drive of any location in Maryland. Admission to the state forests and some of the state parks is free, but some have a nominal entrance or parking fee, usually in the $1–5 range. Many of the state parks have campgrounds and cabins for rent, and backcountry camping is permitted in some of the state forests (see Camping above). Consult the Bicycling, Hiking, Kayaking and Canoeing, and Parks sections in each chapter to find what is available in each region. The Department of Natural Resources–State Forest and Park Service (410-974-3771; 1-800-830-3974; www.dnr.state.md.us) can send you a packet brimming with all kinds of information.

PETS The dog-paw symbol 🐾 appears next to places, activities, and lodgings that accept pets. Always inform a hotel, motel, B&B, or other lodging that you will be traveling with your pet; expect to pay an additional fee.

PICK-YOUR-OWN PRODUCE There's just something about a strawberry, tomato, or peach picked ripe off the plant that grocery-store produce can't match. Farms and orchards that invite the public into their fields and orchards are listed in each chapter. Unless you don't mind just taking a drive in the country, it is a wise idea to call ahead to confirm what is ripe and at what time and day you may come out to pick.

The Maryland Direct Farm Market Association (410-665-0154), 2526 Proctor Lane, Baltimore, 21234, publishes a directory of pick-your-own places and farms that have their own fruit and vegetable stands.

POPULATION The state's population was 5,296,486 according to the 2000 federal census.

RAILROAD RIDES AND MUSEUMS Rail fans, and children, enjoy the excursions offered by the **Walkersville Southern Railroad** near Frederick and **Western Maryland Scenic Railroad** in Cumberland and Frostburg.

Baltimore's **B&O Railroad Museum** has 40 acres of locomotives, cars, and artifacts. Built around 1830, the **Ellicott City B&O Railroad Station Museum** is the oldest railroad terminal in America. **Brunswick Railroad Museum** features a model layout of the B&O line from Washington, DC, to Brunswick. Hagerstown's **Roundhouse Museum** is from the days when five different lines converged on the city.

SAILING LESSONS Three excellent sailing schools make Annapolis, "the Sailing Capital of America," their home port. **Annapolis Sailing School** is one of the world's most well-respected institutions of sailing knowledge. **AYS Charters and Sailing School** offers sailing instructions and charter-certification courses. **Womanship, Inc.**, has sailing instruction taught by and for women.

Rock Hall has the **Maryland School of Sailing and Seamanship**. North of Baltimore in Havre de Grace is **BaySail**. In western Maryland, you can learn to hoist a sail on a lake at the **Deep Creek Sailing School**.

SCENIC BYWAYS I had originally intended to point out quite a number of Maryland's scenic drives (and I do include a few), but when I discovered the excellent *Maryland Scenic Byways* book and accompanying "Scenic Byways Map," it seemed that the effort would be superfluous.

First of all, the 192-page book is free and can be obtained from most local tourism offices, state welcome centers, the **Maryland Office of Tourism Development** (see *Information*), or the **Maryland Scenic Byways, Office of Environmental Design** (1-877-MDBYWAY; www.sha .state.md.us/oed/bywaysprogram.htm).

Second, the book gives directions for more than 30 drives throughout the state with detailed background information on the human and natural history of the area driven through, sites along the route, recreational opportunities, and even side trips worth taking. The shortest byway is 5 miles in Baltimore; the longest is several hundred miles and stretches from the Atlantic Ocean to the Appalachian Mountains.

This a great explorer's resource— and remember, it is available free for the asking.

SEA NETTLES A jellyfish with long tentacles, and known as a sea nettle,

increases in number as the temperatures of summer warm the Chesapeake Bay, its tributaries, and the Atlantic Ocean. Its sting can be a source of irritation for many hours. Alcohol, vinegar, baking soda, or meat tenderizer may help relieve the pain, but some people have severe allergic reactions that require them to be hospitalized.

SKIING, CROSS-COUNTRY **New Germany** and **Herrington Manor State Parks** have trails groomed and tracked just for cross-country skiing. The parks also provide ski rentals and warming huts. Information on the many miles of ungroomed trails around the **Deep Creek Lake** area can be obtained from the **Garrett County Chamber of Commerce** (301-387-4286; www.garrettchamber .com).

    Piney Run Park near Sykesville, the **Catoctin Mountain Park**, **C&O Canal**, and **Appalachian Trail** all make for good cross-country ski outings when enough snow falls to cover the roots and rocks.

SKIING, DOWNHILL **Wisp Ski and Golf Resort**, at Deep Creek Lake, is the state's only downhill skiing spot. It has what is considered to be one of the best snowmaking systems in the world, so all that is really needed is cold weather for the trails to be open. Snowboarding, cross-country skiing, tubing, night skiing, and children's programs are also available.

SNOWMOBILING The Deep Creek Lake area welcomes snowmobilers. **Deep Creek Lake**, **Garrett State Forest**, **Potomac State Forest**, and **Savage River State Forest** have a combined total of 75 miles of marked

trails open for backcountry travel. The **Garrett County Chamber of Commerce** (301-387-4286; www.garrett chamber.com) can supply detailed information.

STAR-SPANGLED BANNER TRAIL A 100-mile scenic and historic driving tour that follows the route taken by the British when they invaded the Chesapeake Bay area in the 1814. The trail takes in numerous sites that highlight the events leading up to the Battle of Baltimore, which inspired Francis Scott Key to write the words that became America's national anthem. Some sites are identified by little more than a marker, others include extensive museums, while still others take in entire towns and cities, such as St. Michael's and Annapolis. A detailed, full-color brochure can be obtained from most state visitors centers or from the **Maryland Office of Tourism Development** (see *Information*).

TAXES The state sales tax is 5 percent; lodging, meals, and amusement taxes can be well in excess of 10 percent.

WATERFALLS Swallow Falls State Park near Oakland has a 1.5-mile circuit hike that will lead you to four different waterfalls. **Muddy Creek Falls** is considered the highest in the state, **Lower Falls** and **Swallow Falls** are on the Youghiogheny River, and there is a sandy beach at **Toliver Falls**.

    The round-trip journey to **Cunningham Falls** near Thurmont is an easy 1-mile hike. **Falling Branch**, in Rocks State Park near Jarrettsville, and **Great Falls** in the Potomac River, are on the fall line where the piedmont meets the Coastal Plain.

can be the most pleasant times of the year, as days warm up to a comfortable degree, nights cool down for easy sleeping, and crowds are fewer.

Snow is common in the mountains, moderate in the Capital and Central Regions, and quite infrequent in southern Maryland and the Eastern Shore. When heat and humidity have taken the joy and fun out of the eastern portion of the state, the mountains will beckon with temperatures that can be 10 or more degrees lower. Exploring Maryland can be a year-round activity.

Incidentally, despite the name, there are no waterfalls in Gunpowder Falls State Park. *Falls* was a colonial term for "river."

WEATHER Maryland can have a wide range of temperatures and conditions. Winters can be unpredictably cold or relatively mild, while summers can become hot and humid or may be rather temperate. Spring and autumn

WHITEWATER RAFTING Precision Rafting in Friendsville is the premier Maryland company that runs the Upper Youghiogheny River as it passes through a narrow, 5-mile gorge with nearly continuous Class IV and V rapids. **River and Trail Outfitters** in Knoxville and **Outdoor Excursions** in Boonsboro have runs along the (usually) calmer Potomac River.

The Eastern Shore

MARYLAND'S SEABOARD—Ocean City, Assateague Island, and Berlin

TANGIER SOUND AREA—Crisfield and Princess Anne

SMITH ISLAND

SALISBURY

CAMBRIDGE AND VICINITY

ST. MICHAELS, EASTON, AND OXFORD

AROUND THE BAY BRIDGE AND KENT ISLAND

CHESTERTOWN AND ROCK HALL

AT THE HEAD OF THE BAY—Chesapeake City, Elkton, and North East

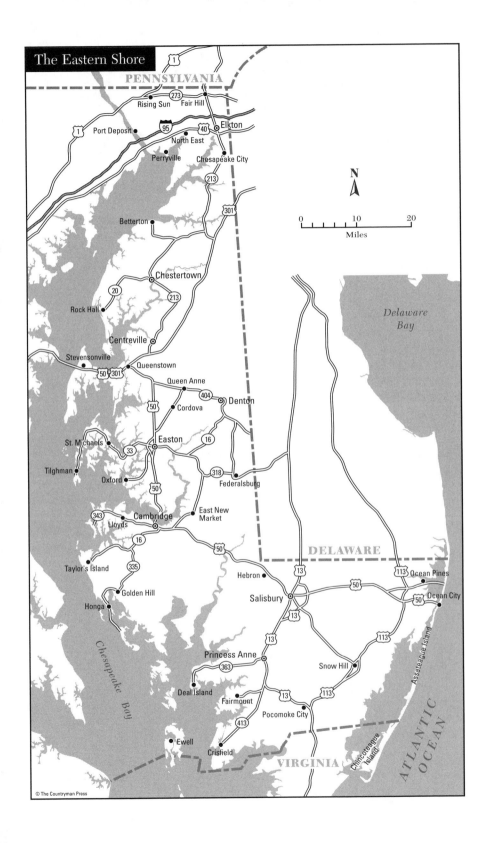

The Eastern Shore

PENNSYLVANIA

1

273 Rising Sun Fair Hill

1 Port Deposit 95 40 Elkton

North East

Perryville Chesapeake City

213

Betterton 301

Chestertown

20 213

Rock Hall

Centreville

Stevensonville Queenstown

50 301 Queen Anne

404 Denton

50 Cordova

Easton 16

St. Michaels 33

Tilghman Oxford 318

50 Federalsburg

Cambridge East New Market

343 Lloyds

16 50 DELAWARE

Taylor's Island 335 Hebron 13 113 Ocean Pines

Golden Hill 50 Ocean City

Honga Salisbury 50

13

Princess Anne 13 113

363 Snow Hill

Deal Island 13 113

Fairmount

413 Pocomoke City

Ewell

Crisfield VIRGINIA

Chesapeake Bay

Delaware Bay

ATLANTIC OCEAN

Assateague Island

Chincoteague Island

N

0 10 20

Miles

© The Countryman Press

THE EASTERN SHORE

Maryland's Eastern Shore is a land where time has stood still—or at least slowed down considerably.

In search of flounder, crabs, clams, oysters, and other delicacies of the deep, watermen still rise before dawn to venture onto the Chesapeake Bay or the Atlantic Ocean. Moving about in small craft often with a crew of just one or two people, they use many of the same techniques that their fathers and grandfathers used decades ago.

The area is unmarred by huge malls and strips of fast-food restaurants; the only industry in many of the unpretentious fishing villages are small seafood-processing plants at water's edge. Thriving downtown districts still exist in a number of small towns. Blessed with a long growing season and fertile soil, the flat fields surrounding the towns produce a rich harvest of corn, beans, tomatoes, peppers, and other vegetables.

The completion of the Bay Bridge in 1952 opened the Eastern Shore to a rush of travelers and new residents. Although rising amounts of traffic and tourism have resulted in subtle changes in Eastern Shore lifestyles, outside influences have also helped bring about an increased awareness of the need to preserve the natural world.

Migrating shorebirds, waterfowl, raptors, and songbirds—including sandpipers, plovers, dowitchers, knots, whimbrels, ducks, geese, herons, egrets, swans, pelicans, falcons, and ospreys—make use of the islands, marshlands, and fields as major resting areas. Thousands of waterfowl, such as snow geese, black ducks, mallards, and pintails, winter here.

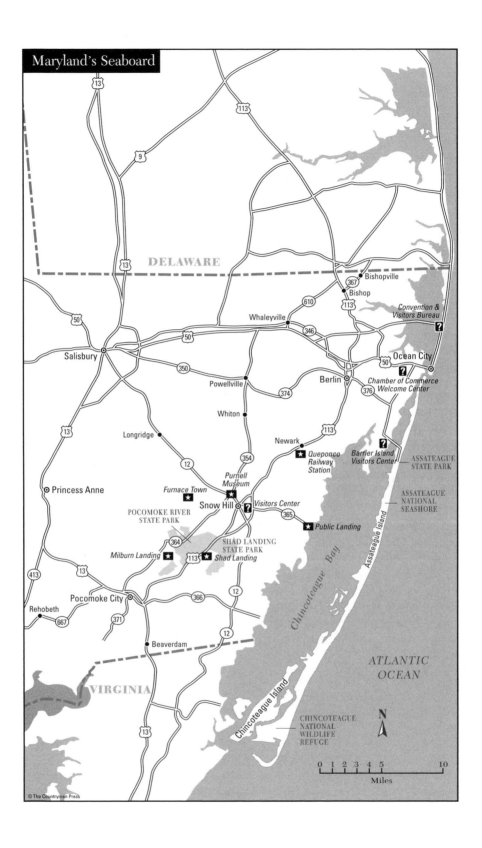

Maryland's Seaboard

13

113

9

DELAWARE

13

Bishopville

367

Bishop

610

113

Convention & Visitors Bureau

50

Whaleyville

346

50

50

Ocean City

Salisbury

350

Berlin

Chamber of Commerce Welcome Center

Powellville

374

376

Whiton

13

Longridge

Newark

113

12

354

Queponco Railway Station

Barrier Island Visitors Center

ASSATEAGUE STATE PARK

Purnell Museum

ASSATEAGUE NATIONAL SEASHORE

Princess Anne

Furnace Town

Snow Hill

Visitors Center

POCOMOKE RIVER STATE PARK

365

Public Landing

364

SHAD LANDING STATE PARK

Milburn Landing

113

Shad Landing

Chincoteague Bay

413

13

Assateague Island

Pocomoke City

366

12

Rehobeth

667

371

12

Beaverdam

12

ATLANTIC OCEAN

VIRGINIA

Chincoteague Island

CHINCOTEAGUE NATIONAL WILDLIFE REFUGE

N

13

0 1 2 3 4 5   10
Miles

© The Countryman Press

MARYLAND'S SEABOARD—
Ocean City, Assateague Island, and Berlin

When Marylanders, especially those from the Baltimore–Annapolis area, say they are "goin' down'e ocean," they mean they will be spending time on the beach at Ocean City. My wife is a native Annapolitan, and her earliest vacation memories are of packing up the beach blankets and sand buckets and spending a few hours in the car anticipating the first whiff of salty air. It is such an entrenched tradition that generation after generation return here, going so far as to spend their vacation time in the exact same motel or B&B room as their parents or grandparents did.

The area began developing as a resort destination in 1869 when Isaac C. Coffin built the Rhode Island Inn. Within a few years, a group of developers received a land grant, and the Atlantic Hotel—still in operation—was opened in 1875.

The construction of a railroad bridge across the Sinepuxent Bay in 1880 connected the mainland to the resort, which was soon host to more than 5,000 visitors a year. Although Ocean City continued to grow in popularity, the city and surrounding area were struck by a major storm in 1933 that destroyed almost the entire infrastructure and nearly every building and road. The storm cut an inlet into the bay, separating the city from what is now called Assateague Island and creating ideal conditions for commercial and sportfishing. Boats could dock in the quiet waters of the bay but have quick access to the ocean for deep-sea fishing.

A four-lane bridge across the bay was constructed in 1941, and Ocean City has continued to grow in popularity since.

With its 10-mile-long beach, the city has many of the aspects of beach towns farther north, such as a 3-mile boardwalk, amusement parks and arcades next to and close to the beach, and an abundance of saltwater taffy and other goodies stores. Yet its waters are warmer and gentler, like those of the ocean resorts found in South Carolina and Georgia.

The southern end of the boardwalk, with arcades, an amusement park, and many fast-food spots, attracts the most people, while the central portion of the beach and the hotels located there tend to draw a young crowd. Those looking for a family atmosphere on the sand often book motels north of the boardwalk.

Almost everyone who visits Ocean City makes the short drive to Assateague Island to catch a glimpse of the wild ponies made famous by Marguerite Henry's popular series of children's books, beginning with *Misty of Chincoteague* in 1947.

A barrier island, Assateague is the farthest east you can go to take a hike or camp in Maryland. Formed by sand that constant waves have raised from the gently sloping ocean floor, a string of such islands extends along the East Coast from Plum Island, Massachusetts, to Padre Island, Texas. Being prime beachfront property, many have been heavily developed and turned into typical high-rise resort areas.

ADDITIONAL SOURCES OF INFORMATION

A number of publications, such as *Sunny Day Guide to Ocean City*, *Ocean City Visitors Guide*, *Ocean City: Sea for Yourself*, and *Beachcomber*, are available free from the Convention and Visitors Bureau, the welcome center, merchants, and vending boxes on the streets. Not only do they provide up-to-date information on stores, restaurants, events, and points of interest, but some also contain a plethora of coupons that could end up saving you quite a few dollars.

The same thing almost happened to Assateague Island. Having purchased the largest majority of it in Maryland, the Ocean Beach Corporation began subdividing the island into small plots in the 1950s. Within a few years, there was a paved road running down the interior of the island, electric lines had been installed, close to 6,000 plots had been sold, and a number of houses already built.

Then a northeaster that struck the island in March 1962 drove the ocean completely across the island in several places. Almost every house was demolished, the power lines were downed and severed, and the road destroyed, with most of its pavement washed away. Realizing the enormous costs of trying to maintain a modern way of life on the island, private investors began to shy away,

WILD PONIES GRAZE ON ASSATEAGUE ISLAND.

and the federal government was able to establish Assateague Island National Seashore in 1965.

Today the entire island is public land and administered as the national seashore by the U.S. National Park Service, Assateague State Park under the jurisdiction of the Maryland Department of Natural Resources, and, on the Virginia side of the island, Chincoteague National Wildlife Refuge within the auspices of the U.S. Fish and Wildlife Service. What this means to you is that the island's 37-mile beach has been left gloriously undeveloped, with just a few minor amenities, such as couple of campgrounds, visitors centers, and a few nature trails concentrated in two small areas.

COMMUNITIES **Berlin** has retained so much of its small-town look and atmosphere that Hollywood has chosen it as the setting for several movies. Two of the most recent are the Julia Roberts and Richard Gere film *Runaway Bride*, and Disney's 2002 release of *Tuck Everlasting*.

The town dates from a 1677, 300-acre land grant establishing the Burley Plantation. It was not named in honor of the German city; most historians believe the name was derived from a local habit of quickly saying and slurring the name of one of the town's inns, the "Burleigh Inn." Its fortunes were in many ways tied to those of Ocean City, as it slowly prospered by becoming a stopping-over point or an alternate destination for travelers headed to the beach.

Today the Atlantic Hotel, built in the late 1800s, sits in the center of the town's well-preserved historic district. Visitors now come to walk the tree-lined streets, stopping to admire structures dating from America's Federal, Victorian, and 20th-century periods, and look through the hidden treasures to be found in numerous antiques stores.

The town of **Snow Hill** was chartered in 1686, and only 8 years later it was named a Royal Port, reflecting its advantageous location. The Chincoteague Bay and access to the Atlantic Ocean were only 7 miles to the east, while the Chesapeake Bay at Pocomoke Sound was less than 30 miles down the river. Snow Hill retained its prominence long into the 19th century, as the railroad came through the center of town. The town is the seat of government for Worcester County, and many of its old homes

PONY PENNING

One of the most exciting events of the year in this area takes place on the last continuous Wednesday and Thursday of July when Virginia's famous herd of ponies swims across the channel from Assateague Island to Memorial Park on Chincoteague Island in Virginia (call 757-336-6161 for more information). Actually owned by the Chincoteague Volunteer Fire Department, some of the foals are sold at auction, with proceeds aiding firefighting efforts. Legend has long held that the ponies are descendants of mustangs that swam ashore after a Spanish ship wrecked off the coast in the 16th century. More likely, their ancestors were placed on the island by mainland owners wanting to avoid taxation and the expense of fencing.

and other historic structures remain along its tree-shaded streets. The small business district is still located where it always was, close to the river—now a playground for recreational boaters.

Pocomoke City, also located along the Pocomoke River, shares much of the same history as Snow Hill. With deeper water, though, it was able to service much larger ships, which it still does today. The Victorian Costen House helps preserve the town's history, while the 1-mile boardwalked trail in Cypress Park is a great place to enjoy the area's natural habitats.

GUIDANCE The **Ocean City Convention and Visitors Bureau** (410-289-2800; 1-800-OC-OCEAN) operates a large information center adjacent to the Convention Center at 4001 Coastal Hwy., Ocean City.

The **Ocean City Chamber of Commerce** (1-888-OCMD-FUN; www.ocean city.org) has a **welcome center** just a few miles west of the beach on US 50 in West Ocean City.

Exhibits, an aquarium, and brochures about Assateague Island are available at the National Park Service's **Barrier Island Visitor Center** (410-641-1441; 410-641-3030), 7206 National Seashore Lane, Berlin.

The **Worcester County Tourism Office** (410-632-3110; 1-800-852-0335) is located on the corner of Pearl and Market Sts. in Snow Hill.

GETTING THERE *By air:* The **Ocean City Airport** (410-213-2471) is available to private planes, while the **Salisbury/Ocean City Airport** (410-548-4827), which is located about 30 minutes west of the ocean, receives regularly scheduled flights via US Airways (1-800-428-4322).

By car: **US 50** is the route that will bring you into the city from points to the north, west, and south. If possible, plan your arrival for times other than Friday afternoon or evening and Saturday morning, and your departure other than Sunday. Doing so will permit you to avoid miles of bumper-to-bumper cars moving at a snail's pace. **US 113** and **US 13** are the main arteries through Worcester County and provide access to major side routes. US 13 also offers a shorter, less congested travel alternative between Wilmington, Delaware, and Norfolk, Virginia.

By ferry: If coming from New Jersey and other places to the northeast, you can save yourself a number of hours and many miles by taking the **Cape May, New Jersey–Lewes, Deleware, Ferry** (1-800-64-FERRY for schedule and reservations) and driving through Rehoboth Beach to Ocean City.

By bus: **Carolina Trailways** (410-289-9307) has a station at 2nd St. and Philadelphia Ave. in Ocean City.

GETTING AROUND *By car:* Driving (and then parking) at any time during the summer season can be a real aggravation. To save driving into the resort area, you can park your car for free at the **Park and Ride** off US 50 in West Ocean City and take the shuttle bus to the 2nd Street Transit Center in Ocean City for only $1.

If you do drive into the resort area and happen to find a parking space, but don't want to drive anymore, you can ride a bus all the way from the Inlet to the Delaware state line for only $2, all day, 24 hours a day. **Buses** run every 10 minutes from Easter to October, every 30 minutes at other times of the year. Routes include all of the major streets and roadways. Exact change required. Call 410-723-1607 for more information.

By train: The **Boardwalk Train** (410-723-1607), with open-air cars, runs the full length of the 2.9-mile boardwalk throughout the heaviest tourist months. $2.50, one way.

By taxi: **Sunshine Cab** (410-208-2828); **Whites Cab** (410-250-8294); **Ace Taxi** (410-641-4280).

By bus: The local bus service, **Shore Transit** (443-260-2300), has a route that enables you to ride a loop from West Ocean City to Berlin. It is also possible to ride between the three lower shore counties.

PARKING Meters in all municipal lots in Ocean City are in effect 24 hours a day during the main tourist season; those on the street have varying times. No-parking zones are enforced, and businesses can be aggressive in their towing policies.

The Inlet parking lot has a gated time system. You get a ticket when you enter and pay when you leave; no need to worry about feeding the meter. Often fills to capacity early in the day.

PUBLIC RESTROOMS In Ocean City, at the boardwalk at Worcester St.; boardwalk at Caroline St.; 3rd St. and St. Louis Ave. at the Skate Park; boardwalk at 9th St.; boardwalk at 27th St.; and the South Division Street Transit Center.

MEDICAL EMERGENCY *Ocean City:* **10th Street Medical Center** (410-289-6241); **75th Street Medical Center** (410-524-0075); **126th Street Medical Center** (410-250-8000). *Berlin:* **Atlantic General Hospital** (410-641-1100), located at the intersection of US 50 and US 113; available for 24-hour emergency services.

✳ To See

MUSEUMS

Ocean City
⌔ **Ocean City Life Saving Museum** (410-289-4991), boardwalk at the Inlet. Open 7 days a week May 1–Oct. 31; Sat. and Sun., Nov.–Apr. Once a lifesaving station, this museum chronicles the exploits of brave members of the U.S. Life Saving Service and Coast Guard who have saved more than 7,000 lives off the Maryland coast. In addition, there are items from Ocean City history, a whimsical look at bathing-suit styles through the years, several small aquariums, shipwreck items, and, what I found very interesting, over 200 samples of beach sand from around the world. Free kids' programs on the boardwalk during summer.

Wheels of Yesterday (410-213-7329), 12708 Ocean Gateway (US 50). Owner Granville Trimper has been gathering his collection for years and shows about 30 antique cars at a time. One that is always on exhibit is Jack Benny's 1917 Overland. Others on display include the 1904 Oldsmobile used in the 2002 movie *Tuck Everlasting* and one of only 1,200 1962 Corvair pickups manufactured with a side bed entrance.

Newark
Queponco Railway Station (410-632-0950), 8378 Patey Wood Rd. Donations accepted. Open first and third Sat. 1–4, May–Oct. A local group rescued this abandoned passenger station in 1991 and is gradually restoring and outfitting it to look as it did from 1910 to the 1960s.

Snow Hill
Julia A. Purnell Museum (410-632-0515), 201 W. Market St. Small admission charge. Tue.–Sat. 10–4, Apr.–Oct. Ms. Purnell created more than 1,000 needlework pictures during the last 15 years of her 100-year life. The works, most of them depicting the historic homes and buildings of Snow Hill, brought her such worldwide acclaim that she was inducted into the National Hobby Hall of Fame. Since its establishment in 1957, the museum has become a repository not only of her accomplishments but also of many items important to the history of the area. Exhibits include a general store, a tribute to local firefighters, and a display of Native American artifacts. The local museum of my childhood had a pair of dressed fleas that attracted many people from the surrounding area, and I was happy to see that the Purnell Museum also contains a pair, with one of them carrying a parasol! Docents tell me this is the museum's most popular display.

Mt. Zion One Room School Museum (410-632-1265), Ironshire and Church Sts. Small admission charge. Tue.–Sat. 1–4, mid-June through Labor Day. Now moved from its original location, the Mt. Zion school served students from the northern part of the county 1869–1931. Many of the original coat hooks and shelves remain, as well as some of the students' metal lunch pails. Docents provide a short guided tour.

Pocomoke City
Sturgis One Room School Museum (410-957-1913), 209 Willow St. Small admission charge. Wed. and Sat. 1–4, May–Oct. The Sturgis one-room school served Worcester County's African American community 1900–1937. Moved from its original site in the late 1990s, it continues to undergo restoration and outfitting.

THE QUEPONCO RAILWAY STATION

HISTORIC HOMES Calvin B. Taylor House (410-641-1019), N. Main and Baker Sts., Berlin. Donations accepted. Mon., Wed., Fri., and Sat. 1–4, Memorial Day weekend through October. Like so many historic buildings in America, the Taylor House, built around 1832, was slated to be

torn down to make way for a parking lot. Rescued from destruction by the Berlin Heritage Foundation, it opened to the public as a museum in 1983. Guided tours take visitors throughout the period-decorated house and focus on its two most prominent occupants. The Harrison family operated the country's largest mail-order nursery business, shipping seedlings from their fruit trees to destinations the world over. In 1890, Calvin B. Taylor established the bank bearing his name, which is still in business. His bank desk and chair are on display along with other items from the town's history. Most impressive are the original flooring and 1830s quilts in the upstairs bedroom, and the portico's butterfly modillions atop the fluted columns.

Costen House (410-957-3110), 206 Market St., Pocomoke City. Small admission charge. Wed. and Sat. 1–4, May–Oct. Dr. Costen was known throughout the Eastern Shore for his courageous works and travels to treat victims of typhoid fever. Built around 1870, his home now helps present the life of a small town and of the doctor and his family. The Hall-Walton Garden on the property recreates a landscape similar to that of the doctor's days.

HISTORIC SITES Furnace Town (410-632-2032), Furnace Town Rd., Snow Hill. Small admission fee. Open 7 days a week 11–5, Apr. 1–Oct. 31. Off-season the grounds and trails are open for walking during daylight hours. The smelting of iron during the 1800s was a labor-intensive process that required an entire village to support just one furnace. Through living-history demonstrations and reconstructed buildings, those days are brought back. Visit the old furnace, observe the blacksmith at work, or stand on the pulpit of the church and preach a sermon. The broom maker explained to me what a niddy-noddy is; be sure to find out for yourself. The easy, 1-mile Paul Leiffer Nature Trail wanders through the Nassawango Cypress Swamp.

1872 RULES FOR TEACHERS

- Each teacher will bring a bucket of water and a scuttle of coal for the day's session.
- Men teachers may take one evening each week for courting purposes, or two evenings a week if they go to church regularly.
- Women teachers who marry or engage in unseemly conduct will be dismissed.
- Any teacher who smokes, uses liquor in any form, frequents pool or public halls, or gets shaved in a barber shop will give good reason to suspect his worth, intention, integrity and honesty.
- The teacher who performs his labor faithfully and without fault for five years will be given an increase of 25 cents per week in his pay, providing the Board of Education approves.

—from the Worcester County one-room schoolhouses

FURNACE TOWN

HISTORIC CHURCHES

Snow Hill

The **Gothic Revival Makemie United Presbyterian Church** (Market and Washington Sts.) was built in 1890 and serves a congregation that can trace its origin to the end of the 1600s.

There are both Gothic and Victorian aspects to the **All Hallows Church** (Market and Church Sts.), built around 1750. The purple and yellow panes in the roundheaded windows were added near the turn of the 20th century. Take a step inside to see the 1701 Bible printed in London and given to the congregation by Queen Anne.

✳ To Do

AIR RIDES

Ocean City

🖋 **Island Parasail** (410-289-2896), 1st St. and the bay. Certainly not cheap, but a thrill nonetheless, Island Parasail has single and tandem flights for kids and adults. It is Ocean City's original parasail company and has completed over 100,000 flights with a perfect safety record while providing a different perspective on the ocean and the beach.

🖋 **O.C. Parasail** (410-723-1464), 54th St. or Talbot St. Pier. O.C. Parasail also has a perfect safety record.

🖋 **Bay Sports Unlimited** (410-289-2144), 22nd St. and the bay. Bay Sports offers single, tandem, and triple parasail rides. Waverunners are also rented.

Cloud Dancer (410-641-2484), Ocean City Airport. Two-passenger open-cockpit flights over the area in a vintage biplane.

Ocean City Sky Tours (410-289-TOUR; www.ocean-city.com/ocskytours), Ocean City Airport. Day, sunset, and night flights.

ARCADES, AMUSEMENT AND WATER PARKS, GO-CARTS

Ocean City

🖋 **Jolly Roger Amusement Park** (410-289-4902), 30th St. and Coastal Hwy. The city's largest amusement park with the Sky Coaster, Giant Ferris Wheel, and Titanic Slide.

🖋 **Splash Mountain** (410-289-6962), 30th St. and Coastal Hwy. Ten waterslides, a lazy river, and a sea-creature walk. Adjacent to Jolly Roger (see above).

🖋 **65th St. Slide and Ride** (410-524-5270), 65th St. and the bay. In addition to three waterslides, this place has several rides for young children.

Speed World (410-289-6088), 30th St. and Coastal Hwy. Go-carts of every imaginable shape, such as Indy racers, LeMans, midget racers, family tracks, and even a speedboat course. Adjacent to Jolly Roger (see above).

Trimper's Rides (410-289-8617), between S. Division and S. 1st Sts., on the boardwalk. Fans of old carousels will love this amusement park with its 1902 Herschel-Spellman carousel. In continuous operation since its 1912 installation, its hand-carved horses, camels, roosters, tigers, zebras, and more have been maintained in excellent condition. Trimper's is the center of activity on the southern end of the boardwalk in the evening.

BICYCLING

Ocean City

Bicycle riding is permitted on Ocean City's **boardwalk**, but hours vary greatly according to the season, so check the posted signs.

Atlantic Bike Company (410-289-3305), 8th St. and the boardwalk. Bicycle and pedal-surrey rentals.

Jo's Bikes (410-289-4298), 2nd St. and the boardwalk. Rents wheelchairs and strollers in addition to bicycles.

Mike's Bikes (410-289-5404), N. Division and Baltimore Ave., and N. 1st St. and the boardwalk (410-289-4637). Open all year for bike rentals, sales, and service.

The **ViewTrail 100 Bike Trail** follows a circular path along country roads, through farms, woodlands, cypress swamps, and small towns for more than 100 miles in Worcester County. Numerous restaurants, historic sites, and accommodations along the way. See *Guidance* for places to obtain the trail brochure.

THE 1902 HERSCHEL-SPELLMAN CAROUSEL AT TRIMPER'S RIDES

Ocean City
OC Rocket (410-289-3500; www.talbotstreetpier.com/boatrides), Talbot St. Pier. A ride, at times up to 40 miles an hour, on this boat should be able to satisfy anyone's need for speed in the ocean. The 50-minute trip passes through the Inlet and goes along the beach almost to the Delaware state line. Hold on to your seat when you bounce across the waves! YeeHah! Be sure to ask for the discounted price.

✐ Located at the same pier as the *OC Rocket*, and owned by the same company, the **Assateague Adventure** is an easy pontoon-boat ride/nature tour. The boat glides into the Ocean City Fishing Center and along Sinepuxent Bay, and lands on Assateague Island. In addition to possibly seeing the wild ponies and hand-net dipping for crabs and clams, you'll hear naturalists narrate tidbits about island migration, saltwater marshes, sea lettuce, and more. Adults may wish for more depth of information, but it's a good introduction to the local environment.

Sea Rocket (410-289-5887), end of Dorchester St., bayside. Claiming to be the world's largest speedboat, the *Sea Rocket* competes with the *OC Rocket* for customers. It is the one with the large rooster-tail wake.

✐ The **Assateague Island Explorer**, operated by the owners of the *Sea Rocket*, provides trips much like those of the *Assateague Adventure* (see above).

✐ **Sport Crabber** (410-289-7438; www.sportcrabber), Bahia Marina between 21st and 22nd Sts. and the bay. Captain Bill and his crew entertain with genial banter as passengers drop lines baited with chicken necks in the hope of attracting a blue crab or two. Although you don't keep the catch, this is an entertaining (and educational) cruise, especially for younger family members.

BOAT RENTALS

Ocean City
Bahia Marina (410-289-7438), between 21st and 22nd Sts. and the bay. Pontoon and skiff rentals.

Sailing Etc. (410-723-1144), 48th St. and the bay. Sailboats, Windsurfers, and kayaks for rent.

HAND-NET DIPPING FOR CRABS AND CLAMS OFF ASSATEAGUE ISLAND

Bayside Boat Rentals (410-524-1948), 54th St. and the bay. Pontoon boats.

FAMILY ACTIVITIES

Ocean City
✐ **Pirate Adventures on the *Sea Gypsy*** (302-539-5155), at Harpoon Hanna's, 142nd St. in North Ocean City. Young kids really enjoy this cruise on a pirate ship in search of sunken treasure. The crew is in cos-

"WHAT'S THAT?"

The boats with the tall booms and apparatuses that you see in the Ocean City Harbor dredge for clams in the waters around the resort area. Most of the catch is sent to Texas, where Campbell's Soup turns it into canned clam chowder.

CLAM-DREDGING BOATS IN OCEAN CITY HARBOR

tume, the kids get their faces painted, cannons are fired, the boat is attacked, and everyone gets to take home a share of the loot.

✧ ♿ **Frontier Town Western Theme Park** (410-289-7877; www.frontier town.com), 3.5 miles south of US 50 on MD 611. Open 10–6; gate closes at 4:30. When my wife told me how much fun she had as a child coming here in the 1960s, my thought was that the children of today would look upon the theme park as a hokey bore. How wrong I was. Kids up to 12 years old were cheering on the good guy in the Gunfight at the OK Corral, joining in the (authentic) Native American dances, and hooting and hollering at the villain in the Trial of Lopez. The constructed frontier town houses gift shops, a western saloon complete with a cancan show, and stagecoach, steam-train, and pony rides. Separate fees provide access to the Frontier Town Water Park and Frontier Town Campground.

FISHING

Ocean City

Headboats (first-come, first-served) and charter boats (reserved ahead of time) leave almost daily from nearly every marina in the Ocean City area. Most provide or rent the necessary equipment.

Ocean City Fishing Center (410-213-1121), West Ocean City. Just off US 50 on the mainland, the center claims to have the largest charter fleet in Ocean City.

Judith M (410-289-7438), Bahia Marina between 21st and 22nd Sts. Possibly the most recognized headboat around Ocean City, the *Judith M* goes on deep-sea fishing trips twice a day during summer. In the evening she provides narrated 90-minute oceanfront cruises.

Bay Bee (410-213-0158; 1-800-322-3065), US 50 and Shantytown Rd., West Ocean City. In search of sea bass, flounder, trout, snapper, blues, and croaker, the *Bay Bee* runs half-day trips.

Snow Hill

Captain Bruce Wooten (410-632-1431), 6661 Snow Hill Rd. Captain Bruce, a licensed guide, specializes in bass fishing on the Pocomoke, Wicomico, Nanticoke, and Choptank Rivers. There are only one or two anglers on each 8-hour trip, so you will have the river and instruction, if needed, to yourself. Offered year-round.

GOLF

Berlin

The Bay Club (410-641-4081; 1-800-BAY-CLUB; www.thebayclub.com), 9122 Libertytown Rd. 36 holes. The course at Bay Club East is one of the area's newest 18-hole courses. The Bay Club West course has been lauded by the *Washington Times*.

Eagle's Landing (410-213-7277; 1-800-2TEE-TIME), 12367 Eagle's Landing Rd. Dr. Michael Hurdzan designed Ocean City's municipal 18-hole course with a par 72 and a length of 6,163 feet. The first certified Audubon sanctuary in Maryland; *Golf Digest* magazine rated it one of the state's top 10 courses.

Ocean City Golf Club (410-641-1779; 1-800-442-3570), 11401 Country Club Dr. Two courses, one seaside and the other with marshes along Newport Bay.

GOLF VACATIONS

Ocean City has become a golfer's destination, with more than a dozen courses nearby. Contact Ocean City Golf Getaway (410-213-7050; 1-800-462-4653; www.oceancitygolf.com), 9935 Stephen Decatur Hwy., Unit 141, Ocean City, 21842, to help you decide which ones to play—and to arrange special package deals with hotels and restaurants. Ocean City Golf Groups (1-888-465-3477; www.ocgolfgroups.com), 2200 Baltimore Ave., Ocean City, 21842, provides the same type of service.

The Beach Club Golf Links (410-641-GOLF; 1-800-435-9223), 9715 Deer Park Dr. Two 18-hole semiprivate championship courses with inner links of 7,000 yards and outer links of 6,600 yards. Open year-round; tee times recommended.

River Run (410-641-7200; 1-800-733-RRUN; www.riverrungolf.com), 11605
Masters Lane. On this Gary Player Signature Course, the first nine holes bring
to mind Scottish links, while the last nine are set among natural marshes.

Rum Point Seaside Golf Links (410-629-1414; 1-888-809-4653; www.rum
pointe.com), 7000 Rum Pointe Lane. This par-72 course, designed by Pete and
P. B. Dye, overlooks Sinepuxent Bay and Assateague Island.

Bishopville

The Links at Lighthouse Sound (410-352-5767; 1-888-55-HILLS; www
.lighthousesound.com), 12723 St. Martin's Neck Rd. One of the closest courses
to Ocean City, it has views of the resort area's skyline. Par 72 with a 73.3 rating.

MINIATURE GOLF

Ocean City

✍ **Lost Galaxy Golf** (410-524-4FUN; www.planetmaze.com), 33rd St. and
Coastal Hwy. Miniature golf with an outer-space theme featuring spaceships,
meteors, fire, and fog. Laser tag and the largest indoor maze in Maryland are
also at this location.

✍ **Old Pro Golf** (410-524-2645, main phone number; www.oldprogolf.com).
Old Pro has eight miniature-golf courses throughout the city. People appeared to
have the most fun at the Lost Civilization theme at 23rd St. and at the new
indoor Under Sea course at 68th St.

✍ **Lost Treasure Golf** (410-250-5678), 140th St. and Coastal Hwy. Caves,
waterfalls, and ancient ruins.

KAYAKING AND CANOEING Several inns and B&Bs have banded together to
form the **Inn-to-Inn Canoe Trail** along the Pocomoke River. Tours are 3 or 5
days long, and everything is included: canoes, shuttles, three meals a day, and
evening accommodations. All you have to do is paddle leisurely along the river
enjoying the scenery and wildlife, knowing that soft beds await you. I can't imagine a better way to get to know the interior lands of the Eastern Shore. The
River House Inn (410-632-2722; www.riverhouse.com), 210 E. Market St.,
Snow Hill, makes the arrangements. Tours begin at $600 for two people.

Pocomoke River Canoe Co. (410-632-3971), 312 N. Washington St., Ocean
City, not only provides livery service for the inn-to-inn trips, but also provides
shuttle service and rents canoes and kayaks for those wanting to explore the river
on their own.

KITEBOARDING **Kite Loft** (410-289-6852; 1-800-682-5483; www.kiteloft.com),
511 Boardwalk. In addition to selling all manner of kites, the Kite Loft can teach
you how to strap your feet on to a board, hang on to a giant kite, and go zipping
across ocean water at amazing speeds. Gain experience and you can launch yourself 30 feet upward while doing intricate aerial acrobatics.

Ocean City

Action Watersports, Ltd. (410-524-4769; www.actionwatersportsltd.com), 106 52nd St.

Island Jet Ski (410-289-2896), 1st St. and the bay.

Odyssea Watersports (410-723-4227), 50th St. and Coastal Hwy.

Inlet Sea-Doos (410-289-1488), on the Inlet.

SKATING Roller skating is permitted on the boardwalk in Ocean City, but hours vary greatly according to the season, so check the posted signs. Be aware that skateboards and scooters are prohibited at all times.

Alfred Memorial Park (410-250-0125), 3rd St., Ocean City. Within this city park is the Ocean Bowl Skate Park, open to skateboarders and in-line skaters. Facilities include a bowl, a half-pipe, ramps, and a concrete streets area.

TENNIS Public courts are located at 3rd St. and the bay; 61st St. bayside; 94th St.; and 136th St. in Ocean City.

WALKING TOURS Ocean City. A walking-tour brochure describing some of the older structures and sites along the southern end of the Ocean City boardwalk is available from the Convention and Visitors Bureau. It's nice to learn the stories behind the Violets Are Blue House, the Tarry-A-While, and St. Mary's of the Sea Catholic Church.

Berlin. The **Historic District of Berlin** contains structures from the 1790s to the early 20th century, and a walking-tour brochure available in the town offices (10 William St.) will direct you to the most historically and architecturally significant. Be sure to seek out the **Burley House** and its narrow brick chimneys atop a steep gable roof.

Snow Hill. The *Snow Hill Walking Tour* brochure points out more than 50 historically or architecturally important structures within the town limits. Available from the Worcester County Tourism Office.

✳ Green Space

BEACHES All 10 miles of the **Ocean City** beach are free and open to the public 6 AM–10 PM. Beach Patrol members are on duty 10 AM–5:30 PM.

&. Access points to the beach for the physically challenged are identified by blue signs along Coastal Hwy.

There are patrolled beaches in both the state park and national seashore on **Assateague Island** that are much less crowded than those in Ocean City. If you want a primitive beach experience, just walk a few hundred yards away from these designated areas and there is a good possibility of having the sand and surf all to yourself.

A small strip of beach in the settlement of **Public Landing** is open to the general public, yet very few people ever take advantage of it.

PARKS Northside Park, 125th St. and the bay, Ocean City. The park's 58 acres situated at the northern end of town on the bayside enable you to escape the noise and congestion of the rest of the resort area.

Pocomoke River State Park (410-632-2566), 461 Worcester Hwy., Snow Hill. Canoeing, swimming, hiking, fishing, and two campgrounds.

WALKS Herring Creek Nature Trail (410-632-2144), Keyset Point Rd., West Ocean City. An easy-to-get-to escape from the resort area. The 1-mile loop trail passes by a pond and creek, through forested wetlands, and onto a small pine island with picnic tables.

Assateague Island. Within **Assateague State Park** and **Assateague Island National Seashore** are miles of unspoiled beaches on which to walk. Three short interpretive trails—Life of the Dunes, Life of the Marsh, and Life of the Forest—are close to the National Seashore Campground. Those wanting a longer hike should consult *50 Hikes in Maryland* (Countryman Press), which describes a 2-day backpacking trip along the beach.

HIKING  About a 30-mile drive from Ocean City, the 1-mile circuit **Bald Cypress Nature Trail** in the Milburn Landing area of **Pocomoke River State Park** is the place to take the kids after they have had enough of sun, surf, and sand and are badgering you about what to do next. The easy walk takes you by a few small swamps and underneath dozens of bald cypress trees, oddities within the world of trees. They are coniferous, meaning they develop cones like pines, firs, and hemlocks—all trees with evergreen needles. Yet while they may look like needles, the leaves of the bald cypress drop off as the weather turns colder, just as those on deciduous trees do. In addition, even though it is called a cypress, the bald cypress is actually a member of the redwood family. It is also a tree more common to the swamps of the South, just barely able to survive here at its very northern limits on the Eastern Shore.

PONIES SHARE THE BEACH WITH SUNBATHERS ON ASSATEAGUE ISLAND.

✴ Lodging

MOTELS AND HOTELS

Ocean City, 21842

Atlantic Hotel (410-289-9111; 1-800-3-ATLANTIC; www.atlantichotel ocmd.com), Wicomico St. and the boardwalk. There are no swimming pools, Jacuzzis, fitness rooms, or private balconies here. If you can accept this, you will enjoy staying in one of the oldest hotels in Ocean City with its sundeck overlooking the beach, six-over-six sash windows, and historic lobby. Do not come here looking for opulence, but do take advantage of the low rates. Owned by the same family since 1922. $140.

&. **Crystal Beach Hotel** (410-289-7165; 1-866-232-2421; www.crystal beachhotel.com), 25th St. and the boardwalk. All rooms are efficiencies and have private balconies—some with a side view, some with ocean view. It's your vacation, so spend the few extra dollars and enjoy an ocean-view room. $239–269.

&. **Dunes Manor Hotel** (410-289-1100; 1-800-523-2888; www.dunes manor.com), 2800 Baltimore Ave. The only hotel in the city with all its rooms facing the ocean. Invoking the grandeur of 19th-century seaside resorts, the Dunes Manor is furnished with antiques and decorated in a Victorian theme. The suites are exceptionally large. Without being pretentious, everything in the hotel is done with a touch of class. Only one block north of the boardwalk. Indoor/outdoor pool. $229–375. See *Dining Out* for the hotel's restaurant, the Victorian Room.

✿ &. **Dunes Motel** (410-289-4414), 2700 Baltimore Ave. Owned by the same people as Dunes Manor, this is my sister's family's choice when they come to Ocean City. It is reasonably priced and caters to families (Disney Channel on TV and a kids' wading pool). It is on the very north end of the boardwalk, which does not have the commercial activity and crowds found on the southern end. Ocean view, pool view, and efficiencies available. $149–299.

✿ &. **Holiday Inn Hotel and Suites** (1-866-627-8483; www.ocsuites.com),

PEOPLE-WATCHING ALONG THE OCEAN CITY BOARDWALK

1701 Atlantic Ave. An all-luxury-suite hotel directly on the ocean with Jacuzzi tubs and private balconies. Two elevated swimming pools overlooking the beach and a children's activity pool. $359–369.

🏄 ♿ **Holiday Inn Oceanfront** (410-524-1600; 1-800-837-3588; www.ocmdhotels.com/holidayinn), 6600 Coastal Hwy. Indoor/outdoor pools with baby pools. Oceanfront, ocean-view, and garden-view rooms and suites. Free children's summertime activities. $150–310. See *Dining Out* for Reflections, the hotel's restaurant.

♿ **Princess Royale Oceanfront Hotel** (410-524-7777; 1-800-4-ROYALE; www.princessroyale.com), 9100 Coastal Hwy. One of the city's newer all-suite facilities. Oceanfront, ocean-view, and one- to three-room suites overlooking the Olympic-sized pool and atrium are available. Guests can have food delivered to them on the beach, and the kids can have fun playing rooftop miniature golf. $149–319.

INNS

Ocean City, 21842
♿ **Lighthouse Club Hotel** (410-524-5400; 1-888-371-5400; www.fagers.com), 56th St. On-The-Bay. The custom-made Lawrence Peabody furniture and water views give this lighthouse-shaped inn the feel of a Caribbean resort. Certainly one of the most luxurious and romantic spots in Ocean City, with a balcony, marble bath, whirlpool Jacuzzi, terry robes, and refrigerator in each suite. Even if you don't get a bay-view room, you can still enjoy a view of herons, geese, and ducks wandering around the inland marsh. To keep up with its growing clientele, the management

opened **The Edge at the Lighthouse**, a hotel next door with the same amenities. All of this is part of the Fager's Island Restaurant/Lighthouse Club Hotel complex (see *Dining Out*). $245–295 includes continental breakfast.

Berlin, 21811
Atlantic Hotel (410-641-3589; 1-800-814-7672; www.atlantichotel.com), 2 N. Main St. The Atlantic Hotel was built in 1895 and has been faithfully maintained with its Victorian features. The impressive staircase adds a bit of grandeur to the small entranceway. Each of the 16 rooms is furnished with antiques and period pieces. I liked watching Berlin's life unfold from the windows of my second-floor front room, while another visit in one of the back rooms was a quiet one removed from the bustle of Main Street. Private bath, air-conditioning, television, and phone are in each room; deluxe rooms can accommodate up to five people. $115–180. Continental breakfast included. See *Dining Out* for the hotel's restaurant.

Snow Hill, 21863
🐾 🏄 ♿ **River House Inn** (410-632-2722; www.riverhouse.com), 210 E. Market St. Larry and Susanne Knudsen have been such successful innkeepers that they have added more buildings on their riverfront property just to keep up with guests'

demands. The East and West Rooms in the 1860 Gothic Revival house are large and bright, and a screened-in porch overlooks the lawn, which slopes downs to the Pocomoke River. The 1834 cottage houses two suites, while the private accommodations in the 1890 Carriage Barn include a whirlpool tub. My favorite spot is the upstairs suite in the Riverview Hideaways. Not only can you enjoy the river from the 28-foot-long porch, but when you retire at night, the clouds painted on the bedroom ceiling provide a serene atmosphere to lull you to sleep. Furnishings in the older structures fit the period, while the decor of newer rooms is modern. The inn is a member of the Inn-to-Inn Canoe Trail (see *To Do*); canoes and kayaks are available for rent, and guests have free use of bicycles. Children and pets are welcome. All rooms have air-conditioning and private bath. $250.

BED & BREAKFASTS

Ocean City, 21842

🐾 **Atlantic House B&B** (410-289-2333; www.atlantichouse.com), 510 N. Baltimore Ave. The front porch with an ocean view, a homestyle breakfast buffet, and outdoor hot tub are all compelling reasons to stay in the 1920s Victorian home. It is one of the most convenient and lower-cost places to stay right on the boardwalk. The oceanside rooms let you watch the sunrise, while the bayside rooms catch the sunset's glow. $110–225.

Inn on the Ocean (410-289-8894; 1-877-466-6662; www.innontheocean .com), 1001 Atlantic Ave. The city's only other B&B is also located on the boardwalk. All six rooms have private bath, TV, VCR, and air-conditioning.

The Veranda Room opens directly onto the wraparound porch (where breakfast is often served), while my favorite, the Oceana Room, has a private balcony overlooking the ocean. Bicycles, beach equipment, and afternoon refreshments are complimentary. $230–325.

Berlin, 21811

🦢 **Holland House B&B** (410-641-1956; www.hollandhousebandb.com), 5 Bay St. Jan and Jim Quick have been operating their B&B for well over a decade and have its operation down to a T. They both have outside jobs, but you would never know it. One or the other will serve you breakfast, and it seems that they are always around when a guest has a question. (They are a great repository of knowledge on where to eat or what to do in the area.) The Holland House was a doctor's residence at the turn of the 20th century, and the size of the rooms and the decor reflect the physician's middle-income status. Many guests enjoy coffee and the morning paper on the front porch. An outside shower enables you to wash off beach sand before dressing for dinner. Children are welcome, which adds to the family atmosphere. $90–125.

Snow Hill, 21863

Chanceford Hall (410-632-2900; www.chancefordhall.com), 209 W. Federal St. The gardens with the second oldest black walnut tree in Maryland, weeping cherry trees, magnolias, boxwoods, and hollies, along with the lap pool, make Chanceford Hall's backyard a visually pleasing yet relaxing place to read a selection from the B&B's extensive library. Host Alice Kesterson works in the publishing industry, so she is constantly adding new books to the collection. Her hus-

band, Randy, is often the one to prepare the large gourmet breakfasts.
Not only are they great conversation-
alists, but Alice and Randy also possess a great knowledge of area history
and attractions. Rooms in the 18th-
century manor house, built by the
family of Robert Morris, financier of
the American Revolution, are spacious and furnished with antiques.
The luxurious feel of a pima cotton
robe and 230-count sheets on the
poster beds made me look forward to
the end of the day. All 10 of the fireplaces are in working condition, so
there is no doubt that you will be
comfortable as you wander through
the house appreciating the elaborate
crown moldings, chair rails, paneled
doors (with the original hardware),
and wide-planked wood floors. Bicycles are free for guests' use. $150.

The Mansion House (410-632-389;
www.mansionhousebnb.com), 4436
Bayside Rd., Public Landing. There
are two things I remember about the
Mansion House: sunrise bathing the
entire house, with its golden glow
reflected off the waters of Chincoteague Bay, and an abundance of fireplaces. Not only does each guest
room have a working fireplace, but
there are also fireplaces on each end
of the living room. The 1800s building
has lots of common space, including a
swing on the upstairs porch, in which
to relax after a swim in the bay or a
walk along the beach. $140–160.

VACATION RENTALS If you plan to
spend a week or more in Ocean City,
you will probably save quite a few
dollars by renting a cottage, house,
or condominium. Among the agencies handling these properties are
O'Conor, Piper and Flyn (1-800-

633-1000), **Ocean City Weekly
Rentals** (1-800-851-8909), and **Coldwell Banker** (1-800-289-2821).

CAMPING

Ocean City, 21842

🐾 **Ocean City Campground** (410-
524-7601; www.occamping.com),
105 70th St. The only campground
in Ocean City is open year-round
(limited winter facilities) and has 200
sites, a laundry, and a small playground.

🐾 🦴 **Frontier Town** (410-641-0880;
1-800-228-5590; www.frontiertown
.com), on MD 611 south of Ocean
City. Only a 10-minute drive from
Ocean City, this 500-site campground
is part of the Frontier Town Western
Theme Park complex. There are tons
of activities for the kids, a free shuttle
to the beach, free access to the large
waterslide park, a choice of primitive
or deluxe sites, and even some trailers
and cabins for rent. The cost of the
primitive sites is a bargain given all
the extras guests are entitled to.

Whaleyville, 21872

🐾 🦴 **Fort Whaley Campground**
(410-641-9785; www.fortwhaley.com),
11224 Dale Rd. A companion campground to Frontier Town (see above),
it has primitive and deluxe sites. Free
admission to the miniature-golf
course and Frontier Town's Water
Park.

Berlin, 21811—Assateague Island

Assateague State Park (410-641-
2120; 1-888-432-2267), 7307 Stephen
Decatur Hwy. Apr. 1–Oct. 31. More
than 300 sites are situated among the
sand dunes; almost 40 have hookups.
Bathhouse and concession building.

**Assateague Island National
Seashore** (410-641-3030), 7206

National Seashore Lane. The National Park Service operates two campgrounds—one near the ocean, the other next to the bay—that offer more of a rustic experience than the other sites listed here. There are no hookups and only chemical toilets and cold showers. Some sites are open year-round. Primitive backcountry sites are available to those willing to walk anywhere from 4 to 11 miles. *50 Hikes in Maryland* (Countryman Press) describes the hike in detail.

Snow Hill, 21863

Pocomoke River State Park (410-632-2566), 461 Worcester Hwy. The **Shad Landing Campground** (off US 113) has a swimming pool, marina, camp store, hookups, a dump station, and a playground.

✿ Also within the park, the **Milburn Landing Campground** (off MD 364) is a bit more primitive, but it does permit pets.

✳ Where to Eat

DINING OUT

Ocean City

🍴 ♿ **Fager's Island Restaurant** (410-524-5500; www.fagers.com), 60th St. on the bay. Open every day, all year, Fager's brings daylight hours to a close with the 1812 Overture. The music starts about 5 minutes before sunset and ends at the exact moment the sun drops out of view. Meals, either indoors or on the deck, can start with corn and crab fritters ($9) with vodka cocktail sauce and basil pesto aioli, progress to bronzed salmon ($24) or prime rib with shaved horseradish ($34), and end with an Italian coffee (amaretto, Galliano, and whipped cream, topped with blue curaçao; $5.50). Fager's is

part of the Lighthouse Club Hotel complex.

♿ **Fresco's** (410-524-8202; www.ocfrescos.com), 8203 Coastal Hwy. Native Italian Pino Frachetti opened this place in 2001 after cooking for more than 20 years in other people's Ocean City restaurants. The variety at lunch is limited, but the quality of the evening entrées makes this the resort town's obvious choice for Italian food. Forget the usual spaghetti and meatballs or lasagna; think more along the lines of penne with crabmeat ($17.95) or chicken Piccata ($17.95). The linguine Portofino (clams, mussels, calamari, scallops, and catch of the day in a red broth sauce served over linguine; $23.95) is one of the signature dishes, while the veal and lobster tail sautéed with shallots and wild mushrooms, deglazed with champagne, and finished with butter and cream ($29.95) is an exceedingly rich indulgence. Sunsets over the bay cast a reddish glow through the restaurant's picture windows. Fresco's was endorsed by a fellow B&B guest, a visitor from Florence, Italy, no less.

Galaxy Bar and Grill (410-723-6762; www.ocgalaxy.com), 6601 Coastal Hwy. Ocean City native John Trader operated his wine shop, Liquid Assets, for more than a decade before opening the Galaxy, and its extensive wine list, ranging from $4 glasses to $550 bottles, reflects his knowledge of the vintner's craft. Yet everything is right on the mark here—not only the freshly inventive dishes, but everything from the mosaic floor in the dining area to the appealing decor in the restrooms. John and his staff collaborate to create items such as melon gazpacho; herbed mushroom pancakes served with goat cheese and vanilla balsamic glazed greens; and mustard seed and jack cheese encrusted catfish. The menu is ever-evolving. Leave room for the raspberry cheesecake set in a raspberry crème fraîche ($9). Lunch items $11–14; dinner entrées $20–40. Currently my favorite Ocean City restaurant; it takes on a nightclub atmosphere late at night.

✦ **Harrison's Harbor Watch** (410-289-5121), South Boardwalk overlooking the Ocean City Inlet. The pleasant view of the Inlet and Assateague Island complements the seafood dishes that are prepared fresh daily. Also on the menu are homemade pastas, breads, and muffins. Has one of the area's most outstanding raw bars. $15–39.

✦ **The Hobbit Restaurant** (410-524-8100), 81st St. and the bay. The Hobbit has been under the same ownership and management since it opened in 1977, decades before the 2001 *Lord of the Rings* movie was even thought about. With a few figurines and paintings depicting characters from J. R. R. Tolkien's fantasy masterpiece decorating the walls, it is a favorite of Newt Gingrich and other Baltimore and Washington, DC, politicos and celebrities. Casual fare in the café, such as the Hobbit burger or chicken sandwich, is $7.95–13.95, while the more formal menu in the dining room has items like roast duckling or prime rib up to $31.95.

✦ **Mario's** (410-289-9445), 22nd St. and Philadelphia Ave. Dinner only. Restaurants come and go, but Mario's has been serving Ocean City since 1954. All meats are cut on the premises. Traditional Italian cooking making use of local seafoods. $9.95–30.99.

✦ **Reflections** (410-524-5252), 67th St. oceanfront. One of the most upscale and formal dining experiences in the city. The small fountain and low, golden lighting make it a place couples come to for a romantic setting. The ever-changing Continental menu has tableside flambé cooking, along with variations on seafood, pasta, and steak from $23 to $35. My early-bird special (5–6 PM) filet mignon ($13.95) was charbroiled to my liking and covered with bordelaise sauce. Inside the Holiday Inn.

✦ **Victorian Room** (410-289-1100; www.dunesmanor.com), 28th St. and the oceanfront. Located in the Dunes Manor Hotel. American cuisine with items from the sea and the land. $13.95–21.95.

Berlin
Atlantic Hotel (410-641-3589; 1-800-814-7672; www.atlantichotel .com), 2 N. Main St. Reservations are strongly suggested. The Atlantic is a winner of the *Wine Spectator* Award of Excellence. Its formal dining decor and the fresh ingredients in the seafood and beef dishes keep locals coming back whenever they have a special occasion to celebrate. The rockers on the front porch are a nice place to let things settle and digest. $26–32. Across the hall in the hotel is the **Drummer's Café**, with a more casual atmosphere and a lighter menu of soups, sandwiches, and some entrées. $6–15. Open for lunch and dinner.

Snow Hill
Tavern on Green Street (410-632-5451; www.tavernongreenstreet.com), 208 W. Green St. I placed Tavern on Green under the *Dining Out* heading because dinners are sumptuous affairs of veal Marsala ($18.95), filet mignon and crabcake ($21.95), or sautéed

scallops ($17.95). However, do not overlook this place for lunch; the menu at that time is more casual and lower in price. If you are a longtime visitor to the area and were disappointed when Jim Washington closed the well-respected Snow Hill Inn, you will be happy to know that this is his newest culinary endeavor.

EATING OUT

Ocean City

 **Angler Restaurant** (410-289-7924), Talbot St. and the bay. Breakfast, lunch, and dinner. The Angler gives a free coastline cruise with every evening meal. You are going to eat dinner anyway, so why not take them up on the offer? The daily catch (market price) can be prepared blackened, amandine, island-style, or several other ways. There are 10 early-bird entrées under $12. Dinner entrées $14–28.

Atlantic Stand Diner (410-289-7203; www.atlanticstand.com), Wicomico St. and the boardwalk. With some dishes less than $3.50, Atlantic has some of the lowest-cost

breakfasts, lunches, and take-out food in the city. The most expensive item is a jumbo lump crabcake for less than $9. In the same location since 1933.

The Bayside Skillet (410-524-7950; www.baysideskillet.com), 77th St. and the bay. The place for out-of-the-ordinary breakfasts. Choose a hot fudge sundae or peach melba crêpe, a seafood frittata (crab, shrimp, and scallops with marinara sauce), or pan-fried potatoes sautéed with bacon, onions, mushrooms, and cheddar cheese. The four-egg omelets are so large that the management recommends sharing (at no extra charge!). I ate about two-thirds of my Spanish omelet and did not eat again until late in the evening. Expect to spend $6–9 at this place, which is easily recognized by its bright pink exterior and lines of people waiting to get in from early morning on. Lunch and dinner are also served.

The Dough Roller. There are five locations in Ocean City: S. Division St. and the boardwalk (410-289-3501); 3rd St. and the boardwalk (410-289-

TALBOT STREET PIER IN OCEAN CITY

2599); 41st St. and Coastal Hwy. (410-524-9254); 70th St. and Coastal Hwy. (410-524-7981); 125th and Coastal Hwy. (410-250-5664). My sister, by far one of the most severe of pizza critics, says Dough Rollers is the best "fast-food pizza" in the city. Eat in or pick up only; no deliveries.

✍ ⌖ **Phillips Crab House and Seafood Festival Buffet** (410-289-6821; www.phillipsfoods.com), 21st St. and Philadelphia Ave. It seems that every ocean resort area in America now has the obligatory all-you-can-eat seafood buffet restaurants, and Ocean City is no exception. With decades of knowledge in the commercial fishing industry, Phillips is the best of the lot, and is one of the few still offering steamed crabs on the buffet. Arrive around 4 PM to save a couple of dollars on the $29 charge. Kids' and regular menus available.

⌖ **Seacrets Bar and Restaurant** (410-524-4900; www.seacrets.com), 49th St. and the bay. Seacrets capitalizes on its reggae theme by providing 14 indoor and open-air bars. Most of the items on the menu, such as veggie, tuna salad, and spicy chicken sandwiches, or ribs and red snapper platters, have a bit of Jamaican heritage to them. Eat under palm trees or lounge on rafts in the water and have your food brought to you. There is live entertainment year-round, but when bands come to play at the height of the season, this place hops so much you might think you've walked into an MTV spring break party. Entrées $7–15.

✍ **The Shark** (410-723-1221; www.thesharkonthebay.com), 46th St. and the bay. The Shark puts a bit of a different twist on the typical Ocean City beach bar food. Try the crab bru-

schetta as your appetizer and the Creole rockfish as the entrée. Sandwiches (from $6.95) and other entrées are available. Most entrées are $16.95–26.95.

Weitzel's Restaurant (410-524-6990), 51st St. and Beach Hwy. Where the locals go for breakfast (creamed chipped beef, $6.75; western omelet, $6.50) and lunch (grilled ham and cheese, $3.50; marinated tuna steak, $5.50). The jalapeño poppers, mahi on a stick, and breaded crab claws ($4.95 each) are good choices to carry out to the beach.

✍ ⌖ **The Wharf Restaurant** (410-250-1001), 128th St. and Coastal Hwy. The emphasis here is on the seafood, much of which is obtained fresh daily from the Seafood and Spirits market next door. A raw bar, award-winning crabcakes, and separate adult and kid-friendly dining rooms. $13.95–27.95.

Snow Hill

Court House Cafe (410-632-2545), 104 W. Green St. With just six tables in a downtown location, the Court House Cafe serves a full breakfast and a lunch menu of soups, salads, and sandwiches.

CRABS

Ocean City

⌖ **Bahama Mamas** (410-289-0291), 221 Wicomico St. The outside deck overlooking Assateague Island is the appropriate place to be cracking open jumbo steamed blue crabs (market price)—obtained fresh from the restaurant's affiliated seafood outlet market just a few miles up the beach. Happy hour 4–7 PM.

✍ ⌖ **Crab Alley** (410-213-7800), 9703 Golf Course Rd., West Ocean

City. Owned and operated by a local waterman and family. If you don't mind driving back onto the mainland, you will probably find some of the freshest steamed blue crabs here (market price). They serve other seafood (such as tuna steak, $18.95; seafood platter, $23.95) when available fresh. I like the children's menu—it simply says, "Half the food, half the price."

Captain's Galley (410-213-2525), 12817 Harbor Rd., West Ocean City. Fresh seafood purchased directly from the docks. It's great fun to sit on the outside deck overlooking the harbor and crack open steamed crabs by the dozen (market price).

Berlin

Assateague Crab House (410-641-4330), MD 611. The post office address is Berlin, but you will find this restaurant on your way to Assateague Island, just south of the MD 611/MD 376 intersection. This is a typical crab house, so the decor is minimal, but the price on the crab-cake sandwich served with french fries is certainly reasonable ($9). All-you-can-eat crabs and shrimp available at market prices.

SNACKS AND GOODIES

Ocean City

Dumser's Dairyland Drive-In (410-524-1588; www.beach-net.com/dumsers), 49th St. and Coastal Hwy. Dumser's has been serving subs, burgers, and fries in Ocean City since 1939, but the real attraction is the ice cream made on the premises that is sold within a few hours of manufacture. The Hawaiian delight—cherries, pineapples, and bananas in vanilla ice cream—is one of the best sellers. A three-dip super sundae ($5.25) could easily fill up two hungry kids.

Candy Kitchens (1-800-60-FUDGE), 5301 Coastal Hwy. Ocean City's saltwater taffy connection for more than 50 years has multiple kitchens located throughout the resort area. Also offers homemade fudge, hand-dipped chocolates, and one of the newest features, "make-your-own ice cream sundae."

✷ Entertainment

MUSIC **The Globe Theater** (410-641-0784; ww.globetheater .com), 12 Broad St., Berlin. Mostly acoustic jazz, folk, classical, and rock music are presented on the weekends in a coffeehouse-type setting. Talent ranges from local to international. The bulk of the audiences come from the surrounding area, so this is the place to mingle with the natives.

NIGHTLIFE

Ocean City

Club 24/Embers Nightclub (410-289-3322), 24th St. and Coastal Hwy. Laser light show and DJs nightly.

Caribbean Bar and Grill (410-289-0837), 2nd St. and the boardwalk. Live funk, reggae, or jazz bands nightly.

The Shark (410-723-1221), 46th St. and the bay. The Shark features live jazz, blues, and acoustic music presented on its private beach.

Shenanigan's Irish Pub (410-289-7181), 4th St. and the boardwalk. Irish entertainment each night on the oceanfront deck during the summer season.

The OC Jamboree (410-213-7581; www.ocjam.com), MD 611 and Mar-jan Lane, West Ocean City. Open all year, the jamboree tries to appeal to families with its Opryland/Branson-type variety musical entertainment.

THEATERS Beach House Restaurant (410-289-6846), 38th St. and the boardwalk, Ocean City. The restaurant produces a Murder Mystery Dinner every Thursday throughout summer. Reservations required.

✳ Selective Shopping

ANTIQUES

Berlin

Town Center Antiques (410-629-1895), Main St. A gallery-type shop with over 125 antiques dealers.

Stuart's Antiques (410-641-0435), Pitts St. It would take a full afternoon to look over all the furniture, glass figures and animals, estate jewelry, china, and silverware crammed into this shop.

ART GALLERIES

Ocean City

The Art League of Ocean City (410-524-9433; www.artleagueof oceancity.org), 94th St. Monthly exhibits of works primarily by members and other local artists.

Ocean Gallery World Center (410-289-5300; www.oceangallery .com), 2nd St. and the boardwalk. There is no mistaking this building, as its exterior is a most amazing hodge-podge of pieces of other buildings from around the world that fans of the gallery have donated to it. The inside is just as convoluted. There are thousands works of art, some by well-known painters, others of ambiguous origin and quality, stacked one against the other over four different floors.

The experience is worth the visit. While taking a lighthearted look at art, you just may find a hidden masterpiece.

Berlin

Worcester County Arts Council (410-641-0809; www.worcestercounty artscouncil.org), Jefferson St. Closed Sat. The council's small retail shop is an outlet for a variety of local artists and craftspeople. This is a chance to bring home something that has not been mass produced.

Waterline Gallery (410-641-9119), 2 S. Main St. The upstairs gallery exhibits monthly fine art shows by regional artists, while the downstairs gallery offers fine-arts prints and cards depicting regional scenes.

BOOKSTORES

Snow Hill

ALICE (410-632-4050), 310 N. Washington St. A selection of books, coffee, and gourmet candies.

Also see *Special Shops—Berlin.*

SPECIAL SHOPS

Ocean City

Donald's Duck Shoppe and Gallery (410-524-9177; 1-877-623-8257; www.donaldsduckshoppe.com), 11515 Coastal Hwy. New items that arrive almost daily include unique decoys and gift items with an emphasis on those pertaining to the coast, ocean, and Eastern Shore.

✐ **The Kite Loft**. With three locations in Ocean City: 5th St. and the boardwalk (410-289-6852); 45th Street Village (410-524-0800); 131st St. and Coastal Hwy. (410-250-4970). Box, wind, diamond, airplane, bird shaped, you name it; this shop has more—and different kinds—of kites than anywhere else in Maryland. Prices range from single to almost triple digits.

Berlin

Dennisons Trackside Hobbies (410-641-2438), Main St. A shop for railroad and model enthusiasts. Not only is there a large selection of trains of all scales, new and used, but you will also find model and remote-control boats, cars, and airplanes.

Ta-Da (410-641-4430), William St. Patty Falck markets a diverse collection of hand-painted furniture and glassware. Many locals come in to get her customized vases as wedding gifts.

Sassafras Station (410-641-0979), Main St. Closed Sun. and Mon. A combination gift store, antiques shop, and local artists' gallery.

Findings (410-641-5049), 11538 Gum Point Rd. Although it has a Berlin address, Findings is located on the north side of US 50 off MD 589. Good-quality primitive handcrafted cottage furniture and garden accessories.

Globe Theater (410-641-0784; www .globetheater.com), 12 Broad St. Three different shops are crammed into the confines of Berlin's historic theater, each with a caliber of items not often found in tourist areas. On the upper floor is the **Balcony Gallery** of paintings, sculpture, jewelry, and pottery work. Many of the items are high-quality one-of-a-kinds. The **Globe Café** serves light-fare food not often found in this part of Maryland. The gourmet sandwiches and soups are about as healthful as they are tasty. The Eastern Shore has a dearth of bookstores, so **Duck Soup Books and Gifts**, with no more than 10

square feet of books, can be a welcome spot.

Snow Hill

Pusey's Country Store (410-632-1992), 5313 Snow Hill Rd. There's a little bit of everything here: wooden buckets, handmade brooms, roasted peanuts, ammo boxes, jellies and preserves, an impressive selection of 50 microbrew beers, and, most importantly, the friendly members of the Pusey family.

OUTLETS Ocean City Factory Outlets (1-800-625-6696; www.ocfactory outlets.com), Ocean Gateway (US 50) and Golf Course Rd., West Ocean City. Includes outlets for Ann Taylor, Bugle Boy, Carter's for Kids, Tommy Hilfiger, Levi's, Dress Barn, and more than 30 other manufacturers.

FARMER'S MARKETS Berlin. Located at N. Main St. Held Wed. and Fri. from 1 PM till sold out, May–Oct.

Pocomoke City. Apr.–Nov., find fresh produce and other farmer's market items Mon.–Sat. 8–6 at Market St. next to Cypress Park.

PICK-YOUR-OWN FARMS Milton's Produce (410-632-2633), 6230 Worcester Hwy., Newark. A variety of fruits and vegetables is available for picking, 7–7, during their seasons.

✳ Special Events

January: **Nautical and Wildlife Art Festival**; **North American Craft Show** (410-524-9177). Both held in the Convention Center, 40th St., Ocean City.

March: **St. Patrick's Day Parade** (410-289-6156). From 61st St. to 44th St., Ocean City.

April: **Easter Arts and Crafts and Kids Fair** (410-524-7020), Convention Center, Ocean City. Egg hunts, clowns, storytellers, and the Easter Bunny. **Ward World Championship Wildfowl Carving Competition** (410-742-4988), Convention Center, Ocean City. Not to be missed by those who have the slightest interest in decoy art. The largest and, without a doubt, the most prestigious competition of wildfowl art. More than 150 exhibitors and artists.

May: **Springfest** (410-289-2800), Inlet Parking Area, Ocean City. A 4-day arts and crafts festival under big-top tents.

June: **Strawberry Day** (410-632-2032), Furnace Town, Snow Hill. Lots of food created from strawberries; contests and tastings.

July: **Annual Ocean City Tuna Tournament** (410-213-1121), Ocean City Fishing Center. **Greek Festival** (410-524-0990), Convention Center, Ocean City. Greek food and goodies, dancing, and entertainment. **Penning of the Ponies** (757-336-6161), Chincoteague Island, nearby in Virginia (see the sidebar on page 41). Watch the ponies swim across the channel from Assateague Island to Chincoteague Island. Draws extremely large crowds.

August: **White Marlin Open** (410-289-9229; www.whitemarlinopen .com), Ocean City. Offshore fishing competition for white and blue marlin, tuna, and shark. This is not a small-time event; prize money totals well over $1 million. **Worcester County Fair** (410-632-1972), Furnace Town, Snow Hill.

September: **Sunfest** (410-289-2800), Inlet Parking Area, Ocean City. Autumn's equivalent of the Springfest. Includes the **Kite Festival,** considered by many to be America's largest gathering of kite fliers. Competitions and aerial exhibits.

November–early January: **Winterfest of Lights** (410-289-2800), Ocean City. Holiday lights and animated displays throughout the city. In addition, there are over 800,000 lights at Northside Park (410-250-0125), where you can ride the Winterfest Express through a mile of animated ornaments.

THE WILD PONIES OF ASSATEAGUE ISLAND

TANGIER SOUND AREA—Crisfield and Princess Anne

In *Beautiful Swimmers*, William W. Warner aptly describes Crisfield as "A town built upon oyster shells, millions of tons of it." And he is right, both figuratively and literally.

When large beds of oysters were discovered in Tangier Sound in the mid-1800s, John W. Crisfield recognized the importance of the find. He brought the railroad from Salisbury so that the oysters could be economically transported to the important markets of the Northeast. In order to bring the tracks right to the water's edge, the land was artificially extended upon a base of compacted oyster shells.

In its heyday, Crisfield's population numbered well over 10,000, and more sailing ships were registered here than in any other port in the country. Close to 150 seafood-processing plants, many of them also built upon oyster shells, clustered around the water. Agricultural packinghouses and a sewing industry also moved into the area to take advantage of the railroad.

When the oysters began to play out, the watermen turned their attention to blue crabs and other seafood. Even though the bay's bounty has declined in recent years, Crisfield remains essentially a working town—and this is the reason to visit. Observing the activity on the city dock could occupy you for a full day. Ferries come and go to Smith Island, tons of seafood are unloaded, and sportfishermen head out with hopes high. Do not expect fancy shops, gourmet food, or theme parks, but the opportunity to observe an industrious way of life.

Princess Anne was chartered in 1733 and became the Somerset County seat in 1742. Until the turn of the 20th century, large ships were able to sail up the Manokin River, bringing growth and prosperity. Many of the town's historic mansions and homes, most notably Teackle Mansion, have been well preserved and make a walking tour of the city worthwhile, while the University of Maryland–Eastern Shore attracts visitors with its cultural events.

COMMUNITIES The small fishing villages of **Deal** and **Wenona** on Deal Island are worth driving through just to catch a glimpse of a lifestyle that may be on its way out.

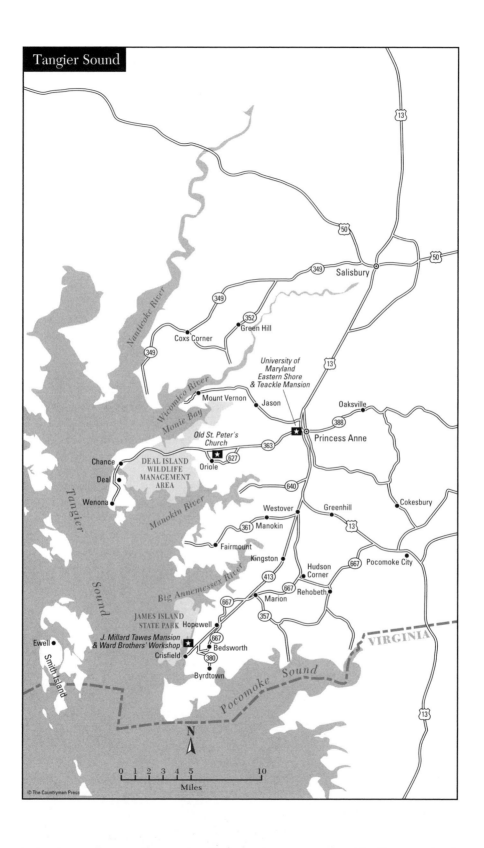

Tangier Sound

13

13

50

50

349
Salisbury

349

349

352
Green Hill

Coxs Corner

Nanticoke River

349

13

Wicomico River

University of Maryland Eastern Shore & Teackle Mansion

Mount Vernon   Jason

Oaksville

Monie Bay

388

Old St. Peter's Church   363   Princess Anne

Chance   DEAL ISLAND WILDLIFE MANAGEMENT AREA   627
Oriole

Deal

Wenona   640

Tangier

Manokin River

Westover   Greenhill   Cokesbury

361   Manokin   13

Fairmount

Kingston   Hudson Corner   667   Pocomoke City

Sound

Big Annemessex River   413   667   Rehobeth

667   Marion

JAMES ISLAND STATE PARK   Hopewell   357   VIRGINIA

J. Millard Tawes Mansion & Ward Brothers' Workshop   667

Ewell   Bedsworth

Crisfield   380

Smith Island   Byrdtown

Pocomoke Sound

13

N

0 1 2 3 4 5   10
Miles

© The Countrymen Press

GUIDANCE **Somerset County Tourism** (410-651-2968; 1-800-521-9189) maintains offices at 11440 Ocean Hwy., Princess Anne, 21853, and inside the **J. Millard Tawes Museum** (410-968-2501), Somers Cove Marina, Crisfield, 21817.

GETTING THERE *By car:* **US 13** is the route that will bring you into the area, with **MD 413** going south to Crisfield.
By bus: **Carolina Trailways** (410-289-9307) makes a stop at the Chevron station, 106 Somerset Ave., Princess Anne, 21853.

GETTING AROUND The **Crisfield Trolley** (410-968-2501). In operation Memorial Day–Oct., the trolley-shaped bus makes a circular route through Crisfield to provide transportation around town. At 1 PM, it picks up passengers at the J. Millard Tawes Historical Museum to begin a guided trolley tour of the area, making stops at a number of the places listed in the *To See* section below.

MEDICAL EMERGENCY **McCready Health Services** maintains a full-service hospital in Crisfield (410-968-1200), and clinics in Princess Anne (410-651-5883) and Dames Quarter (410-651-0585).

✳ To See

COLLEGES Founded as the Delaware Conference Academy in 1886, the **University of Maryland–Eastern Shore** (410-651-2200) in Princess Anne is the cultural hub of the area. Its library contains more than 150,000 books, and diverse programs are presented in the **Ella Fitzgerald Performing Arts Center**. The 700-acre campus can be a quiet place for an afternoon's walk.

MUSEUMS **J. Millard Tawes Museum** (410-968-2501), Somers Cove Marina, Crisfield. Small admission charge. Mon.–Sat. 9–4:30, Oct.–Apr.; Mon.–Sat. 9–6,

THE CRISFIELD CITY DOCK

May–Sep. J. Millard Tawes was a native of Crisfield and Maryland's 54th governor. In addition to paying homage to his life, the museum chronicles the history of the area, from Native Americans to how the catch of the watermen gradually moved from oysters to crabs. The decoys of the Ward Brothers, models of various boats that worked Tangier Sound, and a mural that provides a sweeping overview of Chesapeake Bay chronology make the museum worth the small price of admission.

TEACKLE MANSION, PRINCESS ANNE

HISTORIC HOMES **Teackle Mansion** (410-651-2238), 11736 Mansion St., Princess Anne. Small admission charge. Wed., Sat., and Sun. 1–3, April through mid-December; Sun. 1–3, mid-December through March. The home of Littleton Teackle, prominent educator, banker, and statesman, is so large it took from 1802 to 1819 to complete. Its center has a Flemish-bond brick facade and decorative plasterwork above the door and first-floor windows. The adherence to Federal-style architecture, with its strict sense of symmetry, is as amusing as it is amazing. The house is furnished in period pieces, many from the Teackle family, and tour guides point out the family Bible, prints by artists Teackle met in England, banknotes, and a "Report of the State's Bank."

HISTORIC SITES **Ward Brothers' Workshop**, Crisfield. Crisfield natives Steve and Lem Ward are generally acknowledged as being the ones who elevated decoy carving into an art form. Their workshop, which was rapidly deteriorating, has been stabilized, but not glamorized. Wood chips from the brothers' work remain on the floor, their ripped vinyl chairs have not been replaced, and even the color of the walls remains the same. This is one of the few historic places in which you get a real feel for what went on inside. This is a highly recommended stop, but you must contact the J. Millard Tawes Museum (see *Museums*) to gain access.

HISTORIC CHURCHES Within the **Asbury United Methodist Church** in Crisfield is a painting of Daniel in the lion's den done by Lem Ward. However, he did not like the way it turned out, so he signed it as having been done by "Balkuaves."

The old **St. Peter's Church** in Oriole was founded in 1782, and the congregation is still going strong.

The original congregation of the **Metropolitan United Methodist Church** (30522 E. Broad St., Princess Anne) consisted entirely of slaves. The present building was erected in the late 1800s.

GUIDED TOURS **The Port of Crisfield Escorted Walking Tour** is sponsored by the J. Millard Tawes Historical Museum (see *Museums*). It makes the usual stops at historic sites, churches, and homes, but the tours of the seafood-processing plants are the big treat. At the **Metompkin Bay Oyster Company**, you can watch the amazing ability of workers who shuck hundreds of oysters per hour, while the walk through **Southern Connection Seafood** will enlighten you on how soft-shell crabs are harvested.

Also see the **Crisfield Trolley** under *Getting Around*.

✳ To Do

BICYCLING **Adrenaline High** (410-749-2886; www.adrenalinehigh.com). Stan Shedaker has more than 10 years' experience planning and leading group trips and, along with his wife, Rachael, operates a touring company that puts together customized bicycle and kayak tours in and around Somerset County. Tours include some equipment, shuttles, accommodations, and meals.

BIRDING Woodlands, bay shoreline, and brackish marshes are the reason that **Deal Island Wildlife Management Area** (410-543-8223; MD 363 west of Princess Anne) has such a diversity of bird life: bald eagles, short-eared owls, tundra swans, marsh wrens, black rails, the rare peregrine falcon, and Maryland's only nesting population of black-necked stilts.

FISHING

Crisfield
Tangier Sound has some of the best fishing on the bay, with flounder, striped bass, drum, trout, croaker, and perch being the catch for sportfishermen. Among the many charter-boat captains operating out of Crisfield are **Keith Ward** (410-968-0074; www.crisfield.com/prim), **Gilbert Howard** (410-968-0291), **Vernon Ricker** (www.crisfield.com/naturesbest), and **Curtis Johns** (410-623-2310).

Captains Joe and John Asanovich (410-957-2562; www.crisfield.com/barbara) operate headboats that leave at 7 AM daily from the Somers Cove Marina.

Somerset County Tourism can provide you with a list of additional charter captains operating in and around Tangier Sound.

GOLF ⛳ **Great Hope Golf Course** (410-651-5900; 1-800-537-8009; www.co .somerset.md.us/greathope/index.html), 8380 Crisfield Hwy., Westover. Closed only on Christmas Day. Five sets of tees at each hole allow you to pick your challenge on the 7,049-yard golf course designed by Dr. Michael Hurzdan. A children's discount is available.

HIKING See *Green Space*.

KAYAKING AND CANOEING **Tangier Sound Outfitters (TSO)** (410-968-1803; www.crisfield.org/TSO.html),

> "You have to think like a crab if you want to catch a crab."
> —Charles Bradshaw of Southern Connection Seafood

27582 Farm Market Rd., Marion. A certified partner in the state's Nature Tourism program, TSO offer lessons, rentals, sales, shuttle services, and guided trips on Tangier Sound, Nassawango Creek, the Pocomoke River, and Smith Island. A rarity on the Eastern Shore, they can arrange for backcountry paddle/camping trips.

Also see **Adrenaline High** under *Bicycling*.

✴ Green Space

BEACHES See *Parks*.

GARDENS The **Boxwood Garden** at the corner of Somerset Ave. and Washington St. in Princess Anne dates from the mid-1800s.

PARKS Janes Island State Park (410-968-1565), 40 Alfred Lawson Dr., Crisfield. The park is divided into two areas, the 300-acre Hodson Memorial Area on the mainland and, separated from it by the Daugherty Creek Canal, Janes Island itself. Within the memorial area are a marina with boat-launch capabilities, a 104-site campground with modern amenities, picnic areas, and rental cabins. Although this area has two hiking trails, each a mile in length, it is the 3,000-acre island that is most worth spending your foot-travel time upon.

Except for a small boat dock and some ruins of a former fishing village on its southern end, Janes Island is completely undeveloped. Bordered by Tangier Sound, it is the quintessential Chesapeake Bay island, with a landscape barely above sea level. You will find windswept beaches, salt marshes, ponds, low-growing vegetation, and an assortment of creatures that exist only in this type of environment. To come here is to be brought back in time, to what many of the islands looked like when Captain John Smith made his famous exploration of the bay in the 1600s.

FISHING FROM THE PIER IN CRISFIELD

✳ Lodging

BED & BREAKFASTS

Crisfield, 21817

Bea's B&B (410-968-0423; www
.beasbnb.com), 10 S. Somerset Ave.
Built in 1909 by the founder of the
Handy Soft Shell Crab Company, the
house has many of the features common to fine houses of its day: pocket
doors, stained-glass windows, and a
grand foyer. The pink rose wallpaper in
the Deborah Room gives it a feminine
touch. The lace curtains in the Jennifer
Room catch the morning sun. $80–90.

My Fair Lady B&B (410-968-0352;
www.myfairladybandb.com), 38 W.
Main St. A stay at My Fair Lady provides a glimpse of the opulence and
prosperity of Crisfield's seafood boom
around the turn of the 20th century.
Relax on the wraparound sunporch or
explore the three-story octagonal
tower before retiring to one of four
period-decorated guest rooms or a
third-floor suite. Rate includes tax
and a full breakfast. $120–255.

Princess Anne, 21853

Hayman House (410-651-1107),
30491 Prince William St. On a quiet
side street just one block from the
Teackle Mansion, Hayman House is
the perfect spot to stay for parents
visiting their student-children at the
nearby University of Maryland–
Eastern Shore. The Victorian parlor
with its cranberry-tiled fireplace is a
gathering place for quiet conversations, and the carved woodwork and
oak floors add a warmth to the interi-
or. Morning coffee is best appreciated
on the porch. Hosts Carol and
Charles Pinkerman enjoy relating the
history of the area—and they prepare
a great breakfast. Choice of private or
shared bath. $80–120.

&. **Waterloo Country Inn** (410-651-
0883; http://waterloocountryinn.com),
28822 Mt. Vernon Rd. I could go on
for pages about what makes the
Waterloo such a splendid place to
stay, but a listing of just a few features
will have to suffice: a historic home
built in the mid-1700s; 317 acres of
working farmland and woods to wander upon; free bicycles and canoes to
explore the countryside; an outdoor
pool; Jacuzzis; a choice of six rooms or
suites, each decorated in appropriate
furnishings but in a manner reflecting
the Swiss origin of the inn's hosts. The
Monie Room, where I stayed, has a
king bed, a desk, a sitting area with
wing chairs, and more. To top it all
off, hosts Theresa and Erwin Kraemer
speak German, French, Italian, and
English, so expect to meet visitors
from a number of other countries.
$105–245.

CAMPING Janes Island State Park
(410-968-1565), 40 Alfred Lawson
Dr., Crisfield, 21817. The state park's
campground has sites on the shoreline
overlooking the water and the island.
Rental cabins also overlooking the
water are often reserved a year in
advance. For a more rugged experience, you could camp in one of the
four primitive sites that are located on
the island and accessible only by boat.

**Lake Somerset Family Camp-
ground** (410-957-9897), 8658 Lake
Somerset Lane, Westover, 21871.
Caters primarily to those with an RV.
You'll find hookups, a general store,
metered propane, miniature golf, a
swimming pool, boat rentals, a 5-acre
fishing pond, and rental cabins and
trailers.

Princess Anne Campground (410-
651-1520), along US 13 south of

Princess Anne, 21853. RV and trailer sites packed together with a few tent sites. Short nature trails, free firewood, and hot showers.

✳ Where to Eat

DINING OUT 🍲 **Watermen's Inn** (410-968-2119; www.crisfield.com/watermens), 901 W. Main St., Crisfield. Closed Mon. and Tue. Chef Brian Julian and partner Kathy Berezoski both have degrees in culinary arts from Johnson and Wales University in Rhode Island, and they must have studied well. Brian only uses fresh local seafood and organically grown produce in his cooking. The baked flounder stuffed with feta cheese and spinach and smothered with hollandaise sauce ($14.50) was one of the best flounder meals I've had on the Eastern Shore. The menu ranges from a two-piece fried chicken dinner ($9.95) to a seafood sampler with soft-shell crab, flounder, shrimp scampi, oysters, and mini crabcake ($19.95). Save room for Kathy's inventive desserts. Breakfast and lunch also served. Do not be misled by the modest exterior; dinner is a fine-dining experience.

EATING OUT

Crisfield
🍴 **Captain's Galley Restaurant** (410-968-3313), Main St. and city dock. With a great view of Tangier Sound, Captain's Galley serves everything from steamed crabs (market price) to stuffed mushrooms ($6.75) to a 24-ounce porterhouse ($21.95). Kids' menu with items under $5.

Tropical Chesapeake (410-968-3622), 712 Broadway. Serves breakfast, lunch, and dinner. Good sandwiches ($4.95–8.95) for a light lunch; try the baked egg sandwich for a different twist on breakfast.

Circle Inn Restaurant (410-968-1969), 4012 Crisfield Hwy. Serves breakfast, lunch, and dinner. This is where the locals come for low-cost home cooking. A full breakfast can be had for less than $4, while the most expensive dinner is $12.95.

Gordon's Confectionery (410-968-0566), 931 W. Main St. This is the place to come if you want to soak up the local color. It opens at 4 AM to serve the watermen, and is known for its coffee, old-fashioned fountain service, and a drink called a Zip (primarily chocolate or strawberry milk served over crushed ice). The ever-present group of guys in the back never tires of discussing fishing or politics.

Princess Anne
Peaky's (410-651-1950), 30361 Mt. Vernon Rd. Serves breakfast, lunch, dinner. Known for their fried chicken ($6.95). Many of the lunch and dinner items, such as broiled flounder ($12.95) or pork chops ($9.95), are the same price at both lunch and dinner.

China Chef (410-651-5768), 12087 Somerset Ave. Open for lunch and dinner. The China Chef has the usual menu for Chinese restaurants, but for something different order the ooey, gooey spareribs ($6.95).

Spike's Pub and Subs (410-651-9124), 30264 Mt. Vernon Rd. This is the local bar, but it does make a variety of good (and filling) subs, and the prices can't be beat: $3–5.

Westover
Caddy Shack (410-651-5900), 8380 Crisfield Hwy. Located within the Great Hope Golf Course, Caddy

Shack offers a range of reasonably priced soups, salads, and sandwiches from $4.95 to $8.95.

CRABS Side Street Seafood Market and Restaurant (410-968-2442), 204 S. 10th St., Crisfield. Open for lunch and dinner. My choice for steamed crabs (market price) in Crisfield. The open upper deck lets the Tangier Sound breezes cool you off as you pull tasty morsels from the shell. The downstairs market will pack up a variety of fresh seafood to take home.

SOFT-SHELL CRABS TO GO Southern Connection Seafood (410-968-3367), 7th St., Crisfield. In addition to packaging live or frozen soft-shell crabs for you to travel with, these friendly folks will take you on a tour of the factory to learn more about crabs.

COFFEE BARS Allegro Coffee and Tea Salon (410-651-4520), 11775 Somerset Ave., Suite 6A, Princess Anne. Open Tue., Thu., and Fri. 9:30–5. In addition to serving the usual coffees and teas, this is also a pleasant little restaurant. An assortment of fresh soups changes daily, and the focaccia bread sandwiches ($5.50) are just right for a light lunch. Cakes, pies, and pastries round out the menu.

SNACKS AND GOODIES Ice Cream Gallery (410-968-0809), 5 Goodsell Alley, Crisfield. Daily 11–9:30. The Gallery's deck overlooking Tangier Sound is the place to enjoy the sunset after a meal at one of the local restaurants.

Rosanini's Gourmet Ice Cream (410-651-3933), 11747 Somerset Ave., Princess Anne. There are the old standards such as vanilla and chocolate, but be adventurous and try one of the exotic flavors that are offered seasonally, such as pumpkin, chai, or cantaloupe. Sandwiches, soups, and coffees are also served.

Sno Biz/Shave Ice (410-651-4548), 12100 Carol Lane, Princess Anne. Closed Sun. Good for a cool, sweet treat on a hot day.

✳ Selective Shopping

ART GALLERIES ♿ **Burton Ave. Gallery** (410-986-2787), 26430 Burton Ave., Crisfield. The outlet for the artwork of members of the local Somerset County Arts Council.

PICK-YOUR-OWN PRODUCE FARMS Vassey's Orchards (410-957-1454), Rehobeth Rd., Rehobeth. Beginning in July, you can pick squash, tomatoes, peaches, apples, and pumpkins during their respective seasons.

✳ Special Events

April: **Annual Daffodil Show** (410-651-9636), Princess Anne. More than 400 blooms and arrangements are on display at the Peninsula Bank.

May: **Annual 1800s Festival** (410-651-0351), Fairmont Academy, Upper Fairmont. An 1800s classroom, old-fashioned spelling bee, food, crafts, and music. **Annual Soft Shell Spring Fair** (410-968-1125), Crisfield. Food, crafts, entertainment, and lots of crab.

July: **Annual J. Millard Tawes Crab and Clam Bake** (410-968-2500; 1-800-782-3913), Somers Cove Marina, Crisfield. All-you-can-eat crabs, clams, fish, corn, and more. Tickets must be purchased in advance. **Somerset County Fair** (410-651-2341), Civic Center, Princess Anne.

September: **Annual National Hard Crab Derby and Fair** (410-968-2500), Somers Cove Marina, Crisfield. Lots of fun with crab races, boat-racing and -docking contests, crab-picking contests, arts and crafts, much seafood, and live entertainment. **Annual Skipjack Races** (410-784-2203), Deal Island Harbor. Food, entertainment, and children's activities in addition to boat races.

October: **Olde Princess Anne Days** (461-651-2238), Princess Anne. Historic home and garden tours, Revolutionary War encampment, period crafts, music, and kids' activities. **Annual Native American Heritage Festival and Powwow** (410-623-2660), Bending Water Park Living Village, Marion.

SMITH ISLAND

Defining the western edge of Tangier Sound and existing in the heart of the Chesapeake Bay—12 miles from Crisfield—is a world unto itself, tiny Smith Island (see the map on page 67). The island is 8 miles long and 4 miles wide, and its highest point is only a few feet above high tide; much of the acreage is marshland. The island was sighted by Captain John Smith and settled by Cornish fishermen in the 1600s, and some of the island's inhabitants retain the Elizabethan accents and idioms of their ancestors. Most still make their living from the waters of the bay, heading out early in the morning from the island's many marshy channels. Crab-shedding shanties built upon stilts rise near the water's edge, resulting in its unofficial title: "soft-shell crab capital of the world."

The island is actually a conglomeration of islands separated by creeks, canals, marshes, and inlets. The towns of **Ewell** and **Rhodes Point** are connected by a roadway, but tiny **Tylerton** can be reached only by boat.

Visitors are usually day-trippers who ferry over to Ewell to stay on the island for a few hours, have a meal, and take a quick walking tour or guided mini-bus tour.

The best way to really appreciate the island's uniqueness, however, is to spend the night. After other tourists have gone, overnight visitors can share unhurried conversations with residents, take a walk along the waterfront, or just enjoy the sunset spread a reddish glow across the marshlands. Spring—when the blossoms of pomegranate, fig, pear, and mimosa trees color the scenery and perfume the air—is a great time to visit. Be sure to look in the stores for fig preserves and pomegranate jellies made by island residents in their homes.

GUIDANCE The **Smith Island Visitor's Center** (410-425-3351), 20846 Caleb Jones Rd., Ewell, 21824, provides information once you are on the island. Before going, you might want to contact **Somerset County Tourism** (410-651-2968; 1-800-521-9189) at 11440 Ocean Hwy., Princess Anne, 21853.

If you want to really understand the history and the people of the island before you arrive, read the book *An Island Out of Time*. Author Tom Horton spent 3 years on Smith Island, and his book is an eloquent and sensitive study.

GETTING THERE The **Captain Tyler** (410-425-2771) leaves from the Somers Cove Marina for a lightly narrated cruise at 12:30 daily, arrives at Smith Island about 1:10, and leaves at 4 sharp.

The **Captain Jason** (410-425-4471; 410-425-5931) departs the Crisfield city dock and follows the same schedule. More a working boat than a tourist boat, it is the one many of the islanders use. Expect to share space with furniture, dog food, cases of paper towels, and other items. The gossip you overhear makes up for the lack of narration.

The **Island Belle II** (410-968-1118) is the island's mail boat and follows the same schedule as the other two. Hauling passengers as well as the mail, it leaves from the Crisfield city dock.

GETTING AROUND Bicycles and golf carts can be rented at the ice cream stand beside the **Bayside Inn**, 4065 Smith Island Rd., Ewell. As an alternative, you can bring your own bike on one of the boats (see *Getting There*) by paying a small freight fee.

PUBLIC RESTROOMS Public comfort stations are found inside the Smith Island Visitor's Center.

✳ To See

MUSEUMS ⅙ **Smith Island Visitor's Center Cultural Museum** (410-425-3351), 20846 Caleb Jones Rd., Ewell. Small admission charge. Open daily noon–4, Apr.–Nov. Sometimes open during the off-season. Murals, interactive displays, full-sized workboats, and occasional live interpreters make this the first place to stop to learn more about your Smith Island visit. The time line puts things in perspective and shows how the vagaries of the seafood harvest have affected the islanders.

✳ To Do

BICYCLING Bicycles can be rented at the ice cream stand beside the **Bayside Inn**, 4065 Smith Island Rd., Ewell. In addition to riding around Ewell, take the 1-mile road through salt marshes and over a wooden bridge to Rhodes Point.

WALKING TOURS The best way to experience Smith Island is by foot, and a small brochure available from the visitors center in Ewell describes the sights you will see in the island's three small towns.

✳ Lodging

MOTELS AND HOTELS **Waterman's Rest** (410-425-3321), 4025 Smith Island Rd., Ewell, 21824. Apr. 15–Oct. 15. The Waterman's Rest is a small cottage available to those who wish an extended stay on the island.

BED & BREAKFASTS ⌀ **Ewell Tide Inn** (410-425-2141; 1-888-699-2141; www.smithisland.net), 4063 Tyler Rd., Ewell, 21824. Certainly the nicest accommodations in Ewell, with four rooms that share two baths. The porch and long front yard overlook the water. Captain Steve Eades welcomes children and provide bikes for island exploration. $75.

Inn of Silent Music (410-425-3541; www.innofsilentmusic.com), 2955 Tylerton Rd., Tylerton, 21866. April to mid-November. The only place to stay in Tylerton and accessible only by the *Captain Jason* (see *Getting There*). Hosts Sherryl Lindberg and LeRoy Friesen offer three rooms with private bath. The entire house overlooks the bay, but the upstairs Drum Point Room has the best water views. Canoes, bicycles, and charter boats are available for sightseeing. Be sure to spend some time in Green House. Akin to a tree house, it overlooks Glennan Marsh and Tangier Sound and is a great place to while away an afternoon in peace and solitude. The seafood dinners ($20) Sherryl offers have become legend among former guests. $105–125.

✳ Where to Eat
EATING OUT

Ewell
Bayside Inn (410-425-2771), 4065 Smith Island Rd. The Bayside Inn has picture windows overlooking the town dock and is the place most

tourists eat lunch, with platters starting at $11.99.

Ruke's Seafood Deck (410-425-2311), 20840 Caleb Jones Rd. Be adventurous and pass up the tourist environment of the Bayside Inn in favor of Ruke's, the local restaurant of choice. If you don't mind the rather dull and dingy decor of this grocery/general store, you can dine on sandwiches, french fries, or crabcakes made from local crabs ($7.95) on a screened porch overlooking the marsh. Better yet, sit inside with everyone else and overhear conversations about who is dating who at the high school, how the seafood harvest is going, or the latest prank played by one islander on another.

✳ Selective Shopping
SPECIAL SHOPS

Ewell
♿ **Smith Island Visitor's Center Cultural Museum**. The museum's gift shop stocks a number of locally made items and handicrafts.

Bayside Gifts (410-425-2771), 4065 Smith Island Rd. The shop, a part of the Bayside Inn (see *Eating Out*), has a nautical theme with decoys, gifts, and books on Smith Island and the bay area.

SALISBURY

Salisbury has been the economic and cultural center of the lower Eastern Shore since its establishment in 1732. Large boats coming up the Wicomico River from the bay were the first to bring trade to the city. Because Salisbury is at the intersection of several railroads, rail lines later figured prominently. Finally, easy access via modern highways brought more commerce to the city. Agriculture has always been important to the area, but today's city owes much to Frank Perdue, whose poultry business is a dominant economic engine.

Devastating fires in 1860 and 1868 almost destroyed the town. As a result, much of Salisbury looks like other modern American cities, with undistinguished strip malls, convenience stores, and fast-food shops. However, pockets of loveliness remain, such as the main downtown area (now a pedestrian mall), the campus of Salisbury University, and the historic district of Newtown with six blocks of magnificent Victorian homes. The park along the South Prong Wicomico River is a quiet place within the city and contains the well-managed Salisbury Zoological Park.

The arts and cultural offerings are sophisticated in this metropolitan area of close to 100,000 inhabitants. Salisbury has its own symphony orchestra, a minor-league baseball team, and a number of museums, while presentations at Salisbury University range from local stage productions to international guest lecturers.

GUIDANCE A modern and spacious welcome center operated by the **Wicomico County Convention and Visitors Bureau** (410-548-4914; 1-800-332-8687; www.wicomicotourism.org), 8480 Ocean Hwy., Delmar, 21875, is located north of Salisbury on US 13. This is more than just a place to obtain information. It is located next to an attractive, large pond and within the greenery of **Leonard's Mill Park**, which has public restrooms, picnic facilities, and canoe-launching capabilities.

GETTING THERE *By air:* The **Salisbury/Ocean City Airport** (410-548-4827), 5485 Airport Terminal Rd., is the second largest airport in the state, averaging close to 150,000 passengers a year. It is currently serviced by regularly scheduled flights via US Airways (1-800-428-4322).

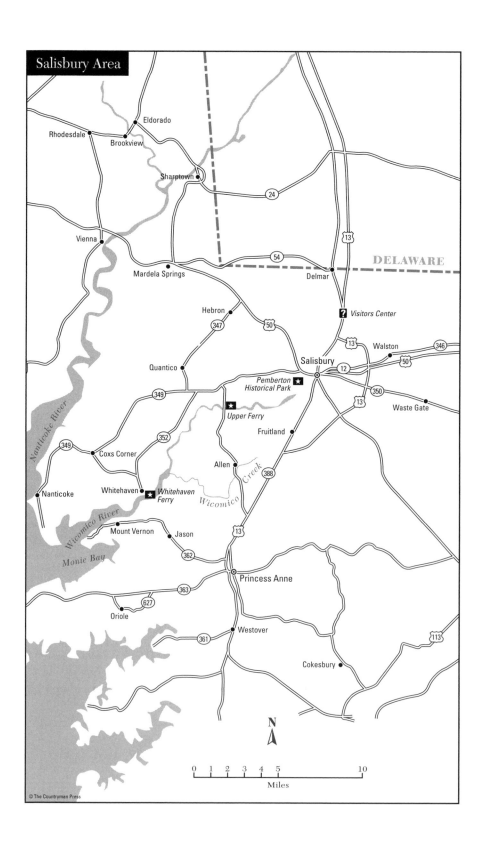

Salisbury Area

Rhodesdale
Eldorado
Brookview
Sharptown
24
Vienna
Mardela Springs
54
DELAWARE
13
Delmar
Hebron
Visitors Center
347
50
13
Walston
346
Quantico
Salisbury
12
50
349
Pemberton Historical Park
350
Upper Ferry
13
Waste Gate
352
Fruitland
Nanticoke River
349
Coxs Corner
Allen
388
Nanticoke
Whitehaven
Whitehaven Ferry
Wicomico Creek
Wicomico River
Mount Vernon
Jason
13
Monie Bay
362
363
Princess Anne
627
Oriole
361
Westover
113
Cokesbury

N

0 1 2 3 4 5   10
Miles

© The Countryman Press

By car: **US 50** and **US 13** intersect in Salisbury and provide access to all points north, south, east, and west. Traffic becomes heavy on US 50 during the summer months as vacationers head to and from Ocean City.

By bus: **Carolina Trailways** (410-749-4121) has a station at 350 Cypress St., Salisbury. **Greyhound** (1-800-229-9424) also has information on bus service to the lower Eastern Shore.

GETTING AROUND *By taxi:* **North End Taxi** (410-546-1477) and **Salisbury Taxi** (410-749-3500).

By bus: The local bus service, **Shore Transit** (443-260-2300), reaches into every sector of the city and the university. Additional routes make it possible to ride to a number of outlying areas such as Princess Anne, Mount Vernon, Crisfield, Berlin, Ocean City, and Cambridge.

MEDICAL EMERGENCY **Peninsula Regional Medical Center** (410-546-6400), 100 E. Carroll St., Salisbury.

✳ To See

COLLEGES **Salisbury University** (410-543-6161; 1-888-543-0184), Camden and West College Aves., Salisbury. Tours of the 125-acre campus, which has been declared a national arboretum and called the most beautiful in Maryland, begin every Mon., Wed., and Fri. at 1:30 at the Admissions House. The campus contains more than 2,100 plant species, pieces of outdoor art, and notable works of architecture. The university is home to the Salisbury Symphony Orchestra, SU Theatre, and several galleries, and has a range of lectures and activities open to the public.

ALONG THE SALISBURY URBAN GREENWAY

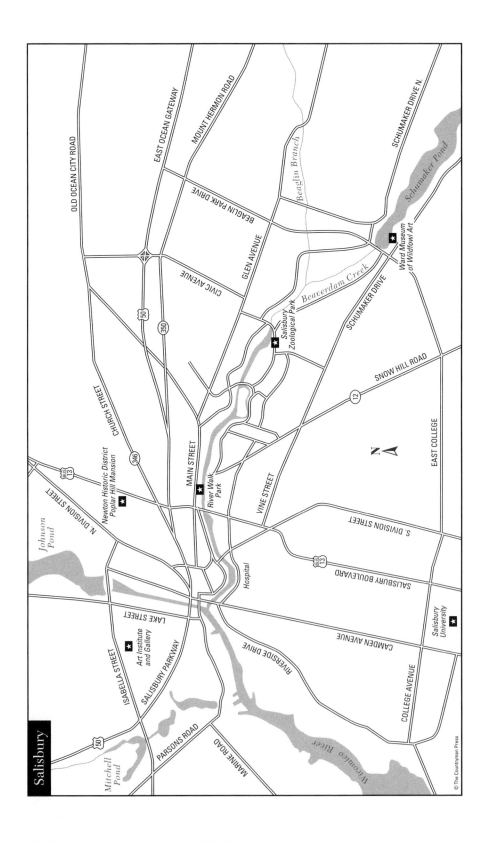

Salisbury

© The Countryman Press

Salisbury

Ward Museum of Wildlife Art (410-742-4988), 909 South Schumaker Dr. Open daily. Adults $7, students $3, seniors $5. The $5.5 million Ward Museum, named for decoy carvers Lem and Steve Ward, opened in 1992. Its 4,000 objects interpret the history and development of decoy carving, from early Native American pieces to the present day. An excellent display shows how specialized decoys were developed for the different North American flyways, while another examines various Eastern Shore hunting methods. The re-creation of Lem and Steve Ward's workshop is an accurate portrayal of their Crisfield business. Do not miss the Championship Gallery, which contains winners from past Ward carving competitions held annually in Ocean City. The detail, beauty, and artistry of these pieces is nothing short of spectacular. One of Elmer Crowell's decoys sold for $319,000. The museum's building is a work of art in itself.

Also see **Ward Brothers' Workshop** under *To See* in "Tangier Sound Area."

HISTORIC HOMES Poplar Hill Mansion (410-749-1776), 117 E. Elizabeth St., Salisbury. Guided tours Sun. 1–4. The oldest house in Salisbury (circa 1805) is the logical starting or stopping point for a walking tour of the **Newtown Historic District** (see *To Do*). Even if you can't get inside to enjoy the period antiques and original brass hardware on the woodwork, the transitional Georgian-style building—with bull's-eye windows, dentil molding, and a second-story Palladian window—is worth walking by.

HISTORIC SITES Pemberton Historical Park (410-860-2447), Pemberton Dr., Salisbury. Small entrance fees are charged for the house and museum. A short drive from downtown Salisbury, this county-operated park includes the home of Isaac and Anne Handy, built in 1741. The Flemish-bond brickwork house still contains the original interior wood paneling. Guided tours are given Sun., May–Sep., but call to make sure someone is there. Handy was a shipowner and captain, merchant, farmer, and justice of the peace, and raised grains, tobacco, and flax on his plantation. The park also includes a re-created 18th-century barn with rotating displays of local history, orchards with dwarf variety apples of the kind that would have been grown in the 1700s, a few picnic tables, and almost 5 miles of nature trails that wind onto Bell Island in the Wicomico River. Side-by-side gardens compare 18th-century crops with those of today. Special events range from canoe trips to maple-sugaring demonstrations to living-history weekends.

PEMBERTON HISTORICAL PARK

ZOO ✍ & **Salisbury Zoological Park** (410-548-3188), 750 S. Park

Dr., Salisbury. Open daily—and parking and admission are free! The Salisbury zoo is one of the prettiest in the Mid-Atlantic region, set within an old pine forest and beside the South Prong Wicomico River. Even though it has 400 examples of 100 species found within the Western Hemisphere, it is not overwhelming like some zoos. Expect to devote a couple of hours to observing animals such as American alligators, Central American black-handed spider monkeys, jaguars, capybaras, and the only bear native to South America, the endangered spectacled bear from the Andes Mountains. The pathways are nearly level, so walking is easy and accessible to everyone. Do not miss this place.

✳ To Do

BICYCLING

Salisbury

The **Wicomico County Convention and Visitors Bureau** has developed an excellent set of maps and descriptions that detail dozens of rides from a few miles to over 100 miles. Short ones are within the city, while others reach to Ocean City, Assateague Island, and Crisfield. A local favorite makes use of the Upper Ferry across the Wicomico River.

The **Salisbury Bicycle Club** (P.O. Box 3512, Salisbury, 21802) and **Salisbury University Bicycle Club** (Campus Box 3046, Salisbury, 21801) welcome guest riders on their outings.

BIRDING

Salisbury

The **Ward Museum of Wildlife Art**, 909 S. Schumaker Dr., and **Salisbury Zoological Park** (see *To See* for both), 750 S. Park Dr., are both located along the Salisbury Urban Greenway next to the South Prong Wicomico River. Cedar waxwings, hummingbirds, woodpeckers, and nuthatches are often seen in the zoo. Schumaker Pond in front of the museum attracts ducks, wigeon, and swans. Scarlet tanagers often breed on-site.

A BISON IN THE SALISBURY ZOO

Open meadows, woodlands, and streambanks attract a variety of bird life to **Pemberton Historical Park** (see *To See*).

FERRIES The **Whitehaven Ferry** (410-873-2862), off MD 352 in Whitehaven, lays claims to being the oldest ferry in continuous operation in the United States. (A ferry in New Jersey is older but has not been in continuous use.) Connected to a fixed line, the ferry's journey across the Wicomico River lasts less than 5 minutes, but offers some of the most free fun you

COMING INTO WHITEHAVEN ON THE WHITEHAVEN FERRY

can have on the Eastern Shore. Operates year-round during daylight hours.

The **Upper Ferry** (410-749-2892), off MD 349 in Upper Ferry, crosses the Wicomico River less than 10 miles west of Salisbury. Like the Whitehaven Ferry (see above), it, too, is free and has the same schedule.

GOLF **Horse Bridge** (410-543-4446), 32418 Mt. Hermon Rd., Salisbury. Open year-round. Ponds, waste bunkers, and drainage ditches make this a challenging course.

Woodcreek Golf Links (410-896-3000; www.golflinks.com), 9080 Executive Club Dr., Delmar. Opened to the public in 2001, it has town houses for sale around the links.

HIKING **Pemberton Historical Park**, Pemberton Dr., Salisbury. The park has almost 5 miles of trails that wind through bottomland forests along the Wicomico River, and deliver you to Bell Island and the site of docks that were once used to load the plantation's crops onto ships.

SWIMMING **Cherry Beach** is a third-of-a-mile-long beach along the Nanticoke River in the small town of Sharptown. Access is free, and there are picnic tables and a playground.

TENNIS A long list of courts located in and around Salisbury can be obtained by contacting the **Wicomico County Department of Recreation and Parks** (410-548-4900), 500 Glen Ave., Salisbury, 21804.

WALKING TOURS A brochure describing a *Walking Tour of Downtown Salisbury* is available from the Wicomico County Convention and Visitors Bureau. Fires in the late 1800s destroyed much of the city, so most of the architecture reflects a later period. The Masonic Temple stands next to the Victorian Court House. The old firehouse and the Brewington Building are two other standouts. Many of the buildings line the Pedestrian Plaza.

The *Newtown Walking Tour* pamphlet is also available from the bureau. The neighborhood of Newtown was built after the fires and has now become the oldest part of town. The Victorian homes found here are magnificent and well taken care of. So many of them would make great B&Bs, but ordinances prohibit such an enterprise. The best time to visit is during the October **Newtown Festival**, when many of the homes are open to tours.

✳ Lodging

MOTELS AND HOTELS

Salisbury, 21801

Ramada Inn (410-546-4400; 1-888-800-7617), 300 S. Salisbury Blvd. About as centrally located as you can get, the Ramada is in the downtown district and has the area's only heated indoor pool. Its spacious rooms overlook the River Walk Park and pedestrian plaza. Complimentary Salisbury airport shuttle.

Sleep Inn (410-572-5516), 406 Punkin Court, 21804. Convenient to US 50. Free continental breakfast and local calls. $99–129.

🐾 **Best Western** (410-546-1300), 1735 N. Salisbury Blvd. On US Business 13 and close to the mall and movie theater. Free exercise room, continental breakfast, and local calls. Pets permitted for extra fee. $120–140. The rates drop by almost 50 percent in the off-season.

🐾 **Comfort Inn** (410-543-4666), 2701 N. Salisbury Blvd. Free continental breakfast, pets permitted, and some two-bedroom suites. $90–140.

BED & BREAKFASTS ✒ **Whitehaven B&B** (410-873-2194; 1-888-205-5921; www.whitehaven.com), 23844–48 River St., Whitehaven, 21856. Maryen and Carlton Herrett have restored the two side-by-side 1800s homes of the Whitehaven B&B, to which they welcome you with a glass of wine and friendly conversation. The six rooms have antique furnishings, some share a private bath, and all overlook the marshes and waters of the Wicomico River. I had a quiet walk around town (all of Whitehaven is on the National Register of Historic Places), took the Whitehaven Ferry across the river, and read a book on the screened porch as the sun set. It is impossible to find a quieter place in the Salisbury area to spend the night. Next visit, I intend make use of the front-yard hammock under a large maple tree. $90–100.

CAMPING 🐾 **Roaring Point Campground** (410-873-2553), Nanticoke Wharf Rd., Nanticoke, 21840. Apr. 1–Nov. 1. There are lots of amenities at this campground, which sits next to the wide mouth of the Nanticoke River: boat rentals, a sandy beach, horseshoes, hayrides, basketball, a coin laundry, and live country music on some weekends. Crabs, rockfish, flounder, perch, and more are caught from the 35-foot pier. Pets permitted on a leash.

☙ **Woodlawn Family Camping** (410-896-2979), 1209 Walnut St., Delmar, 21875. Mar. 15–Oct. 31. One of the smallest, but lowest-cost, private campgrounds on the Eastern Shore. Free showers. Pets permitted on a leash.

✳ Where to Eat

EATING OUT

Salisbury

✐ **Cactus Taverna** (410-548-1254), 2420 N. Salisbury Blvd. This restaurant is the end store of a small strip mall, so there isn't a lot of atmosphere, but the quality of the Mexican, South American, and Mediterranean dishes makes up for it. The shrimp Cancún with raspberry sauce ($15.95) is a house favorite, as is the lamb shank roasted in a Spanish red sauce ($14.95). The huge plate of paella ($14.95) I ordered brought back delectable memories of travels to Spain. Lots of appetizers, vegetarian selections, Mexican specialties, and a children's menu could keep you coming back often. Low-key live entertainment some evenings.

✐ **Brew River Restaurant and Bar** (410-677-6757), 502 W. Main St. The atmosphere and food remind me of an Applebee's or T.G.I. Friday's. The scenery is nice, as the restaurant sits at the end of River Walk Park on the Wicomico River; lots of seating on the outside deck. BBQ ribs (half rack, $14.95) are a favorite. The seafood selection is extensive; shrimp (from $14.99), scallops ($15.99), flounder (from $15.99), crab (market price), and a seafood medley ($22.99). Children's menu.

Flannery's Cajun Café (410-546-2570), 327 E. Main St. The flavor of New Orleans. Jambalaya, red beans, slow-cooked ribs, chicken, muffuletta, and alligator. Dinner $11–23.

Goin' Nuts Café (410-860-1164), 947 Mt. Hermon Rd. As the name implies, the atmosphere makes this a fun place to eat. More than 20 sandwiches to choose from ($4–7.95). Entrées are also extensive: vegetable stir-fry ($11.95), curried honey shrimp ($15.95), and Thai-seasoned seafood ($16.95). A signature item is the City Slicker Chicken—mozzarella and prosciutto on chicken breast simmered in a garlic cream sauce ($14.95).

Dayton's (410-548-2272), 909 Snow Hill Dr. The breakfast place of choice; low-cost meals. $3–12.

Lombardi's (410-749-0522), 315 Civic Ave., Twilley Centre. Offers a typical Italian menu of pasta, *strombolis*, and subs. The pizza is the best item, as it is cooked in a stone oven. The cannoli come from Little Italy in Baltimore. $3.50–15.

Hebron

Hebron Diner (410-749-9955), 201 S. Main St. Hearty country cooking. $4–15.

Pittsville

Pittsville Dinette (410-835-2541), 34200 Old Ocean City Rd. Plain, but good, traditional Eastern Shore food. $4–14.

CRABS ✐ **Waterman's Cove** (410-546-1400), 925 Snow Hill Rd., Salisbury. Owned and operated by a local waterman, so you know the seafood is fresh. Steamed crabs (market price) are available by the dozen; fried soft-shell crabs are served in-season at lunch and dinner. The poached flounder Piccata in lemon butter with crabmeat and capers melts in your mouth (lunch $7.99, dinner $16.99). Evening meal prices are about $14.99–19.99.

&. **The Red Roost** (410-546-5443; www.redroost.com), 2670 Clara Rd., Whitehaven. Although it does not sit right on the water, the Red Roost is a classic Eastern Shore crab house. The roof is tin, long wooden tables are covered in brown paper tablecloths, and bushel baskets serve as lamp shades. The all-you-can-eat steamed crab special (market price) brings the locals in by droves, but another favorite, which I tried and really enjoyed, is the chicken cordon bleu ($16.95) with lump crabmeat. The Sampler ($17.99) gives you about everything: crab, shrimp, snow crab, and chicken. Portions are large, and desserts are homemade. Be sure to pick up a pamphlet to learn the restaurant's colorful history.

TAKE-OUT **Downtown Deli** (410-749-0611), Plaza Gallery Building, downtown Salisbury. Fresh-baked breads, breakfast and lunch sandwiches, coffee, and special desserts.

COFFEE BARS **Aesop's Table** (410-546-4471), 124 N. Division St., Salisbury. Open weekdays 8–3. Inside this antiques dealer's shop is a small coffee bar that also serves light fare.

✳ Entertainment

FILM **Hoyts Cinema Centre** (410-543-0902), 2312 N. Salisbury Blvd., Salisbury, shows first-run movies.

MUSIC Making use of performance facilities at Salisbury University in Salisbury, the **Salisbury Symphony Orchestra** (410-548-5587) has a full set of concerts scheduled each year.

THEATERS Although the **SU Theatre** (410-543-6000) is affiliated with Salisbury University in Salisbury, the cast of most productions is composed of students, faculty, and community members.

SPORTS The **Delmarva Shorebirds** (410-219-3112), 6400 Hobbs Rd., Perdue Stadium, Salisbury, are the Class A affiliates of the Baltimore Orioles. Thanks to the wealth of poultry king Frank Perdue, the stadium they play in is one of the plushest you will find of any minor-league team. Admission cost, though, is still a pittance compared with that in the majors. A great way to spend a summer evening.

✳ Selective Shopping

ANTIQUES

Salisbury
Holly Ridge (410-742-4392), 1411 S. Salisbury Blvd. A large selection of 18th- and 19th-century items.

Market Street Antiques and Collectibles Center (410-749-4112), 150 W. Market St. Almost 90 dealers under one roof.

Parker Place (410-860-1263), 234 W. Main St. Three floors of antiques.

All Manor of Things (410-546-4471), 12 N. Division St.

ART GALLERIES

Salisbury
The **Atrium Gallery** and the **University Gallery** at Salisbury University feature the works of students and professors, and traveling exhibits.

Art Institute and Gallery (410-546-4748), 212 West Main Street Gallery Building on Downtown Plaza. Changing exhibits of original works by local and regional artists. Sponsors classes, field trips, and free film programs. As an interesting aside, the walls outside the gallery are adorned with old photos of Salisbury.

Salisbury Art and Framing (410-742-9522; www.artcafe.net/salisart), 213 N. Salisbury Blvd. A mix of paintings, pottery, decorative art, and handmade jewelry.

BOOKSTORES Market Street Books (410-219-3210), 146 W. Market St., Salisbury. A great collection of used and out-of-print books of interest to adults and children.

CRAFTS Chesapeake East Handmade Ceramics (410-546-1534; 1-800-320-7829; www.chesapeake east.com), 501 W. Main St., Salisbury. Dana Simson creates original and bright designs, which she incorporates onto ceramic bowls, plates, pitchers, vases, drawer pulls, and more. A multitalented artist, she creates stationery items, decor products, and gift books, and writes the award-winning children's "Legendbook" series. I thought this would be just another pottery shop, but Ms. Simson's works are refreshingly new and different. Also, ask for the brochure that describes the building's extraordinary past.

SPECIAL SHOPS Country House and Country Village (410-749-1959; www.thecountryhouse.com), 805 E. Main St., Salisbury. Claims to be "the Largest Country Store in the East." With 23,000 square feet of display space for ever-changing merchandise, they may be right.

OUTLETS Salisbury Pewter (410-546-1188; 1-800-824-1469), N. Salis-

bury Blvd. (US 13), Salisbury. Mon.–Sat., and sometimes Sun. A small glass window lets you watch crafters at work before you purchase pewter items at factory prices.

MALLS The Centre at Salisbury (410-548-1600), 2300 N. Salisbury Blvd., Salisbury. Contains many of the usual national chains found in most malls.

FARMER'S MARKET Salisbury. Located on the city parking lot on the corner of US 13 and Calvert St. Sat. 8–1, Apr.–Nov.

PICK-YOUR-OWN PRODUCE FARMS Peach Blossom Farm (410-742-6545), 27616 Little Lane, Salisbury. A retail stand, and pick-your-own cantaloupes and watermelons.

Strawberry Fields Forever (410-835-8586), 4820 Powell School Rd., Parsonsburg. Strawberries for the picking from mid-May through mid-June.

Garden of Eden Orchards (410-546-0081), 4380 Upper Ferry Rd., Eden. Retail stand and pick-your-own fruits.

Catalpa Grove Farms (410-546-0006), 8398 Riggin Rd., Mardela Springs. A wide variety of pick-your-own fruits and vegetables.

✳ Special Events

Contact the **Wicomico County Convention and Visitors Bureau** for more information on all of these events.

March: **Pork In The Park**, Winterplace Park, Salisbury. The National Bar-b-que Cook-off has food, music, children's activities, and crafts, as well as the culinary competition.

May: **Salisbury Festival**, Salisbury. Entertainment, triathlon, carnival, children's activities, and lots of food.

June: **Seaside Memorial Horse Show**, Equestrian Center, Winterplace Park, Salisbury.

July: **Sunday Night Concerts**, City Park, Salisbury. Free concerts by the Community Band each Sunday evening in July.

August: **Great North American Turtle Races**, Cedar Hill Park, Bivalve.

September: **Pemberton Colonial Fair**, Pemberton Historical Park, Pemberton. Music, games, sports, crafts, demonstrations, food, and other activities of the 18th century.

October: During the **Newtown Festival**, visitors can tour the magnificent Victorian homes in Salisbury's historic district. Includes music, crafts, and walking tours. **Chesapeake Wildlife Showcase**, Ward Museum of Wildlife Art, Salisbury. Auctions and sales of antique wildlife decoys.

November: **Salisbury Kennel Club Dog Show**, Salisbury. Competition and judging.

CAMBRIDGE AND VICINITY

Cambridge's location on the southern bank of the wide Choptank River makes its setting one of the prettiest on the Eastern Shore. Author James Michener has praised its maritime heritage, shaded streets, and lovingly cared-for homes. A walk down High Street (with a brochure from the Dorchester County Department of Tourism) brings you past one beautiful Victorian home after another, while the public park and wharf at street's end give a sweeping vista of the river.

Despite Cambridge's waterfront location, agriculture was the area's first important business. By the mid-1800s, lumber and flour mills were established, which in turn led to the building of ships to transport goods. The late 1800s saw a rise in oyster harvesting. Local lore claims skipjacks were so tightly packed in Cambridge Creek Harbor that you could walk completely across it on their decks.

Seafood and other packinghouses came to the fore in the early 1900s and, despite some decline, still dot Cambridge's landscape. Visitors of today find a community that is waking up to its appeal to the outside world. Museums, boat trips, and outdoor adventures on the water and land are bringing in increasing numbers of tourists. The opening of the Hyatt Regency Chesapeake Bay Golf Resort Spa and Marina in 2002 provided Cambridge with the area's first destination resort.

COMMUNITIES **Church Creek** received its name from Old Trinity Church, the oldest Episcopal church in continuous use in the United States. The community is believed to have been in existence as early as the late 1600s.

On the banks of the Nanticoke River, **Vienna** was settled by 1669. Once a thriving port, its size diminished as main roadways passed it by. A brochure available from the **Visitor Center at Sailwinds Park** describes a walking tour of the now quiet town.

Hurlock began as a railroad station and is now the second largest town in Dorchester County. The train station has been restored and hosts occasional train trips.

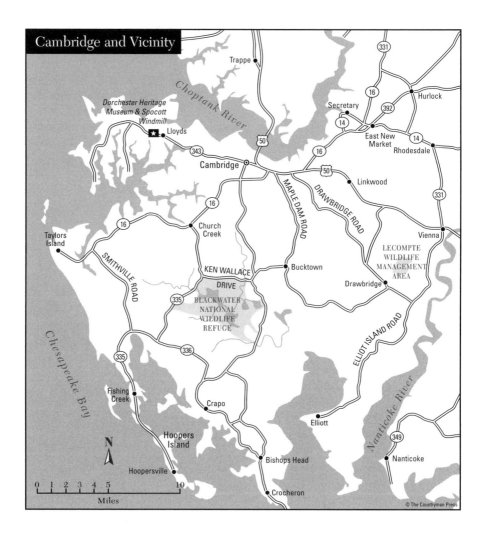

Cambridge and Vicinity

Choptank River

Trappe

Dorchester Heritage
Museum & Spocott
Windmill
Lloyds

331

16

Secretary
14

Hurlock
392

East New
Market
16

14

Rhodesdale

343

50

16

Cambridge

50

Linkwood

16

331

Church
Creek

16

MAPLE DAM ROAD

DRAWBRIDGE ROAD

Taylors
Island

SMITHVILLE ROAD

KEN WALLACE

DRIVE

335

BLACKWATER
NATIONAL
WILDLIFE
REFUGE

Bucktown

Vienna

LECOMPTE
WILDLIFE
MANAGEMENT
AREA

Drawbridge

Chesapeake Bay

335

336

ELLIOT ISLAND ROAD

Nanticoke River

Fishing
Creek

Crapo

Elliott

N

Hoopers
Island

Bishops Head

349

Nanticoke

Hoopersville

0 1 2 3 4 5   10
Miles

Crocheron

© The Countryman Press

Taylors Island is a traditional waterman's village. Marinas, docks, and activity around the water are the reasons to visit.

Hooper Island, another waterman's settlement, is actually three islands and is even more removed from the mainstream than is Taylors Island. The community quietly goes about harvesting and processing thousands of pounds of catch from the bay annually.

A pamphlet available from the **Dorchester County Department of Tourism** points out the historic aspects of **East New Market**, a town whose four entrances are each marked by a church. The entire town is on the National Register of Historic Places.

GUIDANCE & Overlooking the Choptank River beside US 50, the **Visitor Center at Sailwinds Park** and the **Dorchester County Department of Tourism**

(410-228-1000; 1-800-522-8687; www.tourdorchester.org), 2 Rose Hill Place, Cambridge, 21613, have one of the most scenic settings of any welcome center in the state. A gigantic Teflon-coated fiberglass sail makes the spot even more dramatic, while a whimsical outdoor sculpture provides additional charm. There's also a short boardwalk trail to the river and a handicapped-accessible playground.

GETTING THERE *By car:* **US 50** bisects the region with a north–south orientation.

By air: You can fly your own plane into **Cambridge Dorchester Airport** (410-228-4571), 5223 Bucktown Rd., Cambridge. Otherwise, the closest commercial airport is **Salisbury/Ocean City Airport** in Salisbury.

By bus: **Carolina Trailways** (410-289-9307) makes a stop at the Sunburst Mobil Station in Cambridge (410-228-4626) at US 50 and Bucktown Rd.

By water: If you own or rent a boat, the Choptank River provides easy access from the Chesapeake Bay. A number of marinas in Cambridge have transient slips.

GETTING AROUND Other than **US 50**, which nearly becomes bumper-to-bumper with Ocean City traffic on summer weekends, the roadways in this area are lightly traveled and provide pleasant, unhurried driving experiences.

By taxi: **Moxey's Taxi** (410-221-0689); **Streeter's Taxi** (410-228-8791).

By bus: The **Dorchester city bus** (410-221-1910) routes also include part of the surrounding countryside. If you wish to go farther afield, **Shore Transit** (442-260-2300) can take you to most places on the lower Eastern Shore, including Salisbury and Ocean City.

PUBLIC RESTROOMS Restrooms available to anyone are at the Visitor Center at Sailwinds Park and in the Police Department on Academy St. in Cambridge.

MEDICAL EMERGENCY Dorchester General Hospital (410-228-5511), 300 Bryn St., Cambridge.

✳ To See
MUSEUMS

Cambridge
Brannock Maritime Museum (410-228-6938), 210 Talbot Ave. Fri. and

THE OUTDOOR SCULPTURE AT SAILWINDS PARK AND VISITOR CENTER ON THE CHOPTANK RIVER

Sat. 10–4, Sun. 1:30–4. (If nobody is there, ring the doorbell.) Donations accepted. It is the guided tour by founder and curator Earl Brannock that makes this small museum stand out. There is much to see—old photos of Chesapeake Bay steamboats, information on bay activity during the two world wars, dozens of boat models, the compass from Admiral Byrd's yacht, shipwright's tools, displays about the oyster navy—and Mr. Brannock has a story about each one.

DISCOVER DORCHESTER
Pick up a copy of *Discover Dorchester.* It gives not only some practical information about the area but also detailed descriptions of water trails for canoeists and kayakers, and routes for bicycling.

The **Dorchester County Historical Society** (410-228-7953), 902 LaGrange Ave., oversees the **Meredith House**, **Neild Museum and Herb Garden**, and **Goldsborough Stable** within a small complex along a residential street. Mon.–Fri. 10–1. Items in each building reflect the history of the area and include Native American artifacts, a McCormick reaper, and household items from the 18th, 19th, and 20th centuries.

Richardson Maritime Museum (410-221-1871), 401 High St. Wed., Sat., and Sun. 10–5. Dedicated to the boatbuilders of the Eastern Shore, exhibits include dozens of wooden scale models (some are spectacular in detail), a mural depicting Cambridge in the early 1900s, and boatbuilding implements. Of particular interest are the works of local master builder Jim Richardson. All of this is housed in what is believed to be the oldest bank building in town.

Dorchester Heritage Museum (410-228-5530), 1904 Horn Point Rd. Sat. and Sun. 1–4:30, Apr. 15–Oct. 30. The collection of local-history items in the museum began when a teacher asked students to bring in items that pertained to their grandparents. It is now housed in a former airplane hangar a few miles west of town, and the number of items has grown to include watermen's tools (the eel fishing implements are interesting), airplane engines, and Native American artifacts.

HISTORIC CHURCHES **Christ Church**, Historic High St., Cambridge. Erected in 1693, it is an outstanding example of American Gothic Revival architecture. Gaze upward to see the interesting gargoyles on the tower. The cemetery contains the graves of Revolutionary and Civil War heroes and five Maryland governors.

Bazzel Church, Bestpitch Ferry Rd., about 1 mile south of Greenbrier Rd. (which is about 12 miles south of Cambridge). This small wooden structure is where Harriet Tubman's family worshiped in the mid-1800s.

St. Mary, Star of the Sea, on MD 335 on the way to Hooper Island. The second oldest Catholic church on Maryland's Eastern Shore.

Old Trinity Church (410-228-2940), 1716 Taylors Island Rd., Church Creek. Built in the late 1600s, this is the oldest Episcopal church in continuous use in the United States. The floor tiles, altar table, and exterior brick walls are original.

OTHER SITES—WINDMILL Spocott Windmill, MD 343, 7 miles west of Cambridge (no phone). Daily 9–5. Free admission. No, you are not in Holland! Taking on a different kind of project, master boatbuilder James B. Richardson designed and crafted the fully operating English-style post windmill, which can be turned in any direction to face prevailing winds. This is such a novelty that you have to stop by. Even if a docent is not present, you can still look inside at gears and millstones. Also on site is the Tenant House of Adeline and Columbus Wheatly, who worked on Spocott Farm from 1880 to 1930, and a historic one-room schoolhouse.

GUIDED TOURS

Cambridge

Harriet Tubman Museum (410-228-0401), 424 Race St. The museum, with African and Jamaican artifacts, is open Tue.–Sat. 10–2. Tours must be arranged in advance and are available to just a few individ-

THE SPOCOTT WINDMILL CAN BE ROTATED TO FACE ANY DIRECTION.

uals at a time. The museum has a brochure describing a self-guided driving tour, but the excellent narrated van tours take you to many nearby sites to relate the story of Harriet Tubman, who led more than 300 slaves to freedom along the Underground Railroad. The site of her childhood, the place she first stood up to her slave masters, and churches used as stops on the railroad are included. Such an inspiring person and story should not be missed. The tour also provides insight and background on African American experiences around the Dorchester area. Just gaining a different perspective on what went on in the town's historic homes makes the tour worthwhile.

Brooks Barrel Co. (410-228-0790; 1-800-398-2766; www.brooksbarrel.com), 5228 Bucktown Rd. Call in advance to schedule your $5 tour (children over 12 are $3; under 12 are free). One of the few remaining slack cooperages in the country. The barrels were originally designed as meat and seafood shipping containers and are not watertight, which allows runoff from melting ice to escape. Today most of the barrels are used for decorative purposes. This interesting tour, often provided by company president Ken Knox, shows the entire barrel-making process, still done on equipment from around the turn of the 20th century. You can purchase products at reduced prices after the tour.

SCENIC DRIVES A marked route, the **Cambridge Scenic Drive**, is 1.5 miles long and takes you from High St. to Maple Ave. along the Choptank River. Some of the residential homes along the tree-shaded streets are nearly as beautiful as the water views.

✴ To Do

BICYCLING The **Dorchester County Department of Tourism** in Cambridge prints a map pamphlet with more than 100 miles of cycle routes within the immediate area. The scenery is great, and the flat terrain, paved roads, and light traffic are bonuses. Places to eat are identified on the maps.

BIRDING According to the *Birdwatcher's Guide to Delmarva*, **Blackwater National Wildlife Refuge** (see *Green Space*), 12 miles south of Cambridge, is the best place on the Eastern Shore to see bald eagles; it has the largest nesting population on the East Coast north of Florida. There is also the possibility of seeing golden eagles and scores of other bird species.

The **LeCompte Wildlife Management Area** (410-376-3236) near Vienna rewards visitors with species most often found in upland forests and shrubby areas. Also be on the lookout for the endangered Delmarva fox squirrel.

The **Municipal Basin** on the Choptank River in Cambridge is a great place to watch visiting waterfowl from fall to early spring.

BOAT EXCURSIONS

Cambridge

Nathan of Dorchester (410-228-7141; www.skipjack-nathan.org.), docked at Long Wharf at the foot of High St. Cruise times vary; call for schedule. The skipjack was built and is sailed by volunteers whose enthusiasm surpasses that found on many commercial boat rides. Learn a thorough history of the bay, skipjacks, oystering, charts, crabs, and boatbuilding. Observe the raising and lowering of the sail, and rake for oysters. *The* boat trip to take if you have time for only one.

Cambridge Lady (410-221-0776), Trenton St. Dock on Cambridge Creek. Operates May 15–Oct. 31; call for daily schedule. Narrated sightseeing cruises on the Choptank, Trappe Creek, and Tred Avon Rivers on a classic yacht-style wooden

THE *NATHAN OF DORCHESTER* IN CAMBRIDGE

passenger boat. Also has an extensive schedule of theme cruises.

Hurlock
Choptank River Queen and the Dorothy & Megan (410-943-4775), 6304 Suicide Bridge Rd. Call for schedule. Sightseeing and lunch and dinner cruises aboard an authentic early-20th-century paddle wheeler.

FISHING No license is required to fish from **Long Wharf** at the end of High St. in Cambridge.

CHARTER FISHING Among the many charter boats in the area are **Sport Fishing Charters** (410-228-7837), 311 Nathan Ave., Cambridge; **Sassy Lady Charter** (410-397-3578), 2513 Old House Point, Fishing Creek; Double A (410-943-1124), 6311 Suicide Bridge Rd., Hurlock; **B&J Charters** (410-376-0370), 2248 Ellicott Island Rd., Vienna; and **Sawyer Charters** (410-397-3743), 1345 Hooper Island Rd., Church Creek.

GOLF See *Lodging—Resort*.

KAYAKING AND CANOEING A guide to canoe and kayak launches, boat ramps, and facilities is available from the Dorchester County Department of Tourism. An excellent map identifies hundreds of miles of paddleable waterways.

SWIMMING ✿ **Dorchester County Public Pool** (410-221-8535), Virginia Ave., Cambridge. Memorial Day–Labor Day.

> ### THE SKIPJACK WAY OF LIFE
> Skipjacks became so popular because they were one of the easiest boats to build, and many a waterman spent his off-season building a boat of his own. By tradition, the owner of the boat received one-third of the catch, and the crew would have to split the rest, with the captain receiving two shares. So the captain came out way ahead if he was also the boat's owner.

FISHING THE CHOPTANK RIVER FROM LONG WHARF IN CAMBRIDGE

TENNIS James Busick Tennis Courts, Glasgow St., Cambridge. **Secretary Park**, Linden Ave., Secretary. Public tennis courts.

☀ Green Space

GARDENS Harriet Tubman Memorial Garden, US 50, Cambridge. Interpretive signs, landscaped gardens, and a mural are a tribute to the Underground Railroad's "Moses of Her People."

PARKS Great Marsh Park (410-228-2040), Somerset Ave., Cambridge. There are picnic tables, short walking paths, a playground, fishing, and a boat ramp on a bit of land jutting into the Choptank River.

WALKS See *Wildlife Refuges.*

WILDLIFE REFUGES Blackwater National Wildlife Refuge (410-228-2677; blackwater.fws.gov), 2145 Key Wallace Dr., about 12 miles south of Cambridge. Just about every Marylander knows that in late fall and early winter, the refuge is the place to observe hundreds, even thousands, of migratory waterfowl, especially Canada geese. An important resting and wintering spot for birds that travel the Great Atlantic Flyway from Canada to the Gulf of Mexico, the 28,000-acre area is composed primarily of tidal marshes, evergreen and deciduous forests, freshwater ponds and impoundments, and some cropland. Taking the 5-mile scenic **Wildlife Drive**, walking the short but rewarding trails, bird-watching, and paddling upon multiple miles of flatwater are the favored activities here.

☀ Lodging

RESORT ⚓ Hyatt Regency (410-901-1234), 100 Heron Blvd., Cambridge, 21613. The Hyatt is the area's first destination resort, and is being touted as an economic savior. On 342 acres beside the Choptank River are 400 rooms, a golf course, a 150-slip marina with boat rentals and cruises, a European-style spa, five restaurants, and indoor and outdoor pools with slides, a river ride, and waterfalls. Many different package rates available.

BED & BREAKFASTS

Cambridge, 21613
Cambridge House (410-221-7700; www.cambridgehousebandb.com), 112 High St. All rooms in this grand Queen Anne–style sea captain's mansion feature period decor, fireplace, and private bath. The Dorchester and Garret Rooms open onto the back porch overlooking the Victorian gardens. The Garden Room caught my fancy with its poster bed and original 1847 bathtub, sink, and curved wood walls. A full breakfast, with sweet breads, is cooked to order. A short walk from the river and town wharf. $120.

Glasgow Inn B&B (410-228-0575), 1500 Hambrooks Blvd. Glasgow was built in 1760 as the home of William Vans Murray, statesman, ambassador, and friend of George Washington, John Adams, and James Madison. He is believed to have set the stage for the Louisiana Purchase. The B&B

offers seven rooms (two with shared bath, $100; the other five with private bath, $150), six fireplaces, and a Christian atmosphere.

Hurlock 21643

North Fork B&B (410-943-4706; 1-800-N-FORK-BB), 6505 Palmers Mill Rd. Andrea and Frank Feltz welcome guests to their quiet 7-acre retreat on Marshyhope Creek. The main house has a suite ($140) and rooms with private bath ($120). The creek-view room is the one to ask for. A separate guest house has three rooms; you may rent one or all ($180–240). The second night in any room is about half off. Free use of rowboat and other facilities.

Vienna, 21869

☙ **The Tavern House B&B** (410-376-3347), 111 Water St. The Tavern House is one of the oldest structures on the Eastern Shore, predating 1800 and overlooking the Nanticoke River. Harvey and Elise Altergott have restored its colonial countenance. A somewhat plain exterior disguises the simple elegance of the interior. Numerous fireplaces, carved woodwork, authentic colors, and white lime, sand, and hair plaster evoke yesteryear. Rooms, with shared baths, are in period decor. The best parts of my stay, though, were the great conversations with Harvey and Elise during evening refreshments and breakfast. $75.

COTTAGES **Commodore's Cottage** (410-228-6398; 1-800-228-6398), 215 Glenburn Ave., Cambridge, 21613. Shirley and Earl Brannock have created their own 3-acre compound in a residential section of town. Encircling Shirley's prizewinning garden are the Brannocks' home, the Carriage House (living room, kitchen,

and bedroom, $85), the Commodore's Cottage (living room, kitchen, and two bedrooms, $95), and the Brannock Maritime Museum (see *To See*). It's like having your own home, but with a generous continental breakfast delivered to you each morning.

✳ Where to Eat
DINING OUT

Cambridge

Canvasback Restaurant and Irish Pub (410-221-5177), 420 Race St. Tony and Marion Thomas have taken an old storefront and turned it into one of the region's best dining experiences. Lunch is a casual affair, with sandwiches, salads, pasta, and pizza. Dinner entrées change frequently and are clever variations on familiar themes. Undeniably good when I visited was the fried pecan-coated soft-shell crab served with whiskey-lemon butter ($24.95). Then there was lobster ravioli ($17.95) and chicken scaloppine stuffed with crabmeat and cheese ($22.50).

Hurlock

Suicide Bridge Restaurant (410-943-4689; www.suicidebridge.com), 6304 Suicide Bridge Rd. The region's special-occasion restaurant, it has picture windows and a deck overlooking Cabin Creek. Nautical charts on the tabletops, wood paneling, and a stone fireplace add to the chimerical atmosphere. A local native, owner Dave Hickerson has been in the seafood business for close to two decades, so dishes such as Chesapeake rockfish ($15.95) and crab imperial ($19.95) reflect his experience. Daily specials are an extra value. The restaurant's name reflects true incidents; ask for the explanation.

Cambridge

✍ **Snappers Waterfront Cafe** (410-228-0112), 112 Commerce St. Crabcakes (market price) and other seafood (from $13.95). The Crab Skins, potato skins stuffed with crab and cheese, are worth the $6.95 price. Large picture windows provide a view of Cambridge Creek Harbor. Becomes a busy local watering hole on summer and weekend evenings. *Please note:* Ownership changed just as this book went to press, so expect some menu changes.

✍ **Spicers** (410-221-0222), Woods Rd. Owners, and natives of the area, Guy and Jennifer Edgar have retained some of the recipes of former owner Becky Spicer while developing some of their own. Adding a different feel to the usual seafood house are Guy's mounted trophies of deer, ducks, and swordfish. Sandwiches (from $4.95), seafood ($12.95–18.95), chicken and steaks ($8.95–15.95), and homemade desserts. All entrées come with moist corn bread, a vanishing Eastern Shore tradition. There is also a fresh seafood counter for take-out.

Cambridge Diner (410-228-8898), 2924 Old US 50. Open 24 hours every day. Good diner food, with a menu that is seven pages long. Breakfast starts at $3 and sandwiches at $3. Entrées ($7.95–25.95) include Italian specialties, seafood, steaks, chops, and just about everything in between.

CRABS ✍ **Portside** (410-228-9007), 210 Trenton St., Cambridge. A characteristically casual seafood restaurant with wooden tables and vinyl-covered booths. The outside deck is beside Cambridge Creek. Steamed crabs (market price) are, of course, a favorite. The shrimp scampi with pasta ($15.95) I sampled was hot and spicy, while my companion liked the teriyaki tuna steak ($14.95). Sandwiches (from $5.95), salads (from $6.50), and a host of calorie-laden appetizers (from $4).

COFFEE BAR **The Place on Race Café** (410-228-0833), 421 Race St., Cambridge. An espresso bar that also serves sandwiches, soups, and pastries at a former soda fountain. Shares space with the Lilyfield Gallery (see *Selective Shopping*).

✴ Entertainment

Sailwinds Park in Dorchester is the site of concerts, plays, festivals, carnivals, community events, and more. Contact the Dorchester County Department of Tourism for a schedule of events.

✴ Selective Shopping

ANTIQUES

Cambridge

Heirloom Antiques Gallery (410-228-8445), 419 Academy St. A cooperative for several dealers of furniture, pottery, clocks, jewelry, and other antique items.

Packing House Antiques (410-221-8544), 411 Dorchester Ave. More than 135 dealers under one roof.

ART GALLERIES

Cambridge

Dorchester Art Center (410-228-7782), 120 High St. Ever-changing gallery exhibits of local artists and craftspeople. Paintings, pottery, baskets, quilts, sculptures, books, and more for sale in the gift shop. Sponsors concerts, plays, and lectures.

Gallery 447 (410-228-7177), 447 Race St., Suite 201. Several artists have studios inside this building and exhibit their works in the gallery.

Lilyfield Gallery (410-228-0833), 421 Race St. The works of numerous local artists and craftspeople share space with the Place on Race Café (see *Where to Eat*). A "meet the artist" event is held Fri. evening.

(see *Where to Eat*)

SPECIAL SHOPS

Cambridge

Alternative Gift Gallery (410-228-0360; www.alternativegiftgallery.com), 533 Poplar St. Offers items not found in the average gift shop. One-of-a-kind originals, contemporary and modern art, and imported and local handcrafted textiles.

Joie de Vivre (410-228-7000), 410 Race St. Artist-owner Joy Staniforth has assembled an impressive diversity of her own works and that of other local and international artists. Joy mostly works with textiles, but you will also find jewelry, wall hangings, and stained glass. Not just another run-of-the-mill store; there are some unique and distinctive items here.

Bay Country Shop (410-221-0700; 1-800-467-2046), 2709 Ocean Gateway (US 50). A nice mix of quality clothing, books, gifts, and artwork by local and regional artists and craftspeople. The wildlife decoys, boat models, and paintings are worth seeing, even if you don't intend to purchase anything.

Craig's Drug Store (410-228-3322), 409 Race St. Of interest because it has been serving the community since 1867.

✳ Special Events

February: **National Outdoor Show** (410-397-8535), Golden Hill. Muskrat skinning, trap setting, oyster shucking, exhibits, and competitions.

March: **Harriet Tubman Day** (410-228-3106), Elk Lodge on Pine St., Cambridge. Annual event celebrating the life of Ms. Tubman. Includes dinner and tours of her birthplace.

April: **Nanticoke River Shad Festival and Kayak Adventure Paddle** (410-543-1999), Vienna. Old-fashioned river festival and paddle course. **Annual Flower Fair** (410-228-1000), Cambridge. Outdoor festival with seedlings, flowers, hanging baskets, arts and crafts for sale. Also lots of food such as oyster fritters, crabcakes, and homemade ice cream, cakes, and candies.

May: **Antique Aircraft Fly-In** (410-228-1899), Cambridge. Antique planes from across the country arrive for judging and exhibits at the Dorchester Heritage Museum.

July: **Bay Country Festival** (410-228-7762), Cambridge. A 4-day July 4 celebration at Sailwinds Park on the Choptank River. **Annual Power Boat Regatta** (410-228-7920). Races and information booth. Great Marsh Park, Cambridge.

September: **Nause-Waiwah Band of Indians Native American Festival** (410-376-3889), Sailwinds Park, Cambridge. **Dorchester Arts Showcase** (410-228-7782), High St., Cambridge.

December: **Christmas Garden of Trains** (410-22-4220), all month in the Cambridge Rescue Company fire hall, Cambridge.

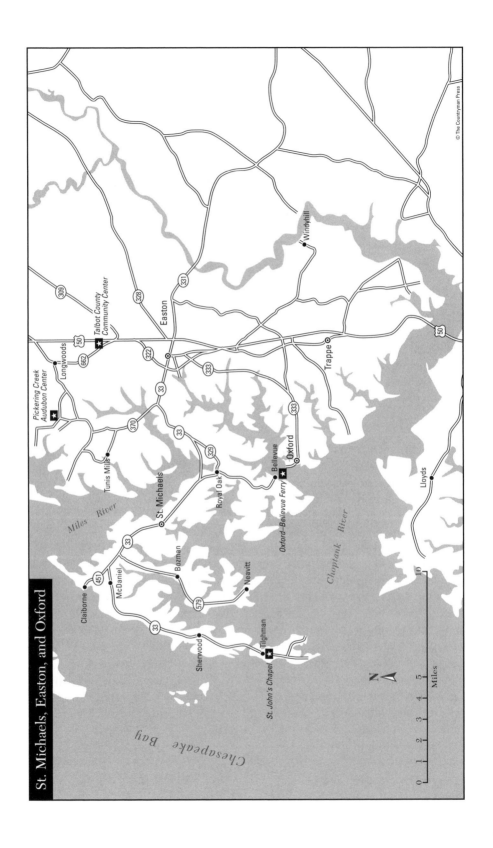

St. Michaels, Easton, and Oxford

Chesapeake Bay

Miles River

Claiborne
McDaniel
451
Bozman
St. Michaels
33
Sherwood
Tilghman
Neavitt
579
St. John's Chapel
Royal Oak
329
Bellevue
Oxford
Oxford-Bellevue Ferry
333
Choptank River
Lloyds
Tunis Mills
370
Pickering Creek Audubon Center
309
Longwoods
662
50
Talbot County Community Center
322
33
333
Easton
328
33
Windyhill
Trappe
50

N

0 1 2 3 4 5 Miles 10

© The Countryman Press

ST. MICHAELS, EASTON, AND OXFORD

My wife, a native Annapolitan, can remember in the not-too-distant past when St. Michaels was a quiet Eastern Shore waterman's village with just a couple of stores and restaurants. Then recreational boaters on the Chesapeake Bay started sailing up the Miles River and discovered the pleasures of eating steamed crabs at the Crab Claw Restaurant. Other establishments soon followed, and St. Michaels is now a trendy destination with dozens of upscale shops, boutiques, B&Bs, antiques stores, numerous festivals focusing on boating and/or the bay, and some of the finest restaurants in Maryland. The Chesapeake Bay Maritime Museum, with exhibits indoors and out, has become a must-see stop.

Many visitors still come by water, but the automobile traffic is also so great that driving the few blocks of the business district is a slow proposition on nice weekends throughout the year.

All of this activity in St. Michaels has begun to spill over into Easton, just a few miles away. Entrepreneurs have recently opened quality boutiques and galleries, and innovative chefs are creating an abundance of delicious dining choices for townspeople and the increasing numbers of tourists. Retirees and other emigrants are coming here to live and creating a lively atmosphere for the arts, as evidenced by the restoration of the historic Avalon Theater and the quality of works to be found in the Academy Art Museum.

Easton had its beginnings in 1682 when the Third Haven Friends Meeting House (now the oldest religious frame structure in the United States) was erected. Organized as a town in 1788, its significance grew so quickly

THE TOWN THAT FOOLED THE BRITISH

On August 10, 1813, residents of St. Michaels learned that British barges planned to attack the town. They tricked the naval forces by hanging lanterns in the masts of ships and in the tops of trees (and blacking out any other lights), causing the cannons to overshoot the town. The ruse was so effective that only one house was hit by a cannonball.

after the Revolutionary War that it was dubbed "the Capital of the Eastern Shore." In ensuing years, it was home to the first newspaper, first bank, first gas plant, and first steamboat connections to Baltimore. A walking tour takes in several buildings dating back to the 1800s.

Bordered on three sides by water, Oxford was once Maryland's largest port, with tobacco and slaves from the West Indies being two of the most important commodities exchanged by companies based in England. The Revolutionary War, and the increasing importance of Baltimore as a port, struck a blow to the town. After the Civil War, oystering, crabbing, and fish processing and packing became the mainstays of commerce, but the town has never regained its busy prominence.

Which is probably fine with its citizens of today, and is certainly okay with travelers who find a quiet village with tree-lined streets, a few shops, several restaurants and lodging choices, and the Oxford–Bellevue Ferry across the Tred Avon River.

A side trip not to be overlooked is the short drive from St. Michaels to Tilghman Island. A slender strip of land surrounded by water, the island is home to the largest remaining commercial fleet of skipjacks in the world, sailing the water for oysters, crabs, and other seafood. Sportfishermen come here for charter boats, while other visitors come for the quiet scenery and good restaurants.

GUIDANCE The **Talbot County Office of Tourism** (410-770-8000; www .tourtalbot.org) is located at 11 S. Harrison St. in Easton.

There is a small information shed with brochures at the corner of N. Talbot and Mill Sts. in **St. Michaels**, and a booth with brochures at the entrance to **Tilghman Island**.

GETTING THERE *By air:* The closest airports with commercial service would be either **Baltimore/Washington International Airport** (1-800-I-FLY-BWI) near Baltimore, or the **Salisbury/Ocean City Airport** (410-548-4827) in Salisbury.

By car: The **Bay Bridge** near Annapolis provides access from the west. **US 50** is the main route through the area; **MD 33** takes you to St. Michaels and Tilghman Island. **MD 322** and **MD 333** lead to Oxford.

By bus: **Trailways** services its station (410-822-5045) at 9543 Ocean Gateway (US 50) in Easton.

GETTING AROUND *By taxi:* **Giant Luxury Taxi Service** (410-822-1201), **Bay Country** (410-770-9030), and **Scotty's** (410-822-1475) are based in Easton.

PARKING Parking in St. Michaels is free on the street, but good luck finding a spot on the weekends. A **free town parking lot** is located on the corner of N. Talbot and Mill Sts.

PUBLIC RESTROOMS In **Oxford**, you can find restrooms at the Oxford–Bellevue Ferry dock, at the parking lot near the end of The Strand, in the public library on N. Morris St., in Causeway Park located on Oxford Rd. (MD 333), and in the town hall.

✳ To See

MUSEUMS

Oxford

Oxford Museum (410-226-0191; www.oxfordmuseum.org), 100 N. Morris St.
Among the many items of local history is the oldest known log canoe still in existence, the "Glide," built in 1864. Also look for original papers on indentured servants, and photos of students from the nearby Maryland Military and Naval
Academy who revolted against the strict discipline of the late 1800s.

Easton

Historical Society Museum (410-822-0773; www.hstc.org), 25 S. Washington
St. Tue.–Fri. 11–3, Sat. 10–4. Guided house tours ($5) are given Tue.–Sat. at
11:30 and 1:30. The museum contains more than 40,000 artifacts, documents,
and photographs pertaining to local history. The items pertaining to the history
of African Americans, the original deeds of property transfers, and an unusual
portrait of Richard Hughlett caught my attention.

The guided "Tour of Three Centuries" takes you through the Federal-period
Neall House (circa 1810), Joseph's Cottage (circa 1790), and The Ending of
Controversie—a reconstruction from the 1600s. The garden, with 100 boxwoods,
is a quiet spot and open to anyone.

St. Michaels

🖉 **Chesapeake Bay Maritime Museum** (410-745-2916; www.cbmm.org),
Mill St. Open daily except New Year's Day, Thanksgiving, and Christmas. $10
adults, $5 children, $9 seniors. Possibly the finest maritime museum in the
Mid-Atlantic; expect to devote a couple of hours. With some open-air displays,
the story is told of the bay, the life of the watermen, and the region's history of
fishing and hunting. The short film about oystering is very interesting, and don't
overlook the opportunity to walk through the restored 1879 **Hooper Straight
Lighthouse**. Several hands-on activities for the kids, and the museum store is a
great stop, too (see *Selective Shopping*).

St. Mary's Square Museum (410-745-9561), Mullberry St. Sat. and Sun. 10–4,
Apr.–Oct. A small museum that showcases the St. Michaels of the 1800s.

HISTORIC CHURCHES

Easton

Third Haven Meeting House (410-822-0293), 405 S. Washington St. Built in
1682 by the Religious Society of Friends (Quakers), this is the oldest frame religious building in continuous use in the United States. You are welcome to walk
the grounds (no pets, please) and go into the building, which has no heat, electricity, or water. The wooden shutters are closed to separate men and women for
business meetings, but the sexes worship together. The adjacent brick building
was built in 1880 and is used in winter.

THIRD HAVEN MEETING HOUSE

Christ Church (410-822-2677), 111 S. Harrison St. This early-English-style church was built in the 1840s and features a tower and spire.

Tilghman Island
St. John's Chapel. Constructed in 1891 of lumber transported by skipjack from North Carolina.

✹ To Do

BICYCLING The **Talbot County Office of Tourism** has maps of lightly traveled routes perfect for cycling.

St. Michaels
St. Michaels Marina (410-745-2400; www.stmichaelsmarina.com), 305 Mulberry St.; the **St. Michaels Harbour Inn Marina** (see *Lodging*); and **Wheel Doctor Cycle and Sport, Inc.** (410-745-6676; www.wheeldrbicycle.com), 1013 S. Talbot St., rent bikes for the day. For a small charge, Wheel Doctor will deliver the bike to you.

Tilghman Island
Tilghman Island Marina (410-886-2500; www.tilghmanmarina.com), 6140 Mariners Court. Bicycle, kayak, and boat rentals by the hour, half day, or day.

BIRDING See **Pickering Creek Audubon Center** under *Hiking*.

BOAT EXCURSIONS

St. Michaels
⅘ *Patriot* (410-745-3100; www.patriotcruises.com), Maritime Museum dock. Rates vary. Cruises at 11, 12:30, 2:30, and 4. One-hour narrated tours of the St. Michaels area and the Miles River.

☙ **The St. Michaels Harbor Shuttle** (410-745-2198), town dock at Mulberry St. The boat leaves every 30 minutes. A 25-minute overview of St. Michaels Harbor. $5 adults, $2 children; pets free.

Tilghman Island
⅘ *Express Royale* (410-886-2643; www.cruisinthebay.com), 21604 Chicken Point Rd. Call for reservations, as schedule and fees vary. Two-hour environmental tours and 90-minute champagne sunset tours.

Also see *Sailing*.

FERRY **Oxford–Bellevue Ferry** (410-745-9023; www.oxfordmd.com/obf). Closed Dec., Jan., and Feb.; $8 one way (car and passenger); $12 round trip (car and passenger); other vehicle passengers are $1 per person. The ferry makes it easy to complete a circular driving tour of Easton, Oxford, and St. Michaels by making a crossing of the Tred Avon River about every 20 minutes—as traffic demands. Established in 1863, it is the oldest privately owned ferry in the United States. You are permitted to get out of your car and enjoy the scenery as you traverse the wide expanse of the river.

BOAT RENTALS

Tilghman Island

Tilghman Island Marina (see *Bicycling*). Bicycle, kayak, and boat rentals by the hour, half day, or day.

BOWLING Easton Bowling Center (410-822-3426), Easton Plaza.

FAMILY ACTIVITIES ✔ **Talbot County Community Center** (410-770-8050), 10028 Ocean Gateway (US 50), Easton. The spot to go for in-line and ice skating, and to try your hand at curling.

✔ **Big Mario's Sport Center** (410-822-7345), 4313 Ocean Gateway (US 50), Trappe. Miniature golf, batting cages, driving range, and putting green.

FISHING On Tilghman Island, **Captains Buddy Harrison and Buddy Harrison Jr.** (410-886-2121) are continuing the traditions of their ancestors of more than 100 years ago by being a one-stop shop for anglers. The **Harrison House** furnishes the lodging, while **Harrison's Restaurant** provides the sustenance. The Harrisons offer the largest sportfishing fleet on the bay and accommodate groups large or small. The Harrison House lounge is the place to gather for evening drinks and entertainment. The Harrisons' good fishing reputation ranges far beyond the Eastern Shore. Many package deals available.

In search of rockfish, Spanish mackerel, croaker, bluefish, sea trout, and more, other charter and headboats also operate out of Tilghman Island and St. Michaels.

A VIEW FROM THE OXFORD–BELLEVUE FERRY

THE *LADY PATTY* ON TILGHMAN ISLAND

The **Talbot County Office of Tourism** in Easton can supply you with a list of competent captains.

GOLF

Easton
Hog Neck (410-822-6079; www.hogneck.com), 10142 Old Cordova Rd. *Golf Digest* rated this par-72 course as one of the top 25 public courses in the country.

Easton Club (410-820-9100; 1-800-277-9800; www.eastonclub.com), 28449 Clubhouse Rd. The par-72 course has over 6,700 yards and great water views.

St. Michaels
Harbourtowne Golf Resort and Conference Center (see *Lodging*). With views of the Chesapeake Bay, this Pete Dye–designed course offers ponds, walls, railroad ties, and protected greens.

HIKING Pickering Creek Audubon Center (410-822-4903; www.pickering creek.com), 11450 Audubon Lane, Easton. The center's nature trail begins in a hardwood forest, crosses several bogs, and ends next to a demonstration garden. You can walk the gravel road back to your car instead of retracing your steps on the trail. This is an easy round-trip walk to possibly see hawks, warblers, woodpeckers, owls, thrushes, and bluebirds. Also see *Green Space* for more information about the center.

St. Michaels

Sirius (410-745-6203), docked at St. Michaels Marina on Mulberry St. This 36-foot sailing catamaran takes passengers on 2-hour cruises on the Miles River Apr.–Oct. Daily departures, but call for the varying schedule and fees.

Tilghman Island

Lady Patty (410-886-2215; 1-800-690-5080; www.sailladypatty.com), Knapps Narrows Marina. Champagne sunset cruises; call for schedule. The 2-hour sunset sails on this 35-foot bronze and teak Bay Ketch are not billed as ecotours, but I learned more about the bay, pound nets, ospreys, and environmental issues than on most nature-oriented boat trips I've taken. The champagne, the sunset, and Captain Mike Richards's tales of the *Lady Patty*'s engaging history will remain in my mind for a long time. $30.

Rebecca T. Ruark (410-886-2176; 410-829-3976), Dogwood Harbor. Built in 1886, this is the oldest skipjack to still be sailing. Captain Wade Murphy, with more than 40 years of oystering experience, gives 2-hour cruises on which you can hoist the sail, steer the boat, dredge for oysters, or throw a line. Walk-ons accepted, but it is best to make a reservation. $30 adults, $15 children.

HORSEBACK RIDING County Comfort Farm (410-745-3160), 23720 St. Michaels Rd., St. Michaels. Indoor and outdoor arenas, and 70 acres for trail rides with experienced guides and horses.

KAYAKING AND CANOEING Tuckahoe Creek near Tuckahoe State Park (see "Around the Bay Bridge and Kent Island") in Queen Anne has well over 10 miles of water bordered by farmlands and forested swamps. The book *Hiking, Cycling, and Canoeing in Maryland*, by Bryan Mac Kay, gives an excellent description of the route and what to watch for.

A brochure describing the **Tilghman Island Water Trail** is available from the Talbot County Office of Tourism. The brochure has maps detailing 10 suggested paddling routes around and near the island that permit you to explore the area and maybe see crabs, schools of fish, oyster reefs, swans, geese, gulls, and other bird life, and observe the watermen going about their business of harvesting the bounty of the Chesapeake Bay. The routes, which are not marked and require a degree of skill and caution, are a great way to spend a morning, afternoon, or full day on the water, but be alert to wind direction and speed, tides, and sudden changes in the weather.

Easton Point Marina (410-822-1201), 975 Port St., Easton. Kayaking the slow-moving streams of the Eastern Shore is one of the best ways to enjoy and come to know the area. The marina rents kayaks for the day or longer, and will even deliver a kayak to your location. Guided tours are also available.

St. Michaels Harbour Inn Marina (see *Lodging*), St. Michaels, rents canoes and kayaks by the hour or day.

Tilghman Island Marina (see *Bicycling*), Tilghman Island. Bicycle, kayak, and boat rentals by the hour, half day, or day.

SPECIAL CLASSES Sign up for a flight lesson at Easton Airport (410-822-8560) with **Easton Aviation** (410-822-8181), Easton.

✳ Green Space

PARKS See "Around the Bay Bridge and Kent Island."

NATURE PRESERVES ✍ **Pickering Creek Audubon Center**, Easton. Open daily. Free admission. There's a lot to do on the 400 acres of forests, marshes, wetlands, and shoreline. Hiking on several nature trails, a canoe launch onto the creek, 150 species of birds to watch, a tool museum, and a wonderful Children's Imagination Garden. Canoe trips, bird-watching walks, lectures, and other programs are offered on a scheduled basis (some fees may apply). This is an oasis in an area where very little land is open to the public for outdoor pursuits.

WALKS See *Nature Preserves.*

✳ Lodging

RESORT ✍ **Harbourtowne Golf Resort and Conference Center** (410-745-9066; 1-800-446-9066; www .harbourtowne.com), MD 33 at Martingham Dr., St. Michaels, 21663. More than 100 standard motel-type rooms at the water's edge of the Chesapeake Bay, each with private balcony and some with fireplace or wood-burning stove. The draws here are the views, bicycling, an outdoor pool, several restaurants, a Pete Dye–designed golf course, and the 153 acres of open space. Very family-friendly; breakfast buffet included. $160–290.

MOTELS AND HOTELS **St. Michaels Harbour Inn, Marina and Spa** (410-745-9001; 1-800-955-9001; www .harbourinn.com), 101 N. Harbor Road, St. Michaels, 21663. Luxury waterfront suites and rooms, many with spas and extra features. Outside pool and waterfront spa. $295–525.

INNS

Oxford, 21654
✍ **Robert Morris Inn** (410-226-5111; www.robertmorrisinn.com),

Morris St. Apr.–Nov.; weekends only, Dec.–Mar. Within view of the Tred Avon River, the inn was built in the early 1700s by ship's carpenters. The 16 rooms have elegant country furnishings such as four-poster beds. Private baths. Some have side water-view balconies. $130–290. James Michener proclaimed the restaurant's crabcakes to be a 9.2 on a scale of 10. About half a block away is the inn's **Sandaway Lodge**, with a small private beach and waterfront porch. $350.

✍ **Oxford Inn** (410-226-5220; www .oxfordmd.com/oxfordinn), 506 S. Morris St. Sue and Rick Schmitt receive rave reviews from their former guests. Most of the 11 rooms have private bath and pleasing furnishings. The third-floor Tavern Hall Room has four window seats with views of Town Creek, yet the lower-cost Chesapeake Room on the second floor provides the same view. $90–150.

Easton, 21601
✍ **Tidewater Inn** (410-822-1300; 1-800-237-8775; www.tidewaterinn .com), 101 E. Dover St. The Tidewater is in the heart of town and,

BLACK-EYED SUSANS, MARYLAND'S STATE FLOWER

although built in 1949, reflects the Eastern Shore's earlier period. Mahogany doors, 18th-century reproductions, and open fireplaces. A favorite place for gentlemen sport hunters, it has a rustic elegance about it. Pay the few extra dollars to stay away from the smaller rooms, as most of the rooms are ample sized and decorated nicely. The inn's restaurant (see *Dining Out*) is renowned for its seafood. $150–295.

Royal Oak, 21662
☙ **The Oaks** (410-745-5053; www .the-oaks.com), MD 329 at Acorn Lane. Built in 1748, The Oaks retains its original exterior appearance but has been remodeled with modern amenities on the inside. Rooms look onto either Oak Creek or the formal gardens. Room 27 has its own deck near the water and a fireplace. $175–325.

St. Michaels, 21663
Five Gables Inn and Spa (410-745-0100; 1-877-466-0100; www.five gables.com), 209 N. Talbot St. All of the rooms have private bath, whirlpool tubs, and gas log fireplaces.

Besides being in the middle of town and close to all the activity, the inn offers another enticement: a spa with herbal bath treatments, massages, facials, and body polishes. The setting is elegant, yet quite casual. Many different packages available. $250–395; about $100 less during the week.

The Inn at Perry Cabin (410-745-2200; 1-800-722-2949; www.perry cabin.com), 308 Watkins Lane. A part of the worldwide chain of exclusive Orient-Express properties, The Inn at Perry Cabin became even more exclusive and luxurious with a $15 million renovation and expansion in 2002. The 19th-century mansion now has 82 rooms and suites on 25 acres, and more lavish amenities than ever. The stay is magnificent and the food world-class, but it is not a place for those who must ask how much. Rates, from $295 to over $625, are quoted once you have made your reservation.

☙ **Wades Point Inn** (410-745-2500; 1-888-923-3466; www.wadespoint .com), Wades Point Rd. Chickens in the yard let you know that you will be staying in country comfort. Located on 120 acres, the inn was built in 1819 on a point of land jutting into the bay. Water-view rooms, screened porches overlooking the water, balconies, and a 1-mile nature trail let you enjoy the setting. Children welcome, but no facilities for very young infants. $140–240.

Tilghman Island, 21671
Tilghman Island Inn (410-886-2141; 1-800-866-2141; www.tilghman islandinn.com), Coopertown Rd. Closed Jan. Spacious and modern rooms and suites with views of the Narrows. Continental breakfast included, and there is an excellent

restaurant on the premises (see *Dining Out*). $250–300.

BED & BREAKFASTS

Oxford, 21654
The 1876 House (410-226-5496), 110 N. Morris St. Furnished in Queen Anne decor, this B&B also features 10-foot ceilings and wide-planked pine floors. All the rooms have a private bath. Continental breakfast in the formal dining room. Complimentary transportation from local marinas or Easton Airport. $110.

✿ **Combsberry** (410-226-5353; www .combsberry.net), 4837 Evergreen Rd. A half-mile tree-lined driveway brings you into the 10-acre estate of Combsberry, built in 1730 along Island Creek. Luxury, quiet, and beauty are the emphases. The Waterfront Room in the Manor House has the best view, while the Garden Room looks onto the Victorian Gardens, which are lit at night. Four luxury cottages (the Oxford Cottage is pet-friendly, with a fenced-in area) provide privacy but still let you interact with other guests on the grounds or during breakfast served by innkeepers Cathy Magrogan and Donna Smith. The house's architecture, the luxurious furnishings, the perfectly cared-for grounds, the hammock on the lawn, and the creek make for a grand place to stay. $250–395.

Easton, 21601
The Bishop's House (410-820-7290; 1-800-223-7290; www.bishops house.com), 214 Goldsborough St. This 1860s Victorian home is romantically furnished in period pieces and is located within the town's historic district. Sit on the wraparound porch and watch the world go by. All rooms

have private bath. Bicycle rentals for guests. $110–125.

St. Michaels, 21663
Two Swan Inn (410-745-2929; www .twoswaninn.com), foot of Carpenter St. Right at the water's edge, with a small lawn in front. Built in 1790, it retains the original pine floors, and all rooms have private bath. The first-floor front room overlooks the water, and upon the walls are official duck stamp prints. The upstairs room on the left has an heirloom bed from the Du Pont family and a sunrise view. $165.

Victoriana Inn (410-745-3368; 1-888-316-1282; www.victorianainn .com), 205 Cherry St. Within sight of the Maritime Museum, the Ionic-columned porch of this 1865 home overlooks the excitement of the harbor. The Tilghman Room and the Junior Suite also have views onto the water. A parlor and sunporch are nice spots for quiet conversation or reading. Complimentary wine, tea, and hors d'oeuvres on weekends. $189–319.

Kemp House Inn (410-745-2243; www.kemphouseinn.com), 412 S. Talbot St. Carved mantels, beaded baseboards, and a central-hall staircase hark back to 1807 when the Federal-style Kemp House was built. The rooms are decorated with period pieces such as four-poster rope beds and Queen Anne tables. Close to the center of activity in town. $110–145.

The Parsonage Inn (410-745-5519; 1-800-394-5519), 210 N. Talbot St. On the main street in town, the Parsonage Inn was built in 1883 and the furnishings in its eight guests rooms reflect the period. Hosts Bill and Char Wilhelm serve up breakfasts of stuffed French toast, egg casseroles, and Belgian waffles. $125–195.

Bay Cottage (410-745-9369; 1-888-558-8008; www.baycottage.com), 24640 Yacht Club Rd. Close to town, but on secluded property, the cottage has six guest rooms and is located on a quiet point of land with water views. $185–295.

Tilghman Island, 21671
Chesapeake Wood Duck Inn (410-886-2070; 1-800-956-2070; www.wood duckinn.com), Gibsontown Rd. at Dog-wood Harbor. Built in the 1890s, the inn has been a boardinghouse, bordello, and waterman's family residence. Kim and Jeff Bushey have operated the B&B since 2000. Many original items remain, such as the wood floors, but their personal touch is evident in many small things: fresh flowers, scented towels, and original art- work by Jeff's mother. The green-themed Shirley G Room overlooks the harbor. I stayed in the Narrows, also with a harbor view, as Kim feels it is the most masculine-feeling room in the house. Kim's breakfasts are always a delectable adventure. Be prepared for crab, sweet corn, and spinach pie; an egg puff with asparagus, apples, raspberry coulis, and key lime mustard sauce; or banana bread French toast with peach and cinnamon cream. $149–229.

Lazyjack Inn (410-886-2215; 1-800-690-5080; www.lazyjackinn.com), 5907 Tilghman Island Rd. Two suites and two rooms with views of Dog-wood Harbor or the inn's gardens. The front porch lets you watch the sailing fleet leave in the morning and return at sunset. $159–269.

Black Walnut Point Inn (410-886-2452; www.tilghmanisland.com/black-walnut), Black Walnut Rd. At the very southern tip of Tilghman Island, the inn is located within a 57-acre wildlife refuge and bordered on three sides by water. All the rooms in the main house have water views, while a baby grand piano fits in with the downstairs decor. For privacy, I liked the Choptank North Cottage, which lets you stay in bed and watch the sunrise. Hammocks in the yard, a swimming pool, and tennis courts. $120–225.

COTTAGES

St. Michaels, 21663
Cygnet House (410-745-2929), 201 Carpenter St. Run by the folks at Two Swan Inn, the cottage has two and a half bedrooms. There is nothing fancy here, the furnishings are simple, but there is a fireplace and it's a good arrangement if you have children, pets, or a group of up to six. The rate starts at $150 for two and goes up to $325 for six; it drops the longer you stay.

Harris Cove Cottages (410-745-9701; www.bednboat.com), 8080 Bozman-Neavitt Rd. Apr.–Oct. This "village" of six cottages has 400 feet of waterfront on Harris Creek. With the feel of a family campground, there is a fishing pier, boating activities for the kids, and boats for rent. The cottages can accommodate two adults and two children. $175–210.

CAMPING See *Green Space* in "Around the Bay Bridge and Kent Island."

✳ Where to Eat
DINING OUT

Oxford
Latitude 38 (410-226-5303), 26342 Oxford Rd. The distinct dishes make this a local favorite. The appetizer to

try is the polenta-fried soft-shell crab with melon salsa and prosciutto-wrapped greens ($9.95). Where else can you have grilled wahoo on white bean hummus served with jicama and nectarine salad and roasted jalapeño corn *mole* ($20.95)? Other meat, seafood, and chicken dishes are just as unusual. Bistro atmosphere with a small fireplace.

Easton

Out of the Fire (410-770-4777; www .outofthefire.com), 22 Goldsborough St. Several Easton restaurants are introducing new cooking styles, and owner-chef Amy Haines is helping lead the way. Her Mediterranean-influenced menu changes seasonally; desserts change daily as well. My appetizer of California champagne grapes and blue cheese complemented a medley of lettuce greens. There were so many vegetables in the risotto primavera that it had a different taste with each bite. Chocolate hazelnut gelato ended the meal perfectly. Other dishes include Caribbean spiced pork, wild mushroom penne, and pizzas (from $13) cooked in a wood-burning stone oven. Bright murals and works of local artists make this a fun place. Currently my favorite Easton restaurant. Entrées $18–26.

The Inn at Easton (410-822-4910; www.theinnateaston.com), 28 S. Harrison St. Wed.–Sun. 5:30–9:30. Another innovative restaurant to appear on the Easton scene. Culinary Institute of America graduate Andrew Evans spent several years working in Australian restaurants before coming to Easton. His signature appetizer, Three Treasures of the Bay, includes a crabcake with tomato confit and tartar sauce, oyster poached in white truffle cream with sevruga caviar, and

teriyaki-glazed fish. The slowed-cooked lamb sirloin with Dijon herb crust is representative of the entrées ($19–34). You can also choose a prix fixe dinner for $65 on Fri. and Sat.

General Tanuki's Restaurant (410-819-0707; www.generaltanuki.com), 25 Goldsborough St. Lunch 11–2; dinner 5–9. Closed Tue. Further evidence that Easton is experiencing a rise in good eating, General Tanuki's brings the foods of the Pacific Rim to town. $12–28.

✂ **Tidewater Inn** (410-822-1300), 101 E. Dover St. Open for breakfast, lunch, and dinner. The Tidewater has been known for its traditional Eastern Shore snapper turtle soup and crabcakes for more than 50 years. Other seafood, meat, and poultry dishes are also well prepared. Choose from elegant surroundings in the dining room or rustic appeal in the lounge. Entrées $19–32.

St. Michaels

Bistro St. Michaels (410-745-9111), 403 S. Talbot St. Open for dinner Thu.–Mon. Chef David Stein, a graduate of the Baltimore Culinary Institute, combines a bit of Paris with the Eastern Shore. In a true bistro atmosphere, you can start with jicama, cucumber, watermelon, and fresh mint inside a mango soup ($8). The pan-roasted venison chop, with sweet potatoes, sautéed rapini, and red currant sauce ($28), is representative of the entrées. Other main dishes range $24–30.

208 Talbot (410-745-3838; www .208talbot.com), 208 N. Talbot St. Open for dinner 5–9 Sun., Wed., and Thu.; 5–10 Fri. and Sat. Casually elegant atmosphere; coat and tie welcome but not necessary. Paul Milne graduated first in his class at the Culinary Institute of America and has been winning awards since. He uses fresh seafood and local produce to make baked oysters, sauté of snail, peppered rockfish, and grilled salmon. $20–35. Saturday-night dinner is prix fixe for $50.

Tilghman Island
Tilghman Island Inn (410-886-2141; www.tilghmanislandinn.com), Coopertown Rd. The picture windows and outside deck provide views of Knapps Narrows. Executive chef David McCallum's dishes have been winning awards and accolades for the inn since the late 1980s. The black-eyed pea cakes with tomato salsa is one of his signature appetizers. The rockfish Norfolk I had was a thick fillet smothered by crab, prosciutto, sherry, and succotash. Pasta, paella, beef, duck, and more are served with similar flair. $19–32.

St. Michaels
Town Dock Restaurant (410-745-5577; 1-800-884-0103; www.towndock.com), 125 Mulberry St. Yes, you can get steamed crabs (market price) here, but chef Michael Rork is known for much more. The crab bisque ($5.95) or oysters Rockefeller ($9.50) should be your appetizer—I had both. Choosing among the potato-crusted rockfish sautéed with shrimp and green tomato piccalilli ($22.95), roast free-range chicken ($19.95), and southern-style shrimp with grits and andouille sausage ($23.95) is tough. A complimentary chocolate-covered strawberry comes with all meals. Inside seats and outside deck overlook the harbor.

Tilghman Island
Bay Hundred (410-886-2126), 6178 Tilghman Island Rd. Breakfast, lunch,

THE HOOPER STRAIGHT LIGHTHOUSE AT THE CHESAPEAKE BAY MARITIME MUSEUM

and dinner. The picture windows look out upon the boat activity of Knapps Narrows. Mussels Aegean and clam picante are chef Brian Bennett's signature appetizers. Sandwiches, beef, chicken, and seafood fresh from the bay. $6.95–23.95. Ask about the history of the restaurant's name.

So Neat Café (410-886-2143), Black Walnut Rd. A small shop with specialty omelets, French toast, Belgian waffles, and quiches for breakfast and lunch. The Baltimore omelet with crab, asparagus, and hollandaise sauce starts the day deliciously. Most meals $10 or less.

CRABS

St. Michaels

⚓ St. Michaels Crab and Steak **House** (410-745-3737; www .stmichaelscrabhouse.com), 305 Mulberry St. Owner-chef Eric Rosen turns out a crab dip ($7.95) that is a superb, melt-in-your-mouth appetizer, while his crab balls (95¢ each) are, refreshingly, broiled and not fried. Steamed crabs (market price) are available by the dozen or half dozen. I have sampled several different entrées here and was well satisfied with all of them ($10.95– 24.95). The 1830s former oyster-shucking house on the waterfront makes this an appropriate setting for the restaurant.

⚓ **The Crab Claw** (410-745-2900), on the waterfront. Open daily 11–10, Mar.–Nov. This place could almost be credited with turning St. Michaels into a tourist town—and establishing what an Eastern Shore crab house should look like. Pleasure boaters and

sailors have been pulling up to its dock since 1965 to feast upon bushels of fresh-steamed crabs (market price) on the outside deck. Oysters on the half shell and steamed cherrystone clams are also popular. Entrées start at about $14.

TAKE-OUT

Easton

Captain's Ketch Seafood (410-820-7177; 1-800-318-4749; www.captains -ketch.com), 316 Glebe Rd. Fresh seafood packed for take-home, travel, or shipment.

Railway Market (410-822-4852), 108 Marlboro Rd. A gourmet supermarket with organic produce, fresh breads and pastries, sushi bar, juices, and espresso.

St. Michaels

Gourmet by the Bay (410-745-6260), 415 S. Talbot St. This small store is about a block from the main shopping area, so many people never stop by to taste the wonderful fresh breads, pâtés, mousses, and fresh fudges. The flavors of the homemade ice cream by the pint remind you of what ice cream is supposed to be. Sidney and Jim Trond will also make you a picnic basket filled with seasonally available items.

COFFEE BARS

Easton

🐾 **Coffee East** (410-819-6711), 5 Goldsborough St. Coffees, teas, shakes, pastries, candies, salads, and sandwiches. A small shop with just a few seats that does a brisk breakfast and lunch business. The "Andrew" sandwich ($5.29) I enjoyed had low-fat ham, cucumbers, red peppers, and mango chutney. They are pet-friendly and even give free doggy treats. Internet access also.

St. Michaels
Blue Crab Coffee Co. (410-745-4155), 211 N. Talbot St. Full-service espresso bar and other specialty coffees. Pastries and desserts.

SNACKS AND GOODIES

Easton
Old Towne Creamery (410-820-5223), 9B Goldsborough St. Ice cream, frozen yogurt, shakes, sundaes, and Italian ices.

Sweet Nina's (410-763-9272), 37 Dover St. A place to warm up with Italian espresso and cool off with wonderful flavors of gelati.

St. Michaels
St. Michaels Candy Co. (410-745-6060; 1-888-570-5060; www.candyisdandy.com), 216 S. Talbot St. Maryland handmade chocolates and truffles, cookies, jelly beans, and gourmet-candy gift baskets.

Justine's (410-745-5416), 106 N. Talbot St. Ice cream and yogurt.

✳ Entertainment
FILM Tred Avon Movies (410-822-5566), Tred Avon Square, Easton. First-run movies.

Also see *Theaters* for vintage and nonmainstream films.

THEATERS Avalon Theater (410-822-0345), Dover and Harrison Sts., Easton. A wide range of plays, symphonies, variety shows, musicals, dance, movies, and arts is presented within this historic art deco theater. Worth a peek inside even if you are not attending a function.

✳ Selective Shopping
ANTIQUES

Easton
There are so many antiques shops in Easton that it would be impossible to list them all in this book. A small guide available from the **Easton Business Management Authority** (410-822-0065; www.eastonmd.org), 14 S. Harrison St., describes what more than a dozen dealers offer.

Tharpe Antiques (410-822-0773), 30 S. Washington St. A consignment shop operated in the late-1800s Mary Jenkins House by the Talbot County Historical Society.

St. Michaels
Canton Row (410-745-2440), 216-C Talbot St. Antiques of every shape and form from more than a dozen dealers.

Pennywhistle (410-745-9771), 408 S. Talbot St. In business for more than two decades.

ART GALLERIES

Easton
Academy Art Museum (410-822-2787), 106 South St. Small admission fee. By far one of the best local arts councils in Maryland. They sponsor lecture series, dances, music, theater events, and a host of classes for children and adults. In addition to national touring exhibits, the museum offers changing displays that showcase the talents of local artists—and the quality is above what you often find through an arts council.

Troika Gallery (410-770-9190; www.troikagallery.com), 9 S. Harrison St. Laura Era, Dorothy F. Newland, and Jennifer Heyd Wharton present their works and those of other artists.

✑ **South Street Art Gallery** (410-770-8350; www.southstreetartgallery .com), 5 South St. Works of local and national artists—and a children's gallery room.

BOOKSTORES

Easton
News Center (410-822-7212), 218 N. Talbot St. Newspapers, magazines, and the area's largest bookstore.

St. Michaels
Chesapeake Bay Maritime Museum Store. One of the best and largest collections of maritime and local books and authors to be found on the Eastern Shore. There are also quality selections of children's toys, nautical items, and artwork. (Also see *To See*.)

USED BOOKS Janet Fanto (410-763-9030), 13 N. Harrison St., Easton. Used books and antiques.

Unicorn Book Shop (410-476-3838), US 50, Trappe. Rare and secondhand books bought and sold. Maps, too.

WINDOW-SHOPPING IN ST. MICHAELS

SPECIAL SHOPS

Oxford
Oxford Mews Emporium (410-820-8222), 105 S. Morris St. Gourmet foods, original art, clothes, boating supplies, books about the bay, and best sellers. I'll let you decide how to categorize this store.

Easton
Vintage Chic (410-822-2317), 12 N. Washington St. Very interesting shop with ethnic art, memorabilia, furniture, clothing, and international artifacts.

✑ **Cracker Jacks** (410-822-7716), 7 S. Washington St. Children's books and some engaging toys.

St. Michaels
Flamingo Flats (410-745-2053; 1-800-HOT-8841), 100 Talbot St. More than 900 hot sauces, 600 mustards, 200 BBQ sauces, 75 salsas, 50 kinds of olives, and 800 cookbooks. Throw in cigars, pastas, Maryland souvenirs, Haitian art, and 300 flamingos in hundreds of different poses and you have a one-of-a-kind store.

Chesapeake Trading Co. (410-745-9797), 102 S. Talbot St. A few books, a few CDs, clothing, and an espresso bar.

Captain's Wheel (410-745-6763), 110 N. Talbot St. Gifts with a nautical theme.

Galerie Française (410-745-6329), 211 N. Talbot St. A bit unexpected on the Eastern Shore—vintage French posters and antique furniture from Provence.

The Mind's Eye (410-745-2023), 210 S. Talbot St. A great collection of unique, playful, and useful "things" from more than 200 American craftspeople. A fun store just to walk through.

✿ **Calico Gallery** (410-745-5370), 212 S. Talbot St. Be sure to go upstairs for some interesting children's toys.

🐾 **Flyin' Fred's** (410-745-9601), 202 N. Talbot St. Gifts for pets and animal lovers. They welcome your dog and will give him a free treat. I like their motto: "Come spoil man's best friend."

FARMER'S MARKETS **Easton Farmer's Market** (410-822-0065), N. Harrison St. Open on Sat. and Wed. afternoon during the season (which varies from year to year).

✳ Special Events

May: **Historic Homes and Gardens Tours** (410-770-8000), St. Michaels. Takes place every other year.

April: **St. Michaels Food and Wine Festival** (1-800-808-7622), St. Michaels.

June: **Eastern Shore Chamber Music Festival** (410-819-0380). Various venues throughout the area. **Boat Bumm's International Cardboard Boat Races** (410-820-4104), Oxford. Build a boat and enter the race or just see which boats stay afloat. **Antique and Classic Boat Festival** (410-745-2916), St. Michaels. A rendezvous of more than 100 antique boats and automobiles.

July: **Talbot County Fair** (410-822-8007), Talbot County Fairgrounds, Easton. **Crab Days** (410-745-2916), St. Michaels. Possibly the largest celebration of the blue crab on the Eastern Shore. Crab races, crabbing demonstrations, and lots of crab to eat.

October: **Arts Marketplace** (410-822-2787), Easton. **Tilghman Island Day** (410-866-2677), Tilghman Island. Boat races, oyster-shucking and crab-picking contests, music, and food.

November: **Waterfowl Festival** (410-822-4567), Easton. Attracts close to 20,000 visitors. Wildlife arts, duck-calling contests, music, lots of kids' activities, demonstrations. Proceeds benefit Atlantic Flyway migratory bird projects. **Festival of Trees** (410-819-FEST), held at the Tidewater Inn and the Academy Art Museum, Easton. **Oyster Fest** (410-745-2916), St. Michaels. Learn how oysters are caught, shucked, and eaten.

December: **Christmas in St. Michaels** (1-888-465-5428), St. Michaels. House tours, parade, Santa, concerts, and activities throughout town.

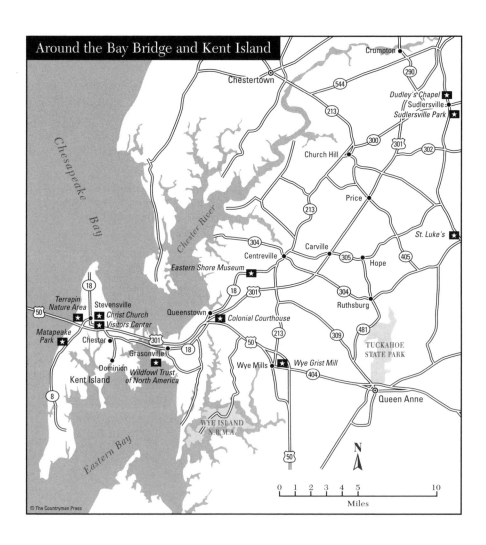

Around the Bay Bridge and Kent Island

Crumpton
290
Chestertown
544
213
Dudley's Chapel ★
Sudlersville ★
Sudlersville Park ★
300
301
302
Church Hill
213
Price
Chesapeake Bay
Chester River
304
Carville
305
St. Luke's ★
Centreville
Hope
405
Eastern Shore Museum ★
18 301
304
Ruthsburg
18
Queenstown ★ Colonial Courthouse
481
Terrapin
Nature Area ★ Stevensville
50 ★ Christ Church
★ Visitors Center
309
TUCKAHOE
STATE PARK
Matapeake
Park ★ Chester 301
18
50
213
Grasonville ★
Dominion Wildfowl Trust
Kent Island of North America
Wye Mills ★ Wye Grist Mill
404
8
Queen Anne
WYE ISLAND
N.R.M.A.
Eastern Bay
N
50

0 1 2 3 4 5   10
Miles

© The Countryman Press

AROUND THE BAY BRIDGE AND KENT ISLAND

The completion of the Bay Bridge, which connects Annapolis with Kent Island, in 1952 opened the Eastern Shore to a rush of travelers and new residents (sometimes referred to as "come here-ers" by older Eastern Shore citizens). In a way, history was just repeating itself, as the island had been in the vanguard several centuries before.

A narrow strip of land that juts far into the waters of the upper Chesapeake Bay, Kent Island was the first place to be settled on the Eastern Shore. Soon after William Claiborne established a fort on its western edge in 1631, the fertile soils of the island were being used to raise tobacco, the most important cash crop of the day. Additional settlers pushed their way inland, establishing large plantations that, around the time of the American Revolution, began to switch over to grain crops and dairy farming. When steam-powered boats made the rapid transit of goods possible, oystering, crabbing, and other commercial fishing became viable occupational choices.

Even today there are several large packinghouses clustered around Kent Narrows, and watermen still ply the bay and inlets, capturing large amounts of blue crabs and soft-shell clams. (It is said that the clams grow three times faster in the bay than they do in the North Atlantic.) With its access to the large populations of Annapolis, Baltimore, and Washington, DC, the area has become a center of activity for pleasure sailors and sportfishermen.

COMMUNITIES Little is left of the early days on the main part of Kent Island. The communities have been swallowed by modern-day America, and about all that is visible from US 50/301 are strip malls, restaurants, and motels. However, get off the four-lane and you will discover little gems, such as **Stevensville**. Developing out of a couple of farms owned by James and Charles Stevens in 1850, the town began to grow, as it was the center of the steamboat trade of the late 1800s. The arrival of the railroad made the town thrive even more, but growth came to an end when rail service stopped in the mid-1900s and the main highway bypassed the town.

Today Stevensville is a small town worthy of a short and easy walking tour. Many of its older buildings are in remarkably good shape, and its historic district was placed on the National Register in 1986. An artists' colony began to develop in the 1990s, and numerous studio-galleries and a couple of nice restaurants have opened and blended in well with the town's character.

Within **Queenstown** is the oldest continuously used courthouse in the state. As with Stevensville, this small village is worth a visit to walk through its historic streets.

A mill has been operating at **Wye Mills** from at least the late 1600s, making it the Eastern Shore's (and maybe even Maryland's) oldest frame gristmill. A small community consisting of blacksmiths, farmers, merchants, and schools, shops, and churches grew up around the mill.

As settlers moved farther inland from the bay, citizens needed a more centrally located county seat, so the legislature moved it from Queenstown to **Centreville** in 1782. A walking tour (brochure available from Queen Anne's County Office of Tourism; see *Guidance*) takes you by many of the buildings still standing from those early days. Styles range from early Federal to late Victorian, providing an architectural view of the town's development. The main business district is along Commerce and Liberty Streets, and it is here that you will find one of the best independently owned bookshops on the Eastern Shore and an agreeable meal at a good café. A nice diversion from the city streets is the Nature Walk along the south bank of the Corsica River.

Church Hill is home to St. Luke's Episcopal Church and the Church Hill Theatre, a cultural treasure for the Upper Eastern Shore.

Many people know **Sudlersville** for it famous son, baseball great Jimmy Foxx. He hit 58 home runs in 1932 while playing for the Philadelphia Athletics, and the town erected a life-sized bronze statue of the Baseball Hall of Fame member in 1997.

GUIDANCE ✐ The **Queen Anne's County Office of Tourism** (410-604-2100; 1-888-400-RSVP; www.qac.org), 425 Piney Narrows Rd., Chester, 21619, has a visitors center just a few miles east of the Bay Bridge and is accessed from US 50 Exit 41. Also known as the **Chesapeake Exploration Center**, it has interactive displays that are informative for adults, but geared toward teaching children about the natural and human history of the Chesapeake Bay and Eastern Shore. A lookout tower provides views of the bay and inlets.

GETTING THERE *By car:* **US 50/301** crosses the bay just east of Annapolis, making this route the gateway to the Eastern Shore. For travelers from Philadelphia, New York, and other points in the Northeast, US 301 is the most efficient and easy route into the area.

By air: The nearest airport with scheduled flights is **Baltimore/Washington International Airport** (1-800-I-FLY-BWI) between Baltimore and Annapolis.

By bus: **Carolina Trailways** (410-749-4121) makes several stops along the US 301 corridor. **Greyhound** (1-800-229-9424) crosses the Bay Bridge and makes one stop in Stevensville. **Annapolis Transit** provides commuter service to Annapolis, Baltimore, and Washington, DC. Contact **Queen Anne's County Office of Tourism** for a copy of the very complicated schedule.

GETTING AROUND *By car:* Within a few miles of crossing the Bay Bridge, US 50/301 splits. **US 301** heads to the northeast on its way to Wilmington, Delaware, and passes through the dairy farms and croplands of Queen Anne's and Kent Counties. (**MD 213** is a smaller, less traveled route that turns to the west toward Chestertown.) **US 50** drops to the south and then turns to the east, providing the quickest route to Salisbury and the Ocean City area.

By bus: **County Ride** (410-758-2357), 104 Powell St., Centreville, 21617, has routes throughout Kent Island and connections with Grasonville, Queenstown, and Centreville.

By taxi: **Dart Cab** (410-643-2466).

PUBLIC RESTROOMS Public restrooms can be found at Queen Anne's County Office of Tourism in Chester; Prime Outlets in Queenstown; and at the Matapeake Trail and Pier in Stevensville.

MEDICAL EMERGENCY Around Kent Island, the closest hospital is in Annapolis: **Anne Arundel Medical Center** (410-481-1000), 2000 Medical Pkwy. For emergencies in the northern part of this area, go to **Kent and Queen Anne's Hospital** (410-778-3300), 100 Brown St. in Chestertown.

✳ To See

MUSEUMS **Museum of Eastern Shore Life** (410-822-6109), 126 Dulin Clark Rd., Centreville. Sat. and Sun. 1–4, Apr.–Oct. Free admission. A collection of tools, implements, and other items from bygone times.

HISTORIC SITES **Colonial Courthouse** (410-827-7646), MD 18 and Del Rhodes Ave., Queenstown. The first courthouse built in Queen Anne's County, the circa-1708 structure was restored in the late 1900s using most of the original studs, diagonal braces, and doorjambs and headers. A simple one-room wooden building, it is furnished with authentic reproductions. Interestingly, the gavel is made from one of the building's original beams. The attached brick building was added as a kitchen sometime in the mid-1800s; it is now used for administrative offices. Check with office personnel for a tour of the courthouse.

HISTORIC CHURCHES **Christ Church** (410-643-5921), 117 E. Main St., Stevensville. This Gothic church, with its steep slate roof and stone foundation, was constructed—using wooden pegs instead of nails—in 1880. The oldest established congregation in the state, founded in 1631, worshiped here until it moved to a location south of US 50.

St. Luke's Episcopal Church (410-556-6644), 401 Main St., Church Hill, was constructed in 1732 and is believed to be the oldest intact brick church in the state. In an example of how important tobacco was in colonial days, the congregation did not pay for the church with money, but with 140,000 pounds of tobacco.

Dudley's Chapel (410-827-4810), Benton Corner Rd., Sudlersville. Constructed in the late 1700s, this brick structure is the oldest Methodist church still standing in the United States. The first Native American Methodist minister, Freeborn Garrettson, preached here.

OTHER SITES **Wye Grist Mill** (410-827-6909), just a few hundred feet south of the MD 662/MD 213 intersection, Wye Mills. Open weekends from mid-April through early November; sometimes during the week. With flour being shipped to Europe, South America, and the West Indies, the late 1700s were the halcyon days for wheat on the Eastern Shore. The Wye Grist Mill is a bit of that time still in existence. A small museum contains many items from the miller's trade, and when all of the gears, millstone, and wheel are in motion, you will be amazed at how little water is required to operate it.

✳ To Do

BICYCLING See *Walks*.

BOAT EXCURSIONS **B & B Yacht Charters** (410-643-1529), 206 Holly Court, Stevensville. The 40-foot sloop *Captiva* takes passengers onto the Chesapeake Bay for 3-hour ($35–45) and 6-hour ($40–55) sailing cruises. Also weekend and weeklong chartered trips.

⌁ **Grabacrab Charters** (410-758-1837), 433 Kent Narrows Way at Harris Crab House, Grasonville. This is an outing for as many as 26 passengers, and designed for the whole family, with crabbing for the kids. The cruise includes a feast of crab dip, shrimp, corn, and crabs. Reservations required.

Orrell's Maryland Beaten Biscuits (410-827-6244; 410-822-2065; www .beatenbiscuits.com), about 1.5 miles south of Wye Mills on MD 622—watch for the sign. There is no storefront here; just knock on the kitchen door. Open Tue. and Wed.; call ahead to arrange a quick tour. The phrase *a throwback to another time* has never been as appropriate as when describing this place. Beaten-biscuit making is at least 300 years old, dating from when leavening was hard to come by. The dough was beaten with a hammer—for at least 30 minutes—to get it to rise. Using a rolling machine to take the place of beating, the Orrell family has been selling the biscuits since the 1930s. After the dough has been rolled, five women (several have been with Orrell's for decades), sitting around an old vinyl table, hand-form each biscuit. Cooked in an oven—not a commercial one, but like the one you have in your kitchen—they are crunchy, but chewy inside. A place with a lot of character that should not be missed.

Schnaitman's Boat Rental (410-827-7663), 12518 Wye Landing Lane, Wye Mills. Full-day rentals of 16-foot wooden rowboats for fishing and crabbing along the Wye East River.

FISHING

Stevensville

& **Matapeake Pier** (410-974-2149), about 3 miles south of US 50 on MD 8. The 900-foot handicapped-accessible pier is open for public fishing 24 hours a day.

Pocomoke Pier, located at the southern end of MD 8. Open for fishing and crabbing sunrise–sunset, May–Oct.

Chester

Island Queen (410-827-7737). This 65-foot headboat takes anglers on a first-come, first-served basis and leaves daily from the Captain Meredith Seafood Restaurant in Kent Narrows at 7 AM and 3 PM, Apr.–Dec. Can accommodate more than 100 passengers.

Also contact the **Queen Anne's County Office of Tourism** for a listing of other licensed charter-boat captains.

GOLF **Blue Heron** (410-643-5721), 101 Queen's Colony High Rd., Stevensville. Operated by Queen Anne's County Parks and Recreation, and open 7 AM–dusk, the course is open to the public on a first-come, first-served basis.

Queenstown Harbor Links (410-821-6611; 1-800-827-5257), 310 Links Lane, Queenstown. Two courses. The 18 holes on the River Course are often within view of the Chester River, while the scenery along the other 18-hole course centers upon a series of lakes.

HIKING See *Walks* and *Parks*.

KAYAKING AND CANOEING **The Choptank and Tuckahoe Rivers Water Trail** is a 60-mile route that runs along the narrow, cypress-tree-lined Tuckahoe River and the more open waters of the Choptank River. An excellent guide to this trip—which provides not only route descriptions but also access points, interpretive information, and cultural aspects along the way—can be obtained from the Old Hartford Town Maritime Center (410-241-8662; www.riverheritage .org), 10215 River Landing Rd., Denton, 21629.

TENNIS Public courts can be found in **Mowbray Park** on MD 8 south of Stevensville, **Grasonville Park** on Perry's Corner Road in Grasonville, **Round-top Park** on Roundtop Road in Chester Harbor, and **Love Point Park** on Old Love Point Road in Stevensville.

A VIEW OF BENNETTS POINT FROM FERRY POINT ON WYE ISLAND

✳ Green Space

BEACHES See **Matapeake Trail and Pier** under *Parks*.

NATURE PRESERVES ✇ **Chesapeake Bay Environmental Center** (410-827-6694; www.wildfowltrust.org), 600 Discovery Lane—US 50 and 301 Exit 43B or Exit 44A, Grasonville. Open 9–5. Small admission fee. The 500-acre headquarters of the Wildfowl Trust of North America. I have always been rewarded with something during my walks on the 4 miles of trails: trumpeter swans coming in for a landing on one of the ponds, an osprey swooping down to grasp a fish in its talons, a black snake warming itself in the sun. There are also canoeing opportunities, kids' exhibits and programs, an enclosed aviary, and special events.

Wye Island Natural Resource Management Area (410-827-7577), 632 Wye Island Rd., Queenstown. Open sunrise–sunset. When Wye Island was threatened with development, many people objected. To prevent future such attempts and to preserve the nature of the locale, the state purchased most of it in the mid-1970s. Because of the foresight of others, a visit here gives you the chance to explore an island that has been used for agricultural purposes for three centuries. The Department of Natural Resources administers the approximately 2,450 acres and still manages them for agricultural uses. There are about 30 miles of shoreline, while virgin stands of timber serve as habitat for the endangered Delmarva fox squirrel. Three short pathways wander through fields, meadows, and woodlands to views of the Chesapeake Bay. If you feel like exploring beyond the trails, you are also permitted to walk the grassy buffer strips between cultivated fields and woodlands.

♿ **Adkins Arboretum** (410-634-2847; www.bluecrab.org), 12610 Eveland Rd., Ridgely. Daily 9–5. Many arboretums are artificially created places, but much of the Adkins Arboretum, a part of Tuckahoe State Park, has been left in its natural state. Walking trails, many with informational signs, and service roads wind through the 400 acres of wooded swamps, upland forest, created meadows, and ornamental plantings. The visitors center has maps and information about guided tours. Service roads and some trails could easily be negotiated in a wheelchair.

PARKS

Stevensville
✿ ♿ **Matapeake Trail and Pier** (410-758-0835; www.qac.org), on MD 8 south of US 50 Exit 37. Open dawn–dusk. A small area on the bay operated by Queen Anne's County Parks and Recreation. There is a free public beach, boat ramp, picnic area, fishing pier, and two short pathways—one of them designated as a dog trail.

♿ **Terrapin Nature Area** (410-758-0835), 191 Log Canoe Circle. Open dawn–dusk. A nearly level trail winds through meadows, wetlands, and forest on its way to tidal pools and an isolated sandy beach along the bay with a view of the Bay Bridge. A nice place to escape to, and especially quiet during the week. Also a small picnic area and portable restroom facilities.

Queen Anne
Tuckahoe State Park (410-820-1668), 13070 Crouse Mill Rd. About 20 miles east of Wye Mills, and bordered by tranquil wooded swamplands, Tuckahoe Creek forms the dividing line between Queen Anne's and Caroline Counties. Just as it has done with many of its other streams and rivers, the state has wisely protected much of this riparian habitat by establishing 3,700-acre Tuckahoe State Park. Within this tract is a 35-site campground with modern facilities, a 60-acre lake providing fishing and canoeing opportunities (canoe rentals available), a ball field, an archery range, and two picnic areas. Naturalist programs are available through spring and summer. All of this is centered in the northern section of the park, which leaves the southern portion—where several pathways wander—undeveloped and natural.

TUCKAHOE LAKE IN TUCKAHOE STATE PARK

Denton
♿ **Martinak State Park** (410-820-1688), 137 Deep Shore Rd. Mid-March through mid-November. Most people come to Martinak to take advantage of the boating on the Choptank River and Watts Creek. The 60-site campground has flush toilets and a dump station.

Stevensville–Kent Narrows

& **Cross Island Trail** (410-758-0835). Open dawn–dusk. Completed in 2001, this is one of the nicest things to happen to Kent Island in years. The paved pathway, open to walkers, cyclists, skaters, and wheelchairs, is nearly 6 miles long. Starting at the Terrapin Nature Area (see *Parks*) next to the bay, it passes through farmland, small forested areas, meadows, marshes, and beside US 50 to come to an end overlooking Kent Narrows. Access to restrooms, dining, lodging, and the Chesapeake Exploration Center makes this a great resource that is a part of the American Discovery Trail, which crosses the United States from the Atlantic to the Pacific.

✳ Lodging

MOTELS AND HOTELS ☙ **Comfort Inn** (410-827-6767), 3101 Main St., Grasonville, 21638. Nice water views are what set this Comfort Inn apart from the many others in this international chain. Also, this establishment is pet-friendly. $109–199.

✍ **Sleep Inn** (410-827-5555), 101 VFW Ave., Grasonville, 21638. Agreeable rooms with refrigerators, ironing boards, and oversized showers. Continental breakfast, free local calls, and a free scoop of ice cream in the evening. $80–130.

INNS ✍ **Kent Manor Inn and Restaurant** (410-643-7716; 1-800-820-4511; www.kentmanor.com), 500 Kent Manor Dr., Stevensville, 21666. This country manor house (circa 1820) has been added onto, providing the inn with 24 guest rooms. It would be hard to tell which are original, as each room has been constructed and decorated in keeping with the feel of country elegance. All rooms have a private bath, and many feature a fireplace with an Italian marble mantel. The inn's 226 acres invite investigation by the provided bikes and paddleboats, or along the quiet lanes. Many special events and packages available. The restaurant (see *Dining*

Out) has a fabulous reputation. $170–235.

BED & BREAKFASTS

Grasonville, 21638
Land's End Manor on the Bay (410-827-6284), 232 Prospect Bay Dr. The twists and turns you have to make while driving to this B&B make it a place you have to really want to get to. With 17 acres bordered on three sides by water, it truly is at land's end. There are only two large guest rooms (a third smaller one is used for overflow); the Swan Room was my favorite with its down bed and view of the water. The wood throughout the manor house, which was once a private hunting lodge, adds richness to each room, while the elliptical staircase and eight working fireplaces hark back to another era. Bicycles, a canoe, pedal boat, and rowboat are available for guest use, as is a swimming pool. Of course, you could just sit in the stone-floored sunroom and watch the daylight play upon the water, or become mesmerized by the fireplace flames in the great room. $125–175.

Queenstown, 21658
& **Queenstown Inn** (410-827-3396; www.queenstowninn.com), 7109 Main

St. Located on a quiet residential street, the inn offers five rooms, each with its own decorating theme, and all with a private bath, air-conditioning, and ceiling fans. Two rooms have private entrances. Guests often gather on the screened porch with its view of the flower gardens. $100–160.

CAMPING See *Parks.*

✳ Where to Eat

DINING OUT **Julia's** (410-758-0471), 122 N. Commerce St., Centreville. Lunch served Mon.–Fri., dinner Wed.–Sat. Centreville natives David and Valerie Clark both worked at a number of Eastern Shore restaurants before opening Julia's, named for their dog, a shepherd-chow mix. Cuisine is American with an Asian accent. Crab summer rolls—perfect with rice paper wraps, shredded vegetables, and lump crab—are just one item on the appetizer menu. Veal scallops and sweet shrimp tossed with pasta and cream is a deliciously rich choice for a main dish. Lighter in calories, but not in taste, is the red snapper accompanied by mashed avocado, lobster-stuffed wontons, and a spicy Chinese mustard. Finish dinner with blueberries in creamy lemon curd. Entrées are in the $25–30 range.

🍴 **Love Point Café** (410-604-0910; www.lovepointcafe.com), 401 Love Point Rd., Stevensville. Fine dining in a pleasant, casual atmosphere. Fresh ingredients are used in creative ways. One of the most popular appetizers is the baked Brie with honey almonds served with seasonal fruit and French bread ($8.95). For a taste of local Chesapeake Bay delicacies, have the stuffed rockfish ($22.95), a 6-ounce fillet broiled with a jumbo lump crab-

cake and crab imperial. Lower in price but also flavorful is the blackened chicken breast with glazed seasonal fruit. Other entrées and sandwiches $6.95–21.95. Extensive wines and beers.

Kent Manor Inn and Restaurant (410-643-5757), 500 Kent Manor Dr., Stevensville. Open for lunch and dinner. Within the setting of four Victorian dining rooms with working fireplaces, chef Kent Tilton and staff offer the area's finest dining. Forgoing other delicious appetizers, start your meal with the lemon pepper calamari ($8) dusted with Asiago cheese and served on spicy roasted tomato coulis and chive aioli. You could order crabcakes (market price), twin lobster tails ($38), or wild mushroom chicken penne ($19) for dinner. A signature dish is crispy skin rockfish ($27), a fillet of pan-seared wild rockfish served over lobster pureed potatoes, baby rainbow Swiss chard, and topped with fresh pineapple and mango salsa. All I can say is yum!

EATING OUT

Stevensville
Hemingway's (410-643-2711), Pier One Rd. (US 50/301 Exit 37). After many years of working with the Clyde's Corporation of Restaurants, Bianna Arentz took over the reins of this seafood restaurant with a commanding view of the bay and Bay Bridge. She grew up in Puerto Rico, and she summers in Spain—thus the restaurant's name. Bianna personally oversees the wine list, and she and the staff are continually trying new recipes. The crab dip was fresh and tasty ($9.50). Just as tasty was the Atlantic salmon with sautéed spinach, mushrooms, and shallots. Downstairs

is Lola's (see *Nightlife*), a bar and grill.

♪ & **Kentmorr Restaurant** (410-643-2263), 910 Kentmorr Rd. (US 50/301 Exit 37, south 5 miles on MD 8). Casual dining with a deck and picture windows overlooking the Chesapeake Bay and Kentmorr Harbor Marina. The tuna salad with chunks of fresh fish ($6.50) filled me up for lunch. Dinner selections include flounder ($14.99), rib-eye steak ($19.99), and half a rack of ribs with chicken breast ($15.99). All-you-can-eat crabs (market price) when available.

Grasonville

Annie's (410-827-7103), 500 Kent Narrows Way (US 50/301 Exit 42). At the Marina in Kent Narrows, Annie's serves steaks ($12.95 and up), seafood (from $13.95), and Italian dishes (crab fettuccine, $19.95).

Holly's (410-827-8711), US 50 and Jackson Creek Rd. In business since 1955, Holly's serves home-cooked breakfasts, lunches, and dinners and is the kind of place that everyone ends up at eventually. The Shoreman's Breakfast ($5.95) contains pancakes, eggs, bacon, and sausage. The Shore Special ($19.95) is three pieces of fried chicken and a crabcake. Sandwiches, soups, and homemade ice cream.

CRABS ♪ **Harris Crab House** (410-827-9500), 433 Kent Narrows Way (US 50/301 Exit 42), Grasonville. The Harris family has been purchasing seafood directly from watermen since 1941, and opened their oystering-paraphernalia-decorated restaurant in 1981. Because it is impossible to find seafood any fresher, it draws many people over the Bay Bridge to devour dozens of steamed and soft-shell crabs (market price) cooked in the Harrises' own hand-tossed spices. The Seafood Basket, with five items and corn, is only $24.95. Rockfish stuffed with crab imperial is $24; other seafood, meat, and chicken entrées $12.95–24. The Harris family also works with the Chesapeake Bay Foundation and the Oyster Recovery Project to study ways to preserve the waters their restaurant overlooks.

SEAFOOD TAKE-OUT

Grasonville

Fisherman's Seafood (410-827-7323), 3036 Kent Narrows Way S. All items are cleaned and steamed or packed in ice at no extra charge.

Hunter's Seafood (410-827-8923), MD 18 and Station Lane. Steamed crabs by the dozen or the bushel. Hunter's also has a complete line of other seafood.

✳ Entertainment

NIGHTLIFE

Stevensville

Lola's. Open from the end of April through October. This downstairs bar area of Hemingway's (see *Eating Out*) serves a full menu with a Caribbean flair. The fun spills outside on the sand when live bands entertain Thu.–Sun. night.

Verna's Island Inn (410-643-2466; 1-800-360-1202), 800 Main St. DJs on Thu. and Fri.; live music on Sat., 9:30 PM–2 AM.

Grasonville

Fisherman's Crab Deck (410-827-6666), 3036 Kent Narrows Way S. Cocktails and live bands on the weekend.

THEATERS

Church Hill Theatre (410-758-1331), 103 Walnut St., Church Hill. Music, plays, films, workshops, and other cultural events are presented inside this art deco theater by professional and amateur groups. Call for schedule.

✳ Selective Shopping

ANTIQUES Stevensville Antiques (410-643-8130), Historic Stevensville. Several dealers of antiques and other collectibles.

Chesapeake Antique Center (410-827-6640), US 301, Queenstown. Daily 10–5. The outlet for a number of dealers.

Dixon's Furniture (410-928-3006), Dudley Corner Rd., Crumpton. In addition to having an almost incomprehensible amount of antiques, Dixon's holds auctions every Wed. beginning at 9 AM.

ART GALLERIES Kent Island Federation of Art (410-643-7424), 405 Main St., Historic Stevensville. Tue.–Fri. 1–4, Sun. noon–4. In addition to featuring works of local artists in its gallery, the federation sponsors art sales, museum exhibits, and dinner-theater bus trips.

Queen Anne's County Arts Council (410-758-2520), 206 Commerce St., Centreville. Changing displays of local artisans and craftspeople. Classes, workshops, concerts, lectures, and more.

CRAFTS

Historic Stevensville
The Glassburg (410-643-5021). Stroll in and watch stained glass being made and displayed in the studio-gallery.

Paul Reed Smith Guitars (410-758-5366; 1-800-723-9096), 380 Log Canoe Circle. The manufacturing home for the well-known brand of electric guitars. Factory tours are given by reservation Tue.–Thu. at 1:30.

SPECIAL SHOPS ⋧ Ye Olde Church House (410-643-6227), 426 Love Point Rd., Stevensville. Fri.–Sun. 10–6. More than just an antiques shop located in a former church. Owner Janet Denny also offers 18th-century crafts items such as hand-spun yarn, handmade soap, herbal vinegars, and dried-flower arrangements. There are also some sheep and goats for children to feed.

OUTLETS Prime Outlets (410-827-8699), at the split of US 50 and 301 N., Queenstown. Outlets for Bass, Liz Claiborne, Brooks Brothers, Bugle Boy, Dockers, Geoffrey Beene, Lenox, and other nationally recognized brands.

PICK-YOUR-OWN PRODUCE FARMS ⋧ Kent Fort Farm (410-643-1650), 10 miles south of US 50 via MD 8 to Kent Point Rd., Stevensville. Mid-April through October, Tue.–Sun. Berries, fruit, and pumpkins. Also the site of the annual **Peach Festival** in August, with a petting zoo, hay- and pony-cart rides, face painting, and homemade peach ice cream.

Erickson's Farm (410-758-1655), 171 Strawberry Lane, Centreville. U-pick strawberries in-season.

G. H. Godfrey Farms (410-438-3501), 130 Blueberry Lane, Sudlersville. Strawberries (mid-May through mid-June) and blueberries (late June through late July).

✳ Special Events

March: **Annual Artists of the Chesapeake Art Auction** (410-758-2520), Chesapeake College, Wye Mills.

April: **Tuckahoe Easter Egg Hunt** (410-820-1668), Tuckahoe State Park, Queen Anne. The Eastern Shore's largest Easter egg hunt. **Spring Festival** (410-758-1419), Centreville. Tractor pulls and other activities; also quilting, weaving, chair caning, and other crafts.

May: **Annual Open-Judged Art Show** (410-643-7424), Stevensville. **Annual Bay Bridge Walk** (1-877-BAY-SPAN). The one day of the year when people are permitted to walk across the 4.3-mile span. Strollers and wheelchairs allowed. A big event on both sides of the bay that attracts close to 50,000 people. My wife was the first person to walk across the bridge and back during the first bridge walk several decades ago. **Waterfowl Weekend** (410-643-7226), **Chesapeake Bay Environmental Center**, Grasonville. Carving competition, exhibits, food, and vendors inside the 500-acre preserve. **Kent Island Days** (410-643-5969), Stevensville. Commemorating the 1631 founding of the island's settlement with historic displays, entertainment, food, crafts, and an 18th-century encampment.

June: **Waterman's Festival** (410-604-2100), Grasonville. Celebrates the waterman's livelihood with docking and anchor-throwing contests, crab races, children's activities, food, and entertainment. **Annual Tuckahoe Triathlon** (410-820-1668), Tuckahoe State Park. A 10-mile bike ride, 2-mile run, and 1-mile canoe course. **Wheat Harvest Fair** (410-822-1910), Wye Mills. A festival celebrating the ways of the past. Oxcart rides, blacksmiths, woodworkers, candle makers, and more. Colonial and Civil War reenactments.

July: **Annual Fireman's Carnival** (410-604-0650), Kent Island.

August: **Queen Anne's County Fair** (410-758-0267), Centreville. Annual **Peach Festival** (410-643-1650) at Kent Fort Farm in Stevensville.

September: **Annual Rockfish Tournament** (410-643-8530), Kentmorr Harbor Marina, Stevensville. **Wetlands Fest** (410-827-6694), **Chesapeake Bay Environmental Center**, Grasonville. Games, exhibits, live-animal programs, hiking, and bird-watching.

October: **Annual Country Fair** (410-758-0620), Gunston Day School, Centreville. Children's games, dog show, baked goods, and more.

November: **Holiday Lighted Boat Parade** (410-643-4101), Kent Narrows.

December: **Heck with the Malls!** (410-758-2520), Centreville. This annual event provides an alternative to mall shopping for mass-produced goods. The crafts show and townwide open house feature crafts, artists' tables, and opportunities to meet the creative talents.

CHESTERTOWN AND ROCK HALL

The word *quaint* is found so often in travel books that I resist using it. However, in the case of Chestertown I must break my hesitancy. For *quaint* is certainly the right word to describe a place with an Italianate-style courthouse, a hotel that has managed to hang on to its early-20th-century attractiveness, and one after another of stately and well-maintained Victorian homes. The downtown has not been abandoned, turned over to national chain stores, or relegated to parking buildings. Rather, you will find small, independently owned shops, businesses, and restaurants lining laid-brick sidewalks.

There are so many buildings of historic and architectural significance that it takes six columns of a walking-tour brochure (available from the Kent County Office of Tourism Development—see *Guidance*) to briefly describe them. The town is also home to a college, but not one of those huge universities that takes over the character of a place. Washington College has barely more than 1,000 students and blends in so well because much of its campus is a maintained arboretum.

The Chester River does not figure in economic importance, as it did several centuries ago when Chestertown was a Royal Port of Entry and later the center of an agricultural and seafood area shipping its wares by steamboat. Although watermen still pursue catches within its waters, it is now a stream of pleasure for recreational boaters and sailors—or just plain beautiful scenery when viewed from the town dock or the riverside Wilmer Park.

Rock Hall is one of the few places on the Eastern Shore that has been able to hit a balance in preserving its traditional watermen's way of life while providing the amenities and attractions travelers want and need. If fact, you can observe this balance every day during summer when visitors gather in Rock Hall Harbor about 5 PM to watch the watermen unload their daily catches. Less than an hour later, the crowd moves over to P. E. Pruitt's dock to witness the charter boats bring in the sportfishermen's trophies of the day.

A small watermen's museum provides a glimpse of what it once took to survive this rugged occupation, while a drugstore is a reminder of what many small towns in America were like in the early 1900s.

As befits a town bordered on three sides by water, Rock Hall has numerous marinas catering to recreational boaters, dozens of charter-boat captains, and

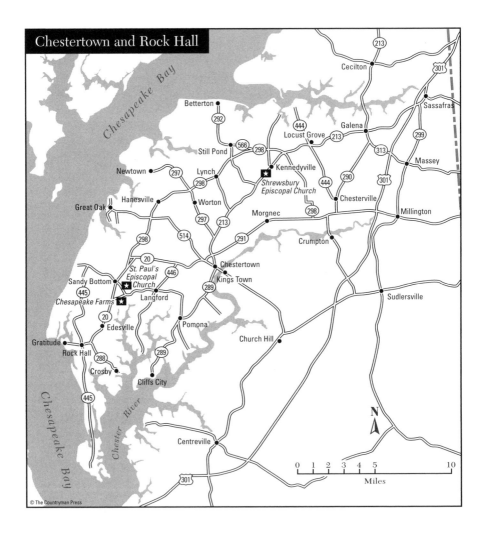

Chesapeake Bay

213

Cecilton

301

Betterton

292

Sassafras

444

Galena

299

Locust Grove

213

566

298

313

Still Pond

Massey

Newtown

297

Lynch

Kennedyville

290

301

298

Shrewsbury
Episcopal Church

444

Hanesville

Worton

Chesterville

Great Oak

Morgnec

298

Millington

297

213

298

514

291

Crumpton

20

Chestertown

St. Paul's
Episcopal
Church

446

Kings Town

Sandy Bottom

445

289

Sudlersville

Chesapeake Farms

Langford

20

Pomona

Edesville

Church Hill

Gratitude

Rock Hall

289

288

Crosby

N

Cliffs City

445

Chesapeake Bay

Chester River

Centreville

0 1 2 3 4 5   10

Miles

© The Countryman Press

sailing-excursion operators. The many waterfront restaurants serve up the fresh catches of the day.

COMMUNITIES **Betterton** was a thriving beach resort in the days of steamboat travel. Although visitors are now far fewer in number, its small beach remains the only place in the Chesapeake Bay that you can swim without fear of brushing up against a sea nettle (jellyfish).

The site of a silver mine before the War of 1812, **Galena** is a small crossroads town with a number of antiques shops and stores. Its dogwood-tree-lined streets come aglow with pink and white blossoms in spring.

GUIDANCE The **Kent County Visitor Center** (410-778-9737) is located at 122 N. Cross St. in Chestertown and is open daily. The **Kent County Office of Tourism Development** (410-778-0416; www.kentcounty.com/tourism) has an office at 400 High St., Chestertown, 21620.

GETTING THERE *By car:* **US 301** crosses in a north–south direction in the eastern part of the area, while the smaller **MD 213** swings to the west to pass through Chestertown.

By air: The nearest and largest airport with scheduled flights is **Baltimore/Washington International Airport** (1-800-I-FLY-BWI), located between Baltimore and Annapolis.

By water: If you have your own boat, the Chesapeake Bay, of course, is the way to get to the area; the Chester and Sassafras Rivers give you access to inland waters.

GETTING AROUND *By car:* **US 301** and **MD 213** are the major thoroughfares. However, **MD 298** parallels MD 213 several miles to the north, has much less traffic, and passes through some beautiful countryside. **MD 20** is the major link between Chestertown and Rock Hall.

By trolley: The **Rock Hall Trolley** (1-866-RH-TROLY; www.rockhalltrolleys .com) makes a complete tour of Rock Hall, covering the town from one end to the other and making nearly 20 stops. It's a fun ride, as its passengers are a good mix of locals and visitors. Ride all day for $2. Weekdays it operates 3–10 PM, Sat. 9 AM–10 PM, and Sun. 9 AM–7 PM.

PARKING There are four lots in Chestertown, all accessed from Cannon St., in which you can park for free 7 days a week. The meters along the streets have a 2-hour limit but are free after 4 and on Sat. and Sun.

PUBLIC RESTROOMS The public is free to use the restrooms in Chestertown's library on High St., the courthouse on Cross St., the Kent County Visitor Center, and the town hall at the corner of Cross St. and Maple Ave.

MEDICAL EMERGENCY **Kent and Queen Anne's Hospital** (410-778-3300), 100 Brown St., Chestertown.

✳ To See

COLLEGES **Washington College** (1-800-422-1782; www.washcoll.edu), 300 Washington Ave., Chestertown. Washington College was founded in 1782, making it the first college chartered after the founding of the United States, the oldest in Maryland, and the 10th oldest in the country. It is named for George Washington, who visited the institution in 1784. A walk on campus takes you through the **Virginia Gent Decker Arboretum** and by several buildings dating from the early 1800s. Lectures, exhibits, and other entertainment are presented in the **Gibson Performing Arts Center**.

MUSEUMS

Chestertown
Geddes-Piper House (410-778-3499; www.kentcounty.com/historicalsociety), 101 Church Alley. Small admission fee; children under 10 free. Sat. and Sun.

1–4, May–Oct. The only 18th-century home in Chestertown open to the public on a regular basis. Guided tours bring you to each room of the house to appreciate the slate fireplaces, original kitchen utensils in the basement, and changing exhibits reflecting the region's history. The Victorian room with a number of quilts, the children's room with a dollhouse, and the fan collection make for interesting examinations.

Rock Hall

Waterman's Museum (410-778-6697), 20880 Rock Hall Ave. Free admission. If the museum is not open, you can obtain the key from the Haven Harbor Marina's Ditty Bag shop store next door. Exhibits on oystering, crabbing, and fishing, with carvings and with a reproduction of a shanty house. It's a small museum, but that makes it easy to see everything; many items donated by local watermen.

Tolchester Beach Revisited (410-778-5347), Oyster Court. Sat. and Sun. 11–3. A small museum put together by Bill Betts, containing memorabilia from the Tolchester Beach Amusement Park, which was a popular resort from 1877 to the mid-1900s.

HISTORIC CHURCHES **St. Paul's Episcopal Church**, 7579 Sandy Bottom Rd., accessed from MD 20 between Chestertown and Rock Hall. The parish was established in 1693. The present building, with a semicircular apse and Flemish-bond brickwork, dates from 1713, making it one of the oldest continuously used churches in the state. Wander around the 19-acre churchyard shaded by boxwood trees and you will find the final resting place of actress Tallulah Bankhead.

Emmanuel Episcopal Church, Cross St. and Park Row, Chestertown. Built in 1767, the large, two-story nave measures 66 feet by 44 feet. Also take note of the Tiffany window on the south wall, and the bell tower, which was added in 1905.

Shrewsbury Episcopal Church, MD 213, Kennedyville. Completed in 1832, this building was constructed using bricks from one of the earlier churches built on this site in 1722. The churchyard dates from the Revolutionary War and contains the graves of veterans from all U.S. wars. Of particular note is the grave of Revolutionary War hero Brigadier General John Cadwalader.

SCENIC DRIVES **Chesapeake Farms** (410-778-8400), 7319 Remington Dr. (off MD 20 between Chestertown and Rock Hall), Chestertown. Open during daylight hours, Feb. 1–Oct. 10. Free admission. A brochure, available in the farm office, tourism office, or visitors center, is keyed to different signed stops along the way on this 3,300-acre farm. From it you will learn how the ponds, fields, hedgerows, and forests are designed to develop, evaluate, and demonstrate agricultural and wildlife management techniques. It should easily take less than an hour if you stop to read everything (you must stay in your car), but it is still a worthwhile drive if you just want to enjoy the scenery.

A section of Maryland's only **National Scenic Byway** follows portions of MD 20, MD 213, and MD 445.

Also see the **Eastern Neck Wildlife Refuge** sidebar on page 139.

BICYCLING Maps of a number of bicycle tours in Chestertown using lightly traveled roads are available from the **Kent County Office of Tourism Development** and the **Kent County Visitor Center**.

Swan Haven Rentals (410-639-2527), 20950 Rock Hall Ave., Rock Hall. In addition to renting floatable transportation devices, they will also provide you with a bike for an hour or a day.

BOAT CHARTERS **Gratitude Yachting Center** (410-639-7111; www.gratitude yachting.com), 5990 Lawton Ave., Rock Hall. Boats of varying shapes and sizes are available for charter by the day or week. Since you are your own captain and crew, you must provide some evidence of your sailing proficiency.

Southern Cross Charters (410-778-4460), Great Oak Landing Marina, Great Oak. You don't need to know a thing about sailing, as Southern Cross provides a captain for you on their 41-foot ketch. Sit back and enjoy the ride, but expect to pay several hundred dollars for the privilege of being inactive.

BOAT RENTALS **Chester River Boat Rental** (410-778-2240), US 213 south of town, Chestertown. Rentals of outboard motorboats, aquacycles, and pedal boats.

Swan Haven Rentals (410-639-2527), 20950 Rock Hall Ave., Rock Hall. If it floats, these folks seem to have it for rent: Kayaks, canoes, johnboats, daysailers, Windsurfers, and more.

FISHING CHARTERS

Rock Hall

As seems natural for an area close to so much water, there are many captains who take sportfishermen out onto the bay and local rivers. Among the many are **Captain Marc Van Pelt** and **Captain Bob Ritchie** (410-639-7063; www .fishfearus.com); **Captain Larry Simns** (410-639-2966; www.dawnii.com); and **Captain Greg Jetton** (410-639-7127; www.gregjetton.com).

The Kent County Office of Tourism Development can provide a listing of many other Coast Guard–certified charter operators. The amount of fishing time and fees vary greatly, so be sure to check specifically how long your trip is, what is provided, and the total costs.

HORSEBACK RIDING ✐ **Crimson Stables** (410-778-7304), Morgnec Rd., Chestertown. Trail rides, pony rides, and hayrides.

KAYAKING AND CANOEING ✐ **Chester River Kayak Adventures** (410-639-2001; www.crkayakadventures.com), 5758 Main St., Rock Hall. These folks not only provide kayak lessons but also lead guided tours upon the local waters for individuals or groups. The half-day tour is $50, or $40 for children older than 10; the full-day tour is $90, or $75 for children older than 10; and the sunset trip is $40, or $32 for children older than 10. It would be wise to make reservations to ensure your time and place.

SAILING *Kathryn* (410-639-9902), docked at Rock Hall Harbor at the foot of Bayside and Caroline Aves., Rock Hall. Captains Bruce and Kathy Meeks take passengers onto the bay on their 43-foot ketch. The 2-hour sail ($25) leaves at 10 AM; the 3-hour cruise ($35) sets sail at 1:30 PM.

SAILING LESSONS **Maryland School of Sailing and Seamanship** (410-639-7030; www.mdschool.com), 21035 Spring Cove Marina, Rock Hall. From Basic Sailing through Ocean Touring Courses, the school can turn any landlubber into an old salt in just a few lessons. Students can become certified by the American Sailing Association. All classes last at least a few days; fees vary. You can take your classes on the bay or travel to exotic locations, such as the Caribbean, with the school.

SWIMMING ✐ The swimming pool in a small county-operated park in Millington is open to the public Memorial Day–Labor Day.

TENNIS Public courts in Worton are available on a first-come, first-served basis in Worton Park.

✳ Green Space

ARBORETUMS **Virginia Gent Decker Arboretum** (410-778-7726; 1-800-422-1782, ext. 7726), Washington College campus, Chestertown. The arboretum was established in 1996 and is based upon the model found at George Washington's Mount Vernon. Building upon the existing trees and shrubs, the college is continually adding to their number and diversity. Although many of the plants are marked by identifying labels, your experience will be enhanced if you pick up an arboretum brochure in Dunning Hall off Campus Ave.

BEACHES **Rock Hall**'s small beach has great sunsets framed by the Bay Bridge to the southwest.

A 3.2-acre sandy beach in **Betterton** is the only swimming area on all of the Chesapeake Bay side of the Eastern Shore that is free of stinging jellyfish. There is also a fishing jetty, boat ramp, and bathhouse. Lifeguards are on duty on Sat. and Sun. during the usual swimming season, but even then the number of people is rather light.

NATURE PRESERVES **Sassafras River Natural Resource Management Area** (410-778-1984), on MD 448 about 3 miles north of Kennedyville. Open sunrise–sunset. This area contains close to 1,000 acres of farmland, marshes, forests, beaches, and tidal pools whose access is limited to those on foot, bicycle, or horseback. Expect to see lots of waterfowl, deer, beaver, and maybe a bald eagle. The adjoining Turner's Creek is a recreation area with a public boat ramp, fishing, and picnic facilities. If time permits, do not miss the historic tree grove and farm museum.

PARKS **Wilmer Park** is Chestertown's waterfront park on the Chester River and is just one block from the historic district.

Eastern Neck National Wildlife Refuge (410-639-7056), 1730 Eastern Neck Rd., Rock Hall. Open year-round. From October through mid-March, thousands of migratory waterfowl winter in the Chesapeake Bay region, many of them on this 2,285-acre refuge. The most common species that have been documented here include as many as 20,000 Canada geese, more than 7,000 tundra swans, over 15,000 canvasback ducks, and an assortment of thousands of others, such as mallards, wigeons, pintails, and buffleheads. Seen throughout much of the year are great blue herons, great and snowy egrets, turkey vultures, ospreys, and bald eagles. In addition, close to 250 other species—ranging from common bluebirds and chickadees to rarely observed peregrine falcons and American woodcocks—have been identified.

Why else should you come here? How about a couple of short trails where you might see white-tailed deer, diamondback terrapins, muskrats, beavers, red foxes, eastern gray squirrels, and the endangered Delmarva fox squirrel? Or sift your hands through mounds of huge shells of oysters shucked by Native Americans more than a millennium ago. Then again, you could come to the refuge just for the quiet beauty of a typical Chesapeake Bay landscape of marshes, croplands, loblolly forests, and grass fields surrounded by sun-speckled water.

Getting to Eastern Neck National Wildlife Refuge can be an enjoyable outing in itself—the federal and state governments consider the drive to be so picturesque that it has been designated as part of Maryland's only **National Scenic Byway.** The island can be reached by leaving MD 213 in Chestertown and driving southward on MD 20 for nearly 13 miles to Rock Hall. Turn left onto MD 445 and cross the bridge onto the island 6 miles later.

A BOARDWALK STRETCHES OVER THE MARSH AT EASTERN NECK NWR.

✳ Lodging

MOTELS AND HOTELS The Imperial Hotel (410-778-500; 1-800-295-0014; www.imperialchestertown.com), 208 High St., Chestertown, 21620. Built in 1903, the Imperial has been renovated to give it modern amenities but retain its earlier charm. Its double verandas—one on the first floor, the other on the second—are inviting spots to sit and watch the world go by. All of the deluxe guest rooms ($135) have a private bath and are decorated with period furnishings. The Parlor Suite ($200) occupies the entire third floor and has its own veranda. (Also see *Dining Out.*)

INNS

Rock Hall, 21661
The Inn at Osprey Point (410-639-2194; www.ospreypoint), 20786 Rock Hall Ave. It almost looks like a modern-day hotel when you drive up, but each of the seven guest rooms is nicely decorated. Some overlook the water and marina, while others have a view of the woods. $135–170. The inn's restaurant (see *Dining Out*) draws people from many miles around.

Georgetown, 21930
Kitty Knight House (410-648-5200; www.kittyknight.com), 14028 Augustine Herman Hwy. (US 301). In 1813, when the British were torching many Eastern Shore towns, Kitty Knight convinced them to spare the two houses (one was the home of an invalid friend) that now make up the inn and restaurant (see *Dining Out*). Purchased and renovated by Joe and Jo Ann Thompson, owners of the largest thoroughbred standards farm in the country, the house has 11 guest

rooms. Some overlook the activity of the harbor on the Sassafras River; all have private bath. Room 1 ($160) is the largest; it has its original pine floors and a private deck. Room 5 may be smaller, but it still has a water view and is only $95. Breakfast in the restaurant is included. $95–160.

BED & BREAKFASTS

Betterton, 21610
🦐 ✄ **Lantern Inn** (410-348-5809; 1-800-499-7265), 115 Ericsson Ave. Just one block from Betterton Beach. Built as a hotel in 1904 when Betterton was a resort destination, the Lantern has been an inn or boardinghouse ever since. There are 13 rooms, some with private bath. Room 15 is bright and overlooks the backyard; Room 9 on the third floor has rich wood furniture; and Room 5 is referred to as the Cinderella Room for its feminine furnishings. Room 1 is the deal—it is large with lots of space and a view of the street. Children over 10 welcome; younger children are accepted on an individual basis after conference with parents. $75–90.

Chestertown, 21620
🦐 **Widow's Walk** (410-778-6455; 1-888-778-6455; www.chestertown/widow), 402 High St. Built around 1877, the Victorian Widow's Walk is named for the lookout on its roof on which fishermen's wives would stand looking for their husbands to come home from the bay or sea. Innkeepers Bob and Sue Lathroum have made the home a genial place to stay by placing family treasures among the antique furnishings. All three suites ($125) have a sitting area and private bath; the two upstairs rooms ($100) share a bath. Its central location

makes it easy to walk just about anywhere in Chestertown.

John L. Stam House (410-778-1926), Washington Ave. Mike and Marta Girone purchased a 200-year-old stained-glass window from a church in England and said they would buy the first house it fit into. A search across the United States brought them to this American Gothic Victorian home. In addition to mounting the window, they replastered, put up period reproductions of wallpaper, and restored the original flooring. Four guest rooms with antique furnishings were completed when I visited (I liked the Stam Room, whose windows looked onto Washington St.), and they had plans to open two more to guests. $100–120.

Pratt-Perry House (410-718-2734; www.prattperryhouse.com), 224 Washington Ave. My taste in art must be the same as innkeeper Carolyn Perry's. The furnishings she purchased on her world travels fit in well with the atmosphere of the Victorian home, and the classically beautiful artwork on the walls is reason enough to visit here. The bed in the Dean Jones Room was made for an English nobleman, and the table is a replica of the one in Winston Churchill's birth room. The wonderfully stocked library, gardens, full breakfast, and afternoon hors d'oeuvres add to the graciousness of a stay. $100–150. There is a two-bedroom accommodation for families with responsible children.

Parker House (410-778-9041; www.chestertown.com/parker), 108 Spring St. Within easy walking distance of downtown and Washington College. Private bath in each guest room—which is appropriate, as this was the first house in Chestertown to have an indoor bathroom. The Gemini II Room has its own screened porch. $110–125.

✿ **Lauretum Inn** (410-778-3236; 1-800-742-3236), 945 High St. Constructed in 1881 and listed on the National Register of Historic Places, Lauretum sits on a 6-acre tree-covered knoll on the outskirts of town. Rooms with semiprivate bath ($75), some with private bath ($115), and a couple of suites ($130–140). Well-behaved children are welcome, and those under 10 are free.

✿ **April Inn** (410-778-5540), 407 Campus Ave. Built in the mid-1900s, the home is furnished in 19th-century antiques. Within a quiet residential neighborhood, it has some of the lowest B&B rates in the area. $65–85.

✿ ✿ **Claddaugh Farm** (410-778-4894; www.claddaughbb.com), 160 Claddaugh Lane. Children and outdoor pets are welcome at this late-19th-century farmhouse about 2 miles south of Chestertown. Three of the rooms have queen-sized beds (two with sleigh beds) and private bath. The two rooms on the third floor share a bath between them. $85–95.

Great Oak Manor (410-778-5943; 1-800-504-3098; www.greatoak.com), 10568 Cliff Rd. Constructed in the 1930s, this manor house has the mien of an older Georgian mansion surrounded by 12 acres. Lots of common areas, a wonderful library with many good books, a grand staircase, and a private beach on the Chesapeake Bay. All guest rooms have a private bath and are appropriately decorated by hosts Don and Dianne Cantor. Free bicycle use and passes to the adjacent nine-hole golf course. $125–235.

Rock Hall, 21611

✎ **Moonlight Bay and Marina** (410-639-2660), 6002 Lawton Ave. Each of the five rooms in the Main Inn has a view of the Chesapeake Bay and private bath. The Garden Moon Room ($120) and Blue Moon Room ($135) are the ones that caught my fancy. The West Wing, built in 1997, is even closer to the water and offers five rooms ($155) decorated in a Victorian Queen Anne style, each with its own whirlpool tub. Rooms 8 and 9 have the most spectacular views. Private beach and afternoon high tea included.

COTTAGES **Bayview Beach House** (410-639-2596), 5783 Beach Rd. Rock Hall, 21611. Nothing fancy here—modern furniture in a mid-1900s-style small cottage. But it can accommodate four adults, has spectacular views of Chesapeake Bay sunsets, and is across the street from Rock Hall Beach. Available for $185 a night or $880 a week.

✳ Where to Eat
DINING OUT

Chestertown
Blue Heron Café (410-778-0188), 236 Cannon St. Open for lunch and dinner, Mon.–Sat. After running restaurants in New York and California and the Byard House for the Du Pont family in Chesapeake City, Paul Hanley opened his own place in Chestertown. Building upon local seafood and produce, his recipes let the tastes come through while leaving your mouth feeling refreshed and clean. The shrimp quesadilla ($9.50) is a good appetizer for dinner but is large enough to be served as a lunch entrée. The lump crab frittata ($9.25) is also great for lunch, but if you come here for dinner, do not overlook the cioppino ($23). This stew is packed with lobster, mussels, clams, shrimp, crab, and finfish in an herb and tomato broth. Meat entrées include veal sweetbreads ($20) and grilled duck breast ($19).

Imperial Hotel (410-778-5000), 208 High St. Open for lunch and dinner. Quality food in turn-of-the-20th-century elegance. Start with the chilled avocado soup ($7) or Thai-fried soft-shell crab ($12) and move on to the mushroom phyllo ($16) or the pecan and peanut encrusted rack of lamb ($28).

Harbor House Restaurant (410-778-0669), Buck Neck Rd. at Worton Harbor. Dinner only; closed Mon. Out in the boonies, a cinder-block building and a gravel parking lot cluttered with old boats mask some of the Eastern Shore's finest dining. The owner is a graduate of the Culinary Institute of America, a former owner of Kitty Knight House in Georgetown, and a gregarious and resourceful chef.

Meals begin with baked breads ranging from dinner rolls to cranberry bread to chocolate bread. The crab imperial ($28) is by far the most delicious, and different, that I've had. Huge lumps of crab are baked atop a flavorful and light sauce. The menu changes daily, but representative entrées include filet mignon ($22.50), rubbed spareribs ($19), and scallops ($20) served with a crispy casino and bacon topping. The crabcakes ($23) are all crab with just a light seasoning. Once you've had the homemade tiramisu ($5), you will never again order what The Olive Garden serves up as authentic. Wednesday is Mystery Dinner night and could be anything. After you eat, you pay what you think it's worth.

Call for reservations a few days ahead (ask for directions), and dishes on the menu will be named for you the evening you dine.

Georgetown

Kitty Knight House (410-648-5200), 14028 Augustine Herman Hwy. (US 301). One of big draws here is the commanding view of the Sassafras River. Chef Michael Dilks used to own the Colonel's Choice in Aberdeen, and his menu is traditional Eastern Shore—crabcakes ($20.95), fried jumbo shrimp ($15.95), and oyster-stuffed chicken breast ($12.95). The dish I really enjoyed was the shrimp and crab penne in basil cream with sun-dried tomatoes ($17.95). Luncheon entrées include crab salad ($10.95), Reuben grill ($8.95), and a sassafras burger with onions, peppers, mushrooms, and melted mozzarella ($6.25).

Live music on the awning-covered deck Fri. and Sat. nights, with more laid-back acoustic music presented Sun. afternoon. As an added bonus to those traveling by water, the kitchen will make up and deliver food baskets to boats tied at the dock.

Rock Hall

Osprey Point Restaurant (410-639-2762), 20786 Rock Hall Ave. A warm and romantic colonial atmosphere seems like the right setting for the restaurant's traditional dishes, enhanced for modern palates. Oysters Osprey ($9.95) with prosciutto, crab, spinach, and sherry sauce is the signature appetizer. The fillet of beef ($22) is topped with a Madeira wild mushroom demiglaze. Duck breast ($19), rockfish with a bourbon maple butter

sauce ($20), and crabcakes ($21) are other entrée choices.

EATING OUT

Chestertown

✍ **Black-eyed Susan** (410-778-1214), Washington St. Lunch and dinner. Has something for everyone. Home cooking with chicken potpie ($7) or liver and onions ($8.95). Specialty dishes include peanut-crusted lamb chops ($18.95) and onion-roasted rockfish ($16.95). For something different, try the snapper soup ($5.95) with creamed sherry or the honey-touched alligator ($7.95). Sandwiches, southwestern dishes, and kids' menu are also available.

La Ruota (410-778-9989), 323 High St. Using recipes taught to him by his Sicilian mother, chef Sal Evola changes his menu nightly depending on what is fresh and available. The night I was there he was featuring scaloppine alla Toscano ($20), veal with peas and served in a vermouth sauce, and spaghetti alla Siciliana ($17) with tomato, baby shrimp, and toasted bread crumbs. Every once in a while, Sal emerges from the kitchen to serenade diners with contemporary Italian songs.

Bayside Bagels (410-778-1101), 4 Washington Square. Mon.–Sat. 7–2, Sun. 8–noon. A great place to grab a quick bite. Breakfast bagels (from $1.69), bagels and cream cheeses (from $1.45), and lunch bagels (from $3.49).

Ellen's (410-810-1992), 205 Spring Ave. Open 6 AM–2 PM Mon.–Wed. and Sat.; 6 AM–8 PM on Tue. and Fri.; 6 AM–1 PM on Sun. The local breakfast spot. Ham and cheese omelet with home fries is only $3.05, while two pancakes are just $1.75. Lunch is sandwiches from $1.80, and dinner is home-cooked items such as pork chops ($6.95) and fried chicken ($5.95).

Rock Hall

Swan Point Inn (410-639-2500), Coleman Rd. and Rock Hall Ave. Open for lunch and dinner. There is no doubt the appetizer to have is the Angels on Horseback ($8.95)— broiled bacon-wrapped shrimp laced with horseradish and served with homemade dipping sauce. Three choices of veal entrées (from $16.95), several other meat dishes (up to $22.95), and local seafood (from $15.95) prepared a variety of ways are included in the dinner menu.

Bay Wolf (410-778-6855), Rock Hall Ave. Open for lunch and dinner. It is unexpected to run into an Austrian/ Eastern Shore restaurant in tiny Rock Hall. Dine like you are in the Alps with Wiener schnitzel ($16.95), Schweinsbraten ($16.95), and apple strudel ($3.95). Or return to the Chesapeake Bay with more local dishes such as crab-imperial-stuffed flounder ($17.95) or the broiled seafood combo ($24.95) with a whole lobster, crabcake, shrimp, and scallops.

Ford's Seafood Restaurant (410-639-2032), 6262 Rock Hall Rd. After many years in the wholesale business shipping clams and operating an oyster-shucking house, Nevitte and Sharon Ford opened their restaurant on the approach into town. The menu contains sandwiches (from $4), soups (from $3), and full dinners. The seafood is caught daily and includes rockfish ($15.95), flounder ($15.95), and a sampler ($17.95) with a crabcake, a fish fillet, and fried oysters. Live entertainment on Fri. and Sat.

evenings. The recipes for the crabcakes ($18.95), crab imperial ($14.95), and crab bisque ($5) are Sharon's.

Millington

Dutch Family Deli (410-778-0507), intersection of US 301 and MD 291. Open 24 hours. An alternative to McDonald's, Hardee's, and other fast-food/road-food restaurants. They serve a quick, real breakfast (not on a biscuit) starting at $3.99; lunch is your choice of burgers ($2.99) and other sandwiches. Dinner is home-cooked ham, chicken, steak, or seafood, $6–12.

CRABS Waterman's Crab House (410-639-2261), at the foot of Sharp St., Rock Hall. Recreational boaters come here to enjoy mounds of steamed blue crabs by the dozen or the bushel (market price). Tue. and Thu. nights feature all-you-can-eat crabs (market price). Waterman's is also known for its full rack of ribs ($15.99) and ice cream drinks, such as the Polar Bear ($5.50): ice cream, Kahlúa, and vodka. Live entertainment on the waterfront deck on Fri. and Sat. nights and Sun. afternoon.

TAKE-OUT Chestertown Natural Foods (410-778-1677), 214 Cannon St., Chestertown. One of the few natural foods and products stores on the Eastern Shore.

J & J Seafood (410-639-2325), MD 20, Rock Hall. The crabs, clams, and other seafood are purchased fresh directly from the watermen. J & J will even steam your crabs for you.

COFFEE BARS Play It Again Sam (410-778-2688), 108 S. Cross St., Chestertown. What a deal. All espresso drinks, none of which costs more than $2.75, are made with double shots. Teas, sandwiches, and lots of baked goodies are other reasons to visit.

SNACKS AND GOODIES Durding's Store (410-778-7957), Main and Sharp Sts., Rock Hall. Enjoy myriad ice cream concoctions while you sit at the marble counter in this authentic 1930s shop. The stainless-steel fountain is original. In step with modern times, Durding's also offers fat-free, sugar-free ice creams.

✳ Entertainment
FILM

Chestertown
Chester Theatres (410-778-2227), Washington Square. First-run movies.
Washington College (410-778-7849). The college's many different clubs, disciplines, and the Office of Campus Events sponsor several film series, festivals, and programs throughout the year, many of them with topics not found anywhere other than a college campus.

MUSIC Gibson Performing Arts Center (410-778-7849), Washington College campus, Chestertown. Concerts, plays, lectures, and more are presented.

NIGHTLIFE Andy's (410-778-6779), 337½ High St., Chestertown. Andy's is a popular nightspot with live entertainment that serves a light fare of soups ($3), salads (from $3), and entrées such as the beef burrito ($5.75).
P. E. Pruitts (410-639-7454), Bayside Ave., Rock Hall. In addition to having crowds show up for their weekend

waterside live entertainment, they also have a full menu of local dishes and New Orleans–style seafood.

Also see **Waterman's Crab House** under *Where to Eat—Crabs*.

✳ Selective Shopping
ANTIQUES

Chestertown
Chestertown Antique and Furniture Center (410-778-5777), 1 mile south of town on MD 213. Old and new furniture sold under the same roof.

Galena
Firehouse Antique Center (410-648-5639), Main St. A multidealer shop.

ART GALLERIES

Chestertown
Washington College's Tawes Gallery (410-778-7849), Washington College campus. Ever-changing exhibits of local and student artists, and some nationally touring programs.
Chester River Artworks (410-778-6300), 306 Parks Row. Open 11–2; closed Mon. Changing exhibits of local and regional works. Classes on every type of arts and crafts.
Chestertown Arts League (410-778-5789; www.chestertown.com/artsleague), 312 Cannon St. Formed shortly after World War II, the league provides classes for those who want to learn arts and crafts as well as exhibits of local talent.

Rock Hall
Rueben Rodney Gallery (410-639-2494), 5761 Main St. Presents works of local artists in acrylics, pottery, watercolors, photography, woodcraft, and other artists' works.

Chestertown

The Compleat Bookseller (410-778-1480), 301 High St. There are so few bookstores on the Eastern Shore that walking into this one is a pleasure. A small shop with an extensive choice, and employees are true book lovers.

Chestertown Used Bookstore (410-778-5777), 1 mile south of town on MD 213. Located inside the Chestertown Antique and Furniture Center, it claims to have more than 80,000 used books.

FARMER'S MARKETS Chestertown Farmer's Market. In Fountain Park on Sat. 9–noon, Apr.–Dec.

✳ Special Events

May: **Annual Chestertown Tea Party** (410-778-0416), Chestertown. Celebrates May 23, 1774, when local residents boarded the *Geddes* and dumped its load of tea into the Chester River.

June: **Rockfish Tournament** (410-639-7611), Rock Hall.

July: **July 4th Sassafras Boat Parade** (410-648-5510), Georgetown

Harbor, Georgetown. Fireworks and a parade of decorated boats. **Kent County Fair** (410-778-1661), Kent Agricultural Center, Tolchester.

August: **Betterton Beach Day and Parade** (410-348-5239), Betterton.

September: **Art in the Park** (410-778-0416), the sale of works by artists and craftspeople. **Rock Hall Fall Fest** (410-778-0416), Rock Hall. Arts and crafts, music, foods, a Kid's Kourt of children's activities, oyster-shucking contest, and boat show. **Candlelight Walking Tour** (410-778- 3499), Chestertown. An annual peek into many of the town's historic homes.

October: **Chester River Wildlife Exhibition and Sale** (410-778-0416), Chestertown. Decoy carving, duck-and goose-calling contests, retrieving contests, live raptor exhibit, entertainment, food, and nature and wildlife films and slide programs.

November: **Sultana Downrigging** (410-778-0416), Chestertown. Traditional sailing vessels from around the Chesapeake will visit Chestertown to help the schooner *Sultana* celebrate the close of her season under sail.

AT THE HEAD OF THE BAY—
Chesapeake City, Elkton, and North East

I t is said that life on the Eastern Shore is determined by the water around it. At the head of the bay, where the Eastern Shore meets mainland Maryland, the land itself is defined by water.

Along its western edge is the wide Susquehanna River, delivering the water it has collected during its long journey from humble beginnings near Cooperstown, New York. At its mouth, where it empties into the bay, are the Susquehanna Flats, shallow waters that attract nearly 90 percent of the waterfowl traveling the Atlantic Flyway. The unique style and heritage of the hunters attracted to these flats more than 100 years ago are preserved in the Upper Bay Museum in North East.

The Chesapeake Bay rings the area with miles of shoreline, while the land at the southern edge is cut by not just one, but three, waterways: the Sassafras and Bohemia Rivers and the Chesapeake & Delaware (C&D) Canal.

As early as the mid-1600s, Augustine Herman proposed a canal that would reduce water travel by nearly 300 miles between Philadelphia and Baltimore. More than a century passed before surveys were done, and it was not until 1829 that the canal was completed. Today it is the third busiest canal in the world, permitting oceangoing vessels easy passage to the bay, as well as providing scores of pleasure boaters a protected and scenic passage along the Intracoastal Waterway.

As for the land in the area, the Kentucky bluegrass has nothing on this gently rolling, coastal plain. Some of the largest and most prestigious horse farms in the country have produced a succession of thoroughbred and standardbred champions. Even if the names Kelso, Northern Dancer, Bet Twice, and Two Punch mean nothing to you, you can still enjoy a ride through the countryside. Miles of wooden fences wrap around acres of lush, green fields, accented by the flying manes and rippled haunches of galloping future champions.

COMMUNITIES The history and fortunes of **Chesapeake City** are tied to the C&D Canal. As construction on the canal progressed, the town sprang up as a

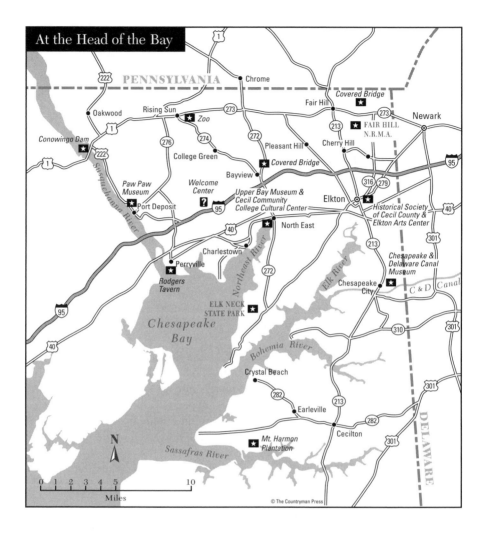

PENNSYLVANIA

Chrome

Oakwood

Rising Sun

★ Zoo

Covered Bridge ★

Fair Hill

Newark

Conowingo Dam ★

★ FAIR HILL
N.R.M.A.

Pleasant Hill

Cherry Hill

College Green

★ Covered Bridge

Bayview

Paw Paw
Museum

Welcome
Center

Upper Bay Museum &
Cecil Community
College Cultural Center

Elkton

Historical Society
of Cecil County &
Elkton Arts Center

★ Port Deposit

★ North East

Charlestown

Perryville

Chesapeake &
Delaware Canal
Museum

Rodgers
Tavern

Chesapeake
City ★

C & D Canal

ELK NECK
STATE PARK ★

Chesapeake
Bay

Bohemia River

Crystal Beach

Earleville

Ceciliton

N

Sassafras River

Mt. Harmon
Plantation

DELAWARE

0 1 2 3 4 5   10

Miles

© The Countryman Press

Susquehanna River

Northeast River

Elk River

place to house workers and supply needed materials. For a while, the canal actually supplied the construction material for the town, as many of its buildings were built from the lumber of dismantled "Susquehanna Arks" that had come across the Chesapeake Bay but were too large to pass through the locks. Chesapeake City's importance as a port faded once the federal government purchased the canal, widened and deepened it, and removed the locks in the early 20th century. Its growth was even more stunted when the construction of the arched bridge on MD 213, which soars 135 feet above the canal, enabled traffic to bypass the town.

Yet it is still one of the most picturesque spots in the area. Many of its buildings date from the early 1800s, and a walking-tour brochure available from Cecil County Tourism provides insight into them. The view of traffic upon the wide waters of the canal makes for a stunning backdrop from the small but active "downtown" area. The Chesapeake and Delaware Canal Museum provides an

accounting of the canal's and town's history, while several good restaurants and
an abundance of B&Bs are reason enough to visit.

The origin of **North East** (its motto is, "Not just a direction . . . it's a destination") is also tied to water. In this case, it is the Northeast River, which supplied
the needs of several early mills and an ironworks. Most of its buildings are from
the late 1800s and early 1900s, and many of them still stand in the busy business
district—along with antiques stores, restaurants serving regional foods, and interesting shops—on Main Street.

Built upon a narrow strip of land between the Susquehanna River and towering
cliffs, the entire town of **Port Deposit** is on the National Register of Historic
Places. Many of its buildings are constructed from granite quarried from the
cliffs; their history is revealed in a walking-tour brochure available from the Paw
Paw Museum in town or from Cecil County Tourism.

Perryville gained importance in colonial days, as it sits on the eastern shore of
the Susquehanna River and became a stopover for travelers taking the ferry
across the river. George Washington was just one of the many people passing
through here on their way to Philadelphia or Baltimore.

Elkton, with a population of close to 10,000, is the economic hub of the area.
Some of its earliest structures remain to remind you of the past, although they
have become mixed in with the office buildings, storefronts, and strip malls of
modern America. The local historical society and art gallery are definitely worth
stopping for.

GUIDANCE Cecil County Tourism (410-996-6290; 1-800-CECIL-95; www
.seececil.org), 1 Seahawk Dr., Suite 114, North East, 21901.

GETTING THERE *By car:* **I-95** is the main route into the region, providing easy
access from Baltimore and the rest of Maryland, and from Delaware and
Philadelphia. **MD 213** is the quickest roadway for those arriving from the southern portion of the Eastern Shore.

By air: **Baltimore/Washington International Airport** (1-800-I-FLY-BWI),
located between Baltimore and Annapolis, is about an hour's drive to the southwest of the Chesapeake City area. Located to the northeast, **Philadelphia
International Airport** (215-937-5400) is also about an hour's drive away.

By bus: **Greyhound** (1-800-229-9424) has a station and makes stops in Elkton.

By train: **MARC** (1-800-325-RAIL), the commuter train from Baltimore, makes
its final stop at Perryville on its northeastern run.

By water: If you own a boat or are chartering one, the Chesapeake Bay is the
obvious way to come from mainland Maryland. Also, the Chesapeake &
Delaware Canal is a part of the Intracoastal Waterway and provides access from
the Delaware River and other points to the east.

GETTING AROUND *By car:* **I-95** is the way to get around quickly, but using
US 40 will give you a chance to see more of the towns along the way. Lightly

traveled **US 222** and **US 1** run through the more rural northern portions of the area, while **MD 213** takes you into the southern region to the C&D Canal and Sassafras River. You can have a scenic drive and get to know this latter area intimately by purchasing the $5 **Historic Driving Tour** audiotape and map from a number of shops or from Cecil County Tourism.

By taxi: **Cox's Cab** (410-287-2797) and **Joe's Taxi** (410-287-2697) are headquartered in North East. **Maryland Cab** (410-378-4300) operates out of Port Deposit.

PARKING Municipal parking lots in North East are located off Main St. between West St. and Wallace Ave.

PUBLIC RESTROOMS In **Chesapeake City**, a public restroom is located beside the Franklin Hall building on Bohemia Ave.

In **North East**, restrooms can be found in the North East Community Park off Walnut St. at the southern end of town.

MEDICAL EMERGENCY **Union Hospital of Cecil County** (410-328-4000), 106 Bow St., Elkton, is a full-service facility with an emergency room.

✳ To See

COVERED BRIDGES Spanning a waterway within the Fair Hill Natural Resources Management Area in Fair Hill is the **Big Elk Creek Covered Bridge**. An interesting tidbit: Construction cost for the bridge in the 1860s was $1,165; its 1992 renovation came in at an amazing $152,000.

About 3 miles north of North East on MD 272 is the 1860 **Gilpin Falls Covered Bridge**. The arches of this 119-foot bridge—the longest covered bridge still standing in the state—are made from single timbers that were gradually

THE BIG ELK CREEK COVERED BRIDGE

THE SUSQUEHANNA RIVER AS SEEN FROM RODGERS TAVERN IN PERRYVILLE

warped into shape by balancing them on a pivot and pulling down on each end with cables and restraints.

MUSEUMS **Chesapeake and Delaware Canal Museum** (410-885-5621), 2nd St. and Bethel Rd., Chesapeake City. Mon.–Sat. Free admission. Exhibits, displays, and models provide a glimpse into the canal's past. One of the models is of the James Adams Floating Theater, which worked the C&D Canal and was the inspiration for the musical *Showboat*. (Yes, *Showboat* took place on the Mississippi, but it was this boat that piqued the composer's imagination.) A computer screen shows the location of ships—in real time—as they travel the canal. Also on museum grounds is a replica of the Bethel Bridge Lighthouse—and sweeping vistas of the canal.

Historical Society of Cecil County (410-398-1790; www.cchistory.org), 135 E. Main St., Elkton. Mon. noon–4 PM, Tue. 6–8 PM, Thu. 10 AM–4 PM, and the fourth Sat. of each month 10 AM–2 PM. Free admission, but donations accepted. Housed in a former bank building (circa 1830), the society maintains exhibits relating to colonial furnishings, Victorian dollhouses, a country store, an Early American kitchen, military items, and a log house.

Upper Bay Museum (410-287-2675), Walnut St. at the North East Community Park, North East. Sat. and Sun. 11–3, but hours and days have been variable. Housed within two large buildings, the museum has a collection of materials reflecting the history of commercial and recreational hunting and fishing on the upper Chesapeake Bay. The size of the decoy collection is impressive when you realize the museum is sponsored and maintained by the local Cecil-Harford Hunters Association. The punt guns, sculling oars, and sink boxes (ask if you don't know what these are—they're interesting) sketch a vivid picture of the heady age of bay waterfowl hunting.

HISTORIC HOMES

Mount Harmon Plantation (410-275-8819), Mount Harmon Rd. (off Grove Neck Rd.—MD 282), Earleville. Tue. and Thu. 10–3 and Sun. 1–4, May–Sep. Small admission fee. In 1963, Mrs. Harry Clark Boden IV purchased the early-1700s tobacco plantation home of her ancestors. She had it restored (which included installing beautifully hand-painted Chinese wallpaper) and furnished with American, English, Irish, and Scottish antiques of the period.

A 2-mile, tree-lined drive brings you to the three-story, five-bay brick manor house. Tour guides point out the Italian marble fireplaces (the screens kept sparks and fire off ladies' dresses), the master-of-the-hunt chair, and the wooden panels along the staircase. The furnishings and artwork are some of the nicest I've seen. Make sure you see the portrait of Lady Arabella Stuart. It reminds me of a modern holograph: The image changes depending on the angle it is viewed from—but it was painted in the 1500s! (Also quite remarkable are the extraordinarily ornate bathrooms installed in the mid-1900s.) Tours also take in the plantation kitchen and the tobacco prize house. A "prize" is a large wooden screw used to compress tobacco into half its volume for more efficient shipment.

Afterward, you are free to wander around the plantation's 200 acres, enjoying the formal boxwood and wisteria gardens, or following maintained pathways along fields, forests, and creeks (ask for a trail brochure). The entire plantation is a nature preserve that protects several rare species of plants.

This is an example of historic preservation at its best.

Paw Paw Museum (410-738-3086), 98 N. Main St., Port Deposit. Open 1–5 on the second and fourth Sun. of the month, May–Oct. Items relating to the history of Port Deposit include letters from Civil War soldiers and photographs of the town in the 19th and 20th centuries. Ask for the story about the signature quilt, which came into being as punishment for "acting up in church."

HISTORIC SITES **Rodgers Tavern** (410-642-6066), 259 Broad St., Perryville. Hours vary; call for times. George Washington, Marquis de Lafayette, Thomas Jefferson, and James Madison are just a few of the luminaries to make a stop at Rodgers Tavern. Built in the early 17th century, it served passengers using the ferry to get across the wide mouth of the Susquehanna River. Guided tours take you through the lightly furnished basement tavern, first-floor parlor and office, and second-floor sleeping accommodations. George Washington truly did sleep here! The view from the lawn is spectacular.

GUIDED TOURS **Chesapeake Horse Country Tours** (410-287-2290; 1-800-874-4556; www.uniglobehilltravel.com), 135 S. Main St., North East, 21901.

Offered for two to seven people by reservation Mon.–Sat. Wayne Hill has put together a tour that provides an overview of life, in his words, "at the peak of the Chesapeake." After a walking tour of Chesapeake City, a guided van trip explores Maryland's largest land preserve, which encompasses many of the horse farms in the area. In addition to enjoying the scenery, you will learn of the Du Pont family's role in reviving the horse industry here, travel through their Bohemia Stables Farm, and make a stop at the grave of Kelso, a champion stallion who was Horse of the Year an unprecedented five times. Upon his gravestone are the words WHERE HE GALLOPS, THE EARTH SINGS.

ZOO ✿ **The Zoo at Plumpton Park** (410-658-6850; www.plumptonparkzoo
.org), 1416 Telegraph Rd. (MD 273), Rising Sun. Daily 1–5, Mar. 2–Sep. 30;
Thu.–Mon. 10–4, Oct. 1–Mar. 1, weather permitting. Adults $6.75; children
2–12, $3.50; over 60, $5.75. This small zoo had its beginnings as a haven for
injured animals. Since then, it has accepted exotic and endangered species confiscated by U.S. Customs, and animals no longer wanted or on loan from other
zoos. Because of this, there is no real theme to the park, but you do get the
chance to see more than 250 animals from around the world. There are also picnic facilities, a children's playground, and a nature trail.

✳ To Do

AUTO RACING **Cecil County Dragway** (410-287-9105), 1573 Theodore Rd., Rising Sun. Mar.–Nov., you can listen to the roar of engines as various vehicles head down the quarter-mile track in Federal Mogul Points, rocket, and street races.

BOAT RENTALS **Elk River Outfitters** (1-866-LQID-FUN), 145 River Rd., Elkton. Located at Locust Point Marina, a short distance north of Chesapeake City. Canoes, kayaks, day-fishing boats, and Sunfish sailboats available for rent for $20 (half day) or $40 (full day).

THE BOHEMIA STABLES OF WOODSTOCK FARM NEAR CHESAPEAKE CITY

North East and Rising Sun

Chesapeake Bay Golf Club North East (410-287-0200), 1500 Chesapeake Club Dr., and **Chesapeake Bay Golf Club Rising Sun** (410-658-4343). These two 18-hole courses are under the same management and are only 6 miles apart. The North East course is a bit more rolling and wooded than the Rising Sun course. Discounts are given if you play both of them. The food at Knicker's Grille (at the North East course) is of higher quality than that found at many other golf clubs.

Elkton

Brantwood (410-398-8848), 1190 Augustine Herman Hwy. (MD 213). Championship 18-hole course with clubhouse and pro shop.

Elkton Club at Patriot's Glen (410-392-9552; 1-800-616-1776; www.patriots glen.com), 300 Patriots. One of the newest courses in the area, it has a par 72.

HIKING **Elk Neck State Park** (410-287-5333), 4395 Turkey Point Rd., North East. Upland forests just a short distance away from the shorelines of the Chesapeake Bay and Elk River provide some of the most diverse environments found in a park on the Eastern Shore, and the best way to explore them is via the park's pathways.

The easy 1.5-mile **Red Trail** passes through a forest of beech, tulip poplar, and red, white, and chestnut oak. A hike along the 1-mile **Green Trail** overlooks a

THINGS TO LOOK FORWARD TO
Principio Iron Works (410-642-2358), Perryville, and **Elk Landing** (410-651-9213; www.elklanding .org), Elkton, are being developed as historic sites. The Iron Works were most active before the Revolutionary War, but production continued into the 1900s. Although not in the best of shape, the manor house, furnace, and some outbuildings remain.

At the confluence of Little Elk and Big Elk Creeks, Elk Landing played a role in the colonies' earliest transportation corridor. There are big plans for both of these

THE MANOR HOUSE AT PRINCIPIO IRON WORKS

places, including living-history demonstrations. Check with Cecil County Tourism to find out what is available while you are in the area.

small lake and a marsh. The 2-mile **Black Trail** provides access to the shoreline of the Elk River, where you can take a swim (at your own risk—no guards). The white-blazed **Thackery Swamp Self-Guiding Nature Trail** is only three-quarters of a mile long, with an interpretive booklet available at the camper registration office.

The trail I enjoy most is the 2-mile **Blue Trail**, which passes through field and forest on its way to the **Turkey Point Lighthouse** and a 100-foot-high cliff overlooking the Chesapeake Bay and Elk River. There is absolutely no better way to greet a new dawn than to be sitting on one of the benches next to the lighthouse and watching the source of earth's warmth rise inch by inch into the eastern sky.

Also see **Fair Hill Natural Resources Management Area** under *Green Space*.

HORSEBACK RIDING Fair Hill Stables (410-620-3883; www.fairwindsstables .com), accessed from Entrance 3 in Fair Hill State Park on MD 273, Fair Hill. Operated by Ted and JoAnn Dawson, hosts of Tailwinds Farm. Guided 1-hour trail rides ($25; $20 for children 8–12) through the woods and fields of Fair Hill Natural Resources Management Area. Pony rides (only $2) every Sat. and Sun., noon–3. The Dawsons also offer riding lessons, and carriage and hayrides.

SUMMER CAMPS ✿ **Sandy Hill Camp** (410-287-5554; www.sandyhillcamp .com), 3380 Turkey Point Rd., North East. June–Aug. This residential camp for boys and girls 8–16 years of age is located on 216 acres overlooking the Chesapeake Bay. There are weekend and weeklong sessions of equestrian activities, sailing, sports, English for international travel, a counselor-in-training program, and traditional camp activities. Eight campers and two counselors share a rustic cabin.

✳ Green Space

BEACHES Crystal Beach (410-275-8083), Earleville. Admission fee. A small, sandy public beach located along the Elk River at the end of MD 282.

PARKS Fair Hill Natural Resources Management Area (410-398-1246), 300 Tawes Dr., Elkton. Open sunrise–sunset. At 5,613 acres, this is one of the largest pieces of public land on the Eastern Shore. Approximately 40 miles of trails open to hikers, bicyclists, and horseback

EARLY MORNING AT TURKEY POINT LIGHTHOUSE

riders wander through its wood and fields and across its many water runs. A very popular place for the local equestrian community. Facilities include the Fair Hill Training Center for racehorses and a turf course, where steeplechase and flat races are held.

Elk Neck State Park (410-287-5333), 4395 Turkey Point Rd., North East. In addition to a network of hiking trails, the state park offers picnic areas, a boat launch (bring your own vessel or rent one), fishing, a naturalist program, rental cabins, and a campground with bathhouses. Bordered by the Elk River and the Chesapeake Bay, it is a place of grand sunrises and sunsets.

WALKS The shoreline **Riverwalk** in Port Deposit is a part of the proposed Lower Susquehanna Heritage Greenway, which will include multiple miles of trail along both sides of the Susquehanna River.

❋ Lodging

MOTELS AND HOTELS ❦ Crystal Inn (410-287-7100; 1-800-631-3803), 1 Center Dr. (MD 272 at I-95 Exit 100), North East, 21901. Spacious rooms, each with microwave, refrigerator, and free local calls. Indoor pool, whirlpool, spa, fitness room, and deluxe continental breakfast. A short drive to North East, Elk Neck State Park, Elkton, and outlet shopping. One of the more pleasant motels I've stayed in. Pets permitted with deposit. $89–109.

BED & BREAKFASTS

Chesapeake City, 21915
❧ ⚹ **Blue Max Inn** (410-885-2781; www.bluemaxinn.com), 300 Bohemia Ave. Less than two blocks from the waterfront and main business area. The large porch invites guests to just sit and watch small-town life unfold as they listen to the sounds of the grand player piano coming from the living room. There are seven guest rooms; I liked the rich blue color of the Randall Room with its own balcony. The Lindsey Room on the first floor is handicapped-accessible. Owner Christine Mullen serves a large breakfast in the solarium or the fireside dining room—and then provides afternoon tea and cookies. Children 10 and over welcome. $120–225.

If you are wondering about the name, it comes from a former occupant, Jack Hunter, who wrote *The Blue Max*. A best seller, the book was adapted as a major motion picture.

❧ **Inn at the Canal** (410-885-5995; www.innatthecanal.com), 104 Bohemia Ave. Emigrating from the Philadelphia area, Mary and Al Ioppolo opened their B&B, the first such establishment in Cecil County, in the late 1980s. They greet you upon arrival to their 1870s home with refreshments, and serve a full breakfast in the morning. Each of the six guest rooms has its own decorating theme and private bath. Far from minding the few wooden steps I had to go down to get to the bathroom in my room, I felt that it just added another historical and unique aspect to my stay. My after-dinner lounging was done on the front porch, watching the boats on the C&D Canal. Children over 10 may be welcome; call to make arrangements. $90–225.

⚹ **Ship Watch Inn** (410-885-5300; www.shipwatchinn.com), 410 1st St.

All eight suites in this 1920s water-front inn have private whirlpool bath and private balcony. Room 5 is the largest, but my choice would be Room 6 because you can see the water without even having to sit up in bed. Room 2 is handicapped-accessible. A nice touch is the binoculars to watch the boats on the canal. $145–190.

North East, 21901

Tailwinds Farm (410-658-8187; www.fairwindsstables.com), 41 Tailwinds Lane. Children over 8 are welcome. This has the feel of what B&Bs started out as. You share the Victorian farmhouse with a family—Ted and JoAnn Dawson and their children. Of two guest rooms, I liked the Blue Room with its bed in a recessed alcove. A good place to relax and enjoy the quiet beauty of a 50-acre working farm. You may bring your own horses and stable them overnight in the 17-stall barn. The Dawsons also own the Fair Hill Stables. In fact, some of their horses were featured in Oprah Winfrey's film *Beloved*—and JoAnn has been an actress in such films as *Twelve Monkeys* and *The Sixth Sense*. $75.

North Bay (410-287-5948; www.northbayinc.com), 9 Sunset Dr. Four contemporary, antiques-accented guest rooms (one with private bath) on the headwaters of the bay. The Captain's and Harbor Rooms have their own water views. $65–95.

Elkton, 21921

Long Creek View (410-885-2012), 1702 Augustine Herman Hwy. (MD 213). Two rooms with private bath in a quiet retreat within its own woodlands. Gardens and a nature trail. $85–110.

Elk Mills, 21920

Elk Forge B&B Inn and Retreat (410-392-9007; 1-877-ELK-FORGE; www.elkforge), 807 Elk Mills Rd. An intriguing place whose core is a centuries-old home, but whose additions, while modern, provide very pleasant and interesting guest rooms (each with a private bath). Harry and LeAnn Lenderman engaged artists Jeanette Robison and Vitale Sem to paint pictures in each room. Robison created one in a 1920s art deco style and painted angels floating on clouds in one of the hallways. Sem's works are more classical, such as the stunning action scene depicting George Washington at the Battle of Brandywine.

The solarium, which overlooks the yard and woodlands and contains a stained-glass window from a Pennsylvania church, is so big that a large water fountain is dwarfed inside it. LeAnn's breakfasts, served in the solarium, have portions to match the size of the room. The many miles of pathways within Fair Hill Natural Resources Management Area can be accessed directly from the side yard.

LeAnn also operates a spa within Elk Forge that is just one more reason to stay in this most relaxing, inviting, and unique B&B. There are many thoughtful amenities for business travelers, too. $115–185.

COTTAGES **The Old Wharf Cottage** (410-885-5040; 1-877-582-4049; www.bayardhouse.com), 10 Bohemia Ave., Chesapeake City, 21915. You cannot get any closer to the water than in this small cottage administered by the Bayard House next door. At the very edge of the land, it has served as an icehouse, tailor shop, and cargo-storage place. It is in the center of activity in town, so expect to have many passersby. $150; discounted rates for multiple-night stays.

VACATION RENTALS Liquid Fun (1-866-LQID-FUN; www.liquidfun .com), 145 River Rd., Elkton, 21921. Liquid Fun is the umbrella name used to cover a number of businesses, including a marina, river outfitters, and vacation rentals on the Elk River and the C&D Canal. All of the rental houses have nice views, and each has its own special amenities. One house sleeps two, four of the houses sleep six, and the one on the canal can accommodate four. Weekly rentals are $900–1,500.

Elk Neck State Park (1-888-432-2267), 4395 Turkey Point Rd., North East, 21901. Rental cabins are available from the first weekend in May through the second weekend in October. Some are equipped with electric-ity, refrigerator, stove, and running water; others are more rustic with just electricity. Both types make use of a central bathhouse and are popular, so make reservations as soon as possible.

CAMPING Riverside Ponderosa Pines (410-642-3431), 1435 Carpenter's Point Rd., Perryville, 21903; **Riverview** (410-642-6200), 1200 Frenchtown Rd., Perryville, 21903; and **Woodlands** (410-398-4414), 265 Starkey Lane, Elkton, 21921, cater primarily to those with RVs.

☙ For a more rustic experience, check into the campground at **Elk Neck State Park** (see *Hiking*). Pets on a leash are permitted in certain sites.

✳ Where to Eat

DINING OUT

Chesapeake City
Bayard House (410-885-5040; www .bayardhouse.com), 11 Bohemia Ave.

Sinking Springs Herb Farm (443-553-4618; www.sinkingsprings.com), 234 Blair Shore Rd. (enter from 843 Elk Forest Rd.), Elkton, 21921. A visit to the Sinking Springs Herb Farm is like stepping into a chapter of Jethro Kloss's *Back to Eden.* There is a little bit of New Age mixed in with a lot of just good old country living. Ann and Bill Stubbs's Wellness Retreats focus on stress, health issues, nutrition, and gardening, and include yoga, massage therapy, regression hypnosis, and more. You do not have to participate in a retreat to enjoy a stay in the small and rustic, but cozy, Garden Cottage B&B ($105) or to make arrangements for family-style lunch with Ann and Bill in their 1700s home. The quiche, bread, and vegetables (all with fresh herbs) I had were a welcome taste of delicious home-cooked food after I'd been on the road for a long time.

Within a couple of outbuildings are a gift shop offering the Stubbs's herbs and dried-flower arrangements, and the studio of painter Carol Mangano. Walking trails wander around the herb and flower gardens and throughout the farm's 130 acres. Be sure to stop and pay homage to the huge sycamore tree next to the house. It was already full grown when Shakespeare was but a teenager.

Open for lunch and dinner. Some of the most pleasurable dining in the area is found in this structure, built decades before the construction of the C&D Canal. Once a private home, it has been a restaurant or tavern since 1829 and was restored in 1985. Its ambience, quality of food, and sweeping water vista make it a favorite "special-occasion" restaurant.

The award-winning Maryland crab soup ($6) is spicy without being hot, and is full of crab. One of the most popular entrées, the Anaheim peppers ($25) are stuffed with lobster, crabmeat, and shrimp and baked with green chile salsa and cheddar cheese. They are simply luscious. Even side dishes are prepared with thought. The au gratin potatoes are made rich and creamy by adding sour cream, cheddar cheese, chives, and smoked bacon.

Other entrées include salmon with watercress and artichokes ($23) and broiled crabcakes ($29). Especially indulgent are the twin filets mignons ($26), one topped with a crabcake, the other with a lobster cake. If with a group, try the petits fours ($4.75) for dessert. Each of you will get to try a variety of flavors, textures, and tastes.

Chesapeake Inn (410-885-2040; www.chesapeakeinn.com), 605 2nd St. Open for lunch and dinner. Upscale waterfront dining with a bit of a Mediterranean flavor to the menu. Popular items are the crab ravioli ($19) and the encrusted ahi tuna with candied walnuts over a pineapple risotto with coconut cream sauce ($28). I made a full lunch out of the seafood quesadilla ($13).

Elkton

Fair Hill Inn (410-398-4187; www .fairhillinn.com), at the intersection of MD 213 and MD 273 north of Elkton. Open for lunch and dinner. Anthony Grazianof and son Peter have been offering Eastern Shore fare with a bit of a French-Italian twist for more than two decades inside this mid-1700s inn. Although the inn was restored, many original items remain, such as the huge stone fireplace and the original pass-through.

The pasta, garlic, and wilted greens ($13.95) reminded me of dishes my Italian-descent mother used to make. My dinner companion enjoyed his jumbo shrimp served in curry cream sauce ($19.95). We split the flavorful appetizer of crabmeat-stuffed mushroom caps ($7.50). Other meat, poultry, seafood, and pasta entrées range $13.95–27.95.

The dining area is actually four rooms, so you never feel like you are in a crowd. For an even more romantic setting, order the Classic for Two dinner and have your seafood Beatrice ($58), châteaubriand ($56), or rack of lamb ($58) prepared tableside.

North East

✎ **Windows on Main** (410-287-3512), 101 S. Main St. Open for lunch and dinner. After operating the **Tavern on Main** (410-287-8761) for a number of years, Barbara and Ed Landis opened this restaurant next door to offer customers a bit more refined dining. It is a comfortable place with heavy wood tables, and books scattered about for you to leaf through. The two tables in the window alcoves are the coveted seats. The lunch sandwiches and soups ($3.95–5.95) are offered at dinner. The 24-ounce porterhouse steak ($18.95) doused in a Jack Daniels pepper-and-mushroom sauce was moist and tasty, but so large that I left with more than half of it in a doggy bag. The folks at the next table enjoyed their rockfish with crab imperial ($18.95) and fish-and-chips ($11.95). Other entrées $11.95–19.95.

Port Deposit
Union Hotel (410-378-3503; www .unionhotel-restaurant.com), 1282 Susquehanna Rd. Open for lunch and dinner. Closed Mon. The hotel was built of hemlock logs around 1783 to cater to the needs of travelers on the Susquehanna Canal. Janet Dooling has been overseeing the restaurant a little over 20 years, serving soups, salads, sandwiches, and light entrées for lunch. I was here with three others, and we all agreed on the watercress and spinach quiche ($7.95). Dinner is a bit more formal and hearty. Sambuca shrimp and scallops ($19.50) is popular, as is the grilled rack of lamb ($22.95). A couple of dishes reflect the hotel's earlier days: sautéed veal liver with bacon and onions ($15.95) and maple-mustard pork loin ($16.95).

EATING OUT

Chesapeake City
Yacht Club Restaurant (410-885-2267; www.yachtclubrestaurant.com), 225 Bohemia Ave. Open for lunch and dinner. Chef Gary Klunk has no formal training, yet most of the Yacht Club's savory offerings are his recipes. It was hard deciding which appetizer to try: the escargot ($8.95) over a pastry puff, sautéed spinach, and hazelnut butter, or the crab and corn chowder ($5.95). The gazpacho with lump crab ($5.95) I settled on did not disappoint. The chicken Chesapeake ($14.95) was rubbed in Old Bay seasoning and topped with crabmeat in a luscious cream sauce—a nice variation on an old standard. Sandwiches

(from $7.95) are served at lunch, and seafood ($15.95–22.95), meat (up to $25..95), and pasta dishes (around $15.95) at dinner.

I liked the waiters' attentive but non-intrusive service, as well as the old photos of Chesapeake City on the walls. Gary and co-owner Cheri Wilson did such a good job of renovating that you would never imagine you are eating in a former hardware store. As a nice touch, you are treated to a horse-drawn carriage ride if you leave your car at the public parking lot under the MD 213 bridge on Fri., Sat., or Sun. night.

North East
Pier One (410-287-6599), 1 N. Main St. Pam and Vinny Cirino have been operating this popular diner-style place since the late 1990s. Like most diners, it has an extensive menu of sandwiches, pastas, meats, and seafoods. $10.95–22.95.

CRABS ✿ **Woody's Crab House** (410-287-3541; www.woodyscrab house.com), 29 S. Main St., North East. Open for lunch and dinner. A classic Maryland crab house with brown paper tablecloths and a concrete floor (on which you are expected to throw the shells from the complimentary peanuts served with every meal). Steamed crabs in Woody's own spice blend (market price) are the obvious choice, but people also come here for the steamed sack of 50 shrimp ($15.95) or big bucket of little-neck clams ($15.95). My dining mate and I couldn't decide, so we ordered the Net Buster ($27.95), with enough lobster, crabcake, crab imperial, two varieties of shrimp, clams, and fresh fish to satisfy us both. A crowded, noisy, and fun atmosphere.

COFFEE BARS Beans, Leaves, Etc.
(410-287-8033), 33 S. Main St., North
East. Coffees, teas, and gourmet foods.

**SNACKS AND GOODIES Canal
Creamery** (410-885-3314), 9
Bohemia Ave., Chesapeake City. With
outdoor seating right on the waterfront, this is the best spot for homemade ice cream on a hot afternoon or
as an after-dinner treat. Also serves
light lunch and dinner items.

✳ Entertainment
THEATERS

North East
**Cecil Community College Cul-
tural Center** (410-287-1037), I-95
Exit 100. Dance, music, and theatrical
productions are presented here. The
local Covered Bridge Theatre Company does at least three presentations
annually, two of which are musicals.

✳ Selective Shopping
ANTIQUES

North East
5 and 10 Antique Market (410-287-
6565), 115 S. Main St. Eighty dealers
housed within a former hotel (which
was also a five-and-dime store).
North Chesapeake Antique Mall
(410-287-3938), 2288 Pulaski Hwy.
Another multidealer shop, this one is
on US 40 north of town.

ART GALLERIES

Chesapeake City
Neil's Artwork (410-885-5094), 226
George St. Neil's works focus on the
scenery of the upper Chesapeake Bay.

Elkton
Elkton Arts Center (410-392-5740;
www.cecilcountyartscouncil.org), 135

E. Main St. The home of the
extremely active Cecil County Arts
Council. Their calendar of events
includes changing exhibits of regional
artists and craftspeople, classes, concerts, dance recitals, readings, lectures, and more.

North East
**Chesapeake Gallery and Frame
Shop** (410-287-5300), 2718 Turkey
Point Rd. Primarily a frame shop, but
it does feature the works of some very
competent local artists.

USED BOOKS Bookseller's Antiques
(410-287-8652), 35 S. Main St., North
East. Used books and old papers.

**CRAFTS England's Colony on the
Bay** (410-287-5575), 505 S. Main St.,
North East. There are many touristy
items in here, but be sure to stop in
to take a look at the decoys and birds
carved by local artisans.

SPECIAL SHOPS

Chesapeake City
Back Creek General Store (410-885-
5377), 100 Bohemia Ave. It is worth it
to step into this shop, which has been
restored to its 1800s makeup with
original shelving and glass cabinets.

North East
Day Basket Factory (410-287-6100;
www.daybasketfactory.com), 714 S.
Main St. Although no longer owned
by the Day family, the factory is still
making baskets in the same manner it
has done for more than 125 years.
Each piece of local white oak is split
and woven by hand into utilitarian
and ornamental baskets. If the craftspeople are at work, ask to take a quick
tour, and you will see why these baskets, which have only copper and

brass fittings—not steel—put those marketed by Longaberger to shame. Day baskets are also guaranteed for life.

OUTLET **Prime Outlets** (410-378-9399), I-95 Exit 93, Perryville. Includes the outlet shops of Nike, L'eggs, Van Heusen, OshKosh B'Gosh, Book Cellar, and more than 35 other nationally known names.

PICK-YOUR-OWN PRODUCE FARMS

Elkton

✎ **Milburn Orchards** (410-398-1349; www.milburnorchards.com), 1945 Appleton Rd. (MD 316). The orchards have been in the Milburn family for more than 100 years, and the Milburns have learned a few things about growing and marketing produce. Their U-pick selections include cherries in early summer, peaches in midsummer, and apples in early fall. Lots of fun kids' activities throughout the season with a playground, petting zoo, and barnyard animals. Hayrides, crafts shows, corn maze, and other activities in fall. The farm market (open July 5 through the last Saturday in January) sells not only produce but also some delicious home-baked goodies.

Walnut Springs Farm (410-398-3451), Blue Ball Rd. U-pick fruits and seasonal events.

✳ Special Events

April: **Red Heart American Indian Festival** (410-885-2800), Fair Hill Fairgrounds, Fair Hill.

May: **Spring Fling** (410-642-6066), Rodgers Tavern, 259 Broad St., Perryville. Entertainment, crafts, food, and exhibits. **Highland Gathering** (410-885-2005), Fair Hill Race Track, Fair Hill. A gathering of the clans for dance, piping, drumming, sheepdog demonstrations, and food.

June–July: **Summer Music in the Park** (410-392-5740), Pell Gardens, Chesapeake City. Free outdoor concerts ranging from bluegrass to rock 'n' roll. Sun. at 6 PM.

June: **Annual Mid-Atlantic Chevelle Show** (410-879-7893), Community Park, North East. Scores of Chevelles from 1964 to 1987. **Canal Day** (410-885-3132), Chesapeake City. A street festival with arts, crafts, food, and music.

July: **Cecil County Fair** (410-398-8544), Fair Hill Fairgrounds, Fair Hill.

September: **Annual Juried Exhibition** (410-392-5740), Elkton Arts Center, 135 E. Main St., Elkton. Works by regional artists. **Yesterdays** (410-287-5801). North East celebrates its heritage with street entertainment, demonstrations, children's activities, crafts, music, and an evening ghost walk.

October: **Annual Upper Bay Rockfish Tournament** (410-392-3833), Community Park, North East. **Festival in the Country** (410-755-6065), Fair Hill Natural Resources Management Area, 376 Fair Hill Dr., Fair Hill. International-level equestrian championships and dog agility trials.

Central Maryland

HARFORD COUNTY—Havre de Grace,
Aberdeen, and Bel Air

NORTH OF BALTIMORE—Owings Mills,
Hunt Valley, Westminster, and Taneytown

BALTIMORE

WEST OF BALTIMORE—Ellicott City
and Columbia

ANNAPOLIS AND VICINITY

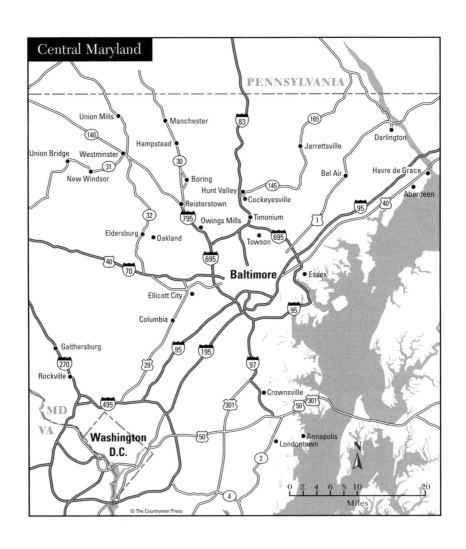

Central Maryland

PENNSYLVANIA

Union Mills • Manchester • (83) (165)
(140) Hampstead • Jarrettsville • Darlington •
Union Bridge • Westminster • (30) Bel Air • Havre de Grace •
(31) Boring (145) Aberdeen •
New Windsor • Hunt Valley • Cockeyesville
(32) Reisterstown • Timonium (1)
Eldersburg • (795) Owings Mills • (695)
• Oakland Towson • (695)
(40) (695)
(70) Baltimore • Essex
Ellicott City •
Columbia • (95)
Gaithersburg •
(270) (95) (195)
Rockville • (29) (97)
MD (495) Crownsville •
VA (301) (50) (301)
Washington (50) • Annapolis
D.C. • Londontown
(2)
(4) N

0 2 4 6 8 10 20
Miles

© The Countryman Press

HARFORD COUNTY—Havre de Grace, Aberdeen, and Bel Air

H arford County is a place of transition. Its southern portion lies on the Coastal Plain, with the low, flat type of terrain and access to the Chesapeake Bay most often associated with the Eastern Shore. Yet north of I-95, the land rises quickly to the Piedmont Plateau, a landscape of rolling hills and deep gorges created by swiftly moving streams and waterfalls.

Water used to play a more important part in citizens' livelihoods than it does today. During the 1800s, the Susquehanna & Tidewater Canal carried timber, wheat, coal, and other products from Wrightsville, Pennsylvania, to Havre de Grace, but use of the canal declined with the coming of the railroads. Some of the best waterfowl hunting in the world was along the Susquehanna Flats, where the Susquehanna River meets the Chesapeake Bay. Many local residents became commercial hunters, and many more catered to the thousands of sport hunters who flocked to the area. The decline in waterfowl populations and needed strict regulations brought that way of life to an end in the 1960s.

Like all metropolitan areas, Baltimore is ever-expanding, and Harford County started becoming one of its bedroom communities around the 1970s. In fact, a large percentage of the population is now employed in the Baltimore metro area or is engaged in meeting the needs of those who are. It only takes a short drive on a country road to see how quickly living in housing developments is becoming the norm.

Yet a quick drive, especially into the northern and eastern reaches of the county, will also reveal that much of the beauty of the land survives. Susquehanna and Rocks State Parks preserve thousands of acres along waterways, and large farms still provide large, pleasing-to-the-eye, open spaces.

Havre de Grace's location next to the water would have, by itself, ensured that it was the county's most scenic town. But it has also managed to become a 21st-century travel destination without damaging its earlier architecture and small-town atmosphere. Elegant Victorian homes line Union Avenue, waterfront parks abound, and independent businesses—not national chains—still occupy the downtown area.

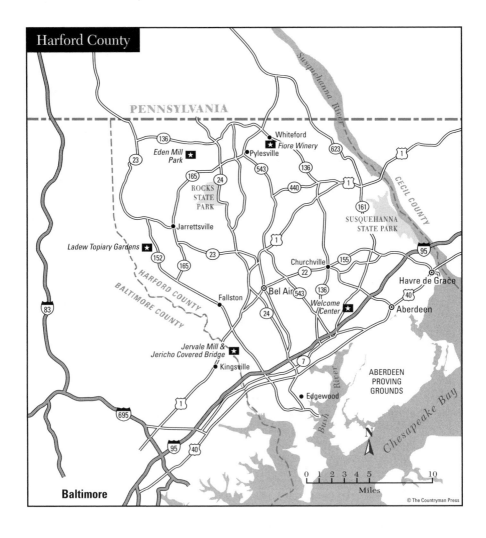

Havre de Grace has dubbed itself "the Decoy Capital of the World," and its Decoy Museum goes a long way in substantiating that claim. The Susquehanna Museum chronicles the days when the town was the southern terminus for the Susquehanna & Tidewater Canal, while the Maritime Museum tells the story of the waters around the town. A favorite activity of residents and visitors alike is the simple joy of walking The Promenade, a boardwalk along the shoreline.

COMMUNITIES Aberdeen was originally called Hall's Cross Roads but was renamed when the Wilmington & Baltimore Railroad's first station manager asked that it be changed to the name of his hometown in Scotland. It was an important transshipment center but truly began to grow after the establishment of the military's Aberdeen Proving Grounds in 1917. Aberdeen's best-known site celebrates the town's favorite son, baseball legend Cal Ripken Jr.

Bel Air is the county seat, which, in addition to its administrative functions, primarily serves as a retail hub for the thousands of homes and housing developments that began to ring around it in the late 1900s. The nearby community college has an active Center for Cultural Arts, and the Ma and Pa Railroad Trail provides a pleasant diversion from urban activity.

GUIDANCE **The Discover Harford County Tourism Council** (410-575-7278; 1-800-597-2649; www.harfordmd.com) has a visitors center located in a downtown location at 3 W. Bel Air Ave., Aberdeen, 21001.

Information specific to the Havre de Grace area can be obtained through the **Havre de Grace Tourism Commission** (410-939-8810; 1-800-851-7756; www .hdgtourism.com), 712 Giles St., Havre de Grace, 21708.

A state visitors center, the **Maryland House Travel Center** (410-272-0176), is on I-95 between Exits 80 and 85, and can provide information on the local area as well as the entire state.

GETTING THERE *By car:* **I-95** is the main route into the region, providing easy access from Baltimore and the rest of Maryland, and from Delaware and Philadelphia.

By air: **Baltimore/Washington International Airport** (1-800-I-FLY-BWI), located between Baltimore and Annapolis, is less than an hour's drive to the southwest. Located to the northeast, **Philadelphia International Airport** (215-937-5400) is a bit more than an hour's drive away.

By bus: **Greyhound** (1-800-229-9429) has a station and makes stops in Aberdeen.

By train: As a part of its Washington, DC–New York route, **Amtrak** (1-800-USA-RAIL) has a station in Aberdeen and makes a stop there. **MARC** (1-800-325-RAIL), the **commuter train** from Baltimore, makes stops in Edgewood and Aberdeen.

By water: If you own a boat, or are chartering one, the Chesapeake Bay is the obvious way to arrive. Also, the Chesapeake & Delaware Canal is a part of the Intracoastal Waterway and provides access from the Delaware River and other points to the east.

GETTING AROUND *By car:* **I-95** is the way to get around quickly. **US 40** is also a four-lane highway, but it has a tendency to bring you by the faded parts of the county. **US 1** runs through the more rural, central portions of the area, while **MD 136** in the very northern part of the county is a designated **State Scenic Byway**.

By bus: **Harford County Transportation Services** (410-612-1621) has several bus routes that operate in towns along the I-95/US 40 corridor, and one that runs into Bel Air.

By taxi: In Havre de Grace, you can call **DP Cab** (410-939-1133), **Montville Taxi** (410-939-0900), or **Poole's Taxi** (410-939-2506). **Victory Cabs** (410-272-0880), **Dollar Cab** (410-273-6099), and **Aberdeen Cab** (410-272-3200) operate out of Aberdeen.

PARKING In Havre de Grace, parking lots are located near the water at the foot of Franklin St., in town at the corner of N. Union and Pennington Aves., and at the Havre de Grace Yacht Basin next to Millard E. Tydings Memorial Park.

PUBLIC RESTROOMS In Havre de Grace, you can find public restrooms in Millard E. Tydings Memorial Park along the southern end of The Promenade, and in small Hutchins Memorial Park at the foot of Congress Ave. near the center of town.

MEDICAL EMERGENCY Harford Memorial Hospital (410-843-5000), 501 South Union St., Havre de Grace.

Upper Chesapeake Medical Center (410-643-1000), 500 Upper Chesapeake Dr., Bel Air.

✳ To See

COLLEGES Harford Community College (410-836-4000; www.harford.cc .md.us), 401 Thomas Run Rd., Bel Air. Most community colleges go about their business of providing an education but are not known for their cultural arts offerings to the local community. Not the case here. The **Center for Cultural Arts** is very active in presenting concerts, plays, musicals, dance theater, and a changing gallery of works of art.

COVERED BRIDGES See **Jerusalem Mill** under *Historic Sites*.

MUSEUMS

Havre de Grace

Havre de Grace Decoy Museum (410-939-3739; www.decoymuseum.com), 215 Giles St. Open daily 11–4. Small admission fee. The excellence and quantity of decoys here rivals that of the larger Ward Museum of Wildlife Art in Salisbury on the Eastern Shore (see "Salisbury"). The exhibits include working decoys (hand carved and factory produced), decorative decoys, and those made by local, but nationally known, craftspeople. Do not overlook the superb diorama of a decoy carver's shop or the upstairs picture windows' sweeping view of the bay.

Susquehanna Museum of Havre de Grace (410-939-5780), Erie and Conesto Sts. Sat. and Sun. 1–5, May–Oct. Small admission fee. The Susquehanna & Tidewater Canal provided a water transportation system between Philadelphia and Baltimore from the early 1800s to 1900. Although much has changed at this site, which was the canal's southern terminus, you can still get a feel for the early days by walking along a short section of the towpath and across the pivot bridge. Volunteers take visitors into the lock house furnished with Victorian-period reproductions. The 1782 survey map of the town also helps bring things into perspective.

Havre de Grace Maritime Museum (410-939-4800), 100 Lafayette St. One of the newest cultural assets in Havre de Grace, the Maritime Museum preserves the heritage of the area with artifacts, photographs, and memorabilia. It is also home to the **Chesapeake Wooden Boat Builders School** (see *To Do*).

Steppingstone Museum (410-939-2299), 461 Quaker Bottom Rd. (accessed from I-95 Exit 89). A stone farmhouse and several outbuildings preserve and demonstrate the 1880–1920 rural lifestyle and crafts of the region. (Also see *To Do—Special Classes*.)

Aberdeen

U.S. Army Ordnance Museum (410-278-3602), Maryland and Aberdeen Blvds., on the Aberdeen Proving Grounds. Open daily 10–4:45; the outside exhibits are open during daylight hours. Free admission. An amazingly extensive collection of military hardware that is sure to be of interest to military-history students. Inside are technological breakthroughs that made history, such as body armor, the Gatling gun, and a V-2 rocket. Many items are the last ones of their kind. The 225-acre lot contains more than 200 tanks and vehicles from around the world, dating from World War I to the present.

Bel Air

Hays House Museum (410-838-1213; www.harfordhistory.net), 324 Kenmore Ave. Sun. 1–4. Donations accepted. Currently the repository for the Historical Society of Harford County's collection of artifacts, furniture, and other items. The house still has its original staircase, mantels, woodwork, and shutters.

HISTORIC SITES Rock Run Grist Mill, in Susquehanna State Park, north of Havre de Grace. Located next to the Susquehanna River, the Rock Run Grist Mill was built by John Stump in 1794. It still works, and grinding demonstrations are presented on a scheduled basis. The building to the left of the parking area is the Jersey Toll House, built for the toll collector of the Susquehanna River Bridge, which was destroyed by ice floes in 1856. It is now the information center for the park. To get a better understanding of the mill and its heyday, pick up

TANKS ON DISPLAY AT THE U.S. ARMY ORDNANCE MUSEUM

the historic walking-tour brochure from the information center. On the easy 45-minute journey you will learn how the mill operated, and pass by the springhouse, the miller's home, and the stone Rock Run House.

Jerusalem Mill (410-877-3560; www.JerusalemMill.org), 2813 Jerusalem Rd. (off MD 152), Kingsville. The Friends of Jerusalem Mills have restored the 18th-century mill and several other buildings that were a part of a Quaker settlement that prospered for two centuries. A small museum, and living-history demonstrations presented from time to time, provide background information. The circa-1865 **Jericho Covered Bridge** is nearby and was an important part of the community.

HISTORIC CHURCHES

Churchville
Calvary United Methodist Churche (410-734-6920), 1321 Calvary Rd. The oldest continuously operating original Methodist church on Maryland's western shore, it still has many of its 1821 features—including the slave gallery.

LIGHTHOUSE Concord Point Lighthouse (410-939-0768), Concord and Lafayette Sts., Havre de Grace. Sat. and Sun. 1–5, Apr.–Oct. No admission fee; donations accepted. Built of nearby Port Deposit granite in 1827, this is one of the oldest continuously operating lighthouses in the United States, and possibly the oldest in Maryland. Other than its electric light, it has been restored, with lighthouse-keeper furnishings and other accoutrements, to appear as it did in the 19th century. Being at the end of The Promenade and overlooking the point where the Susquehanna River meets the Chesapeake Bay, this is a great spot to sit, walk, or picnic even if the lighthouse is not open.

ROCK RUN GRIST MILL

BOAT EXCURSIONS **Skipjack** *Martha Lewis* (410-939-4078; 1-800-406-0766), at the Concord Point Lighthouse, Concord and Lafayette Sts., Havre de Grace. The *Martha Lewis*, owned by the Chesapeake Heritage Conservancy and one of the last remaining oyster dredge boats, offers 75-minute Discovery Cruises to the public. Cruises depart at noon, 1:30 PM, and 3 PM on Sat. and Sun., Apr.–Oct. Reservations are not needed, but be mindful that the sailboat is limited to 28–30 passengers.

BOATBUILDING SCHOOL **Chesapeake Wooden Boat Builders School** (410-939-4800), 100 Lafayette St., Havre de Grace. Located within the Havre de Grace Maritime Museum. Here is a chance to learn a true craft whose product is just as useful and beautiful today as it was in decades past. Classes include antique canoe repair and restoration, model-ship building, and basic wooden-boat building. There are always a number of boats in various stages of construction, so stop by to see the process even if you are just visiting the museum.

BOWLING **Bowl Harford Lanes** (410-272-3555), 20 Custis St., Aberdeen.

GOLF **Bulle Rock** (410-939-8887; 1-888-285-5375), 320 Bleinheim Lane, Havre de Grace. Bulle Rock is a Pete Dye course that opened in the late 1990s to favorable reviews from numerous golfing magazines.

Beechtree (410-297-9700; 1-877-233-2487; www.beechtreegolf.com), 811 S. Stepney Rd., Aberdeen. Designed by Tom Doak to make use of the natural lay of the land. The front nine are played in rolling, open meadows, and the back nine wander through woodlands.

MINIATURE GOLF 🎯 **Churchville Golf and Baseball** (410-879-5357; www.churchvillegolf.com), 3040 Churchville Rd., Churchville. Batting cages and miniature golf.

HIKING A 20-mile section of the 190-mile **Mason-Dixon Trail System**, which branches off the **Appalachian Trail (AT)** in Cumberland County, Pennsylvania, passes through Harford County and Susquehanna State Park

CONCORD POINT LIGHTHOUSE

SKIPJACK *MARTHA LEWIS* MOORED IN HAVRE DE GRACE

(see below). Some of it follows roadways, yet it is a scenic hike with a number of views of the Susquehanna River. More information can be obtained by writing 719 Oakburne Rd., West Chester, PA 19382.

As it comes through the county, the Mason-Dixon Trail System shares its footpath with a portion of the **Lower Susquehanna Heritage Greenway**, a proposed system of trails that will include multiple miles of pathways along both sides of the Susquehanna River. Approximately 10 miles of the trail that run from Havre de Grace to Susquehanna State Park (see below) have been marked and are easy to follow. The Lower Susquehanna Heritage Greenway, Inc. (410-475-2182; www.marylandhistoricaltrust.net/ha-lsusq.html), 4948 Conowingo Rd., Darlington, 21304, can provide maps and up-to-date information.

Susquehanna State Park (410-557-7994), north of Havre de Grace along the Susquehanna River on Stafford and Rock Run Rds. The waters of the Susquehanna River rise in Otsego County, New York, and flow for more than 400 miles to empty into the head of the Chesapeake Bay, close to where the river separates central Maryland from the Eastern Shore. Protecting a portion of the river's drainage just before it meets the bay is 3,600-acre Susquehanna State Park.

A network of approximately 15 miles of pathways enables you to explore this varied topography of riverside vegetation, heavy forest cover, lightly flowing brooks, rock outcrops with grandstand views of the river, and interesting history (see *Historic Sites*). In addition, the park offers a campground with restrooms and hot showers, a picnic area, boat-launch facility, and evening interpretive programs.

Rocks State Park (410-557-7994), 3318 Rocks Chrome Hill Rd., Jarretsville. Deer Creek has cut a gorge into the Piedmont Plateau, creating a rugged scenery of large boulders, interesting rock formations, and steep cliffs. The park's trail system winds through the irregular landscape, going down to the creek and up to the heights. Don't miss the route to the **King and Queen's Seat**. These rock outcrops, close to 200 feet above the creek, look down onto some pretty dramatic views.

Located nearby, and administered by the state park, are **Hidden Valley Natural Area** with additional trails, and **Falling Branch**, the state's second highest vertical waterfall.

Also see *Parks* and *Walks*.

SAILING **BaySail** (410-939-2869; www.baysail.net), 100 Bourbon St., Tidewater Marina, Havre de Grace. BaySail is a one-stop sailing shop. Their school, which offers courses for beginners on up to bareboat-charter certification, is certified by the American Sailing Association. Once you gain a bit of proficiency, you can set out on your own cruise with a charter boat rented by the half day, day, or week—or buy a boat of your own from BaySail. If you don't have the time to gain the needed expertise, just ask them to include a captain with your charter boat.

SPECIAL CLASSES **Steppingstone Museum** (410-939-2299), 461 Quaker Bottom Rd. (accessed from I-95 Exit 89), Havre de Grace. The museum sponsors historical crafts workshops in early spring, usually in May. (Also see *Museums*.)

SWIMMING Deer Creek passes through **Rocks State Park** in Jarretsville, within the deep gorge it has cut into the land, and is a popular swimming and tubing stream. Be aware that you are on your own; there are no lifeguards.

TENNIS Courts open to the public are located in a number of the parks operated by the Harford County Department of Parks and Recreation. Among the many are **Francis Silver Park** on Shuresville Rd., **Churchville Recreation Complex**,

THE SUSQUEHANNA RIVER AS VIEWED FROM SUSQUEHANNA STATE PARK

Forest Hill Recreation Complex, and **Norrisville Recreation Complex**. More information can be obtained by calling 410-638-3572.

✳ Green Space

PARKS ✇ ⅋ **Eden Mill Park and Nature Center** (410-836-3050; www.eden mill.org), 1617 Eden Mill Rd., Pylesville. The Nature Center, located in an old mill building, is one of the most impressive I have seen in a county-operated park. Lots of good displays for the kids and a very active volunteer group that presents programs on a wide variety of topics. The park's trail system is well thought out. In just 2 miles, it can take hikers through a variety of environments along Deer Creek, into small meadows, and over a low ridge. There are also several public canoe-launch sites; one is handicapped-accessible.

WALKS **The Promenade** in Havre de Grace is a half-mile boardwalk along the waterfront with interpretive signs explaining the natural and human history of the area. Because it starts at **Millard E. Tydings Memorial Park**, goes by the **Decoy** and **Maritime Museums**, and ends at the **Concord Point Lighthouse**, it is a convenient way to see the sites without having to drive. Looking out upon the Chesapeake Bay, it is also a great place to be for sunrise and sunset. This is surely one of the nicest gifts the citizens of Havre de Grace have given themselves and visitors to enhance the quality of town life.

The Ma and Pa Trail in Bel Air follows an easy, nearly level old railroad grade through the town of Bel Air and out into the countryside. Several miles are usable now; when completed, it will total 7 miles in length.

✳ Lodging

MOTELS AND HOTELS

Edgewood, 21040
✇ ⅋ **Comfort Inn** (410-679-0770; 1-800-221-2222), 1700 Van Bibber Rd. (accessed from I-95 Exit 77). Within easy driving distance of many area attractions. Lots of extras, including complimentary deluxe continental breakfast, HBO, in-room coffee-makers, and an outdoor pool. Children 18 and under stay free. $69–109.

🐾 **Best Western** (410-679-9700), 1709 Edgewood Rd. (accessed from I-95 Exit 77). Operated by the same management corporation as the Comfort Inn, it offers the same amenities but also has an exercise room and permits small pets (with an additional deposit). $69–99.

INNS

Havre de Grace, 21078
✇ **Vandiver Inn** (410-939-5200; 1-800-245-1665; www.vandiverinn .com), 301 S. Union Ave. Built in 1886 by Murray Vandiver as a wedding gift to his wife, Annie. The opulence of the house reflects his political career, which included serving in the Maryland House of Delegates, as state treasurer, as mayor of Havre de Grace, and an appointment to the IRS by President Cleveland. The chandelier and stained glass in the parlor are original, as are many items in the nine large guest rooms. The two houses next door to the inn have eight rooms available to guests. Children over the age of 6 are welcome. $99–149.

GARDENS

✍ **Ladew Topiary Gardens** (410-557-9570; www.ladewgardens.com), 3535 Jarretsville Pike, Monkton. Mon.–Fri. 10–4, Sat. and Sun. 10:30–5, mid-April through October 31. Admission to the gardens and nature walk is $8 adults, $7 seniors/students, and $2 children. Admission for the gardens, nature walk, and a guided tour of the house is $12 adults, $11 senior/students, and $4 children.

Expect to spend several hours to appreciate all that is here. In fact, bring your lunch or eat in the Ladew Café and devote half a day to walking, relaxing, and enjoying the gardens' 22 acres and house.

Between 1929 and 1971, Henry S. Ladew developed 15 gardens, each with a different theme, form, and color. Among them are the Woodland Garden (the first to bloom in spring), the Berry Garden (designed to be bright and colorful in winter and to provide forage for birds), and the Yellow Garden (with its variety of yellow blossoms throughout the season). I found that as I walked from one to the other, the landscaping created angles of vegetation that were pleasing to the eye and drew me along in anticipation of what was around the next bend.

The centerpiece, of course, is the Topiary Garden with its sculpted unicorn, sea horses, Churchill's top hat and victory sign, birds in flight, and more. Very young children will enjoy the animal sculptures, while older teens will appreciate the work and talent that went into creating them.

The Manor House is also a tribute to Ladew's vision. It was nothing more than a farmhouse when he purchased it in 1929. It is now a place of such architectural character and lavishness, tempered with an eye toward quality, that one of its rooms, the Oval Library, is included in the book *100 Most Beautiful Rooms in America*.

FANCIFUL SHRUBBERY AT LADEW TOPIARY GARDENS IN MONKTON

🍴 **Crazy Swede** (410-939-5440; www
.crazyswederestaurant.com), 400 N.
Union Ave. The Crazy Swede offers a
number of suites in several different
buildings and houses. All come with a
private bath, continental breakfast in
the room, and 20 percent off meals
purchased in the Crazy Swede
Restaurant (see *Dining Out*). Some
suites have full kitchen and/or Jacuzzi.
The size of the rooms and their elegant furnishings are a good deal for
the price. $99–159.

BED & BREAKFASTS

Havre de Grace, 21078
Currier House (410-939-7886;
1-800-827-2889; www.currier-bb
.com), 800 S. Market St. In 1996,
Jane Currier Belbot opened a B&B in
the 1760 house that has been in her
family since 1861. I truly felt more
like I was visiting someone's home
than I did in any other establishment
in Harford County. The house is
decorated with heirlooms, family furniture, original Currier and Ives litho-
graphs, and photos of ancestors and
the glory days of Havre de Grace.
All four guests rooms have a private
bath, and two of them have a balcony
overlooking a grand magnolia tree,
the Concord Point Lighthouse, and
the bay. I was especially taken by
the milieu of the Crawford Room's
cedar-wood-lined bathroom. The full
watermen's breakfast includes oysters
and Maryland stewed tomatoes (in-
season). $95–125.

La Clé D'or (410-939-9562; 1-888-
HUG-GUEST; www.lacledorguest
house.com), 226 N. Union Ave. This
place should have a motto something
like, "Live in opulence for a while
without spending a fortune." The
1868 home is loaded with gorgeous

antiques and has 17 Strauss crystal
chandeliers. The guest rooms are decorated with their own theme. Breakfast is served on a variety of fine china
accompanied by gold utensils, the
brick-walled garden is entered
through a wrought-iron gate, and the
outdoor whirlpool Jacuzzi is large
enough to handle a party of 10.
Refreshments and a cookie jar are
always available. $120–140.

🛏 **Spencer Silver Mansion** (410-
939-1097; 1-800-780-1485; www
.spencersilvermansion.com), 200 S.
Union Ave. Children welcome. One
of the most beautifully restored Victorian mansions I've seen. Guests rooms
are lavishly furnished with oak and
mahogany antiques of the period; a
stone two-story carriage house is
available for those wishing privacy.
$70–140.

CAMPING See **Susquehanna State
Park** under *Hiking*.

✳ Where to Eat
DINING OUT

Havre de Grace
🍴 **MacGregor's** (410-939-3003;
1-800-300-6319; www.macgregors
restaurant.com), 331 St. John St.
Open for lunch and dinner. Seafood is
the definite specialty of this restaurant, which has a casually elegant
atmosphere. Crabcakes (market
price), stuffed flounder ($21.95), and
the shrimp and chicken stir-fry
($17.95) make use of the local catch.
The older portion of the restaurant is
inside a former bank building, while
the newer glass-enclosed section provides memorable views of the Susquehanna River. The tavern serves light
fare and has live entertainment on the
weekends.

HAVRE DE GRACE

Note to film and history buffs: The MacGregor name comes from owner Daniel Lee, a direct descendant of Rob Roy MacGregor.

Tidewater Grill (410-939-3313), 300 Franklin St. Open for lunch and dinner. The dining room and two outside decks overlook the Susquehanna River. Seafood, much of it mixed with pasta, occupies at least half of the menu, with chicken, beef, and chops making up the rest of the entrées. Meat lovers will enjoy the American Mixed Grille with a petite fillet, breast of chicken, loin lamb chop, and "An Do We" sausage ($25.95). $14.50–25.95.

Crazy Swede Restaurant (410-939-5440; www.crazyswederestaurant .com), 400 N. Union Ave. Within the old 1893 Chesapeake Hotel building (where Al Capone once dined), you will find a refined preparation of seafood, poultry, beef, and pasta served in a casual atmosphere. My

crab dip appetizer ($9.75) was remarkably creamy, while the shrimp stuffed with crabmeat and topped with the restaurant's own imperial sauce ($21.95) was even richer and creamier. Entrées $14.95–24.95; sandwiches and soups start at $6.95.

The Crazy Swede also operates an inn with a number of suites available (see *Inns*). The moniker, by the way, comes from a former owner, who named it for "that crazy Swede chef" he once employed.

EATING OUT

Havre de Grace
✿ **The Bayou Restaurant** (410-939-3565), 927 Pulaski Hwy. (US 40). Open for lunch and dinner. You know that family-owned restaurant near you that has been around for decades and that everyone in town patronizes from time to time? Well, this is Havre de Grace's version. Expect friendly service and honest home cooking. All of

the soups, breads, and pies are made from scratch. The seafood combo ($15.95) of flounder, crabcake, oysters, shrimp, and scallops is available broiled or fried. A filling, healthful, and low-cost entrée is the vegetarian fettuccine ($6.95). Many choices of beef, veal, poultry, and other seafood entrées fill the menu ($6.50–24.95). Lunch buffet ($5.95) Tue.–Fri.

Aberdeen

The New Ideal Diner (410-272-1880), US 40. Open for breakfast (served all day), lunch, and dinner. Established in 1931. The present structure is the restaurant's fourth dining car in the same location. The gleaming stainless-steel and green-enamel striped car was manufactured by Jerry O'Mahony, Inc., and transported to the site in four sections in 1952. A very popular local favorite, it is always crowded for breakfast and lunch. Dinner selections include seafood, meats, and pasta. $6.45–18.95.

✺ **Olive Tree** (410-575-7773), 1005 Beards Hill Rd. Open for lunch and dinner. Since the pasta is made fresh before your eyes inside the glass "pasta booth," it only makes sense to order a dish containing one of its many forms. Choose a pasta entrée by itself or accompanied with crab, chicken, or beef. $8–18.

✺ **Japan House** (410-272-7878), 984 Beards Hill Rd. Open for lunch and dinner. Fresh sushi and sashimi ($3–9) are what bring diners in. Items from the teppanyaki grill, such as salmon ($13.95) and sesame chicken ($11.95), are also popular.

Edgewood

✺ **Vitali's** (410-671-6370), 1709 Edgewood Rd. (accessed from I-95 Exit 77). Open for breakfast, lunch,

and dinner. The atmosphere and quality of food are nicer than what you usually find in a restaurant next to a motel. Seafood, chicken, beef, and veal entrées are prepared with an Italian slant. The pasta dishes, with plenty to choose from, are among the most flavorful offerings. $9.95–19.95.

COFFEE BARS **Java by the Bay** (410-939-0227), 118 N. Washington St., Havre de Grace. Coffees and teas by the cup or the pound. Lots of goodies to choose from, such as a bagel, muffin, or Danish, to go with your drink.

SNACKS AND GOODIES

Havre de Grace

Bomboy's (410-939-2924; www .bomboyscandy.com), 329 Market St. Closed Mon. The chocolate candies created at Bomboy's, available by the piece or the pound, are made fresh daily using old family recipes. Fresh fudge and sugar-free chocolates are also available. If candy is not your fancy, **Bomboy's Homemade Ice Cream** is directly across the street.

Ritz (410-939-5858), 100 N. Washington St. With the atmosphere of a coffeehouse, Ritz serves desserts, pastries, beverages, and Edy's ice cream. There is also a good selection of sugar-free treats.

✳ Entertainment

FILM **Beards Hill Movies 7** (410-272-6770), 963 Beards Hill Rd., Aberdeen, is the place to see movies in and around town.

The Campus Hills Cinema 7 (410-836-2111), Campus Hill Shopping Center, and the **Tollgate Movies 7** (410-838-7077), 615 Baltimore Pike, both in Bel Air, show first-run movies.

✳ Selective Shopping

ANTIQUES There are so many antiques shops clustered along St. John St., N. Union Ave., and N. Washington St. in Havre de Grace that the area has come to be known as **Antique Row**.

Memory Makers (410-877-0450), 1804 Harford Rd., Fallston. Tue.–Sun 11–6. Antique wood furniture and porcelains and china are found in abundance here.

Spenceola Antique Center (410-803-0011), 1445 Rockspring Rd., Bel Air. Over 22,000 square feet of display space and more than 150 dealers showing their wares. You should be able to find just about anything you want, if you can just wade through that much merchandise.

Bayside Antiques (410-939-9397), 232 N. Washington St., Havre de Grace. An antiques mall with a number of dealers offering upscale merchandise.

ART GALLERIES The **Picture Show Art Gallery** (410-939-0738), 301 St. John St., Havre de Grace. Features Chesapeake Bay sculpture and artwork.

USED-BOOK STORES

Havre de Grace
Washington Street Books (410-939-6215), 131 N. Washington St. Wed.–Mon. noon–6. More than 35,000 used, rare, and out-of-print books. A small selection of new books.

Courtyard Book Shop (410-939-5150), 313 St. John St. Open every day. A selection of used and antiquarian books.

SPECIAL SHOPS **National 5 and 10** (410-939-2737), 232 N. Washington St., Havre de Grace. Like the five-and-dimes of yore, National sells toys, clothing, housewares, hardware, and souvenirs.

FARMER'S MARKETS **Havre de Grace Farmer's Market**. 9–noon, May–Oct., you can find seasonal offerings at the market on Pennington Ave.

Bel Air Farmer's Market. Produce stands are set up at the Harford Mall, MD 24 and US 1, on Sun. 10–2, Apr.–Oct.

Edgewood Farmer's Market. You can purchase the bounty of the seasons in Edgewood in the lot across from the MARC station on Thu. 3:30–7 PM, June–Oct.

PICK-YOUR-OWN PRODUCE FARMS
✐ **Applewood Farm** (410-836-1140), 4425 Prospect Rd., Whiteford. You can pick your own pumpkins, gourds, and mums during Sep. and Oct. Special events during the year include a petting zoo, hayrides, a maze, and train displays.

WINERIES
Fiore Winery (410-879-4007; www.fiorewinery.com), 3026 Whiteford Rd. (MD 136), Pylesville. Open for tours and tastings Wed.–Sat. 10–5, and noon–5 Sun. Vintner Mike Fiore was born in Calabria, Italy, and grew up in a family whose experience in winemaking goes back more than 400 years. Coming to this sloping hillside in northern Harford County, he planted his first grapes in 1977. Besides the tour and the tastings, you are also permitted to enjoy the scenery and the vineyards. Fiore sponsors several annual fun events, such as its well-attended jazz and arts festival.

✳ Special Events

May: **Annual Decoy and Wildlife Art Festival** (410-939-3739). For 3 days in May, Havre de Grace hosts one of the largest and longest-running festivals to honor decoy carving and other forms of wildlife art. **ArtQuest** (410-638-5974), Bel Air. Food and live entertainment accompany the works of local professional and amateur artists.

June: **Annual Evening of Wine and Jazz** (410-939-5780), Susquehanna Museum, Havre de Grace. **Scottish Festival** (410-939-2299), Stepping-stone Museum, Havre de Grace. A full day of pipe-band music, sheep herding and shearing, spinning and weaving, and lots of Scottish food and fashions. **Harford County Farm Fair** (410-838-8663), Bel Air.

August: **Annual Arts and Crafts Show** (410-939-9342), Millard E. Tydings Memorial Park, Havre de Grace. For more than four decades, the local chapter of Soroptimist International has been sponsoring this 2-day event. Arts, crafts, food, demonstrations, and music. **Antique St. Fest** (410-939-9397), Franklin St., Havre de Grace.

September: **Annual Duck Fair** (410-939-3739), Havre de Grace. Wildlife artists and carvers, retriever demonstrations, and many children's activities.

December: **Candlelight Tour** (410-939-3947), Havre de Grace. A yearly event in which businesses, churches, B&Bs, and historic homes open their doors to visitors.

NORTH OF BALTIMORE—Owings Mills, Hunt Valley, Westminster, and Taneytown

Baltimore's neighbors to the north, especially those within 15 miles or so of the I-695 beltway, are becoming ensnared in the city's sprawl. Long strings of strip malls, fast-food restaurants, and convenience stores meld into one another. It's hard to tell where some towns, such as Pikesville, Owings Mills, Towson, Lutherville, and Timonium, begin or end.

This does not mean you should overlook these places in your quest to explore the best that Maryland has to offer. Just off the beltway in Towson is Hampton, the first property to be accepted into the National Park Service system on architectural, and not necessarily historic, merit in 1948. The Fire Museum of Maryland in Lutherville, with more than 60 vehicles dating from the early 1800s, has one of the largest collections of its kind in the country. The last remaining serpentine grasslands in the state, Soldier's Delight National Environmental Area, are located just outside Owings Mills, while more than one-fourth of all of Maryland's horse farms occupy large amounts of acreage between I-83 and MD 140/MD 30.

Also providing quick escapes from the density of Baltimore are Oregon Ridge, a regional park whose pathways provide impressive views of Hunt Valley, and the North Central Railroad Trail with a level route stretching for 20 miles from the Pennsylvania border to Cockeysville. More than 100 miles of trails snake around the varied terrain of 17,000-acre Gunpowder Falls State Park.

Farther afield, and a bit to the west, Carroll County has more land devoted to agricultural purposes than any other county in the state. A drive on just about any of its two-lane roadways yields a scenery of rolling meadows freckled by grazing cattle and poultry farms. All of those open fields means the county is also the least forested, but places like Piney Run and Hashawha Parks help preserve large stands of mature trees for present and future generations.

Substantial population growth in the last few decades has not robbed the communities of their small-town personalities. On the outskirts of Westminster, the county seat, MD 140 is lined with big-box discount stores and shopping

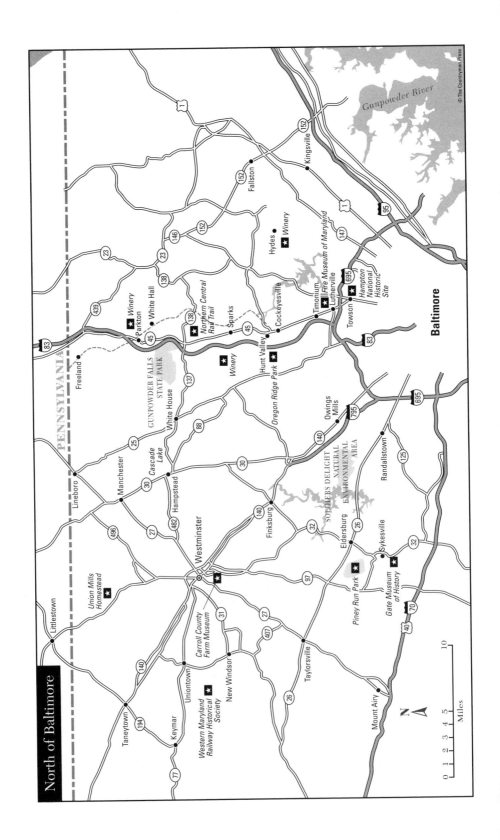

North of Baltimore

Baltimore

PENNSYLVANIA

GUNPOWDER FALLS STATE PARK

SOLDIER'S DELIGHT NATURAL ENVIRONMENTAL AREA

Gunpowder River

© The Countryman Press

Littlestown

Taneytown

Keymar

Union Mills Homestead

Uniontown

Western Maryland Railway Historical Society

New Windsor

Taylorsville

Mount Airy

Lineboro

Freeland

White Hall

Parkton

Winery

Manchester

Cascade Lake

Hampstead

Westminster

Carroll County Farm Museum

Finksburg

Owings Mills

Randallstown

Eldersburg

Sykesville

Piney Run Park

Gate Museum of History

White House

Winery

Northern Central Rail Trail

Sparks

Cockeysville

Hydes

Winery

Fire Museum of Maryland

Timonium

Lutherville

Hampton National Historic Site

Towson

Hunt Valley

Oregon Ridge Park

Fallston

Kingsville

N

Miles

0 1 2 3 4 5   10

centers, yet the historic district around Main Street remains packed with structures from the 1800s, many mom-and-pop businesses, and a 1920s art deco theater—home of the local arts council.

Nearby Taneytown, most scenically reached via MD 832 instead of MD 140, is the county's oldest town. George Washington visited the Adam Good Tavern in 1791, when a sign above it read, A DAMN GOOD INN, ENTERTAINMENT FOR MAN AND BEAST. Undoubtedly much more upscale, the Antrim 1844 Inn takes in today's travelers.

Mount Airy has always been a place along America's busiest transportation routes. First, it was the Old National Pike in the early 1700s, then the Baltimore & Ohio Railroad in the 1800s, and US 40 in the early 1900s. High-speed motorists on I-70 now tend to zip by, missing its antiques shops and nearby wineries.

An interesting chapter in Sykesville's history is Betsy Syke's wedlock to Napoleon Bonaparte's brother, Jerome. Napoleon was against the marriage and refused to allow Betsy to enter France, and she never saw Jerome again. The town is one of the many old railroad towns in Maryland that thrived when the trains came through, but withered away once they left. The train station now houses a restaurant whose live folk and jazz entertainment attracts many locals and Baltimoreans on the weekend.

Uniontown has no such commercial establishments; its claim to fame is its historic district with a diversity of 18th-, 19th-, and 20th-century structures. An easy walking tour of 20 minutes will take you past an abundance of architectural delights decorated by cupolas, cornices, dormers, and hipped roofs.

GUIDANCE **The Carroll County Visitor Center** (410-848-1388; 1-800-272-1933) shares space with the Historical Society of Carroll County and is located at 210 E. Main St., Westminster, 21157.

Information can also be obtained from the **Carroll County Office of Tourism** (410-386-2983; www.carr.org/tourism), 224 N. Center St., Room 100, Westminster, 21157.

The Baltimore County Conference and Visitors Bureau (410-296-4886; 1-877-STAY-N-DO; www.visitbacomd.com) is located in the Towson Town Center Mall, second level, Towson, 21204, and at 118 Shawan Rd., Hunt Valley Mall, Hunt Valley, 21030.

GETTING THERE *By car:* **I-83** heads directly north of Baltimore after it branches off the **Baltimore Beltway (I-695)** at Exit 24 near Lutherville. The largest percentage of listings and attractions in this section are is located in Carroll County, which can be reached by taking **I-795** from Baltimore and then continuing along **MD 140**.

By air: **Baltimore/Washington International Airport** (1-800-I-FLY-BWI), located between Baltimore and Annapolis, is about an hour's drive to the southeast.

GETTING AROUND *By car:* Traffic along any of the roads within 15 miles of the **Baltimore Beltway (I-695)** is extremely heavy during the morning and evening rush hours. There are not any good alternatives, so just turn on the radio and accept it. During the middle of the day, **I-83** becomes a fairly rapid way to head directly north into Baltimore County.

The situation is much better in Carroll County. **MD 140** is a good four-lane highway that becomes a two-lane country road north of Westminster. Other roads are lightly traveled during the middle part of the day.

By rail: The **Central Light Rail Line** (410-832-1200, ext. 3990), the commuter train service out of Baltimore, basically parallels I-83 and makes stops at Lutherville, Timonium Business Park, and Timonium. Trains run about every 15 minutes and operate until 11 PM; 7 PM on Sun. The **MARC** rail service (1-800-325-RAIL) makes stops in Owings Mills and Hunt Valley.

By taxi: One phone number—410-486-4000—puts you in contact with taxicabs based in Owings Mills, Reisterstown, and Pikesville. Near Towson you can call **Jimmy's** (410-837-7200), and in Overlea contact **Overlea Cab** (410-665-1300).

PARKING In Westminster, parking meters are free after 5 PM and all day Sat. and Sun.

MEDICAL EMERGENCY **St. Joseph Medical Center** (410-337-1226), 7601 Osler Dr., Towson.

Northwest Hospital Center (410-521-2200), 5401 Old Court Rd., Randallstown.

Carroll Hospital Center (410-848-3000), 200 Memorial Ave., Westminster.

✳ To See

COLLEGES **McDaniel College** (410-848-7000), Westminster. A liberal arts college, McDaniel has been educating students for more than 135 years. It could also be considered the cultural engine for the area with its **Esther Prangley Rice Gallery** and various vocal and instrumental groups, lectures open to the public, and its sponsorship of **Common Ground on the Hill** and **Theatre on the Hill**.

MUSEUMS

Westminster
Historical Society of Carroll County (410-848-6494; www.carr.org/hscc), 210 E. Main St. The society's Shriver-Weybright Exhibition Gallery displays items from its permanent collection illustrating the history of the county. The exhibits are constantly changing, so there will probably be something new each time you visit.

Union Mills Homestead (410-848-2288), 3311 Littlestown Pike (about 7 miles north of Westminster on MD 97). Tue.–Fri. 10–4, and Sat. and Sun. noon–4, June 1–Sep. 1. Small admission fee. Because all of the furniture and artifacts in this 1797 clapboard farmhouse belonged to the Shriver family, visitors get a true picture of what life was like when the Shrivers lived here. Things that caught my

UNION MILLS HOMESTEAD

eye were the letter to David Shriver from Thomas Jefferson, the 1863 Steinway piano, and an original WANTED poster for runaway slaves. The gristmill, built with bricks made on the property, still works. Guided tours are given of the house and mill.

Sykesville
Gate House Museum of History (410-549-5150), 7283 Cooper Dr. Wed. and Sun. 1–6, Fri. 2–8. Donations accepted. A small collection of objects from the town's history.

Union Bridge
Western Maryland Railway Historical Society (410-775-0150), Union Bridge Station (MD 75). Sun. 1–4, Wed. 9–noon and 1–3. Housed in the 1902 station is a collection of artifacts and memorabilia from the 125-year history of the Western Maryland Railroad.

Freeland
& **Morris Meadows Historic Preservation Museum** (410-329-6636), Freeland Rd. Associated with the Morris Meadows Campground (see *Lodging*); you may need to go to the campground to get someone to open the museum. Old tractors, dolls, farm machinery, and displays of a schoolhouse, general store, kitchen, and gristmill. The sheer volume of items becomes even more impressive when you realize it is the private collection of Clive and Virginia Morris.

Lutherville
✍ & **Fire Museum of Maryland** (410-321-7500; www.firemuseummd.org), 1301 York Rd. (accessed from I-695 Exit 26B N.). Tue.–Sat. 11–4, June–Aug.; Sat. only, Sep.–May. Adults $6; seniors and firefighters $5; children 3–18 get in for $4. Presents the history of firefighting from the colonial days to the present. Children especially enjoy sitting in the 1938 fire-engine driver's seat.

🖋 ♿ **Carroll County Farm Museum** (410-876-2667; 1-800-654-4645), 500 S. Center St., Westminster. Apr.–Oct. Small admission fee. Was I ever mistaken when I thought all I would see was a few old farm implements! This 140-acre complex does contain a few of those, but it provides a much broader picture of 1800s farm life with its completely furnished farmhouse, wagon shed, kitchen, smokehouse, and springhouse. Artisans within the living-history center practice the crafts of yesteryear that would have supplied the farm with many of its necessary items. Be sure to walk over to the barnyard full of chickens, cows, turkeys, pigs, horses, goats, and lambs. Bring a picnic lunch and plan to spend a few hours. This is one of the best re-created farms I have ever seen—especially in light of the small amount of change it costs to get in.

HISTORIC HOMES Hampton National Historic Site (410-823-1309), 535 Hampton Lane (just a few moments' drive from I-695 Exit 27B), Towson. Open daily 9–5. Small admission fee. Hampton was the largest house in the country when constructed in the late 1700s. Guided tours take you through this grand house, which is furnished almost exclusively with items that belonged to the six generations of the Ridgely family. Afterward, walk over the rest of the grounds to the family cemetery, slave quarters, dairy house, and gardens.

GUIDED TOURS The **Carroll County Visitor Center**, 210 E. Main St., Westminster, has put together a number of walking-tour brochures for Westminster, Uniontown, and other nearby sites. For a fun time, pick up the one for the ghost walk through Westminster. There are also driving-tour pamphlets to the Civil

HAMPTON NATIONAL HISTORIC SITE

War sites and one that takes you to places important to the birth of American Methodism.

✳ To Do

BICYCLING **Liberty Bike Shop** (410-549-9258; www.libertybikeshop.com), 1912 Liberty Rd., Eldersburg. If you are riding around in the area and your bike develops a problem, these folks have a complete center that services all makes and models.

CIVIL WAR The rolling terrain of this area north of Baltimore saw a lot of troop movement and battle activity during the Civil War, especially when Robert E. Lee was trying to gain a foothold in Northern territory. That movement was, of course, halted at Gettysburg in the summer of 1863. Brochures available from the **Carroll County Visitor Center** map out a couple of driving tours to the site of a cavalry skirmish that took place in Westminster and other places that played a part in the Gettysburg drama.

FAMILY ACTIVITIES 🖉 **Cascade Lake** (410-374-9111), 3000 Snydersburg Rd., Hampstead. Open 10–7; the season is usually from around Memorial Day through close to Labor Day. This 6-acre spring-fed lake has a gently sloping sandy bottom and a large roped-off swimming area watched over by certified lifeguards. The kiddie area has a number of fun things to do and is well guarded. There are several waterslides, floating rafts, and a high-dive platform. Within the 25-acre property are fishing and boating areas (boat rentals), picnic tables, a playground, and a hiking trail. Popular with local families.

ROAD BIKING CARROLL COUNTY

A brochure available from the **Carroll County Visitor Center** details 10 rides throughout the county. Conceived by a group of local cyclists, the outings range from 8 miles to 33 miles and take in scenic farmlands, lightly traveled country roads, and small towns. Three are designed to bring you past ice cream shops, some go by historic sites, and others enable you to leave the bike for a while and take to a hiking trail. All of the rides are circular, so you always return to the starting point, where you are permitted to park your car.

I like the 15-mile **Westminster South route,** which not only delivers me to Hoffman's Ice Cream Shop but also enables an exploration of the **Carroll County Farm Museum** (see the sidebar on page 186). Then there is the 30-mile **Taneytown tour** with lots of great scenery and diversions. Open meadows are often dotted with deer, small Pipe Creek bubbles beside the road, and the public pool in Taneytown Memorial Park beckons when the asphalt begins to release the heat it has soaked up on a sunny day.

Westminster

Wakefield Valley (410-876-6662; www.wakefieldvalley.com), 1000 Fenby Farm Rd. Three 9-hole courses make up Wakefield Valley's 27 holes. The Green Course has long par 5s, and the White Course covers hilly terrain. Combined, the courses have the second highest slope rating in the state.

McDaniel College Golf Course (410-848-7667). This nine-hole course was built on the college campus in 1935 by students and faculty and is one of the oldest courses in the county. Open to the public; students, faculty, and staff play for free.

Finksburg

Francis Scott Key Golf Club (410-526-2000; www.fskgolfclub.com), 1900 River Downs Dr. A par-72 Arthur Hills–designed course on very rolling, wooded countryside.

White Hall

Greystone (410-887-1945), 2115 White Hall Rd., less than 10 minutes from I-83 Exit 31. An abundance of tall trees and other vegetation, ponds, and wetlands add a challenge to this Joe Lee–designed course.

Timonium

Longview (410-887-7735), 1 Cardigan Rd. A scenic and open course that is considered to be friendly to beginning golfers. Fees are lower here than at many other courses in the area.

MINIATURE GOLF ✐ **Four Seasons Sports Complex** (410-239-3366), 2710 Hampstead–Mexico Rd., Hampstead. There are fast-pitch baseball and slow-pitch softball batting cages in addition to the 18-hole Play-A-Round Miniature Golf Course.

HIKING Gunpowder Falls State Park (410-592-2897), 2813 Jerusalem Rd., Kingsville. Cool, shaded spots by a small swimming hole. Wildflower and pine fragrances wafting through the air. Owl hoots breaking the stillness of early evening. Muskrat and raccoon paw prints stamped into soft mud. Hazy silhouettes of deer foraging in the morning mist.

These are not descriptions of things you must travel to western Maryland to enjoy, but rather some of the delights to be found in Gunpowder Falls State Park, located a short drive from Baltimore. More than 100 miles of trails wander through the park's 17,000 acres, which are divided among four areas that are separated from one another. *50 Hikes in Maryland* (Countryman Press) describes a hike in each area.

Soldier's Delight National Environmental Area (410-461-5005), 5100 Deer Park Rd., Owings Mills. Looking at the types of vegetation in Maryland today, it may be hard to imagine that grasslands once spread across tens of thousands of acres of this landscape. Prior to colonial settlement, much of Baltimore and Harford Counties, and adjacent counties in Pennsylvania, was covered by open

Northern Central Railroad Trail (administered by Gunpowder Falls State Park; see above). The northernmost parking area for this trail is on MD 108 at Freeland, and the southern terminus is on Ashland Rd. in the Ashland Village housing development off MD 45 in Hunt Valley. The Rails-to-Trails Conservancy, the association generally recognized as spearheading the nationwide movement to convert abandoned railroad rights-of-way into trails, was formally organized in 1986. Nearly a decade before that, though, the state of Maryland, Baltimore County, and a group of local citizens were already laying the groundwork for the Northern Central Railroad Trail.

From 1838 to 1972, the Northern Central Railroad connected Baltimore with York, Pennsylvania, providing a major link for small communities along the way. Union troops made use of the railroad during the Civil War, and Abraham Lincoln traveled it on his way to deliver his famous Gettysburg Address. The construction of the interstates—and the resulting increase in truck and automobile transportation—marked the railroad's decline. Floods from Hurricane Agnes in 1972 dealt the final blow by washing out trestles and miles of track.

Never far from civilization, yet with long stretches of detachment from the humanized world, this 20-mile route is a great place to introduce someone to the joys of outdoor walking, without subjecting them to the rigors, and fear, of a harsh or isolated terrain. The pathway is level, and road crossings are fairly frequent if the need for help should happen to arise. In addition, public restrooms are situated at seven sites, with drinking water available beside three of the road crossings. The historic aspects of the railroad are an added bonus. This is a multiuse trail, also open to bicyclists and equestrians, so always walk to the right and avoid walking two abreast. Pets must be on a leash.

spaces not unlike the prairies found in the Midwest. At 2,000 acres, Soldier's Delight preserves the largest remaining serpentine grasslands in the state. A network of trails lets you explore the area to enjoy the open scenery and wide skyscape, and to find interesting plants and flowers such as the sandplain gerardia and fringed gentian.

HORSEBACK RIDING Brochures and maps available from the **Carroll County Department of Enterprise and Recreation Services** (410-386-2103; 1-888-302-8978), 225 N. Center St., Room 100, Westminster, 21157, point out the many miles of trails and locations in the county available to equestrians.

SKIING, CROSS-COUNTRY See *Green Space*.

TENNIS Six of the parks in Carroll County have courts that are open to the public. Call 410-386-2103 for locations and availability.

✳ Green Space

PARKS ❅ ♂ よ **Hashawha Environmental Center** (410-848-9040), 300 John Owings Rd., Westminster. Open sunrise–sunset. So much land is devoted to agricultural purposes (and lately housing developments) that Carroll County is the least forested county in the state. Knowing that may help you to appreciate even more so the woodlands that the pathways of Hashawha wander through. The trails are open to hikers, bikers, and cross-country skiers; one is handicapped-accessible. **Bear Branch Nature Center** (410-848-2517), inside the park, has a number of interpretive displays and sponsors a variety of outings and programs on- and off-site.

❅ ♂ よ **Piney Run Park** (410-795-3274), 30 Martz Rd., Sykesville. Apr. 1–Oct. 31, 6 AM–sunset. Small vehicle entrance fee. Nov.–Mar. visitors may park outside the gate, hike the trails, fish from the banks, and visit the nature center.

In addition to fishing and boating opportunities on the 300-acre lake, there is a network of trails on the surrounding 500 acres. One of the trails is open to mountain bikers and another to equestrians; all trails are open for cross-country skiing in winter. If your time is short, follow the **Field Trail**, as it will lead you into a variety of environments in only two-thirds of a mile. Canoes, sailboats, rowboats, kayaks, and electric-powered fishing boats are available for rent during the season. The nature center has several small exhibits and offers a host of programs for children and adults. Pets on leashes are permitted.

❅ **Oregon Ridge** (410-887-1815), 13555 Beaver Dam Rd., Cockeysville. Oregon Ridge is an excellent model of a county or regional park that has been able to meet many of the diverse recreational needs of a growing local population, yet

PINEY RUN PARK

still keep the vast majority of the land undisturbed. Within the park's 1,036 acres are tennis courts, picnic areas, a dinner theater and lodge, an outdoor stage (the summer home for the Baltimore Symphony Orchestra), a swimming lake and sandy beach, and a bathhouse and snack bar. A network of marked pathways meanders through the undeveloped part of the park, rising to the main forested ridgeline and descending into a narrow creek valley. The nature center, with exhibits relating to local natural and human history, sponsors one of the best and most active interpretive programs available anywhere in Maryland—pick up a schedule and take part in an activity. Pets permitted on leashes.

✳ Lodging

INNS **Westminster Inn** (410-876-2893), 5 S. Center St., Westminster, 21157. Here's a twist: This is an old schoolhouse that has been turned into an inn with luxury rooms (each with a Jacuzzi) and a complete fitness club. Close to the center of town. $100–200.

✍ ⟨ **Antrim 1844** (410-756-6812; 1-800-858-1844; www.antrim1844 .com), 30 Trevanion Rd., Taneytown, 21787. It is almost hard to grasp that small Taneytown contains one of the most celebrated inns in all of America.

The constant attention to details, lavish furnishings, and impeccable service are rarely found in such a perfect combination. The 29 guest rooms and suites are furnished with canopy featherbed, fireplace and/or Jacuzzi (my room had a pedestal Jacuzzi, a bidet, and a private balcony), and antiques appropriate to the inn's antebellum history.

Everything has been arranged to be pleasing to the eye, even the 23 acres of grounds. The gardens are reminiscent of those found in European estates, the croquet lawn is perfectly

ONE OF MANY RELAXING SPOTS ON THE 23 ACRES OF ANTRIM 1844

manicured, and the swimming pool and its gazebo are surrounded by hedgerows. The quality of the restaurant's meals (see *Dining Out*) matches that of the inn. $160–375.

BED & BREAKFASTS Yellow Turtle Inn (410-635-3000; www.yellowturtle inn.com), 111 Springdale Ave., New Windsor, 21776. Several years ago, Joan Bradford had a dream about opening an inn. She became convinced it was her destiny when, a few days later, someone else said they, too, had had a dream about her and an inn—and the inn looked exactly the same in both dreams.

Sitting on 3 acres, the 1800s house is decorated in an amazing amount of Victorian furnishings and items. Each guest room is unique: The Windsor Vineyard Room has a curved wall, there is a mural in the Mary Cole Room, and the Queen's Chambers has a bed constructed of tree branches.

The grounds include an interesting seven-circuit meditation labyrinth. If a full-body massage and herbal tea are not enough to relax you, the view of the 100-acre preserved farmland from the wraparound porch surely will. $105–165.

✍ ♿ **Wood's Gain** (410-775-0308; www.woodsgain.com), 421 McKinstry's Mill Rd., Linwood, 21791. Open weekends Sep.–June and daily July–Aug. The 1866 brick house, with five fireplaces and four stairways, is the oldest structure in tiny Linwood village. Beverly and Steve Kerkam have expertly restored the house while adding modern fixtures and amenities. All guest rooms have a private bath. The Keeping Room, in the oldest section of the home, is fully handicapped-accessible. I thought the

decor in the Grandmother's Room, which had belonged to both sets of grandparents, was a loving tribute to family. However, I enjoyed an evening in the Summer Kitchen, a detached two-room cottage with a sitting room, fireplace, and whirlpool tub.

Guests often gather around the old upright piano and phonograph in the parlor, or sit in the rose garden or on the porch to watch the evening unfold. Supervised children 7 and older are welcome. $95–155.

CAMPING ✍ Ramblin' Pines Campground (410-795-5161; 1-800-550-8733; www.ramblinpines.com), 801 Hoods Mill Rd. (3 miles from I-70 Exit 76), Woodbine, 21797. As much a destination resort as it is a campground. Besides RV (with full hookups) and tent sites, there's a swimming pool, a playground, a miniature-golf course, hiking trails, and planned activities such as hayrides, bingo, and live entertainment. Sites are somewhat close together, but the property is rambling and spread out. Cabins and trailers available for rent.

Morris Meadows (410-329-6636; 1-800-643-7056), 1523 Freeland Rd., Freeland, 21053. Located just a couple of minutes' drive from I-83 Exit 36. The campground is on land that has been in the Morris family since 1793; the original deed, written on goatskin, is on display in the registration lobby. This is a mini family resort with tent and RV sites, rental cabins, a swimming pool, miniature golf, fishing, and the most extensive list of planned activities (Apr.–Oct.) I've ever seen in a commercial campground. (Also see *Museums*.)

✳ Where to Eat

DINING OUT 🌸 ✑ **Paradiso Ris-torante** (410-876-1421), 20 Distillery Dr., Westminster. Open for lunch and dinner. Salvatore and June Romeo serve traditional Italian dishes in what was once the dryer house for a distill-ery. The large windows allow the sun to light the attractive atmosphere. The cheese tortellini rose ($12.50) with mushrooms, sun-dried tomatoes, and prosciutto is a taste I will always remember. My dining partner raved about her veal medallions sautéed in cognac sauce with mushrooms and spinach ($17.50). The service, setting, and quality make the prices a bargain. Other entrées $9.50–19.

♿ **Antrim 1844's Smokehouse Restaurant** (410-756-6812; 1-800-858-1844), Taneytown. Open for din-ner. Reservations are mandatory. *The* place to go to really celebrate a spe-cial occasion. The six-course prix fixe ($65 per person) dinner is determined each evening by renowned chef Michael Gettier from a menu of re-gional cuisine accented with a French flair. Hors d'oeuvres delivered to you in the parlor by a butler, a wine list with more than 1,000 selections, large fireplaces, and a warm-hued brick floor complement the experience.

🌸 **Rudy's 2900** (410-833-5777; www .rudys2900.com), 2900 Baltimore Blvd., Finksburg. There are only about five dozen Certified Master Chefs and Master Pastry Chefs. Rudy Speckamp is one of them, and the prices you pay here (entrées are $16.95–28.95, and a three-course prix fixe dinner is only $21.95) are a bar-gain to sample what a master can do with Continental and contemporary cuisine. Many of the dishes are even heart healthy, such as the seafood

brochette ($18.95) and the veal scaloppine with artichoke, mush-rooms, and capers ($18.95). There is also a menu of moderately priced items like game sausage with onions and greens ($9.95), and salmon with warm onion torte ($11.95).

EATING OUT

Westminster
Johanssons (410-876-0101), 4 W. Main St. Open for lunch and dinner. Johanssons makes its own beers, and the aroma of the brewing process spreads throughout the restaurant. The Honest Ale was to my liking, flavorful but not heavy. Lunch, with sandwiches and salads, also includes English pub items like fish-and-chips ($8.95), shepherd's pie ($9.95), and bratwurst and mashed potatoes ($8.95). I decided on something a little lighter—the vegetable turnover ($7.95); the shell would do any pastry chef proud. Various forms of seafood, meats, and chicken are offered for dinner. $15.95–22.95. Ask for a window seat to watch the traffic go by on MD 27. **The Down Under Bar and Grill** downstairs is a festive place with billiard tables, a game room, and live entertainment on the weekend.

✑ **Harry's Main Street Grille** (410-848-7080), 65 W. Main St. Harry's has a full breakfast, lunch, and dinner menu, but its real claim to fame are the Coney Island–style hot dogs ($1.75) covered with chili, mustard, and onions. Soups, salads, and other sandwiches are served for lunch. I stopped by for dinner, as the grill is also known for baby back ribs that are marinated for 7 days, simmered for hours, and char-grilled with Harry's BBQ sauce. The half rack ($8.95) filled me up, but you could also order a full rack ($14.95). Other options for dinner are pastas, seafood, beef, and 8-ounce burgers. $4.95–15.95.

🦐 🍴 **Baugher's** (410-848-7413), 289 W. Main St. Extension (junction of MD 31 and MD 32). Open for breakfast, lunch, and dinner. You know this place—it has vinyl chairs and Formica tabletops, serves home-cooking-style food, and attracts everybody in town. The prices on the breakfast plates ($1.85–3.40) and lunch sandwiches ($1.50–5.30) may make you think you have entered a time warp. And where else can you get four pieces of fried chicken, two vegetables, a roll, and a beverage for only $6.90? Similar entrées run $4.50–11.50. Save room for homemade ice cream or a slice of pie.

Ma Baugher began selling pies and other baked goods to supplement a meager income during the Depression. The operation today includes more than 1,000 acres of farmland, a packinghouse, fields of produce, a farm stand, and the restaurant.

Rafael's (410-840-1919), 32 W. Main St. Open for lunch and dinner; closed Sun. A pleasant place that, in addition to a usual menu of sandwiches and entrées with meat, serves a number of healthy vegetable dishes. Try the veggie brochette appetizer ($6) or the veggie kebabs for dinner ($9). Entrées $7–18.

Taneytown

Bart's Place (410-756-6001), 465 E. Baltimore St. Open for breakfast, lunch, and dinner. Bart is the host of *Cooking with Bart* on a Baltimore cable channel, so you know you're getting good food from a practiced chef. Sandwiches, salads, and dishes

using regionally available seafood and poultry. Entrées $4.95–16.95.

Mount Airy

Brick Ridge (301-829-8191; www .brickridge.com), 6212 Ridge Rd. Hours vary slightly each day, but it is open for lunch on Fri. and Sat., and for dinner Tue.–Sun.; Sunday brunch 11–2. The menu changes often at the Brick Ridge, as the culinary team strives to provide contemporary cuisine from every state in America. A sample of a dinner menu includes filé gumbo ($4.95), horseradish-encrusted beef ($18.95), and Porterman's pie ($13.95), a slight variation on shepherd's pie. The restaurant's building began its life in the late 1800s as a school for children from the ages of 6 to 20 years.

CRABS **Gary and Dell's Crab House** (410-346-7652), 2820 Littlestown Pike, Westminster. Like all crab houses, Gary and Dell's serves steamed crabs by the dozen (market price), but the real deal here is the all-you-can-eat crab special for only $21.95. And you are permitted to eat for 3 hours if you wish! Sandwiches, other seafood, and meats round out the menu. $4–25.95.

Tangier Crab House (410-549-1161), 1945 Liberty Rd., Eldersburg. Sandwiches, crabcakes, and seafood platters are available inside the restaurant ($6.75–27.95), but a large portion of the business is the take-out seafood. Live or steamed crabs are available by the dozen, and half and full bushels. You can also purchase crabmeat and fresh fish by the pound.

COFFEE BAR **Irish Moon Coffee House** (410-756-6556), corner of MD 194 and MD 140, Taneytown.

Coffee, food, and live Irish entertainment on the weekends.

TAKE-OUT Giulianova Groceria
(410-876-7425), 11 E. Main St., Westminster. The grocery part of the store carries everything you could want to make your own Italian meal. If you don't feel like cooking, you can always order a hoagie, hot entrée, or Italian-style soup to go. Don't miss getting a cannoli for dessert—the pastry shell is not stuffed until you order it.

MICROBREWERY Johanssons (410-876-0101), 4 W. Main St., Westminster. Johanssons brews its own beers within its historic 1800s restaurant (see *Eating Out*). There are always at least five different brews to choose from at any time.

SNACKS AND GOODIES

Westminster
Baugher's (410-848-7413), 289 W. Main St. Extension (junction of MD 31 and MD 32). Baugher's makes homemade pies (47 different kinds) and ice cream (20 flavors), both available for eat-in or take-out. Ask them to heat a piece of pie and top it with ice cream and you will be in sweets heaven. (Also see *Eating Out.*)

Heinz Bakery (410-848-0808), 42 W. Main St. This family-owned bakery, turning out pastries and breads, has been a downtown mainstay for many years.

Treat Shop (410-848-0028), 400 N. Center St. Open daily. The Treat Shop has been making fresh candy and fudge daily in Westminster for close to 50 years. It is almost impossible to walk by without being drawn in by all the delicious creations displayed in the window.

Hoffman's Home Made Ice Cream (410-857-0824), 934 Washington Rd. Open until 10 PM every day. Jeff, Linda, and Lori Hoffman are using the same recipes that their grandfather used when he started making ice cream in 1947. There are at least 30 different flavors available daily.

✳ Entertainment

FILM Carrolltown Movies 6 (410-795-7744), 6405 W. Hemlock Rd., Eldersburg. Each theater has digital sound and rocking chairs.

Loews Theatre Valley Center 9 (410-363-4194), 9616 Reistertown Rd., and **General Cinema** (443-394-0060), 10100 Mill Run Circle. Both are in Owings Mills and show first-run movies.

Hoyts Hunt Valley Cinema (410-329-9800), 11511 McCormick Rd., Hunt Valley. Mainstream films.

MUSIC Common Ground on the Hill (410-857-2771), McDaniel College campus, Westminster. The organization takes its name from its mission, which is to promote learning experiences for artists, musicians, and craftspeople while searching for a common ground among ethnic, gender, and racial groups. Sponsors workshops and the annual **American Music and Arts Festival** during summer.

THEATER ♪ Theatre on the Hill (410-857-2448), McDaniel College campus, Westminster. This professional theater company presents a number of productions—musicals, dramas, comedies, and children's shows—throughout the summer months.

✳ Selective Shopping

ANTIQUES

Westminster
Sidetracked Antiques and Design
(410-876-8680), 10 E. Main St. The
store combines two of the owner's
passions—antiques and estate jewelry—with a selection of fine wines.
Patricia Keener (410-848-2018), 10
E. Main St. Ms. Keener displays 18th-
and 19th-century furniture, paintings,
Oriental rugs, and estate jewelry
inside an early-19th-century building.

Mount Airy
&. **Shops of Yesteryear** (301-829-
0330), 102 Center St. An antiques
marketplace in which more than 90
dealers show their wares.

ART GALLERIES

Westminster
&. **Carroll Arts Center** (410-848-
7272; www.carr.org/arts), 91 W. Main
St. Within a refurbished 1928 art
deco movie house, this is much more
than just an art gallery displaying
changing exhibits. The theater is the
setting for films, concerts, lectures,
theatrical productions, and recitals.

Classes in all of the various arts are
available.
Ain't That a Frame (410-876-3096),
31 W. Main St. An art gallery,
antiques shop, and custom framing
store.
Esther Prangley Rice Gallery (410-
857-2595), Peterson Hall, McDaniel
College campus. The gallery is the site
of changing exhibits in a variety of
media from students, professors, and
local and national artists. There is also
the continuous display of the Albert
and Eva Blum Collection of Art from
Five Continents.

BOOKSTORES **Locust Books** (410-
876-1620), 9 E. Main St., Westminster. In addition to best sellers and
classics, Locust is a great resource for
books concerning the local area and
all of Maryland.

GENEALOGY BOOKSTORE **Willow
Bend Books** (410-876-6101; www
.willowbendbooks.com), 65 E. Main
St., Westminster. Willow Bend is the
largest genealogy bookstore in the
world. Its thousands of titles provide
history and genealogy information on

A Greater Gift (410-635-8711), 500 Main St. (MD 31), New Windsor. This nonprofit organization, started by the Church of the Brethren in the late 1940s,
buys crafts at fair prices from more than 30 countries and the United States.
These purchases help to provide a small bit of security for what would
otherwise be hundreds of underprivileged people. The items here are not
only of high quality but would be hard to find anywhere else: textiles, pottery, furniture, candles, musical instruments, wood carvings, jewelry, and
much more. If you're going to buy a gift or something for yourself, why not
get it here and put money into the hands of a person instead of a faceless
multinational corporation? A highly recommended stop; the peaceful setting
on a knoll overlooking the countryside will do your soul some good, too.
Mail-order catalogs available.

all 50 states and Canada. It has become the number three tourist attraction in Carroll County and a must-stop for anyone interested in the subject. Check out the Web site if you are unable to make it to the store, as the majority of the company's sales are through mail order.

CRAFTS **Carousel Stained Glass** (410-848-2968), Liberty St., Westminster. Roger Lewis has been a stained-glass artist for more than 30 years, and his works are installed in churches, mausoleums, and hundreds of homes. Most pieces are custom-designed. He also does carved and etched glass and restorations.

SPECIAL SHOPS

Westminster
Gypsy's Tea Room (410-857-0058), 111 Stoner Ave. Afternoon tea with scones by reservation Tue.–Sat. 11–4.

FARMER'S MARKETS ♿ Carroll County **Farmer's Market**. Operates from mid-June through early Septem-

ber in the Agricultural Center at 702 Smith Ave. on Sat. 8–1; additional farm products can be found at the DownTown Westminster Farmers Market, Conaway parking lot (Railroad Ave. and Emerald Hill Lane), 8–noon on Sat., from early June through late October. Both are handicapped-accessible.

PICK-YOUR-OWN PRODUCE FARMS
✿ **Baugher's** (410-848-5541), corner of MD 140 and Baugher Rd., Westminster. The season begins in late May with strawberries and peas. Cherries come in late June and early July. Pumpkins can be picked on Sat. and Sun. in October, when hayrides will take you to and from the patch. The kids will enjoy the variety of animals in the petting zoo, which is open throughout the season. (Also see *Eating Out*.)
✿ **Shady Hill Farm and Orchard** (410-875-0572), 2001 New Windsor Rd. (MD 31), New Windsor. A variety of apples become ripe from mid-September through October. The

BAUGHER'S RESTAURANT AND PRODUCE STAND IN WESTMINSTER

orchard has 600 dwarf and semidwarf trees, so it's a perfect outing for young children. There are also free hayrides on Sunday for pick-your-own customers.

WINERIES

Manchester

Cygnus Wine Cellars (410-374-6395; www.cygnuswinecellars), 3130 Long Lane. Tours, tastings, and sales on Sat. and Sun. noon–5. Sparkling and red and white table wines.

Mount Airy

The three wineries of Mount Airy are so close to one another that you could almost walk from one to the other—which is what you may want to do after tasting all they have to offer.

Berrywine Plantations Linganore Winecellars (410-795-6432), 13601 Glissans Mill Rd. Weekdays 10–5, Sat. 10–6, and Sun. noon–6. A selection of more than 25 wines; lots of special annual events.

Elk Run Vineyards (410-775-2513), 15113 Liberty Rd. (MD 26). Wed.–Fri. noon–4, Sat. 10–5, and Sun. 1–5. Best known for its ice wine, champagne, and summer concerts.

BOORDY VINEYARDS IN HYDES

Loew Vineyards (301-831-5464), 14001 Liberty Rd. (MD 26). Tours, tastings, and sales Sat. 10–5 and Sun. 1–5. Estate-bottled wines.

Sparks

Basignani Winery (410-472-0703; www.basignani.com), 15722 Fall Rd. Wed.–Sat. 11:30–5:30 and Sun. noon–6. Bertero Basignani was an amateur winemaker for 15 years before establishing his own winery in 1986. His low-key operation employs traditional cellar methods and produces about 5,000 gallons a year from grapes that are estate grown and bottled.

Parkton

Woodhall Wine Cellars (410-357-8644; www.woodhallwinecellars.com), 17912 York Rd. Tours, tastings, and sales are available Tue.–Sun. noon–5. Woodhall was started by three amateur winemakers in 1983 and moved to its present scenic location next to the Gunpowder River in 1995. The largest percentage of grapes comes from outside sources.

Hydes

Boordy Vineyards (410-592-5015; www.boordy.com), 12820 Long Green Pike. Open for tastings and sales Mon.–Sat. 10–5, Sun. 1–5. Tours on the hour daily 1–4. Maryland's oldest winery was established in 1945. The vines you see were planted in the 1960s, and the winery began bottling in the 1980s. The 19th-century fieldstone barn is a pleasant atmosphere for tastings and serves as the focal point for the winery's many annual events.

✳ Special Events

Year-round: **Movie Night** (410-848-7272). Sponsored by the Carroll Arts Center in Westminster on the fourth Saturday of each month.

March: **Maple Sugarin' Festival** (410-848-9040), Hashawha Environmental Center, Westminster. A day of maple syrup demonstrations, taste testing, kid's activities, and country crafts. **Annual Toy Show and Sale** (410-756-6253), Taneytown. New and antique farm and collectible toys for sale. **Annual Music Show** (410-848-9080), Westminster High School, Westminster. A full day of gospel music featuring nationally known talent.

April: & **Earthworks Festival** (410-848-2517), Bear Branch Nature Center, 300 John Owings Rd., Westminster. Family fun, children's activities, presentations, native gardening, entertainment, and food. **Annual Flower and Plant Market** (410-848-2288), Union Mills Homestead, 3311 Littlestown Pike, Westminster. Food. Fee for tours of the house and mill.

May: & **Westminster Flower and Jazz Festival** (410-848-9393), E. Main St., Westminster. Plants, crafts, music, and food. **Annual Carroll Kennel Club All-Breed Dog Show** (410-549-3646), Agriculture Center, 700 Agriculture Center Dr., Westminster.

June: **Annual Strawberry Festival** (410-795-8959), Sykesville. Celebrates the ripening of the berry with food, crafts, kids' games and entertainment, and hayrides. **Art in the Park** (410-848-7272), Westminster. An annual outdoor festival of performing and visual arts. **Fiddlers' Convention** (410-876-2667), Carroll County Farm Museum, Westminster. A competition of bluegrass musicians with awards, crafts, and farmhouse tours.

July: **Carroll County 4-H and FFA Fair** (410-386-2760), Carroll County Agricultural Center, Westminster.

Annual Ice Cream Sundae Social (410-848-2288), Union Mills Homestead, Westminster. Lots of fun for the kids, with face painting, pony rides, a clown, and tours of the mill.

August: **Annual Car Show** (410-756-6253), Taneytown. A gathering of antique, rod, and custom cars and trucks. There is also lots of food, music, raffles, and games.

August–September: **Maryland State Fair** (410-252-0200), State Fair Grounds, Timonium.

September: **Maryland Wine Festival** (410-876-2667; 1-800-654-4645), Carroll County Farm Museum, Westminster. The largest celebration of the fruit of the vine in the state. Thousands attend for the tastings, wine seminars, crafts, food, and strolling entertainers.

October: **Fall Festival** (410-549-7868), Sykesville. A banquet of arts, crafts, food, and entertainment in a small-town atmosphere. **Fall Harvest Days** (410-876-2667), Carroll County Farm Museum, Westminster. Bring the kids and yourself for scarecrow making, wagon rides, puppet shows, country food and crafts, and—the best of all—the milk mustache contest.

November: **Random House Book Fair** (410-386-8155), Carroll Community College, Westminster. Book signings by authors, silent auctions of signed and first-edition books, workshops, and children's stories.

December: **Festival of Wreaths** (410-848-7272), 91 W. Main St., Westminster. The annual display and silent auction of more than 100 handmade theme wreaths that benefits the Carroll Arts Center.

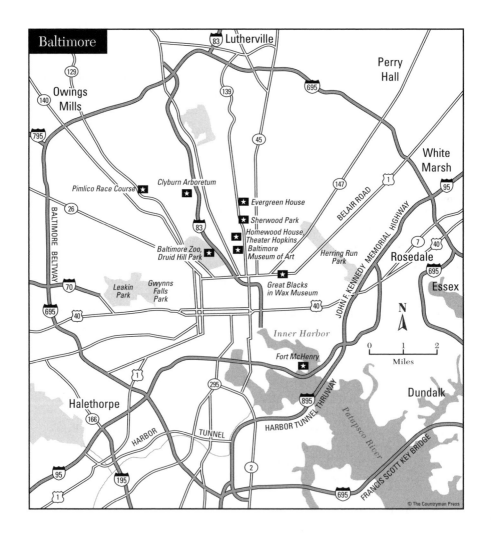

BALTIMORE

Baltimore grew from a small tobacco-producing community to a major shipping center in less than 100 years. By the mid-1700s, it was exporting flour, grains, iron, tobacco, and produce, and importing sugar, molasses, rum, slaves, and manufactured goods. It came into true prominence during the Revolutionary War, when members of the Continental Congress met in the city for 2 months after signing the Declaration of Independence.

Privateers, sailing in sleek clipper ships built in the city's harbors, took advantage of the turmoil to prey upon British merchant ships. Within a few years, they had made off with booty estimated at more than a million English pounds. They infuriated the British once more by resuming the practice during the War of 1812. Detained upon an English ship, Francis Scott Key watched Great Britain's forces exact revenge by bombarding the harbor area throughout the early morning of September 14, 1804. When the sun's first rays illuminated the large flag flying over Fort McHenry, signifying that the fort and city had held, Key was inspired to write what would become the U.S. national anthem.

It was primarily settlers from Germany and the British Isles, along with their African slaves, who first shaped the city, but soon immigrants from other parts of the world began to arrive. Italians, Russians, Ukrainians, Poles, and Lithuanians poured in, attracted by Baltimore's flourishing shipbuilding and shipping industries, transportation services, and cannery factories. In the last few decades, the majority of newcomers have been Hispanic, Caribbean, and Near Eastern in origin. The many cultural backgrounds are celebrated with a series of ethnic festivals throughout the summer months.

Just as the city's population is composed of diverse groups of people, so too are its neighborhoods. Many still reflect the origins of their inhabitants, while others possess a personality and atmosphere all their own.

Inner Harbor was the focus of an intense revitalization program that began in the late 1970s. What was once a place of decaying factories and warehouses is now a vibrant showplace attracting thousands daily. Water taxis cross the water, taking commuters and visitors all around the harbor. There is almost always some kind of outside entertainment going on, and the Harborplace pavilions are full of shops and restaurants. The strikingly triangular-shaped National Aquarium of Baltimore is topped by glass pyramids and contains more than 10,000 species

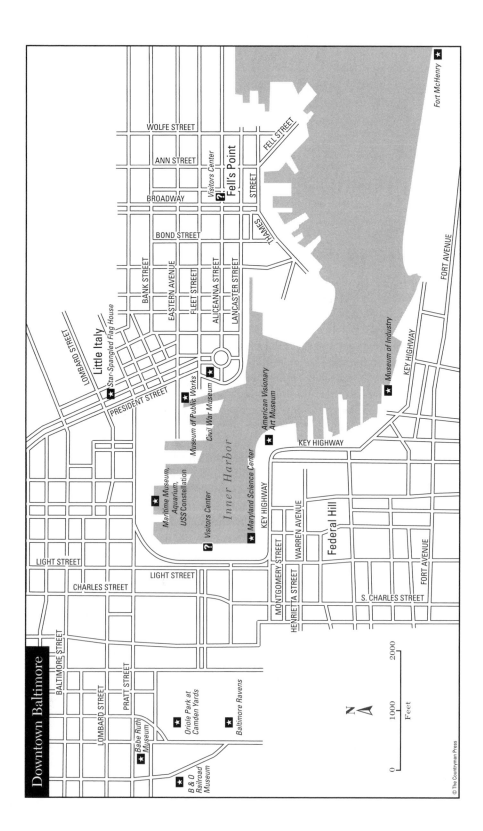

Downtown Baltimore

WOLFE STREET

ANN STREET

BROADWAY

BOND STREET

Visitors Center ⓘ

Fell's Point

FELL STREET

STREET

THAMES

LOMBARD STREET

Little Italy

Star-Spangled Flag House

BANK STREET

EASTERN AVENUE

FLEET STREET

ALICEANNA STREET

LANCASTER STREET

PRESIDENT STREET

Museum of Public Works ★

Civil War Museum ★

FORT AVENUE

Museum of Industry ★

KEY HIGHWAY

American Visionary Art Museum ★

Inner Harbor

Maritime Museum, Aquarium, USS Constellation ★

Visitors Center ⓘ

Maryland Science Center ★

KEY HIGHWAY

KEY HIGHWAY

MONTGOMERY STREET

HENRIETTA STREET

WARREN AVENUE

Federal Hill

FORT AVENUE

LIGHT STREET

CHARLES STREET

LIGHT STREET

S. CHARLES STREET

BALTIMORE STREET

LOMBARD STREET

PRATT STREET

Babe Ruth Museum ★

Oriole Park at Camden Yards ★

Baltimore Ravens ★

B & O Railroad Museum ★

Fort McHenry ★

N

2000

1000

0

Feet

© The Countryman Press

of marine life. Tours of the USS *Constellation*, the last all-sail vessel built by the U.S. Navy, and other historic ships tie into the harbor's past seafaring life.

Along the eastern edge of Inner Harbor is the Power Plant, a huge brick building the city obtained from the Baltimore Gas and Electric Company in 1977. It now houses a large Barnes & Noble bookstore, an ESPN Zone restaurant, and a Hard Rock Café, and has proven to be a magnet for the harbor area. Reflected in the water are the soaring, modern, high-rise steel and glass structures of a number of national hotel and motel chains.

I'm convinced you gain weight just by breathing in the aromas that waft through the 12 blocks of Little Italy. Dozens of restaurants, some quite formal and others very casual, line the streets and employ and expand the culinary arts that have made Italian food a world favorite. Take a walk through the neighborhood and you may feel like you've been transported to the Old Country. Good-natured, accent-flavored arguments arise from the games of bocce ball.

Fell's Point was established as a shipbuilding center in 1730, making it Baltimore's first port and one of the country's oldest waterfront communities. It soon developed a rough and rowdy reputation as sailors came ashore for rest and relaxation. Many of the rather seedy buildings were condemned to make way for an interstate in the late 1960s. However, locals banded together, defeated the idea, and embarked upon a revitalization program. Their efforts have been more or less successful, as the best way to describe the area would be "shabby chic." Hip restaurants, live theaters, and upscale lodging spots are interspersed among coffeehouses and shops that sport bohemian atmospheres. By the way, so that you won't be marked as an outsider, you need to pronounce *Thames* (Street) just as it is spelled, not as they say it in London.

Jubilant citizens went to one of the highest points in their city to mark Maryland's ratification of the U.S. Constitution in 1788 with celebrations and fireworks; it's been referred to as Federal Hill ever after. A park upon the promontory provides one of the best views of the city. The area was settled by blue-collar workers and still retains much of that feel, as many of the homes are two-story row houses. The Baltimore Museum of Industry, the innovative American Visionary Art Museum, an assortment of antiques shops, and a variety of restaurants are reasons to visit.

Mount Vernon, laid out in 1831, was once the most in-vogue address in town. The movers and shakers of Baltimore's politics and businesses took up residence in many of the largest homes and row houses. With their money came an array of cultural diversions, including the Walters Art Museum, Peabody Conservatory of Music, Lyric Opera House, and, later, Joseph Meyerhoff Symphony Hall. Charles Street, known as "Restaurant Row," is packed with culinary offerings from what seems like every nation in the world. The street also leads to the neighborhood's central point, the Washington Monument. A climb up the 228 steps will help work off some of the calories consumed for lunch. Baltimoreans claim that the structure, which was conceived in 1809 and completed in 1829, is the first one that was dedicated to the Father of Our Country. However, the citizens of Boonsboro, Maryland, completed their Washington Monument in 1827 and assert that theirs was the first.

GUIDANCE Information about all of Baltimore can be obtained from the **Baltimore Area Convention and Visitors Association** (410-659-7300; 1-800-343-3468; www.baltimore.org) at 100 Light St., 12th Floor, Baltimore, 21202.

Located on the waterfront in Inner Harbor is the **Baltimore Visitor Center** (1-877-BALTIMORE).

The **Fell's Point Visitor Center** (410-675-6750; www.preservationsociety.com/visitorcenter.html) at 808 S. Ann St., Baltimore, 21213, is open daily 10–4.

The **Mount Vernon Cultural District, Inc.** (410-605-0462; www.mvcd.org), at 217 N. Charles St., 21201, does a good job in highlighting what many people think is the city's cultural center.

The *Destination Planning Guide* will help you plan your trip, while *Discover Baltimore* is a guide to the city's African American attractions. Both publications can be obtained from the **Baltimore Area Convention and Visitors Association** or the **Baltimore Area Visitor Center**.

The *City Paper*, available free from newspaper boxes, provides a lot of art, dining, and entertainment information as well as an alternative view of the city.

GETTING THERE *By car:* Like the spokes on a pinwheel, interstate highways come into Baltimore from many different directions. **I-95** is the major East Coast highway that runs from Florida to Maine and is the way people driving from the northeast (Philadelphia, Pennsylvania, New York City) or the southwest (Washington, DC, and Richmond, Virginia) will probably arrive. (The **Baltimore–Washington Parkway** is a slightly more scenic alternate from DC.)

I-83 comes in from due north and ends near Inner Harbor. Travelers from the west (Frederick, Maryland, and Pittsburgh, Pennsylvania) will find that **I-70** is the most direct route. **I-795** connects the suburbs of the northwest with the city, while **I-97** is the fastest way from Annapolis and the Eastern Shore.

By air: **Baltimore/Washington International Airport** (1-800-I-FLY-BWI) is just about 10 miles south of Baltimore and has interstate, MARC and Amtrak (see *By train*, below), and limousine connections with the city.

By bus: **Trailways** (703-691-3052) and **Greyhound** (1-800-229-9429) will deliver you to the Baltimore Travel Plaza (410-633-6389) in the eastern part of the city at the intersection of I-95 and O'Donnell St. There is also a Greyhound terminal at 210 W. Fayette St., a few blocks north of Inner Harbor.

By train: **Amtrak** (1-800-USA-RAIL) at Penn Station (410-231-2222), at the intersection of I-83 and N. Charles St., is close to the University of Baltimore and has received a major face-lift in the last few years.

MARC (1-800-325-RAIL) provides commuter rail service between Washington, DC, and Baltimore on weekdays.

GETTING AROUND *By car:* **I-695 (Baltimore Beltway)** encircles the city, giving access to each of its neighborhoods and suburbs. Going into Mount Vernon, Inner Harbor, and Federal Hill, Charles St. completely intersects the city in a north–south direction. **US 40** goes through the city in a west-to-east orientation.

Like all big cities, Baltimore has a traffic problem during rush hours, but it is surprisingly easy to get around during other times of the day. This is especially true in the downtown/Inner Harbor area—as long as you pay attention to the many one-way streets. Luckily, street and directional signs are plentiful and well placed.

By bus, by subway, and by rail: The **Mass Transit Authority** (MTA) (410-539-5000; 1-800-543-9809) operates bus, subway (closed Sun.), and rail lines that reach into every nook and cranny of the city, and many nearby areas and counties, making it possible to leave your hotel, go to dinner, and then attend the theater without having to drive. Maps and timetables can be obtained at the visitors center in Inner Harbor or by calling MTA. A daily pass is available that is good on any MTA system; exact fare is required to ride the bus.

By taxi: The companies servicing the city are **Yellow** and **Checker Cab** (410-685-1212); **Diamond Cab** (410-947-3333); **Arrow Cab** (410-484-4111); and **Royal Cab** (410-327-0330).

By water: Among the most fun, and certainly most scenic, ways to reach many sites along Baltimore's waterfronts are the water shuttles and taxis. Coming to each stop at about 15-minute intervals (40 minutes off-season), they will take you to Inner Harbor, Fell's Point, Canton, Federal Hill, and Fort McHenry. You also get ever-changing views of the city from the water, something many visitors miss. **Ed Kane's Water Taxi** (410-563-3901; 1-800-658-8947; www.thewater taxi.com) is the city's original water service ($8 adults, $4 children 10 and under, for an all-day, unlimited-use pass).

PUBLIC RESTROOMS In the downtown/Inner Harbor area, restrooms can be found in the Pratt St. and Light St. Pavilions.

MEDICAL EMERGENCY Baltimore has more than a dozen hospitals with emergency rooms. Among them are:

THE FUN (AND FASTEST) WAY TO GET AROUND INNER HARBOR

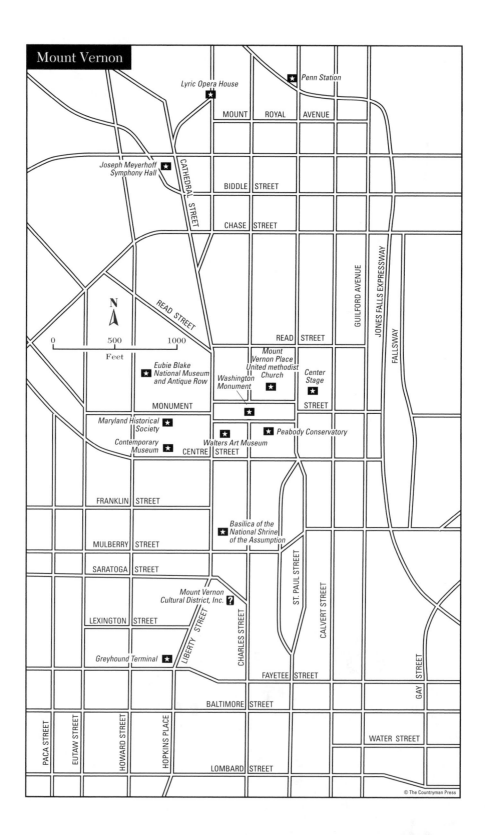

Mount Vernon

Lyric Opera House

Penn Station

MOUNT ROYAL AVENUE

Joseph Meyerhoff Symphony Hall

CATHEDRAL STREET

BIDDLE STREET

CHASE STREET

GUILFORD AVENUE

JONES FALLS EXPRESSWAY

FALLSWAY

READ STREET

READ STREET

N

0   500   1000
Feet

Eubie Blake National Museum and Antique Row

Mount Vernon Place United methodist Church

Washington Monument

Center Stage

MONUMENT

STREET

Maryland Historical Society

Peabody Conservatory

Contemporary Museum

Walters Art Museum

CENTRE STREET

FRANKLIN STREET

Basilica of the National Shrine of the Assumption

MULBERRY STREET

ST. PAUL STREET

SARATOGA STREET

Mount Vernon Cultural District, Inc.

CALVERT STREET

LEXINGTON STREET

LIBERTY STREET

CHARLES STREET

Greyhound Terminal

FAYETEE STREET

GAY STREET

BALTIMORE STREET

PACA STREET

EUTAW STREET

HOWARD STREET

HOPKINS PLACE

WATER STREET

LOMBARD STREET

© The Countryman Press

University of Maryland Medical Center (410-328-6722), 22 S. Greene St. The state's largest hospital. On the corner of Baltimore and Greene Sts., about seven blocks west of Inner Harbor. **Mercy Hospital** (410-332-9477), 301 St. Paul Place—at the corner of Saratoga and Light Sts. About seven blocks north of Inner Harbor. **Church Home Hospital** (410-522-8505), 100 N. Broadway. On the corner of Fayette St. and Broadway about 1.5 miles northeast of Inner Harbor. **Johns Hopkins Hospital** (410-955-2280), 600 N. Wolfe St. Located near the intersection of Orleans St. and Broadway about 2 miles northeast of Inner Harbor.

Mount Vernon
Maryland General Hospital (410-225-8100), 827 Linden Ave. On the western edge of Mount Vernon next to Madison St.

Northern part of the city
Good Samaritan Hospital (410-532-4040), 5601 Loch Raven Blvd. About 3 miles south of I-695 Exit 29.

Northwestern part of the city (Park Heights)
Sinai Hospital (410-601-8800), 2401 Belvedere Ave. Accessed from I-83 Exit 10.

✳ To See

MUSEUMS

Downtown/Inner Harbor
Baltimore Civil War Museum (410-385-5188; www.mdhas.org), 601 President St. Open daily; small admission fee. Inside the old President Street Depot, which served rail customers from the mid-1800s to the mid-1900s, the Maryland Historical Society presents the role Baltimore played in the Civil War and the Underground Railroad. It is a small museum; an available cassette will take you on a 10-minute guided tour if your time is limited.

✍ **Baltimore Museum of Public Works** (410-396-5565), 751 Eastern Ave. Tue.–Sun. 10–4. Small admission fee. Many people complain about paying taxes; here's a fun place to discover what some of those funds accomplish. The museum takes you behind the scenes with displays and interactive exhibits about roads, bridges, sewage treatment, creating clean water, and waste disposal. You and the kids will enjoy negotiating the outdoor maze created from pipes and drains.

✍ ♿ **Maryland Science Center, Davis Planetarium, and IMAX Movie Theater** (410-685-5225; www.mdsci.org), 601 Light St. Open daily. Adults $14; seniors $13; children 3–12 are $9.50; IMAX is an extra fee. There is much to keep you and the children involved and learning for hours. Three floors with hundreds of interactive exhibits and hands-on displays relating to the bay, mathematics, energy, space, and other scientific discoveries. Pay whatever it costs to see a movie in the five-story IMAX theater, especially if the presentation is in

✍ ⚓ **National Aquarium in Baltimore** (410-576-3800; www.aqua.org), 501 E. Pratt St., downtown/Inner Harbor. Open 9–8 daily in July and Aug.; 10–5 Sat.–Thu. and 10–8 Fri., Nov.–Feb.; 9–5 Sat.–Thu. and 9–8 Fri., Mar.–June and Sep.–Oct. Adults $17.95; seniors $16.95; children 3–11 are $10.95.

I admit to being somewhat of a skinflint when it comes to paying admission charges, but I urge you to pay whatever they are asking to experience the National Aquarium. I've never been anywhere that does a better job of displaying the underwater world with live specimens and then explaining it with vivid exhibits.

A gently sloping walkway takes you along one tank after another, letting you linger as long as you want to observe the more than 10,000 creatures housed in the seven-story structure. There are sharks, dolphins, sea horses, frogs, eels, piranhas, stingrays, and turtles. The kids will love the touch tank and the dolphin show within the 1.2-million-gallon water-tank theater.

Be aware that baby strollers are not permitted and that long lines can form early in the day, especially during the summer months and in fall when school classrooms fill the aquarium with hundreds of kids. Allow a minimum of 2 to 3 hours to experience it all. I felt rushed when I spent more than 3 hours there—and that was *before* the aquarium had completed an expansion that nearly doubled its size.

3-D. The IMAX 3-D films pull the images off the screen and put you in the middle of the action—the experience is unforgettable.

✍ ⚓ **Babe Ruth Museum and Birthplace** (410-727-1539; www.baberuth museum.com), 216 Emory St. Open daily, Apr.–Oct., 10–5 PM, and until 7 PM on all Orioles home game days; Nov.–Mar., 10–4. Adults $6; seniors $4; children 5–16 are $3. The Sultan of Swat was born in this humble home in 1895 and went on to become baseball's greatest player (without the controversial steroid use of today's players). Tours take you through the home and its collection of memorabilia.

✍ ⚓ **Sports Legends at Camden Yards** (410-727-1539, ext. 3011; www.sports legendsatcamdenyards.com), north end of the Camden Yards complex. This $16 million attraction was opened in 2005 to house the memorabilia collection that had become too large for the Babe Ruth Museum to contain. The 22,000-square-foot structure has exhibits relating to Babe Ruth, Johnny Unitas, Maryland Terrapins, Baltimore Orioles and Colts, and the city's Negro Leagues.

✍ **B&O Railroad Museum** (410-752-2490; www.borail.org), 901 W. Pratt St. (10 blocks from Inner Harbor). Open daily 10–5. Adults $14; seniors $10; children 3–12 are $8. Free parking. The huge 1844 brick-and-glass 22-sided polygon roundhouse is a familiar landmark to Baltimoreans and the largest circular industrial building in the world. You don't have to be a train buff to appreciate the spectacular 40-acre collection of locomotives, railcars, models, and artifacts, which is purported to be the most comprehensive collection of railroad artifacts in the Western Hemisphere. The kids' (and your) imaginations will bring the glory days back to life when you actually get to board some of the engines and walk through the cars.

Great Blacks in Wax Museum (410-563-3404), 1601–3 E. North Ave. (about 3 miles north of Inner Harbor). Closed Mon. Adults $6.80; seniors and students $5.75; children 12–17 are $4.25; children 2–11 are $3.75. The country's first-and-only wax museum of African American history has more than 100 life-sized figures. A replica of a slave ship is also featured.

Federal Hill

✄ **Baltimore Museum of Industry** (410-727-4808; www.thebmi.org), 1415 Key Hwy. (between Federal Hill proper and Fort McHenry). Closed Mon. Hands-on exhibits revisit the Industrial Revolution's impact on Baltimore, the bay, and the rest of Maryland. Includes the **Museum of Incandescent Lighting** with more than 50,000 lightbulbs and related objects, such as some of Thomas Edison's earliest experimental bulbs.

American Visionary Art Museum (410-244-1900), 800 Key Hwy. Closed Mon. The museum showcases the talents of innovative, self-taught artists, so the works you see here are almost always different, often unique, and probably found nowhere else.

Fell's Point

✄ ♿ **Fell's Point Maritime Museum** (410-732-0278; www.mdhs.org/explore/ maritime), 1724 Thames St. Housed in a block-long building that was once the barn for the area's horse-drawn trolley service, the museum traces the influence

♿ **Baltimore Museum of Art** (410-396-7100; www.artbma.org), N. Charles and 31st Sts. (3 miles north of Inner Harbor), Uptown. Opens at 11 AM Wed.–Sun. Adults $7; seniors and students $5; children 18 and under are free. No charge on the first Thu. of every month. Everything about the museum requires a superlative: As the state's largest art museum, it houses more than 100,000 objects that range from the ancient to the contemporary. The museum has one of the broadest Andy Warhol and other modern artists' collections; multiple galleries devoted to European masters such as Raphael and Rodin; art of Africa, Asia, the Americas, and Oceania; an American wing with paintings, furniture, and more from the 1700s to the present; and one of the country's most expansive outdoor sculpture gardens.

The Cone Sisters' collection of more than 500 works of art is considered to be one of the most important in the world. Because of them, you are able to appreciate the talents of Matisse, Picasso, Gauguin, van Gogh, Renoir, Cézanne, and others. Even the building is a work of art, having been designed by John Russell Pope, designer of the National Gallery of Art in Washington, DC.

THE USS *CONSTELLATION* IN INNER HARBOR

that the fast-sailing Baltimore clipper schooners had on the local economy, worldwide trade, and the sailing industry. The collection of artifacts and maritime objects is impressive.

Mount Vernon
🐾 ♿ **Walters Art Museum** (410-547-9000; thewalters.org), 600 N. Charles St. Closed Mon. Small admission fee. The Walters contains 55 centuries of art displayed in a manageable way. With just one or two visits, you can experience much of its Egyptian, Roman, Greek, Etruscan, and ancient Near East collection. A recent renovation has made the exhibit spaces flow into one another, enhancing what each has to offer. The cost of admission is a bargain when compared with that of other art museums—many of which are not even close to being on par with the Walters.

Maryland Historical Society (410-685-3750; www.mdhs.org), 201 W. Monument St. Closed Mon. Small admission fee. The original manuscript of the "Star-Spangled Banner" is probably the most famous of the five million objects in the society's collection. You will also find furniture, costumes, uniforms, and more that relate to the state's past. The gift shop has many handmade items.

Eubie Blake National Museum and Cultural Center (410-225-3130; www .eubieblake.org), 847 Howard St. Honors the life and music of this jazz great and Baltimore native. Also highlights others, such as Cab Calloway and Billie Holiday, who were also from Baltimore. Changing exhibits focus on many aspects pertinent to the city's African American community.

Contemporary Museum (410-783-5720; www.contemporary.org), 100 E. Centre St. Changing exhibits of contemporary art in a variety of media.

Downtown/Inner Harbor

USS Constellation (410-539-1797; www.constellation.org), Pier 1, Pratt St. Handheld audio devices take you on a guided tour of the 1854 *Constellation*, the last all-sail vessel built by the U.S. Navy. I liked learning about the history and operation of the ship, but most amazing was the number of levels below the main deck.

Baltimore Maritime Museum (410-396-3453; www.baltimoremaritime museum.com), Pier 3, Pratt St. Open daily. Adults $7; seniors $6; children 6–14 are $4. There are no real walls to this museum, as it consists of three ships docked about a block from one another. The U.S. submarine *Torsk* was the last ship to sink an enemy boat in World War II; the *Taney* is the only ship still afloat that was in Pearl Harbor, and the *Chesapeake* served as a lightship for more than 29 years. Tickets also give you admission to the **Sevenfoot Knoll Lighthouse**, the oldest screw-pile lighthouse in the state.

HISTORIC HOMES

Little Italy

The Flag House and Star-Spangled Banner Museum (410-837-1793; www .flaghouse.org), 844 E. Pratt St. Tue.–Sat. 10–4. Free parking. Small admission fee. The 1793 home, furnished in Federal-period antiques, was the home of Mary Pickersgill, who sewed by hand the flag that inspired Francis Scott Key's famous poem. The museum next door chronicles the War of 1812.

Uptown

Evergreen House (410-516-0341), 4545 N. Charles St. Open daily to 4 PM; tours offered on the hour. Adults $6, seniors $5, students $3. Surrounded by 26 acres, the Italianate Evergreen House was built in 1840, and its 48 rooms are filled with decorative arts, antiques, and Tiffany glass. The house and grounds have been restored to reflect the time when Ambassador John Garrett's family resided here, from 1878 to 1942.

Homewood House (410-516-5589), 3400 N. Charles St. Open to 4 PM; tours on the hour. Closed Mon. Adults $6, seniors $5, students $3. The Federal-architecture

---

SAVE A FEW DOLLARS

Harbor Pass (1-877-BALTIMORE; www.baltimore.org) provides admission to the **National Aquarium** in Baltimore, the **Maryland Science Center, Port Discovery,** and the **Top of the World Observation Level** on the World Trade Center, as well as a 1-day pass for **Ed Kane's Water Taxi.** It also gives various discounts to a number of other harbor attractions, such as **Baltimore Orioles** games, **Baltimore Maritime Museum,** and the **USS *Constellation.*** The pass is good for 3 days and can be purchased over the phone, online, or from the Baltimore Visitor Center in Inner Harbor. Adults $46; children 3–12 are $25.

1801 house was a wedding gift from Charles Carroll to his son and is now on the campus of Johns Hopkins University. Many of the pieces in the home belonged to the Carroll family. Be sure to visit the brick outhouse, which has graffiti from when the house served as a boys' school.

HISTORIC SITES &. **Fort McHenry** (410-962-4290), E. Fort Ave. Open daily; small admission fee. After witnessing 25 hours of vehement bombardment by the British, the flag flying over this fort on the morning of September 14, 1814, inspired Francis Scott Key to pen the "Star-Spangled Banner." Star-shaped Fort McHenry has been restored to its pre–Civil War appearance with cannons, barracks, and jail cells. Be sure to watch the presentation in the visitors center, and remember that the place is a great spot to watch ships going in and out of the harbor.

HISTORIC CHURCHES

Mount Vernon
Basilica of the National Shrine of the Assumption (410-727-3564), Cathedral and Mulberry Sts. The 1821 basilica was the first Roman Catholic cathedral built in America and was designed by Benjamin Henry Latrobe, the architect of the U.S. Capitol. Many consider it to be one of the best neoclassical structures in the world. Guided tours are provided after the Sunday 10:45 Mass.

Mount Vernon Place United Methodist Church (410-685-5290), 10 E. Mount Vernon Place. The ornately carved interior of the 1874 church contains an organ with 3,287 pipes and a labyrinth nearly a mile long. The green serpentine and gray stone church is on the site where Francis Scott Key died in 1843.

SEVENFOOT KNOLL LIGHTHOUSE IN INNER HARBOR

GUIDED TOURS African American Cultural Tours (410-727-0755) and **Renaissance Productions and Tours** (410-728-3837) conduct tours highlighting contributions, landmarks, institutions, and individuals of significance to African Americans.

OBSERVATION POINT Top of the World Observation Level (410-837-8439), 401 Pratt St. Sun.–Wed. 10–6 winter; 10–9 summer. Adults $5, children $3. Located on the 27th floor of the World Trade Center, the world's tallest pentagonal building (423 feet above the harbor), designed by architect I. M. Pei. The observation level

FORT McHENRY

has expansive windows that provide vistas onto the Inner Harbor, the surrounding city, and the Chesapeake Bay. Guides provide information and facts about the city and surrounding area. A great place to be as the sun sets and the harbor's waters reflect its golden glow and those of the thousands of electric lights that brighten Baltimore at night. The observation level also has rotating art, history, and cultural exhibits and events.

ZOO 𝄂 ⅄ **The Maryland Zoo in Baltimore** (410-366-LION; www.baltimore zoo.org), Druid Hill Park, Uptown (accessible from I-83 Exit 7). Open daily. Free parking. Adults $15; seniors $12; children 2–11 are $10. Opened in 1867, this is the third oldest zoo in the country and home to more than 2,000 animals from six continents. There are the exotic species such as polar bears, lions, and leopards, as well as the locally familiar turtles, barnyard animals, and owls. This is a very child-friendly place, as most of the exhibits are arranged so that even the smallest of visitors can see the animals. Lots of special events for children, too.

✳ To Do

BICYCLING Bicycle trails wend their way through the green landscape of **Herring Run Park** (see *Green Space*).

𝄂 **Light St. Cycles** (410-685-2234), 1015 Light St., Federal Hill. A bicycle may just be the best way to tour the downtown/Inner Harbor/Federal Hill area, and these folks will rent you one for an hour or a day.

LESSER FLAMINGOS IN THE MARYLAND ZOO IN BALTIMORE

BIRDING See *Nature Preserves.*

BOAT EXCURSIONS

Inner Harbor

Clipper City (410-539-6277; www.sailingship.com), docked between the Light St. Pavilion and the Science Center. The 158-foot, two-masted schooner takes 2-hour sailing tours of the harbor daily Apr.–Nov. Adults $20; children under 10 are $5. Times vary, so consult the Web site or call for a current schedule. There are also special-theme and Sunday-brunch cruises.

Harbor Cruises (410-727-3113; 1-800-695-BOAT; www.harborcruises.com), 301 Light St. (close to the Light St. Pavilion). Offers daily lunch, dinner, sightseeing, and evening cruises on three different boats. Departure times, costs, and itineraries vary widely, so call to obtain the latest information.

Ride the Ducks Baltimore (410-727-DUCK). Adults $24; children 3–12 are $14. A most interesting way to see the waterfront area. These 1945 army DUKWs have been converted into passenger vehicles. As they are amphibious, part of your 80-minute tour is on the water, while the other portion takes you to sites along waterfront roadways. Open Apr.–Oct.

BOAT RENTALS

Downtown/Inner Harbor

✒ **Trident Electric Boat Rentals** (410-539-1837), located between the World Trade Center and the National Aquarium. Boats of various shapes and sizes are available for rent so that you can explore the harbor on your own.

ALONG THE WATERFRONT PROMENADE IN INNER HARBOR

FAMILY ACTIVITIES ✑ ⚅ **Port Discovery** (410-727-8120; www.portdiscovery .com), 35 Market Place, downtown/Inner Harbor. Open daily. Adults $11; children 3–12 are $8.50. The kids will just think they're having fun deciphering hieroglyphics, piecing together clues, or crossing the rope bridge, but Walt Disney's Imagineers designed the activities for children 6–12 to teach goal setting, problem solving, and creative thinking. Allow 1–2 hours.

Also see *Zoo*.

FISHING Captain Don Marani (410-342-2004; www.captdonscharters.com), 1001 Fell St., Fell's Point. June–Dec., Captain Don heads into the bay from Henderson's Wharf Marina in search of rockfish, bluefish, croaker, spot, and more. Charters range from $220 (2 hours) to $425 (full day).

GOLF There are five courses within the municipal boundary of Baltimore. Information on all five can be obtained by calling 410-444-4933 or visiting www .bmbcgolf.com.

HORSE RACING ⚅ **Pimlico Race Course** (410-542-9400), Hayward and Winner Aves., Mount Washington (northwestern part of the city). Pimlico is home to the second jewel in thoroughbred racing's Triple Crown, the Preakness Stake. The Preakness is run annually on the third weekend in May, but you can attend other races here throughout the warmer months of the year.

WALKING TOURS Frederick Douglass Walking Tour (410-675-6750), 808 S. Ann St., Fell's Point. Sponsored by the Preservation Society, the guided walk travels to sites that enslaved Africans, free blacks, runaways, and Frederick Douglass called home. The society also sponsors a general-history **Fell's Point Walking Tour**.

The Mount Vernon Cultural District, Inc. (see *Guidance*), Mount Vernon, has several brochures describing different walks throughout the neighborhood, taking in the cultural, historic, and retail aspects of each.

✳ Green Space

GARDENS Sherwood Park (410-323-7982), Stratford Rd., Guilford (northeastern part of the city). Open dawn–dusk daily. Free admission. It is small, but loaded with azaleas, boxwoods, cherries, dogwoods, magnolias, and wisterias. The most spectacular time to visit is late Apr.–early May, when the 80,000 tulips are in bloom.

NATURE PRESERVES ⚅ **Clyburn Arboretum** (410-396-0180), 4915 Greenspring Ave., Mount Washington (northwestern part of the city). Grounds open 6 AM–9 PM daily; mansion and museum open 8 AM–3 PM Mon.–Fri. Free admission. Signs identify hundreds of plants and trees throughout the 170 acres. There are marked trails, a garden of senses for the physically impaired, and a number of flower gardens. The 1888 Clyburn Mansion contains a commendable nature museum.

This is one of the Baltimore Bird Club's favorite sites. Great horned owls are year-round residents, and a variety of thrushes and warblers pass through during migrations. Come here in midspring and you'll see (or at least hear) sparrows, scarlet tanagers, finches, and yellow-bellied sapsuckers.

PARKS ☙ **Druid Hill Park** (410-396-6101), Druid Park Lake Dr., Hampden (accessed from I-83 Exits 7 and 8). One of the largest urban parks in America, Druid Hill was set aside as public space in 1688. Tennis courts, a public swimming pool, and lots of picnic tables. The main draws are the large amount of open ground on which to wander and several points overlooking various parts of the city. Pets permitted on a leash.

☙ **Herring Run Park** (410-396-6101), Belair-Edison (northeastern part of the city). A linear urban park along the waters of Herring Run. A few picnic tables and several streamside trails make this green space a neighborhood escape. Parking is available at Sinclair Lane and Harford and Belair Rds. Pets permitted on a leash.

☙ **Gwynns Falls–Leakin Parks** (410-396-6101), Edmonson Village (western part of the city). Officially they are separate parks, but they are side by side and their pathways connect. Altogether they provide more than 1,200 acres of preserved land within the city limits. One trail follows the route of an old millrace along Gwynns Falls, while others wind through the deep cleft created by Dead Run. Pets permitted on a leash.

WALKS The **Waterfront Promenade** in the downtown/Inner Harbor area runs for more than 7 miles, taking in the best that the waterfront has to offer. By starting at one end, you could walk through Canton, Little Italy, Inner Harbor, and Federal Hill, and end up at Fort McHenry.

✳ Lodging

RESORTS ☙ ✐ **Gramercy Mansion B&B** (410-486-2405; 1-800-553-3404; www.gramercymansion.com), 1400 Greenspring Rd., Stevenson, 21153. It calls itself a B&B, but with a swimming pool, a tennis court, formal and herb gardens, an organic farm, and trails winding through its 45 acres, I call it a resort. Guest rooms in the antiques-furnished, fireplace-rich 1902 Tudor-style mansion house range from spacious three-room suites with whirlpool tubs and private sunporches to basic rooms with shared bath. The basic "back-hall" rooms are a real deal, as they are less than half the cost of other rooms.

Because all the amenities were still available to me, I didn't feel like I was missing a thing. $100–350.

MOTELS AND HOTELS

Downtown/Inner Harbor, 21202
☙ ✐ ♿ **Pier 5 Hotel** (410-539-2000; www.harbormagic.com), 711 Eastern Ave. The Pier 5 is one of Baltimore's few boutique hotels—its art deco style is a splash of colors—and it is the only Inner Harbor hotel situated right next to the water. This permits you to walk to all of Inner Harbor's attractions without having to cross any busy streets.

PIER 5 HOTEL IN INNER HARBOR

Staff are gracious and very attentive to your needs, but the more than 60 spacious rooms let you attain large-hotel anonymity if you wish. Some rooms have water views, while others have views of the city; my room had both, as it overlooked the harbor and National Aquarium. Terry-cloth robes permitted me to lounge in comfort, while nightly turn-down service let me know someone cared. Parking fee. Pets permitted; must be brought into the hotel in a travel crate. $299–439; many packages available. (Also see McCormick and Schmick's under *Dining Out*.)

Baltimore Marriott Waterfront (410-385-3000; www.marriotthotels .com), 700 Aliceanna St. The Marriott is one of Inner Harbor's newest hotels, and most of its more than 700 rooms on 32 floors have views of the water. Indoor pool, exercise room. $279–349.

✇ ♿ **Harbor Court Hotel** (410-234-0550; www.harborcourt.com), 550 Light St. The Harbor Court is a modern hotel with a feel from another era. The grand staircase sweeps up from the oak-paneled lobby, while the concierge staff cater to your needs. Most rooms are elegantly appointed and overlook the harbor. The fitness facilities are extensive. Child care available. Parking fee. $290–650.

Hyatt Regency (410-528-1234; 1-800-233-1234; www.baltimore .hyatt.com), 300 Light St. The gleaming glass-and-steel Hyatt towers over Inner Harbor, reflecting the water, sky, and surrounding buildings. Amenities include an extensive health club, a recreation deck with jogging track, a putting green, tennis courts, and almost 500 guest rooms with great views. Concierge service. Parking fee. $270–340.

✇ ♿ **Renaissance Harborplace** (410-547-1200; 1-800-HOTELS-1; www.renaissancehotels.com), 202 E.

Pratt St. Another towering steel-and-glass structure overlooking the harbor, the Renaissance has more than 600 rooms (some without a water view). Connected to the Gallery Mall, it has a swimming pool and exercise room. Children under 18 stay free in the same room with parent. Parking fee. $239–389; some suites are available, ranging $600–3,500.

Sheraton Inner Harbor (410-962-8300; www.sheraton.com/innerharbor), 300 S. Charles St. Its location is perfect for families with dedicated sports fans and other members who would rather shop or see the sights. It is located just one block from Inner Harbor, two blocks from the Orioles' Camden Yards, and a few more blocks from the Ravens' new M&T Bank Stadium. Some rooms have water views; amenities include pool and fitness room. Free on-site parking. $255–325.

☀ ♿ **Tremont Plaza Hotel** (410-685-7777; www.tremontsuitehotels.com), 222 St. Paul Place. Located about halfway between Inner Harbor and Mount Vernon. Italian marble and mahogany add a touch of distinction to the lobby. All of the more than 200 guest accommodations are suites with separate living and sleeping rooms and fully equipped kitchens. Parking fee; pets permitted with extra fee. $164–354.

Note: Many more hotels and motels are located near the Baltimore/Washington International Airport and almost every exit along the I-695 beltway. Among the lower-cost national chains are **Days Inn** (1-800-544-8313; www.daysinn.com); **Comfort Inn** (1-800-228-5150; www.comfort inn.com); **Red Roof Inn** (1-800-

RED-ROOF; www.redroof.com); **Courtyard by Marriott** (1-888-236-2427; www.courtyard.com); and **Microtel** (410-865-7500; www .microtelinn.com). The **Homestead Village Guest Studios** (410-691-2500), 939 International Dr., with low-cost studio efficiencies, is close to the airport.

INNS

Fell's Point, 21231
☀ ♂ ♿ **The Admiral Fell Inn** (410-522-7380; www.admiralfell.com), 888 S. Broadway. The European-style Admiral Fell Inn's main building originally served as a seamen's hostel. Today guests sip complimentary coffee or tea next to the lobby's fireplace or retire to rooms decorated with Federal-period furnishings. My room had a canopy pencil-post bed and overlooked the fading VOTE AGAINST PROHIBITION sign painted on the building next door. Specialty rooms and suites have deep dormers, original wood floors, Jacuzzis, and balconies. A complimentary house breakfast is included. (Also see True under *Dining Out*). Dogs permitted with extra fee; free parking nearby. $225–450.

♟ ♂ ♿ **Inn at Henderson's Point** (410-522-7777; 1-800-292-4667; www.hendersonswharf.com), 1000 Fell St. The inn was originally constructed in 1893 as a tobacco warehouse. Many of the large guest rooms retain the original 3-foot-thick brick walls, providing them a warm radiance. Some rooms overlook the water, others face the cobblestoned inner courtyard. Continental breakfast included. A good value when compared with the hotels in Inner Harbor. $199–209.

Fell's Point, 21231

Ann Street B&B (410-342-5883), 804 S. Ann St. Joanne and Andrew Mazurek were active in revitalizing Fell's Point when it was on the skids several decades ago. The B&B is the same row house Andrew grew up in, and they have restored the luster of the original hardwood floors and staircase, and maintained all 12 fireplaces. Only three guest rooms ensure an intimate stay, and the meticulously maintained garden (which the upstairs back room overlooks) is the place to relax after a meal at one of Fell's Point's many restaurants. $100–110.

Celie's (410-522-2323; 1-800-432-0184; www.celieswaterfront.com), 1714 Thames St. There are seven guest rooms in this large row house (long and narrow like most of Baltimore's row houses). Some have fireplaces, others whirlpool tubs; all have a TV and VCR. The ground-floor room has its own private courtyard and is handicapped-accessible. Walk up the steps to the roof deck for a small view of the harbor. Children over 10 are welcome. $159–249.

Federal Hill, 21230

Scarborough Fair (410-837-0010; www.scarborough-fair.com), 1 E. Montgomery St. This is the place to stay if you want to be close to Inner Harbor (it is only two blocks away) but don't want the impersonal service (or higher prices) of a hotel. Ellen and Ashley Scarborough offer six period- and/or reproduction-furnished guest rooms in their 1801 home; each has a private bath, and four have working fireplace. Refreshments and treats available, and the Scarboroughs promise you will not go away hungry

from breakfast. Free off-street parking. $159–189.

Mount Vernon, 21201

Aunt Rebecca's B&B (410-625-1007; www.auntrebeccasbnb.com), 106 E. Preston St. Within their 1870s brownstone town house, Becky and Joe Pitta offer three large (12-foot ceilings) guest rooms furnished in Victorian style. Each room has individually controlled air-conditioning, and the bathrooms retain the original claw-foot tubs for relaxing soaks. Off-street parking available. $95–140.

Abercrombie Badger B&B (410-244-7227; 1-888-9BADGER; www.badger-inn.com), 58 W. Biddle St. This 1880s row house is conveniently located in Mount Vernon, close to many of Baltimore's cultural offerings. The 12 guest rooms have private bath, while guests meet and greet one another in the parlor on the first floor. Well-mannered children over 10 are welcome. $115–155.

Bolton Hill, 21217

Mr. Mole B&B (410-728-1179; www.mrmolebb.com), 1601 Bolton St. Mr. Mole is just a few blocks away from its companion B&B, Abercrombie Badger. There are five guest rooms decorated with 18th- and 19th-century English-style antiques in the mid-1800s row house. Three are suites. Well-mannered children over 10 are welcome; be sure you understand the cancellation and check-in and check-out policy. $119–175.

✳ Where to Eat

DINING OUT

Downtown/Inner Harbor

McCormick and Schmick's (410-234-1300), 711 Eastern Ave. (in the

Pier 5 Hotel) at Inner Harbor. Open for lunch and dinner daily. Walls of dark wood, stained glass, and a mahogany bar embellish the view of the harbor. This Portland, Oregon–based chain came to Baltimore in 1998 with a changing menu featuring more than 30 varieties of fish from both of America's oceans. There can be as many as 10 different appetizers on the half shell, and the menu tells you where the fish came from that day. Wanting to stay somewhat local, I had the mackerel, from New Jersey, grilled with tomatoes and capers. Entrées $14–32.

& **Charleston** (410-332-7373; www .charlestonrestaurant.com), 1000 Lancaster St. (between Inner Harbor and Fell's Point). Open for dinner 5:30–10 Mon.–Sat. Reservations strongly advised. Considered by many to be one of Baltimore's finest dining experiences. Chef Cindy Wolf prepares a daily changing selection of American cuisine with bits of southern and French influences. Recent menus have included pan-roasted salmon dusted with marcona almonds and served with cauliflower and chervil beurre blanc ($36), and grilled pork tenderloin with butternut squash, andouille sausage risotto, and local apple cider reduction $32. A prix fixe menu of several courses is $79; with wines to match each course, $119.

Purple Orchid (410-837-0080), 729 E. Pratt St. (on the corner of Pratt and President Sts.). Open for lunch 11:30–2:30 Mon.–Fri. Dinner is served 5:30–10:30 Mon.–Fri., and 5–11:30 Sat. and Sun. Known for its sushi and French and Oriental seafood. The oven-roasted rockfish with flying-fish roe is popular, as are the spicy sweet prawns in an orange

and plum sauce. Angus beef, veal, and fowl are also available ($17–39).

Little Italy
Da Mimmo Ristorante (410-727-6876; www.damimmo.com), 217 S. High St. Open for lunch Mon.–Fri.; dinner daily. Reservations strongly advised. Low lights, candles on the table, and a tuxedoed wait staff in a 200-year-old building—the idyllic setting to savor Chef Mimmo's irreproachable preparations. The pasta fagioli was like my mother's, while the taste of the gnocchi alla Napolitana almost made me believe my Italian grandfather had come back to life. An order of veal chops could serve a small army, as could the filet mignon alla Rossini. As a bonus, Da Mimmo is the only restaurant in Little Italy with its own parking lot. $14–30.

& **Dalesio's** (410-539-1965), 829 Eastern Ave. Dalesio's forte is northern Italian cuisine, which, by its nature, has a bit of a French character to it. The frutti di mare all Mediterranea is shrimp and scallops with mushrooms in a creamy Marsala sauce. Not quite as heavy is the capellini al Carciofi, with artichoke hearts, tomatoes, and a touch of Chianti. Veal, chicken, and duck dishes $16–24.

& **La Scala** (410-783-9209; www .lascaladining.com), 1012 Eastern Ave. Italian cooking that is inspired by the whole country and not just one region. The prices on the pasta dishes, such as the capellini al pomodoro, are great deals at $12.95–19.95. Chicken, veal, beef, and seafood entrées are only slightly higher.

Fell's Point
& **True** (410-522-2195), 888 S. Broadway. Open for lunch Mon.–Fri., dinner

Mon.–Sat., brunch Sun. Fine dining inside the historic Admiral Fell Inn (see "Inns—Fell's Point"). The seasonal menu includes local seafood (crabcakes and their accompaniment are exceptional—$24), organic beef fillets ($32), and seafood ragout ($25). The warm crab and Brie (blue crab and creamy organic Brie in a light puff pastry, baked and served with seasonal berries—$10) is almost as good for dessert as it is an appetizer.

&. **The Black Olive** (410-276-7141; 1-877-916-5483; www.theblackolive .com), 814 S. Bond St. Open for dinner daily. Dimitris, Pauline, and Stellos Spiliadis use only organic produce, milk products, flour, and sugar in their Greek restaurant. The fish offerings, such as arctic char, sea bream, and Dover sole, arrive fresh from around the world, and are filleted tableside. Lamb, veal, and several vegetarian selections are also prepared with care. Entrées $25–48.

&. **Kali's Court** (410-276-4700; www .kaliscourt.com), 1606 Thames St. Open for lunch and dinner daily. Like The Black Olive (see above), Kali's offers fish from around the world. Many dishes, like the Australian swordfish ($22.95) and the bouillabaisse ($27.50), are cooked in a brick oven for a bit of a different taste. Appetizers range from the brick-oven oysters ($8.95) to an ounce of beluga caviar served with minced egg ($52).

&. **Pierpoint** (410-675-2080; www .pierpointrestaurant.com), 1822 Aliceanna St. Open for lunch Tue.–Fri., dinner Tue.–Sun. Chefowner Nancy Longo has been attracting customers into her small space since the late 1980s. The smoked crabcakes (market price) established her reputation as someone who does

things differently. The BBQ duck egg rolls ($8.50), corn-fried oysters ($22), and Maryland-style cioppino ($23) are just a few other examples.

Federal Hill

&. **Corks** (410-752-3810; www .corksrestaurant.com), 1026 S. Charles St. Open for lunch and dinner, but hours vary each day; closed Mon. Reservations strongly recommended. An outstanding wine list paired with an ever-changing discriminating menu served inside a Baltimore row house. The veal, fish, beef, and fowl are almost always prepared a bit differently each time you visit. Entrées $24–30.

Mount Vernon

&. **Tio Pepe** (410-539-4675), 10 E. Franklin St. Open for lunch Mon.–Fri., dinner daily; hours vary slightly each day. Jacket and tie required; reservations strongly recommended. The dining rooms in which Tio Pepe serves its authentic Spanish food are in one of Baltimore's famous row houses. Black bean is the soup to go with. The veal chops in black truffle sauce are truly decadent, while the paella for two could probably feed four. Entrées $17–45.

EATING OUT

Downtown/Inner Harbor

&. **ESPN Zone** (410-685-3776), 601 E. Pratt St. (in the Power Plant). Open for lunch and dinner. Home run, three-pointer, touchdown, goal! More than 220 video monitors (they are even in restroom stalls) ensure that you will never miss a moment of action of any game, in any sport, being played at any moment in history. ESPN, the sports network, has gone into the restaurant business, although the food is almost secondary to fans glued to the monitors or having fun in 10,000 square feet of interactive and electronic sports games. Appetizers, soups, sandwiches. Pasta (such as Cajun fettuccine), beef (like a 10-ounce fillet), and seafood entrées (salmon) range $10–22.

✍ ✆ **Hard Rock Café** (410-347-7625; www.hardrock.com), 601 E. Pratt St. (in the Power Plant). The Baltimore location of the international café chain serves traditional American food (burgers, steak, and pasta) amid a profusion of rock 'n' roll memorabilia. Entrées $8–20.

✍ ✆ **City Lights** (410-244-8813), 301 Light St. (in the Light St. Pavilion), Inner Harbor. Open for lunch and dinner daily. Seafood with a view of the water. Flambéed scallops, fried fisherman's platter, and roast chicken are representative of the menu. Live entertainment on the weekend. $14.95–26.95.

Attman's (410-563-2666; www .attmans.com), 1019 E. Lombard St. In the same location and serving a taste of New York deli sandwiches since 1915. Reubens ($5.95), pastrami ($4.95), kosher hot dogs ($2.49), cream cheese and lox on a bagel

($5.75), liverwurst ($4.49), and more. Combination sandwiches $4.95–9.95. They even have rice and bread puddings ($1.95) for dessert.

Marconi's (410-727-9522), 106 W. Saratoga St. (between downtown and Mount Vernon). Marconi's has been in the same townhouse location since 1920, and is possibly the longest-running restaurant in Baltimore. The traditional American menu has stayed much the same, too: Italian fare, seafood, and meats. For something different, dine on the broiled sweetbreads with mushrooms. Most entrées are $14–30.

Little Italy

✍ **Chiapparelli's** (410-837-0309; www.chiapparellis.com), 237 S. High St. Serving southern Italian cooking since the 1940s. Many people come just for the house salad (served with each entrée), which is topped by Chiapparelli's dressing of garlic, oregano, Parmesan cheese, eggs, and pepperoncini. Pastas, chicken, veal, beef, and seafood dishes available. $15–28.

Federal Hill

✍ ✆ **Mother's Federal Hill Grille** (410-244-8686; www.mothersgrille .com), 1113 S. Charles St. Open for breakfast, lunch, and dinner daily. Brothers Dave and Adam Rather took an old bakery and turned it into a local gathering spot. Crabcakes ($20.95) and other seafood are favorites, but don't overlook the ribs ($14.95), tuna wrap ($9.95), or Mediterranean pasta ($9.95). A number of bottled microbrews and homemade ice cream are other reasons people like Mother's.

Blue Agave (410-576-3938; www .blueagaverestaurant.com), 1032 Light St. Michael Marx brought

THE HARD ROCK CAFÉ IN INNER HARBOR

authentic food from the heart of Mexico and Baja peninsula to Federal Hill several years ago. Don't look for bland fajitas or chimichangas. Instead, try the mahimahi Veracruzana ($16.50) with sauce made from tomatoes, poblano chile, lime, olive, garlic, and oregano. Or maybe the quail stuffed with *huitlacoche* (often called Mexico's truffle), and served with green chili and sautéed spaghetti squash ($18). Other entrées $13.95–22.95.

& **Bandaloops** (410-727-1335; www .bandaloops.com), 1024 S. Charles St. A restaurant and tavern setting. The crab and artichoke in garlic Parmesan cream sauce ($8.95) is *the* appetizer. Salads and sandwiches are available, but try the rack of lamb topped with mango chutney ($19.95) or maple-glazed duck breast ($16.95).

& **One World Café** (410-234-0235), 904 S. Charles St. Open for breakfast, lunch, and dinner daily. Organic vegetarian fare and a few seafood dishes. Repeat customers often go for the cheese and bean burrito. Coffee, teas, and delicious treats. Most entrées are less than $12.

Mount Vernon

& **Sascha's 527** (410-539-8880; www .saschas.com), 527 N. Charles St. Closed Sun. Sascha's has grown from a lunch-delivery-only service to serving cafeteria-style for lunch and employing a wait staff at dinner. With a hip and upbeat personality and world-inspired dishes, it has some of the most refreshing foods I've encountered. How about shredded duck and apple ragout over an apple onion pancake ($7.50) for lunch? Instead of french fries (which are also available), get the portobello fries with peach ketchup and gingered soy ($5.50). Big sandwiches, a host of sal-

ads and veggie offerings, daily plate specials, and designer *pizettes* will make you want to come back again. Entrées $6.50–19.50.

Donna's Café and Coffee Bar (410-385-0180; www.donnas.com), 2 W. Madison St. at Charles St. Popular with the local bohemian crowd, Donna's is most often thought of for gourmet coffees ($2–4.25) and rich desserts ($1–7). Also served are pizzas, salads, a wonderful variety of sandwiches, and full dishes (after 5 PM). Entrées $6.50–21.95.

& **Woman's Industrial Exchange** (410-685-4388; www.womans industrialexchange.org), 333 N. Charles St. Open for breakfast and lunch 9–3 Mon.–Fri. You'll spend money to eat out anyway, so let it do some good at this nonprofit group (see *Selective Shopping*). The prices are very reasonable; the most expensive breakfast is about $4. Lunch is salad and sandwiches (they're famous for chicken salad): $3.25–7.95. Finish the meal with a slice of sweet potato pie ($1.95). *Please note:* The business was coming under new ownership as this book went to press; call to find out current status.

Uptown

& **Gertrude's** (410-889-3399; www.johnshields.com), 10 Art Museum Dr. Open for lunch and dinner Tue.–Sun. The setting could certainly not be any more aesthetically pleasing, as Gertrude's is located inside the Baltimore Museum of Art. However, many people come just for the flavorful Chesapeake-style food. Lots of seafood dishes, such as herb-encrusted rockfish (market price), crabmeat quiche ($10.95), and gumbo with six different seafoods and andouille sausage ($16.50). There are also "platters from the land" and several veggie offerings. The panini smothered in peppers, onion, field greens, caponata, and fresh mozzarella ($7.95) I had was an outstanding blend of tastes.

CRABS ✐ ♿ **Obrycki's** (410-732-6399; www.obryckis.com), 1727 E. Pratt St., Fell's Point. Open for lunch and dinner; closed during winter. A classic crab house with crabs (market price) steamed in Obrycki's own spice mix, crabcakes ($27.95—rumored to be Oprah Winfrey's favorites), crab soup ($5.95), and other seafood and entrées ranging $7–29.95. If you like what you ordered, they have a mail-order business that ships worldwide.

✐ **Bo Brooks** (410-558-0202; www.bobrooks.com), 2701 Boston St. (inside the Baltimore Marine Center), Canton. There have been several owners since Mr. Brooks began his business in the 1940s, but steamed crabs (market price) have remained a constant. The latest owner has expanded and updated the menu to include a crab quesadilla ($11), other seafood ($12–30), and sandwiches ($6–14).

TAKE-OUT **Viccino** (410-576-0266), 1315 N. Charles St., Mount Vernon. It is only a carry-out, but you'll get some of the city's best pizza. Try the Pizza Viccino and you may never want another kind. Salads, pasta, and huge calzones. $5–16.

COFFEE BARS

Fell's Point
Funk's Democratic Coffee Spot (410-276-FUNK), 1818 Eastern Ave. The name says it—a funky little spot

with books to read and board games to play.
The Daily Grind (410-558-0399), 1726 Thames St. A local hot spot that attracts the bohemian/shabby-chic local crowd. At times it is next to impossible to get in, but the coffee is good enough that you should try.

MICROBREWERIES ✐ ♿ **Capital City Brewing Company** (410-539-PINT), 301 S. Light St. (in the Light St. Pavilion), Inner Harbor. Open for lunch and dinner until 2 AM daily. A clamorous and bustling place with decor befitting a microbrewery. Overlooks the harbor. The menu recommends the beer to complement each entrée. The Pale Rider Ale is suggested for the stuffed shrimp platter ($19.95), and the Amber Waves Ale for the brew master's chicken breast ($12.95). Other entrées and sandwiches $7–23.

SNACKS AND GOODIES **Cheesecake Factory** (410-234-3990), 201 E. Pratt St. (inside the Pratt St. Pavilion), downtown/Inner Harbor. Yes, this national chain has a full menu, but the desserts are the real reason to visit. The thick slices of cheesecake ($5.75–6.95) are available in more than 30 varieties. The espresso drinks ($2–4.50) are a good complement.

Vaccaro's (410-685-4905), 222 Albemarle St., Little Italy. Some of the best Italian sweets to be found in the eastern United States. The tiramisu melts in your mouth, the cream in the éclairs is surely rich enough to clog your arteries after two bites, and the cannoli are stuffed to order. To really indulge, have your pastry topped with a dip of gelato.

Maggie Moo's Ice Cream (410-276-4556), 821 S. Broadway, Fell's Point.

The ice cream is made fresh daily in the shop.

✴ Entertainment

FILM & **Charles Theater** (410-727-3456), 1711 N. Charles St., Charles Village (a few blocks north of Penn Station). This neighborhood theater is the place to go to see the foreign, art, independent, and documentary films that never seem to make it to the cineplexes.

& **The Senator** (410-435-8338), 5904 York Rd., Homeland (northern part of the city). The 1939 Senator shows first-run movies in its opulent art deco atmosphere and has been named one of the top movie theaters in the country.

MUSIC

Mount Vernon
& **Baltimore Opera Company** (410-494-2712; www.baltimoreopera .com), Lyric Opera House, 140 W. Mount Royal Ave. The opera has been producing hits for more than 50 years, and features international singers and conductors. Operas are performed in the original language with projected English subtitles.

& **Baltimore Symphony Orchestra** (410-783-8000; www.baltimore symphony.org), Joseph Meyerhoff Symphony Hall, 1212 Cathedral St. A wide variety of classical, pops, and family entertainment is presented throughout the year in the near-perfect symphony hall.

& **Peabody Conservatory of Music** (410-659-8124), 1 E. Mount Vernon Place. Operas, symphonies, and recitals performed by student and guest artists. Many of the performances are free.

Downtown/Inner Harbor
Have a Nice Day Café (410-385-8669), 34 Market Place. Thu.–Sat. Claims to be "Baltimore's Grooviest 70s and 80s Nightclub."

Howl at the Moon (410-783-5111), 34 Market Place. Claims to be "the World's Best Dueling Piano Rock-and-Roll" bar.

Improv Comedy Club (410-727-8500), 6 Market Place. The Baltimore location of the nationally known comedy club that has given many professional comedians their start. Reservations suggested.

Fell's Point
The Horse You Came In On Saloon (410-327-8111), 1626 Thames St. It says it was established in 1775, which would make it the country's oldest saloon. The saloon has a bit of an English pub atmosphere. Local live music is presented nightly.

Latin Place (410-522-6700; www .latinplace.com), 509 Broadway. Closed Mon. Learn the merengue or salsa as you dance the night away to Latin and international music.

Belair-Edison (northeastern part of the city)
& **Café Tattoo** (410-325-7427), 4825 Belair Rd. Open 4 PM–2 AM Tue.–Sat. Live jazz and blues in the bar downstairs, which serves an extensive list of imported and microbrews. Tattoo parlor upstairs.

THEATERS & **The Vagabond Players** (410-563-9135), 806 S. Broadway, Fell's Point. All of the actors and stagehands are volunteers, but this does not stop them from presenting professional-caliber theater. Productions have included *Prelude to a Kiss*, *Inherit the Wind*, and *Blood Brothers*.

CenterStage (410-685-3200; www .centerstage.org), 700 N. Calvert St., Mount Vernon. The **State Theater of Maryland** mounts productions ranging from Broadway hits to works by new artists. Previous presentations have included *A Raisin in the Sun*, *Three Tall Women*, and *The Pajama Game*. The season usually runs Oct.–June.

Hippodrome Theatre at the France-Merrick Performing Arts Center (410-837-7400; www.france -merrickpac.com), 12 N. Eutaw St. Now restored to its original 1914 appearance, the historic vaudeville theater has more than 2,000 seats from which to enjoy productions of Broadway shows such as *Mamma Mia*, *The Lion King*, and *The Phantom of the Opera*.

& **Theater Hopkins** (410-516-7159), The Merrick Barn at Johns Hopkins University, Uptown. An ever-changing and entertaining schedule of major American, British, and Irish plays is presented in the 1804 brick barn.

SPORTS & & **Oriole Park at Camden Yards** (410-685-9800; www .theorioles.com), 333 W. Camden St. (about six blocks west of Inner Harbor). The American League Baltimore Orioles have been playing in Baltimore since 1954 and in Camden Yards since it was built in the early 1990s. All of the seats in the stadium provide a clear view of the action, and, amazingly in this day and age, bleacher seats are still a bargain.

& & **Baltimore Ravens** (410-986-5225; www.baltimoreravens.com), Hamburg St. (a couple of blocks south of Camden Yards). The Browns changed their name to the Ravens to honor Edgar Allan Poe when they moved from Cleveland to Baltimore in the mid-1990s. Their new M&T Bank Stadium is a luxurious place compared with the old Memorial Stadium—and ticket prices reflect the cost to build it.

& **Baltimore Arena** (410-347-2020; www.baltimorearena.com), 201 W. Baltimore St. Home for the Baltimore Blast (410-732-5278; www.baltimore blast.com), members of the Major Indoor Soccer League.

Baltimore Bayhawks (410-666-0200; www.baltimorebayhawks.com). Major-league lacrosse is played in the M&T Bank Stadium.

Baltimore Burn (410-768-1383; www .baltimoreburn.com), CCBC Dundalk Field at 7200 Sollers Point Rd. This Women's Professional Football team started playing in spring 2001.

✳ Selective Shopping

ANTIQUES

Fell's Point

There are close to 30 antiques dealers within a few blocks of one another in Fell's Point, so just about everything imaginable is available. I found artwork, lamps, furniture, handcrafted pieces from around the world, architectural items, memorabilia, and more. A map and brochure of the shops is available from the **Fell's Point Antique Dealers' Association** (410-675-4776). The association can also supply information about the **Antique Market** held on the second Sunday of every month Apr.–Oct.

Federal Hill

Antique Center at Federal Hill (410-625-0182), 1220 Key Hwy. Open daily. More than 25 dealers display their wares in room settings instead of the usual large warehouse atmosphere.

Mount Vernon

The 700 and 800 blocks of Howard St. are known as Baltimore's **Antique Row**. There are close to 40 shops that, very appropriately, are located in somewhat revitalized antique buildings. A brochure available from the Mount Vernon Cultural District, Inc., describes what each shop has to offer.

ART GALLERIES

Fell's Point

Art Gallery of Fell's Point (410-327-1272), 1716 Thames St. Open daily. A cooperative of more than 40 artists working in a variety of media.

Conrad-Miller Studios and Gallery (410-563-3190), 2007 Fleet St. Step inside to watch Melvin Miller create his latest maritime scene, or Nancy Conrad paint one of her many floral works. The works of other local artists are also featured in the gallery.

Federal Hill

Tradestone Gallery (410-752-8085; www.tradestonegallery), 803 Light St. Closed Mon. Offers paintings of Russian artists and other items—such as nesting dolls and painted eggs—of Russian origin.

Montage Gallery (410-752-1125; www.montagegallery.com), 925 S. Charles St. Tue.–Sat. Monthly exhibits of artwork from recognized and new regional, national, and international artists.

THE SHOPS AT FELL'S POINT

Downtown/Inner Harbor

Barnes & Noble (410-385-1709), 601 E. Pratt St. (in the Power Plant). Yes, this is the chain store, but its location in Inner Harbor makes it very convenient. It is also one of the largest and busiest in the chain.

Fell's Point

Mystery Loves Company (410-276-6708; 1-800-538-0042), 1730 Fleet St. Closed Mon. The name says it all. The little shop is packed with mystery books, old and new. Among them you may find first editions or author-signed copies.

Mount Vernon

✂ **Drusilla's Books** (410-225-0277), 817 Howard St. Tue.–Sat. A place to bring back childhood reading memories, as Drusilla's specializes in children's and illustrated books, both old and rare.

Clayton Fine Books (410) 752-6800; www.claytonfinebooks.com), 317 N. Charles St. Out-of-print and rare books as well as today's best sellers and books of all genres.

Federal Hill

Global Village Market (410-230-3540), 700 Light St. Much like Ten Thousand Villages (see below) in Fell's Point, this shop carries fairly traded handicrafts from around the world.

Fell's Point

Ten Thousand Villages (410-342-5568; www.villages.com), 1621 Thames St. This is the local outlet for the international nonprofit organization by the same name that purchases fairly traded handicrafts from around the world. A number of unique items.

Mount Vernon

Woman's Industrial Exchange (410-685-4388), 333 N. Charles St. The nonprofit exchange was established in 1880 to benefit financially ailing women by providing a place to sell their handcrafted goods. The purpose is still the same, except some of the items are now produced by men. The quality items you find here may not be available anywhere else—and the money you spend helps others.

KIDS CAN PADDLE A SEA MONSTER TO EXPLORE INNER HARBOR.

FARMER'S MARKETS Baltimore Farmer's Market (410-752-8632), Saratoga St. (between Holiday and Gay Sts.), downtown/Inner Harbor. You will find thousands of people shopping for fresh produce 8–noon on Sunday morning June–Dec. Lots of parking space underneath I-83.

Waverly Street Farmer's Market (410-889-8095; www.32ndstreet market.org), 400 block of E. 32nd St., Charles Village. This place almost becomes a street fair every Sat., 7–noon, throughout the year, as people come out to eat goodies and watch the entertainment in addition to buying produce.

✴ Special Events

Late February and/or March: **American Craft Council Craft Show** (877-BALTIMORE), Baltimore Convention Center, 1 W. Pratt St. Usually features more than 800 craftspeople form across the country. All artists are selected through a jury process, so the quality of work and originality is excellent.

May: **Film Festival** (1-877-BALTI-MORE), various locations. A week of lectures, screenings, and events that highlight the city's contributions to the movies. **The Preakness Celebration** (410-837-3030) is held in different places. The running of the Preakness race is preceded by a week of events including a parade, a hot-air balloon race, the Pee Wee Preakness, boat races, and a concert.

June: **African American Heritage Festival** (410-318-8286; www.aahf .org). The festival is so large (usually attracting close to 400,000 people over the 3-day event) that it takes place in Camden Yards. **Hispanic Festival** (410-558-8419), Patterson Park, downtown. A celebration of Hispanic heritage.

July: **Artscape** (1-877-BALTIMORE), Mount Royal (in the northern part of the city). Thought to be the largest arts festival in the country.

July–August: **Little Italy Open-Air Film Festival** (1-877-BALTIMORE), Little Italy. If you saw *Cinema Paradiso*, you will love this festival, which projects movies onto an outdoor screen every Fri. at 9 PM.

September: **Book Festival** (1-877-BALTIMORE), various locations in Mount Vernon. The annual event includes author readings and signings, children's writers and storytellers, and book vendors. **Ukrainian Festival and Carnival** (410-682-3800), Patterson Park, downtown. Dances, songs, and Ukrainian Easter eggs and crafts.

October: **Annual Fun Festival** (410-675-6750; www.preservationsociety .com), Fell's Point. Food, drink, dancing, and a plethora of local bands. **Annual Maryland Craft Beer Festival** (410-377-5523; www.federal hillevents.com), Federal Hill. Food, crafts, retail vendors, and a chance to sample two selections from every microbrewery in the state. **Annual Chocolate Festival** (410-685-6169), Lexington Market. The city's bakeries and confectioners come together to present a bewildering array of chocolate treats, from truffles to cakes to coated fruits.

November–December: **Zoo Lights** (410-366-LION; www.baltimorezoo .org), Baltimore Zoo. Annual display of more than 750,000 lights. Active and passive light sculptures and displays.

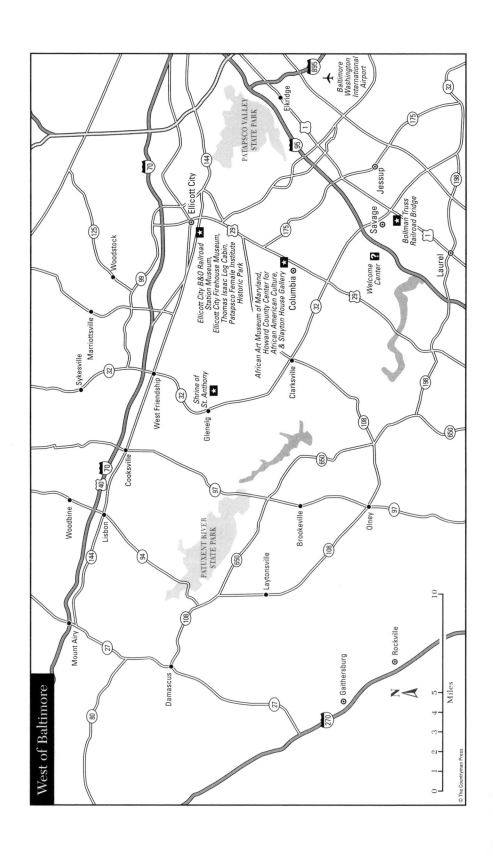

West of Baltimore

Baltimore Washington International Airport

PATAPSCO VALLEY STATE PARK

Elkridge

Jessup

Savage

Bollman Truss Railroad Bridge

Laurel

Welcome Center

Ellicott City

Ellicott City B&O Railroad Station Museum, Ellicott City Firehouse Museum, Thomas Isaac Log Cabin, Patapsco Female Institute Historic Park

African Art Museum of Maryland, Howard County Center for African American Culture, & Slayton House Gallery

Columbia

Woodstock

Marriottsville

Sykesville

West Friendship

Shrine of St. Anthony

Glenelg

Clarksville

Cooksville

PATUXENT RIVER STATE PARK

Woodbine

Lisbon

Brookeville

Olney

Mount Airy

Laytonsville

Damascus

Gaithersburg

Rockville

N

Miles

0 1 2 3 4 5   10

© The Countryman Press

WEST OF BALTIMORE—Ellicott City and Columbia

Three Quaker brothers, John, Andrew, and Joseph Ellicott, traveled from their Pennsylvania home and settled along the banks of the Patapsco River in the 1770s. Deeper and stronger than it is today, the river provided the power needed for the brothers' mill to grind wheat produced by local farmers. The town, known as Ellicott City (first called Ellicott Mills), that grew up around their business soon became the largest flour-milling center in the American colonies. Although it gave life to the settlement, the Patapsco River has been a harsh benefactor, periodically flooding nearly the entire town. Markers on the railroad bridge show the dates of the floods and how high the water has reached.

The country's first railroad terminal was built in Ellicott City in 1831, to service the first 13 miles of track laid in America. Soon afterward, Andrew Jackson became the first president to ride a train, taking it from the city into Baltimore. The station is now a museum, providing insight into the past.

In fact, much of the town, now bypassed by four-lane US 40, is like a museum. Buildings within the historic district have been well preserved. Some of today's restaurants were former mills, and shops along Main Street are filled with antiques that would have suited the town's glory days. Tongue Row, a small specialty-shop area off Main Street, was once owned by Ann Tonge as rental property. Local tradition says the spelling of its name changed because so many "miller's wives would lean out of windows to gossip with one another."

Columbia's birth as one of America's first planned communities in 1966 was conceived and directed by developer James Rouse. He envisioned a city that would give residents a sense of belonging by having a variety of houses set up in small communities, with each clustered around its own neighborhood social center. The city would provide a large portion of its own jobs, shopping, health care, education, cultural resources and activities, and recreation. Commercial and industrial development would be balanced by permanently designated parks and green spaces.

For the most part, his dream has retained its original ideas. Columbia is now a city of about 100,000 residents (with average family income well over $80,000), living in a number of designated villages. Cultural venues abound, from art classes and exhibits at several community centers and in the African Art Museum of Maryland to the city's own orchestra, a professional theater troupe, and an endless procession of festivals, celebrations, and free concerts and movies. More than 5,300 acres (well over one-third of the city's land) have been set aside for parks, playgrounds, and natural areas, and close to 88 miles of walking and biking trails provide alternatives to getting around by automobile.

COMMUNITIES The Patapsco River was a major means of transportation during our nation's early history, and trade vessels would ply its waters to the bustling port town of **Elkridge**. Now much shallower—due to erosion and siltation—the river is no longer a busy thoroughfare but a quiet waterway protected by long and narrow Patapsco Valley State Park. The town's fortunes have followed those of the river, and despite some recent housing development around it, its stately Victorian homes give it an air of a slow-moving small town.

Savage grew up around its namesake textile mill, which operated from the early 1800s to the mid-1900s. Many of the modest mill workers' homes are still occupied by today's residents. The mill has been converted to a major antiques, specialty-shop, and artisans' workshops attraction.

GUIDANCE The entrance to **Howard County Tourism, Inc.** (410-313-1900; 1-800-288-TRIP; www.visithowardcounty.com), is a side door on the ground floor of the Ellicott City Post Office at 8267 Main St., Ellicott City, 21043.

Maryland **welcome centers** are located on I-95 between Exits 35 and 38. The phone number for the one near Savage is 301-490-1333. You can contact the other, near Laurel, by calling 301-490-2444.

GETTING THERE *By car:* **I-70** cuts across the northern portion of this part of Maryland. It arrives from Baltimore in the east and Frederick in the west. **I-95** and **US 1** run along the area's eastern section, as they connect Baltimore with Washington, DC.

By air: **Baltimore/Washington International Airport** (1-800-I-FLY-BWI) is about a 20-minute drive from the eastern part of this region.

By rail: **Amtrak** (1-800-USA-RAIL) makes stops in Baltimore and Washington, DC. Local buses and **MARC** commuter trains (see *Getting Around*) can then deliver you to several points in the Ellicott City–Columbia area.

GETTING AROUND *By car:* **I-70** runs east–west along the north, while **I-95** and **US 1** run north–south in the eastern part of this region. Four-lane **US 29** is the quickest route between Columbia and Ellicott City. **MD 144** is only a two-lane road, but it goes through some of the smaller towns.

By bus: **Howard Transit Service** (410-313-1919) makes multiple stops in Columbia, Ellicott City, the BWI airport terminal, the MARC/Amtrak station, and along the US 1 corridor. **MTA** (1-800-543-9809) has buses that will take you into Baltimore and Washington, DC, on a scheduled basis.

By rail: The **MARC** commuter trains (1-800-325-RAIL) make stops in Savage, Jessup, Dorsey, and St. Denis as they run between Baltimore and Washington, DC.

By taxi: **Howard County Yellow Cab** (410-381-1818).

PARKING In Ellicott City, parking is free in the municipal lots on the corner of Ellicott Mills Dr. and Main St., on Courthouse Dr. above the main part of the city, and in the Oella Lot located across the Patapsco River. Some of the spaces in the lot behind the post office are free; other spaces have meters. Check the signage for the on-street parking, as some spots have 1-hour limits and others have 2-hour limits.

MEDICAL EMERGENCY **Howard County General Hospital** (410-740-7890), 5755 Cedar Lane, Columbia.

✳ To See
MUSEUMS

Columbia
African Art Museum of Maryland (www.africanartmuseum.org), 5430 Vantage Point Rd. (inside Historic Oakland). Tue.–Fri. 10–4, Sun. noon–4. Small admission fee. Within its small quarters, the museum presents permanent and changing exhibits of masks, sculptures, textiles, musical instruments, jewelry, baskets, and items of everyday life from the entire African continent. I was especially impressed by the intricacy of work on the gold weights made by the lost-wax method (which may or may not be on display when you arrive).

✔ **Howard County Center of African American Culture** (410-715-1921), 5434 Vantage Point Rd. Tue.–Fri. noon–5, Sat. noon–4. Small admission fee. A dining room, kitchen, and living room are furnished to represent the 19th-century lifestyle of county African Americans. Other exhibits include sports and military memorabilia, hands-on exhibits for children, and an extensive collection of early and contemporary African American artwork, inventions, and musical recordings.

Ellicott City
✔ **Ellicott City B&O Railroad Station Museum** (410-461-1944), 2711 Maryland Ave. Hours vary. Small admission fee. The oldest railroad terminal in America, it was built circa 1830 to accommodate freight service and expanded for passengers in 1856. Amazingly, almost 50 percent of all of the supplies and soldiers that participated in the entire Civil War passed through the town on the railroad.

Exhibits chronicle its history, but there is much more to see and experience here. Living-history demonstrations are presented on an irregular basis, and the HO model layout of the railroad from Baltimore to Ellicott City is elaborate and detailed. Special exhibits come and go on a scheduled basis. One of the most entertaining past exhibits chronicled the exploits of Owney, the mascot of the Railway Mail Service. A stray dog who was adopted by postal workers, he rode the trains on top of mailbags. At each stop workers would attach tags to commemorate his visit. He collected more than 1,000 and traveled to far-flung places in the world such as China and Japan.

Firehouse Museum (410-313-1413), Main St. and Church Rd. Sun. 1–4 in summer, by appointment other times. Donations accepted. The firehouse was built on an incline above the town to give the firemen "a running start." Artifacts include a horse-drawn hose cart, the original fire-alarm bell that was loud enough to be heard across town, and a whimsical display of toy fire equipment.

HISTORIC SITES

Ellicott City

Thomas Isaac Log Cabin (410-313-1413), Main St. and Ellicott Mills Dr. Mon., Tue., and Thu. 10–5. Donations accepted. Living historians relate the story of the National Road and what life was like in the late 1700s. The cabin is the oldest surviving structure in the city.

& **Patapsco Female Institute Historic Park** (410-465-8500), 3961 Sarah's Lane. Sun. 1–4. Guided tours are given at 1:30 and 3. Small admission fee. On a hilltop overlooking Ellicott City, the institute opened in 1837 as a finishing school for young women. It was one of the first places in America to teach math and science to women. The building was used for various venues after the school closed in 1891 but eventually fell into ruin.

It is now the site of what is believed to be one of the few stabilized ruins in the country, and elevated walkways lead visitors through the building's shell to imagine what the living quarters, classrooms, and kitchen would have looked like. Next door, **Mt. Ida**, the 1828 home of William Ellicott, serves as the park's visitors center.

Savage

Bollman Truss Railroad Bridge, 8600 Foundry St. (next to Historic Savage Mill; see *Selective Shopping*). This style of wrought-iron and cast-iron semi-suspension bridge was once used throughout the United States and Europe. This B&O Railroad bridge from the 1860s is the last of its kind left in the world.

HISTORIC CHURCHES St. Paul's Catholic Church, St. Paul St., Ellicott City. The 1830s church was the site of Babe Ruth's first wedding, in 1914.

OTHER SITES Shrine of St. Anthony (410-531-2800), 12300 Folly Quarter Rd., Ellicott City. Originally, this was part of the 18th-century country estate of Charles Carroll, the last surviving signer of the Declaration of Independence. Folly Quarter is now the site of a Franciscan friary and chapel dedicated to St. Anthony, patron saint of the lost. The public is welcome, and I enjoy visiting the extensive grounds, taking a quiet walk on the meditative nature trails, and appreciating the architecture of the chapel and other buildings.

✳ To Do

BALLOONING Friendship Hot Air Balloon Company (410-442-5566), 12465 Barnard Way, West Friendship. Sunrise and sunset flights over central Maryland.

BICYCLING Columbia Association Welcome Center (410-715-3000), 10221 Wincopin Circle, Columbia. The association publishes "A Path Runs Through It," a map of the 80 miles of biking and hiking trails that wind through natural areas and connect the city's villages with one another. Some of those miles pass through parklands, while many are roadway or sidewalk connectors.

Also see the **Patapsco Valley State Park** sidebar on page 236.

BOAT RENTALS Columbia Association Welcome Center (410-715-3000), 10221 Wincopin Circle, Columbia. The center rents a variety of small boats during the summer months, enabling visitors to explore the 25 acres of Lake Kittamaqundi.

Centennial Park (410-313-4700), MD 108, Ellicott City. Visitors can rent small boats May–Aug. and enjoy the park's 52-acre lake.

FAMILY ACTIVITIES ✎ **Rounding 3rd Family Entertainment Center** (410-796-0800; www.roundingthird.baweb.com), 6600 Amberton Dr., Elkridge. Miniature golf, go-carts, batting cages, and an arcade.

GOLF The Timbers at Troy (410-313-GOLF; www.timbersgolf.com), 6100 Marshalee Dr., Elkridge. The par-72 course has over 6,650 yards from the back tees, and is bordered by streams and mature woodlands.

Waverly Woods (410-313-9182), 2100 Warwick Way, Marriottsville. The Arthur Hill–designed course follows the natural contours of the land with minimal bunkering. Five sets of tees range from 4,808 yards to 7,024 yards.

Willow Springs (410-442-7700; www.willowspringsgolfcourse.com), 12980 Livestock Rd., West Friendship. Opened in the 1990s and designed by Al Janis. Walkons are welcomed and will be accommodated as soon as possible.

Also see **Turf Valley Resort and Conference Center** under *Lodging.*

MINIATURE GOLF See *Family Activities.*

WALKING TOURS Columbia Association Welcome Center (410-715-3000), 10221 Wincopin Circle, Columbia. The association publishes a pamphlet describing the sites to be seen along Lake Kittamaqundi. Most interesting are the outdoor sculptures, especially that of Pierre du Fayet.

✹ Green Space

GARDENS Mill Stone Park, Ellicott Mills Dr., Ellicott City. Millstones rescued from the Patapsco River are bordered by a small garden maintained by local volunteers.

PARKS See the **Patapsco Valley State Park** sidebar on page 236.

HIKING

✎ **Patapsco Valley State Park** (410-461-5005), 8020 Baltimore National Pike (US 40), Ellicott City. Surprisingly detached from the signs of civilization surrounding it, this park is an exquisitely beautiful area with trails beside tumbling streams and along quiet hillsides. The park is more than 40 miles long and is developed in several separate sections.

The 5-mile **Switchback Trail** (a favorite with mountain bikers) and its numerous side routes in the McKeldin area lead into a wonderfully isolated valley in which the river rolls down picturesque **South Branch Rapids.** Trails in the **Daniels Dam** area (off Old Frederick Rd. in Ellicott City) provide easy miles of walking to discover the ruins of a former river town. About 3 miles of trails wind along the hillside and connect the campground (see *Lodging*) to the river in the Hollofield area.

Within the Hilton and Avalon–Orange Grove areas are easy trails along the river that are favorites with families with small children, while the routes that wind onto the hillside attract mountain bikers. **Buzzard Rocks** overlooks the river, and **Cascade Falls** tumbles down the hillside. Be aware that the hillside trails in these areas may have few signs, meager markers, rugged terrain, and rough footing.

CASCADE FALLS

✳ Lodging

RESORTS Turf Valley Resort and Conference Center (410-465-1500; www.turfvalley.com), 2700 Turf Valley Rd., Ellicott City, 21042. The 1,000-acre resort has two 18-hole golf courses to choose from, two restaurants, more than 200 hotel rooms, several golf villas, swimming pools, and a full European spa. Most amenities require an additional fee, but many available packages can be structured to include the amenities without any additional fees. $150 and up.

MOTELS AND HOTELS

Columbia, 21045

Hampton Inn (410-997-8555; www.hamptoninn.com), 8880 Columbia 100 Pkwy. Indoor pool, fitness center, and complimentary deluxe continental breakfast. The common areas are large and nicely furnished. $99–175.

⛄ **Sheraton** (410-730-3900; 1-800-638-2817; www.sheratoncolumbia.com), 10207 Wincopin Circle, 21044. Overlooks 25-acre Lake Kittamaqundi in Columbia's Town Center. Fitness room, pool, and in-room coffee. $109–245.

🐾 ✎ ⛄ **Staybridge Suites** (410-964-9494; 1-800-238-8000), 8844 Columbia 100 Pkwy. Designed for extended-stay business travelers, the studio, one-bedroom, and two-bedroom/two-bath suites also appeal to families with children. Complimentary breakfast. $125–200.

Elkridge, 21075

Best Western (410-796-3300; 1-800-528-1234), 6755 Dorsey Rd. (accessed from I-95 Exit 43). Just a few minutes away from Baltimore/Washington International Airport. Fitness center, indoor pool, sauna, and free morning newspaper. $89–189.

Ellicott City, 21043

🐾 ⛄ **Residence Inn by Marriott** (410-997-7200; 1-800-331-3131; www.residenceinn.com), 4950 Beaver Run. Most of the guest accommodations are like small apartments. One or two bedrooms, kitchen, and a separate sitting room. Small pets permitted with a substantial deposit. $150 and up.

Forest Motel (410-465-2090; 1-877-606-6424), 10021 Baltimore National Pike (US 40). A simple but clean motel on the main highway with only 25 rooms. Reminiscent of the 1950s and 1960s. Pool. $60–75.

Jessup, 20794

Holiday Inn (410-799-7500), 7900 Washington Blvd. Characteristic Holiday Inn rooms with in-room coffee and pay-per-view movies. Swimming pool and coin laundry. $130–175.

Super 8 (410-796-0400), 8094 Washington Blvd. Nothing fancy, but one of the lowest rates in a high-rate area. $75–99.

BED & BREAKFASTS Clarksville Inn (410-531-5332), 11746 MD 108, Clarksville, 21029. The 5,000-square-foot 1985 California contemporary home has lots of wood inside and large picture windows to look onto the hillside forest. Six decks and a teahouse enable you to get even closer to the trees. The inn markets itself to extended-stay corporate travelers but also accepts guests for single nights if possible. The seven suites have private baths, desk and chair, and satellite TV. $100–225.

Commodore Joshua Barney House (301-362-1900; 1-800-475-7912; www.joshuabarneyhouse.com),

7912 Savage Guilford Rd., Savage, 20763. Commodore Joshua Barney was the only American officer to win acclaim in both the Revolutionary War and the War of 1812. His 1760s home, listed on the National Register of Historic Places, now serves as a gracious B&B, with guest rooms and suites available (all with private bath). Antiques, fine art, and a host of amenities make stays here luxurious, while the 6 landscaped acres along the Little Patuxent River provide a quiet and restful atmosphere. A favorite of business travelers. $175–225.

Peralynna Manor at Rose Hill (410-715-4602; 1-877-PERALYNNA; www.peralynna.com), 10605 Clarksville Pike, Columbia, 21044. Like Clarksville Inn (see above), Peralynna Manor caters primarily to extended-stay corporate travelers but also accepts guests for single nights if possible. And what a place to stay. The 14,000-square-foot contemporary manor, located next to a 1,100-acre farm, has a great room bigger than my entire home. Guest suites are large, have private balconies, and are packed with amenities geared for those on business trips. Exercise equipment, hot tub, and food provided to make your own breakfast. $180–315.

Wayside Inn (410-461-4636; www.waysideinnmd.com), 4344 Columbia Rd., Ellicott City, 21042. The field-stone inn was built in the late 1700s as a plantation manor, and local lore claims it was visited by George Washington and John Quincy Adams. The three suites and two guest rooms have private bath. My choice would be the Ellicott Room with fireplace, sleigh bed, and view of the landscaped back-yard. $135–175.

CAMPING 🐾 ♿ **Patapsco Valley State Park** (410-461-5005; call 1-888-432-CAMP for reservations), 8020 Baltimore National Pike (US 40), Ellicott City, 24102. More than 70 RV and tent sites are available in the Hollofield area of the park next door to Ellicott City. A special loop is reserved for those with pets. The season usually runs late Mar.–late Oct.

Ramblin' Pines (410-795-5161), 801 Hoods Mill Rd., Woodbine, 21797. More than 150 RV sites and about 20 tent sites. A dump station, showers, a pool, and miniature golf; facilities limited in winter. Short nature trails wind through the 45 acres.

✳ Where to Eat

DINING OUT ♿ **Tersiguel's** (410-465-4004; www.tersiguels.com), 8293 Main St., Ellicott City. Open for lunch Mon.–Sat. 11:30–2:30; lunch Sun. 10:30–2:30; dinner Mon.–Thu. and Sun. 5–9; dinner Fri. and Sat. 5–10. Dinner reservations recommended. French country fare based upon Fernand and Odette Tersiguel's original home in Brittany. Served in the 1800s home of one of Ellicott City's mayors. The hors d'oeuvres menu takes up a full page; *saumon fumé* ($9.95) is a local favorite. Lamb, steak, duck, chicken, pork, and seafood entrées are well presented. Entrées $23.95–36.95. Daily specials and prix fixe menu also available.

♿ **Elkridge Furnace Inn** (410-379-9336; www.elkridgefurnaceinn.com), 5745 Furnace Ave., Elkridge. Open for lunch Tue.–Fri. 11:30–2; open for dinner Tue.–Fri. 5–9, Sat. 5–10; open Sun. for brunch 10–2, dinner 4–8. Dinner reservations recommended. Meals can be peaceful and relaxing in this 1700s country manor home and restaurant on the banks of the Patapsco River. Chef-owner Dan Wecker changes his French-cuisine menu almost every month. Appetizers have included *gâteau au fromage*—walnut-topped blue cheese and cream cheese cake filled with bacon and house-cured salmon, served with a tomato relish ($9); entrées might range from fennel and pine nut tortellini ($15) to trout fillet ($26) and *filet de boeuf* ($34).

EATING OUT

Columbia

🍴 ♿ **Clyde's** (410-730-2828; www.clydes.com), 10221 Wincopin Circle. Open for lunch and dinner daily. Picture windows overlook Columbia's Lake Kittamaqundi, and the Victorian bar is decorated with circus and travel posters. Sandwiches and light entrées for lunch ($7.95–11.95). I liked the vegetable frittata ($8.95). Dinner entrées are a bit heavier, with pork chops ($15.95), BBQ platter ($15.95), and pan-roasted halibut ($16.95) being some of the favorites. Extensive wine list.

♿ **P. F. Chang's China Bistro** (410-730-5344), 10300 Little Patuxent Pkwy. (at The Mall in Columbia). Open daily for lunch and dinner. Possibly the most impressive things about this chain are the huge sculptures at its restaurants' entrances. They are interpretations of 11th-century BC sculptures unearthed in China in the 20th century. The menu draws from major regions of the country. The beef à la Szechwan is twice-cooked with celery and carrots; the mu shu pork is served with hoisin sauce and thin pancakes; lemon-pepper shrimp is stir-fried with chives and bean sprouts. Entrées $8.95–17.95.

🌿 ♿ **The Mango Grove** (410-884-3426; www.themangogrove.com), 6365B Dobbin Rd. Open for lunch and dinner; closed Tue. Authentic southern Indian vegetarian food served in a plain interior at amazingly low prices. The wait staff will be happy to explain if you do not know what Samosas, *dosas*, and curries are. The most expensive dinner entrée is less than $10.

♿ **La Madeleine French Bakery and Café** (410-872-4900), 6211 Columbia Crossing. Open for breakfast, lunch, and dinner daily. This national chain sends each new café manager to France to learn the country's ways. Breakfast is light baked goods, lunch is sandwiches and pizza, and dinner has many choices like goat cheese ravioli and pasta Française. Dinner entrées $8–17.

Ellicott City

The Trolley Stop (410-465-8546), 6 Oella Ave. Open for breakfast, lunch, and dinner. Yes, the trolley did stop at this tavern constructed in 1833, and the brick walls and exposed beams hark back to the building's earliest days. Lots of soups (the Maryland crab has a definite homemade taste), salads, and sandwiches ($4.95–9.95) for lunch. A few entrées are also served for lunch, with more on the dinner menu. The chicken *riggie* with artichoke and shallots ($12.95) is a standout. Other entrées $11.95–16.95.

🍴 ♿ **Crab Shanty** (410-465-9660), 3410 Plumtree Dr. Fresh seafood in its many forms makes up the bulk of the menu, with a few meat items. If you are on a tight budget, go for the shrimp-and-fish combo ($13.95); if money is no object, then the two New Zealand lobster tails are for you ($46.50). Most entrées range

$13.95–26.95. Almost every item in the decor has a story, which is related on the back of the menu.

♿ **La Palapa** (410-465-0070), 8307 Main St. Open daily for lunch and dinner. The fajitas, chimichangas, enchiladas, and tacos are joined on the menu with house specialties such as chili verde ($12.95); chicken mole ($13.95); trout grilled with tomatoes, onion, capers, olives, and wine ($13.95); and a *muy delicioso* vegetarian burrito ($10.95). Live music on the weekend turns out the crowds for quite the party. Most entrées are $6.95–18.95.

Jessup

♿ **Frank's 24-Hour Diner** (410-799-8198), 7395 Cedar Ave. and US 1. Nothing fancy here; the name describes it well. Breakfast is always available, so it is the place for when you feel the need for eggs, pancakes, bacon, or sausage. Lunch and dinner are the usual sandwiches and diner entrées. Meat loaf is a specialty. Dinner entrées $7–15.

♿ **Log Cabin** (410-799-9874), 8126 Washington Blvd. Mon.–Fri. 6 AM–7 PM. The same family has owned the restaurant for about half a century. Come here if you are familiar with chitterlings, pig's feet, maws, and fried eggplant. Better yet, come here if you don't know about them and learn why the restaurant has such a loyal following. By the way, be sure to order the extremely cheesy macaroni and cheese as a side dish. Entrées $6–10.

COFFEE BARS Bean Hollow (410-465-0233), 8059 Main St., and **Kirinyaga Coffee and Specialties** (410-203-2743), 8381 Merryman St., Ellicott City.

Also see **Old Mill Bakery Café** under *Snacks and Goodies*.

SNACKS AND GOODIES Sarah and Desmond's (410-465-9700), 8198 Main St., Ellicott City. Homemade pastries, cakes, and breads, along with lite vegetarian fare and locally roasted coffee.

Old Mill Bakery Café (410-465-2253), 4 Frederick Rd., Ellicott City. The espressos, cappuccinos, and lattes are superb complements to the many goodies. The éclairs, Danishes, rolls, muffins, and cookies are baked in-house. The gourmet pastries are made by "various chef friends" who bake for Washington, DC, embassies and hotels.

✳ Entertainment

FILM

Columbia

Marvelous Movies and More at the Slayton House Gallery (410-730-3987), Wilde Lake Village Green. A series of classic movies from the 1920s through the 1950s is presented throughout the year. Most of the films are unavailable in video, and a discussion and dessert bar are held after each showing. A most interesting way to spend an evening.

Loews Columbia Palace (410-730-4600), 8805 Centre Park Dr., and **Snowden Square Stadium** (410-872-0670), 9141 Commerce Center Dr., are the area's first-run movie houses.

MUSIC

Columbia

Columbia Orchestra (410-381-2004; www.columbiaorchestra.org). The orchestra began life as a small chamber music group in 1978 but grew quickly to include well over 50 members. It now presents a season of full orchestral works and numerous small "candlelight concerts" at various area venues.

Sundays at Three (410-381-3240), Christ Episcopal Church (corner of Oakland Mills and Dobbin Rds.). Chamber music concerts presented in an intimate setting on selected Sunday afternoons. The audience is invited to mingle with the guest artists after the performances.

THEATERS

Columbia
🌢 **Rep Stage** (410-772-4900), 10901 Little Patuxent Pkwy., Howard Community College. The theater offers professional productions at low ticket prices; the troupe has received a multitude of Helen Hayes awards and nominations. Past performances have included O'Neill's *A Moon for the Misbegotten* and Albee's *Three Tall Women*.

Toby's (410-730-8311; 1-800-88-TOBYS; www.tobysdinnertheatre .com), 5900 Symphony Woods Rd. Toby's is a dinner theater "in the round" that has presented productions such as the *Wizard of Oz*, *It's a Wonderful Life*, and *Joseph and the Amazing Technicolor Dreamcoat*. Performances are accompanied by live music.

Also see **Howard County Arts Council** and **Slayton House Gallery** under *Selective Shopping*.

✱ Selective Shopping
ANTIQUES

Columbia
Mimi's Antiques (410-381-6862; 1-888-368-6862; www.mimisantiques

.com), 8763 Carriage Hills Dr. Specializes in 18th- and 19th-century porcelains, furniture, and paintings.

Ellicott City
Ellicott City's Country Store (410-465-4482), 8180 Main St. Open daily. There are four floors of antiques within the historic Walker-Chandler Building, believed to be the country's first duplex.

Taylor's Antique Mall (410-465-4444), 8197 Main St. Open daily. Four floors of possible hidden treasures.

Ballindullagh Barn Antiques (410-988-8002), 2410 Woodstream Court. European pine and hardwood furniture from the 18th century.

Wagon Wheel Antiques (410-465-7910), 8061 Tiber Alley. Be sure to go upstairs to see the 1850s Easton's Funeral Hearse that owner Ed Growl has restored.

Elkridge
Flea Market World (410-796-1025), 6675 Amberton Dr. Sat. and Sun. 8–4. More than 300 vendors under one roof.

ART GALLERIES

Columbia
Slayton House Gallery (410-730-3987), Wilde Lake Village Green. The nonprofit organization provides space for classes, and theatrical and musical performances. Its two galleries have changing exhibits from local artists working in various media.

Ellicott City
Howard County Arts Council (410-313-ARTS; www.hocoarts.org), 8510 High Ridge Rd. The county's arts council offers a gallery for changing exhibits of local and regional artists. Its **Black Box Theatre** provides a

venue for emerging groups, and theatrical and musical productions. A great place to not only catch locals "in the act" but also see works not found anywhere else.

Margaret Smith Gallery (410-461-0870; 1-888-227-8670; www.margaret smithgallery.com), 8090 Main St. Works of local artists, and an affiliate for animation art from Disney, Warner Bros., and other studios.

BOOKSTORES **Daedalus Books** (410-309-2370), 9645 Gerwig Lane, Columbia. Warehouse outlet with most books at least 50 percent off.

USED BOOKS **Gramp's Attic Books** (410-750-9235), 8304 Main St., Ellicott City. Used, old, and rare books in many different categories.

SPECIAL SHOPS ✍ **Forget-Me-Not Factory** (410-465-7355), 8044 Main St., Ellicott City. The building once served as an opera house and vaudeville theater, and is rumored to be where John Wilkes Booth gave his theatrical debut. It is now filled with items such as fairy crowns, bubble wands, wind banners, toys, and other whimsical things of interest to both children and adults. Ask them to let you see where the hillside bedrock was incorporated into the structure when it was originally built as the Patapsco Hotel.

Historic Savage Mill (1-800-788-MILL; www.savagemill.com), 8600 Foundry St., Savage. One of the most interesting venues for a shopping center you will ever visit. The mill operated as a weaving business from 1822 to 1947, and its 200,000 square feet are now home to more than 50 specialty shops (primarily antiques or art

shops) with more than 250 dealers. Part of the amusement in visiting here is negotiating the maze of convoluted great rooms, halls, and stairways to discover a nearly hidden treasure store or an artist painting a life-sized portrait. The **Bollman Truss Railroad Bridge** is next to the mill.

Stillridge Herb Farm (410-465-8348), 10370 Old Frederick Rd. (MD 99), Woodstock. This is a pick-your-own place, but instead of fruits and vegetables you pick flowers and herbs. Walking between the rows, you can choose strawflowers, zinnias, celosias, basil, chives, sage, and much more. The gift shop is full of items that incorporate the farm's harvest.

PICK-YOUR-OWN PRODUCE FARMS **Triadelphia Lake View Farm** (410-489-4460), 15155 Triadelphia Mill Rd., Glenelg. Pick your own vegetables from mid-July through September.

✍ ♿ **Larriland Farm** (410-442-2605; 301-854-6110), 2415 Woodbine Rd. (MD 94), Woodbine. The Moore family invites people to pick a very wide variety of fruits and vegetables from midspring into fall. October activities include hayrides and a straw maze. Choose and cut your own tree at Christmastime.

❋ Special Events

March: **Annual Teddy Bear and Doll Show and Sale** (301-498-6871), Historic Savage Mill.

March or April: **Easter Egg Hunt and Bonnet Contest** (410-465-8500), Patapsco Female Institute Historic Park, Ellicott City.

April–November: **Ghost Tours** (410-313-1900), Ellicott City. The first Fri.

and Sat. of each month, guides tell true tales of hauntings in the city.

May: **Maryland Sheep and Wool Festival** (410-531-3647), fairgrounds, West Friendship. Nationally known festival with sheepdog demonstrations, shearing, spinning and weaving, arts and crafts, and more than 1,000 woolly animals. **Wine in the Woods** (410-313-PARK), Merriweather Post Pavilion, Columbia. Samples of Maryland's wines, foods, and arts and crafts.

June: **Columbia Festival of the Arts** (410-715-3044), various locations in Columbia. A 2-week celebration with entertainers, children's activities, and many works of arts and crafts.

June–September: **Summer Lakefront Festival** (410-715-3000), Columbia. Music, movies, and other events every night of the week.

July–November: **Ghost Walks** (410-313-1900), Savage Mill. Every Fri. and Sat., guides tell true tales of hauntings and happenings in the historic mill.

August: **Howard County Fair** (410-442-1022), fairgrounds, West Friendship.

September: **Annual Heritage Day** (410-465-8500), Patapsco Female Institute Historic Park, Ellicott City. Relive the Victorian days when the institute was in its prime. Family games, lectures, music, and dance. **Maryland State Quarter Horse Show** (410-747-0363), fairgrounds, West Friendship. **Annual Farm Heritage Days** (410-465-8877), Mt. Pleasant Farm, Woodstock. Vintage farm equipment, antique cars and trucks, wagon rides, music, and crafts.

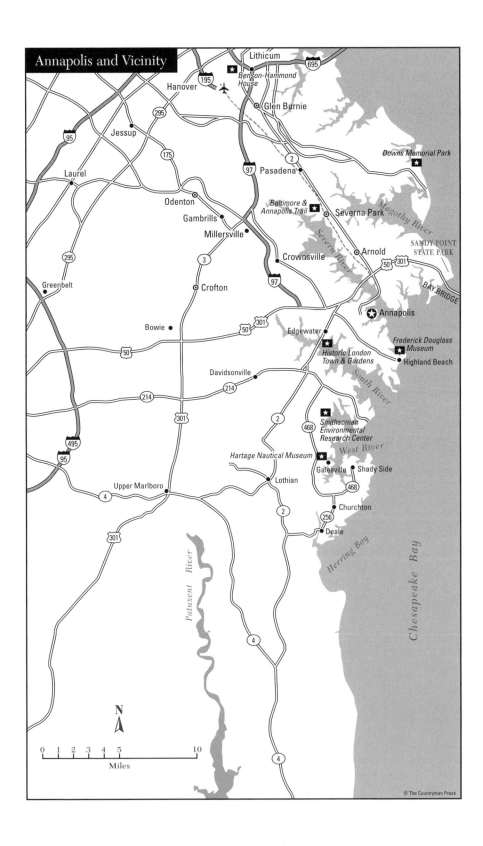

Annapolis and Vicinity

Lithicum
695
Benson-Hammond House
Hanover
195
Glen Burnie
295
Jessup
95
175
Laurel
97 Pasadena
Downs Memorial Park
Odenton
Baltimore & Annapolis Trail
Gambrills
Severna Park
Nagothy River
Millersville
Severn River
Arnold
SANDY POINT STATE PARK
295
3
Crownsville
50 301
Greenbelt
97
BAY BRIDGE
Crofton
Bowie
50 301
Annapolis
Edgewater
Frederick Douglass Museum
Historic London Town & Gardens
Highland Beach
Davidsonville
214
South River
214
301
2
Smithsonian Environmental Research Center
468
495
Hartage Nautical Museum
West River
95
Galesville Shady Side
Upper Marlboro
Lothian
468
4
2
Churchton
256
301
Deale
Patuxent River
Herring Bay
Chesapeake Bay
4
N
0 1 2 3 4 5   10
Miles
4

© The Countryman Press

ANNAPOLIS AND VICINITY

Annapolis has come to be a special place for me. It is where my wife was born and raised, and we have spent many a blithe hour or day revisiting the places of her memories. She has brought me to the woods where she and her friends would ride bikes and transport themselves to their imaginary worlds of cowboys and Indians, knights in shining armor, and the jungles of Tarzan. I have seen her favorite swimming hole, the high school she graduated from, her old family home, and the preferred haunts of her teenage years.

Although the town she grew up in has changed—former cow fields are now shopping malls, housing developments have replaced woodlands, and four-lane highways reach into previously isolated locales—much has remained the same.

The waterfront has been the focal point of activity since 1649, when a group of Puritans wandered northward from Virginia in search of religious tolerance. Within a year, their settlement along the Severn River was part of the new Anne Arundel County, named for the wife of Cecil Calvert, second Lord Baltimore. Around 1695, the town became the capital of the Maryland colony and was renamed Annapolis in honor of Princess Anne, heiress in the British monarchy.

The protected harbor soon enabled the city to become a major international shipping center, with goods flowing to and from England, Africa's west coast, and the West Indies. Prosperous merchants built their Georgian-style town houses just a block or two from the water. A stroll in the area will take you through what the federal government proclaims is "the greatest concentration of 18th-century homes anywhere in America." All four of Maryland's signers of the Declaration of Independence lived here, and three of their homes are open for public tours.

The merchants of today occupy the same storefronts as their predecessors. Except for a few changes for modern serviceability, the buildings look as they did centuries ago, while the streets they line are as narrow as they were in horse-and-buggy days. The plaque dedicated to Kunta Kinte was placed at the water-front in 1981 and commemorates the day that Alex Haley's ancestor arrived in America aboard a slave ship.

The U.S. Naval Academy was established in the mid-1800s, and its presence almost overshadows everything else in Annapolis. Much of the life in the city revolves around the academy's calendar, and the town becomes loaded with proud parents in late May when midshipmen graduate to become fully commissioned

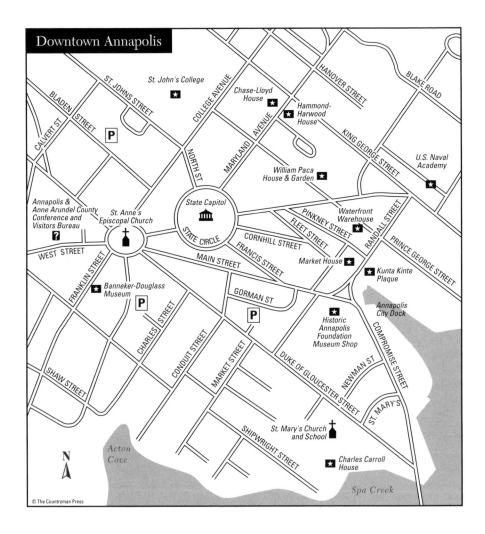

Downtown Annapolis

St. John's College
Chase-Lloyd House
Hammond-Harwood House
St. Johns Street
Bladen Street
Calvert St
College Avenue
Hanover Street
Blake Road
King George Street
U.S. Naval Academy
North St
Maryland Avenue
William Paca House & Garden
Annapolis & Anne Arundel County Conference and Visitors Bureau
St. Anne's Episcopal Church
State Capitol
Waterfront Warehouse
Pinkney Street
Fleet Street
Randall Street
Prince George Street
West Street
State Circle
Cornhill Street
Main Street
Francis Street
Market House
Kunta Kinte Plaque
Banneker-Douglass Museum
Gorman St
Annapolis City Dock
Franklin Street
Charles Street
Conduit Street
Market Street
Historic Annapolis Foundation Museum Shop
Duke of Gloucester Street
Newman St
Compromise Street
St. Mary's
Shaw Street
Shipwright Street
St. Mary's Church and School
Charles Carroll House
Acton Cove
Spa Creek
N
© The Countryman Press

naval officers. There are no professional sports teams in Annapolis, but that doesn't matter, as the academy's football, lacrosse, soccer, and other athletic endeavors provide a full roster for spectators year-round. The academy, and St. John's College—one of the country's oldest—create an atmosphere of culture, sophistication, and artistic endeavor often found lacking in towns of similar size.

The City Dock is no longer crowded with warehouses of goods waiting to be sent to foreign lands. Yet the Naval Academy, recreational boaters, and sailing schools keep the harbor so busy that the town has been dubbed "the Sailing Capital of the United States." One of the most pleasant, and absolutely free, things to do in Annapolis is to walk down Main Street and watch the glow of a morning or evening sun light up the water to highlight the scores of sailboats wending their way in and out of the harbor.

COMMUNITIES The **Eastport** neighborhood of Annapolis developed as a farming and maritime community around the time of the Civil War, and is now a vibrant residential and dining spot.

The area around **Spa Creek** is a quick walk or water-taxi ride from the City Dock and is full of marinas and popular restaurants.

Highland Beach began as the state's first incorporated African American settlement when the son of Frederick Douglass subdivided 44 acres south of Annapolis. Many of the families that live on this beautiful stretch of land along the Chesapeake Bay are descendants of the original homeowners.

Arnold, **Severna Park**, **Pasadena**, **Glen Burnie**, **Linthicum**, and other neighborhoods strung along MD 2 serve as bedroom communities for the Washington, DC/Baltimore/Annapolis metro area.

The southern portion of Anne Arundel County belies its proximity to such a large population center. Here the small towns of **Galesville**, **Deale**, and **Shady Side** still go about the business of harvesting the fruits of the Chesapeake Bay. This is the place to go if you want to catch a glimpse of the way life used to be along the bay but don't have time to visit the Eastern Shore.

GUIDANCE Information can be obtained by contacting or stopping by the **Annapolis and Anne Arundel County Conference and Visitors Bureau** (410-280-0445; www.visitannapolis.org), 26 West St., Annapolis, 21401. The adjacent parking garage offers 1-hour free parking.

There is also a **Visitors Information Booth** open seasonally in the harbormaster's office on the City Dock.

ANNAPOLIS ROW HOUSES

Inside Annapolis Magazine, available free from newspaper-type boxes, is published bimonthly with articles about life in and around the city. The free *What's Up* magazine features much of the same type of information.

GETTING THERE *By car:* **US 50/301** is the main four-lane highway access to Annapolis and connects the city with Washington, DC, and the Eastern Shore. **I-97** comes southward from Baltimore and connects with US 50/301 just west of Annapolis.

By air: The **Baltimore/Washington International Airport** (1-800-I-FLY-BWI) is located in the northwestern part of Anne Arundel County and is less than a 30-minute drive from Annapolis. Interstate highways, rail, bus, taxi, and limousine services can transport you just about anywhere you wish to go from the airport.

By bus: **Greyhound** (1-800-231-2222; www.greyhound.com) stops in Annapolis at the Department of Transportation at 308 Chinquapin Round Rd. seven times a day, 7 days a week. The **Maryland Mass Transit Administration** (410-539-5000; 1-800-543-9809; www.mtamaryland.com) operates both rail and bus routes that permit you to travel to Annapolis and northern Anne Arundel County from Baltimore, Washington, DC, and the Eastern Shore without having to drive a car.

By rail: See *By bus.*

GETTING AROUND *By car:* The streets within the Annapolis downtown/City Dock area were created in the 17th century for horse-and-buggy travel and have not changed much since then. There are many narrow, one-way streets and traffic circles, so pay attention to the signs and avoid the short rush times in the mornings and evenings. Traffic is tolerable the rest of the day.

The **Governor Ritchie Highway (MD 2)** is the local route between Annapolis and Baltimore, but you will probably make better time using **US 50** and then **I-97**. MD 2 is known as **Solomons Island Rd.** as it travels south of Annapolis. It is an efficient and scenic way to get into the southern portion of Anne Arundel County.

By bus: **Annapolis Transit** (410-263-7964) serves the city and much of the surrounding area with regular bus routes that have more than 150 stops.

By taxi: **Annapolis Cab** (410-268-0022; 410-268-1323), **Checker** (410-268-3737), **Neet-N-Kleen** (410-320-3374), and **Reliable Cab** (410-268-4714).

By water: Although it does not provide quite the extensive service that its counterparts in Baltimore do, **Jiffy Water Taxi** (410-263-0033) is still a fun and efficient way to get around to many of the waterfront areas—and to do some sightseeing along the way.

PARKING In Annapolis, parking meters are in effect 10 AM–7:30 PM daily and have only a 2-hour time limit. You are permitted to park free on residential streets, but again the limit is only 2 hours. This rule is strictly enforced.

In the downtown area, the **Gotts Court Garage** off Calvert St. or Northwest St., and the **Hillman Garage** off Main St., provide free parking for the first hour. Fees imposed hourly after that. Be sure to get your ticket stamped for a discount if you make a purchase at a participating **Park and Shop** store.

You can avoid the headache of parking downtown by leaving your car at the **Navy–Marine Corps Memorial Stadium** and taking a shuttle into the historic district. Parking is about $5, and the shuttle is about $1 (it is free on the way back).

PUBLIC RESTROOMS In Annapolis, public restrooms are located in the Harbor Masters Building at the City Dock, in the State House on State Circle, and in the Annapolis and Anne Arundel County Conference and Visitors Bureau at 26 West St.

MEDICAL EMERGENCY **Anne Arundel Medical Center** (410-481-1000), 2001 Medical Pkwy. (off Jennifer Rd.), Annapolis.
North Arundel Hospital (410-787-4000), 301 Hospital Dr., Glen Burnie.

✳ To See

COLLEGES **St. John's College** (410-263-2371; www.sjca.edu), 60 College Ave., Annapolis. In a city filled with historic sites, St. John's is one of the most historic. It traces its origins all the way back to 1696 with the founding of King William's School. McDowell Hall was built in the mid-1700s for the colonial governor and housed the entire college when given to the school in the 1800s. The exhibits in **Mitchell Art Gallery** (see *Selective Shopping*) are open to the public. Known today for its fine liberal arts education, the school has an unusual curriculum that features the study of "great books of the ages."

Also see **U.S. Naval Academy** under *To See*.

MUSEUMS

Annapolis
&. **Banneker-Douglass Museum** (410-216-6180), 84 Franklin St. Tue.–Fri. 10–3, Sat. noon–4. Free admission; donations accepted. The small museum maintains a collection of artifacts and photographs relevant to black life in Maryland, along with African and African American art, documents, and rare books. The former Mount Moriah African Methodist Episcopal Church, which houses the museum, is a Victorian Gothic structure worthy of being named a National Historic Landmark in 1973.

Waterfront Warehouse (410-267-7619; www.annapolis.org), 4 Pinkney St. Exhibits within the 1800s warehouse focus upon Maryland's early tobacco trade with Great Britain.

Galesville
Hartage Nautical Museum (410-263-4683), Hartage Boat Yard, Church Lane. Open daily. Free admission. The models, photos, and artifacts in the private museum commemorate the more than 150 years of boat designing and building that have taken place in the small Chesapeake Bay town.

THE FREDERICK DOUGLASS MUSEUM AND CULTURAL CENTER, HIGHLAND BEACH

HISTORIC HOMES

Annapolis

♿ **Hammond-Harwood House** (410-269-1714; www.hammondharwood house.org), 19 Maryland Ave. Open daily; last tour begins at 3. Small admission fee. The carved entranceway, large and elegant formal rooms, and grand scale of Matthias Hammond's 1774 home are a testament to his wealth and architect William Buckland's talent. Guided tours take guests throughout the house, furnished with 18th- and 19th-century decorative arts and Peale family portraits. Be sure to go into the gardens to enjoy the boxwoods and to appreciate the house's design and 15-inch-thick walls.

Chase-Lloyd House (410-263-2723), 22 Maryland Ave. Mon.–Sat., Mar.–Dec. Small admission fee. Guided tours of the 1769 Georgian mansion of Samuel Chase, a signer of the Declaration of Independence.

William Paca House and Garden (410-263-5553; www.annapolis.org), 186 Prince George St. Open daily, but hours are limited in Jan. and Feb. House and garden admission is $8 for adults, $7 for seniors, $5 children 6–17, or a family rate of $15. Fees are less to visit either just the house or just the garden. The restored 1760s Georgian mansion of William Paca, a signer of the Declaration of Independence, contains period furnishings. The garden, laid out around 1770, is one of the most relaxing places in the downtown area.

♿ **Charles Carroll House** (410-269-1737; www.carrollhouse.com), 107 Duke of Gloucester St. Tours by appointment. The waterfront home of Charles Carroll, the only Catholic and last surviving signer of the Declaration of Independence, was built in several stages over the course of 100 years. The partially restored home has little furniture but does retain its original flooring and many drawings from the days when George Washington and General Lafayette were regular visitors.

Highland Beach

Frederick Douglass Museum and Cultural Center (410-295-7233), 3200 Wayman Ave. Small admission fee. Many places that are open only by appointment have been left out of this book, but abolitionist/orator/publisher Frederick Douglass is such an important and inspiring figure in our nation's history that it would have been a disservice to ignore this small home and museum. Douglass's former summer home overlooks a small beach along the bay (with a grand view of the water), and contains a number of items that belonged to him. The impressive woodwork in the modest home is original, while displays and exhibits provide insight into the man, the experiences of other African Americans, and a bit of history on the local community.

Linthicum

Benson-Hammond House (410-768-9518), 7101 Aviation Blvd. Tue.–Sat. 11–3. Small admission fee. The Anne Arundel County Historical Society saved this farmhouse from destruction by the expansion of the Baltimore/Washington International Airport in the mid-1970s. Made of clay bricks from the farm, the original four rooms were constructed in the 1820s. Some of the floors are still original, and the period furnishings reflect the times when the Hammond family occupied the house, from the 1880s to the 1940s.

HISTORIC SITES **Historic London Town and Gardens** (410-222-1919; www .historiclondontown.com), 839 Londontown Rd., Edgewater. The house is closed

HISTORIC LONDON TOWN

for tours Jan.–Mar., but the gardens are open Tue.–Sat. During the rest of the year, the house is open Tue.–Sun. Admission fee for house and garden $7 adults; $5 seniors; children 7–12 are $3. The fee is less if you wish to tour just the garden or just the house. Established along the South River in 1863, London Town was a major tobacco-exporting center by the early 1700s. William Brown—carpenter, ferry master, and tavernkeeper—built his large brick home around 1760. He used convict labor to operate a tavern and inn in part of the house, and a guided tour takes visitors through the restored home, which reflects those days. Ongoing archaeological digs are uncovering more of the history of the town, and future plans call for reconstructed buildings and living-history demonstrations. A walk through the extensive gardens, filled with tree peonies, daylilies, cherry trees, bloodroot, trillium, and many shrubs, takes you down to the banks of Almshouse Creek and is the way I like to relax and end my visits here.

HISTORIC CHURCHES

Annapolis
Asbury Methodist Church (410-268-9500), 87 West St. This 1888 Gothic Revival church stands on the site of an earlier 1803 church, which was home to one of the earliest African American congregations in Annapolis.

St. Anne's Episcopal Church (410-267-9333), Church Circle. The present structure, built in the late 1800s, is the third church to stand on this site. The stained-glass window by Tiffany and Company won first prize for ecclesiastical art in the 1893 World's Fair, and the silver communion service presented to the congregation by King William III in 1695 is still in use.

St. Mary's Church (410-263-2396), Duke of Gloucester St. The Victorian Gothic church dates from the 1860s. Be sure to go inside the rib-vaulted interior to view the wonderfully hand-carved altar screen.

GUIDED TOURS

Annapolis
Maryland State House (410-974-3400), 91 State Circle. Free guided tours of the country's oldest continuously used statehouse are given every day at 11 AM and 3 PM. (Adults must show photo ID.) The only statehouse to also serve as the nation's capital, it was built between 1772 and 1779 and occupies the highest point in the city. The tour takes you into the Old Senate Chamber where Congress ratified the Treaty of Paris, giving America its independence from Great Britain.

✄ **Discover Annapolis Minibus Tours** (410-626-6000; www.discover-annapolis .com) depart from the Annapolis and Anne Arundel County Conference and Visitors Bureau at 26 West St. Adults $15; children 11–15 are $7; children 10 and under are $3; preschoolers are free. The 1-hour narrated tour of the city in air-conditioned/heated buses runs daily Apr.–Nov. and on most weekends Dec.–Mar.

& **U.S. Naval Academy** (410-263-6933; www.usna.edu or www.navyonline .com), 52 King George St. (entrance is at Gate 1), Annapolis. The grounds and visitors center are open to the public 9–5 (9–4, Jan. and Feb.); the chapel and crypt close at 4. Several tours are given daily, but times vary with the season. The first tour always begins at 10; be aware that it is quite tight to get everything in before closing time if you take the 3 PM tour. Adults $7; seniors $6; children in 1st–12th grade are $5. (Adults must show photo ID.) The 338-acre academy along the banks of the Severn River was established in 1845 and is the undergraduate college of the U.S. Navy. There is much to see here, and the best way to do it is to take one of the guided tours that originate at the Armel-Leftwich Visitor Center. You will walk through 33-acre Bancroft Hall to see a typical midshipman's dorm room, the Tripoli Monument (oldest military statue in the United States), Memorial Hall, the Academy Museum, chapel, and the crypt of Revolutionary War hero John Paul Jones. If you are here around noon on weekdays during the school year, you will witness the formation of all midshipmen as they march off to lunch.

Watermark Cruises and Annapolis Tours (410-268-7601; www.annapolis-tours .com), 48 Maryland Ave. Twice daily, Apr.–Oct.; once only on Sat., Nov.–Mar. Adults $11, students $6. I enjoyed following the colonial-garbed guide, taking in the many historic sites in the city and the U.S. Naval Academy. However, I was most entertained by the guide's explanations of phrases we use in our everyday conversations:

Put your best foot forward: Colonial women enjoyed looking at men's well-developed calves, so a man would stand with one foot in front of the other, which accentuated his calf muscle.

Mind your P's and Q's: Tavern revelers would run a tab; in order not to come up short of money, a barmaid had to keep track of who had drunk how many pints and quarts.

Crack a smile: Beeswax was used as a facial cosmetic, which you would crack if your smile was too large. Also the origin of *Mind your own beeswax.*

Not playing with a full deck: The king put a tax on playing cards, but it only applied to the ace of spades. So people would purchase a deck without that card.

Straitlaced: Respectable ladies would keep their bodices tightly laced. On the other hand, a female who wanted to show a bit of her bosom would not pull the laces quite so tight. She soon became known as a "loose" woman.

Putting on the dog: Affluent members of society would have slippers made out of the family dog's hide and fur after it died.

✳ To Do

BICYCLING

Annapolis

Annapolis has been called one of the most walker-friendly cities in the country, but it has not forgotten bicyclists. A 38-mile system of designated bike routes along city streets and grade-separated trails lets you explore on two wheels instead of four. The **City Planning and Zoning Department** (410-263-7961) can provide more information. All buses in the city have racks that will hold two bikes; there is no additional charge for this service.

The **Baltimore and Annapolis Trail** is a paved pathway that follows the route of an old railroad bed close to Governor Ritchie Hwy. (MD 2) for more than 13 miles. Although it does pass by busy streets, housing developments, and a mall or two, it can be a nice ride, especially along the least-developed 3 miles closest to Annapolis. The trail begins near the Baltimore/Washington International Airport (where it connects with another paved trail encircling the airport) and ends on MD 2 just as it enters Annapolis. More information and a map can be obtained from the **Anne Arundel County Department of Recreation and Parks** (410-222-6244).

Also see **Quiet Waters Park** and **Truxton Park** under *Parks*.

BOAT EXCURSIONS

Annapolis

Watermark Cruises (410-268-7601; 1-800-569-9622; www.watermarkcruises .com), Slip 20 at the City Dock. Narrated tours of 40 minutes (adults $8; children 3–11 are $4) and 90 minutes (adults $16; children 3–11 are $8) are provided Mar.–Dec. Days and times vary throughout the season, so call for the latest information.

🎵 **Schooner *Woodwind*** (410-263-7837), 80 Compromise St. (at the Marriott Hotel). Closed Mon. Times and rates vary. Most cruises are around $25–30 for adults and $15 for children under 12. The 74-foot sailboat, beautiful with its mahogany woodwork and chrome trim, offers daily sailing cruises. Most of the trips last about 2 hours and take in Annapolis harbor, the Naval Academy, and a portion of the Severn River. You can be passive or take a turn at the wheel or hoist the four sails.

BOAT RENTALS South River Boat Rentals (410-956-9729), located at Pier 7 Marina, Edgewater. Hourly, daily, overnight, and weekly rentals of a variety of motor- and sailboats. No experience needed. Rates range from $30 an hour up to $400 per day.

Also see **Quiet Waters Park** under *Green Space*.

FISHING Charter fishing excursions are offered by a number of outfitters in the Annapolis area. Among the many are:

Bounty Hunter (1-800-322-4039; www.bountyhuntercharter.com), 8076 Windward Key Dr., Chesapeake Beach, MD 20732. Captain Glenn James takes groups of 6–49 onto the water on the 55-foot *Bounty Hunter*.

Captain Clyde's Charters (410-974-4314; www.captclydes.com), 1058 Deep Creek Ave., Arnold. More than 20 years of fishing and cruising experience.

Mallard **Charters** (410-798-1119), 3742 Bay Dr., Edgewater. Groups of up to six can go along with Captain Steve Vierkorn on his 42-foot *Mallard.*

GOLF Dwight D. Eisenhower Golf Course (410-571-0973), Generals Hwy. (MD 178), Crownsville. You will need to reserve your tee time at this public course.

South River Golf Links (1-800-767-4837), 3451 Solomons Island Rd., Edgewater. The closest course to Annapolis is set amid a dense forest with dramatic elevation changes on the links.

☙ **Severna Park Golf Center** (410-647-8618), 1257 Governor Ritchie Hwy., Arnold. A nine-hole course and a driving range with sheltered and heated tees. Miniature golf and batting cages for the kids.

MINIATURE GOLF See **Severna Park Golf Center** under *Golf.*

KAYAKING AND CANOEING Amphibious Horizons (410-267-8742; 1-888-I-LUV-SUN; www.amphibioushorizons.com), 600 Quiet Waters Park Rd., Annapolis. Not only will the staff here rent you a kayak and instruct you on how to use it, but they can also arrange guided kayaking tours of Annapolis harbor or set up camping and B&B kayaking trips throughout the Chesapeake Bay region.

SAILING Sunsail Sailing Vacations (1-800-327-2276; www.sunsail.com), 980 Awald Rd., Suite 302, Annapolis. The largest charter-boat company in the world, with operations as far flung as Turkey and Tahiti, offers bareboat and crewed charters on which you choose the time, pace, and destination.

SAILING LESSONS

Annapolis
☙ **Annapolis Sailing School** (410-267-7205; 1-800-638-9192; www.annapolissailing.com), 601 6th St. One of the best-respected institutions of sailing knowledge, Annapolis Sailing is also the oldest and largest sailing school in the country. Courses of various duration are designed for basic, cruising, and advanced sailing, and for those interested in preparing for a bareboat charter or coastal navigation and piloting. There are also classes for children 5–15 years aboard 12- to 14-foot sailing dinghies.

AYS Charters and Sailing School (410-267-9151), 7416 Edgewood Rd. Charter trips (captained or bareboat) and sailing instructions on 28- to 42-foot sailboats. Charter certification courses are offered every weekend.

Womanship, Inc. (1-800-342-9295; www.womanship.com), 137 Conduit St. Sailing instruction taught by and for women. Their courses are for novice to advanced sailors. I like their motto: "Nobody yells!"

Annapolis Powerboat School (410-267-7205; www.annapolispowerboat.com), 601 6th St. Several different hands-on, on-the-water classes are offered. One of the most popular is the 5-day instruction course, which cruises around the bay, enabling you to spend evenings at various waterfront inns.

SKATING **Dahlgren Hall Ice Rink** (410-293-2350; www.usna.edu/NAFPRODV/Icerink), U.S. Naval Academy, 52 King George St. (entrance is at Gate 1), Annapolis. Adults will need a photo ID. Adults $5, children $4, skate rental $2.50. The season usually begins by mid-October.

Also see **Quiet Waters Park** under *Parks.*

SWIMMING See *Tennis* and **Truxton Park** under *Green Space*.

TENNIS The **Anne Arundel County Recreation and Parks Department** (410-222-7300), 1 Harry S. Truman Pkwy., oversees more than 30 regional parks with tennis courts open to the public on a first-come, first-served basis, and four parks with swimming available to the general public. Contact them for more information.

Also see **Truxton Park** under *Green Space.*

WALKING TOURS Annapolis boasts more than 35 homes and sites of historical significance within a few blocks of one another in the downtown/City Dock area of the city. These sites are described in the *Annapolis and Anne Arundel County Visitors Guide*, which is available from the Annapolis and Anne Arundel County Conference and Visitors Bureau. Pick up a copy and take an easy stroll into the city's past.

✷ Green Space

BEACHES See the **Sandy Point State Park** sidebar on page 257.

GARDENS ♿ **Helen Avalynne Tawes Garden** (410-260-8189), next to the Tawes State Office Building on Taylor Ave., Annapolis. Open daily dawn–dusk. Expect to see a number of state employees escaping bureaucratic headaches when you walk through this 6-acre park. One of the nicest free city botanical gardens on the East Coast, it has sections representing Eastern Shore habitats, mountain forestland, and streamside environments. An abundance of birds and small wildlife make their home in the garden.

PARKS

Annapolis

✐ ♿ **Quiet Waters Park** (410-222-1777), 600 Quiet Waters Park Rd. Open 7 AM–dusk; closed Tue. This 336-acre park is easily accessed from Bay Ridge Rd. in the Eastport neighborhood of the city and has been called the finest county-operated park in the state. It is bordered by Harness Creek and the South River, so much of the recreational emphasis is on water sports, with a variety of boats for rent from spring through fall. There are also more than 6 miles of hiking/biking trails through wetlands and shoreline, picnic facilities, a visitors center (with two art galleries), a large playground, and even an outdoor ice rink open during the colder months. A great place to make a quick escape from the city traffic and noise.

✄ **Truxton Park** (410-263-7958), Hilltop Lane. Only 77 acres in size, the park is a city playground with tennis and basketball courts, a swimming pool, bike routes, and picnic facilities. Small fee for swimming.

Pasadena

Downs Memorial Park (410-222-6230), Johns Down Loop. Small parking fee. A small shoreline park that offers biking opportunities, picnicking, interpretive programs, and outdoor concerts.

WALKS ✄ **Smithsonian Environmental Research Center** (443-482-2200), 647 Contees Wharf Rd., Edgewater. An easy pathway works its way to a re-created Piscataway Indian village, by dairy farm implements and exhibits about tobacco plantations, and across a marsh. A great escape spot from noisy highways and cities.

✳ Lodging

Annapolis Accommodations, Inc. (443-482-2200; 1-800-715-1000; www .stayannapolis.com), 41 Maryland Ave., Annapolis, 21401. Represents hotels, motels, inns, and B&Bs in and around Annapolis and will make recommendations and reservations based upon your needs.

MOTELS AND HOTELS

Downtown and close to downtown, 21401

🐾 ♿ **Loews Annapolis Hotel** (410-263-7777; 1-800-23-LOEWS; www .loewsannapolis.com), 126 West St. One of the closest hotels to the waterfront and the City Dock. Large, luxurious rooms and an attentive staff

---

✄ ♿ **Sandy Point State Park** (410-974-2149), 800 Revell Hwy. (off US 50/301), Annapolis. Open year-round for day use. Less than 10 miles northeast of Annapolis, the park's beaches (guarded Memorial Day–Labor Day) are considered among the finest along the Chesapeake Bay and are favored by local families. Rowboats and motorboats are available for rent, and close to 5 miles of trails course through woodland and marsh. The varied habitat makes for good bird-watching and, being on the Atlantic Flyway, attracts a large number of migratory waterfowl. Some facilities are handicapped-accessible.

Of the more than 4,600 miles of shoreline around the bay, less than 2 percent is accessible to the public; the rest is privately owned—a fact that is almost impossible to accept. Maybe we should utter a word of thanks that the state was wise enough to preserve the open land of Sandy Point in the 1950s.

have enabled the Loews Annapolis to be designated a AAA four-diamond hotel for more than a decade. The common areas are bright and airy. Pets permitted. $125–299.

☛ ♿ **Annapolis Marriott Waterfront Hotel** (410-268-7555; 1-800-336-0072; www.annapolismarriott .com), 80 Compromise St. The Annapolis location of this national chain is the city's only downtown hotel to be located directly on the water. Pets permitted. $240–699.

♿ **O'Callaghan Hotel Annapolis** (410-263-7700; www.ocallaghanhotels -us.com), 174 West St., Annapolis. Located in the downtown area, it is within walking distance of the Naval Academy and City Dock. The convenient location is matched by the attentive service and luxurious style. $280–400; additional parking fee adds about $20 per overnight/day stay.

Note: Many more hotels and motels are located near the Baltimore/Washington International Airport and along many state roads between Annapolis and Baltimore. Among the lower-cost national chains are **Days Inn** (410-224-4317; 1-800-544-8313; www .daysinn.com); **Courtyard by Marriott** (410-266-1555; 1-888-236-2427; www.courtyard.com); and **Microtel** (410-865-7500; www.microtelinn .com). **The Comfort Suites** (410-691-1000; 1-800-228-5150) at 815 Elkridge Landing Rd. in Linthicum is within a couple of minutes' drive of the airport. $119–199.

INNS

Downtown, 21401
♿ **Gibson's Lodgings** (410-268-5555; 1-877-330-0057; www.gibsons lodgings.com), 110 Prince George St.

Features a variety of guest rooms in two historic homes and another structure built in 1988. Close to most of the downtown/City Dock attractions. $89–169.

Scotlaur Inn (410-269-6737; www .scotlaurinn.com), 165 Main St. Wallpaper, quilts on metal beds, throw rugs, and windows looking onto the bustle of Main St. give the 10 rooms above Chick and Ruth's Deli (see *Eating Out*) the feel of a neighborhood hotel or tourist home from the turn of the 20th century. Central heating and air-conditioning. $80–150.

Historic Inns of Annapolis (410-263-2641; 1-800-847-8882; www .annapolisinns.com.), 58 State Capital Circle. The Historic Inns are actually three inns operated under the same management group. The **Governor Calvert House**, facing the State Capitol, was built in 1727 for the colonial governor. The **Robert Johnson House**, also facing the capitol building, was constructed as a private residence in 1765. The **Maryland Inn**, on State Circle, is the only one of the three that was originally built to cater to travelers. The Treaty of Paris restaurant (see *Dining Out*) downstairs has been serving patrons for more than 200 years. Each inn offers a wide variety of accommodations, with many different amenities. $159–249.

BED & BREAKFASTS

Downtown, 21401
✐ **Flag House Inn** (410-280-2721; 1-800-437-4825; www.flaghouseinn .com), 26 Randall St. The location couldn't be any better. The City Dock and the main Naval Academy gate are only one block away, and the B&B has private off-street parking. All six guest

rooms in the restored 1870 Victorian home have a private bath, TV, and air-conditioning. There were so many things I enjoyed about my stay here: the two-sided fireplace that heated the living and dining rooms; the front porch to lazily sit on and watch the rest of Annapolis hurry by; and Charlotte and Bill Schmickle's large English breakfast. The guests I shared breakfast with came from many corners of the globe. Children over 10 welcome. $120–250.

Randall House (410-263-4970; www.randallhousebandb.com), 30 Randall St. Just a couple of doors down from the Flag House Inn (see above), the Randall House shares the same great location. Each guest room in the mid-1800s house has a private bath; the back room has a deck overlooking the garden. $140–180.

✂ **Chez Amis** (410-263-6631; 1-888-224-6455; www.chezamis.com), 85 East St. Chez Amis was a corner grocery store when the 20th century began and, as the B&B home of Don and Mickie Deline, retains the original Georgia pine floors, tin ceiling, and an oak display counter. All rooms have private bath, TV, and down comforters on the brass beds. Children over 10 welcome. $150–180.

The Annapolis Inn (410-295-5200; www.annapolisinn.com), 144 Prince George St. Alex DeVivo and Joseph Lespier have turned the home of Thomas Jefferson's physician into the modern personification of pampering and luxury. Crystal chandeliers, etched-glass shower and pocket doors, sumptuous furniture, cedar guest closets, and a heatable tumbled marble bathroom floor are just a few of the niceties. Yet they have kept much of the old, such as original crown moldings and medallions, and the horsehair plaster on the walls. $310–475.

THE MARYLAND INN IN ANNAPOLIS

Two-O-One (410-268-8053; www
.201bb.com), 201 Prince George St.
All of the guest quarters in this Georgian home have four-poster beds and
are elegantly furnished, but I am particularly smitten by the Crow's Nest
Suite on the third floor. There is just
something about the large tiles and
woodwork in the bathroom that provides a rich and sensuous experience.
The large gardens are a nice respite
from the noise of the city. Off-street
parking. $170–220.

1908 William Page Inn (1-800-364-
4160; www.williampageinn.com), 8
Martin St. Native Annapolitan Robert
Zuchelli has been operating his B&B
for more than 15 years and is one of
the most composed hosts I have met.
He personally redesigned and refurbished the 1908 home and has created
a place of soothing elegance. The
home is on a quiet cross street that
creates the illusion of being in a much
smaller town. Off-street parking.
$140–270.

55 East (410-295-0202; www.55east
.com), 55 East St. Matt and Tricia
Herban have renovated their 1864
home (originally a grocery store) and
decorated it with fabulous heirlooms
and furnishings, such as Matt's grandfather's Las Cruces desk and spectacular pieces from China in the sitting
room. However, what I remember
most from my visit are the luscious
corn and pecan waffles served at
breakfast. All three guest rooms have
a private bath and sitting area.
$185–225.

Gatehouse B&B (410-280-0024;
www.gatehousebb.com), 249 Hanover
St. The Georgian-style B&B home of
Carol and Jim Woller overlooks the
Naval Academy and is furnished in
period reproductions. Most rooms

have a private bath; all come with
fresh flowers to brighten the day, and
soft robes for comfortable lounging.
Breakfasts are wonderful variations on
old standards, such as cream cheese
and ice cream French toast or Italian-
style quiche. $180–285.

Georgian House (410-263-5618;
1-800-557-2068; www.georgianhouse
.com), 170 Duke of Gloucester St.
Innkeeper Sandy Mayer's breakfasts
of fresh breads and hot entrées are
reason enough to stay here. There is
also her masterful decorating of the
guest rooms and common areas of the
1747 home. $175–220.

Close to downtown, 21401
❦ ✑ **The Barn on Howard's Cove**
(410-571-9511; www.bnbweb.com/
howards-cove.html), 500 Wilson Rd.
Just minutes away, but seemingly a
world apart, from the activity of
downtown, Libbie and Graham
Gutsche have been quietly operating
their B&B for two decades. You
would never know that the house,
with two guest suites—each with private bath and entrance—was the barn
for a mid-1800s farm. Porches, decks,
and large windows overlook a quiet
cove of the Severn River. Canoes and
a kayak are available to explore the
waterway, and a full breakfast will
give you the energy to do so. Children
welcome. $125.

❦ ✿ **Meadow Gardens** (410-224-
2729; www.bnbweb.com/meadow
gardens/index), 504 Wilson Rd. There
is only one guest suite in this modern
home B&B operated by the daughter
of the folks at the adjacent Barn on
Howard's Cove (see above). This
means you will not only have her
undivided attention, but also have
access to the boats and water at the
Barn, as well as a swimming pool and

hot tub. The sunroom, where an ample breakfast is often served, overlooks the 6.5 acres of gardens and meadows. Pets welcome. $95.

Eastport neighborhood of Annapolis, 21403

The Inn at Spa Creek (410-263-8866; www.innatspacreek.com), 417 Severn Ave. This very contemporary home was a bachelor's party house until Rick and Jeanne Brown made it a B&B in the late 1990s. The open floor plan, flowing from one room to the next, still lends itself to socializing—which fits in with the milieu of the neighborhood. Jeanne says that she lives in "the Key West of Annapolis." I like the huge windows that let you look out on the action. $150–250.

VACATION RENTALS Leisure Management, LLC (410-224-3257; www.leisuremanagementllc.com), 2007 Tidewater Colony Dr., #1A, Annapolis, 21401. If you will be in the area with a large group or family for an extended period, you might consider contacting these folks, who operate a four-bedroom, two-and-a-half-bath modern house in the Eastport neighborhood. A group of eight can rent the entire house for $1,400 for a 3-day weekend. Weekly and monthly rentals also available.

CAMPING ❀ Capital KOA (410-923-2771), 768 Cecil Ave., Millersville, 21108. Late Mar.–Nov. 1. This is the closest campground to Annapolis, and one of the closest to Washington, DC. Free daily shuttle to DC Transit. Expect the many amenities found in this national chain: pool, dump station, playground. Pets permitted.

❀ Duncan's Family Campground (410-741-9558; 1-800-222-2086), 5381

Sands Rd., Lothian, 20711. Open year-round; limited facilities in winter. Located in the southern part of Anne Arundel County, close to the bay and Patuxent River Park. Free transportation to Washington, DC, metro services. Pool, miniature golf, tent sites. Small pets permitted.

✳ Where to Eat

DINING OUT

Annapolis

Ristorante Piccola Roma (410-268-7898), 200 Main St. Silvana Recine left her homeland more than 30 years ago, but her cooking shows that her Roman roots remain strong. All of the dishes served here are from her recipes, with many adapted to make use of local products. I started my meal with the crab, prosciutto, and artichoke in a cream sauce. The salmon with orzo, sun-dried tomatoes, and zucchini baked in parchment paper may be the most succulent fish I've had. Pasta dishes range $16–21; other selections are $17–29. In true Romanesque style, salad is served after the entrée. Save room for the ever-changing selection of desserts. The wait staff are friendly, knowledgeable about the extensive wine list, and attentive. When time allows, Silvana mingles with her guests. Without a doubt, this is currently my favorite Annapolis restaurant.

Treaty of Paris (410-216-6340), Church Circle and Main St. (inside the Maryland Inn). Nouveau French cuisine served within the gracefully restored inn. A lunch buffet is available, but you will certainly enjoy the food—and appreciate the kitchen's abilities—more if you order from the menu. Entrées $18–27.

Yin Yankee Café (410-268-8703; www.yinyankee.com), 105 Main St. Brings the foods of the Pacific Rim to Annapolis's City Dock area. Lots of seafood and vegetable dishes. Expect to pay about $25–30 per person for a meal.

Close to downtown

🍴 ♿ **Les Folies** (410-573-0970), 2552 Riva Rd. It sometimes seems like you have to take out a second mortgage to enjoy a meal at a good French restaurant. Not at Les Folies. Manager Alain Matrat and chef Jean-Claude Galan, both born in France, provide a Parisian atmosphere and quality food at rational prices. The recipes of the ever-evolving menu reflect distinct regions of France: Paris, Gascony, Provence, Alsace, Lyon, and others. Expect an appetizer of crabmeat custard with lobster sauce on one visit, and garlic sausage over lentil salad on another. The fish and pasta dishes are some of the most popular entrées, and, of course, you cannot leave with having one of the special desserts. My second favorite Annapolis dining spot. Entrées $14–24.

Northwood's (410-268-2609), 609 Melvin Ave. Open daily for dinner only. The place that couples come to when they are looking for a romantic spot. The menu has a definite Mediterranean flavor, so start the meal with a *zuppa de pesce* and continue with a seafood bisque. Entrées range $20–26.

Eastport neighborhood of Annapolis

🍴 **Boatyard Bar and Grill** (410-216-6206; www.boatyardbarandgrill.com), 400 4th St. Much local color here, as this is where the area's resident sailors, boaters, fishermen, and boat-yard workers hang out. Open daily for lunch and dinner; also serves breakfast on weekends. The menu has influences from the Chesapeake Bay, Caribbean, and Key West. Dressings and soups are made from scratch. Standouts include crab dishes, conch fritters, jerk chicken, Key West steamed shrimp, and daily specials. Entrées $11–22. Drinks by the pint.

Carrol's Creek (410-263-8102; www.carrolscreek.com), 410 Severn Ave. Steaks and other meats are available at this waterfront restaurant, but it would be a mistake not to go for the seafood. The cream of crab soup is thick and rich, but you might also want to try the curried zucchini and shrimp soup. The crabcakes (market price) are delicious, as is the rockfish served over Parmesan polenta. Most entrées run $14–30.

EATING OUT

Annapolis
McGarvey's Saloon and Oyster Bar (410-263-5700; www.mcgarveys.net), 8 Market Space. Open for lunch and dinner Mon.–Sat.; Sunday brunch at 10. The festive, publike atmosphere and location at the City Dock has made McGarvey's a popular eatery since it opened in 1975. Obviously, oysters prepared many different ways are a specialty, but there is also light fare ($4.95–8.95), sandwiches ($6.95–11.95), and a few entrées such as filet mignon. The rich wood-and-brick interior created a pleasant place to enjoy the fillet béarnaise sandwich I ordered. Entrées to $29.95.

🍴 **Buddy's Crabs and Ribs** (410-626-1100; www.buddysonline.com), 100 Main St. Open for lunch and dinner daily. A typical crab house, and close to the City Dock. Many people choose the buffet bar, but you will probably be more satisfied with ordering from the menu. Entrées $8.99–37.99.

49 West Coffeehouse (410-626-9796; www.49westcoffeehouse.com), 49 West St. Open daily for breakfast, lunch, and dinner. I thought long and hard on how to describe this place to you. I came up with: It is a funky-chic place that appeals to the sophisticated beatnik/vegetarian meat eater/yuppie/coffee lover in all of us. The interior is a funky blend of an old brick wall on one side, a 1950s dropped acoustic tile ceiling above, and a plaster wall covered in artwork for sale on the other side.

The menu is as varied. Baked goods, a Belgian waffle ($5.95), quiche ($7.25), and egg dishes ($4.95) for breakfast. Sandwiches range from melted ham and cheese ($7) to vegetarian burgers with soy cheese ($7.50). Entrées served after 6 PM include crab scampi over pasta ($14.95) and honey-garlic pork ($15.95). Everything is well prepared.

Galway Bay (410-263-8333; www.galwaybayannapolis.com), 61–63 Maryland Ave. Open daily for lunch and dinner. Authentic Irish food prepared according to the recipes of owner Michael Galway, who left his native Kilkenny in southeast Ireland in 1986. My potato-leek soup served with hearty baked bread was creamy and tasty, while the seafood pie, crammed with salmon, shrimp, crabmeat, scallops, and clams, was a nice variation on the traditional shepherd's pie. Steak, chicken, and other seafood ($14.95–19.95) prepared the Irish way are also available. Bread pudding, rhubarb and strawberry tart, and Irish whiskey cake are just a few of the desserts ($2.95–5.95).

✍ ♿ **Chick and Ruth's Deli** (410-269-6737; www.chickandruths.com), 165 Main St. Open daily for breakfast, lunch, and dinner. Chick and Ruth have been gone for some time now, but their family continues to serve up solid deli and diner food. A long menu complete with 16 kinds of omelets ensures that this is the place to start your day. As a bonus, you can join the staff as they recite the Pledge of Allegiance each morning. Entrées $4.50–15.95.

Annapolis Gourmet (410-263-6115), 116 Annapolis St. The Leano family has been in the deli business for more than 65 years, so they know a thing or two about making sandwiches, soups, and salads. The chicken salad has become a local tradition. Entrées $4–14.

✍ **Middleton Tavern** (410-263-3323; www.middletontavern.com), 2 Market Space. Open daily for lunch and dinner. Traditional American/Maryland cuisine inside the historic tavern on the City Dock. Many seafood items from the raw bar and appetizer menu. Pasta, sandwiches, meats, and seafood entrées. Broiled rockfish with lemon butter ($27.95) is a house specialty. Other entrées are $16.95–33.95.

Eastport neighborhood of Annapolis
The Main Ingredient Café (410-626-0388; www.themaingredient.com), 914 Bay Bridge Rd. (at Georgetown Plaza). Open for breakfast, lunch, and dinner. It is in a strip mall, but the sunlight and bright decor can help you overlook that fact. The food will, too; there is a light touch on everything, even the fried onion rings ($2.99) and the Thai chicken quesadilla ($10). Lots of healthy items like applewood-smoked

salmon ($9), bruschetta ($9), and three-bean chili ($3.99). Heartier appetites might go for the fish-and-chips ($13), meat loaf ($15), or pesto shrimp ($20).

Forest Plaza Shopping Center

Jalapeños (410-266-7580; www.jalapenosonline.com), 85 Forest Dr. Open for lunch Mon.–Fri.; dinner daily. Gonzalo Fernandez and Alberto Serranco serve up foods from Spain and Mexico, and you can choose items from either or both countries in one meal. A house favorite is the *Gambas alajillo*—shrimp sautéed in olive oil, garlic, tomatoes, and dry sherry. Paella, enchiladas, and other entrées $9.95–19.95.

CRABS *⚓* **Cantler's Riverside Inn** (410-757-1311; www.cantlers.com), 458 Forest Beach Rd., near Annapolis. Open daily for lunch and dinner. Cantler's own boats bring the seafood in daily, so you know it is fresh. Many B&B owners directed me to this scenic Mill Creek spot when I inquired about the best place in Annapolis for steamed hard-shell crabs (market price). There are also many types of fresh fish and meat entrées to choose from. $8.95–22.95.

Mike's Bar and Crab House (410-956-2784; www.mikescrabhouse.com), 3030 Old Riva Rd., Edgewater. On the South River waterfront, Mike's serves steamed crabs by the dozen or by the bushel (market price). Other seafood available for lunch and dinner ($10.95–29.95). Takes on a festive atmosphere on the outside deck every day in summer, and has live music on Fri. night.

⚓ **Skipper's Pier** (410-867-7110; www.skipperspier.com), 6158 Drum

CHICK AND RUTH'S DELI IS A LOCAL INSTITUTION.

Point Rd., Deale. A favorite with recreational Chesapeake Bay boaters who come here to enjoy steamed crabs (market price) on the waterfront. Light fare and full entrée choices are also available. $8.95–28.95.

COFFEE BARS

Annapolis

The Pony Espresso (410-280-6160), 33½ West St. Baked goods and specialty coffees just across the street from the Annapolis and Anne Arundel County Conference and Visitors Bureau.

Seattle Coffee Company (410-263-9747), 71 Maryland Ave. Enjoy a cappuccino as you sit on the window couch watching the rest of Annapolis walk by.

Also see **49 West Coffeehouse** under *Eating Out*.

SNACKS AND GOODIES

Annapolis

✿ **Fudge Kitchen** (1-800-898-9701), 112 Main St. They make all of their items—fudge, cookies, peanut brittle, lemonade, and more—from scratch, and you can watch them do it.

✿ **Storm Brothers Ice Cream Factory** (410-263-3376), 130 Dock St. A wide variety of flavors in a family-owned business at the waterfront.

Great Harvest Bread Co. (410-268-4662; www.greatharvest.com), 208 Ridgely Ave. Closed Sun. and Mon. The owners and employees are up and working early in the morning to deliver more than a dozen types of baked goodies (the caramel chip scones are great!) by 7 AM and at least two dozen varieties of bread by 9 AM. (Not all are available each day.) Great Harvest grinds its own wheat fresh every day.

✳ Entertainment

DANCE ♿ **Ballet Theatre of Maryland** (410-263-8289; www.btmballet.org), 801 Chase St., Annapolis. The professional troupe's season usually runs from October into April and consists of at least four different programs. The ballet has been offering live music along with its dance performances during a few of its presentations over the last few seasons.

FILM

Annapolis

Crown Theaters of Annapolis (410-224-1145), 2474 Solomons Island Rd., and **Annapolis Mall XI** (410-571-2796), Annapolis Mall, show first-run movies.

The Annapolis Cinema Grill (410-266-8437), Forest Plaza, is the place to head if you miss a flick first time around. The price is lower, and you can have lunch or dinner with the movie.

MUSIC

Annapolis

Annapolis Opera (410-267-8135; www.annapolisopera.com), Maryland Hall for Arts, 801 Chase St. The season runs from September into April. There are usually two or three full operas (with electronic English subtitles) and several other concerts during the season. *La Bohème* and *Don Giovanni* are a couple of past productions.

Annapolis Symphony Orchestra (410-269-1132; www.mdhallarts.org/ASO.html), 801 Chase St. The city's professional music organization offers classical, pops, family, and chamber music presentations throughout the year.

Annapolis

Rams Head Tavern and Fordham Brewing Company (410-268-4545; www.ramsheadtavern.com), 33 West St. Open daily. You can enjoy a good meal, a Fordham microbrew, and a nationally known act all in the same location. Past performers have included Arlo Guthrie, Livingston Taylor, Richie Havens, José Feliciano, Spyro Gyra, and Leon Redbone. Dinner/show combos are available.

King of France Tavern (410-216-6340), inside the Maryland Inn. The live music presented each weekend usually falls within the jazz or big-band genre.

THEATERS

Annapolis

Annapolis Summer Garden Theatre (410-268-9212; www .summergarden.com), 143 Compromise St. Comedies and musicals are presented in an outdoor setting Thu.–Sun. in the evening Memorial Day–Labor Day.

Colonial Players (410-263-0533), 108 East St. This acting troupe's season usually runs from September into April. This is a great place to see theatrical works that are well known but not presented that often on stage. Past productions have included *The Trip to Bountiful, Hay Fever,* and *To Gillian on Her 37th Birthday.*

✳ Selective Shopping

ANTIQUES

Annapolis

Bon Vivant (410-263-9651; www .bonvivantantiques.com), 104 Annapolis St. Furniture, glassware, dolls, toys, plus designer pieces by local artists.

Hobson's Choice Antiques (410-280-2206), 58 Maryland Ave. Closed Tue. Chinese porcelain, silver, 18th- and 19th-century furniture, along with nautical items and Lionel trains.

ART GALLERIES

Annapolis/downtown/City Dock

✐ **Mitchell Art Gallery** (410-626-2556; www.sjca.edu/main.html), 60 College Ave. Closed Mon. St. John's College's art gallery features changing exhibits of high-quality works in a variety of media. Also sponsors tours, lectures, and children's programs.

Annapolis Marine Art Gallery (410-263-4100; www.annapolismarine art.com), 110 Dock St. Open daily. Befitting the Sailing Capital of the World, the gallery presents only marine art—paintings, graphics, ship models, scrimshaw, and more—produced by living artists.

La Petite Galerie (410-258-2425), 39 Maryland Ave. Closed Mon. and Tue. Works by Chinese, French-Russian, American, and local artists.

Maria's Picture Place (410-263-8282), 45 Maryland Ave. Maria's lays claim to having the largest selection of Annapolis scenes anywhere.

Dawson Gallery (410-269-1299), 44 Maryland Ave. Mon.–Sat. and some Sundays. Most commercial galleries emphasize works by contemporary artists, but you will find the paintings of 19th- and early-20th-century American and European artists in the Dawson Gallery.

Aurora Gallery (410-263-9150), 67 Maryland Ave. Changing exhibits by local and regional artisans in a variety of styles and media.

Maryland Federation of Art Gallery on the Circle (410-268-4566), 18 State St. Closed Mon. The exhibits in all media by local and regional artists change monthly in the nonprofit organization's gallery. A good place to catch rising or promising artists early in their career.

McBride Gallery (410-267-7077; www.mcbridegallery.org), 215 Main St. Open daily. The city's largest gallery contains seven rooms of landscapes, wildlife paintings, and nautical scenes.

ArtFX (410-990-4540), 45 West St. Closed Mon. A cooperative venture of approximately 25 artists, so you will find items in just about every medium possible. You can meet a new featured artist on the first Sunday of every month 6–9 PM.

BOOKSTORES & U.S. Naval Institute Bookstore

(410-293-2108; www.usni.org), Preble Hall, U.S. Naval Academy, 52 King George St. (entrance is at Gate 1), Annapolis. The number of books pertaining to seamanship and naval history, American and worldwide, is just short of phenomenal.

CRAFTS

Annapolis/downtown/City Dock
League of Maryland Craftsmen (410-626-1277), 216 Main St. Closed Tue. This outlet for the statewide organization is where you will find the output of some of the state's finest artists and craftspeople. Works are done in watercolor, oils, glass, pottery, metal, and textiles.

♂ **Annapolis Pottery** (410-268-6153), 40 State St. Owners Bill and Genevieve McWilliams, along with

other potters, so enjoy sharing their craft with others that they have installed benches inside their studio so that you can watch them create various items. They are happy to converse with you and are especially friendly to inquisitive children.

MALLS

Annapolis
Annapolis Harbour Center (410-266-5857; www.lernerenterprises.com), US 50 Exit 22. Contains a Barnes & Noble bookstore, other national chains, and a multiplex.

Westfield Shoppingtown Annapolis (410-266-5432; www.shoppingtown.com), 2002 Annapolis Mall. Located 4 miles from downtown.

Hanover
Arundel Mills (410-540-5110; www.millscorp.com), at the intersection of I-295 and MD 100 (near the Baltimore/Washington International Airport). The area's largest mall attracts shoppers from Baltimore, Annapolis, and Washington, DC.

SPECIAL SHOPS

Annapolis
Historic Annapolis Foundation Museum Store (410-268-5576; 1-800-639-9153), 77 Main St. This little shop gets my vote as the best place to obtain mementos of your visit to the area. In addition to pottery, jewelry, glassware, and books, the store offers many items that relate to the history of Annapolis.

Annapolis Treasure Company (410-263-7074), 161 Main St. A full line of nautical gifts such as ship models, brass bells, lanterns, and nautical jewelry.

Plat du Jour (410-269-1499; www
.platdujour.com), 210 Main St. You
would have to travel to Italy or
France to find the selection of linens,
glassware, ceramics, and artwork that
you can purchase here.

FARMER'S MARKETS **Anne Arundel
County Farmer's Market** (410-570-
3646), Riva Rd. and Harry S. Truman
Pkwy., Annapolis. Apr.–early Dec.
Usually on Sat. 7–noon and Thur. 3–6.
Days and hours may change late in
the season.

Deale Farmer's Market (410-570-
3646), Deale–Churchton Rd., Deale.
Produce dealers bring their wares to
the Cedar Grove Methodist Church
parking lot in the southern part of
Anne Arundel County on Thu. 4–7,
July–Oct.

Piney Orchard Farmer's Market
(410-672-4273), Stream Valley Rd.
(off MD 170), Odenton. Wed. 2–6:30,
June–Oct.

Severna Park Farmer's Market
(410-841-5770), MD 2 and Jones Station Rd., Severna Park. Look for fresh
fruits and vegetables Sat. 8–noon from
mid-April through late November.

PICK-YOUR-OWN PRODUCE FARMS
Mt. Airy U-Pick (410-798-0838), 832
Mt. Airy Rd., Davidsonville. Planters
Jim and Tim Hopkins request that
you call first before heading out to
choose your own strawberries from
mid-May through mid-June.

✳ Special Events

April: **Maritime Heritage Festival**
(410-268-7676; www.aaaccc.org),
Annapolis City Dock. Crafts, entertainment, historic home and site
tours, lots of boats and maritime-

history displays. **County Fair Craft
Show** (410-923-3400; www.aacounty
fair.org), fairgrounds, Crownsville.
More than 100 artists and crafts-
people show their wares. **The Great
Kite Fly** (410-626-2530; www.shca
.edu), St. John's College, Annapolis.
Kite-flying contests, ballets, and
stunts. **Annual Wildlife Art Show
and Sale** (301-497-5789), Patuxent
Research Refuge, National Wildlife
Visitor Center.

May: **Annual Bay Bridge Walk**
(1-877-BAY-SPAN). The one day out
of the year that the public is permitted to walk the 4.3-mile US 50/301
bridge across the bay. **Annual Open
House for Nature** (443-482-2218),
Smithsonian Environmental Research
Center, Edgewater. Guided riverboat
and canoe trips, forest canopy visits,
hayrides, face painting, seining, crabbing, and checking out the oyster
reefs.

June–August: **Concerts at Banneker-
Douglass Museum** (410-366-5008),
Annapolis. Free live concerts on Thu.
night by young musicians from the
Heifetz International Music Institute.

August: **Rotary Crab Feast** (410-
841-2841; www.annapolisrotary.com),
Annapolis. Thought to be the largest
crab feast in the world. So many
people attend that it is held in the
U.S. Navy–Marine Corps Stadium.
Kunta Kinte Celebration (410-349-
0338; www.kuntakinte.org), Annapolis.
A 2-day celebration of African American history, arts, and entertainment.
Children's tent and ethnic foods.

September: **Anne Arundel County
Fair** (410-923-3400; www.aacounty
fair.org), fairgrounds, Crownsville.
Annual Maryland Seafood Festival
(410-268-7862; www.mdseafood
festival.com), Sandy Point State Park,

⚓ **Maryland Renaissance Festival** (410-266-7304; 1-800-296-7304; www .rennfest.com), on Crownsville Rd. in Crownsville. Held every weekend late Aug.–late Oct. Adults $17; seniors $15; children 7–15 are $8; special prices for multiday visits. Go back in time to 16th-century England and watch knights in armor joust on horseback, eat a turkey leg so big that it would have choked even King Henry, and watch comedies and tragedies unfold on 10 theatrical stages. The atmosphere of this festival is one of grand celebration. Visitors, as well as volunteers, show up in period dress and never break character for a moment. Many children's activities and much food and music from those merry old days.

Annapolis. Arts and crafts, petting zoo, beach golf, and lots of other family-oriented activities in addition to mounds of Chesapeake Bay seafood prepared various ways. **USNA Artists Authors Fair** (410-263-6933; www.navyonline.com), U.S. Naval Academy, Annapolis. Meet authors, craftspeople, and artists whose works pertain to the navy, Annapolis, and the Chesapeake Bay. **Deale Bluegrass Festival and Car Show** (410-867-6707), Herrington Harbor North Marina, Deale.

October: **United States Sailboat Show and United States Powerboat Show** (410-268-8828; www .usboat.com), Annapolis City Dock. These shows run back to back over two weekends and are the country's oldest and largest in-water boat shows. They attract tens of thousands of vendors and enthusiasts from around the world. **Anne Arundel Scottish Highland Games** (410-849-2849), Anne Arundel Fairgrounds,

Crownsville. A clans' gathering that includes dancing, piping, fiddling, sheepdog demonstrations, children's games, and livestock exhibitions. A variety of Scottish goods for sale, too. **Fall Crafts Festival** (410-923-3400; www.aacountyfair.org), fairgrounds, Crownsville. More than 100 crafters, entertainment, flower and pumpkin sales.

November: **Annapolis by Candlelight** (410-267-7619; www.annapolis .org), Annapolis. An annual self-guided tour of private homes and public sites in the city's historic district.

December: **Bed and Breakfast Holiday Tour** (410-268-7070), Annapolis. B&Bs in the heart of the city open their doors for guided tours. **Eastport Yacht Club Lights Parade** (410-263-0415), Annapolis Harbor. The state's oldest lighted boat parade usually has more than 70 lighted boats.

Capital Region

LAUREL, COLLEGE PARK, BOWIE, AND
UPPER MARLBORO

SILVER SPRING, BETHESDA, ROCKVILLE,
AND GAITHERSBURG

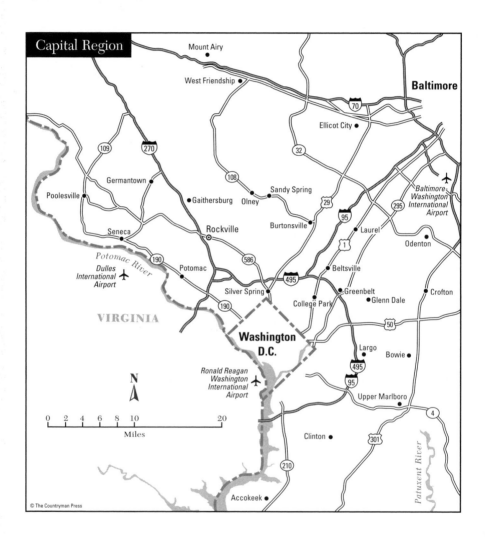

Capital Region

CAPITAL REGION

Getting a handle on just what is available, and where it is located, can be difficult in the Capital Region, that portion of Maryland around Washington, DC. An ever-expanding population, spurred on by ever-increasing federal and state bureaucracies, has transformed the once agrarian landscape. It is now a place of sprawling housing developments, large business parks and office buildings, and scores of malls and other shopping centers. Town lines have blurred, and it is often hard to tell where one ends and another begins.

This can be a good thing for travelers and explorers, however. You are, of course, right next door to Washington, DC, and can make quick forays into the city without having to pay its inflated lodging rates. You also don't have to drive very far to take in most of the Capital Region's museums, galleries, parks, restaurants, shopping areas, and other attractions.

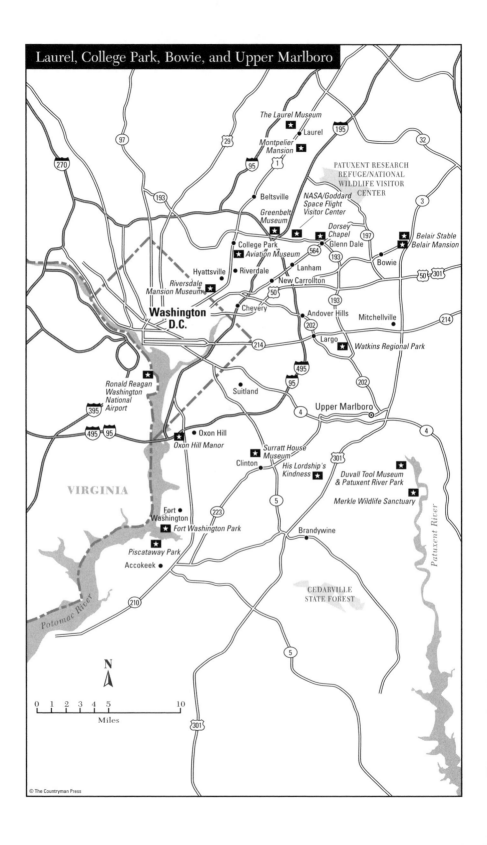

Laurel, College Park, Bowie, and Upper Marlboro

The Laurel Museum
Laurel
Montpelier Mansion
PATUXENT RESEARCH REFUGE/NATIONAL WILDLIFE VISITOR CENTER
Beltsville
NASA/Goddard Space Flight Visitor Center
Greenbelt Museum
Dorsey Chapel
Belair Stable
Belair Mansion
College Park
Aviation Museum
Glenn Dale
Bowie
Hyattsville
Riverdale
Lanham
New Carrollton
Riverdale Mansion Museum
Washington D.C.
Chevery
Andover Hills
Mitchellville
Largo
Watkins Regional Park
Ronald Reagan Washington National Airport
Suitland
Upper Marlboro
VIRGINIA
Oxon Hill
Oxon Hill Manor
Surratt House Museum
Clinton
His Lordship's Kindness
Duvall Tool Museum & Patuxent River Park
Merkle Wildlife Sanctuary
Fort Washington
Fort Washington Park
Brandywine
Piscataway Park
Accokeek
Patuxent River
CEDARVILLE STATE FOREST
Potomac River
N

0 1 2 3 4 5   10
Miles

© The Countryman Press

LAUREL, COLLEGE PARK, BOWIE, AND UPPER MARLBORO

Laurel was one of the area's first industrial centers. Early in the 1800s, members of a prominent Quaker family, the Snowdens, developed iron mines and furnaces, and operated grist- and cotton mills. The Laurel Museum helps preserve those times. By the early 1900s, most of these businesses had closed; but due to Laurel's proximity to Washington, DC, the town's population has only continued to grow and is now dominated by shopping centers, restaurants, and other services associated with bedroom communities.

Life in College Park focuses upon the University of Maryland, and businesses clustered around the school reflect the liberal lifestyles of the 35,000 students. The university's Clarice Smith Performing Arts Center is a theatrical showplace that provides the town with a cultural event of some kind or another almost every day of the year.

Unbeknownst to many of the state's citizens, Bowie is Maryland's fifth largest municipal entity. It quickly grew as a transportation center around two railroad lines that junctioned here soon after the Civil War. Although the city has expanded to encompass 16 square miles, the old part of town has retained its early charms. A brochure detailing a self-guided tour of historic sites is available from the Prince George's County, Maryland, Conference and Visitor's Bureau, Inc.

Although it is the county seat of Prince George County, the municipal boundary of Upper Marlboro is quite small. Once a thriving center of trade for the tobacco grown around it, the town lost some of its prominence when large-scale plantations began to fail and modern highways passed it by. Those roadways did, however, enable scores of housing developments to spring up on former agricultural lands.

For a region with such a dense population, the area has a surprising amount of land set aside for recreational and open-space use. Patuxent Research Refuge encompasses 13,000 acres; 6,000 acres along the Potomac River are preserved by Piscataway Park; and state and regional parks, forests, and preserves ensure that thousands of other acres will escape any future development.

GUIDANCE The **Prince George's County, Maryland, Conference and Visitor's Bureau, Inc.** (301-925-8300; www.visitprincegeorges.com), is located in a modern office building within a business park at 9200 Basil Court, Suite 101, Largo, 20774. There is ample free parking, but you may have to drive around the building to find an open space.

GETTING THERE *By car:* **US 50** cuts across the northern part of this region, arriving from Washington, DC, in the west and continuing to the Eastern Shore in the east. The **Baltimore–Washington Parkway (I-195)** connects those two cities and provides access to the northwestern part of the region. **US 301** crosses the Potomac River on a toll bridge, arriving from Virginia's Northern Neck.

By air: **Ronald Reagan Washington National Airport** (703-417-8000; www.mwaa.com/national) in northern Virginia and **Baltimore/Washington International Airport** (1-800-I-FLY-BWI) between Baltimore and Washington are within a 30-minute drive. Both have bus and rail connections that can bring you into this region.

By rail: **Amtrak** (1-800-USA-RAIL) makes a stop in New Carrollton during its New York–Washington, DC, run.

GETTING AROUND *By car:* **I-495 (Capital Beltway)**, **I-195**, **US 50**, **US 301**, and **MD 201** are four-lane highways, but expect heavy traffic on all of them throughout most of the daylight hours.

By bus: **MTA** (1-800-543-9809; www.mta.maryland.com) buses connect and make stops in all of the major cities and towns in the region. **The Prince George's County Bus System** (301-324-BUSS) provides service on a more local level, enabling you to visit most of the attractions listed in this region without having to drive to them.

By rail: **MARC** commuter rail service enables you to visit many of the towns in this area, as well as Baltimore and Washington, DC, without the hassle of driving a car. **Metro** rail (202-637-7000) provides the same service from Capitol Heights, Cheverly, Landover, New Carrollton, College Park, and a few other sites. (Also see *By bus.*)

MEDICAL EMERGENCY A number of hospitals have the facilities to handle an emergency should one arise:

Greater Laurel Beltsville Hospital (301-497-7954), 7300 Van Dusen St., Laurel.

Doctor's Community Hospital (301-552-8665), 8118 Good Luck Rd., Lanham.

Prince George's Hospital Center (301-618-3750), 3001 Hospital Dr., Cheverly.

Southern Maryland Hospital Center (301-899-4500), 7503 Surratts Rd., Clinton.

✳ To See

COLLEGES **University of Maryland** (301-314-9866; www.maryland.edu), College Park. The university began as an agricultural college in the mid-1800s; in 1988 it joined a statewide system that includes numerous other campuses with a total enrollment of more than 130,000 students. The school offers a full range of graduate and undergraduate courses, but possibly its most interesting facet for a visitor is the **Clarice Smith Performing Arts Center**. Opened in 2001, the $130 million, 318,000-square-foot center has performance halls, galleries, studios, and rehearsal rooms. See *Entertainment* for information on performances presented by the various art disciplines.

MUSEUMS **Laurel Museum** (301-7225-7975), Main and 9th Sts., Laurel. Wed. 10–2. Free admission. The 1830 mill workers' house contains photographs, tools, personal belongings, and other items depicting the town as a thriving mill center in the early 1800s.

✈ **College Park Aviation Museum** (301-864-6029; www.pgparks.com), 1985 Corporal Frank Scott Dr., College Park. Open daily; small admission fee. The museum is adjacent to **College Park Airport**, the world's oldest continuously operating airport, and celebrates its many aviation firsts: the first American female passenger, the training of the first military pilots (by Wilbur Wright), the first U.S. Postal Air Mail service, and more. There is a multitude of kid-friendly interactive exhibits and a number of historic aircraft—like the plane Gus McCloud flew over the North Pole. You are even permitted to sit in a Taylorcraft airplane. The upstairs contains changing exhibits and a balcony to view the aircraft from a different angle.

& **Greenbelt Museum** (301-507-6582), 10-B Crescent Rd., Greenbelt. Sun. 1–5. Free admission. The small museum is actually one of the planned community's original houses (for more information on this community, see Greenbelt Park under *Parks*). It lends insight into the lives of those who lived here when Greenbelt first opened during the Great Depression. The two bedrooms, bath, living room, and kitchen are decorated with the original furniture constructed specifically for the community. Within walking distance is the art deco–style community center, with friezes on the outside wall depicting the preamble to the Constitution and exhibits inside pertaining to life in Greenbelt.

& **Duvall Tool Museum** (301-627-6074), 16000 Croom Airport Rd., Patuxent River Park, Upper Marlboro. Sun. 1–4. W. Henry Duvall scoured the countryside for more than 50 years, buying old farm, home, and hand tools used during the 1800s. His collection of 1,000 pieces is now housed in this museum.

Surratt House Museum (301-868-1121; www.surratt.org), 9118 Brandywine Rd., Clinton. January 1 through mid-December, Thu. and Fri. 11–3; and Sat. and Sun. noon–4. Small admission fee. Period-dressed guides present a balanced account of the role John and Mary Surratt played in Lincoln's assassination. Their middle-class home was a tavern, post office, inn, and safe house in southern Maryland's Confederate underground. John Wilkes Booth stopped here during his escape from Washington, DC, to retrieve weapons and supplies, and the upstairs bedroom is furnished as it would have been at that time. The museum also sponsors a 12-hour bus trip, the John Wilkes Booth Escape Route Tour, which makes stops at significant sites on his flight through Maryland. Dates, times, and fees vary; call for the latest information.

LEARNING HISTORY AT THE SURRATT HOUSE

HISTORIC HOMES Montpelier Mansion (301-953-1376; www.pgparks.com/places/artsfac.html), Muirkirk Rd. and MD 197, Laurel. Tours given on the hour Sun.–Thu. noon–3 (at 1 and 2 Jan. and Feb.); please note that this schedule has been known to change frequently. Small admission fee. Guided 60-minute tours take visitors through the late-1700s Georgian home of Thomas and Anne Ridgely Snowden. Furnished with period pieces based upon an 1831 inventory of their belongings. The dining room contains some original family pieces; also on display is the wedding dress of the Snowdens' granddaughter. If not discussed during your tour, ask your guide to show you the secret trapdoor and hidden stairway.

The **Montpelier Cultural Arts Center** (301-953-1993) is adjacent to the mansion. Free guided tours (daily 10–5) enable visitors to watch sculptors, painters, printmakers, and other craftspeople at work.

Riversdale Mansion (301-864-0420), 4811 Riverdale Rd., Riverdale. Sun. noon–4. Small admission fee for a 60-minute guided tour. A National Historic Landmark, the five-part, stucco-covered plantation home of George Calvert, grandson of the fifth Lord Baltimore, has been restored and furnished to reflect the early 1800s. The mahogany handrail and some of the furnishings are original, and be sure to ask a docent to provide background on the scenic wallpaper in the study.

♿ **Belair Mansion and Stable Museum** (301-809-3089), 12207 Tulip Grove Dr., Bowie. Days and times that this attraction is open seem to change constantly, but it has always been open Sun. 1–4. Small admission fee; stable museum is free. Self-guided tours of the 1700s five-part Georgian mansion take in many original pieces of furniture that help interpret its 300-year history.

The largest cucumber tree of its kind in the state (planted in 1820) is located on the terraced grounds leading down to the stables. From the 1930s to the 1950s, this was one of the premier racing stables in the country and was the home of Gallant Fox and Omaha, the only father-and-son horses to win the coveted Triple Crown. Individual stalls contain separate and distinct displays chronicling thoroughbred racing in America.

Poplar Hill on His Lordship's Kindness (301-856-0358; www .poplarhillonhlk.com), 7606 Woodyard Rd., Clinton. Thu. and Fri. 10–4; Sun. noon–4. Small admission fee for self-guided tour. This National Historic Landmark was named by Colonel Henry Darnell in gratitude for the

BELAIR STABLES IN BOWIE

7,000-acre land grant given to him by Lord Baltimore. The architecture and many features in the house are original; however, it is furnished as it would have been in the 1950s when the last owners, John and Sarah Walton, lived there.

SITES ALONG THE POTOMAC RIVER There is a succession of protected lands strung along the east bank of the Potomac River. They preserve and interpret bits of history, and provide spectacular views across the wide river to Washington, DC, and Alexandria and Mount Vernon in Virginia. They can all be accessed from **MD 210**, and from north to south are:

Oxon Hill

✍ **Oxon Cove Park/Oxon Hill Farm** (301-839-1176; www.nps.gov), 6411 Oxon Hill Rd. Free admission and parking. The 512-acre property is operated as a working farm of the late 1950s by the National Park Service. It is a great place

HIS LORDSHIP'S KINDNESS

for urban children to find out about country life. I've watched entire groups become amazed when a ranger reaches under a cow and squeezes some milk into a pail. Chickens, sheep, and donkeys wander around in pens next to fields of corn, sorghum, and wheat. The farmhouse, barn filled with historic agricultural equipment, and a visitors center help round out the story. The horses stabled here are the ones that pull the White House tree through the streets of Washington, DC, at Christmastime. Short hiking and biking trails wind into fields and woods, and down to the river. Great views of Alexandria, Virginia.

Fort Foote Park, Fort Foote Rd. A small picnic area on the site of a pre–Civil War fort. A few of the old ramparts and guns remain. Nice views across the river.

Fort Washington

Fort Washington Park (301-763-4600; www.nps.gov/fowa), 13661 Fort Washington Rd. Open daily. Small entrance fee per car. You can take a self-guided tour or a ranger-narrated walk (times and dates vary) of the early 1800s fort, built on the site of an earlier one destroyed by the British in the War of 1812. Cannons, ramparts, earthworks, and displays in the visitors center help interpret the fort's important history as the first line of defense of the nation's capital. As a journalist once remarked, "We know our country is safe as long as we see the garrison flag at Fort Washington." Impressive view of Washington, DC.

Accokeek

✦ **National Colonial Farm and Piscataway Park** (301-283-2113; www.nps .gov/pisc; www.accokeek.org), 3400 Bryan Point Rd. Tue.–Sun., mid-March through mid-December; open on weekends the rest of the year. Small admission fee. The farm is operated by the nonprofit Accokeek Foundation as a living-history demonstration of a typical 1800s farm owned by a colonial family of modest

LEARNING TO MILK A COW AT OXON HILL FARM

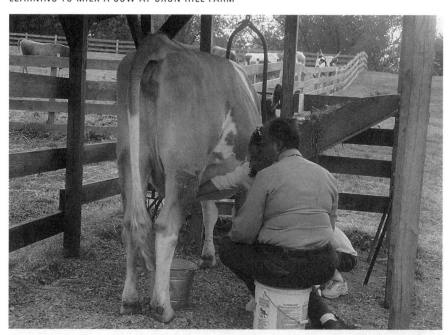

means. Many of the plants and animals are heritage breeds—meaning they are no longer part of mainstream farming and are in danger of disappearing.

Self-guided tours (or guided tours on weekends) take you by structures and gardens, all built and tended with period practices and implements. A ferryboat (a replica of an 1800s riverboat) crosses the Potomac to Mount Vernon, Virginia, on weekends to provide insight into how the upper classes fared during colonial days. The foundation also sponsors an eco-farm, on which local volunteers work to create organic produce.

The colonial farm is within the 6-mile-long, 4,000-acre **Piscataway Park**, created by the National Park Service to protect the views of Mount Vernon. Numerous trails, some along the Potomac River, meander through the property and provide easy escapes from the modern world.

HISTORIC CHURCHES **Dorsey Chapel** (301-464-5291), 10704 Brookland Rd., Glen Dale. Open the first and third Sunday of each month. Small admission fee. The small frame meetinghouse-style church was in use by the local African American community throughout most of the 1900s.

OTHER SITES ✍ **National Wildlife Visitor Center in Patuxent Research Refuge** (301-497-5580; www.fws.gov), 10901 Scarlet Tanager Loop, Laurel. (Also see the sidebar on page 285.) Open daily. Free admission. The National Wildlife Visitor Center is by far the largest and best facility of its kind that I have ever seen. The quality and quantity of its displays and exhibits outshine many museums for which you pay a fee to visit. Hands-on activities, multimedia presentations, and life-sized dioramas not only portray the natural drama of the refuge but also examine global environmental issues, different habitats around the world, and the behavior of a wide variety of animals. Be sure to allot a few hours to take it all in; what you learn here will add greatly to outings you happen to take anywhere in the natural world.

A COSTUMED DOCENT AT THE NATIONAL COLONIAL FARM

✍ ⅙ **NASA/Goddard Space Flight Visitor Center** (301-286-8981; www.gsfc.nasa.gov), Explorer Rd., Greenbelt. Open daily 9–4. Free admission. Guided tours Mon.–Sat. at 10:30 and 1:30, and Sun. at 11 and 2. Goddard is the center of NASA's spaceflight-tracking activities. There are many presentations, interactive displays, programs, and the opportunity to view the working areas of communications operations, satellite control, and spacecraft construction.

GUIDED TOURS See **Surratt House Museum** under *Museums*.

SCENIC DRIVES ✿ **Chesapeake Bay Critical Area Driving Tour** (301-627-6074), 16000 Croom Airport Rd., **Patuxent River Park** (see *Green Space*), Upper Marlboro. Open to automobiles Sun. 10–3; open to walkers and bicycles Sat. Originating at the entrance of the Jug Bay Natural Area of Patuxent River Park, the 4-mile, self-guided drive highlights the natural resources of the river and the Chesapeake Bay. Passing over wetlands on an elevated boardwalk, it provides tidal marshes, forests, a 40-foot observation tower with a grand view of the river, and glimpses of wildlife. I think this is one of the best and, since you are driving and not walking, easiest introductions to a variety of the state's environments.

✷ To Do

BICYCLING Washington, Baltimore, and Annapolis Trail (301-699-2407). The 5.6-mile trail follows an old railroad grade from Glen Dale to the Patuxent River.

Anacostia Trails (301-210-3788; www.anacostiatrails.org). A system of trails, multiple miles in length, is open to bikers and hikers along the Anacostia River and a number of its tributaries. Some trails are nicely isolated while others go through urban areas, but they all are pleasant alternatives to driving in this region.

Also see *Scenic Drives*; *Hiking*; and the **Patuxent Research Refuge** sidebar on page 285.

FAMILY ACTIVITIES ✿ **Six Flags America Theme and Water Parks** (301-249-1500; www.sixflags.com/america), Central Ave., Largo. Open limited days Apr.–May and Sep.–Oct., and daily June–Aug. A 1-day ticket is about $35–40; the ticket grants admission to both parks. From humble beginnings as a small animal safari park, Six Flags America has grown to 140 acres (and still owns 300 acres on which to expand). Live shows, special small-children's rides in Looney Tunes Movie Town, and numerous roller coasters. The Wild One is 85 years old, the Superman has a 200-foot crest and reaches 70 miles an hour on its 1.5-mile track, and you ride facing the ground on the Batwing.

✿ **Watkins Regional Park** (301-249-9220), 301 Watkins Park Dr., Upper Marlboro. The 1,800-acre park provides a great variety of activities for the family. In addition to a small campground and several miles of nature trails, there are tennis courts, a miniature-golf course, and a miniature train that winds through woodlands and by the **Old Maryland Farm**. The farm is a petting zoo that provides the chance to visit livestock, participate in nature activities, and walk through organic gardens. Close to the farm is the **Chesapeake Carousel**, an early-1900s Dentzel carousel with hand-carved animals. All of these attractions are open on various days and times; contact the park office for details.

GOLF Henson Creek (301-567-4646), 7200 Sunnyside Lane, Fort Washington. The nine-hole course is open to the public with no advance tee times—first come, first served.

Paint Branch (301-935-0330), 4690 University Blvd., College Park. Like Henson Creek (see above), Paint Branch is a nine-hole course with no advance tee times. Its links are short and flat, and have small greens.

Enterprise Golf Course (301-249-2040), 2802 Enterprise Rd., Mitchellville. The par-72 course is constructed on the site of a former dairy farm and is open daily 6:30 AM–dark.

Marlton Golf Club (301-856-7566), 9413 Midland Turnpike, Upper Marlboro. Open to the public with bent-grass fairways, water hazards, and many sand bunkers.

MINIATURE GOLF See **Watkins Regional Park** under *Family Activities.*

HIKING **Cedarville State Forest** (301-888-1410), MD 310 and Cedarville Rd., Brandywine. Harboring some of Maryland's rare and endangered species such as the bald eagle, red-bellied woodpecker, and diamondback terrapin, **Zekiah Swamp** is the state's largest freshwater swamp. Stretching to the southwest for approximately 20 miles, from Cedarville State Forest to the Wicomico River, it is almost a mile wide in some places.

Within the boundary of the state forest, miles of trails cross and parallel headwater streams, where the extra moisture enables the vegetation to become lush and thick. This provides a wonderful feeling of walking along a swamplike environment but without having your boots become mired in several inches of mud and ooze. In addition, the deep forest filters out much of the noise from the outside world, creating a quiet sense of isolation. Trails are also open to mountain bikers and equestrians.

OLD MARYLAND FARM IN WATKINS REGIONAL PARK

Also see **Oxon Cove Park/Oxon Hill Farm** and **National Colonial Farm and Piscataway Park** under *To See*; *Bicycling*; **Merkle Wildlife Sanctuary** under *Nature-Watching*; the **Patuxent Research Refuge** sidebar on page 285; and *Green Space*.

KAYAKING AND CANOEING See **Patuxent River Park** under *Green Space*.

NATURE-WATCHING Merkle Wildlife Sanctuary (301-888-1410), 11704 Fenno Rd., Upper Marlboro. The center opens at 10 daily; trails are open sunrise–sunset. Rover and Fido must be left at home. Continuing the dream of Edgar Merkle, the 2,000-acre sanctuary provides habitat for Canada geese. Trails go by ponds, wetlands, upland and bottomland forest, cultivated fields, and creeks, which provide a variety of scenery as well as habitats for plants and animals. It takes a six-page pamphlet to catalog all of the birds observed here, while raccoons, rabbits, squirrels, skunks, foxes, and white-tailed deer have been spotted making quick dashes from field to forest. A list of flowers blooming in just one month, July, contains nearly 100 species. Exhibits in the visitors center focus on the goose and local human history. An observation deck with telescopes overlooks Merkle Pond, and an extensive schedule of interpretive programs is offered throughout the year.

RACING Rosecroft (301-567-4000; 1-877-818-WINS; www.rosecroft.com), 6336 Rosecroft Dr., Fort Washington. Admission $2. Free parking. Live harness racing every Thu.–Sat. starting at 7:20 PM.

✳ Green Space

PARKS Greenbelt Park (301-344-3948), 6565 Greenbelt Rd. (accessed from I-495 Exit 22), Greenbelt. It is ironic that a bureaucratic housing project ended up saving the natural environment of Greenbelt Park. The land was acquired in the 1930s by the federal government to be part of Greenbelt, one of a number of model towns within a belt of open space to be developed around the District of Columbia. Although some housing was constructed, the project never progressed as hoped, and the government sold the buildings to a local cooperative. Most of the remaining land became a component of the National Park Service in 1950.

Although the park is bordered by four-lane highways on three sides, its network of more than 8 miles of trails enables you to make a quick escape from urban landscapes to sweet gum trees, blueberry bushes, and small wetlands areas. The park also has a campground and sponsors nature walks and evening programs.

Patuxent River Park (301-627-6074), 16000 Croom Airport Rd., Upper Marlboro. Located along its namesake, the 6,000-acre park contains marshes, swamps, and forests with many miles of trails. Also available are fishing piers, canoe and kayak rentals, and a number of organized hikes, boat excursions, and special events.

Also see **National Colonial Farm and Piscataway Park** under *To See*.

☀ Lodging

MOTELS AND HOTELS ♿ **Fairfield Inn** (301-572-7100), 4050 Powder Mill Rd. (accessed from I-95 Exit 29), Beltsville, 20705. Fairly low rates for being this close to Washington, DC, and having a swimming pool and exercise room. $89–149.

🐾 ✆ **Comfort Suites** (301-206-2600; 1-800-628-7760), 14402 Laurel Place, Laurel, 20707. Surrounded by restaurants and shopping opportunities, and close to Patuxent Research Refuge. Indoor pool and fitness center. Kids stay free in parent's room; small pets welcome with a deposit. $99–249.

Marriott Inn and Conference Center (301-985-7300; http://marriott .com/property/propertypage/wasum), University Blvd. and Adelphi Rd., College Park, 20740. Original paintings and sculptures fill the spacious public areas and hallways, calling to

THE BOARDWALK IN PISCATAWAY PARK IN ACCOKEEK MAKES A GREAT OUTDOOR CLASSROOM.

mind an upscale resort more than a hotel interior. Within a few short blocks of the University of Maryland's Clarice Smith Performing Arts Center, it has its own fitness room, golf course, and jogging and walking trails. $139–249. (See also The Garden Restaurant under *Dining Out*.)

🐾 ✆ **Patuxent Research Refuge** (301-497-5580; www.fws.gov), 10901 Scarlet Tanager Loop, Laurel. President Franklin D. Roosevelt established the refuge in 1936, and it has grown from an original 2,670 acres to nearly 13,000 acres. It supports a diversity of wildlife in a typical Maryland landscape of meadow, wetland, and forest habitats. Although the more than 200 species of birds that are known to be in the refuge at one time or another receive the greatest share of visitors' attention, deer, beavers, squirrels, muskrats, snakes, lizards, turtles, frogs, salamanders, raccoons, rabbits, and mice are also part of the environment.

The refuge is divided into three areas. The **North Tract** offers over 10 miles of roads and trails that are open to hikers, bikers, and horseback riders. The **Central Tract** contains offices and study sites, and is closed to the public. The **South Tract** is probably the most visited portion, with a network of scenic trails (open only to foot travel), two large lakes, and a visitors center. Pets are permitted on the trails, but must be leashed. Sadly for those who enjoy early-morning or early-evening strolls, when wildlife is most active, the South Tract is open to the public only 10–5:30. (The North Tract has longer hours; check at the visitors center.)

& **Hampton Inn** (301-809-1800; 1-800-HAMPTON), 15202 Major Lansdale Rd., Bowie, 20716. All rooms have a large desk and chair, in addition to an iron and a hair dryer. Swimming pool. Close to Six Flags America. $99–199.

& **Doubletree Club Hotel** (301-773-0700; 1-888-444-CLUB; www.clubhotels.com), 9100 Basil Court (accessed from I-495 Exit 17A), Largo, 20774. Large and comfortable lobby and other public areas, nicely appointed rooms, heated indoor pool, exercise facility and sauna. Within a few minutes' drive of USAir Arena, and downtown Washington, DC. $99–199.

🐾 **Forest Hills Motel** (301-627-3969), 2901 Crain Hwy., Upper Marlboro, 20774. Nothing fancy here—no swimming pool or fitness center—but they will let you take your pet into the room with you. $75–85.

& **Colony South Hotel and Conference Center** (301-856-4500; www.colonysouth.com), 7401 Surratts Rd. (accessed from I-495 Exit 7A), Clinton, 20735. With a Cape Cod–like exterior and lush wooden interior, this place feels more like a country lodge than a hotel that is less than 5 miles from Pennsylvania Ave. and downtown Washington, DC. Rooms are quite large, there is a full-service fitness center with indoor pool, and free shuttle service is provided to and from Ronald Reagan Washington National Airport in Virginia and a Metro station. $149–229. (Also see Wayfarer under *Dining Out*.)

Best Western Potomac View (301-749-9400), 6400 Oxon Hill Rd. (accessed from I-495 Exit 3A), Oxon Hill, 20745. Indoor pool, weight room, and oversized guest rooms. Very reasonable rates given its close proximity to the attractions of Washington, DC. $99–149.

CAMPING 🐾 & **Cherry Hill Park** (301-937-7116; www.cherryhillpark.com), 9800 Cherry Hill Rd., College Park, 20740. The closest RV campground to Washington, DC, its 60 acres have a heated swimming pool, miniature golf, and modern facilities. A dog-walking service is offered, as well as guided tours of the nation's capital. Metro buses also make several stops a day to take visitors into Washington, DC.

🐾 **Greenbelt Park** (301-344-3948), 6565 Greenbelt Rd. (accessed from I-495 Exit 22), Greenbelt, 20770. Just 12 miles from the downtown attractions of Washington, DC. The setting of the 174 spaces is a bit more forested than those found in Cherry Hill Park (see above). Other than traffic noise from nearby four-lanes, this is usually a quiet, laid-back experience. Pets permitted.

Watkins Regional Park (park office 301-249-9220; campground 301-249-6900), 301 Watkins Park Dr., Upper Marlboro, 20774. Located next door to Six Flags America, this small campground has just over 30 sites with a restroom/shower facility in the middle of it. Be aware that there are neither hookups nor a dump station for RVs.

🐾 **Cedarville State Forest** (301-888-1410), MD 310 and Cedarville Rd., Brandywine, 20613. The wooded camping area, with a central bathhouse, is open late Mar.–early Dec. A couple of sites are reserved for campers with pets.

Cosca Regional Park (301-868-1397), 11000 Thrift Rd., Clinton 20735. A small campground with a central comfort station.

✳ Where to Eat

DINING OUT **The Garden Restaurant** (301-985-7300; http://marriott .com/property/propertypage/wasum), University Blvd. and Adelphi Rd., College Park. Open for breakfast, lunch, and dinner. The restaurant's small space inside the large Marriott Inn and Conference Center belies the quality of its slightly French-influenced foods. My wild mushroom vol-au-vents ($6) were in some of the crispiest pastry shells I've had, and my entrée of grilled lamb chops with herbes de Provence ($22) was succulent. Duck ($20), filet mignon ($24), and seafood ($18–22) are also on the menu.

✐ **Wayfarer** (301-856-4500), 7401 Surratts Rd., inside the Colony South Hotel, Clinton. Open for breakfast, lunch, and dinner. Consistent with the country-lodge feel of the hotel, the restaurant's decor includes a fireplace and beamed ceilings. The menu focuses on northern Italian dishes such as veal Piccata ($17.50), chicken Romana ($13.50), and penne with crabmeat and spinach (market price). A lunch buffet is offered Mon.–Fri.

EATING OUT

Laurel

Café de Paris (301-490-8811), Laurel Lakes Center, 14252 Baltimore Ave. Recalling a French bistro of the mid-1900s with wooden floors and posters on the wall, the café has a menu that is an ever-changing variation on French country cooking. The onion soup ($3.95) is good, as are the seafood offerings. Dinner entrées $19–25.

✐ **Pasta Plus** (301-498-5100), Central Plaza Shopping Center, 209 Gorman Ave. The name as well as this restaurant's exterior do not do justice to its warm interior and quality of food. The pizzas ($7.95–14.95) have a great taste because they are cooked in a wood-burning stove, and most of the other dishes are delicious because the pasta and sauces are made fresh daily on the premises. Veal and seafood round out the menu. $9–20.

Beltsville

Kay's Diner (301-595-3002), 10973 Baltimore Ave. Open 6 AM–5 PM. Closed Sun. How can you go wrong when the average price of a complete breakfast is less than $5? Most lunches, such as sandwiches, burgers, and a few entrées, will not cost you more than $7.

College Park

✐ **94th Aero Squadron** (301-699-9400), 5420 Paint Branch Pkwy. Open for lunch and dinner. Overlooking the College Park Airport, the restaurant is built to resemble how a distressed French countryside farmhouse would have looked after experiencing the troubles of World War I. Lots of aviation memorabilia inside, and the wait staff is in period dress. Steaks ($17.95–28.95) are the specialty, with a few seafood ($17.95–23.95) and "farmhouse favorites" (meat loaf $12.95; pot roast $14.95) mixed in. Entrées $12–25.

✐ **R. J. Bentley's Filling Station** (301-277-8898), 7323 Baltimore Blvd. Open for lunch and dinner. Located within in a 1920s gas station, Bentley's has been a favorite with University of Maryland students and alumni for several decades. Signed jerseys of university athletes who went on to become professionals adorn the walls. The menu features what I call "bar food," lots of burgers and sandwiches ($5.95–8.95) with a few chicken, pasta, and steak dinner entrées ($8.95–18.95).

CRABS ♂ **Captain Jerry's** (301-604-CRAB), 143 Bowie Rd., Laurel. Open daily for lunch and dinner. The all-you-can-eat crabs (market price) are the way to go when available. If they're not, then try a soft-shell crab sandwich ($8.95) for lunch, or one of the many seafood entrées for dinner ($12.95–27.95). The crabcake dinner special ($16.95) is a deal.

Pop's Seafood and Carry Out (301-459-4141), 7437 Annapolis Rd., Landover Hills. You come here for the hard- and soft-shell crabs (market price), not for the atmosphere, but Pop's has been serving to the locals for more than two decades.

COFFEE BARS **Year of the Rabbit Coffee Pub** (301-809-0979; www .ourbowie.com/yotr), Hilltop Plaza, 6700 Race Track Rd., Bowie. Open daily. Nestled in an alleyway, the pub offers hot and cold coffees, a variety of beers and wines, pastries, and live regional entertainment Thu.–Sun.

SNACKS AND GOODIES **Simple Pleasures Ice Café** (301-809-5880), 6948 Laurel–Bowie Rd., Bowie. Closed Mon. Santamaria Perrin and Terri Russell, mother and daughter, offer homemade ice cream, cakes, sorbets, and gourmet coffees and teas. Sugar-free items also available.

✳ Entertainment

DANCE **School of Dance** (301-405-ARTS; www.claricesmithcenter.umd .edu), University of Maryland, College Park. The school sponsors performances throughout the school year, many of them by professional troupes, and several student presentations each semester.

FILM All of the following show first-run movies:

Sony Theatres (301-937-0742), 4001 Powder Mill Rd., Beltsville.

Showcase Market Place Cinema (301-464-1702), 3208 Superior Lane, Bowie.

AMC Academy (301-474-0077), 6198 Greenbelt Rd., Greenbelt.

Old Greenbelt Theater (301-474-9744), 132 Centerway Rd., Greenbelt.

P&G Laurel Towne Center (301-776-2500), 13314 Laurel Bowie Rd., Laurel.

Laurel Lakes Cinema (301-490-8001), 929 Fairlawn Rd., Laurel.

AMC Carrollton (301-459-6999), 7828 Riverdale Rd., New Carrollton.

AMC Rivertown (301-389-9571), 6075 Oxon Hill Rd., Oxon Hill.

Andrews Manor (301-736-6373), Andrews Manor Shopping Center, Suitland.

MUSIC **Maryland Presents** (301-405-ARTS; www.claricesmithcenter.umd .edu), University of Maryland, College Park. Maryland Presents is the theatrical arm of the **Clarice Smith Performing Arts Center**, which presents a wide range of programs throughout the year. Performances include solo artists, full orchestras, quartets, popular music, Broadway and theatrical productions, and student and faculty recitals. Since all of the arts disciplines are housed in the center, artists from each discipline often work together on the productions.

THEATERS **University of Maryland Department of Theater** (301-405-ARTS; www.claricesmithcenter.umd.edu), University of Maryland, College Park. Performances have included many Broadway standards, such as *The Music Man*, along with newer works like George F. Walker's *Problem Child*. The productions include members of the school's faculty, students, and local actors—professional and amateur.

& **Publick Playhouse** (301-277-1710), 5445 Landover Rd., Cheverly. Located just 10 minutes from downtown Washington, DC, the playhouse—a converted 1940s movie theater—presents everything from jazz and gospel to modern dance, and from musical theater to historic drama.

SPORTS **University of Maryland Terrapins** (301-314-7070), College Park. The university's student teams provide action for spectators in basketball, baseball, soccer, lacrosse, swimming, and other sports.

Washington Redskins (301-276-6000), FedEx Field, Landover. The professional NFL team plays its home games in the 83,000-seat FedEx Field.

✍ **Bowie Baysox** (301-805-6000; 1-800-956-4004), Prince George's Stadium, 4101 North East Crain Hwy., Bowie. Come watch a possible future Baltimore Oriole as the AA team plays its season Apr.–Sep.

Washington Power Lacrosse (301-324-1755), Capital Center, Largo. Professional indoor lacrosse.

✷ Selective Shopping

ART GALLERIES **Harmony Hall Regional Center** (301-203-6060),

10701 Livingston Rd., Fort Washington. A converted elementary school provides arts classes and an exhibition gallery.

Also see **Montpelier Mansion** under *To See.*

FARMER'S MARKETS **Main St. Farmer's Market** (301-262-6200), Gallant Fox Lane and MD 197, Bowie. Start the week with fresh produce by stopping by on Sunday between 9 and 1 during the season of May–Oct.

Prince George's Plaza Farmer's Market (310-627-0977), MD 410, Hyattsville. Strawberries are some of the first things to appear when the season opens in May, while pumpkins close it out in November. Open Tue. 3–6.

USDA Farmer's Market (301-504-1776; 1-800-384-8704), 5601 Sunnyside Ave., Beltsville. This market should offer some of the best fruits and vegetables around, as it is adjacent to the Beltsville Agricultural Research Center. Open Thu. 10–2, June–Sep.

College Park Farmer's Market (301-262-8662), 5211 Calvert Rd., College Park. Stands are temporary and quite informal, as everything is set up in a swimming-pool parking lot on Sat., May–Nov. Things crank up at 7 AM and get pretty quiet by noon.

PICK-YOUR-OWN PRODUCE FARMS **Cherry Hill Orchard** (301-292-4642), 12300 Gallahan Rd., Clinton. The season starts in mid-May with red raspberries and continues well into fall with other berries, fruits, and a very wide variety of vegetables.

Miller Farms (301-297-5878), 10140 Piscataway Rd., Clinton. The strawberries are usually ripe by mid-May;

return about a month later to choose and pick your own vegetables.

❧ **Robin Hill Farm Nursery** (301-888-1849), 15800 Croom Rd., Brandywine. Bring the kids out to choose a pumpkin so that they can carve their own jack-o'-lantern.

✳ Special Events

February: **Annual Choreographers' Showcase** (301-405-ARTS), Clarice Smith Performing Arts Center, College Park.

March: **Annual Jewelry, Mineral and Fossil Show and Sale** (301-297-4575), Fort Washington. Also includes the **Family Wildlife Art Festival** with performances, music, workshops, and kids' activities.

April: **Play Festival** (301-322-0444), Prince George's Community College, Largo. Annual presentation of new theatrical works and talent from the region.

May: **Spring Festival Horse Show** (301-952-7999), Upper Marlboro. A-rated hunter/jumper horse show.

Montpelier Spring Festival (301-776-2805), Laurel. Arts and crafts, several stages presenting music and dance, pony rides, and kids' parade. **Harlem Renaissance Festival** (301-918-8418; www.prgeoharlem renaissancefestival.org), Landover. Several stages of music, dance, poetry, and theater, with other activities for all ages. **Marlboro Day and Parade** (301-952-9575), Upper Marlboro. Parade, food, crafts, vendors, and entertainment.

June: **Main St. Antique, Arts and Craft Show** (301-725-7539), Laurel. Juried show featuring regional artists and antiques dealers. Appraisals and entertainment.

September: **County Fair** (301-579-2598), Equestrian Center, Upper Marlboro.

November–early January: **Winter Festival of Lights** (301-699-2545), Watkins Park, Upper Marlboro.

SILVER SPRING, BETHESDA, ROCKVILLE, AND GAITHERSBURG

Francis Preston Blair was out riding his horse in the mid-1800s when his mount became spooked, throwing him to the ground. With his face in the mud, he noticed he had landed next to a spring, whose mica deposits shone like silver in the bright sunshine. He purchased the land around the water source, built his home, and Silver Spring was born.

Although it is not an incorporated city, its downtown area was a major shopping point in the mid-1900s but lost favor as the 20th century came to a close. A $400 million revitalization program has reversed the trend, and shops, restaurants, and businesses have returned. The National Capital Trolley Museum is just a few miles away and chronicles the days before automobiles ruled the roadways.

Numerous research centers, such as the National Institutes of Health, National Naval Medical Center, National Cancer Institute, and software development and telecommunications firms make Bethesda the state's second largest employment center. The money generated by these enterprises has transformed the city into a sophisticated and trendy place. The shopping district is crowded with some of the most upscale stores—both locally owned and national chains—in the Washington, DC, area.

Bethesda is also a great patron of the arts, especially with its Art in Public Spaces Discovery Trail. A stroll along urban streets and byways will reveal more than 40 indoor and outdoor works of art, and McCrillis Gardens and Gallery presents a changing array of exhibits. The written word is also valued here, evidenced in the number of new and used bookshops.

Rockville began with the establishment of Owen's Ordinary, an inn and tavern, around 1750. A few years later, in 1774, citizens gathered in another inn, Hungerford's Tavern, to discuss their outrage over Britain's blockade of Boston Harbor and called for a Maryland boycott of trade with England. From those early days, Rockville has become Maryland's second largest city in area, occupying more than 13 square miles.

Much of its history is preserved in the architecture of the downtown area and within the 1800s Beall-Dawson House, open for public tours. F. Scott Fitzgerald,

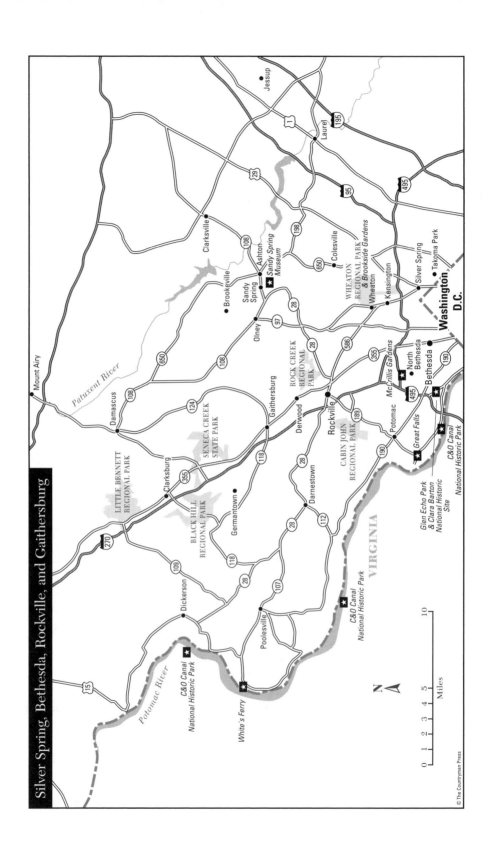

Silver Spring, Bethesda, Rockville, and Gaithersburg

Jessup

Laurel

195

1

29

95

495

Clarksville

108

198

Ashton

Sandy Spring Museum

650

Colesville

WHEATON REGIONAL PARK & *Brookside Gardens*

Wheaton

Kensington

Silver Spring

Takoma Park

Brookeville

Sandy Spring

28

Washington, D.C.

Olney

97

28

McCrillis Gardens

Mount Airy

Patuxent River

650

108

ROCK CREEK REGIONAL PARK

586

355

North Bethesda

190

108

124

Gaithersburg

Derwood

Rockville

189

Potomac

495

Bethesda

Damascus

Great Falls

C&O Canal National Historic Park

SENECA CREEK STATE PARK

CABIN JOHN REGIONAL PARK

LITTLE BENNETT REGIONAL PARK

Clarksburg

355

118

28

Darnestown

190

BLACK HILL REGIONAL PARK

Germantown

28

112

VIRGINIA

270

118

Glen Echo Park & Clara Barton National Historic Site

C&O Canal National Historic Park

109

28

107

C&O Canal National Historic Park

15

Dickerson

Poolesville

Potomac River

C&O Canal National Historic Park

White's Ferry

N

Miles

0 1 2 3 4 5   10

© The Countryman Press

his wife, Zelda, and other family members are buried in the cemetery of nearby St. Mary's Church. Those wishing to escape the urban environment can drive just a few miles to Rock Creek Regional Park along the city's northern border, or Cabin John Regional Park to south.

Gaithersburg began as a small agrarian community known as Log Town in the mid-1700s. The arrival of the Baltimore & Ohio Railroad in 1873 allowed the farmers to reach a wider market and enabled travelers to escape the summer heat in Washington, DC. These earlier days are recalled in the exhibits of the now restored B&O Railroad Station. The arrival of the interstates, specifically I-270, in the late 20th century put an end to the farming way of life, and the city now functions as a bedroom community for the Washington, DC, metropolitan area.

COMMUNITIES Towns removed just a few miles from the I-270 corridor are also growing but so far have escaped rapid urbanization. **Sandy Spring** was settled by Quakers in 1725, and the Sandy Spring Museum documents its history.

Close to the Potomac River, **Poolesville** was settled in 1783 and retains much of its rural, farming roots. It is believed that **Clarksburg** can trace its roots back to a Native American trading post. Much of the green space that would have surrounded the small Indian settlement has been preserved by Little Bennett Regional Park.

GUIDANCE Contact the **Conference and Visitors Bureau of Montgomery County, Maryland, Inc.** (301-482-9702; 1-800-925-0880; www.cvbmontco .com), 12900 Middlebrook Rd., Suite 1400, Germantown, 20874, for information, brochures, and other travel advice.

GETTING THERE *By car:* **I-270** makes an almost arrow-straight run through the middle of the region, and connects with **I-70** at Frederick to the northwest and with the **Capital Beltway (I-495)**, which encircles Washington, DC, to the southeast.

By air: This area is blessed with being serviced by three major airports. The two closest are **Ronald Reagan Washington National Airport** (703-417-8000; www.mwaa.com/national) and **Dulles International Airport** (703-572-2700) in northern Virginia. Located between Baltimore and Washington, DC, is the **Baltimore/Washington International Airport** (1-800-I-FLY-BWI).

By rail: **Amtrak** (1-800-872-7245) makes a stop at the Rockville Metro Station, which means you can arrive here by train from any other place that has Amtrak connections.

By water: **White's Ferry** (301-349-5200), US 15. The only remaining ferry across the Potomac River permits you to come into Maryland near Poolesville from US 15 just north of Leesburg, Virginia. Although the ferry is a utilitarian boat, the ride across the river can be a scenic and enjoyable one as you watch waterfowl and other birds wing their way above the water. You will also get a chance to look at the river and the Chesapeake & Ohio (C&O) Canal from the same perspective as the folks who took the ferry in the 1800s did. It operates daily 5 AM–11 PM and costs about $3 one way; $5 round trip.

GETTING AROUND *By car:* **I-270** and **I-495 (Capital Beltway)** are the major limited-access highways. The interstates are extremely crowded and slow during morning and evening travel hours, and at lunchtime; automobile travel on local highways can be frustratingly slow at any time of day. Just accept it, go with the flow, and give yourself twice as much time as you think you need to get to your destination. Here's an insider's tip: It is not always true, but many times **MacArthur Blvd.** and **Clara Barton Pkwy.** along the Potomac River are blessedly free of traffic when other roadways are bumper-to-bumper.

By bus: The **Metrobus** (202-637-7000) system has routes on every major roadway in the region and can also transport you into Washington, DC, and Baltimore.

Ride On (240-777-7433; www.rideonbus.com), the Montgomery County bus system, has more than 80 routes with thousands of stops. Its buses also connect with the Metro system to provide transportation throughout the Washington, DC–Baltimore area.

The **Bethesda Trolley** (301-656-0868; www.bethesdatransit.org) has a figure-8 route that takes the trolley through the downtown business and office area. It runs until midnight Mon.–Thu., and until 2 AM Fri. and Sat.

By rail: The **Metro** (202-637-7000) subway rail system operates out of Washington, DC, and makes 13 stops in this region. The line is just a bit east of the I-270 corridor it parallels.

By taxi: Among the many taxi companies operating in and around Silver Spring, Bethesda, Rockville, and Gaithersburg are **Montgomery Taxicab** (301-762-2001), **Action Taxi** (301-840-1222), **All-County Cab** (301-924-4344), and **Regency Cab** (301-990-9000).

&. **Taxi Plus** (301-984-1900) has wheelchair-accessible mini vans.

MEDICAL EMERGENCY **Suburban Hospital** (301-896-1000), 8600 Old Georgetown Rd., Bethesda.

Montgomery General Hospital (301-774-8882), 18101 Prince Phillip Dr., Olney (close to Rockville and Gaithersburg).

Shady Grove Adventist Hospital (301-279-6000), 9901 Medical Center Dr., Rockville.

Holy Cross Hospital (301-754-7000), 1500 Forest Glen Rd., Silver Spring.

✳ To See

MUSEUMS **Dennis and Philip Ratner Museum** (301-897-1518; www.ratner museum.com), 10001 Old Georgetown Rd., Bethesda. Sun. 10–4:30. Free admission. Provides a visual depiction of the Hebrew Bible through sculpture, drawings, paintings, and other works of art—primarily those of Philip Ratner. Although this is a private museum based upon the scriptures of the Jewish faith, everyone is welcome, the atmosphere is low-key (in other words, no proselytizing like that found in some other religious museums), and the artwork is interesting and worthwhile.

Community Museum (301-258-6160; www.gaithersburghistorical.org), 5 S. Summit Ave., Gaithersburg. Thu.–Sat. 10–2. Donations accepted. Exhibits inside the restored 1884 B&O Railroad Station chronicle local rail history and the city's movement from a farming community to the present day. The outdoor rail yard has a number of locomotives and other railcars.

Sandy Spring Museum (301-774-0022; www.sandyspringmuseum.org), 17901 Bentley Rd., Sandy Spring. Closed Tue. and Fri. Much to see and do here. The **Farquhar Gallery** features changing traveling exhibits, a guided tour explains the museum's historic aspects and furnishings, and a stables and blacksmith shop reflect the life of earlier times. Musical concerts of various types presented throughout the year.

C&O CANAL NATIONAL HISTORICAL PARK

Around the turn of the 19th century, individual canals afforded access around waterfalls and rapids, providing an easy water route between a young America's eastern coastline and areas west of the Blue Ridge Mountains. Taking a cue from ideas expressed by George Washington and Thomas Jefferson, construction of the Chesapeake & Ohio Canal began on July 4, 1828.

Originally projected to extend 360 miles, the canal never lived up to its investors' dreams. Mounting costs, coupled with the other problems, caused financial backers to decide in 1850 that enough was enough, and that Cumberland was the farthest west the canal would be constructed—a distance of 184.5 miles.

Dry spells, floods, winter freezes, and competition from the B&O Railroad (which coincidentally began construction on the very same day) kept the canal from operating at a profit. A tremendous flood in 1924 destroyed so much of the infrastructure that the canal never reopened. Canal owners turned it over to the federal government for $2 million in 1938.

The canal was proclaimed a national monument in 1961 and named a national historical park in 1971. Today the towpath is open to hikers, bikers, and (except for a short section) horseback riders, and camping is permitted at designated sites. The park service has an abundance of informational handout sheets at its **Great Falls Visitor Center** (301-299-3613; www.nps.gov/choh), 11710 MacArthur Blvd., Potomac, 20854. Exhibits within the center illustrate the history of the canal, while Mike High's book *The C&O Canal Companion* covers the subject in great detail.

Also see *Hiking*.

⌘ **National Capital Trolley Museum** (301-384-6088; www.dctrolley.org), 1313 Bonifant Rd., Silver Spring. Open year-round, but days and hours vary greatly. Small admission fee. *Clickety-clack, clickety-clack.* Take a ride on one of the electric trolley cars that serviced the area for nearly 100 years to relive the days of screeching wheels and swaying cars. The museum has interactive displays, a model streetcar layout, and dozens of vehicles that serviced the area "from Lincoln to Kennedy."

HISTORIC HOMES Clara Barton National Historic Site (301-492-6245), 5801 Oxford Rd. (off MacArthur Blvd.), Glen Echo. Open daily. Free admission and parking. Almost before artillery stopped firing and bullets ceased whistling through the air, Clara Barton was on the battlefield attending to the wounds of Civil War soldiers. Guided 1-hour tours take you through the home of this founder of the American Red Cross. The 1891 house, which was built along the lines of a Red Cross relief structure, contains many items that once belonged to Barton. Adjacent to Glen Echo Park.

Beall-Dawson House (301-340-2825; www.montgomeryhistory.org), 103 W. Montgomery Ave., Rockville. Small admission fee. Guided tours provide insight into early-1800s life. Many of the items in the house (such as the pianoforte and the interesting tin bathtub) belonged to the Beall family. Mr. Beall came and went often, so most of the time the house was inhabited and run by women and slaves. Rotating exhibits on the second floor focus on local Rockville history. Located on the lawn is the small **Stonestreet Museum of 19th-Century Medicine**. The Gothic Revival office was built for Dr. Stonestreet in 1852 and contains many items from his practice.

OTHER SITES F. Scott Fitzgerald Burial Place (301-428-9702), corner of Rockville Pike (MD 355) and Viers Mill Road, Rockville. In what could be interpreted as a summation of the human condition, Fitzgerald wrote in *The Great Gatsby*, "So we beat on, boats against the current, borne back ceaselessly into the past." These words are now engraved upon his St. Mary's Church cemetery tombstone, located at a busy highway intersection next to a Metro rail station. His wife, Zelda Sayre, lies next to him.

✳ To Do

BALLOONING Fantasy Flights (301-417-0000; www.airtravel.com/fantasy), 823 Quince Orchard Rd., Gaithersburg. Sunrise and sunset hot-air balloon rides over the countryside.

BICYCLING Capital Crescent Trail (202-234-4874). The packed-surface rail-trail connects local communities from Georgetown in Washington, DC, to Silver Spring—for a distance of about 11 miles. It does pass through heavily populated areas, but by making use of the C&O Canal, a country club, and a couple of parks, the trail ride can be a pleasant one. One of the highlights is the Delecarlia Tunnel, whose brick-faced portals are a testament to the masons' expertise.

Rock Creek Trail (301-495-2525). This mostly paved route follows Rock Creek for 21 miles from Lake Needwood in Rockville to the heart of Washington, DC.

✦ **Glen Echo Park** (301-492-6282), 7300 MacArthur Blvd., Glen Echo. Open daily. Free admission and parking. It almost feels as if you have walked into the middle of a *Twilight Zone* story. The bumper-car pavilion and the arcade still stand, and the horses of the carousel are freshly painted, but no one is there to operate the rides or entice you to play a game of ring toss.

The land was first developed in 1891 by the National Chautauqua Assembly as a center for the sciences, arts, languages, and literature. The Glen Echo Company, operators of trolleys in the Washington, DC, area, purchased the land and operated the amusement park from 1899 to 1968. The federal government acquired it in 1971, and the park is now used, once again, as a place for cultural pursuits. Classes are conducted on nearly every type of art and craft imaginable; children's theater productions are presented throughout the year—The Puppet Company's are a favorite—and the dances (waltz, big-band, contra, square, and popular) in the Spanish Ballroom are attended by hundreds every weekend. The **Discovery Center Children's Museum** is geared for children ages 2–11.

I just enjoy coming here for an early-morning walk or a browse through the bookstore and gift shop, and to take a ride on the carousel when it happens to be operating (contact the office for times and dates). Ranger-conducted tours of the carousel are given at 2 PM on Sunday.

THE REFURBISHED CAROUSEL'S ROUND HOUSE

Most of the time it runs through the woods along the creek or passes through the recreation areas of neighborhood parks. Be careful at the many intersections with busy roadways.

Seneca Creek State Park (301-924-2127), Gaithersburg. The trailhead parking lot is at 14938 Schaeffer Rd., accessed from MD 118 (Germantown Rd.) south of Gaithersburg. In an out-of-the-way section of Seneca Creek State Park, local citizens have cooperated with authorities and put in many volunteer hours constructing and maintaining a 10-mile network of trails. Hikers, mountain bikers, and horseback riders can freely visit over and over again, watching corn and soybean crops advance from tiny seed sprouts to tall mature plants. The variation from open land to wooded tracts ensures a variety of wildlife, and warblers, vireos, meadowlarks, woodpeckers, vultures, and owls have all been seen visiting or living here.

Bicycle Tour of the African American Community, Sandy Spring. Call 301-260-8860 to obtain a map that details this tour.

Also see the **C&O Canal National Historical Park** sidebar on page 295.

BOAT EXCURSIONS ✐ **C&O Canal**, Great Falls. The 1-hour rides originate at the Great Falls Visitor Center and operate Apr.–Oct. Adults $8; seniors $6; children 4–14 are $5. Take a ride on the mule-drawn *Canal Clipper* boat. Rangers, naturalists, and the mule driver dress in period costume, and the *clip-clop* of the mules along the towpath brings back the canal's former days.

Also see **Rock Creek Regional Park** under *Green Space*.

THE *CANAL CLIPPER* PREPARES TO LEAVE LOCK 20.

FAMILY ACTIVITIES See *Miniature Golf*, and **Dave and Buster's** under *Eating Out*.

299

SILVER SPRING, BETHESDA, ROCKVILLE, AND GAITHERSBURG

GOLF **Hampshire Greens** (301-476-7999), 616 Firestone Dr., Ashton. Features bent grass all the way from the tee to the green on all 18 holes. Total distance from the tip tees is almost 7,000 feet.

Little Bennett Golf Course (301-253-1515), 25900 Prescott Rd., Clarksburg. The par-72 course's hilly terrain offers a challenge as well as nice scenery.

Rattlewood Golf Course (301-607-9000), 13501 Penn Shop Rd., Mount Airy. The excellent drainage on this par-72 course makes it the place to go when other courses are too wet to play on.

Trotter's Glen (301-570-4951), 16501 Batchellors Forest Rd., Olney. Ed Ault designed the par-71 course.

Falls Road Golf Course (301-299-5156), 10800 Falls Rd., Potomac. The weekend fee for playing the 18 holes situated around a lake is about $35.

White Oak Golf Course (301-593-6910), 10911 New Hampshire Ave., Silver Spring. The course is only nine holes, but the low cost of a round and the par 32 make it a good choice for beginning or intermediate golfers.

MINIATURE GOLF ✔ **Bohrer Park** (301-258-6240), 506 S. Frederick Ave., Gaithersburg. The park's miniature-golf course is open May–Oct.

HIKING **Seneca Creek State Park** (301-924-2127). Seneca Creek State Park (also see *Bicycling*) provides enough easy trails to make for enjoyable morning or afternoon hikes. The 3.7-mile **Lake Shore Trail** encircles Clopper Lake, passing through fields of wildflowers. **Long Draught Trail** is 2.5 miles long and follows a stream to a wetlands area and onto a laurel-covered hillside. The **Great Seneca** and **Mink Hollow Trails** are each 1.25 miles in length and traverse forested slopes and marshlands. The **Old Pond Trail**, only a third of a mile long, passes by a pond in its last stages of succession. All of these pathways interconnect in some way or another.

C&O Canal, Great Falls (also see the sidebar on page 295). The area around Great Falls has an abundance of hiking trails. One side trail off the main towpath leads to the dramatic scenery of **Great Falls**, where the Potomac River rushes and churns over a series of drops within the narrow confines of the gorge it has etched out of the landscape. Another outing, with only a few short ups and downs, brings you by reminders of gold-mining days and may enlighten you as to just how much wildlife can exist in proximity to large human population centers.

The **Billy Goat Trail** just might have the most awkward and exhausting 1-mile portion of trail in all of Maryland as it climbs over huge boulders and rock outcroppings along the northern bank of the Potomac River.

Also see *Bicycling* and *Parks*.

HORSEBACK RIDING **Wheaton Regional Park** (301-622-3311), Wheaton, **Rock Creek Regional Park** (301-589-9026), Rockville, and the **Maryland**

Horse Center (301-948-8585), Gaithersburg, provide lessons, recreational riding, and some boarding services throughout the year.

You are also permitted to ride your own horse on the trails of many of the regional parks. Contact the **Montgomery County Department of Parks** (301-495-2507), 9500 Brunett Ave., Silver Spring, for the latest information.

Also see the **C&O Canal National Historical Park** sidebar on page 295, and **Seneca Creek State Park** under *Bicycling*.

KAYAKING AND CANOEING Canoes, rowboats, and some paddleboats are available for rent during the warmer months at **Black Hill** (in Boyds) and **Rock Creek** (in Rockville) **Regional Parks**. Most of the paddling is on small lakes or quiet creeks.

One of America's most scenic waterways, the **Potomac River** provides close to 30 miles—from White's Ferry to Great Falls Park—of delightful canoeing and kayaking for paddlers of all skill levels. Below the Great Falls Visitor Center at **Great Falls**, the river reaches its fall line and becomes narrow, swift, and dangerous for anyone but those who possess the most proficient of paddling skills. If you are an expert, however, that stretch of river will give you the thrill of your life, with narrow channels, 90-degree turns, and drops of 22 or more feet.

Anyone attempting to paddle the falls should go with someone who has made a successful run; paddlers are required to register with C&O Canal park rangers in the visitors center before beginning the trip. Have fun, this is a great thrill, but do not take it lightly, as many have lost their lives here.

Canoes for paddling the Potomac River are available for rent by the hour or day at the **White's Ferry store** (301-349-5200), White's Ferry. They will also shuttle you and your canoe if you make reservations ahead of time.

NATURE-WATCHING See *Walks*.

SKATING Skate Park in Bohrer Park (310-258-6350), 506 S. Frederick Ave., Gaithersburg. Open daily; children under 10 must be accompanied by an adult. The 12,300-square-foot park is designed for in-line skating and skateboarding. The ramps and boxes are designed to suit all skill levels, while the ground surface is asphalt.

Cabin John Regional Park (301-365-2246), 10610 Westlake Dr., Rockville. The park's enclosed rink provides ice skating well into June.

Rubini Athletic Complex—Ice Skating Rink (301-649-2703), 1800 Glenallan Ave., Wheaton. Located within Wheaton Regional Park.

SWIMMING The **Montgomery County Department of Recreation** (301-217-6880) operates six public outdoor pools (usually open Memorial Day–Labor Day) and three year-round indoor pools.

Water Park at Bohrer Park (301-258-6445), 510 S. Frederick Ave., Gaithersburg. Open Memorial Day–Labor Day. Small admission fee. The main pool has several different areas, and a double 250-foot waterslide twists and turns into the splash pool.

✳ Green Space

GARDENS **McCrillis Gardens and Gallery** (301-365-5728), 6910 Greentree Rd., Bethesda. Open daily 10–sunset. The time to visit is between April and mid-June when the 5 acres are ablaze with azaleas and rhododendrons. The gallery features changing exhibits from area artists.

Brookside Gardens (301-949-8230; www.mc-mncppc.org/parks/brookside), 1800 Glenallan Ave., Wheaton. Open daily sunrise–sunset. By far one of the most well-maintained, extensive, and prettiest free-admission gardens I have been privileged to visit. A dozen themed gardens, with plants that bloom from early spring into early winter, allow you to enjoy the beauty of the 50 acres. Sculpted ponds add variety to the scenery, as does the maturing forest around the gardens. This is a don't-miss place, and even if outside temperatures drop too low for you in winter, you can always visit the plants and flowers inside the two conservatories.

PARKS ♿ **Rock Hill Regional Park** (301-972-9396), 20930 Lake Ridge Dr., Boyds. Little Seneca Lake, at 505 acres, is the focal point of the park. You can bring your own electric-powered boat, or rent a canoe or rowboat (in-season). Anglers come here for the largemouth bass, tiger muskie, crappie, catfish, and sunfish. A fishing pier is handicapped-accessible. A system of more than 13 miles of trails (3 miles are paved and handicapped-accessible) enable exploration of the surrounding fields and woodlands. Other features include playgrounds, volleyball courts, and a fitness course.

Little Bennett Regional Park (301-972-9222; www.mncppc.org), 23701 Frederick Rd., Clarksburg. Unlike many other parks located close to large population centers, Little Bennett Regional Park is not overdeveloped with swimming pools, amusement centers, skating rinks, basketball courts, and the like. It does offer a campground with hot showers and a camp store, horseshoe and volleyball areas, and a nature center; yet these facilities are concentrated on just a few acres of its southern edge off MD 355 (and are only available to campers).

The rest of the park has been—more or less—left in its natural state, and 14 miles of trails are available to lead visitors onto 3,700 acres of dense forests, open meadows, narrow hollows, low-rising ridgelines, and small stream valleys lush with vegetation.

Rock Creek Regional Park (301-762-1888), 15700 Needwood Lake

BROOKSIDE GARDENS IN WHEATON

Circle, Rockville. Located close to the center of Montgomery County, the park has two distinct sections: The portion around Lake Needwood is quite developed, with an 18-hole golf course, an archery range, picnic shelters, a playground, a snack bar, and a boat shop that rents canoes, rowboats, and paddleboats in-season. There is even a pontoon boat that carries 25 people onto the lake for 20-minute cruises on weekends and holidays throughout the summer season.

In contrast, the section of the park near Lake Frank has been left in a more natural state. A well-designed network of trails goes beside a small pond, comes into contact with several streams and open areas, and swings around the lake. You may be privileged to watch some of the park's inhabitants—such as squirrels, rabbits, white-tailed deer, snakes, frogs, salamanders, raccoons, weasels, foxes, and beavers—go about their daily lives.

WALKS **Woodend Nature Trail** (301-652-9188; www.audubonnaturalist.org), 8940 Jones Mill Rd., Chevy Chase. Woodend is the headquarters of the Audubon Naturalist Society of the Central Atlantic States. The 40-acre property was willed to the society in 1967, and a brochure keyed to stops along the trail describes the wonders of a nature preserve hidden within a major metropolitan area. The walk is easy and should take about 30 minutes. Free guided walks of the trail are given on the third Saturday of each month at 10, and bird-watching and other nature programs are provided on a scheduled basis. Be sure to visit the gift shop for a superb selection of natural-history books.

* Lodging

MOTELS AND HOTELS This area is nearly bereft of B&Bs but is awash with scores of hotels and motels. Any national chain you can think of will have one or more properties here. Some of the standouts that I have stayed in or visited include:

Bethesda, 20814

Bethesda Court Hotel (301-656-2100), 7740 Wisconsin Ave. This boutique hotel has imaginatively appointed rooms and serves a European-style afternoon tea. Exercise room. $125–175.

Gaithersburg, 20879

🐾 ♿ **Holiday Inn** (301-948-8900; 1-800-HOLIDAY; www.holiday-inn.com), 2 Montgomery Village Ave. The many amenities raise the rooms a notch above those typically found in a Holiday Inn. In-room iron and ironing boards, coffeemaker, free movie channel on the TV, dataports, and an unusually large amount of work space. Indoor pool and fitness center are also available. $89 and up.

♿ **Springhill Suites by Marriott** (301-987-0900), 9715 Washingtonian Blvd. All of the guest accommodations are spacious suites with a sofa bed in the outer room. Fitness center, heated pool, whirlpool, and complimentary continental breakfast. $89–150.

Rockville, 20850

🐾 ♿ **Sleep Inn** (301-948-8000; 1-800-753-3746), 2 Research Court. One of the lowest-cost motels in the region, it has an outdoor swimming pool and free continental breakfast. $80–125.

Silver Spring, 20904

♿ **Courtyard by Marriott** (301-680-8500), 12521 Prosperity Dr. Spacious rooms and nicely decorated public areas and landscaped courtyard. Pool, whirlpool, and exercise room. Some rooms have a coffeemaker, refrigerator, and microwave. $150 and up.

BED & BREAKFASTS Longwood Manor (301-774-1002; 1-866-774-1002; www.bbonline.com/md/longwood), 2900 DuBarry Lane, Brookeville, 20833. Once here, you realize that the modern housing development you drove through occupies land that once belonged to the manor house. Situated on 2 of the original 280 acres, the Mount Vernon–like house was the home of Thomas Moore, who had his friend Thomas Jefferson stay with him a number of times.

Hosts Bruce and Lynn Bartlett are proud of their home and love to share its history (ask about its Civil Defense days) and that of the surrounding area. The furnishings reflect its early-1800s origin, and guest accommodations include two suites and a room that can accommodate three people. I enjoyed sitting on the screened porch overlooking the grounds during my stay in the Brookmore Suite, and I look forward to returning in warmer weather to make use of the swimming pool surrounded by century-old trees. $95–155.

🖉 ♿ **The Reynolds of Derwood B&B** (301-963-2216; www.reynolds-bed-breakfast.com), 16620 Bethayres Rd., Derwood, 20855. Just 2 minutes from a Metro subway station, the modern home has two guest rooms, hot tubs, sauna, and putting green. Children are welcome; lots of toys and videos for them. $95.

🐾 🐾 **Park Crest House** (301-588-2845), 8101 Park Crest Dr., Silver Spring, 20910. The 1930s English Tudor brick home is one of closest B&Bs to Washington, DC (which makes its low rate even more of a deal). European antiques fill the one suite and one other guest room, and terraced gardens descend to a neighborhood park. Pets permitted with prior approval. $80–90.

🖉 **Davis Warner Inn** (301-408-3989; www.daviswarnerinn.com), 8114 Carroll Ave., Takoma Park, 20912. Built in the mid-1800s, the 6,400-square-foot inn has four guest rooms. Three share a common bath, and one has its own Jacuzzi bath. The third floor has three bedrooms and is available for families with children under 16 (inquire about the rate). $75–125.

CAMPING Little Bennett Regional Park (301-972-9222; www.mncppc.org), 23701 Frederick Rd., Clarksburg, 20871. The campground is located within one of the largest regional parks in the Washington, DC, area and provides access to miles of trails and 3,600 acres of woodlands. Close to 100 tent and RV sites with showers, dump station, and coin laundry.

Cabin John Regional Park, 7701 Tuckerman Lane, Rockville, 20850. Head to this park for rustic camping at its seven walk-in primitive sites. Water is not available Nov.–Mar. Permits must be obtained in advance by calling 301-495-2525.

Also see **Seneca Creek State Park** under *Bicycling* and *Hiking*.

✳ Where to Eat

DINING OUT ♿ **La Ferme** (301-986-5255), 7101 Brookeville Rd., Chevy

Old Angler's Inn (301-365-2425), 10801 MacArthur Blvd., Potomac. Open for lunch and dinner daily. Reservations recommended for dinner, when semi-formal attire is expected. Old Angler's opened in 1860 to serve C&O Canal travelers and local estate owners. Its popularity with the movers and shakers of the federal government continues to this day, and it is very possible that the person at the next table will be a Washington, DC, politico, an upper-echelon business executive, or a nationally known sports figure.

Olympia Reges has owned the inn for more than 50 years, and many of its recipes are hers. She does, however, let the kitchen staff be a bit adventurous at lunch, while the offerings at dinner are classic French. Sit on the patio in good weather, or use the spiral staircase to reach the second-floor dining area.

I practically melted into my chair when a bite of the crab porcupine with tarragon ($12.50) hit my taste buds. My dining mate smiled when she sampled her tuna carpaccio ($10). We both smiled as we dined on roast guinea hen with rosemary sauce ($26) and the bourride of seafood medley ($28). Other items on the menu sounded equally enticing and ranged $20–32. The menu changes seasonally, so there will always be something new and exciting.

OLD ANGLER'S INN

Chase. Closed for lunch Sat. The traditional French cuisine pairs with an ambience and decor inside an old farmhouse to transport you to the French countryside. Châteaubriand is a house specialty, but many diners claim the fricassee of lobster is the restaurant's pièce de résistance. Prices are very reasonable for a French restaurant. Entrées run $18–28.

EATING OUT

Gaithersburg

❧ **O'Donnell's** (301-519-1650; www.odonnellsrestaurants.com), 311 Kentlands Blvd. Open daily for lunch and dinner. Fresh fish is brought in daily. Most dishes are prepared as Tim O'Donnell prepared them when he founded his restaurants in 1922. Raw bar, crabcakes, steaks, pasta, and chicken. The broiled rockfish with corn, crab aioli, fried green tomatoes, and rice ($18.95) was tasty and nicely presented. And, oh, those rum buns they serve with each meal! They alone make a visit here worth your time. Entrées $13.95–34.95.

❧ **Summit Station Restaurant and Brewery** (301-519-9400; www.summit-station.com), 227 E. Diamond Ave. Open daily for lunch and dinner. Located in Historic Olde Town. The menu is contemporary American with offerings such as crabcakes (market price), marinated strip steak ($17.95), and pan-seared salmon ($14.95). A variety of their own ales is available throughout the year, with stouts and porters brewed seasonally.

North Bethesda

❧ **Dave and Buster's** (301-230-5151; www.daveandbusters.com), 11301 Rockville Pike. Open daily for lunch and dinner. Much like the ESPN Zone restaurant in Baltimore, food is almost secondary to entertainment at Dave and Buster's. The business occupies 60,000 square feet on the third floor of the White Flint Mall, and most of it is devoted to video games, billiard tables, and simulated horse and car racing and golf games. Lunch is busy, but evenings truly attract the crowds—families and singles alike.

The six-page menu is full of salads, sandwiches, seafood, steaks, chicken, and pasta. The Jack Daniels BBQ Cheeseburger ($7.25) is popular for lunch; expect dinner entrées to be around $15–20. I enjoyed the chicken tortilla soup ($4.50).

Poolesville

❧ **Meadowlark Inn** (301-428-8900), 19611 Fisher Ave. Open daily for lunch and dinner. The family-owned restaurant is known for its large portions and country cooking. You will find the usual chicken and beef items, along with crabcakes and other traditional Maryland dishes. It is hard to resist filling up on the warm homemade bread before your meal arrives. Entrées $10–20.

Rockville

❧ **Wurzburg-Haus Restaurant** (301-330-0402), 7236 Muncaster Mill Rd. (inside Red Mill Shopping Center). Open daily for lunch and dinner. The background music and decor fit right in with the robust German cuisine. Dishes like the potato pancakes or the sauerbraten will keep your digestive juices busy for many hours after you have finished eating. The imported beers and wines have been selected to complement the food. Entrées $9–15.

Silver Spring

❧ **Crisfield Seafood Restaurant** (301-589-1306), 8012 Georgia Ave.

Open for lunch and dinner; closed Mon. A local tradition for more than half a century. The decor is, of course, nautical and the atmosphere relaxed. Seafood dishes include crab-stuffed flounder and fried oysters. The creamy seafood bisque is the way to start your meal. Entrées $12–20.

Wheaton

⌀ **Anchor Inn Seafood Restaurant** (301-933-1814), 2509 University Blvd. Open daily for lunch and dinner. Family-friendly. Clam chowder and baked crab imperial are favorites here. However, do not overlook the meats: The filet mignon with béarnaise sauce is so tender, you almost don't need a knife to cut it. A complete meal (minus drink and dessert) will run you somewhere between $10 and $20.

✱ Entertainment

FILM The Cineplex Odeon (301-469-6601), 7101 Democracy Blvd., Bethesda, presents first-run movies.

Montgomery Village Theatres (301-948-9200, 19236 Montgomery Village Ave., and **Loews Cineplex** (301-948-0906), 9811 Washington Blvd., are the places to see the blockbusters in Gaithersburg.

The Olney 9 Cinemas (301-774-0018), 18167 Town Center Dr., Olney, is located in a shopping center north of Rockville and Gaithersburg.

AMC City Place 10 (301-585-3738), 8661 Colesville Rd., and **Apex Aspen Hill Cinemas** (301-460-3010), 13279 Connecticut Ave., in Silver Spring, are usually among the first theaters in the area to show Hollywood's most highly advertised films.

MUSIC See **Sandy Spring Museum** under *To See*, **Strathmore Hall**

under *Selective Shopping*, and **Imagination Stage** under *Theaters.*

NIGHTLIFE Rock Bottom Brewery (301-652-1311), 7900 Norfolk Ave., Bethesda. Open daily. A full restaurant menu of pizzas, steaks, and meats is served alongside the microbrewer's own offerings of lagers, ales, and stouts. Pool tables attract people during the week, and crowds pour in for the live music on the weekends.

Hollywood Ballroom (301-622-5494; www.hollywoodballroom.com), 2126–38 Industrial Pkwy., Silver Spring. Singles and couples show up Wed.–Sun. to practice and participate in new and old dance steps on the 7,200-square-foot floating maple dance floor.

THEATERS The Olney Theatre Center (301-924-4485; www.olney theatre.org), 2001 Olney–Sandy Spring Rd., Olney. One of the two state theaters of Maryland, the Olney is located on 14 acres and has presentations throughout the year. Besides staging 20th-century American classics, it also produces experimental and alternative plays. Recent productions have included *Grease!*, *Candida*, and *Bye Bye Birdie.*

⌀ **Imagination Stage** (301-881-5106), 11301 Rockville Pike (at White Flint Mall), Rockville. The **Bethesda Academy of Performing Arts** produces plays, musicals, and other theatrical events for children throughout the year. Free or very low-cost admission.

✱ Selective Shopping
ANTIQUES

Brookeville
Lessig's Pleasant Valley (301-924-2293), 21000 Georgia Ave. Usually

open daily. Furniture, china, and collectibles.

Gaithersburg
Julia's Room (301-869-1410) 9001-A Warfield Rd. Thu.–Sun. Carol Bills specializes in English and Belgian furniture, silver, and china.

Kensington
You could easily spend a full day enjoying the architecture and investigating the treasures to be found in the five-block **Antique Row** in Old Town Kensington. Among the many places to browse are:

Prevention of Blindness Society Antique Shop (301-942-4707), 3716 Howard Ave. All of the money generated from the shop helps the nonprofit society offer free visual screening and testing, eyeglasses, and other services to those who would go without. Shop here and do a good turn all at the same time.

✄ **Aunt Betty's General Store** (301-946-9646; www.auntbettysgeneral store.com), 3730 Howard Ave. The interior still has its original pressed-tin ceiling and wood flooring. A great gift shop, especially for kids' items such as old-fashioned toys, Hardy Boys and Nancy Drew books, dolls, and a number of handmade items. The friendly staff will take the time to point out and explain items without any hint of pushing you toward making a purchase.

Pritchard's (301-942-1661), 3748 Howard Ave. Stained glass, art deco items, and Mission arts and crafts.

Doll Shop (301-946-4242), 3758 Howard Ave. Antique and collectible dolls and toys.

Kensington Antique Center (301-942-4440), 3760 Howard Ave. More than 10 dealers in one building.

Antique Scientific Instruments (301-384-1394), 3760 Howard Ave. Almost a museum, as it is filled with old-time weather, navigation, and timepieces.

Olney
The Briars Antiques (301-774-3596), 4121 Briars Rd. Thu.–Sun. Two floors of furniture, china, silver, and crystal. An admirable selection of Victorian jewelry.

ART GALLERIES Kensington Gallery (301-946-6577), 3766 Howard Ave., Kensington. Changing exhibits and displays from local artists.

Strathmore Hall (301-530-0540; www.strathmore.org), 10701 Rockville Pike (MD 355), North Bethesda. A dozen major exhibits focusing on artists of the area are presented throughout the year in the early-1900s mansion. Classes on various art disciplines are also provided, along with a series of classical, jazz, and popular music programs.

Gudelsky Gallery (301-649-4454; www.mcadmd.org), 10500 Georgia Ave., Silver Spring. Located at the Maryland College of Art and Design. One goes to the Gudelsky to see tomorrow's art luminaries today. Although there are exhibits by professional artists, some of the most interesting are those from the college's students and faculty.

Also see **McCrillis Gardens and Gallery** under *Green Space.*

BOOKSTORES The chain stores, such as **Barnes & Noble, B. Dalton Bookseller, Tower Books, Waldenbooks,** and **Borders** are well represented in Kensington, Bethesda, Gaithersburg, and Rockville.

Bethesda

✎ **Bookoo Books for Kids** (301-652-2794), 4945 Elm St. Jam-packed with children's books. Also stocks games, science-project kits, and toys not often found elsewhere.

Olsson's Books and Records (301-652-6399), 7647 Old Georgetown Rd. This local chain is known for its extensive selection and active community events such as author signings and talks.

Mystery Bookshop (301-657-2665), 7700 Old Georgetown Rd. Located inside an office building. Books of intrigue, mystery, and whodunit are stacked all the way to the ceiling. Some are used, most are new; and if you don't feel like reading, there is an extensive selection of audio- and videotapes.

Also see **Woodend Nature Trail** under *Green Space*.

USED BOOKS Second Story Books (301-656-0170; www.secondstory books.com), 4836 Bethesda Ave., Bethesda. With more than 86,000 titles in stock, you are sure to find something to your liking.

All Books Considered (301-929-0036), 10408 Montgomery Ave., Kensington. Located at one end of Antique Row, it has an extensive collection of used and rare books.

Bonifant Books, Records & CDs (301-946-1526), 11240 Georgia Ave., Wheaton. Trade in the books you have read for used records and CDs.

SPECIAL SHOPS G Street Fabrics (301-231-8998), 11854 Rockville Pike, Rockville. Open daily. The store is known and visited by people from around the country who prize its wide selection of materials and sewing items.

FARMER'S MARKETS Gaithersburg Farmer's Market (301-590-2823). Be at the corner of E. Cedar and S. Frederick Aves. Thu. 2–6, June–Nov., to make your choice from the offerings.

Silver Spring Farmer's Market (301-590-2823). The Fenton Street Village Parking Lot 3 is the site of crates and boxes full of the bounty of the land for sale Sat. 7–1, June–Oct.

Rockville Farmer's Market (301-309-3335). You will find the market open at the Rockville Town Center, Wed. 11–2 and Sat. 9–1, June–Oct.

PICK-YOUR-OWN PRODUCE FARMS

Germantown

✎ **Butler's Orchards** (301-972-3299), 22200 Davis Mill Rd. A variety of berries is available for picking from late spring through early fall. Call to find out what is in-season when you get ready to go. Butler's also has a pumpkin festival each weekend in October with hayrides, a petting zoo, and entertainment.

✎ **Phillips Farm** (301-540-2364), 13710 Schaeffer Road. Jean Phillips invites people to the farm from mid-summer into autumn to pick hot peppers, nonhybrid varieties of tomatoes, and flowers. Free hayrides to the pumpkin patch during October.

Poolesville

✎ **Homestead Farm** (301-977-3761), 15600 Sugarland Rd. Fruits and vegetables available throughout the entire growing season. Hayrides every weekend in October, and you can return in December to cut your own Christmas tree.

Silver Spring

⚓ **Beacraft's Farm** (301-236-4545), 14722 New Hampshire Ave. (MD 650). Pick strawberries in May and return to choose a pumpkin in October. Weekends in October are quite festive with a corn maze, a pumpkin patch, and kids' games.

✴ Special Events

February: **Annual East Coast Jazz Festival** (301-933-1822), DoubleTree Hotel, Rockville. Concerts, exhibitors, workshops, and competitions.

March: **Gem and Mineral Show** (301-926-7190), fairgrounds, Gaithersburg. An annual exhibit of minerals, gemstones, and fossils. Demonstrations, workshops, and sales from screened and certified reputable dealers.

April: **Annual Sugarloaf Crafts Festival** (1-800-210-9900), fairgrounds, Gaithersburg. A major festival that attracts more than 500 artisans and craftspeople from around the country. **Steam and Gas Show and Civil War Medical Seminar** (301-670-4661), Agricultural History Farm Park, Derwood. A celebration of tractors, trucks, cars, and riding lawn mowers. A kids' tractor pull and—somehow mixed in with all of this—a demonstration of medical practices from the Civil War. **Literary Festival** (301-215-6660), various sites in downtown Bethesda. Annual event that features nearly 50 literary and cultural artists.

May: **Audubon Nature Fair** (301-652-9188), Woodend, 8940 Jones Mill Rd., Chevy Chase. Annual event of juried arts and crafts, live animals, educational games, and entertainment.

June: **Annual Strawberry Festival** (301-774-0022), Sandy Spring Museum, Sandy Spring. Strawberries galore, plus crafts, music, and kids' games.

July: **Silver Screen Under the Stars** (301-565-7300), Georgia Ave. and Ellsworth Dr., Silver Spring. A 3-day event of food, vendors, and movies presented on a large outdoor screen.

August: **Montgomery County Fair** (301-926-3100), Agricultural Center, Gaithersburg. The largest county fair in Maryland.

September: **Shaker Forest Festival** (724-643-6627), Seneca Creek State Park, Gaithersburg. Handcrafted folk, contemporary, and Shaker styles of furnishings. **Germantown Octoberfest** (240-777-6821), Town Center, Germantown. **Takoma Park Folk Festival** (301-589-3717), Takoma Park Middle School, Silver Spring. Six stages of music and dance, crafts, and children's activities.

October: **Antique and Classic Car Show** (301-309-3340), Civic Center Park, Rockville. Car show and automobile-related flea market. **F. Scott Fitzgerald Literary Conference** (301-309-9461), Montgomery College, Rockville. Workshops, discussions, and tours.

November: **Railroad-Transportation Artifacts Show and Sale** (703-536-2954), fairgrounds, Gaithersburg. More than 600 tables of railroad, steamship, bus, and airline memorabilia for sale.

December: **Winter Lights Festival** (301-258-6310), Seneca Creek State Park, Gaithersburg. A 3.5-mile drive through the holiday light show.

Southern Maryland

ALONG THE CHESAPEAKE SHORE—
Chesapeake Beach, North Beach,
Prince Frederick, and Solomons

AT THE MOUTH OF THE POTOMAC—
St. Mary's City and Leonardtown

ALONG THE POTOMAC SHORE—
La Plata, Port Tobacco, and Waldorf

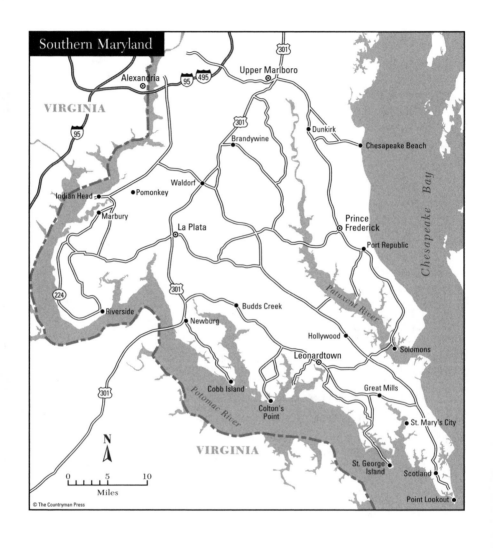

Southern Maryland

VIRGINIA

Alexandria

Upper Marlboro

Dunkirk

Brandywine

Chesapeake Beach

Waldorf

Pomonkey

Indian Head

Marbury

La Plata

Prince Frederick

Port Republic

Chesapeake Bay

Paxuxent River

Riverside

Budds Creek

Newburg

Hollywood

Leonardtown

Solomons

Cobb Island

Great Mills

Colton's Point

St. Mary's City

Potomac River

VIRGINIA

St. George Island

Scotland

Point Lookout

N

0   5   10
Miles

© The Countryman Press

SOUTHERN MARYLAND

A bit off the beaten path, and overshadowed by the Washington, DC–Baltimore metro area, southern Maryland is often ignored as a travel destination by Marylanders and visitors alike. Yet this is where the state had its beginnings when 140 European settlers arrived to found the Maryland Colony in 1634. One of the best-preserved 17th-century town sites in the United States, Historic St. Mary's City is an 800-acre living-history museum on the site of the state's first capital.

History is around every curve in the road. St. Ignatius Church is one of the oldest active Catholic parishes in the country, having served worshipers for more than three centuries. The home of Dr. Samuel Mudd, the physician who treated the broken leg of President Lincoln's assassin, is here, in Waldorf. Several lighthouses from bygone eras are preserved near the shorelines, while it is even possible to scuba dive to the only known World War II rubber-clad German U-boat found within America.

Southern Maryland's lifestyle and low-lying landscape are influenced by the waters of the Chesapeake Bay and those of the Patuxent and Potomac Rivers. Although some of the trappings of the 21st century—such as strip malls and planned communities—are making inroads into the area, many of the old ways remain. In search of flounder, crab, clams, and oysters, many watermen rise before dawn to venture onto the rivers and the bay. Oyster houses and seafood-processing plants along the waterfronts provide employment for those who stay on land.

Numerous tiny towns dot the many miles of shoreline, which, in addition to providing scenic places to rest, can arrange charter excursions for those wanting to cast a line for rockfish or bass. The gently rolling terrain has attracted road bikers for decades, and the local tourist offices have responded by producing a brochure describing various circuit excursions. Finally, no journey into southern Maryland would be complete without a hike to the bay's western shore at Calvert Cliffs State Park to hunt for fossilized shark's teeth.

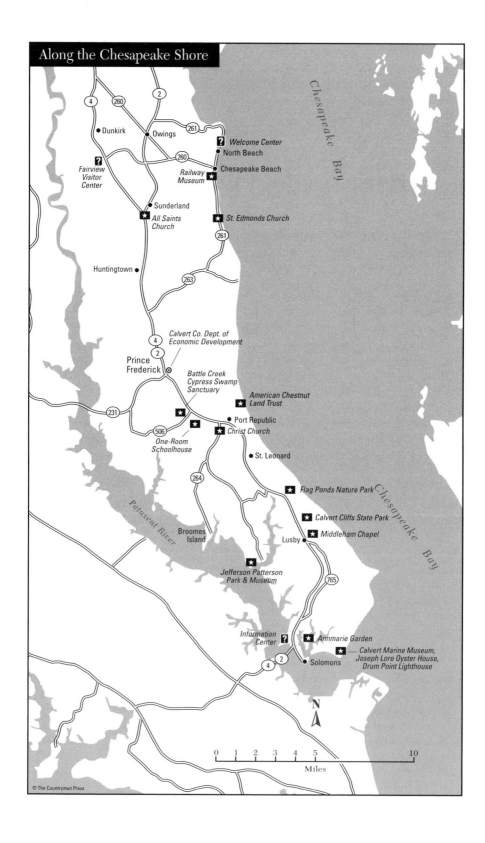

Along the Chesapeake Shore

Chesapeake Bay

Dunkirk
Owings
Welcome Center
North Beach
Chesapeake Beach
Railway Museum
St. Edmonds Church
Fairview Visitor Center
Sunderland
All Saints Church
Huntingtown
Calvert Co. Dept. of Economic Development
Prince Frederick
Battle Creek Cypress Swamp Sanctuary
American Chestnut Land Trust
Port Republic
Christ Church
One-Room Schoolhouse
St. Leonard
Flag Ponds Nature Park
Calvert Cliffs State Park
Middleham Chapel
Lusby
Broomes Island
Jefferson Patterson Park & Museum
Patuxent River
Chesapeake Bay
Information Center
Annmarie Garden
Calvert Marine Museum, Joseph Lore Oyster House, Drum Point Lighthouse
Solomons

N

0 1 2 3 4 5   10
Miles

© The Countryman Press

ALONG THE CHESAPEAKE SHORE—Chesapeake Beach, North Beach, Prince Frederick, and Solomons

Chesapeake Beach began in 1900 as the dream of Colorado railroad baron Otto Mears. By laying railroad tracks from Washington, DC, he hoped to entice people to visit his newly constructed resort town on the western shore of the Chesapeake Bay. For a while his dream was a reality, with scores of people flocking to the amusement park, casino, and hotel along the mile-long boardwalk. Fires, the Great Depression, and easy access to Ocean City on the Eastern Shore brought the dream to an end by the mid-1930s.

Gradually, though, the town has reemerged as a destination spot with a sandy beach, a water park, and several good restaurants.

Due to its proximity to Chesapeake Beach (in fact, it is hard to tell where one town ends and the other begins), the history of North Beach is a parallel of its neighbor's: a rise in tourism in the early 1900s, a decline in the mid-1900s, and revitalization in the late 1900s. A brochure available from the North Beach Welcome Center leads visitors along on a self-guided walking tour of the significant features of the waterfront town. Many people may not take the full tour, but it would be a mistake to overlook the town's boardwalk (now bordered by homes and B&Bs) and its free beach.

Prince Frederick has been the Calvert County seat since 1725, but little remains of its early days. The British burned it in 1814, and another fire in 1884 completed the job of destroying many other buildings. It remains the hub of county services, and has developed into the economic and shopping center of the region.

Solomons has emerged as the area's primary 21st-century destination spot. It was the scenery that first drew me, and many other people, to the small village, located as it is at the wide mouth of the Patuxent River where it meets the Chesapeake Bay. Once here, though, I found many reasons to linger: the excellent exhibits in the Calvert Marine Museum, the Riverwalk boardwalk (from which sunsets are nothing short of spectacular), charter fishing and other boat excursions, and an abundance of B&Bs and restaurants. Nearby, Annmarie Garden and Calvert Cliffs State Park satisfy the need to explore the natural world.

GUIDANCE The **Calvert County, Maryland, Department of Economic Development** (410-535-4583; 1-800-331-9771; www.ecalvert.com), Courthouse, Prince Frederick, 20678, is full of useful information, and its employees are well versed in what to see and do.

The **Solomons Information Center** (410-326-6027), MD 2/4, Solomons, 20688, sits underneath the Governor Thomas Johnson Memorial Bridge and is staffed by information specialists proud of the area in which they live.

Along the North Beach boardwalk is a small structure housing the **North Beach Welcome Center** (301-812-1046), 9032 Bay Ave., North Beach, 20714.

At the very northern end of this area is the **Fairview Information Center** (410-257-5381), 8120 Southern Maryland Blvd. (MD 2), Owings, 20736.

GETTING THERE *By air:* The closest two airports with commercially scheduled flights are **Baltimore/Washington International Airport** (1-800-I-FLY-BWI) near Annapolis and **Ronald Reagan Washington National Airport** (703-417-8000; www.mwaa.com/national) in northern Virginia.

By car: **MD 4** arrives in the region from the Washington, DC, area, while **MD 2** comes in from the north—allowing access from **US 50/301** near Annapolis and the Eastern Shore. (MD 4 and MD 2 combine into one four-lane roadway north of Huntingtown.) The **Governor Thomas Johnson Memorial Bridge** crosses the Patuxent River at Solomons, bringing travelers into the region from St. Mary's County on **MD 2/4.**

By bus: **Calvert County Public Transportation** (410-535-1600; 301-855-1243) operates several commuter buses that could bring you from Washington, DC, to connect with buses continuing on to local sites and towns.

By rail: **Amtrak** (1-800-USA-RAIL) will deliver you to Washington, DC. From there, you could take one of the commuter buses (see *By bus,* above) into the area.

SOLOMONS HARBOR

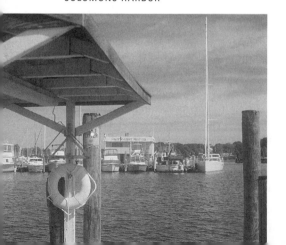

By water: If you own a boat, or are chartering one, the Chesapeake Bay is the obvious way to arrive. There are many marinas along the shoreline to take care of your needs.

GETTING AROUND *By car:* Four-lane **MD 2/4** runs in a north–south direction through the center of this area. Traffic is only moderately heavy, even during rush hours. The smaller two-lane roadways that reach into the more isolated areas are lightly traveled and are great ways to see the local

countryside without feeling harried. **MD 261** through Chesapeake Beach, and
MD 263 to Plum Point, are particularly scenic.

By bus: **Calvert County Public Transportation** (410-535-1600; 301-855-1243) has interconnecting bus routes that reach into nearly every corner of the region. You may have to take a couple of different buses, but you can get to wherever you wish from wherever you are. General fare is $1.50 or less.

By taxi: **Yellow Cab** (410-257-2202), Prince Frederick; **B&B Cab** (410-326-8200), Solomons; and **Calvert Taxi** in North Beach (410-257-2510) and Prince Frederick (410-535-6272).

PUBLIC RESTROOMS In **North Beach**, restrooms (and shower facilities!) are located in the rear of the Welcome Center on the boardwalk.

In **Solomons**, public restrooms can be found along the boardwalk overlooking the Patuxent River and inside the Solomons Information Center.

MEDICAL EMERGENCY **Calvert Memorial Hospital** (410-535-4000), 100 Hospital Rd. (about a mile north of town), Prince Frederick.

Dunkirk Medical Center (410-286-7911), 10845 Town Center Blvd., Dunkirk, and **Solomons Medical Center** (410-394-2800), 14090 Solomons Island Rd., Solomons, have urgent care facilities that can handle minor emergencies.

☀ To See

MUSEUMS ♿ **Railway Museum** (410-257-3892), 4155 Mears Ave. (off MD 261), Chesapeake Beach. Open 1–4 daily, May–Sep.; Oct.–Apr., weekends only, 1–4. Free parking and admission. Exhibits in the 1898 rail station focus on Chesapeake Beach's boardwalk, amusement park, and railroad history.

Port Republic School Number 7 (410-856-0482), Broomes Island Rd., Port Republic. Sun. 2–4, June–Aug. Free. The little one-room schoolhouse served the

THE RAILWAY MUSEUM IN CHESAPEAKE BEACH

✒ ♿ **Calvert Marine Museum** (410-326-2042; www.calvertmarinemuseum
.com), 14200 Solomons Island Rd., Solomons. Open daily 10–5. Small admission fee. It may be smaller in size, but the quality of exhibits and the experience you will have here will easily rival those found in the maritime museum
in St. Michaels on the Eastern Shore. Life-sized boats, models, paintings, and
wood carvings illustrate the life of the watermen, while fossilized remains
and skeletal models of huge sea creatures vividly paint the natural history of
the bay and its tributaries. More than 15 **aquariums** contain live specimens
of the bay's colorful inhabitants. A **children's Discovery Room** has enough
activities to keep even the most rambunctious kid interested and occupied.
Outside exhibits include a re-created salt marsh, live river otters splashing
about in a native habitat site, and a boat basin with vintage vessels.

Don't leave the museum without climbing through the hatch of the **Drum
Point Lighthouse,** one of only three surviving Chesapeake Bay screw-pile,
cottage-style lighthouses. Restored to its original appearance and furnished
as it would have been in the early 1900s, it is a glimpse into the past.

One-hour cruises around Solomons Harbor and the Patuxent River aboard
the **Wm. B. Tennison,** the only Coast Guard–licensed passenger-carrying log-
hulled vessel on the bay, originate from the museum's dock (see *To Do*).

The museum also sponsors shuttle-bus trips ($3; daily June–Aug., week-
ends in May and Sep.) to the **Cove Point Lighthouse,** the oldest continuously
operating lighthouse in the state. Built in 1828, it marks one of the narrowest
parts of the Chesapeake Bay and helps guide ships into the Patuxent River.

THE DRUM POINT LIGHTHOUSE AT CALVERT MARINE MUSEUM

community for more than 100 years, and is now restored and filled with memorabilia.

Joseph C. Lore & Sons Oyster House (410-326-2878), 24430 Solomons Island Rd., Solomons. Open daily 10–5, June–Aug.; 10–5 Sat. and Sun. only in May and Sep. Free. The restored 1934 packinghouse chronicles the boom and decline of the area's seafood business. Tools, equipment, and boats illustrate the lifestyle of the watermen. Free admission.

HISTORIC CHURCHES **St. Edmonds United Methodist Church** (410-535-2506), 3000 Dalrymple Rd., Chesapeake Beach. The original church on this site was built of logs and served as a house of worship and a school for the African American community. It burned in 1893.

Patuxent United Methodist Church (410-535-9819), 3500 Solomons Island Rd., Huntingtown. Built by its African American congregation, the original church on this site burned in 1893 and was replaced with the present structure.

Middleham Episcopal Chapel (410-326-4948), 10210 H. G. Trueman Rd., Lusby. Built in 1784, this is the oldest religious structure in Calvert County. It is also the oldest cross-shaped church in the state. The bell is the oldest one in Maryland.

Christ Episcopal Church (410-586-0565), 3100 Broomes Island Rd., Port Republic. The present structure dates from 1772; be sure to take a walk through its garden of biblical plants.

All Saints Episcopal Church (410-257-6306), at the intersection of MD 4 and MD 2, Sunderland. The Flemish-bond brick church is based upon Georgian ecclesiastical architecture. The baptismal font was imported from England in the early 1700s.

OTHER SITES ✐ **Jefferson Patterson Park and Museum** (410-586-8500; www.jefpat.org), 10515 Mackall Rd., St. Leonard. Wed.–Sun., 10–5, Apr. 15–Oct. 15. Free admission. The museum part of the 544-acre park has a permanent exhibition, 12,000 Years in the Chesapeake, a children's discovery room, and historic farm equipment. Several short trails (brochure available in the museum) go through fields and forest and down to the bank of the Patuxent River.

Chesapeake Biological Laboratory Visitor Center (410-326-7443; www.cbl .umces.edu), Charles St., Solomons. Tue.–Sun. 10–4, Apr.–late Dec. Free. The small visitors center tells the story of the oldest state-supported marine laboratory on the East Coast. Its mission is to increase knowledge about the ecology and natural history of the bay. Free tours of the entire facility are available on Wed. and Fri. at 2, but you must make arrangements in advance.

GUIDED TOURS **Solomons Walkabout** (410-394-0775; www.solomonswalk about.com), Solomons. Reservations required. Tours are given May 3–Oct. 31, Tue.–Sat. 10:30–4 and Sun. after 2. Adult $7; seniors $5; student $3; children under 6 are free. Learn the historic and architectural aspects of Solomons Island during the 2-hour walking tour.

✳ **To Do**

BICYCLING The flat to gently rolling terrain of this region makes it an ideal place to explore by wheel and pedal powder. Most of the side roads are lightly traveled, while the main highway, MD 2/42, has moderately heavy traffic but is blessed with paved shoulders.

The Calvert County, Maryland, Department of Economic Development can supply information on several popular and scenic circuit rides. One of the rides is 37 miles long and passes by the beaches at **Chesapeake Beach**, **North Beach**, and **Breezy Point**, in addition to traversing lightly traveled roads close to the **Patuxent River**. Another, about 15 miles in length, offers the opportunity to get off the bike and do some walking in **Battle Creek Cypress Swamp Sanctuary**, **Flag Ponds Nature Park**, **Jefferson Patterson Park and Museum**, and **Calvert Cliffs State Park**. A third circuit ride is less than 3 miles long and takes in most of the small streets and attractions in **Solomons**.

4 X-Treem Sports (410-257-7858), 3865 Old Town Rd. (at Huntingtown Plaza), Huntingtown. These folks will repair your bike if you happen to run into trouble while touring. They, of course, will be happy to sell you a new one, too.

BOAT EXCURSIONS 🦆 ♪ **Wm. B. Tennison** (410-326-2042), docked at the Calvert Marine Museum, Solomons. Cruises Wed. at 2, May–Oct.; there is an additional 12:30 PM cruise in July and Aug. Small admission fee. The lightly narrated 1-hour trips aboard this 1899, nine-log, chunk-built bugeye (the oldest licensed passenger-carrying vessel of its kind on the bay) take you along Back Creek and onto the wide mouth of the Patuxent River. It's a nice excursion that gives you a different perspective on the land you sail by. The pure white stucco of Our Lady of the Sea Catholic Church stands out impressively against the scenic background.

BOAT RENTALS **Solomons Boat Rental** (410-326-4060), Alexander St. and MD 2, Solomons. If sailboats, canoes, and pontoon boats are too slow for you, these folks rent 15- and 20-foot powerboats in 1-hour, 4-hour, and 8-hour increments.

BOWLING **Lord Calvert Bowl** (410-535-3560), 2275 Solomons Island Rd., Huntingtown, has 22 lanes.

FAMILY ACTIVITIES

♪ **Chesapeake Beach Water Park** (410-257-1404; 301-855-3803), 4079 Gordon Stinnett Ave., Chesapeake Beach. Open Memorial Day through the first day of school. Admission is by height: Guests 42 inches or taller are $14; those shorter (and seniors) are $12. County and town residents are admitted at a reduced rate. It may be small by the standards of water parks in major resort areas, but it still has enough features for a full day's worth of fun. Activity pool, kids' pool, seashell and other slides, and free use of tubes.

FISHING The middle part of the Chesapeake Bay is generally considered to have the best variety of fish species. Charter boats usually take sport anglers onto the water in April in search of rockfish, and in late May and early June for black drum and Atlantic croaker. Bottom fishing for spot, trout, and white perch takes place in July. Bluefish and Spanish mackerel make their appearance in August and are joined by schools of gray trout in September. The season is rounded out by the return of the rockfish in October.

This area of Maryland lays claim to having the largest charter-fishing fleet on the Chesapeake Bay. It is certainly true that there are so many charter boats and charter-boat associations, it is impossible to list them here. **The Calvert County, Maryland, Department of Economic Development** can supply you with information on the associations and individual charter companies.

If you decide to go fishing on the spur of the moment, **Captain Mike Shaw** takes the *Elizabeth S.* (301-997-0852) out of Solomons twice a day. One trip starts at 7 AM, the other at 6 PM. He operates it as a headboat, meaning no reservations are required—just show up. Adults $30, children 12 and under $20.

Other headboats operate out of **Rod 'N Reel** (301-855-8450) in Chesapeake Beach and **Bunky's Charter Boats** (410-326-3241) in Solomons.

GOLF & **Chesapeake Hills** (410-326-4653), H. G. Trueman Rd., Lusby. The par-72 course has tree-lined fairways, doglegs, and a varying terrain. The back nine have a number of water hazards.

& **Mellomar Golf Park** (410-286-8212), 6215 Scaggs Rd., Owings. The nine-hole course has water hazards, sand traps, and bent-grass greens.

& **Twin Shields Golf Club** (410-257-7800; 301-855-8228), 2425 Roarty Rd., Dunkirk. Roy and Ray Shields designed the par-70 course with rolling terrain and water hazards on seven of the holes.

HIKING Flag Ponds Nature Park (410-586-1477), Flag Ponds Pkwy. (MD 4), Lusby, is just a 10-minute drive north of Calvert Cliffs State Park and worth visiting while you're in this area. A network of trails courses through a similar environment and can deliver you to another beach for more fossil hunting.

Also see the **American Chestnut Land Trust** sidebar on page 323.

KAYAKING AND CANOEING Island Creek Outfitters (410-286-0950), 40 Honeysuckle Lane, Owings. They will rent you a kayak by the hour or the day, and will arrange for an instructive class if you are a novice.

✳ Green Space
BEACHES

Chesapeake Beach
Bay Front Park (410-257-2330). There is no admission or parking fee for this small, sandy beach open daily during daylight hours.

& **Breezy Point Beach and Campground** (410-535-0259), Breezy Point Rd. (off MD 261 about 5 miles south of town). Memorial Day–Labor Day. Adults $4;

Calvert Cliffs State Park (301-872-5688), MD 765 (off MD 4/2), Lusby. Open daily sunrise–sunset. Donation requested. Impressively rising to heights of more than 100 feet above the water, Calvert Cliffs was formed millions of years ago when southern Maryland was under a shallow sea. More than 600 species of sea creatures, such as whales, sea cows, porpoises, rays, sharks, seabirds (the size of small airplanes!), crocodiles, mollusks, and reptiles lived in the warm waters.

Since as far back as the 1600s, people have been coming to the base of the cliffs to see what new fossils they would yield. Whale ear bones and skulls, sea cow ribs, crocodile snouts (and fossilized dung), and even peccary scapulas and fossilized pinecones have been uncovered. But it is the thousands of fossilized shark's teeth, some from the extinct great white shark, that have made the cliffs famous and drawn generations of schoolchildren and other visitors to the area.

Today most of the cliffs' 30 miles are privately owned, so you and I are lucky that the state has set aside a short stretch of the shoreline. Here we can walk to the water's edge, study the bay's ecology, search for small paleontological treasures hidden in the sand, or just sit peacefully on the beach. (For visitors' safety, walking on or below the crumbling cliffs is prohibited; and to keep the cliffs from deteriorating any faster, visitors are not permitted to dig for fossils on them.) A network of marked trails takes visitors into uplands forest, through freshwater and tidal marshlands, and beside slowly flowing creeks. It is about 2 miles (one way) to the beach.

CALVERT CLIFFS

seniors and children under 12 are $2; children under 2 are free. This sandy beach on the Chesapeake Bay is about 2,600 feet long; nets protect the swimming area from jellyfish. Popular with the locals for swimming, picnicking, and crabbing from a 300-foot pier.

The campground (additional fee) has waterfront and water-view tent and RV sites with hookups. May 1–Oct. 1.

North Beach

✎ **North Beach Public Beach** (410-257-9618; 301-855-6681). Free. The beach and its bordering boardwalk measure just a bit more than half a mile in length. A fishing and crabbing pier is open 24 hours; the beach is open 6 AM–10 PM. Public restrooms and shower facilities are located in the rear of the welcome center. Since there are no large, rolling ocean waves, the beach is the perfect place to let the kids build a sand castle without fear of it (or them) getting washed away. This gets my vote as the best beach in Maryland after Ocean City.

Also see *Hiking* and the **Calvert Cliffs State Park** sidebar on page 322.

GARDENS **Annmarie Garden** (410-326-4640), Dowell Rd., Solomons. Open daily 10–4. Free. The combination sculpture and botanical garden lends itself to quiet contemplations of artwork and appreciation of the beauty found in nature. The 30 acres are divided into display areas with individual works connected by

---

NATURE PRESERVE

American Chestnut Land Trust (410-586-1570), Scientists Cliffs Rd., Port Republic. Open daily dawn–dusk. Free. Concerned about the detrimental effects Calvert County was experiencing as a result of having the fastest population growth of any county in the Washington, DC, area, a group of far-sighted citizens banded together to form the nonprofit American Chestnut Land Trust. So far, the trust has been able to preserve almost 1,000 acres and has accepted the management of 350 acres owned by the state. Along with adjacent land held by The Nature Conservancy, 2,700 acres of fields, forests, marshes, swamps, and streams are no longer threatened by the modern world.

A network of pathways on these lands is open to the general public. Because they are not well known and are located off main roadways, the trails are blissfully underutilized. About the only other people you may see are trust members on a hike or a local neighbor out for a morning walk. Among the natural features are one of the state's largest living American chestnut trees and Maryland's only known community of sweet pinesap. Parkers Creek, a brackish tidal stream, flows through the last pristine salt marsh on the bay's western shore.

an easy, level path through the woods. I thoroughly enjoy this place and urge you to visit; even the entrance gate and the restrooms are works of art.

WALKS ♂ ♿ **Battle Creek Cypress Swamp Sanctuary** (410-535-5327), Grays Rd., Prince Frederick. Closed Mon. Free. This is a favorite place of mine when I don't have a lot of time to spare but still have a strong urge to return to the natural world. A quarter-mile boardwalk snakes through the 100-acre sanctuary, allowing me to enjoy the abundant wildlife and stately bald cypress trees—which are at their northernmost natural limit here. Exhibits in the nature center explore the area's mysteries (what purpose do cypress knees serve?), and its natural and cultural history.

❋ Lodging

MOTELS AND HOTELS ♿ **Holiday Inn Select** (410-326-6311; 1-800-356-2009), 155 Holiday Dr., Solomons, 20688. More than 300 rooms on a 9-acre waterfront property. Health club, outdoor pool, and tennis and volleyball courts. Modern, clean, well kept, and a friendly staff. $119–269.

BED & BREAKFASTS

North Beach, 20714
Bay Views B&B (410-257-1000; 1-877-245-2223), 9131 Atlantic Ave. With its location directly on the boardwalk and sandy beach, you may

think you are in an Ocean City B&B; but here things are quieter, crowds are fewer, and there is only one guest room and one suite—each with private bath and deck. $120–160.

Prince Frederick, 20679
🌸 **The Cliff House** (410-535-4839; www.bbonline.com/md/cliffhouse), 156 Windcliff Rd. "The Cliff" is right! The modern home is spectacularly perched on the edge of the same cliff face made famous by Calvert Cliffs State Park. The sunrises over the Chesapeake Bay are spectacular, and lounge chairs at water's edge let you enjoy the breezes. Owner Christine Ferrandino was raised in a German *pension* and she has a degree in hotel management, so she knows a bit about hospitality. Only one guest room and one suite ensures a quiet stay. $120.

♿ **Back Creek Inn B&B** (410-326-2022; www.bbonline.com/md/back creek), Alexander Lane and Calvert St. Former navy wives Lin Cochran and Carol Pennock offer landscaped gardens and a goldfish pond, a hot tub, and water-view rooms in their 1880s waterfront home. All rooms have a private bath. The suites and cottage (with its own whirlpool) are additions that provide a bit more privacy with their own entrances. I was

ANNMARIE GARDEN

drawn to the Tansy Room, where you can watch the sun rise over the water in fall. Free bike use for guests. $110–185.

Sedwick House (410-326-0993; www .sedwickhouse.com), 14376 Sedwick Ave. Built in 2002, the luxurious home has a distinctive decor and is only one block from the waterfront. With just two guest rooms, you are assured of having the hosts' attention and help. Afternoon tea or wine, a full breakfast (ask if it is possible for them to fix you the mixed cheese and country sausage strata or stuffed French toast with cream cheese and strawberry jam), and use of bicycles included in the rate of $125–150.

Solomons Victorian Inn B&B (410-326-4811; www.solomonsvictorian inn.com), 125 Charles St. The 1906 Queen Anne Victorian home overlooks Solomons harbor. All guest rooms and suites have a private bath; my favorite was the third-floor Solomons Sunset Suite. Its nooks and lush woodwork made me feel like I was in the cabin of a sailboat. The Carriage House suites have great harbor views. Breakfast is a grand affair with dishes such as shrimp soufflé or a Brie tarragon croissant. $110–195.

Blue Heron Bed and Breakfast (410-326-2707; www.bbonline.com/ md/blueheron), 14614 Solomons Island Rd. The columned Charleston colonial offers two guest suites with balconies overlooking the Patuxent River's confluence with the Chesapeake Bay. Evening wine and hors d'oeuvres and free use of bicycles included. A furnished apartment is also available for weekly or monthly rentals, and by the time you read this they may have completed two additional harbor-view rooms. $200.

COTTAGES **The Cottages of Governors Run** (410-586-2346; 1-877-586-1793; www.baycottages.com), 2847 Governors Run Rd., Port Republic, 20676. Mid-March through October. Two cottages are on a low cliff overlooking the Chesapeake Bay, so great sunrises are assured. A third cottage is only 200 feet away. A small beach is only a minute's walk away. Sue and Steve Kullen have refurbished the 1940s vacation homes and stocked them with everything you need, including linens. One cottage sleeps four to six; the other is designed for two to four. Weekly rates are $850–1,225; weekend and 5-day rates are available.

CAMPING **Patuxent Camp Sites** (410-586-9880), 4770 Williams Wharf Rd., St. Leonard, 20685. Open year-round, but limited sites and facilities in winter. Waterfront sites with hookups, dump stations, and hot showers in the bath facilities. The 100-foot pier is great for fishing or crabbing.

Also see **Breezy Point Beach and Campground** under *Green Space*.

✴ Where to Eat
DINING OUT

Prince Frederick
🌶 ⚓ **Old Field Inn** (410-535-1054; www.oldfieldinn.com), 485 Main St. Open for dinner daily. The winding driveway that goes by manicured lawns delivers you to the 1890s Victorian home and its graciously furnished dining rooms. Seafood is featured prominently on the menu ($16–30), and the fresh fillet of salmon with spinach and Boursin cheese wrapped in puff pastry ($20) is a standout. Or

THE NORTH BEACH BOARDWALK

try the grilled pork tenderloin ($19), or herb cream cheese stuffed filet mignon ($28). A nice place to spend a quiet, romantic evening.

Solomons

&. DiGiovanni's Dock of the Bay (410-394-6400; www.digiovannis restaurant.com), 14556 Solomons Island Rd. Open daily at 5 for dinner. Venetian Anna Maria DeGennaro brings the food of her homeland to this small restaurant overlooking the mouth of Back Creek. Cacciucco alla DiGiovanni, a mélange of six seafoods slowly poached in a shellfish broth ($21.95), is the house specialty. The tasty ravioli di granchio, free-form raviolis with a crabmeat and cheese filling topped with a split of saffron and marinara sauce ($24.95), was different from any pasta dish I've had. Other items based on Anna's recipes, as well as traditional Italian entrées, range $14.95–26.95.

&. Dry Dock Restaurant (410-326-4817; www.zahnisers.com/drydock .htm), C St. in Zahniser's Marina. Open daily for dinner only. Great view of Solomons harbor. The menu changes daily and features seafood purchased fresh from local vendors.

The day I dined, chef Shana Murphy (who started here as a dishwasher before going to culinary school) prepared basil-crusted rockfish with garlic and parsley tossed pasta ($23.95), jumbo lump crabcakes ($27.95), Cornish game hen ($24.95), and cinnamon-crusted oysters ($21.95). Lots of big chunks of meat in the crab soup ($4.95).

&. Lighthouse Inn (410-326-2444; www.lighthouse-inn.com), 14636 Patuxent Ave. Open daily for dinner. Crabcakes and other seafood are the specialties of the two-story restaurant whose huge windows overlook the Patuxent River. The bar, a one-third replica of a skipjack, was designed and built by local craftsperson "Pepper" Langley. Entrées $13–30; sandwiches $7–14.

White Sands

&. Vera's White Sands Restaurant (410-586-1182), 1200 White Sands Dr. Tue.–Sat. 5–9 PM, Sun. 1–9 PM. Closed Oct.–Apr. Live entertainment Thu.–Sun. Vera's extraordinary personality, wardrobe, and decorating style have made this a must-see place for decades. Holding court under a reed-and-bamboo ceiling, she wanders among guests bedecked in pearls, woven headband, and Polynesian-style dress, sipping an endless glass of champagne. Dinner entrées ($14.95–28.95) include beef, poultry, lamb, and seafood. The veal osso buco is simmered in a "provincial" sauce for hours, while the bouillabaisse has an abundance of seafood in a tomato sauce.

EATING OUT

Broomes Island

♂ ᶄ **Stoney's Seafood House** (410-586-1888; www.stoneysseafoodhouse .com), 3939 Oyster House Rd. Open daily for lunch and dinner. The restaurant is next to the Patuxent River, and to get a real feel of being on the water, ask to be seated on the floating deck. Entrées are made with items purchased from Denton's Seafood next door, so everything is as fresh as it can get. The crabcakes (market price) have received accolades for years, while the Neptune's platter ($24.95) gives you a taste of several items. If you are here in the right season, lunch on one of the soft-shell crab sandwiches (market price). Most entrées $12.95–24.95. Steamed crabs by the dozen (market price) are served if locally available. Stoney's has **another restaurant** (410-535-1888) in the Fox Run Shopping Center in Prince Frederick. The menu is the same, but I always miss the atmosphere of the place on the water.

North Beach

♂ ᶄ **Thursday's** (410-286-8695; www.nbeachmd.com/thursdays.html), 9200 Bay Ave. Open daily for lunch and dinner. Thursday's is a local watering hole that serves good, solid food. Appetizers ($4.95–9) and soups ($4.25–7.95) are made from scratch, and prime rib ($13.95) is hand cut and slow-roasted. A few seafood dishes ($10.95–market price) and "south of the border" ($7.95–12.95) items are also on the menu. A dozen draft beers complement meals.

Solomons

ᶄ **The CD Café** (410-326-3877), 14350 Solomons Island Rd. Open daily for lunch 11:30–2:30; dinner

STONEY'S SEAFOOD HOUSE

5:30–9. There is a reason people are willing to sometimes wait a long time to get seated at one of the less-than-a-dozen tables here: Owner-chefs Catherine File and Deborah Witmer create delicious, and for the most part healthful, dishes. The roasted vegetarian sandwich (with house salad; $8.95) I lunched on was full of sweet and flavorful red peppers. The pasta with sun-dried tomatoes, artichoke, feta, and garlic caper sauce ($13.95) I had the next evening was equally satisfying, while my dining mate almost wanted to lick the plate after finishing her honey-blackened salmon ($16.95). Other entrées $7.95–19.95. CD Café is, without a doubt, my choice for Solomons's best taste-bud experience.

& **The Wharf** (410-326-3261), 14442 Solomons Island Rd. Serves lunch and dinner daily in a casual waterfront atmosphere. A dock is available for those arriving by boat. The menu includes steaks ($12.95–15.95) and other entrées ($12.95–17.95), but since you are next to the Chesapeake Bay, go for one of the well-prepared seafood dishes. The she-crab soup (market price) may just be the best and creamiest you will find in all Maryland, and the crab imperial ($19.95) is full of backfin crabmeat.

& **Solomons Pier** (410-326-2424), 14575 Solomons Island Rd. Open daily for lunch and dinner. Located on the pier built in 1919 on the Patuxent River (read about its colorful history on the menu's front cover), so it has a great view of its surroundings. Seafood is the specialty, with a variety of crab dishes (market price), oysters (market price), and crab-imperial-stuffed flounder ($18.95). Chicken, steak, and pasta entrées $9.95–22.95.

CRABS & **Abner's Crab House** (410-257-3689; 301-855-6705), 3748 Harbor Rd., Chesapeake Beach. Open daily for lunch and dinner.

SUNSET AT THE SOLOMONS WATERFRONT

Overlooks the marsh in Fishing Creek Park. Typical crab house with crab balls ($14.95), crabcakes ($14.95), and other fresh catches from the bay ($11.95–18.95). Daily specials and a raw bar.

TAKE-OUT **Dunkirk Seafood Market** (410-257-3000), Lyon's Creek Center (on MD 260), Dunkirk. Open daily. Live or steamed crabs, oysters, and a variety of fish that is available whole or filleted.

Captain Smith's Seafood Market (410-326-1134), MD 4/2, Solomons. Live and steamed crabs, shrimp, seafood, and fresh crabmeat.

COFFEE BARS & **One of a Kind Gallery and Espresso Bar** (410-257-7580), 3725 E. Chesapeake Beach Rd., Chesapeake Beach. The name says it all—coffee amid artwork.

SNACKS AND GOODIES ♂ **Old Town Candy** (410-286-7300), 9122 Bay Ave., North Beach. Lots of things to satisfy the sweet tooth. Individual candy bars or items by the pound.

✴ **Entertainment**

FILM **Apex Theatres** (410-535-0776), Calvert Village Mall, Prince Frederick, shows first-run movies.

✴ **Selective Shopping**

ANTIQUES **Southern Maryland Antiques Center** (410-257-1677), 3176 Solomons Island Rd. (MD 4/2), Huntingtown. Thu.–Sun. A multi-dealer center with items from furniture to china to folk art.

About a dozen antiques dealers, some with their own storefronts and others in a center with several other shops, are located on Bay, 7th, and Chesapeake Aves. in North Beach. All are within easy walking distance of one another.

Dodson's on Mill Creek (410-326-1369), 13690 Olivet St., Lusby. English and nautical antiques.

MAKE YOUR OWN CRABCAKES
Many restaurants proclaim that their crabcakes are 100 percent meat—so that they won't be accused of using filler—but the traditional Maryland recipe included a few extra ingredients:

> 1 cup seasoned bread crumbs (usually Old Bay seasoning)
> 1 large egg
> ¼ cup mayonnaise
> ½ tsp. salt
> ¼ tsp. pepper
> 1 tsp. Worcestershire sauce
> 1 tsp. dry mustard
> 1 lb. crabmeat
> butter or oil for frying

Mix the bread crumbs, egg, mayonnaise, and seasonings together; then mix in the crabmeat. Shape into 6 cakes. Cook in a frying pan with a bit of oil until well browned on each side. Enjoy.

Grandmother's Store Antique Center (410-326-3366), 13892 Dowell Rd., Dowell. Open daily. Inside an old country store are nine rooms of antiques, books, and other items available from various vendors. Be sure to locate the **In the Country** shop to take a look at the "Lilamericans" figurines hand-sculpted by the owner-artist.

Island Trader Antiques (410-326-3582), 225 Lore Rd., Solomons. Closed Wed. A mix of furniture, trunks, linens, and old advertising boxes.

The Chesapeake Marketplace (410-586-3725; 1-800-655-1081), 5015 St. Leonard Rd., St. Leonard. Wed.–Sun. 10–5. More than 80 shops gathered within a 5-acre, former lumberyard complex. The majority are antiques dealers; the others have local crafts, gift items, ceramics, and collectibles.

Nice and Fleazy Antique Center (410-257-3044); 7th and Bay Aves. Several dealers specializing in refurbished oak and Victorian furniture, clocks, vintage slot machines, and nautical items.

ART GALLERIES Calvert County Cultural Arts Council (410-535-0302), 246 Mirrimac Court, Prince Frederick. A small area displays the works of local council members.

BOOKSTORES Bay Books (410-535-9540), 541 Solomons Island Road North, Prince Frederick. Best sellers and local interest.

SPECIAL SHOPS Coffee, Tea and Whimsey (410-286-0000), 9122B Bay Ave., North Beach. You can sip on a cup of coffee while wandering through the gift items.

Main St. Contemporary Art (410-535-3334), 486 Main St., Prince Frederick. Closed mid-February through April 1. The quality of pottery, jewelry, tile, blown glass, and other objets d'art is higher than that often found in similar shops.

Calvert Country Market (410-414-9669; www.calvertcountrymarket .com), 98 S. Solomons Island Rd., Prince Frederick. Located within a refurbished A&P grocery store, the establishment is part farmer's market,

SEA GULL COVE GIFTS, SOLOMONS

part gift shop, part eating establishment. Come here for local produce, meats and seafood, baked goods, arts and crafts, antiques, and people-watching.

Sea Gull Cove Gifts (410-326-7182), 14488 Solomons Island Rd., Solomons. Many nautical and local theme items. Worth a stop to browse and see what is available.

✳ Special Events

February: **Sportfishing Show and Seminar** (301-262-5668), Solomons. Seminars on all bay species taught by experts. Equipment sales, free boat rides, face painting, and casting contests for all ages.

March: **Calvert Artists Showcase** (410-535-7005), Owings. Annual event celebrating the works of local artists. Moneys raised support local nonprofit organizations.

April: **Right of Way Hike** (410-257-3892), Chesapeake Beach. Annual exploration of the old Chesapeake Beach Railway route, by car and by foot. **Celtic Festival of Southern Maryland** (410-257-9003), St. Leonard. Music, dance, bagpiping, children's games, competitions, storytelling, and all things Celtic.

May: **Annual Herb and Wildflower Show** (410-535-5327), Battle Creek Cypress Swamp Nature Center, Prince Frederick. The sale of herbs and native wildflowers benefits local environmental education programs.

June: **Annual African American Family Community Day** (410-535-2730), Jefferson Patterson Park and Museum, St. Leonard. Music, wagon rides, African dancing, kids' activities, crafts, and food.

July: **American Indian Heritage Day** (410-586-8502), Jefferson Patterson Park and Museum, St. Leonard. Dance, music, and other visual and performing arts by American Indians from the region. Hands-on basketry, archery, and stone tool making.

August: **Calvert County Jousting Tournament** (410-586-0565), Port Republic. Oldest tournament in Maryland of the state's official sport. Crafts, country supper, and bazaar. **North Beach Bayfest** (301-855-6681), North Beach. Crafts, Maryland food, pony rides and other children's activities, music, and antique cars.

September: **Artsfest** (410-326-4640; www.annmariegarden.org), Annmarie Garden, Solomons. Juried arts and crafts show, with visual and performing arts. **War of 1812 Reenactment and 19th-Century Tavern Night** (410-586-8502), Jefferson Patterson Park and Museum, St. Leonard. Relive the Battle of St. Leonard during the War of 1812. Reenactors stage the land and water aspects of the skirmish. Recreations of camp life, period crafts, and food. **Calvert County Fair** (410-535-0026), fairgrounds, Barstow.

November: **Hospice Festival of Trees** (410-535-0892), Patuxent High School, Lusby. Marvelously decorated trees, holiday music, and crafts. Benefits Calvert Hospice.

December–early January: **Garden in Lights** (410-326-4640), Annmarie Garden, Solomons.

December: **Solomons Christmas Walk** (410-326-1950; www.solomons .business.com), Solomons. Annual event with candlelit streets, art, entertainment, bell choirs and carolers, a puppet show, and a boat light parade.

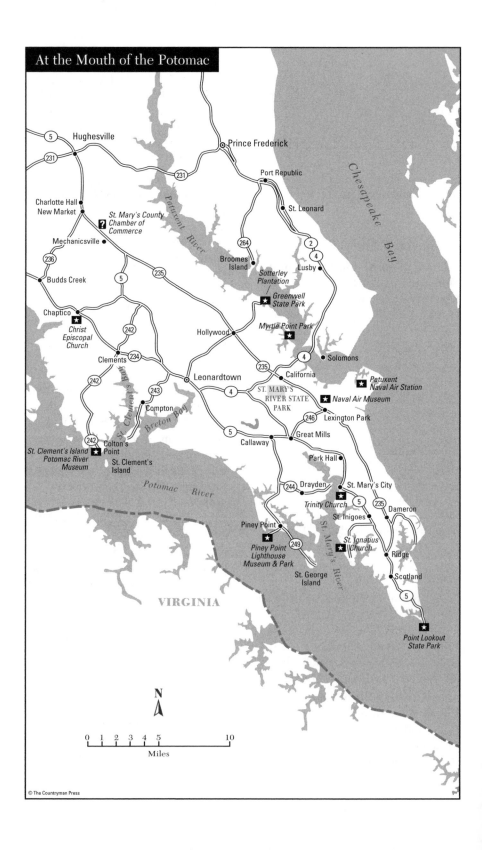

At the Mouth of the Potomac

Hughesville

Prince Frederick

Port Republic

Charlotte Hall
New Market

St. Leonard

St. Mary's County
Chamber of
Commerce

Mechanicsville

Broomes
Island

Lusby

Budds Creek

Sotterley
Plantation

Chaptico

Greenwell
State Park

Christ
Episcopal
Church

Myrtle Point Park

Hollywood

Clements

Leonardtown

Solomons

California

Patuxent
Naval Air Station

Compton

ST. MARY'S
RIVER STATE
PARK

Naval Air Museum

Lexington Park

St. Clement's Island
Potomac River
Museum

Colton's
Point

Callaway

Great Mills

St. Clement's
Island

Park Hall

Drayden

St. Mary's City

Trinity Church

Dameron

St. Inigoes

Piney Point

St. Ignatius
Church

Ridge

Piney Point
Lighthouse
Museum & Park

St. George
Island

Scotland

VIRGINIA

Point Lookout
State Park

Chesapeake Bay

Patuxent River

St. Clement's Bay

Breton Bay

Potomac River

St. Mary's River

N

0 1 2 3 4 5   10
                  Miles

© The Countryman Press

AT THE MOUTH OF THE POTOMAC—St. Mary's City and Leonardtown

Maryland's deepest roots grow here, for this is where the colony that eventually became a state was born.

Maryland's story begins in November 1633. Imagine the courage, fortitude—and desperation—it must have taken for close to 200 British men, women, and children to leave all they had known to venture forth into unclear futures in an unknown land. Longing for a religious tolerance denied to them in their home country, they boarded the *Ark* and the *Dove* to face a 4-month voyage across the Atlantic Ocean. Sailing into the mouth of the Potomac River, these seekers of a new life landed at St. Clement's Island in March 1634. A large wooden cross was erected in thanks, and they prayerfully celebrated the first Roman Catholic Mass in the English-speaking colonies.

Soon afterward, they moved to a more suitable site for a permanent settlement along the St. Mary's River. Their story, and that of the state's early days, is vividly portrayed and preserved for visitors to experience in 800-acre Historic St. Mary's City.

As to be expected on fertile land bordered by two rivers and the Chesapeake Bay, life in the colony developed around large plantations and seafood harvesting. To some degree, many things remain the same today. Yes, housing developments eat into farmland, and strip malls replace tobacco barns; but acres of open meadows still edge quiet country lanes, and new generations of watermen carry on the traditions of their grandparents. And like many American presidents, going all the way back to James Madison, visitors are lured here by the water, the scenery, and a slower pace of life. Montana may be known as Big Sky Country, but to stand on a southern Maryland shoreline surrounded by open fields and gaze to where water meets earth's canopy is to be filled with a sense of immense space.

COMMUNITIES **Leonardtown**, despite being St. Mary's County seat since 1708, still has a population of only about 2,000 people. While retaining a small-town atmosphere—it has a central square bordered by local businesses and the

ST. CLEMENT'S ISLAND

courthouse—it has some of the best upscale restaurants and shops in the region.

The area around **Lexington Park** remained a quiet place until the middle of World War II, when a small naval station expanded into the 6,000-acre Patuxent Naval Air Station. The federal government developed a housing project outside the station for military personnel, and the city has continued to expand. It is now the economic center of the region, and shows all of the signs of rapid modernization, with shopping centers, restaurants, strip malls, and—modest by big-city standards—the heaviest traffic around.

California is basically a suburb of Lexington Park, and its stores and restaurants are the first things people see when they arrive from Solomon's across the MD 4/ Governor Johnson Memorial Bridge.

Like a thin finger jutting into the expanse of water created by the confluence of the Potomac and St. Mary's Rivers, **St. George Island** is connected to the mainland by a two-lane bridge. The life you see here is representative of what you would find if you were to drive many of the region's country lanes to small communities at land's end.

Amish families from Pennsylvania began to move onto farmland around **Charlotte Hall** in the mid-1900s, and it is not an uncommon sight to see a horse and buggy moving along at 18th-century speeds on some of the back roads.

GUIDANCE **St. Mary's County Division of Tourism** (301-475-4200; 1-800-327-9023; www.stmarysmd.com/tourism), 23115 Leonard Hall Dr., Leonardtown, 20650.

The **St. Mary's County Chamber of Commerce** (301-884-5555; www.smc chamber.com), 28290 Three Notch Rd. (MD 5), Mechanicsville, can also supply you with some information.

GETTING THERE *By car:* This is almost a you-have-to-want-to-get-here kind of place. **MD 5/235** is the main highway coming into the area from the north and provides access from Washington, DC, and the interstates. The **MD 4/Governor Thomas Johnson Memorial Bridge** crosses the Patuxent River near California for those coming from Solomons and other points in Calvert County.

By air: The two airports that serve this area with scheduled commercial flights are **Baltimore/Washington International Airport** (1-800-I-FLY-BWI) near Annapolis and **Ronald Reagan Washington National Airport** (703-417-8000) in northern Virginia.

By water: There are no scheduled boats bringing you into the region, but if you own or are renting one, there are scores of marinas to make your stay easier.

GETTING AROUND *By car:* **MD 235** is a four-lane highway that runs in a north–south direction through the region. **MD 5** parallels MD 235 a bit to the south, is primarily two-lane, and travels through smaller towns and scenic countryside.

By bus: The **St. Mary's Transit System** (301-475-5100) has bus routes that make it possible to get to just about anywhere in the area: Leonardtown, Lexington Park, California, Great Mills, Charlotte Hall, and points in between. Most fares are about $1, but some rural routes are up to $3; exact change required.

By taxi: **Friendly Cab** (301-863-8141) in Lexington Park and **Leonardtown Cab** (301-475-9157) in Leonardtown.

MEDICAL EMERGENCY **St. Mary's Hospital** (301-475-8981), 25500 Point Lookout Rd., Leonardtown.

✳ To See

MUSEUMS ⅃ **St. Clement's Island Potomac River Museum** (301-769-2222), 38370 Point Breeze Rd., Colton's Point. Weekdays 9–5 and weekends noon–5, late Mar.–Sep.; noon–4 Wed.–Sun., Oct.–late Mar. Small admission fee; children 12 and under are free. The displays in the small museum do a good job of telling the story of Maryland's first English settlers. By the time I left here, I knew what prompted them to leave their homeland, and the difficulties they faced before and during their ocean voyage. A 20-foot mural celebrates their arrival on St. Clement's Island.

ON DISPLAY AT THE PATUXENT RIVER NAVAL AIR MUSEUM

The museum sponsors boat tours to the 40-acre island on Sat. and Sun. at 12:30, May–Oct. Adults $5; children 12 and under are $3. Now a state park, it has interpretive signs along short pathways that lead to the large cross erected in 1934 to celebrate the 300th anniversary of the settlers' arrival.

& **Patuxent River Naval Air Museum** (301-863-7418; www.paxmuseum.com), MD 235 (next to Gate One of the Patuxent River Naval Air Station), Lexington Park. Open 10–5; closed Mon. Free parking and admission. The only museum in the country dedicated to naval aviation research and testing. Outside are a number of historic aircraft such as an E-2B Hawkeye, F-14 Tomcat, and Grumman A-6 Intruder. The inside exhibits tell of the development of the ejection seat, flight helmet, and the amazingly portable helicopter.

HISTORIC HOMES **Tudor Hall** (301-475-2467), 41680 Tudor Place, Leonardtown. Mon.–Fri. 10–2. Donations accepted. The 1700s Georgian mansion is notable for its inset portico, a new style for its day. The home sat on a 1,000-acre farm and was once owned by members of the Francis Scott Key family. It is now the research repository for the St. Mary's Historical Society. The public is welcome to walk through the house with a member of the society.

HISTORIC SITES & **Sotterley Plantation** (301-373-2280; 1-800-681-0850; www.sotterley.com), on MD 245, Hollywood. Grounds open all year (free), Tue.–Sun. 10–4; guided house tours (small admission fee) given Tue.–Sun., May–Oct. Operates as a working plantation of the 1800s. The house's initial construction began in 1717, making it decades older than other famous homes such as Mount Vernon and Monticello. The extensive grounds sit next to the Patuxent River. One of the most interesting sites is the slave quarters of the Hillary Kane family, the only publicly accessible slave cabin in the state. (Greenwell State Park is just a couple of minutes' drive from here; see *To Do*.)

Old Jail Museum (301-475-2467), 41680 Tudor Place, Leonardtown. The museum is officially open Wed.–Fri. noon–4, but you may need to go to Tudor Hall to find someone to open it for you. A few pieces of furniture and other artifacts depict what the jail would have looked like in the mid-1800s. The jailer's family residence was on the first floor, the small women's cell has a bunk in it, and the larger men's cell is on the top floor.

HISTORIC CHURCHES & **Christ Episcopal Church** (301-884-3451), MD 238, Chaptico. Constructed in 1736. During the War of 1812, the British dug up graves in the yard and stabled their horses inside the church. Members of the Francis Scott Key family are buried here in a family vault.

Dent Chapel (301-884-8171), Old MD 5, Charlotte Hall. Constructed of granite with a brick belt in 1883, it may be one of the best Victorian Gothic structures in the state.

St. Francis Xavier Church (301-475-9885), MD 243, Compton. Constructed in 1731, less than 100 years after the first settlers arrived in the area, it is thought to be the oldest Catholic church in continuous use in English-speaking America.

Historic St. Mary's City (240-895-4990; 1-800-SMC-1634; www.stmaryscity.com), Rosecroft Rd. (off MD 5). Wed.–Sun., late June through mid-September; Tue.–Sat. in spring and fall. Days and hours have changed year to year, so call for the latest schedule. Adults $7.50; students with ID $5.50; children 6–12 are $3.50.

One of the best-preserved archaeological sites in America and certainly the best representation of a 17th-century colonial town in Maryland. Schedule a minimum of half a day to take in everything on this 800-acre living-history site of Maryland's first permanent English settlement. Self-guided tours (with provided map/brochure) lead you to costumed interpreters (who are some of the best I've met in not breaking character) in the reconstructed Woodland Indian settlement, Godiah Spray Plantation, Farthings's Ordinary, State House, and, most spectacularly, a full-sized reproduction of the *Dove*, one of the ships that transported the settlers across the ocean.

THE FULL-SIZED REPRODUCTION OF THE *DOVE*

Williamsburg in Virginia may be bigger, yet Historic St. Mary's is a much more manageable place to get a handle on the big picture—and its admission fee is much less.

Trinity Episcopal Church (301-862-4597), MD 5, Historic St. Mary's City. Constructed in 1829 with bricks that were salvaged from Maryland's first statehouse, which had been built in 1676.

St. Ignatius Church (310-872-5590), Villa Rd. (off MD 5), St. Inigoes. Constructed in 1785, it is believed to house the oldest active Catholic parish in the country.

PINEY POINT LIGHTHOUSE AND MUSEUM

LIGHTHOUSES & **Piney Point Lighthouse and Museum** (301-769-2222), MD 249 and Lighthouse Rd., Piney Point. Grounds open daily sunrise–sunset; the museum is open noon–5 Fri.–Mon., May–Oct. Donations accepted. Built in 1836, the brick tower Piney Point Lighthouse was Maryland's first permanent lighthouse on the Potomac River and is the only accessible such structure on its original location in southern Maryland. The small museum, once the chief petty officer's garage, tells the story of its construction and operation, and the role of the Coast Guard.

Piney Point's beautiful scenery and cool breezes have made it a popular recreation spot for many U.S. presidents, beginning with James Madison. A small beach is available for swimming (no lifeguards). Be here as the glow of a rising or setting sun shimmers upon the broad expanse of water and you will understand why they came.

OTHER SITES **Naval Air Station** (301-757-4814), Lexington Park. The world's premier research, development, testing, and evaluation center for naval aircraft covers 6,000 acres, much of it environmentally and culturally interesting. A pamphlet describing a self-guided tour is available at the entrance gate. *Please note:* Continuing security concerns have led to restrictions on public visitation at military installations; call for the latest information.

✳ To Do

AUTO RACING & **Maryland International Raceway** (301-884-9833; www .mirdrag.com), MD 234, Budds Creek. Races take place on weekends Mar.–Oct. at the International Hot Rod Association (IHRA) quarter-mile drag-racing track.

BICYCLING More and more bicyclists are discovering the pleasures of riding the lightly traveled roadways of the area. The **St. Mary's County Division of Tourism** can provide information on four popular circuit routes.

One trip is almost 26 miles long and concentrates on the sites to be seen near **St. Clement's Bay** and the **Wicomico** and **Potomac Rivers**. Another is a ride of less than an hour that is more centered upon sights to be seen along the **Patuxent River**, such as **Sotterley Plantation** and **Greenwell State Park**. A third journey is just over 40 miles. Its route includes the waterside along **St. George Island** and **Piney Point Lighthouse**. The fourth ride, at 27.5 miles, is historically interesting, as it brings riders into **Historic St. Mary's City** and **Point Lookout State Park**.

St. Mary's River State Park (301-872-5688), Camp Cosoma Rd. (off MD 5), Great Mills. You may not think of the flat land of southern Maryland as having much terrain for mountain bikers. However, the 9-mile singletrack course, built with mountain bikes in mind, encircles a 250-acre lake and can be a good challenge and a nice ride. Also open to hikers.

Mike's Bikes (301-863-7887), 21310-C Great Mills Rd. (at Great Mills Shopping Center), Lexington Park. Closed Sun. They sell skateboards, and also sell and service bicycles.

BIRDING ❀ ♿ **Greenwell State Park** (301-373-9775; 301-373-2731), 25402 Rosedale Manor Lane, Hollywood. Open daily during daylight hours. Free; donations accepted. The many different environments of the park—riparian, wetlands, floodplain, field, and forest—are attractive to a wide variety of feathered creatures. Among the many seen here are great blue heron, bald eagle, osprey, American kestrel, a variety of hawks (primarily red-tailed), and the elusive Swainson's hawk. Barred, great horned, and eastern screech owls are sometimes heard in the early evening, while black vultures soar over the fields—which are home to a bird I see and hear less often than I used to, the bobwhite.

Point Lookout State Park (310-872-5688), MD 5, Scotland. Its location on the tip of land at the confluence of the Potomac River and the Chesapeake Bay ensures the park as a great place to experience the migrations along the Great Atlantic Flyway. Watch for northern gannets, brown pelicans, and others.

BOAT EXCURSIONS See **St. Clement's Island Potomac River Museum** under *To See*.

FAMILY ACTIVITIES ✎ **Bowles Farm Corn Maze** (301-475-2139; www .bowlesfarm.com), Pincushion Rd. (off MD 234), Clements. Fri.–Sun.

NEGOTIATING THE BOWLES FARM CORN MAZE

from mid-September through October. Adults $8; children 6–11 are $6; children under 5 are free. A fun way to spend a morning or afternoon. More than 3 miles of trails twist, turn, and befuddle as the maze takes you through 15 acres of tall, living cornstalks. After making your way through the labyrinth (some folks have had to be rescued!), you can reward the kids by wandering over to the petting zoo and/or picking out your Halloween pumpkin.

✍ **Forest Hill Farm Crazy Corn Maze** (301-884-3086; www.foresthillfarm .com), 39136 Avie Lane, Mechanicsville. Sat. and Sun. from mid-August through October. Corn maze, hayrides, farm animals, picnic area, and local produce.

Also see *Miniature Golf.*

FISHING Fishing in the area starts in late April and continues through December. Charter boats, many providing very personal service by taking only six or fewer passengers, can take you onto the water for rockfish, flounder, sea trout, Spanish mackerel, black sea bass, and more. The **St. Mary's County Division of Tourism** can supply you with a full list of contacts.

Some of the many well-respected captains in the area include:

Ridge
Captain Gary Sacks (301-872-5506; www.maricaii.com), 48862 Curley's Rd.

Captain Randy Powers (301-872-9321; www.shannoniv.com), 16518 Chesapeake Dr.

Park Hall
Captain Scott Russell (1-877-272-2526; www.playtimefishing.com), P.O. Box 331.

Captain Mike Gerek (301-863-2330; paxp.com/sandramarie), 18164 Point Lookout Rd.

GOLF ♿ **Wicomico Shores** (301-884-4601), Aviation Yacht Club Rd. (Wicomico Shores Subdivision), Chaptico. Open daily. The course is scenically located next to the Wicomico River and has many wooded areas with lots of wildlife. The back tees measure 6,397 feet, and 72 is par.

♿ **Breton Bay Golf and County Club** (301-475-2300), 21935 Society Hill Rd., Leonardtown. Open daily. The 18-hole course was designed by J. Porter Gibson and built in 1974. Fairways have Bermuda grass; the greens are planted with bent grass. Lakes and other water come into play.

MINIATURE GOLF ✍ **Hollywood Swing and Swat** (301-373-8858), Mervell Dean Rd., Hollywood. Open daily Mar.–Nov. The 18-hole course is adjacent to a driving range and batting cages.

HIKING 🐾 ♿ **Greenwell State Park** (301-373-9775), 25402 Rosedale Manor Lane, Hollywood. The 600-acre park is on land that was once a part of 4,000-acre Resurrection Manor. A patchwork of open fields, wetlands, and forests keeps the land looking much the way it would have in the 17th century, and about 6.5 miles of trails take visitors out to the far reaches. Most of the routes are easy and level, but if you don't have time to hike all the pathways, I urge you to at least take the one along the Patuxent River. It is a particularly pretty outing, and a portion of it is handicapped accessible. All but two of the trails are also open to bikers and equestrians; pets must be leashed.

Also see **St. Mary's River State Park** under *Bicycling*, and *Green Space*.

SCUBA DIVING U-1105 Black Panther Historic Ship Preserve (301-769-2222), Piney Point. The World War II German Black Panther was the world's first stealth weapon, as its rubber coating made it invisible to sonar equipment. Captured near the end of the war, it was tested by the U.S. Navy and then intentionally sunk in about 100 feet of water in the Potomac River. Expert recreational divers are permitted to dive to the site after obtaining information from the Piney Point Lighthouse and Museum.

✴ Green Space

BEACHES Myrtle Point Park (301-475-4572), Patuxent Blvd., California. Free. The small beach and several short trails have a view onto the Patuxent River and its Governor Johnson Memorial Bridge. No lifeguards.

Elm's Beach (301-475-4572), Forest Rd., Dameron. Free. A county-operated park, Elm's has a nice beach (access open year-round) on the Chesapeake Bay. The bay is so wide here that you could almost convince yourself that you are at an oceanside beach. No lifeguards.

🐾 **Greenwell State Park** (301-373-9775; 301-373-2731), 25402 Rosedale Manor Lane, Hollywood. Swimming is permitted from the park's small beach along the Patuxent River. Remember that you are swimming in a river, so there may be a strong current to contend with. No lifeguards.

PARKS ✐ **Point Lookout State Park** (310-872-5688), MD 5, Scotland. Open daily sunrise–sunset. Small admission fee. The park's location at the mouth of the Potomac River made it a strategic defense point, and it served as a watch post during the Revolutionary War and the War of 1812. During the Civil War, it functioned as a military hospital and prison camp—in which more than 3,000 of the estimated 20,000–50,000 Confederate prisoners died from exposure, starvation, and diseases related to poor sanitation. The park's museum (the original photos of prisoners are vivid relics of the past) and nearby ruins of **Fort Lincoln** tell the story.

POINT LOOKOUT LIGHTHOUSE

THE REAR ENTRANCE OF THE BROME-HOWARD INN, ST. MARY'S CITY

Also in the park are picnic areas, several short nature trails, and a swimming beach and picnic area. The 1830 **Point Lookout Lighthouse** sits at land's end and is open to the public only one day a year, in November.

✷ Lodging

INNS Brome-Howard Inn (301-866-0656; www.bromehowardinn.com), 18281 Rosecroft Rd., St. Mary's City, 20686. Roses on your bed and dresser welcome you to your room in the elegant 19th-century Brome-Howard Inn. All guest rooms and the suite have a private bath. Come here for beautiful St. Mary's River views, miles of hiking trails connecting with those of Historic St. Mary's City, free bicycle use, and the opportunity to enjoy a delicious dinner (see *Dining Out*). Ask how the house came to sit on this particular piece of land—it is an amazing story. $145–185.

BED & BREAKFASTS

Ridge, 20680
Bard's Field B&B (301-872-5989), 15671 Pratt Rd. Host James Pratt grew up in this 1798 small Colonial manor home that overlooks Rawley Bay on the Potomac River. He and his wife, Audrey, refurbished it and offer two large guest rooms that share a bath. The surrounding fields, gardens, and water make for a relaxing stay. Do not leave without having James take you into the basement. It is a virtual museum of items he has collected from days gone by—tools, drills, carpenter's planes, and more. $75.

Scotland, 20687
🍃 **Hale House B&B** (301-872-4558), 49644 Potomac River Dr. The Hales designed and hand-built their impressive contemporary home, which sits at the very mouth of the Potomac River. Many of the interior walls are brick, and each wall facing the river is basically one big window. All rooms, including the two for guests (private baths and entrances), are spacious. A

swimming pool overlooking the river and the 500-foot pier only add to the value of the low rates. $85.

St. Michael's Manor (301-872-4025; www.stmichaels-manor.com), 50200 St. Michael's Manor Way. There are only two guest rooms (with shared bath) in this brick 1805 home sitting alone on 10 waterfront acres, so it has a very homey feel. In addition to cooking a full country breakfast, Nancy and Captain Joseph Dick set out figs, apples, and fruits freshly picked from their garden. A canoe and a pedal boat are available for guest use; the hammock overlooking the water is for relaxing after a dip in the pool. $70–90.

CAMPING ✿ **Take It Easy Campground** (301-994-0494; 1-877-994-0494), 25285. Take It Easy Ranch Rd. (off MD 249), Callaway, 20620. Open year-round. There are tent and RV sites with hookups and a dump station, a swimming pool, and a 7-acre fishing lake on the 200-acre property. Pets permitted.

✿ **Dennis Point Marina and Campground** (301-994-2288; 1-800-974-2288), 46555 Dennis Point Way, Drayden, 20630. Waterfront camping, a short nature trail, a couple of small playgrounds for the kids, a tennis court, a swimming pool, laundry facilities, fishing, canoeing and kayaking, a store, and a restaurant. With all of these amenities, you may never have to leave.

Le Grande RV Sales & Camping Resort (301-475-8550), MD 5 (south of Leonardtown), Leonardtown, 20650. There are a few tent sites, but the obvious clientele is the motorized crowd. Hookups, a dump station, and RV sales and service.

Seaside View Recreation Park & Campground (301-872-4141; www.seaside-view.com), 48593 Seaside View Rd., Ridge, 20680. Tent and RV sites with hookups and a dump station. A restaurant and full-service marina on Jutland Creek are on the premises.

Camp Merryelande (1-800-382-1073; www.campmd.com), MD 249, St. George Island, 20674. Open year-round. Waterfront tent sites overlooking the broad mouth of the Potomac River. A beach and swimming area, crabbing and fishing pier, and laundry. Rental cottages (one to six bedrooms) complete with kitchen, linens, TV, and air-conditioning.

Also see **Point Lookout State Park** under *Green Space.*

✳ Where to Eat

DINING OUT The Tavern At The Village (301-863-3219; www.thetavernatthevillage.com), Wetstone Lane, Wildewood Retirement Community, California. Reservations strongly recommended. Lunch served Tue.–Sat. 11–2; dinner, Wed.–Sat. 5:30–9. Fine dining in a retirement community? Yes. The menu changes frequently and has included pan-seared and baked duck breasts with orange, pomegranate, date palm, orange confit, and a sweet chili glaze ($25.95); pan-seared, Kurobuta-bacon-wrapped filet mignon with Gorgonzola cheese and a marchand de vin sauce ($28.50); and cioppino—Italian bouillabaisse with mussels, clams, fish, crabmeat, scallops, lobster, and shrimp in a fennel tomato broth ($32.95). Other meals $23.95–54.95.

Nook and Monk's (301-475-3020; www.nookandmonks.com), 22695

Washington St., Leonardtown. Open for lunch and dinner Mon.–Sat. Pleasant atmosphere complements the ever-changing menu. A staple is fried tomato with crabmeat ($21.95); other entrées have included crabcakes, coconut-fried shrimp, Cajun jambalaya, and New York strip steak. $15.95–28.95. Sandwiches $7.95–15.95.

& **Brome-Howard Inn** (301-866-0656; www.bromehowardinn.com), 18281 Rosecroft Rd., St. Mary's City. Open for dinner Thu.–Sun. from 5 PM; Sunday brunch 11–2. Reservations appreciated. The menu changes frequently in this gracious manor house, whose two dining rooms have fireplaces, splendid views, and an impeccable wait staff. I think the crabcakes with rémoulade sauce ($22.50) are some of the best I've had in southern Maryland. The folks at the table next to me praised their pork tenderloin with apple cranberry rum sauce ($20.95) and fisherman's stew ($20.95). Entrées $15.95–27.95.

California
Asahi Japanese Steak and Seafood House (301-866-9070), 2576 MacArthur Blvd. (at San Souci Plaza). Open daily for lunch and dinner. The quality of the freshly made sushi and fresh-cooked meals have made this a popular spot with personnel from the Patuxent Naval Air Station, who have dined in many parts of the world. $7.95–21.95.

Hollywood
& **Clarke's Landing** (301-373-8468), Clarkes Landing Rd. Open daily for lunch and dinner; closed Mon., Oct.–May. The restaurant overlooks the Patuxent River, so it stands to reason that the seafood is obtained fresh locally. Steamed and soft-shell crabs are a favorite, but Rusty Shriver (the former head chef of Stoney's in Calvert County) also prepares pastas, soups, and hand-cut steaks. Entrées $8.95–market price.

CLARKE'S LANDING, HOLLYWOOD

Leonardtown

♿ **Café des Artistes** (301-997-0500; www.cafedesartistes.ws), corner of Fenwick and Washington Sts. Lunch, Tue.–Fri. 11–2; dinner, Tue.–Thu. 5–9, Sat. 5–9:30, and Sun. noon–8. Days and hours subject to change. Such a delightful place to find in a small town. All dishes are based upon the French chef's own recipes. The *croque monsieur* (grilled ham and Swiss, $7.95) brought back memories of my travels through the Pyrenees. I returned for dinner, and the filet mignon in a puff pastry and green peppercorn sauce ($20.95) transported me to Paris.

And—ooh, la la—the desserts. Be sinful and have the pastries stuffed with ice cream and covered by warm dark chocolate ($5.95). Lunch entrées $9.95–13.95; dinner entrées $16.95–20.95.

Mechanicsville

♿ **Bert's 50's Diner** (301-884-3837), 29760 Three North Rd. (MD 5). Return to the middle of the 20th century, with lots of neon lights, memorabilia, and hand-dipped ice cream, malts, and milk shakes. Blue-plate specials include meat loaf, hot turkey sandwich, and country-fried steak. Burgers, subs, pizza, and fries. Most full meals will cost you less than $14.

Ridge

Courtney's (301-872-4403), Wynne Rd. The fading cinder-block exterior and old 1950s paneled interior make this the kind of place you might pass up if you didn't know locals congregate here daily for breakfast, lunch, and dinner. The owner is a waterman, so the fish is fresh. His wife, Julia, from the Philippines, does the cooking and provides a bit of a twist to the usual southern Maryland fare. Crab-cake dinner, as well as a variety of broiled fish, chicken, and T-bone steaks are a few of the entrées. $8.95–17.95.

St. George Island

☷ ♿ **Evans Seafood** (301-994-2299; www.evansseafood.com), MD 249. Closed Mon. Obviously, seafood is the specialty. Local steamed crabs are offered in summer, oysters (from Evans's own beds) appear in fall, and shrimp, scallops, and clams are on the menu year-round. Stuffed ham, a true southern Maryland dish, makes its appearance around the Thanksgiving/Christmas season. Entrées $10–28.

CRABS ♿ **Still Anchors** (301-994-2288), Dennis Point Way (at Dennis Point Marina), Drayden. Open for lunch and dinner, Apr.–Oct. 1. Closed Mon. There is a full menu here, but the real reason to come is to enjoy dozens of freshly steamed crabs (market price) in the outside waterfront dining area. Entrées less than $28.

TAKE-OUT American Soft Shell Crab Company (301-872-4444; http://us-news.org/amcrab.htm), 49676 Freeman's Rd., Dameron. Open daily 7–7, Memorial Day–Labor Day. Dale and Mary Scheible take the crabs right off the boat to deliver them fresh to you. Soft- and hard-shell crabs—live or steamed.

Crabknockers Seafood Market (301-475-7830), Leonardtown Center, Leonardtown. A convenient location to pick up crabs and other fresh seafood.

SNACKS AND GOODIES Wildewood Pastry Shop (301-862-4177), 23415

Three Notch Rd. (at Wildewood Shopping Center), California. Pastries, cookies, breads, and candies.

✳ Selective Shopping

ANTIQUES ♿ **Maryland Antiques Center** (301-475-1960; www.paxp .com/mac), MD 5 (about a third of a mile south of the MD 243 intersection), Leonardtown. More than 30 dealers are spread out over 10,000 feet of display area. In addition to the usual antique items, be on the lookout for quality used books, artware, and nautical instruments.

ART GALLERIES ♿ **North End Gallery** (301-475-3130; www.north endgallery.org), Fenwick St., Leonardtown. A cooperative gallery by local artists working in myriad media, including one of the most modern—digital images. There is a feature exhibit and a reception each month.

BOOKSTORES **Bay Books** (301-862-1424), 23415 Three Notch Rd., Wildewood Shopping Center, California. Open daily. This is it—the only full-service bookstore for many miles around. They have large selections of local-interest titles, best sellers, and children's books.

Bowes Books (301-863-6200), 21550 Great Mills Rd., Lexington Park. A combination framing shop, game store, and bookstore.

CRAFTS ♿ **Cecil's Old Mill** (301-994-1510), Indian Bridge Rd., Great Mills. Open Thu.–Sun., mid-March through October; daily November through December 24. An interesting place: 50 craftspeople create and sell their wares among the gears, cogs, and other machinery of the circa-1900 grist- and sawmill. Some of the items are—please forgive the pun—just run-of-the-mill, but much of what is displayed is high quality, different, and worth stopping by to see even if you don't intend to buy anything.

♿ **Toddy Hall Pottery** (301-994-0947), Cherryfield Rd., Hollywood. Open by appointment. I have seen pieces made here by local craftspeople show up on Internet auction sites. They also stock sculptures, paintings, and prints from local artisans.

Olde Town Crafters (301-997-1644), Washington St., Leonardtown. Open Tue.–Sat. 10–5. Many locally

---

MAKE YOUR OWN MARYLAND STEAMED CRABS

    1 large pot with perforated false bottom
    1 cup vinegar
    1 cup water
    1 dozen live crabs
    3 tbsp. salt
    2½ tbsp. seafood seasoning (such as Old Bay)
Bring the vinegar and water to a boil and add the live crabs (do not cook dead crabs, which contain bacteria!), sprinkling a mixture of salt and seasoning between each layer. Allow the water to return to a boil, then let the crabs steam for at least 30 minutes.

made items of arts, crafts, and baked goods.

SPECIAL SHOPS & **Cecil's Country Store** (301-994-9622), Indian Bridge Rd., Great Mills. Across the street from Cecil's Old Mill (see *Crafts*), this place keeps the same hours. It is part antiques shop, part country store. What sets it apart is that many of the items are displayed inside old dairy cases and iceboxes.

FARMER'S MARKETS

Charlotte Hall
North St. Mary's Farmer's Market (301-475-4404), in the library parking lot at the intersection of MD 5 and MD 6. Closed Sun. Fresh produce, along with many products produced by the local Amish community, are available daylight hours May–Oct.

Farmer's Market and Auction (301-884-3966), MD 5. Open year-round. As much of a flea market as it is a produce stand, there are more than 150 vendors here on Wed. and Sat. 8–5. Also a place to find Amish goods.

California
California Farmer's Market (301-475-4404), 22180 Three Notch Rd. (MD 235). Sat. 9–1. The season lasts May–Oct.

✳ Special Events

March: **Maryland Day** (301-769-2222), St. Clement's Island Potomac River Museum, Colton's Point, and at Historic St. Mary's City. A commemoration of the founding of Maryland. Wreath laying, militia musters, and refreshments.

April: **Rod and Classic Spring Fling** (301-475-7285), Leonardtown.

Car and truck show with antiques, food, and activities.

May: **Annual Spring Festival** (301-994-0525), fairgrounds, Leonardtown. Arts and crafts, classic cars, carnival rides, live entertainment, and antiques auction. **Lighthouse Days** (301-769-2222), Piney Point Lighthouse Museum and Park. Decoy carvers, kids' programs, exhibits, and live entertainment. **Annual Quilt and Needlework Show** (301-373-2280; www.Sotterley.com), Sotterley Plantation, Hollywood. Juried exhibition. **Annual Blue and Gray Days** (301-872-5688), Point Lookout State Park. Artillery demonstrations, infantry march, and other living-history activities. Tours of Fort Lincoln.

June: **Crab Festival** (301-475-6910), Governmental Center on MD 245 near Hollywood. Antique car show, crafts, and lots and lots of crabs prepared many ways.

September: **St. Mary's County Fair** (301-475-2256), fairgrounds, Leonardtown. **IHRA President's Cup Nationals** (301-449-RACE; www.mirdrag.com), Maryland International Raceway (MD 234 near Budds Creek). The largest motor-sport event in the state. More than 400 teams.

October: **Annual Blessing of the Fleet** (301-769-2222), St. Clement's Island Potomac River Museum, Colton's Point. Entertainment, arts and crafts, parade and fireworks, the Blessing of the Fleet, and boat rides to the island. **Grand Militia Muster** (301-862-0990; 1-800-762-1634; www.stmarys-city.org), Historic St. Mary's City. Believed to be the largest gathering of 17th-century reenactment units in the country. **Oyster Festival** (301-863-5015; www.usoysterfest.com), fairgrounds,

Leonardtown. Carnival games and rides, arts and crafts, live entertainment, and the **National Oyster Cook-Off** and **National Shucking Championship**.

November: **Lighthouse Open House** (301-872-5688), Point Lookout Lighthouse, Point Lookout State Park, Scotland. The only day of the year visitors can tour the lighthouse. Exhibits about the site, legends, and history. **Unique Boutique** (301-475-2365), Hollywood Volunteer Fire Department Social Hall, Hollywood. An annual juried exhibit of arts and crafts. **Amish Quilt Auction** (301-884-4062), MD 236, Charlotte Hall. A chance to bid on a handmade quilt.

ALONG THE POTOMAC SHORE—
La Plata, Port Tobacco, and Waldorf

As in all of southern Maryland, water has played a major role in defining this area and its way of life. Along its eastern border is the state's longest stream, the Patuxent River, while the wide expanse of the Potomac River outlines the western edge.

Through the centuries, the Port Tobacco River has silted in and become much shallower than it once was. During the early days of colonial settlement, it was the area's most important waterway. Wide and deep enough to be navigated by oceangoing vessels, it enabled Port Tobacco to be Maryland's second largest port throughout most of the 17th and 18th centuries, and to remain an important shipment center well into the 19th century. The coming of the railroads brought about the town's decline, but a visit to Historic Port Tobacco can bring those days back.

If Port Tobacco was the loser, La Plata was the winner when the railroad arrived in 1872. Coming from Baltimore and reaching all the way to the Potomac, the tracks brought prosperity to the town, which really started out as not much more than a post office and general store. Within a few years, the county seat was moved from Port Tobacco to La Plata. The coming of US 301 changed the town again, as its downtown area—now a small place worth a short stroll through—was bypassed. Most of the commerce, primarily strip malls, chain-food restaurants, and convenience stores, is located on the four-lane.

The largest city in the area, Waldorf, also owes its existence to the railroads. But it was tobacco, and not county bureaucracy, that brought money into the municipal coffers. People wishing to escape living in Washington, DC, discovered the city and surrounding countryside in the mid-1900s, and it is now primarily a bedroom community for the metro area, with large shopping malls and other modern conveniences.

COMMUNITIES You need to eschew US 301 and drive the back roads if you really want to explore the area. Leaving the major highway in Waldorf and

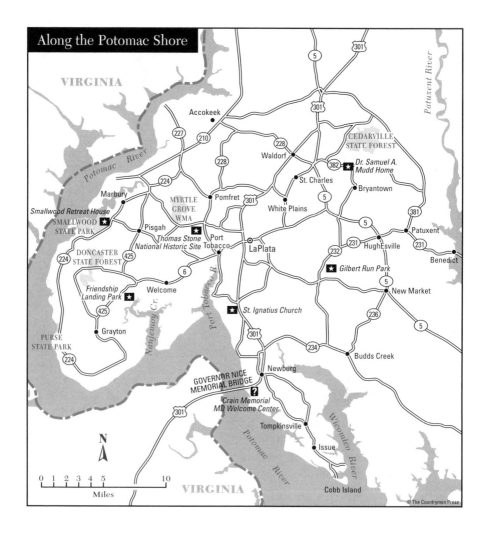

Along the Potomac Shore

VIRGINIA

Patuxent River

Potomac River

Accokeek

Waldorf

CEDARVILLE
STATE FOREST

Dr. Samuel A.
Mudd Home

St. Charles

Bryantown

Marbury

MYRTLE
GROVE
WMA

Pomfret

White Plains

Smallwood Retreat House

SMALLWOOD
STATE PARK

Pisgah

Thomas Stone
National Historic Site

Port
Tobacco

LaPlata

HughEsville

Patuxent

DONCASTER
STATE FOREST

Benedict

Gilbert Run Park

Friendship
Landing Park

Welcome

New Market

PURSE
STATE PARK

Grayton

St. Ignatius Church

GOVERNOR NICE
MEMORIAL BRIDGE

Newburg

Budds Creek

Crain Memorial
MD Welcome Center

Tompkinsville

Wicomico River

N

Issue

0 1 2 3 4 5   10
Miles

VIRGINIA

Potomac River

Cobb Island

© The Countryman Press

driving east on MD 5 can bring you to such out-of-the-way places as the house
where Dr. Mudd, the physician who worked on John Wilkes Booth's broken leg,
lived. He is buried close to his home place in St. Mary's Church cemetery in
Bryantown. Branch off MD 5 at **Hughesville** and you can follow MD 231
to the Patuxent River and **Benedict**. In addition to being the landing site for
British troops that marched westward to burn Washington, DC, during the War
of 1812, the now sleepy community bustled for more than 250 years. Established
as a port in 1683, it continued to attract freight and passengers traveling on
steamboats into the mid-1900s.

GUIDANCE **Charles County Visitors Bureau** (301-645-0558; 1-800-SO-MD-
FUN; www.explorecharlescomd.com), 200 Baltimore St., La Plata, 20646.

The **Crain Memorial Welcome Center** (301-259-2500), US 301, Newburg, is
a state-operated facility and can provide information on all of Maryland as well

as local attractions. It is located 1 mile north of the Governor Nice Memorial Bridge over the Potomac River on US 301.

GETTING THERE *By car:* Four-lane **US 301** will bring you into the area from the north around Washington, DC. It is also the main highway coming in from the south, connecting southern Maryland with Virginia via the Governor Nice Memorial Bridge (toll) across the Potomac River.

By air: The closest airport, **Ronald Reagan Washington National Airport** (703-417-8000), is across the Potomac River in northern Virginia, but it is only about a 30- to 45-minute drive away. In another direction, but just a few minutes' longer drive away, is **Baltimore/Washington International Airport** (1-800-I-FLY-BWI) near Annapolis.

By bus: **Greyhound** (1-800-229-9429) stops in Waldorf on its route between Virginia and other points in Maryland.

By water: The **Charles County Visitors Bureau** can supply you with a long list of marinas that will take care of you if you happen to arrive on your personal boat.

GETTING AROUND *By car:* Except for **US 301**, most of the roadways are lightly traveled.

By bus: The **Charles County Department of Community Services** (301-934-9305) administers six bus routes in the Waldorf and La Plata areas that are in operation Mon.–Sat.

By taxi: **B&J Community Cabs** (301-843-7302), **Cab of Waldorf** (301-638-0696), **Waldorf Cab** (301-843-5400), and **Yellow Cab** (301-645-4316) are all based in Waldorf.

MEDICAL EMERGENCY **Civista Medical Hospital** (301-609-4160), 701 E. Charles St., La Plata.

✳ To See

COLLEGES **College of Southern Maryland** (301-934-7828), 8730 Mitchell Rd., La Plata. The college's **Fine Arts Center** has so many things going on that it has become the cultural hub of the area. The **Walter Grove II** and **Tony Hungerford Memorial Galleries** feature works by students and staff, and the theater offers musicals, dramas, dances, concerts, and lectures throughout much of the year.

HISTORIC HOMES ♿ **Dr. Samuel A. Mudd House** (301-645-6970), Dr. Samuel Mudd Rd. (about 6 miles east of Waldorf via MD 5 and Poplar Hill–Beantown Rd.), Waldorf. Sat. and Sun. noon–4 and Wed. 11–3, Apr.–Nov. Small admission fee. Dr. Mudd became known to the world when he set the broken leg of John Wilkes Booth, Abraham Lincoln's assassin. This private home museum, which has been in the Mudd family since 1694, relates that story in a very personal way. Although some historians believe Mudd knew who Booth was, Mudd maintained his innocence throughout his 3½ years of imprisonment and to his death.

There is a real sense of history here, as many items in the house are original. It is easy to imagine the events when you look at the couch Booth lay on, the room in which he was operated on, Mudd's medical instruments, and furniture Mudd made while in prison.

HISTORIC SITES

Port Tobacco

&. **Historic Port Tobacco** (301-934-4313), Chapel Point Rd. (off MD 6). Sat., Sun., and Wed. noon–4, Apr.–Oct. Small admission fee. Just a short time after the first settlers arrived in the Maryland colony at St. Mary's City, Captain John Smith, founder of Jamestown, founded Port Tobacco. The town soon developed into the second largest port in the state but declined when the railroad arrived in the area in the 1870s.

Costumed docents lead guided tours of the Court House, providing background on the town and some of the sites still recognizable. Upstairs, the model of the town puts things into perspective.

&. **Port Tobacco One-Room School House** (301-932-6064), 7215 Chapel Point Rd. Sat. and Sun. noon–4, Apr.–Oct.; also Wed. noon–4, July and Aug. Free. The school was built in 1876 to serve students in grades one through seven. The furnishings reflect its earliest days.

&. **Thomas Stone National Historic Site** (301-392-1776), 6655 Rose Hill Rd. (between MD 6 and MD 225). Open daily 9–5 Memorial Day–Labor Day; Thu.–Sun. 9–5 the rest of the year. Free. Thomas Stone was a contributor to the Articles of Confederation and one of Maryland's four signers of the Declaration of Independence. Guided tours take you through the five-part mansion, constructed in the 1770s. The house was nearly destroyed by fire in 1977 but has been fully restored. The original kitchen survived, and some of the original furnishings are spread throughout the house. A number of pleasant hiking trails wander through the property.

HISTORIC CHURCHES St. Mary's Catholic Church, Bryantown. The final resting place of Dr. Samuel Mudd (see *Historic Homes*).

Oldfields Chapel (301-934-1424), MD 231, Hughesville. The chapel and surrounding area were used as a campground by the British during the War of 1812. Two soldiers who died there are buried in the cemetery.

Christ Church (301-932-1051), 110 E. Charles St., La Plata. Replacing earlier church structures, this one was originally built in Port Tobacco in 1884. In 1904, it was dismantled and its numbered stones carried by oxcart to La Plata, where it was reassembled next to the courthouse.

St. Ignatius Church (301-934-8245), 8855 Chapel Point Rd., Port Tobacco. Along with St. Ignatius Church in St. Mary's County, this is the oldest Catholic parish in the country. Located on a small knoll overlooking the Port Tobacco River, it houses a Relic of the True Cross, brought by settlers across the Atlantic Ocean on the *Ark* and *Dove*. Be sure to seek out the kneelers that were needle-pointed by local residents and depict scenes of interest to the area.

BICYCLING Less than 25 miles from the nation's capital, this region lures many bicyclists to its quiet country roads. The **Charles County Visitors Bureau** can provide information on three of the most popular circuit rides.

One of the rides, the longest of the three at about 27 miles, is my favorite. It follows roadways close to the **Potomac River** and passes by several opportunities to get off the bike and take to the woods on hiking trails. Another, at 16.5 miles, encounters **Historic Port Tobacco** and the sites in downtown **La Plata.** The third one is about an hour's ride and skirts the eastern edge of **Zekiah Swamp.**

Mike's Bikes (301-870-6600; www.ridemikes.com), 2102 Crain Hwy., and **Bike Doctor** (301-932-9980), 5051 Festival Way, both in Waldorf, can help you with repairs if you run into problems you can't fix yourself.

BOAT RENTALS See **Gilbert Run Park** and **Smallwood State Park** under *Green Space.*

BOWLING ✎ **AMC Lanes** (301-843-1494), 11920 Acton Lane, Waldorf. Automatic scoring and bumper bowling for the kids.

FISHING The **Potomac River** has earned a reputation as a world-class fishery, especially for largemouth bass and striped bass (known in Maryland and Virginia as rockfish). Although fishing is a year-round event in the area, spring and fall are the best times to cast for striped bass.

Also see **Myrtle Grove Wildlife Management Area** under *Hiking* and **Friendship Farm Park** under *Green Space.*

GOLF Swan Point Country and Yacht Club (301-259-0047), 11550 Swan Point Blvd., Issue. A semiprivate waterfront community with an 18-hole course designed by Bob Cupp. Great views of the Potomac River as the course goes through marshes and woodlands.

White Plains Golf Course (301-645-1300; 301-843-2947), at the intersection of DeMarr Rd. and St. Charles Pkwy. (inside White Plains Regional Park), White Plains. The county-operated, tree-lined, 18-hole course is open daily.

HIKING

La Plata
Myrtle Grove Wildlife Management Area (301-743-5161), about 5 miles west of US 301 on MD 225. In an area of the state where large tracts of public land available for outdoor recreation are somewhat sparse, this 900-acre tract provides the opportunity to enjoy natural beauty away from the traffic, strip malls, liquor stores, and other modern-day distractions along US 301. The majority of the 5 miles or so of hiking opportunities follow the routes of service roadways, but there are also a few narrow pathways.

Once home to the Piscataway Indians, the terrain is that of a typical southern Maryland landscape, with gently rolling hills of fields and forest, and natural and created wetlands. Watch for signs of beaver, woodcock, quail, and turkey. Consider bringing along tackle, as small Myrtle Grove Lake contains bluegill, pickerel, catfish, and largemouth bass.

Doncaster Forest (301-934-2282), 13 miles west of La Plata on MD 6. Hiking in this 1,400-acre forest is done on well-established, but sometimes unmaintained or unmarked, pathways most often used by hunters. Do not let that deter you, however. If you have a sense of adventure, you can take these routes, which add up to well over 10 miles, into forestlands and along some very pretty small streams.

Also see *Green Space* and **Thomas Stone National Historic Site** under *To See*.

KAYAKING AND CANOEING Nanjemoy Creek is a tidal waterway with high banks in some places that harbor nesting sites for bald eagles. In other spots, it passes through miles of scenic marshlands with great blue herons trolling for a meal. One put-in place is at the bridge over the creek on MD 6 near **Grayton**; another is the boat ramp at **Friendship Farm Park** (301-932-3470) off MD 425 between Ironsides and Grayton. The paddling is easy, the scenery great, and obstructions few.

SKATING ♂ **Skatepark** (301-645-1300), at the intersection of DeMarr Rd. and St. Charles Pkwy. (inside White Plains Regional Park), White Plains. Small fee. Designed by local skateboarders, in-line skaters, and bikers, the park has various-depth bowls, and lots of street elements such as rails, ledges, and banks.

SMALLWOOD RETREAT HOUSE IN SMALLWOOD STATE PARK

BEACHES See **Purse State Park** under *Parks*.

PARKS

La Plata
Gilbert Run Park (301-932-1083), 1001 Radio Station Rd. (about 6 miles east of La Plata on MD 6). The 180-acre county-operated park offers fishing and boating (rentals in-season) on a 60-acre lake, picnic areas, a nature center, and about 4 miles of trails. Pick up a booklet at the office to learn about what you are seeing along the 1.5-mile self-guided nature route.

Marbury
Smallwood State Park (301-743-7613), 2750 Sweden Point Rd. Open daily; $2 admission on weekends and holidays, May–Sep. Trails of about 4 miles in total length connect at several points to form a continuous loop and pass through hardwood forests and a number of spots of historical interest. The **Smallwood Retreat House** (open Sun., May–Sep.) is the restored 18th-century home of General William Smallwood, Revolutionary War figure and governor of Maryland. Nearby is a 19th-century tobacco barn. Also in the park are boat rentals (in-season), a marina on Mattawoman Creek, and a picnic area. A small campground is usually open Apr.–Oct. and has hookups, a central shower house, and a few small cabins for rent.

Purse State Park (contact is Smallwood State Park; see above), MD 224. Because it is so overused, I refrain from using the phrase *hidden gem*. Until now, that is. There are no improvements here (although the state is talking about some)—just a quarter-mile trail through the forest that delivers you onto an isolated Potomac River beach. Swim (no lifeguards), stroll, search for fossils and centuries-old shark's teeth, or do whatever comes naturally. If you go during the week, it is a good possibility you may be the only person in the entire 90-acre park.

ALONG THE BEACH IN PURSE STATE PARK

Nanjemoy
Friendship Farm Park (301-932-3470), Friendship Landing Rd. The park borders Nanjemoy Creek, providing miles of marshes, scenic water, and access to the Potomac River. A trail system wanders through 235 acres and has two birding observation platforms. The Maryland Department of Natural Resources has designated the park a free fishing area—meaning you don't have to purchase a state fishing license to enjoy the thrill of casting a line into the water.

✳ Lodging

MOTELS AND HOTELS

Indian Head, 20640

✿ **Super 8** (301-753-8100; 1-800-800-8000), Indian Head Highway. Basic rooms and few amenities in the motel, but a low rate. Free continental breakfast. Pets permitted, but you must call the local number for permission. $58–78.

La Plata, 20646

✿ **Best Western** (301-934-4900), 6900 Crain Hwy. Small pool and exercise room. Free continental breakfast. Small pets permitted with a deposit. $95–130.

Waldorf, 20603

ᕕ **Comfort Suites** (301-932-4400), 11765 Business Park Dr. All rooms are suites with irons and in-room coffee. Indoor pool. $129–199.

✿ **Days Inn** (301-932-9200), 11370 Days Court. In-room coffee and irons. Complimentary continental breakfast. Pets permitted. $85–175.

Holiday Inn (301-645-8200), 45 St. Patrick's Dr. (adjacent to the mall). Exercise room, outdoor pool, coin laundry; irons and hair dryers in the rooms. $99–139.

Super 8 (301-932-8957), 3550 Crain Hwy. Basic low-cost motel with basic rooms and some suites. Free continental breakfast, fitness room. $54–78.

BED & BREAKFASTS

Bryantown, 20617

Shady Oaks of Serenity (301-932-8864; 1-800-597-0924; www.bnbweb.com/shadyoaks), 7490 Serenity Dr. Fresh flowers and fruit are placed in the one and only guest room (with its own bath and TV) in this modern Georgian Victorian home. The front porch and back deck overlook the property's 3 acres. $55–125.

La Plata, 20646

Linden Farm B&B (301-934-9003), 8530 Mitchell Rd. Located on a 47-acre working horse farm, in which young horses are always in training, the 1783 house sits on a knoll with a commanding view. Stairs, banisters, fireplaces, floors, and even the door latches are original. The 90-foot porch overlooks the Port Tobacco valley, and miles of trails can take you into woodlands or down to Port Tobacco Creek. Two of the guest rooms share a bath; the other has a private bath. Any one of them you choose will provide almost as a nice a view as that from the porch. Continental breakfast. $95–150.

Part of Plenty Bed & Breakfast (301-934-0707; 1-800-520-0708; www.partofplenty.com), 8664 Port Tobacco Rd. Located in historic Port Tobacco, the two-story house was built around 1850 (renovated 1996), is located on 4 acres and has five guest rooms (all with private bath) with period antiques and reproductions. Outdoor pool. $75–85.

CAMPING ✿ **Goose Bay Marina and Campground** (301-934-3812), 9365 Goose Bay Lane, Welcome, 20693. The full-service marina, which sits on Goose Creek, an inlet of Port Tobacco River, also contains waterfront campsites, hookups, a swimming pool, and a camp store. Pets permitted.

Also see **Smallwood State Park** under *Green Space.*

✳ Where to Eat

DINING OUT 🦞 ✐ **The Crossing at Casey Jones** (301-932-6226; www.thecrossingatcaseyjones.com), 417 E.

Charles St., La Plata. Open for lunch 11–2:30, and dinner from 5 PM; closed Sun. In an area awash with national chains, it is a pleasure to find this place. Chef Gary Fiek, a Culinary Institute of America graduate, ensures that everything is prepared fresh, seafood is purchased direct from suppliers, and meats are organic. His menu changes seasonally and in response to his travels throughout the world in search of new ideas.

Entrées have included mango soy glazed duck, London broil topped with sherry-shiitake reduction; and roast salmon with sauce verge and lemon crème fraîche. I thought I had eaten crab in every form possible until chef Fiek served me his luscious crab and pesto dumplings with a hot tomato coulis accompanied by shrimp, pine nut salad, and toasted orzo. All desserts are made on the premises with only natural ingredients. Entrées $18.95–29.95.

EATING OUT Tony's River House (301-274-4440), 7320 Benedict Ave., Benedict. A local favorite that is situated almost on top of the Patuxent River. The knotty-pine walls give it a mid-1900s feel, and the menu features what could only be called Maryland/American fare. Crabcakes (market price), pork chops, and chicken Chesapeake are always on the menu. There are also daily specials like the tasty snapper sandwich I had for lunch. Most entrées $14–28.

🦀 **Robertson's Crab House** (301-934-3300; www.robertsonscrabhouse .com), 11455 Popes Creek Rd., Newburg. Open daily for lunch and dinner. A family business for several decades, it sits on the very bank of the Potomac River. I really enjoyed the

crabcakes ($29.95) here. Unlike many places that are afraid to add something, these had tiny bits of onion, celery, green pepper, and spices. A very nice change from the commonplace. Other seafood, meats, and entrées range $12.95–23.95 and up to market price.

CRABS 🦀 **Captain John's Crab House** (301-259-2315; www.cjcrab .com), 16215 Cobb Island Rd., Cobb Island. Open daily for breakfast, lunch, and dinner. Located on the waterfront on Cobb Island, Captain John's is the typical Maryland crab house with inside and outside dining, but unlike many others, it is open year-round. The seafood platter ($22.99) has enough food to feed two with a crabcake, fried scallops, fried fish, fried shrimp, fried clams, and either fried oyster or fried soft-shell crab (in-season). Try the broiled seafood platter ($23.99) if you wish to keep your arteries unclogged. Other sandwiches and dinners $2.95–29.99.

TAKE-OUT Randy's Ribs and BBQ (301-274-3525), MD 5 and Gallant Green Rd., Hughesville. Open daily from 10 AM. It is just a roadside stand, but anytime you drive by, there is a line of people waiting to place their order. Beef, pork, chicken, ribs, hot dogs, and a variety of platters are offered. The thing to get, however, is the BBQ sandwich. It may be the tastiest BBQ I've had in Maryland. By the way, do not make the mistake of ordering two—even if you are hungry. The size of one is almost large enough to feed two people. $3.95–11.95.

SNACKS AND GOODIES Walls Bakery (301-645-2833), 2805 Crain Hwy. (US 301), Waldorf. After rising early every morning since 1968 to create their baked goods, George and Christa Walls, to the dismay of many, retired in 2001. However, George found that he was still waking up at the same time each day, and felt he might as well continue baking.

We are the winners. The breads, cookies, and pies here are always worth coming in for. However, it is the pastries, especially the giant éclairs, that cause people and tour-bus-loads of passengers to detour miles out of their way. It is impossible to miss seeing this place as you drive along US 301—an old nightclub/casino shaped like a wigwam.

✳ Entertainment

FILM **Waldorf North** (301-843-9381), 3232 Crain Hwy., Waldorf, shows first-run movies.

Also showing most films when they are newly released is the **St. Charles Town Cinema** (301-645-0818), 100 St. Charles Town Center.

NIGHTLIFE **Spurs** (301-843-9964), US 301 and Mattawoman Beantown Rd., Waldorf. There is a lot of movement happening on the 1,250-square-foot wooden floor, with line-dance, hand-dance, and West Coast swing lessons Wed.–Fri., and live entertainment Fri. and Sat. Pool tables, dartboards, video games, and big crowds on the weekend.

THEATERS **Port Tobacco Players** (301-932-6819), 508 Charles St., La Plata. Housed in an old 1940s movie theater. The Port Tobacco Players formed in 1947 as a way to raise funds for the restoration of Port Tobacco buildings. The troupe stages half a dozen or so productions each year.

Most presentations are American musicals and plays, and past ones have included A *Streetcar Named Desire*, *You Can't Take It with You*, and Rodgers and Hammerstein's *Cinderella*. Most shows take place Fri. and Sat. evening and Sun. afternoon.

Also see *To See—Colleges*.

✳ Selective Shopping

ANTIQUES **The Shops at Heritage Design** (301-932-7379), 3131 Old Washington Rd., Waldorf. A multi-dealer shop.

Hughesville Bargain Barn (301-934-8580), Leonardtown Rd., Hughesville. More than 140 shops crowd into two large barns selling antiques, collectibles, coins, and new and used furniture. Much of the stuff is what you would find in a flea market.

Nostalgia Nook (301-753-6940), 36 Mattingly Ave., Indian Head. Open Sat. and Sun. 9–3. English period and country furniture, and glassware; will do appraisals.

ART GALLERIES **Mattawoman Creek Art Center** (301-743-5159), inside Smallwood State Park, Marbury. Fri.–Sun. 11–4. Set off by itself with woodlands close by, and overlooking where Mattawoman Creek meets the Potomac River; I can't imagine a prettier setting for a gallery. The inside space is illuminated by natural light to accent the high quality of works by local, regional, national, and international artists. A real treasure in an out-of-the-way place.

Also see *To See—Colleges*.

BOOKSTORES Two national chains, **Borders** (301-705-6672), 3304-A Crain Hwy., Waldorf, and **Walden-**

books (301-645-0770), St. Charles Town Center, are located in shopping malls.

USED BOOKS **Ellie's Paperback Shack** (301-843-3676), 2700 Crain Hwy., Waldorf. More than 30,000 used books for sale and trade.

FARMER'S MARKETS **Indian Head Farmer's Market** (301-743-5511), Mildred Rice Rd. Produce arrives at the village green every Tue. and Thu., June–Oct., and is available for purchase 9–1.

La Plata Farmer's Market (301-934-8345), corner of Charles St. and Washington Ave. Produce and other items are displayed on stands in the courthouse parking lot on Wed. 10–7 and Sat. 8–3:30.

PICK-YOUR-OWN PRODUCE FARMS **Hydromont Berry Farm** (301-932-0872), 8020 Hawthorne Rd., La Plata. Show up in May and pick all the strawberries you can right off the vine.

✳ Special Events

March: **Children's Spring Party and Easter Egg Hunt** (301-743-5574), Indian Head village green. Live entertainment, children's activities, and photos with the Easter Bunny.

April: **Annual Potomac River Clean Up** (301-932-3599). Volunteers beautify the Potomac and other area streams. **House and Garden Pilgrimage** (301-934-8819), various sites. Every third year, the local garden club sponsors a tour of the area's best homes and gardens. **Artfest** (301-932-5900), Indian Head. A day

of music, visual arts, theater, and literature. Lots of entertainment.

May: **Charter Day Celebration** (301-6454-0558). Historic sites throughout the area provide free admission, costumed docent tours, and refreshments to mark the county's birthday.

May–September: **La Plata Summer Concert Series** (301-934-8421), La Plata Town Hall, La Plata. A series of outdoor musical concerts presented each Fri. evening 7–9.

June: **Annual Juried Art Show** (301-743-5159), Mattawoman Creek Art Center. Artists from Maryland, Virginia, and Washington, DC, display juried works in a wide variety of media. **Cobb Island Day** (301-259-0160), Cobb Island Field. Crab races, corn-shucking contests, many kids' activities, crafts sales, and fire-engine and carriage rides.

August: **Durham Parish Festival** (301-743-7099), Christ Church, Nanjemoy. This event has taken place each year since 1847! Traditional southern Maryland ham and chicken dinner, children's games, lots of home-baked goodies, and crafts.

September: **Charles County Fair** (301-932-1234), fairgrounds, La Plata.

November: **Annual Holiday Art Show** (301-743-5159), Mattawoman Creek Art Center. Works by local member artists.

December: **Annual Holiday Festival and Craft Fair** (301-743-5574), Indian Head. Live entertainment, door prizes, crafts and children's crafts-making activities, a gingerbread-house contest, and an antique model-train display.

Frederick and
the Catoctin
Mountains Area

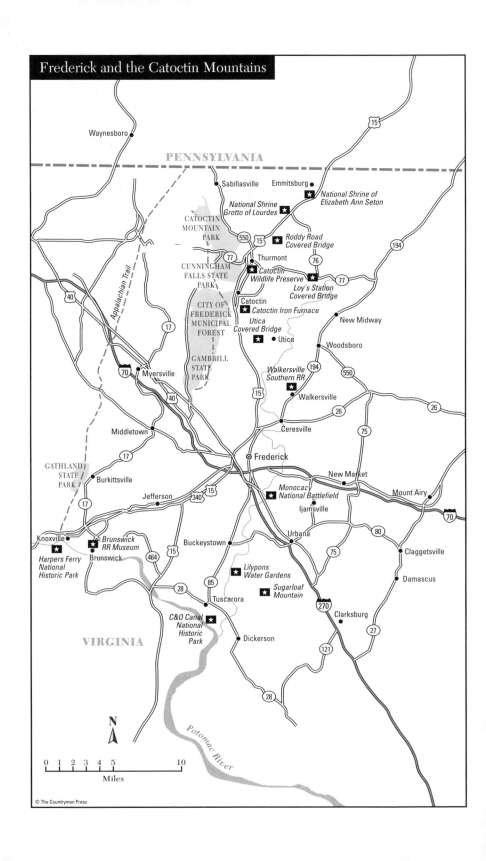

Frederick and the Catoctin Mountains

Waynesboro

PENNSYLVANIA

15

Sabillasville • Emmitsburg •

National Shrine of
Elizabeth Ann Seton

National Shrine
Grotto of Lourdes

194

CATOCTIN
MOUNTAIN
PARK

Roddy Road
Covered Bridge

550   15

76

77   Thurmont

Catoctin
Wildlife Preserve

77

CUNNINGHAM
FALLS STATE
PARK

Loy's Station
Covered Bridge

Appalachian Trail

40

Catoctin

Catoctin Iron Furnace

New Midway

CITY OF
FREDERICK
MUNICIPAL
FOREST

17

Utica
Covered Bridge

• Utica

Woodsboro

GAMBRILL
STATE
PARK

194   550

Walkersville
Southern RR

70   Myersville

15   Walkersville

40

26

Middletown

Ceresville

26

75

GATHLAND
STATE
PARK

Burkittsville

17

New Market

Mount Airy

Jefferson

15

340

Monocacy
National Battlefield

70

Ijamsville

Knoxville •

17

Brunswick
RR Museum

Buckeystown •

Urbana

80

Claggetsville

Harpers Ferry
National
Historic Park

Brunswick

464

15

75

Damascus

Lilypons
Water Gardens

28

85

Sugarloaf
Mountain

270   Clarksburg

C&O Canal
National
Historic
Park

Tuscarora

• Dickerson

27

VIRGINIA

121

28

N

0 1 2 3 4 5   10
Miles

Potomac River

© The Countryman Press

FREDERICK AND THE CATOCTIN MOUNTAINS AREA

Up from the meadows rich with corn,
Clear in the cool September morn,
The clustered spires of Frederick stand,
Green-walled by the hills of Maryland.
—John Greenleaf Whittier, "The Ballad of Barbara Fritchie"

The words of Whittier's 1862 poem are just about as true today as they were then. There may be fewer meadows of corn, but the clustered spires still point skyward, framed by lush, green hillsides.

It seems that cities are always discussing ways to attract people by saving their downtown areas and historic structures; Frederick has accomplished it. Other than Annapolis, which has done an admirable job of preserving its harbor area, Frederick is the most viable, vibrant, and historic-architecture-rich city in the state.

The Historical Society of Frederick County is housed in an 1820s Federal-style mansion; the Barbara Fritchie House—where the events Whittier wrote about occurred—is reconstructed with its original materials; and many of the Victorian town houses are still lived in by families and have not been turned into offices. Yet businesses thrive within the inner city without destroying it: With a minimum of changes, a complex of small shops in Everedy Square and Shab Row occupy what were once 18th- and 19th-century dwellings. Market Street and Patrick Street, the crossroads of the downtown area, are lined by renovated buildings with restaurants, antiques shops, and galleries that entice people to linger after normal business hours have expired.

The city's spirited arts and culture community has also fallen in line with protecting the old. The Delaplaine Visual Arts Education Center makes use of the renovated Mountain Mill, while the Weinberg Center for the Arts, where presentations of all forms are staged throughout the year, is in a lavish 1926 movie palace. And, of course, the steeples, spires, and towers of more than a dozen buildings provide the city with one of its most photographed scenes, its skyline.

Just northwest of Frederick are the Catoctin Mountains. The eastern rampart of the Blue Ridge Mountains, they stretch almost 40 miles from southern Pennsylvania, across Maryland, and into the northern portion of Virginia. Geologists believe the mountains once attained heights comparable to those of the Andes in South America, but wind and water over the course of millions of years have eroded Catoctin into a much lower ridgeline. Today the high point is only about 1,900 feet above sea level, while the lowest spot is a mere 500 feet. The mountain's numerous rock outcroppings are a bit more resistant to erosion, being composed of Catoctin greenstone that developed from lava flows 600 million years ago.

The mountain range's name is a derivation of *Kittocton*, from an Algonquian tribe that once lived near the Potomac River. Linguists believe the word translates to "land of the big mountain" or "land of the white-tailed deer." Native Americans and colonial hunters traipsed through the folded landscape in search of abundant wildlife.

Several parks in the Catoctin Mountains, and on South Mountain a bit farther to the west, along with the Chesapeake & Ohio (C&O) Canal along the southern region, have made this area a mecca for hikers, bikers, kayakers, canoeists, anglers, and others looking to experience and play in the natural world.

THE MORTUARY CHAPEL AT THE NATIONAL SHRINE OF SAINT ELIZABETH ANN SETON IN EMMITSBURG

COMMUNITIES Emmitsburg has been attracting religious pilgrims ever since Father John Dubois founded Mount St. Mary's College, a Catholic 4-year college and seminary, in the early 1800s. One of those attracted was Elizabeth Ann Seton, who began the country's first parochial school in Baltimore before moving to Emmitsburg and establishing the Sisters of Mercy. About 150 years after her death, she was canonized as a saint, the first native-born American woman to be so recognized. A nearby spot on the side of the Catoctin Mountains, now the National Shrine Grotto of Lourdes, was one of her favorite places of meditation.

True to the translation of its name, **Thurmont** is "the Gateway to the Mountains." Nestled on the edge of the Monocacy Valley at the base of the Catoctin Mountains, it began attracting hunters, anglers, and other outdoor types when the railroad arrived in the 1870s. The establishment of Catoctin Mountain Park and Cunningham Falls State Parks in the mid-1900s further enhanced its sylvan appeal. The television age has brought the little town worldwide fame, as it is used as a base camp by news agencies and journalists to keep track of events taking place in nearby Camp David. It is quite common to turn on the evening news and to see Cozy Country Inn or Mountain Gate Restaurant used as a reporter's backdrop.

During one of his many trips to the area, George Washington declared **Middletown** to be "one of the prettiest valleys I've ever seen." The town and surrounding areas are experiencing a building explosion as more and more housing developments take over former farmlands.

Despite interstates and malls growing up a few miles away, **Buckeystown** has managed to retain the look and feel of a Victorian village. Its main street, Buckeystown Pike (MD 85), remains a two-lane roadway passing by many homes and structures from the late 1800s. The town's few commercial enterprises include the upscale Inn at Buckeystown and the Catoctin Inn.

New Market, established in 1793, flourished as a stopover point for 19th-century travelers along the National Road (now US 40). Many of its early structures still exist; today the small town is billed as "the Antiques Capital of Maryland," with dozens of antiques shops occupying a number of historic buildings.

GUIDANCE The **Tourism Council of Frederick County, Frederick Visitor Center** (301-228-2888; 1-800-999-3613; www.fredericktourism.org), 19 E. Church St., Frederick, 21701, is located in one of the city's historic town houses. Signs point the way from every major road access into town.

Maryland state welcome centers, which can provide local and statewide information, are located at mile marker 39 on I-70 near Myersville. The phone number for the center for eastbound traffic is 301-293-2526; the westbound traffic center can be reached at 301-293-4161.

Another **state welcome center** (301-447-2553) is located 1 mile south of the Pennsylvania border on US 15 near Emmitsburg.

GETTING THERE *By car:* All roads may lead to Rome, but almost as many seem to converge on Frederick and this area of Maryland. **I-70** comes from Baltimore in the east and Hagerstown in the west. **I-270** is the way most people drive here from the Washington, DC, area. **US 15** arrives from Pennsylvania to the north, while **US 340** crosses the Potomac River from Virginia and West Virginia.

By air: **Dulles International Airport** (703-572-2700) in northern Virginia is the closest air facility to the area, especially if you are driving a rental car and can cross the Potomac River at either Point of Rocks on US 15, Brunswick, on VA 287, or Harpers Ferry on US 340. Flying into **Ronald Reagan Washington National Airport** (703-417-8000) enables you to take the MARC commuter train (see *By rail*) into the area. Located a little more than an hour away, between Baltimore and Washington, DC, is the **Baltimore/Washington International Airport** (1-800-I-FLY-BWI).

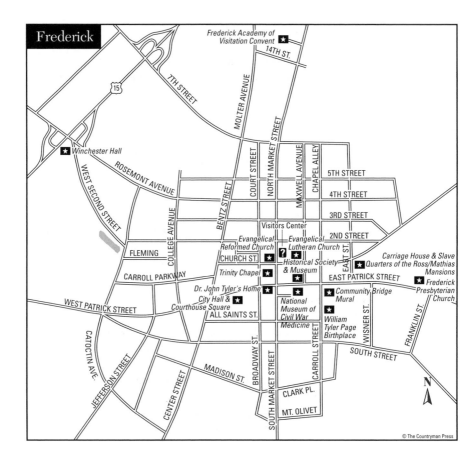

By bus: **Greyhound** (1-800-229-9424) has a terminal on E. All Saints St. (301-663-3311). Unlike many bus terminals, it is not located in some out-of-the-way, decaying part of town but is just a block or two from many of downtown's best attractions and restaurants.

By rail: **MARC** (1-800-325-RAIL) has a commuter train that can bring you to a late-1800s Victorian station in Point of Rocks, to downtown Frederick, or to MD 355 close to many of the city's motels.

GETTING AROUND By car: The main roadways mentioned in Getting There will get you around quickly—except in rush hours—but use the smaller roads, such as **MD 77** and **MD 194** in the north or **MD 85** and **MD 17**, to take you on the more scenic routes.

By bus: The local bus system, **TransIT** (301-694-2065), operates throughout Frederick and its immediate vicinity. Routes also go to Thurmont, Emmitsburg, Brunswick, and Jefferson.

By taxi: In Frederick, you can call **Bowie Taxi** (301-695-0333) or **City Cab** (301-662-2250).

PARKING In Frederick, parking meters are on 9–5 Mon.–Sat. I find the municipal parking decks, especially the one at 44 E. Patrick St., to be convenient for downtown explorations without running back to feed the 2-hour-limit meters. Park and Shop merchants will stamp your ticket to give you a discount. Stop by the Frederick Visitor Center to have your parking ticket validated for 2 free hours in the Church St. parking deck.

PUBLIC RESTROOMS An information station and public restrooms can be found next to Arlene's Antiques at 41 W. Main St. in New Market.

MEDICAL EMERGENCY Frederick Memorial Hospital (301-698-3300), 200 W. 7th St., Frederick.

✳ To See

COVERED BRIDGES All three of the area's remaining covered bridges are located north of Frederick:

Situated off Old Frederick Rd. near Utica, the 110-foot, Burr Arch–design **Utica Covered Bridge** was originally constructed in 1850 over the Monocacy River. It was washed away in 1889, and local citizens salvaged its remains to reconstruct it over Fishing Creek in 1889.

Just south of the intersection of Old Frederick Rd. and MD 77 east of Thurmont is the **Loy's Station Covered Bridge**, built in the mid-1800s. Spanning Owen's Creek, the 90-foot bridge retains its original timbers. A small park with picnic tables and a playground enables you to enjoy the setting while giving the kids something to do.

Less than 2 miles north of Thurmont on Roddy Rd. (off US 15), 40-foot **Roddy Road Covered Bridge** was built in 1856. A small park is adjacent to the single-span Kingpost-design bridge.

You can obtain the itinerary for a self-guided driving tour/route of the covered bridges by logging onto www.fredericktourism.com.

MUSEUMS

Brunswick
🚲 **Brunswick Railroad Museum** (301-834-7100; www.brrm.net), 40 W. Potomac St. Fri.–Sun. Small admission fee. Railroad equipment, photographs, furnishings, toys, and other items tell of the town's early history. Of special interest to rail fans (and children) is the HO model layout of the B&O line from Washington, DC, to Brunswick. In the same building is the C&O Canal Information Center.

Frederick
Historical Society of Frederick County (301-663-1188; www.hsfcinfo.org), 24 E. Church St. Open daily. Small admission fee. Guided tours take you through an 1820s Federal-style mansion furnished with the society's collection of historic memorabilia, such as Barbara Fritchie items, furnishings of the early 1800s, and a superior collection of tall-case clocks.

& **National Museum of Civil War Medicine** (301-695-1864; www.civilwar med.org), 48 E. Patrick St. Open daily. Adults $6.50; seniors $6; children older than 10 are $4.50; children 9 and younger are free. Some of the most realistic life-sized dioramas I've seen tell of the care and healing efforts during the Civil War. More than this, though, the reason to visit is the unfamiliar facts brought to light. Did you know: More than 2,000 women, disguised as men, served as soldiers? About 3,000 horses and mules perished during the Battle of Antietam? Most operations were done under anesthesia and not by "biting the bullet," as portrayed by Hollywood? Nearly two-thirds of the 62,000 soldiers who died did so from disease and not battle injuries? Interesting items include the only surviving field stretcher (and a photo of it in use during the war) and a set of war letters from Union Private P. Bradford.

HISTORIC CIVIL WAR DRIVING TOUR A brochure available from the **Tourism Council of Frederick County, Frederick Visitor Center**, gives directions to, and details of, various sites of significance to the Confederacy's 1862 Maryland Campaign. Battles occurred at Monocacy, Antietam, and South Mountain. Another pamphlet from the visitors center, or the **Central Maryland Heritage League** (301-371-7090), P.O. Box 721, Middletown, 21769, provides additional insight into the Battle of South Mountain. By the way, the drive is just as scenic as it is historic.

HISTORIC HOMES Barbara Fritchie House and Museum (301-698-0630), 154 W. Patrick St., Frederick. Thu.–Mon., Apr.–Sep; Sat. and Sun., Oct.–Nov. Small admission fee.

The story goes that 95-year-old Barbara Fritchie defiantly waved the Union flag from her window as Confederate General Stonewall Jackson's troops marched

MONOCACY NATIONAL BATTLEFIELD

CATOCTIN IRON FURNACE IN THURMONT

through town. John Greenleaf Whittier made her famous in his poem "The Ballad of Barbara Fritchie": "Shoot if you must, this old gray head, / But spare your country's flag, she said."

Did the event really happen? Who knows; does it really matter? It is a great piece of Americana, and the museum (reconstructed out of materials from the original house) is furnished with items from the Fritchie family.

Please note: The Barbara Fritchie House and Museum sustained severe water damage around the turn of the 21st century and was closed as this book went to press. Contact the **Tourism Council of Frederick County** for current information.

Schifferstadt (301-663-3885), 1110 Rosemont Ave., Frederick. Wed.–Sun., April through mid-December. Small admission fee. Built in 1756, the German Colonial home retains much of its original hardware and exposed oak beams. A period garden complements the scene.

HISTORIC SITES & **Monocacy National Battlefield** (301-662-3515; www.nps .gov/mono), 4801 Urbana Pike, Frederick. Open daily Apr.–Oct.; Wed.–Sun., Nov.–Mar. Free. A small visitors center provides perspective on the site of the last Southern push into Union territory. Although Confederate General Jubal Early's troops won the battle on July 9, 1864, they were delayed long enough that Federal reinforcements arrived to block the way to Washington, DC.

Ranger-conducted programs and tours are presented during the summer months, while a pamphlet keyed to numbered sites along a driving-tour route lets you experience the battlefield any time of year. The **Worthington Farm Trail** consists of two connecting loops. One takes you onto **Brooks Hill** for a lesson in forest succession; the other is through bottomland to the site of the **Washington–McKinney Ford** on the Monocacy River. Each loop is about 2 miles in length.

Catoctin Iron Furnace, on MD 806 (off US 15), Thurmont. Administered by Cunningham Falls State Park. Open daily 8 AM–sunset. Free. The iron furnace was in use 1776–1903, making it one of the state's longest-running such enterprises. It has only been about a century since it ceased operating, so its ruins are in fairly good shape; even portions of the ironmaster's home are identifiable.

The furnace is also accessible via a footpath from the state park.

HISTORIC CHURCHES

Frederick

The spires and steeples of Frederick have given the town much of its identity and have been immortalized and praised in words by luminaries such as Dr. Oliver Wendell Holmes and John Greenleaf Whittier. Among the many are:

Trinity Chapel, 10 W. Church St. Its Colonial steeple was designed by Stephen Steiner and constructed in 1807, making it Frederick's oldest spire. The 10-bell chimes are still used by the tower's clock.

Evangelical Lutheran Church, 35 E. Church St. The present German Gothic structure was built in 1854, and its twin spires were among those Whittier referred to when he wrote the 1862 Barbara Fritchie poem that opens this chapter. The west tower contains a bell that was cast in England in 1771.

Evangelical Reformed Church, 15 W. Church St. The church's two open towers, built in 1848, add to the city's skyline.

AT THE NATIONAL SHRINE GROTTO OF LOURDES

Saint John the Evangelist Catholic Church, 116 E. 2nd St. Built in the early 1800s, its spire has a gold-leafed dome and cross, the highest point in the city. *The Crucifixion* by Pietro Gugliardi and *The Ascension* by Baraldi are masterpieces that necessitate a visit inside.

Also see **National Shrine Grotto of Lourdes** and **National Shrine of Saint Elizabeth Ann Seton** under *Other Sites*.

MEMORIALS ♿ **National Fallen Firefighters Memorial Park** (301-447-1365; www.firehero.org), 1682 S. Seton Ave., Emmitsburg. Located on the Federal Training Center grounds, the monument has certainly taken on more meaning and significance since the events of September 11, 2001.

OTHER SITES

Buckeystown

Lilypons Water Gardens (301-874-5133; 1-800-999-5459; www.lilypons.com), 6800 Lilypons Rd. Open daily Mar.–Sep.; Mon.–Sat., Oct.–Feb. Looking at it one way, this is just a commercial aquatic plant nursery that has been in operation since 1917. It can also be a nice outdoor experience, however. You are permitted to follow pathways beside acres of water gardens to enjoy the flowers, cattails, and resident and visiting frogs, dragonflies, and dozens of species of birds including red-winged blackbirds, geese, wild turkeys, sandpipers, and herons. (Ask at the office for the bird checklist—it identifies more that 240 species that have been seen here!) Be aware there is no shade, and walking during hot weather can be uncomfortable.

By the way, I lost my car key on one of my outings here. Please let me know if you find it. Thanks.

Emmitsburg

♿ **National Shrine Grotto of Lourdes** (301-447-5318; www.msmary.edu/grotto), 16300 Old Emmitsburg Rd. Open daily. Free. A short, paved, rhododendron-lined pathway leads to the Western Hemisphere's oldest replica of the Grottoes of Lourdes. The meditative, scenic beauty of the place makes a visit worthwhile, even if you happen to have no interest in the shrine, the artistic quality of the copper-relief Stations of the Cross, or mosaic scenes of the Mysteries of the Rosary along the pathway.

♿ **National Shrine of Saint Elizabeth Ann Seton** (301-447-6606; www.seton shrine.org), 333 S. Seton Ave. Open daily, except Mon., Nov.–Apr. 1. Free admission. In 1975, Elizabeth Ann Seton was the first native-born American woman to be canonized a saint. Her relics lie in the basilica built in her honor in the 1990s. The adjoining museum traces her early life, the founding of the Sisters of Charity of St. Joseph's, and the establishment of the country's first parochial school. The architecture and interior of the basilica alone are worth a stop.

Frederick

The **Community Bridge Mural**, on S. Carroll St. between E. Patrick and E. All Saints Sts. If there is a more impressive work of public art in Maryland, I have

THE *COMMUNITY BRIDGE MURAL* IN FREDERICK

yet to see it. Muralist William M. Cochran spent 5 years transforming what had been a plain concrete bridge. From a distance, it now appears as an old, ivy-covered stone bridge. Even when you're standing right next to it, your eyes are convinced that the stones and other items are truly three-dimensional. Cochran is also the painter of the equally impressive, and somehow calming, *Angels in Architecture* murals you find in the downtown district. More information about him, his work, and the bridge can be obtained from the Frederick Visitor Center.

Mount Olivet Cemetery (301-662-1164), 515 S. Market St. The final resting place for Francis Scott Key, Barbara Fritchie, Thomas Johnson, and more than 800 Union and Confederate soldiers.

ZOO 🐾 ♿ **Catoctin Wildlife Preserve and Zoo** (301-271-3180; www.cwpzoo .com), 13019 Catoctin Furnace Rd. (off US 15), Thurmont. Open daily Apr.–Oct., weekends in Mar. and Nov. Adults $12.95; children 2–12 are $8.95. The 30-acre zoo began as a small snake farm in 1933. Family owned since 1966, it now includes more than 300 animals from Australia and North and South America. Displays and enclosures are arranged to allow to you get as close as possible and still be safe.

✳ To Do

BICYCLING **C&O Canal National Historical Park** (see the sidebar on page 295 for background history and information on the canal). Approximately 20 miles of the Chesapeake & Ohio Canal pass through this area, and some of the highlights are the impressive **Monocacy River Aqueduct**, the **Victorian Railroad Station** at Point of Rocks, and access to the **Railroad Museum** in the town of Brunswick.

Three designated campsites, with vault toilets and water (in-season), are available on a first-come, first-served basis. There are also three public ramps from which you can launch a boat into the Potomac River. The **C&O Canal Visitor Center** in Brunswick (301-582-0813), 40 W. Potomac St., is located within the Brunswick Railroad Museum.

Also see **The Catoctin Trail** under *Hiking*, and **Gambrill State Park** under *Green Space.*

BIRDING See the sidebar on birding, page 399.

Also see **Lilypons Water Gardens** under *To See.*

BREWERY TOUR Frederick Brewing Company (301-694-7899; 1-888-258-7434; www.fredbrew.com), 4607 Wedgewood Blvd., Frederick. The brewer of Wild Goose, Blue Ridge, and Brimstone beer offers free tours and tastings on Sat. and Sun. at 1:30 PM.

FAMILY ACTIVITIES ✐ **The Children's Museum of Rose Hill Manor Park** (301-694-1650; www.rosehillmuseum.com), 1611 N. Market St., Frederick. Open daily, Apr.–Oct.; weekends only in Nov. Costumed docents lead tours through the 1790s Georgian Colonial mansion of Thomas Johnson, Maryland's first governor. Hands-on exhibits invite children to help make a quilt or prepare beaten biscuits. Historic displays—and outbuildings such as the blacksmith shop, icehouse, and log cabin—help young ones gain an understanding of colonial life.

Also see *Zoo* under *To See,* and **Candlelight Ghost Tours** under *Walking Tours.*

FISHING See **Gambrill State Park** and **Cunningham Falls State Park** under *Green Space.*

GOLF Clustered Spires (301-624-1295), 8415 Gas House Pike, Frederick. Open all year. The municipally owned course was designed by Ault-Clark and built in 1991. Look for water hazards on about half of the holes and heavily mounded fairways.

Whiskey Creek (301-694-2900; www.whiskeycreekgolf.com), 4804 Whiskey Court, Ijamsville. A dramatic course with 100-foot drops on some holes. Fees hover around $100 for weekend play.

&. **Musket Ridge** (301-293-9930), 3555 Brethren Church Rd., Myersville. The 150-acre course occupies the highest northern elevation in the Middletown Valley.

Maple Run (301-271-7870), 13610 Moser Rd., Thurmont. The front nine of this family-owned course are in the open, with views of the Catoctin Mountains. The back nine are tree lined, requiring shot-making accuracy.

&. **Worthington Manor** (301-874-5400; www.worthingtonmanor.com), 8329 Fingerboard Rd., Urbana. The 7,000-yard, daily-fee course has been the site of U.S. Open and U.S. Amateur Qualifiers. An Ault-Clark Signature Course, it sits in the shadow of Sugarloaf Mountain.

Glade Valley (301-898-5773), 10502 Glade Rd., Walkersville. Gently rolling terrain, with views of the Catoctin Mountains, harbors the holes, which have numerous tricky sand traps.

HIKING **The Catoctin Trail**. Public lands occupy much of the Catoctin Mountains northwest of Frederick, and in the late 1900s volunteers from the **Potomac Appalachian Trail Club** (703-242-0965), 118 Park St., SE, Vienna, VA 22180, built several miles of pathways to create the 26-mile Catoctin Trail. There are a few road crossings, but for the most part it provides a great sense of isolation. A series of extraordinary views and the opportunity to walk by Cunningham Falls are other reasons to walk the trail. Backcountry camping is not permitted, but you can stay in either of Cunningham Falls State Park's campgrounds.

The trail begins in **Gambrill State Park**, where it soon rises to the ridgeline. Weaving around streams in the **City of Frederick Municipal Forest** (whose trails are also popular with mountain bikers), it enters Cunningham Falls State Park before coming to an end in **Catoctin Mountain Park**. *50 Hikes in Maryland* (Countryman Press) gives a detailed description of the entire route.

Sugarloaf Mountain (301-874-2024), 7901 Comus Rd. (off MD 109), Dickerson. Open sunrise–sunset. No fee. Sugarloaf Mountain is such a significant feature on the rolling lands of Maryland's piedmont that it is easily visible for miles around. A monadnock—a residual hill or mountain that stands alone above a surrounding peneplain—Sugarloaf rises more than 800 feet above the farmland below. Its upper layer is composed primarily of quartzite, an extremely erosion-resistant material that was formed by compression about 500 million years ago. In contrast, the piedmont around it is believed to be mostly metamorphic rock, much more susceptible to the erosive effects of wind and water.

A nonprofit organization, Stronghold, Incorporated, has established a network of more than 13 miles on the mountain, with a roadway leading almost to the top. The quarter-mile **A. M. Thomas Trail** will take you to the summit for spectacular views of the lands to the south and west. The **Northern Peak Trail** leads to other vistas, while other trails wander around the mountainside and onto valley floors. Do not miss coming here.

& **The Trail House** (301-694-8448; www.trailhouse.com), 17 S. Market St., Frederick. Thu.–Sun. An outfitter for hiking, backpacking, cross-country skiing, and rock climbing. Also has an extensive offering of books on these activities and where to do them in the local area.

Also see *Green Space* and the sidebar on **Catoctin Mountain Park** on page 377. In addition, you'll find more hiking information under *To Do* and in the Appalachian Trail sidebar on page 400.

KAYAKING AND CANOEING **River and Trail Outfitters** (301-695-5177; 1-888-I-GO-PLAY; www.rivertrail.com), 604 Valley Rd. (off US 340), Knoxville. One of the most complete outfitters in the state, River and Trail can rent or sell you all the equipment you need to go kayaking, canoeing, rafting, tubing, biking, hiking and backpacking, and cross-country skiing. Better yet, take one of their guided trips and not only learn how to do the activity safely, but also become informed about the natural and human history of the areas you pass through.

Also see *Bicycling*.

TRAIN EXCURSIONS **Walkersville Southern Railroad** (301-898-0899; 1-877-363-9777; www.wsrr.org), 34 W. Pennsylvania Ave., Walkersville. The 1-hour, 15-minute excursions depart Sat. and Sun. at 11 AM, 1 PM, and 3 PM, May–Oct. Adults $7; children 3–12 are $3.50. Passing through the woodlands and farms north of Frederick, the train makes use of a route laid out just a few years after the Civil War. A highlight is the crossing of the reconstructed bridge over the Monocacy River.

WALKING TOURS

Frederick

Guided Walking Tours of Historic Frederick (301-228-2888; 301-845-7001). Tours originate at the Frederick Visitor Center and begin 1:30 on Sat. and Sun., Apr.–Dec. Small tour fee. Certified guides lead the walks to learn of the city's architecture, history, and stories. If your guide neglects to tell you, ask what happened to the state representatives who came to Frederick to discuss secession.

✿ **Candlelight Ghost Tours** (301-845-7001) depart from Brewer's Alley Restaurant at 124 N. Market St. Call for days and times. Adults $8; children 6–12 are $5. Period-costumed tour guides take you through dark streets and alleyways to relate paranormal happenings and stories based on historic fact. A fun way to spend 90 minutes of your evening.

✳ Green Space

PARKS

Frederick

Baker Park, Carroll Pkwy. and 2nd St. The attractive 44-acre park, with Carroll Creek flowing along its southern edge, has a public swimming pool, tennis courts, and playgrounds to provide a respite from downtown noise and traffic. Also the site of many special events and outdoor concerts.

Gambrill State Park (301-271-7574), 8602 Gambrill Park Rd. The park is a gift that a group of conservationists gave to themselves and other citizens of Maryland. After using private funds to purchase land around High Knob, the group donated the tract to the city of Frederick as a municipal park. In 1934, the city turned the 1,137 acres over to the state to develop as part of the state park system.

Developed areas include picnic facilities, a campground with modern restrooms and hot showers, a nature center, a ridgeline roadway with designated overlooks, and a small pond with largemouth bass, bluegills, and channel catfish. Nature walks and campfire programs are held throughout the summer season.

Encircling the top of the mountain is a trail system of about 10 miles that takes you through a predominantly oak and hickory forest, and out to a couple of

Olympian views of the Monocacy Valley. Most of the pathways are also open to mountain biking.

Thurmont

Cunningham Falls State Park (301-271-7574), 14039 Catoctin Hollow Rd. There always seems to be confusion and misinformation when it comes to the height of a waterfall. A state brochure describes Cunningham Falls as a "78-foot cascading waterfall" and the highest in the state. Yet other official sources proclaim the "sparkling water tumbling from a 51-foot ledge" of Muddy Creek Falls in western Maryland to be "Maryland's highest waterfall."

For the most part, these incongruities don't matter to those who enjoy waterfalls, and you can find the narrow grotto that Cunningham Falls flows through in the northwestern corner of the park's 5,000 acres. The **Lower Trail** is the shortest and easiest pathway to it. Other trails wander onto the ridgelines and connect with those in Catoctin Mountain Park. **Hunting Creek Lake** has swimming and boating (paddleboat and rowboat rentals during the summer), and fishing in **Big Hunting** and **Little Hunting Creeks** is permitted with artificial flies and a catch-and-return trout policy. Anglers can also fish for bass, sunfish, catfish, crappie, and bluegills in the lake.

Also see *Hiking* in "The Great Valley and Blue Ridge Region."

CUNNINGHAM FALLS STATE PARK

Catoctin Mountain Park (301-663-9388; www.nps.gov/cato), 6602 Foxville Rd., Thurmont. The federal government purchased land for Catoctin Mountain Park to demonstrate how worn-out lands could be rehabilitated. Earlier owners had clear-cut the forest or employed unsound farming practices. In 1954, 5,000 acres were deeded to Cunningham Falls State Park, while Catoctin Mountain Park retained 5,770 acres.

These lands have grown back to an eastern climax forest, much as they were in the 1700s. Barred owls, pileated woodpeckers, red-tailed hawks, and scores of other animals live in, or pass through, the park's woodlands. Close to 100 species of wildflowers, such as bloodroot, spring beauty, Dutchman's breeches, and nodding trillium, rise from the soil.

Catoctin Mountain Park has a visitors center, picnic areas, a campground, rental cabins, and a scenic drive with viewpoints. Well hidden from view, the U.S. presidential retreat, Camp David, is within the park. **Big Hunting Creek,** along MD 77, is known to anglers for the quality of its trout fishing, and the park has some of the most diverse interpretive offerings I have come across. Programs include cross-country skiing seminars, wildflower walks, and evening programs.

Approximately 15 miles of trail, including the northern portion of the **Catoctin Trail**, reach into every corner. My favorite outings are the 2.2-mile **Chimney Rock Trail,** from which there is an impressive view of the Monocacy Valley, and the short walk to the **Blue Ridge Summit Overlook** with views northward into Pennsylvania.

✳ Lodging
MOTELS AND HOTELS

Frederick, 21703
& **Courtyard by Marriott** (301-631-9030; 1-800-321-2211; www.courtyard.com/wasfd), 5225 Westview Dr. May be reached from I-270 Exit 31B or I-70 Exit 54. Listed for its ease of access and location close to many attractions in and around Frederick. Amenities include work desk and chair, telephones with ports, in-room iron and coffee. Indoor pool and exercise room. $95–175.

Thurmont, 21788
& **Cozy Country Inn** (301-271-4301; www.cozyvillage.com), 103 Frederick Rd. (MD 806). The inn is best known as the place the national and international press, as well as many dignitaries, stay while events take place at nearby Camp David in Catoctin Mountain Park. There are the traditional motel rooms and cottages, but the standouts are the upscale rooms decorated to commemorate the styles of various past presidents.

The Carter Room reflects his penchant for hunting and fishing, the Eisenhower Room is decorated in Mamie's favorite colors, the Roosevelt Room has a bed similar to the one he was born in, and the Kennedy Room has the famous rocker. Other "presidential" rooms are similarly furnished;

all are equipped with nice amenities. A bountiful continental breakfast is included. $70–150. (Also see Cozy Restaurant under *Eating Out*.)

Super 8 (301-271-7888; 1-877-678-9330), 300 Tippin Dr. The motel's amenities are few, but its proximity to Catoctin Mountain Park and Cunningham Falls State Park is the reason to stay. $65–99.

INN **Catoctin Inn and Conference Center**

Catoctin Inn and Conference Center (301-874-5555; 1-800-730-5550; www.catoctininn.com), 3619 Buckeystown Pike, Buckeystown, 21717. The inn has an accommodation for just about any type of traveler. If you enjoy the B&B atmosphere, stay in the 1780 manor house, where each antiques-filled room has its own character. The modern, motel-like rooms in the old stable-hand quarters appeal to business travelers or to those who value their anonymity. The Smoke House, Summer Cottage, and Bucky's Cottage (with two-person whirlpool bath) ensure privacy for the romantically inclined. Breakfast is included with all rooms. $95–150.

BED & BREAKFASTS

Buckeystown, 21717

The Inn at Buckeystown (301-874-5755; 1-800-272-1190; www.innat buckeystown.com), 3521 Buckeystown Pike. Host Janet Wells has filled the 1897 Victorian mansion with period pieces to complement the three working fireplaces, grand chandeliers, and columned front porch. Everything speaks of the elegance and charm of the inn's earliest days.

Some of the rooms and suites have private baths; others share a bath. One of the most compelling reasons to stay here is to partake in one of the inn's

prix fixe dinners (see *Dining Out*). The B&B rate, which includes breakfast, ranges $110–160. Rates with dinner for two included range $175–225.

Frederick, 21701

McCleery's Flat (301-620-2433; 1-800-774-7926; www.fwp.net/mccleerysflat), 121 E. Patrick St. The 1876 Empire-style town house is furnished with period antiques and reproductions. The three rooms and two suites have private baths. I stayed in the Franklin Room because I like the blue-and-white porcelain collection and large library, and the way the two brick fireplace flues come together to form an arch over the four-post bed with rice leaves and fronds carved on it. The Grand Suite overlooks the backyard garden; the Secret Chamber was discovered during renovations. Host Jutta Terrell's breakfasts are what bring many guests for return visits. $115–140.

&. **Tyler Spite House** (301-831-4455; www.tylerspitehouse.com), 112 W. Church St. Andrea Myer has filled her 1814 Federal-style home with historically significant antiques. The Thomas Johnson Room has his shaving mirror, and the chest of John Hanson (elected president by the Continental Congress in 1781) is in the room bearing his name. The parlor piano belonged to the Francis Scott Key family, and the Barbara Fritchie Room has her spinning wheel. Amazingly, the house also contains the desk on which MacArthur signed the peace treaty in the Philippines. $200–250.

Hill House (301-682-4111; www.itlink.com/hillhouse/1.html), 12 W. 3rd St. Within Frederick's historic downtown area, Taylor and Damian Branson offer four guest rooms, each with private bath. The 1870 three-story

Victorian town house is filled with original artwork and many heirloom documents, pieces of furniture, and other items. I enjoy staying in the Steeple Suite on the third floor, where small windows overlook the city's spires and spur thoughts of Whittier's Barbara Fritchie poem. Damian's years of catering and gourmet cooking are evident in the breakfast she will serve to you. $105–150.

Hollerstown Hill Bed & Breakfast (301-228-3630; www.hollerstown hill.com), 4 Clarke Place. Located just a short walk from the main downtown area, this late-Victorian home was built around the turn of the 20th century and reflects that time with carved mantels and fireplaces, period antiques, and a wraparound veranda on which to relax. Guest rooms, which are quite large, contain TV and private bath. Hosts Betty and Phillip LeBlanc prepare a full breakfast of home-baked breads, fresh fruit, tasty casseroles, and more. $115–125.

HOSTEL American Youth Hostel (301-834-7652; www.harpersferry hostel.org), 19123 Sandy Hook Rd., Knoxville, 21758. The hostel is located along the C&O Canal and the Appalachian Trail, which means it is a place to meet some interesting travelers. You do not have to be a member of AYH or international hosteling organizations to stay. There are a couple of private rooms, but, for economy and companionship, most people stay in the bunk room, where you supply your own sleeping bag or linens. As with all such hostels, it is closed to patrons 9 AM–6 PM. $15–20.

VACATION RENTALS ❧ **Above All Else @ Windsong** (301-831-5083;

www.windsongarabians.com), 1313A Old Annapolis Rd., Mount Airy, 21771. The vacation home, with four bedrooms and three baths—and a corral so that you can bring your own horses—sits in a private corner of a large operating horse farm. $200 per couple; $75 each additional person. If you have a group and are staying for a week, the $1,000 charge for up to eight people is a real deal.

CAMPING

Brunswick, 21706
❧ **Brunswick Family Campground** (301-834-8050), adjacent to the C&O Canal. Open early Apr.–early Nov. A municipal facility, it has trailer and tent sites, a playground area, and a bathhouse. The rates are some of the lowest you will find in the state. I like that you can walk out of your tent and onto the canal in just a few steps.

Frederick, 21701
❧ **Gambrill State Park** (see *Green Space*). The campground is located at the base of High Knob and provides access to the park's trail system. There are no hookups, and sites are quite primitive, but this makes a good, low-cost base from which to explore Frederick and the Catoctin Mountains area.

Thurmont, 21788
Catoctin Mountain Park (see the sidebar on page 377). **Owens Creek Campground** sits high on the mountain and is usually open from mid-April through mid-November. There are flush toilets, but no showers. One of the prettiest settings of all the area's campgrounds.

❧ **Crow's Nest Campground** (301-271-7632; 1-800-866-1959), 335 W. Main St. Open year-round. Swimming pool, children's playground, and trails that connect with those in Catoctin Mountain Park.

Cunningham Falls State Park (see *Green Space*). There are two campgrounds within the park. Just off US 15 are the 148 sites of the **Houck Area**. A little more isolated, and certainly quieter, are the 31 sites in the **Manor Area**, close to the falls and the lake. Be forewarned: The showers only have cold water.

Ole Mink Farm Recreation Resort (301-271-7012; www.oleminkfarm .com), 12806 Mink Farm Rd. Open year-round. Many of the 90 sites are leased on a yearly basis to RV owners, but you can still enjoy the place in your tent or in one of the deluxe camping cabins. Swimming pool.

Also see **C&O Canal National Historical Park** under *Bicycling*.

✻ Where to Eat

DINING OUT

Buckeystown
The Inn at Buckeystown (301-874-5755; 1-800-272-1190; www.innat buckeystown.com), 3521 Buckeystown Pike. Open for dinner Thu.–Sun. Reservations are mandatory, as the chef prepares the five-course prix fixe meal based upon who and how many will be dining. The inn is elegant and the food superb, yet the atmosphere is anything but stuffy. Guests are often seated together at one big table, and as the courses (and BYOB bottles) flow one into the other, conversations become more amiable and animated. Expect to be served lamb, duck, steak, pasta, or chicken (sometimes all in the same meal) prepared by a Culinary Institute of America–trained chef. An

experience that will not soon be forgotten. The prix fixe meal is about $40 a person; à la carte menu selections are also available.

Frederick
Isabella's Tavern & Tapas Bar (301-698-8922; www.isabellas-tavern .com), 44 N. Frederick St. Lunch and dinner; closed Mon. Bringing a bit of Spain to Frederick, Isabella's became a local favorite within a short time of opening soon after the turn of the 21st century by providing elegant dining at quite reasonable prices. Tapas (Spanish appetizers) include inventive items such as crispy panko-crusted asparagus "fries" with smoked tomato *aliolo* ($4.95), and fried house-breaded goat cheese with almond fritters and shallot vinaigrette ($5.25). Dinners are equally inventive with a variety of paellas and meat and fish dishes costing $15.95–28.95.

The Tasting Room (240-379-7772; http://pages.frederick.com/dining/ tasting.htm), 101 N. Market St. Lunch and dinner; closed Sun. Owner-chef Michael Tauraso earns accolades from food critics and customers daily. An employee of the Tourism Council of Frederick County says the Sicilian rice ball appetizer—pignoli nuts and Fontinella stuffing ($7.95)—is one of the best things she has ever eaten and that the lobster whipped potatoes ($7.95) are a must-have. She calls the oak-planked rockfish with sherry roasted tomatoes and garlic cream ($22.95) "fantastic" and comments that the cod Mitonnée—oil-seared cod, winter greens, tomato, white beans, wine, and Gruyère croutons ($11.95)—on the lunch menu is "light, but really, really good with lots of flavor." Dinner entrées are $17.95–32.95.

Ijamsville

🍴 ♿ **Gabriel's Inn** (301-865-5500), 4730 Ijamsville Rd. Open for dinner from 3 PM Wed.–Sun. Traditional French cuisine served in a relaxed and casual atmosphere. Each meal is available French-style (including hors d'oeuvres, soup, entrée, vegetables, salad, cheese tray, and dessert; $23–33) or American-style (salad, entrée, and vegetables; $16–23). A $10 menu is available Wed. and Thu. 3–7; Fri. and Sat. 3–5.

New Market

🍴 ♿ **Mealey's** (301-865-5488; www.mealeysrestaurant.com), 8 Main St. Open for lunch Fri. and Sat. 11:30–2:30; dinner Mon.–Sat. 5–9; dinner Sun. noon–8. Antiques fill the 1793 brick building, which has served as a general store and a hotel. The kitchen staff does an admirable job of preparing the typical American/Maryland fare. Prime rib is the specialty, but there are also many seafood choices. The atmosphere and quality of food and service are a special value, as many entrées are less than $25.

EATING OUT

Emmitsburg

♿ **Carriage House Inn** (301-447-2366; www.carriagehouseinn.info), 200 S. Seton Ave. Open daily for lunch and dinner. With a colonial atmosphere inside and out, the inn serves what I call "upscale American" fare. Seafood, steaks, pork, chicken, and pasta all decently prepared and presented. Lots of tasty desserts, such as the chocolate mold with black raspberry ice cream inside. Entrées $14.95–33.95.

Frederick

🍴 ♿ **Venuti's Ristorante** (301-668-2700; www.venutis.com), 16 E.

Patrick St. Open daily for lunch and dinner. The restored interior of the 1880s building, with brick walls and rich wood accents, gives Venuti's an upscale atmosphere, but entrée prices reflect an ownership willing to give value. Traditional Italian dishes of lasagna, veal Marsala, seafood Alfredo, and others cost less than $18.

🍴 ♿ **Brewer's Alley** (301-631-0089; www.brewers-alley.com), 124 N. Market St. Open daily for lunch and dinner; closed for a couple of hours between lunch and dinner on weekdays. Contemporary American pub fare and wood-fired pizzas complement the fresh-brewed beer. The southwestern grilled chicken fajita ($8.95) went well with the ale I chose. Other sandwiches and entrées $7.95–18.95.

🍴 ♿ **Jug Bridge Seafood** (301-228-2722; www.jugbridge.com),

THE TOWN HOUSES OF FREDERICK

909 Baltimore Rd. Open for dinner daily; open for lunch Sat. and Sun. Serving steamed crabs, crabcakes, crab imperial, and other seafood for more than 50 years. Other entrées include steak and chicken, but it is hard to tell you exactly how they will be prepared, as the menu changes frequently to take advantage of seasonal items. $9–30.

✎ **La Paz Mexican Restaurant** (301-694-8980), 18 Market Space. Open daily for lunch and dinner. The local Mexican restaurant serving the traditional dishes found in most American/Mexican establishments. Fajitas, burritos, quesadillas, tacos, and other entrées $6.50–14.

& **Barbara Fritchie Restaurant** (301-662-2500), US 40. Open for breakfast, lunch, and dinner. I have only had breakfast here—and certainly did enjoy it—so I can't advise you on the lunch and dinner entrées, but the menu features country-cooking items at fairly low prices. $5–12.95.

Thurmont

✎ & **Cozy Restaurant** (301-271-7373; www.cozyvillage.com), 103 Frederick Rd. (MD 806). Open daily for breakfast, lunch, and dinner. Established in 1929 by William Freeze and still owned by the Freeze family, the restaurant's fame parallels that of the adjacent Cozy Country Inn. Winston Churchill stopped by to play the jukebox, and Mamie Eisenhower was a frequent visitor to the pub. Display cases contain pictures, autographs, and other memorabilia from these and other famous diners.

Traditional country fare and Maryland seafood specialties are on the reasonably priced menu. The aroma of fresh-baked breads and desserts fills the air. During the growing season, the vegetables at the daily buffet were organically grown in Cozy's own garden. $8.99–15.99.

✎ & **Mountain Gate** (301-271-4373), 133 Frederick Rd. (MD 806). Open daily for breakfast, lunch, and dinner. Large buffets make this the place for hungry families looking for large quantities of country-cooked fare at low prices. Items from the menu include roast beef, fried ham, and a seafood platter. $5.95–16.95.

COFFEE BARS

Frederick

Mudd Puddle Coffee Café (301-620-4323), 124 S. Carroll St. Closed Sun. Specialty coffees and gourmet sandwiches.

Frederick Coffee Company (301-698-0039), 100 N. East St. Live music on weekend evenings.

SNACKS AND GOODIES

Frederick

The Candy Kitchen (301-698-0442), 52 N. Market St. Producing handmade chocolates, truffles, fudges, and more since 1902.

McCutcheon's Apple Products (301-662-3261; www.mccutcheons .com), 13 S. Wisner St. The quality of McCutcheon's cider, preserves, apple butter, juices, relishes, and other jars of tasty victuals is such that Marylanders often give them as gifts.

Middletown

South Mountain Creamery (301-371-4388; www.southmountain creamery.com), 8305 Bolivar Rd. Call for business hours. The milk, yogurt, cheese, ice cream, and other products sold at the retail store, located on the farm, are not only the freshest you will find but are also grown completely organically.

Thurmont

Mom and Pop's Ice Cream Shop (301-271-7800), 19 Water St. One of Mom and Pop's huge snowballs of shaved ice, available in almost 20 flavors, is the way to end a hike in nearby Catoctin Mountain Park.

✳ Entertainment

FILM

Frederick

West Ridge Cinema (301-698-9100), 1037 W. Patrick St. First-run films.

Hoyts Frederick Towne Mall Cinema (301-682-6400), US 40. One of the most expensive (tickets and goodies) first-run theaters I've ever been in.

Holiday Cinemas (301-694-0100), 100 Baughman's Lane. Shows films after they have been out awhile, at nicely reduced prices.

See **Weinberg Center for the Arts** under *Theaters* for classic films.

NIGHTLIFE **Oldies Music Legends** (301-698-2600), 5311 Buckeystown Pike, Frederick. More than 5,500 square feet on which to ballroom dance. Call for days and times.

THEATERS

Frederick

✐ ♿ **Weinberg Center for the Arts** (301-228-2828; www.weinbergcenter .org), 20 W. Patrick St. The renovated 1926 movie palace has developed into the arts and cultural center of the region. Traveling troupes and nationally and internationally known performers present plays, musicals, concerts, and dance throughout the year. The

Weinberg also has a yearly series for families and one of classic movies.

Fredericktowne Players (301-694-6659; www.fredericktowneplayers .org), 306 E. Patrick St. The resident company for the Weinberg Center for the Arts (see above) presents at least four performances Sep.–July. Productions have included *The Seven-Year Itch*, *Run for Your Wife*, and *Joseph and the Amazing Technicolor Dreamcoat*.

Maryland Ensemble Theatre (301-694-4744; www.marylandensemble .org), 15 W. Patrick St. The multi-faceted organization stages a number of performances during its season; most productions are new works by local talent. An added bonus is the comedy sessions presented after the Saturday-night performances. Works by regional artists are located in the lobby.

♿ **Way Off Broadway Dinner Theater** (301-662-6600; www.wayoff broadway.com), Willowtree Plaza (US 40 W.). A dinner buffet accompanies the presentations of musicals, comedies, and mysteries.

SPORTS **Frederick Keys Baseball** (301-662-0013), 6201 New Design Rd., Frederick. The Keys, Class A affiliates of the Baltimore Orioles, provide hometown action on the field of the Harry Grove Stadium Apr.–Sep. The stadium is also the site of professional wrestling, concerts, and other events.

✳ Selective Shopping

ANTIQUES

Frederick

Antique Imports (301-662-6200; 1-800-662-2014), 125 East St. A large selection of British furniture and accessories.

Emporium Antiques (301-662-7099; www.emporiumantiques.com), 112 E. Patrick St. Open daily. More than 100 dealers under one roof.

Cannon Hill Place (301-696-9304), 111 S. Carroll St. The 1700s stone granary houses antiques and collectibles.

Old Glory Antique Marketplace (301-662-9173), 5862 Urbana Pike. Open daily. Close to 110 dealers.

Middletown

Antiques in Middletown (301-371-7380), 100 N. Church St. A multi-dealer shop that is so eager to have you stop by, they offer everyone a free cup of coffee, whether or not you buy anything.

New Market

With more than 30 shops, the small town of New Market, a few miles east of Frederick, has dubbed itself "the Antiques Capital of Maryland." Sometimes, places with such a large number of dealers can be overwhelming, but many of the businesses are housed within historic homes and storefronts, giving you a chance to walk around, enjoy the scenery, and recharge before entering another establishment. All shops are open on the weekend; on other days, a flag flying on a storefront indicates it is open. Information about the shops can be obtained from the **Tourism Council of Frederick County, Frederick Visitor Center**, or by logging onto www.newmarketmd.com.

ART GALLERIES

Frederick

& **Delaplaine Visual Arts Education Center** (301-698-0656; www .delaplaine.org), 20 S. Carroll St. Open daily. A nonprofit organization, the center overlooks Carroll Creek and the *Community Bridge Mural.* The exhibit areas showcase local and regional talent, while the studio spaces are used for instruction and special events.

Museum Shop, LTD (301-695-0424; 1-888-678-0675), 20 N. Market St. Japanese woodcuts, handcrafted items, and original Whistler and Kornemann art.

Gallery Wear (301-662-7100), 116 E. Patrick St. Interesting blend of artist-made jewelry, clothing, ceramics, and furniture.

Thurmont

Her Studio Gallery (301-447-2866), 304 E. Main St. Fri.–Sun. Linda Postelle works with watercolors, acrylics, and painted furniture.

BOOKSTORE Book Center (301-663-1222), US 15 and W. 7th St. (at Frederick Shopping Center), Frederick. A combination book/gift/café shop.

USED BOOKS & **Market St. Books** (301-228-2127), 143 N. Market St., Frederick. Closed Mon. A small selection of new books can be found among the many used volumes.

Quill and Brush (301-874-3200), 1137 Sugarloaf Mountain Rd., Dickerson. A purveyor of signed, limited, and first editions of collectible books. All fields and genres are stocked, but they concentrate on literature and mysteries.

Wonder Book and Video (301-694-5955; www.wonderbk.com), 1306 W. Patrick St., Frederick. A retail outlet for the chain-store company that claims to have more than a million new, rare, and used books available through its Web site.

✄ **I Made This!** (301-624-4030; www.imadethispottery.com), 10-B East St., Frederick. Open daily. Paint your own pottery. A good rainy-day activity.

Catoctin Pottery (301-371-4274; www.catoctinpottery.com), 3205 Poffenberger Rd., Jefferson. Closed Sun. Susan Hanson's studio is located in a former gristmill where she creates her vivid pieces of ceramics, tableware, and lamps.

SPECIAL SHOPS

Frederick

The Shops at Everedy Square and Shab Row, corner of East and Church Sts. The 18th- and 19th-century dwellings that once housed wheelwrights, tinkers, and crafts-people are now a complex of small shops filled with everything from antiques to books to artworks and crafts supplies. As interesting for its history and architecture as it is for the shops.

✄ **Dancing Bear** (301-631-9300; www.dbeartoys.com), 12 N. Market St. Toys, gifts, and music for the kids. I certainly no longer qualify as a kid, but I had a smile on my face as I looked through children's books written and illustrated by Maryland residents.

Hunting Creek Outfitters (301-668-4333), 29 N. Market St. An authorized Orvis dealer with fly-fishing rods and reels, accessories, and clothing.

Thurmont

Cozy Village, across from Cozy Country Inn and Restaurant, is an assemblage of cutesy little shops filled with handcrafted items, antiques, and gift ideas. Most of the shops are open until 5 daily.

FARMER'S MARKETS

Frederick

Everedy Square and Shab Row Farmer's Market (310-898-3183), Church and East Sts. Close to the antiques and shopping center of town, the market is open Thu. 3:30–6:30, early June–late Oct.

Frederick County Fairgrounds Market (301-663-5895), fairgrounds. The area's largest selection of farmer's market items is open year-round 8–2 on Sat.

West Frederick Farmer's Market (301-898-3183), 110 Baughman's Lane. Stands are set up in the Bluecross/Blueshield parking lot 10–1 on Sat., early May–Oct.

PICK-YOUR-OWN PRODUCE FARMS

Maynes Tree Farm (301-662-4320), 3420 Buckeystown Pike, Buckeystown. The strawberries are ripe from mid-May through mid-June, and the pumpkins are ready to pick by mid-September. Return during the holiday season to pick and/or cut your Christmas tree.

Glade-Link Farms (301-898-7131), MD 194, New Midway. The farm grows fruit, vegetables, and gourds, so you can come here early spring–early fall and find something to take home.

Catoctin Mountain Orchard (301-271-2737; www.catoctinmountain orchard.com), 15036 N. Franklinville Rd., Thurmont. The blackberries, blueberries, and cherries all ripen about late June and can be picked into early July.

✳ Special Events

February: **Cabin Fever Festival** (301-898-5466; www.cabinfever festival.com), fairgrounds, Frederick.

The annual event gets you outdoors for a midwinter arts and crafts show.

April: **Farm Museum Spring Festival** (301-694-1650), Rose Hill Manor Park, Frederick. Hayrides, pedal-tractor pull, petting zoo, and children's crafts.

June: **Festival of the Arts** (301-694-9632; www.frederickarts.org), Frederick. Juried arts market, children's activities, and live entertainment along Carroll Creek.

June–August: **Summer Concert Series** (301-694-2489), Baker Park, Frederick. Free outdoor concerts every Sun. evening feature local and regional acts. Expect to hear everything from New Age to country to jazz to urban music.

July: **Battle of Monocacy** (301-662-3515), Monocacy National Battlefield. Living-history portrayals of aspects of the battle.

August: **Country Peddler Show** (941-479-5005), fairgrounds. Annual event featuring folk artists from around the country. Crafts and folk art for sale. **Hunting and Fishing Show** (301-865-3019), fairgrounds.

An annual exposition of outdoor equipment. Classes, exhibits, and live animals.

September: The **Great Frederick (County) Fair** (301-663-5895), fairgrounds.

October: **Oktoberfest** (301-663-3885), Schifferstadt, Frederick. Annual festival with German food, biergarten, and oompah bands. Children's events and juried arts and crafts show. **Maryland Mountain Festival** (301-898-5466; www.marylandmountainfestival.com), Lynfield Complex (north of Frederick). Juried arts and crafts. **Railroad Days** (301-834-7100), Brunswick Railroad Museum, Brunswick. Scenic bluegrass train excursions, and model-railroad exhibits and demonstrations.

December: **Candlelight Tour of Historic Houses of Worship** (301-228-2888; 1-800-999-3613), Frederick. More than a dozen houses of worship participate, with each one providing a different program, such as organ recital, bell-chime demonstration, Christmas pageant, harp ensemble, and choir performances.

The Mountains of Western Maryland

**THE GREAT VALLEY AND BLUE
RIDGE REGION**—Hagerstown,
Antietam, and Hancock

THE ALLEGHENY PLATEAU—
Rocky Gap, Cumberland, and Frostburg

AROUND DEEP CREEK LAKE—
Grantsville, McHenry, Thayersville,
and Oakland

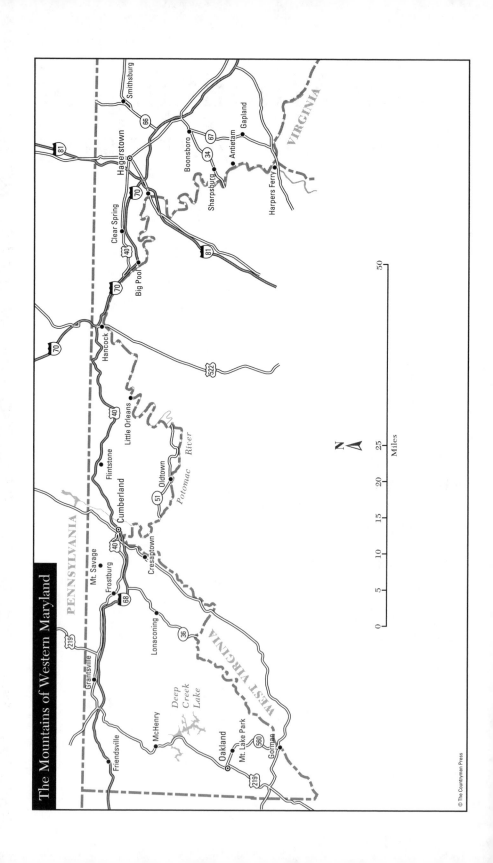

The Mountains of Western Maryland

© The Countryman Press

THE MOUNTAINS OF WESTERN MARYLAND

The mountains of western Maryland are a world apart. Although they were the gateway through which early settlers passed on their way to America's early frontiers, they were the last area in Maryland to be settled. The construction of I-70, I-81, and I-68 has made them more accessible, yet things are still a little rough around the edges—and that is the allure.

Other than in Hagerstown and Cumberland, and their immediate vicinities, malls and supersized discount stores are few and far between; there are only a couple of large luxury resorts; home-style cooking is what you will find in many of the restaurants; and mom-and-pop enterprises are the norm. Two-lane roadways, which snake over heavily forested ridgelines and along swiftly moving mountain streams, connect one sparsely populated community with another.

Traveling along the interstates is more scenic than you would imagine. Valley floors resemble patchwork quilts, made up of cropland, fields of cattle, and meadows all tinted by nature's own hues. West of Hancock, the Allegheny Plateau continues into West Virginia, providing mile after mile of extended mountain vistas. This is Maryland's coalfield. While driving on country roadways, you may look into your rearview mirror to see the grille of an overloaded coal truck barreling down the mountain, just inches from your rear bumper.

Due to the access provided by the interstates, much of this is changing and "economic development" is on the rise. So the time to visit western Maryland is now, before it loses its rough edges, before its roadsides are littered with the parking lots of fast-food restaurants instead of being bordered by modest homesteads. Before other folks learn of the charms of the place and come flocking to an area just waiting to be discovered. Explore now, while public lands are not well visited and can provide rambles and wanderings in relative peace and quiet with few other wayfarers.

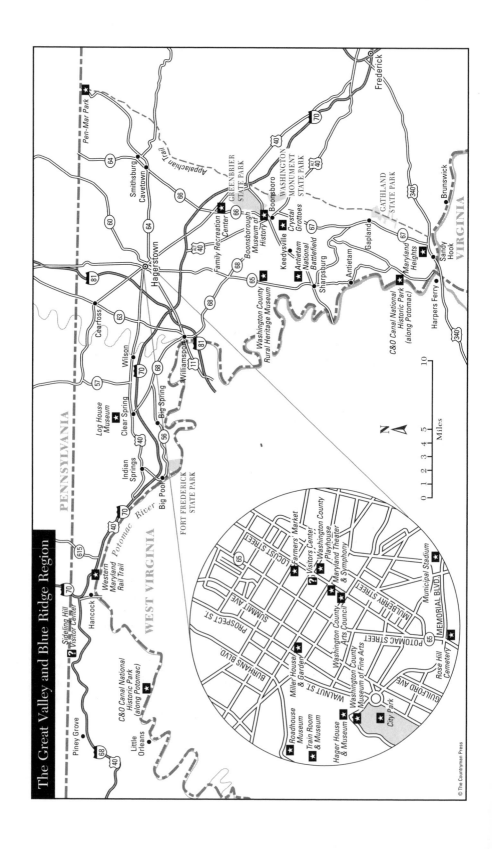

The Great Valley and Blue Ridge Region

PENNSYLVANIA

WEST VIRGINIA

VIRGINIA

Pen-Mar Park

Smithsburg
Cavetown

Appalachian Trail

GREENBRIER
STATE PARK

Boonsboro

WASHINGTON
MONUMENT
STATE PARK

Family Recreation
Center

Boonsborough
Museum of
History

Crystal
Grottoes

Keedysville

Antietam
National
Battlefield

Sharpsburg

Antietam

Gapland

GATHLAND
STATE PARK

Maryland
Heights

Sandy
Hook

Brunswick

Frederick

Hagerstown

Washington County
Rural Heritage Museum

C&O Canal National
Historic Park
(along Potomac)

Harpers Ferry

Cearfoss

Wilson

Williamsport

Big Spring

Clear Spring

Log House
Museum

Indian
Springs

Big Pool

FORT FREDERICK
STATE PARK

Potomac River

Western
Maryland
Rail Trail

Hancock

Sideling Hill
Visitor Center

C&O Canal National
Historic Park
(along Potomac)

Little
Orleans

Piney Grove

N

Miles

0 1 2 3 4 5   10

Farmers' Market

Visitors Center

Washington County
Playhouse

Maryland Theater
& Symphony

Washington County
Arts Council

Miller House
& Garden

LOCUST STREET

SUMMIT AVE

PROSPECT ST

BURHANS BLVD

WALNUT ST

Roadhouse
Museum

Train Room
& Museum

Hager House
& Museum

Washington County
Museum of Fine Arts

City Park

Municipal Stadium

MULBERRY STREET

POTOMAC STREET

MEMORIAL BLVD

Rose Hill
Cemetery

GUILFORD AVE

© The Countryman Press

THE GREAT VALLEY AND BLUE RIDGE REGION—Hagerstown, Antietam, and Hancock

As I-70 rises onto the crest of South Mountain—a part of the Blue Ridge Mountains stretching from northern Georgia to central Pennsylvania—westbound travelers gaze upon the bounteous expanse of the Great Valley.

A miles-wide and relatively flat feature in an otherwise mountainous landscape, the valley extends from mid-Pennsylvania into southern Virginia and beyond. This natural travel conduit is what Jonathan Hager and other German settlers from Pennsylvania followed into the Maryland colony, arriving in the early 1700s to establish new lives on the fertile valley floor.

During the French and Indian War in 1755, British troops (including a young George Washington) under the command of General Braddock built a wagon road through Turners Gap on South Mountain, the valley's eastern barrier. In 1806, the route was designated part of the National Road and became a major thoroughfare to the West.

Hagerstown began to grow where the two routes met, and its strategic location made it a contested site during the Civil War. Maryland was a free state, but there were many Confederate sympathizers in Hagerstown, and escaped slaves were often captured and returned to their Southern owners.

Confederate troops under the command of Robert E. Lee occupied the town prior to the Battle of Antietam in 1862, retreated after the conflict, and returned 9 months later. Lee's push into Northern territory was once more thwarted, with most of the fighting this time taking place on South Mountain. Land on which these hostilities occurred has been preserved, and you can trace the events by visiting Antietam National Battlefield or walking the route of the Appalachian Trail along South Mountain.

The arrival of several railroad lines after the Civil War helped establish Hagerstown as the industrial center of the valley. The construction of I-81 (along the basic course Jonathan Hager followed) and I-70 (which parallels the route of the National Road) solidified its economic status and brought new people into the area. The downtown area, with a blend of old and new buildings, harbors a vibrant arts and cultural community, evident in the many museums, galleries, and theaters within a few blocks of one another. The Washington County Museum of Fine Arts is one of the best of its kind, and the Hager House and Museum preserve the city's former days.

On the western edge of the valley, Hancock began as an early-1700s trading post close to where Native Americans forded the Potomac River. The settlement was later named for Revolutionary War figure Edward Joseph Hancock Jr. and, like Hagerstown, started to grow when the National Road, and later the Chesapeake & Ohio (C&O) Canal, reached the town. It, too, was fought over during the Civil War, with Stonewall Jackson laying siege to it as early as January 1862. Hancock lost much of its importance in the mid-1900s when I-70 bypassed it a bit to the north. Its narrow downtown area, however, has remained an active business district with antiques shops, a C&O Canal Visitor Center, and a number of places catering to canal bikers and hikers.

COMMUNITIES **Boonsboro** was established in 1792 by George and William Boone. Its position along the National Road brought it growth and prosperity, as it lay about halfway between Frederick and Hagerstown. There is now another spurt of growth as the populations of the two cities migrate toward each other. A couple of museums (do not miss the Boonsborough Museum of History!), a commercial cavern, and a couple of the region's finest restaurants have begun to put the town on many a traveler's must-stop list.

Sleepy little **Williamsport** was once considered by George Washington as a potential site for the nation's capital, but its remoteness and inaccessibility caused him to look elsewhere. The town's fortunes grew once the C&O Canal reached it in 1834, yet declined when the waterway closed in the early 1900s. The canal and its history remain focal points, though, as people come to town to access the towpath or obtain information about it at the C&O Canal Visitor Center.

GUIDANCE The **Hagerstown/Washington County Convention and Visitors Bureau** (301-791-3246; 1-888-257-2600; www.marylandmemories.org) is located at Elizabeth Hager Center, 16 Public Square, Hagerstown, 21740, and can provide you with information if you are calling or writing when you are not in the area. The best place for guidance while in town is the bureau's **Welcome Center** at 6 N. Potomac St., Hagerstown.

GETTING THERE *By air:* By way of **Hagerstown Regional Airport** (240-313-2777; 1-800-428-4322), US Airways Express (1-800-428-4322) provides scheduled passenger commuter service to and from **Pittsburgh International Airport** (412-472-3525).

By car: **I-81** comes into the region from Pennsylvania to the north, and West Virginia and Virginia to the south. **I-70** provides access from the east, while **I-68** (which terminates at I-70 in Hancock) is the way to arrive from the west.

By bus: **Greyhound** (1-800-231-2222) will drop you off at its local terminal (301-739-7420) located at 10527 Sharpsburg Pike in Hagerstown.

By rail: A **MARC** (1-800-325-RAIL) commuter train out of Washington, DC, makes stops in Harpers Ferry, which is just across the Potomac River in West Virginia.

GETTING AROUND *By car:* Many streets in Hagerstown are one way; pay attention to the signs.

By bus: The local bus service, **County Commuter** (301-791-3047), has routes to all points in Hagerstown and to a few of the nearby communities such as Funkstown, Maugansville, Smithsburg, Long Meadow, and Williamsport.

By taxi: **Antietam Cab** (301-393-8811), **Antietam Transportation** (301-714-2286), and **Turner Van Service** (301-733-7788) are based in Hagerstown. In and around Hancock, you can call **Valley Cab** (301-678-7767).

MEDICAL EMERGENCY **Washington County Hospital** (301-790-8300), 2511 E. Antietam St., Hagerstown.

✳ To See
MUSEUMS

Boonsboro
Boonsborough Museum of History (301-432-6969), 113 N. Main St. Sun. 1–5, May–Sep. Small admission fee. Doug Bast's late father was a fanatical collector, and Doug has followed in his footsteps. Their assortment of thousands of items is crammed into a two-story structure. It is almost impossible to describe what is here, but it is, by far, one of the most amazing personal museums I have ever seen. There are bullet carvings from the Civil War, a preserved rose from Lincoln's coffin, a pike given to a slave by John Brown, an original letter from Clara Barton, a cane carved by Geronimo, religious items dating from AD 800, and a clay lamp made in 1500 BC. Do not miss this place!

Washington County Rural Heritage Museum (240-420-1712), 7313 Sharpsburg Pike (MD 65). Open Sat. and Sun. 1–4. Small admission fee. I thought I would be visiting a typical farm museum with a few pieces of agricultural equipment. I found this museum, which depicts the struggles and achievements of farmers of the past, to be much more. There are grain reapers, potato graders, and such, but there are also sleighs, buggies, an original Conestoga wagon, a replica of a country store, the complete interior of the old Keedysville post office—and a grain harvester that is believed to have been built in Eastern Europe nearly 1,000 years ago. Future plans include the construction of a rural village.

THE LOG HOUSE MUSEUM IN CLEAR SPRING

Clear Spring

Log House Museum (301-842-2553), 11 S. Mill St. Open by appointment. Small admission fee. A labor of love. Carl Brown restored this 1825 cabin with his own money during the late 1900s. Items of everyday life from the 1800s and 1900s, many of them from the Brown family, fill the two-story cabin. The museum has received scant public funds, which makes it more remarkable that the spinning wheels, washing machines, a sled with sleigh bells, the medical instruments used by a local doctor, and a fireplace with wrought-iron cooking utensils have been preserved.

Hagerstown

& **Washington County Museum of Fine Arts** (301-739-5727; www.washco museum.org), 91 Key St. (in Hagerstown City Park). Open Tue.–Sat. 10–5, Sun. 1–6. Donations accepted. Certainly one of the most impressive free-admission, small-city galleries you will find anywhere. The permanent collection contains more than 7,000 pieces of noted American art, Old Masters, European works, decorative and folk arts, and items by regional and Maryland artists. In addition, the museum brings in some of the world's finest artwork for limited exhibitions. There is also at least one music concert a month. Steel baron William H. Singer donated the building that houses the museum, and its beauty alone makes a stop here worthwhile.

✍ **Roundhouse Museum** (301-739-4665), 300 S. Burhans Blvd. Open Fri.–Sun. 1–5. Small admission fee. At one time, five railroad companies operated in the Hagerstown area, and more than 20 passenger trains a day came into the city. Inside are displays, items, and photographs from those days. The HO and O gauge model-train layouts are impressive, and children are permitted to operate the largest one, which depicts the roundhouse and nearby tracks. The museum sponsors a popular leaf-color train excursion each fall.

Hancock

Hancock Town Museum (301-678-6308), corner of High St. and Pennsylvania Ave. Open 2–4 on the first and third Sun., Apr.–Oct. Donations accepted. Within a small basement area of a former school, the museum chronicles the town's history with photographs (seek out the original *Harper's* magazine prints), transportation exhibits, and an early tool collection. There is even an original letter from Henry Clay postmarked 1827. All in all, it is a great collection of items, especially for a place that charges no admission fee.

HISTORIC HOMES

Hagerstown

Miller House and Garden (301-797-8782; www.mdwchs.com/wchs1.html), 135 W. Washington St. Apr.–Dec., Wed.–Sat. 1–4 (Dec. hours and days may vary). Small admission fee. The town house, built in various stages, is furnished as it would have been in 1825. The spiral staircase and furnishings reflect William Price's desire to let others know he was successful. The gardens are planted in period plants. One of the most interesting items is the original ledger of ransom for Hagerstown from Civil War Confederate General McCausland.

HAGER HOUSE IN HAGERSTOWN

Hager House (301-739-8393), 110 Key St. (within Hagerstown City Park). Tue.–Sat. 10–4 and Sun. 2–5. Small admission fee. Jonathan Hager arrived in frontier Maryland in 1739, built his house of uncut fieldstones (with 22-inch walls), married neighbor Elizabeth Kreshner, and set up a trading post in his home. The building is filled with period pieces, many of them Hager family originals. (Ask the docent to explain the origin of *pop goes the weasel*.) Period plants grow all around the house. The **Hager Museum** next door contains 18th- and 19th-century items found when the Hager House was restored in 1953. I find it amazing that so many of Hager's belongings still exist—such as his *Book of Sermons* (in German) and his waistcoat.

HISTORIC SITES

Big Pool

Fort Frederick State Park (301-842-2155), 11100 Fort Frederick Rd. The park and the fort are open daily; other attractions have varying open dates and times. Free admission to the park; a small fee to enter the fort. The colony of Maryland constructed the fort in 1756 to protect its western frontier during the French and Indian War. It also saw action during the Revolutionary and Civil Wars. With the fort restored to its earliest appearance, its stone walls enclose barracks, catwalks, and parade grounds. Costumed interpreters provide information on displays inside the barracks, and living-history demonstrations are presented on a scheduled basis. (A large reenactment with British, French, and Indian reenactors takes place each Memorial Day weekend.) A self-guided walking-tour brochure is available.

Also within the state park is a visitors center (with an excellent orientation film), a **Civilian Conservation Corps Museum**, seasonal boat rentals, a short nature

FORT FREDERICK

trail, and a small campground scenically located on bottomland between the C&O Canal and the Potomac River.

Hagerstown

Rose Hill Cemetery (301-739-3630), 600 S. Potomac St. The cemetery, which still has plots available, is the final resting place for more than 2,000 Confederate soldiers killed during the Antietam and South Mountain battles. Less than 350 were able to be identified.

Beaver Creek Country School (301-797-8782), 9702 Beaver Creek Church Rd. Sun. 2–5, Apr.–Sep. The 1904 brick building, filled with desks, books, slates, and engaging wall charts, is the third school to stand on this site. The museum room contains artifacts of early rural life. Interestingly, across the street, the refined steeple and stained glass of the 1902 **Beaver Creek Christian Church**, laid out by the same architect who designed the school, stand in stark contrast to the simple lines and windows of the 1845 **St. Matthew's Lutheran Church** next door.

BEAVER CREEK COUNTRY SCHOOL

Sharpsburg

Antietam National Battlefield (301-432-5124). The visitors center is off MD 65 a few miles north of Sharpsburg. Open daily. Small admission fee. When Confederate General Robert E. Lee made his first push into Northern territories in September 1862, his troops clashed with Union soldiers on a battlefield that covered 30 square miles. More men were killed or wounded than on any other single day during the Civil War.

I was impressed with the way the park service had organized visitors' experiences when I first came here many years ago. It was the first Civil War battlefield I had ever visited, and I have never failed to learn something new on subsequent visits. A driving tour takes you by significant battle sites, rangers lead guided walks, and a couple of trails take the more inquisitive into hidden areas of the battlefield's 3,000 acres.

THE BURNSIDE BRIDGE AT ANTIETAM NATIONAL BATTLEFIELD

Antietam National Cemetery is off MD 34 in Sharpsburg. Grand old maple, oak, and Norway spruce trees provide shade for the graves set out in a circular fashion. It is mind-boggling to walk through here and realize that only a portion of those killed during the battle are buried here.

OTHER SITES

Throughout the area

Between 1819 and 1863, more than 30 **stone bridges** were constructed along Antietam and Conococheague Creeks and their tributaries. Many of these impressive and eye-pleasing structures still exist. Information on where they are located can be obtained from the **Hagerstown/Washington County Convention and Visitors Bureau**.

SIDELING HILL

On Interstate 68 west of Hancock, the Washington County–Allegany County line, the interstate makes a long climb over 1,600-foot Sideling Hill. To reduce the length and grade of the ascent, workers spent more than 2 years making a cut 360 feet deep into the mountain's ridgeline (the deepest road cut in Maryland).

The passageway is a great place to learn about the geology of the mountains, so take a few minutes' break from driving to visit the **Sideling Hill Exhibit Center** (301-678-5442), accessed directly from the interstate. The four-story center offers exhibits, displays, and storyboards about many aspects of western Maryland. You will learn that the road cut reveals fossilized plants and seashells from 350 million years ago when the site was at the bottom of an ancient ocean. You can also see how the layers of sedimentary rock were folded as Africa collided with North America about 230 million years ago.

CAVERN TOUR ✎ **Crystal Grottoes Caverns** (301-432-6336), MD 34 about 1.5 miles west of Boonsboro. A 30-minute guided tour takes you through the 250-million-year-old caverns, believed to contain more formations per square foot than any other commercial cavern in the world. Triangular pyramids of calcite have formed eight-sided crystals rarely found anywhere else.

✳ To Do

BICYCLING **Western Maryland Rail Trail** (301-842-2155). The paved, and nearly flat, trail follows the route of the former Western Maryland Railroad. Still in the development stage, the completed portion begins about half a mile west of Fort Frederick State Park and continues westward for 19 miles into Hancock and beyond. A total of 25 miles will be available for riding when completed. The trail parallels the C&O Canal, which makes it possible to do round-trip rides without following the exact same course.

C&O Canal National Historical Park. The **C&O Canal Visitor Centers** in Williamsport (301-582-0813) and Hancock (301-678-5463) can provide you with much detailed information. (Also see the sidebar on page 295 for background history and information on the canal.) Well over 50 miles of the canal pass through this area of Maryland, providing a grand opportunity for hours of easy riding and sightseeing. Some of the highlights include access to the **Appalachian Trail** and **Maryland Heights**, the Big Pool area and **Fort Frederick State Park**, and the rewatered parts of the canal at Williamsport and Hancock. Spaced along the route are a dozen designated campsites, with vault toilets and water (in-season), that are available on a first-come, first-served basis. There are also numerous ramps from which you can launch a boat into the Potomac River.

Hancock
Potomac Outdoor Expeditions (301-678-6718). Amiable John Hess will rent you a canoe or bicycle and shuttle you to just about any point along the C&O Canal within 50 miles or so of Hancock. John has been doing this for so long that he is a true storehouse of knowledge, which he is willing to put to use for you if you ask for help in planning your trip. He will, if his schedule permits, also shuttle you if you wish to use your own bike or canoe.

C&O Bicycle (1-800-678-BIKE), located next to the C&O Canal. Bicycle rentals, sales, and service.

BOAT RENTALS See **Fort Frederick State Park** under *Historic Sites*, and **Potomac Outdoor Expeditions** under *Bicycling*.

FAMILY ACTIVITIES ✎ **Family Recreation Park** (301-733-2333), 21036 National Pike, Boonsboro. Open daily May–Aug.; weekends in Apr., and Sep.–Oct. You may not know what Water Wars is, but your kids do—and they probably can't wait to start propelling liquid-filled balloons into the air. This local hot spot also offers miniature golf, batting cages, attractions for very small children, and three go-cart tracks. The figure-8 is one of the most fun tracks I have ridden in many years.

Also see *Cavern Tour* under *To See*.

Hagerstown

Municipal Golf Course (301-733-8630), 2 S. Cleveland Ave. The nine-hole course was built in the 1930s by citizens who could not afford the fees of a private club. The entire grounds project a maturity and feel not found in newer courses.

Black Rock (240-313-2816; www.blackrockgolfcourse.com), 20025 Mount Aetna Rd. Grand views of the mountains from the par-72, 6,878-yard course.

Yingling's Golf Center (301-790-2494), 20220 Jefferson Blvd. The area's only par-3 course, it is an excellent choice for beginners or those wanting to brush up on their game. Also on the premises are a miniature-golf course and batting cages.

MINIATURE GOLF See **Family Recreation Park** under *Family Activities*, and **Yingling's Golf Center** under *Golf*.

HIKING **Maryland Heights** (304-535-6298), located off Sandy Hook Rd. across the Potomac River from Harpers Ferry, West Virginia. A steep and strenuous circuit hike of 5 miles will take the hardy and adventurous past remnants of Civil War fortifications and out to a spectacular view of the confluence of the Shenandoah and Potomac Rivers. Thomas Jefferson proclaimed the vista to be "one of

BIRDING—THE AUTUMN HAWK MIGRATION

Maryland's portion of the Appalachian Trail (see the sidebar on page 400) has overlooks along South Mountain, which are great areas from which to watch the annual autumn hawk migration. Heated air from rays of the sun striking cliffs and rock outcroppings couples with warm air rising from the lowlands to create forceful drafts, or *thermals,* that the hawks use to soar upward. In addition, by gliding near the crest of the ridges, they take advantage of the northwesterly winds striking the Appalachians, providing more uplift.

Sometimes as early as mid-August, ospreys, American kestrels, and a few bald eagles begin the procession southward. The migration commences in earnest in the middle of September as broad-winged hawks take to the skies. Peak daily sightings of several thousand are not uncommon. In early October, peregrine falcons join the movement, while later in the month one of the smallest hawks, the sharp-shinned, becomes the dominant migrant. Joining the procession are the larger but fewer-in-number Cooper's hawks. Red-tailed hawks, northern harriers, and red-shouldered hawks zip by leafless trees in November. Soaring over an Appalachian Trail that could be covered by December snows, northern goshawks and golden eagles bring the migratory season to a close.

THE APPALACHIAN TRAIL

There may be no better introduction to backpacking and primitive camping than the Appalachian Trail through Maryland. Shelters and campsites are conveniently spaced so that you don't have to do marathon miles to find a place to spend the night, wildlife is abundant, and the trail crosses numerous roads where help may be available in case of an emergency. Even though the route has a good feeling of isolation, there are four places where it is possible to make use of modern restroom facilities—and one spot that offers free warm showers!

The gentle terrain and great scenery are what make this the perfect place to bring the kids for overnight hikes or to break friends into the pleasures of backpacking without introducing them to the rigors of a more rugged topography. Other than a couple of climbs of less than 500 feet, the trail stays along the gently undulating crest of South Mountain for nearly the entire distance, neither losing nor gaining much in the way of elevation. On the rare occasions when winter cooperates by bringing in a blanket of snow deep enough to completely cover all of the rocks and boulders, the trail can be a great cross-country skiing or snowshoeing route.

In addition to its natural beauty, South Mountain has been the scene of numerous activities in American history. George Washington crossed the mountain a couple of decades before the colonies broke from England, the first National Road coursed its way over it, and skirmishes of the Civil War were waged on its heights.

The guidebook *50 Hikes in Maryland* (Countryman Press) gives a detailed description of the trail's 40-mile route through the state.

the most spectacular scenes in Nature, and worth a voyage across the Atlantic." Luckily, you only have to drive here and take a hike to enjoy it.

Also see **Antietam National Battlefield** under *Historic Sites*, and *Bicycling.*

KAYAKING AND CANOEING **Outdoor Excursions** (1-800-77-KAYAK; www .outdoorexcursions.com), P.O. Box 24, Osage Dr., Boonsboro. A one-stop shop for water-sports trips. They can teach you what you need to know and then will take you on guided kayaking, rafting, and tubing trips along the Potomac River. You can choose from day or weekend outings and a number of lesson packages. All instructors are certified by the American Canoe Association. **Antietam Creek Canoe** (301-881-7570; www.antietamcreek.com), 11420 Old Georgetown Rd., Rockville, provides the same basic services, but along a 22-mile section of Antietam Creek.

Also see **C&O Canal National Historical Park** and **Potomac Outdoor Expeditions** under *Bicycling.*

Hagerstown

✦ **Hagerstown Ice and Sports Complex** (301-766-9122), 580 Security Rd. Ice-skating lessons, rentals, and public sessions are available within the 35,000-square-foot structure.

✦ **Family Skating Center** (301-582-2020), 1733 Virginia Ave., and **Starland Roller Rink** (301-739-9844), 800 Park Rd., are both open to the public for roller-skating fun.

SKIING, CROSS-COUNTRY, AND SNOWSHOEING See the **Appalachian Trail** sidebar on page 400.

SWIMMING Claude M. Potterfield Municipal Pool (301-733-2599), 730 Frederick St., Hagerstown. Memorial Day–Labor Day.

TRAIN EXCURSIONS See **Roundhouse Museum** under *To See.*

WHITEWATER RAFTING See *Kayaking and Canoeing.*

✳ Green Space

PARKS

South Mountain at the Frederick –Washington County line

Five parks encompass most of the land along South Mountain's ridgeline and protect Maryland's 40 miles of the Appalachian Trail (see the sidebar on page 400). From south to north they are:

South Mountain State Park (301-791-4767), 21843 National Pike. It is hard to actually tell where this park is, as it was established to safeguard those lands along the mountain that were not already protected by the other parks. Be thankful the state appropriated the funds to purchase these additional acreages.

Gathland State Park (301-791-4767), Gapland Rd. (off MD 67). Open daily 8 AM–sunset. The park is the site of the only monument in the world to war correspondents. Planned

WAR CORRESPONDENTS MEMORIAL, GATHLAND STATE PARK

and built by George Alfred "Gath" Townsend, a journalist and columnist 1866–1910, it memorializes more than 150 reporters and artists who covered the Civil War from both sides of the conflict. The off-balance monument contains a large Moorish arch below three smaller ones of Roman design. Taking the time to look at and read the dozens of inscriptions and view the mythological figures could take up much of an afternoon. Picnic areas; also a small museum open on an irregular basis.

Washington Monument State Park (301-432-8065), accessed from US Alternate 40 east of Boonsboro. Open daily. Home of the original Washington Monument. Built by the citizens of nearby Boonsboro in 1827, the jug-shaped tower was the first structure to be completed in honor of America's first president. Be sure to ascend the inside staircase for a grand view of the rolling Maryland countryside to the west. There are also attractive picnic sites close to the monument.

Greenbrier State Park (301-791-4767), on US 40 about 9 miles east of Hagerstown. The focal point of the park is a 43-acre lake that provides swimming, fishing, and boating. Short hiking trails, a campground, and some great nature interpretive programs are other reasons to stop by.

Pen-Mar Park, in the town of Pen-Mar. Appearing to be not much more than a community picnic grounds today, this spot was an amazingly popular resort between 1890 and 1920. Seven hotels and close to 100 guest cottages were located nearby to cater to daily crowds of 5,000 or more drawn to an amusement park. Gas rationing during World War II forced the park to close in 1943. There is a splendid view of Hagerstown (Great) Valley to the west, and restrooms and water are available in-season.

Hagerstown
✿ **City Park**, located along Virginia Ave. in the city's South End. One of the state's prettiest municipal parks. Three man-made lakes are surrounded by 50 acres of open and forested areas, playgrounds, tennis courts and ball fields, and short walking trails. Within the park are the **Washington County Museum of**

HAGERSTOWN CITY PARK

✳ Lodging

MOTELS AND HOTELS ☗ **Four Points by Sheraton** (301-790-3010), 1910 Dual Hwy. (accessed from I-70 Exit 32), Hagerstown, 21740. Listed here because of its central location and proximity to many of the area's attractions. Exercise room, outside pool, and free continental breakfast. $75–125.

BED & BREAKFASTS

Hagerstown, 21740
Inn on Potomac (301-739-5679; www.innonpotomac.com), 400 N. Potomac St. By removing plastic shower stalls to expose original tile, refurnishing with a blend of antiques, and taking down walls that had turned the house into small rental apartments, Don Tollefson and Harold Walter have returned this home to its early-1900s beauty. When I tired of watching the daily bustle of Potomac Street from the Beige Suite, I closed the original wooden shutters and slid into the Jacuzzi tub. The walk-in bay in the Gold Room catches the morning sun, while the upstairs porch provides a grandstand view of holiday fireworks. The main downtown area is just a few minutes' walk away. $100–150.

If moments in the Jacuzzi are not relaxing enough, make an appointment for a facial or full-body massage with the **Tranquility Day Spa**, located within the inn.

Wingrove Manor (301-733-6328; www.wingrovemanor.com), 635 Oak Hill Ave. The large manor home, with an inviting front porch, sits impressively atop its long, sloping lawn, fitting in perfectly with the other grand

old homes of the neighborhood. A curved wood staircase leading to the four guest rooms, along with the fine furnishings and slate fireplace, exudes elegance and adds a touch of class to your stay. $100–150.

Bed & Breakfast at Lewrene Farm (301-582-1735; www.things-to-do .com/b&b/getaways/md/more7771 .htm), 9738 Downsville Pike. Of the many B&Bs in which I have stayed, this one feels most like being invited into someone's home. The furnishings are not just antiques but items from generations of Lewis and Irene Lehman's families. The couple spent many years on missions to Guatemala and Kenya, so the Colonial-style home is also filled with unique items—such as an intricately carved leather travel case and a hand-built marimba. Although you could wander around the working farm's 125 acres, enjoy the country breezes, or relax in the large parlor, the best use of your time would be getting to know this interesting couple who host not only B&B guests but also a succession of foreign exchange students. $68–95.

Hancock, 21750
Cohill Manor (301-678-7573), 5012 Western Pike. The five guest rooms (which share two and a half baths) are arranged in a circular pattern around the staircase in this 16-room home, whose original wing was built in the mid-1700s. Deborah and John Cohill (a great-grandson of an 1800s owner) have restored it to its original luster. The Cohills and their 16 acres—which support goats, barnyard animals, and

cats—are popular with C&O Canal cyclists. Be sure to ask about the fire and the angel picture—it is a great story. $50–95.

Sharpsburg, 21782

Inn at Antietam (301-432-6601; 1-877-835-6011; www.innatantietam .com), 220 E. Main St. This Eastlake Victorian home, circa 1908, has been receiving accolades since its B&B inception in the 1980s. Charles Van Metre and Bob Leblanc (memorabilia in the solarium chronicle their many years in the theater business) continue to run the inn with a touch of class. Each of the five guest suites has a private bath. I enjoyed the Rose Suite, with its antique four-poster bed and bright walk-in bay overlooking Sharpsburg's Main Street. The Smokehouse Suite is where hams and other meats were cured. Today the stone fireplace remains the focal point of the sitting room, while guests bed

down in an upstairs loft. Although somewhat out of character from the rest of the house, the Penthouse Suite's resemblance to a studio apartment and grandstand view of the surrounding mountains are a great use of the remodeled third-floor attic.

If a walk around the inn's 7 acres or an evening spent rocking on the wraparound porch are too relaxing, you can always exercise your mind by playing chess with the hand-carved Civil War set. $110–175.

Jacob Rohrbach Inn (301-432-5079; www.jacob-rohrbach-inn.com), 138 W. Main St. The 1800 Federal-period inn is named for the man who lost his life defending the property from horse thieves during the Civil War. The Clara Barton guest room is decorated with furniture made by host Paul Breitenbach's grandfather. I thought that the three small steps into the elevated bathroom in the Thomas

INN AT ANTIETAM, SHARPSBURG

Jackson Room added a bit of historical authenticity to my stay. The restored summer kitchen house was a great place to unwind. $114–149.

Rustic Rentals (202-686-5339; 1-877-787-8425). They have a number of cabins (in West Virginia and in this area of Maryland) that are available for rent for the night, weekend, week, or month. Each is fully equipped and can accommodate four to six people.

CAMPING

Boonsboro, 21713
Greenbrier State Park (301-791-4767), on US 40 about 9 miles east of Hagerstown. Usually open early Apr.–late Oct. The large campground has a dump station and flush toilets. Within the state park is a lake for swimming, fishing, and boating (with paddleboat and canoe rentals).

Big Pool, 21711
☙ **Indian Springs Campground** (301-842-3336), 10809 Big Pool Rd. One of the lowest-cost commercial campgrounds in the state. Limited facilities in winter.

♿ **Fort Frederick State Park** (301-842-2155), 11100 Fort Frederick Rd. Apr.–October. Located adjacent to the Potomac River and the Big Pool area of the C&O Canal. Vault toilets and two handicapped-accessible sites.

Gapland, 21779
☙ **Maple Tree Campground** (301-432-5585), 20716 Townsend Rd. Open year-round. A nicely laid-back campground in which RVs and trailers are not permitted; there are only tent sites. Two camping tree houses accommodate up to six people—a fun and different way to enjoy

the woods. Rates are some of the most reasonable you will find anywhere, and the campground backs up to the Appalachian Trail. Pets permitted on a leash.

Hancock, 21750
☙ **Happy Hills** (301-678-7760), 12617 Seavolt Rd. Open all year. The campground's 350 acres are within easy walking distance of the C&O Canal, which means you have access to many more miles of trails in addition to those in the campground. RV and tent sites, pool, miniature golf, and activities building. Camping cabins for rent. Pets on a leash permitted.

Williamsport, 21795
☙ **Antietam Hagerstown KOA** (301-223-7571; 1-800-562-7607), 11579 Snug Harbor Lane. Open year-round. The campground's 24 acres are along scenic Conococheague Creek, and some of the sites are next to the water. Canoe rentals, miniature golf, and many, many planned family activities.

McMahon's Mill (301-223-8778), Avis Mill Rd. (at mile 88.1 on the C&O Canal). The closest campground to Antietam National Battlefield, it has tent and RV sites next to the Potomac River. Flush toilets and hot showers. Also on the premises are a restaurant and the small **Civil War Military and American Heritage Museum** (open Sat. and Sun. 12:30–2:30; $3 admission fee).

☙ **Yogi Bear's Jellystone Park** (301-223-7117), 16519 Lappans Rd. Open all year. Lots of things to do on the campground's 90 acres: pool, playground, basketball and volleyball courts, and miniature golf. Some sites have full hookups. Small camping cabins for rent.

✳ Where to Eat

DINING OUT

Boonsboro

Old South Mountain Inn (301-432-6155; www.oldsouthmountaininn.com), 6132 Old National Pike. Open for lunch Sat. and Sun., dinner Tue.–Sun. Reservations strongly recommended for dinner. The inn was established in 1732, so be sure to read about its eventful past on the back of the menu.

Complimentary cheese and crackers accompany every meal on the menu, which features Maryland dishes influenced by cuisines from around the world. Scallops Provençale ($21), chicken saltimbocca ($19), shrimp Mediterranean ($23), and a couple of vegetarian entrées are just a few of the savory surprises to be found in this restaurant sitting next to the Appalachian Trail. The wait staff are friendly and knowledgeable about the many wines available. Desserts are delectable—and huge.

Heather B's (301-432-5100), 1 S. Main St. Open daily for lunch and dinner; Sunday breakfast. Self-taught chef-owner Beth Lowerey offers a blend of American and Italian dishes, with the pastas being the standouts. Entrées $7.95–23.95.

Hagerstown

🎋 ♪ **Rocco's** (301-733-3724), 501 Liberty St. Open for dinner Tue.–Sat. 5–9 (hours and days have been known to change). Reservations recommended. Tucked within a residential neighborhood, Rocco's reputation is such that many of its customers drive more than 35 miles to enjoy its southern Italian dishes. Washington County's oldest continuously operating restaurant, it has been family owned since 1936. The interior's piazza-like appearance of stone brick walls and a Trevi Fountain mural furnishes a fitting atmosphere for a menu best known for its Italian wedding soup, lasagna, and eggplant parmigiana. $8.95–18.95.

The Rhubarb House (301-733-4399), 12 Public Square. Open 8 AM–3 PM for breakfast and lunch Mon.–Fri.; 5–10 PM for dinner Fri. and Sat. The lunch menu has a wide choice of salads, inventive sandwiches ($4.25–7.95), and soups (the $5.95 cream of seafood is flavorful). Homemade potato chips sprinkled with grated cheese are a house specialty. Seafood Alfredo ($19.95) and chicken and sautéed asparagus over pasta in a champagne cream sauce ($13.95) are standouts for dinner. Ask for the lower dining room if you want the quieter spot during lunch.

EATING OUT

Hagerstown

The Grille at Park Circle (301-797-9100), 325 Virginia Ave. Open for lunch and dinner; closed Mon. Directly across from the city park. It may call itself a grill, but it is much more, with entrées like sautéed scallops and Italian sausage in a tomato cream sauce, and tenderloin smothered in a peppercorn sauce. The chef has labored over stoves in California, Washington, Italy, Australia, and Chile, and the menu shows his experience. Most entrées are $11.95–19.95.

Ron's Deli (301-739-1090), 29 N. Burhans Blvd. Open for lunch and dinner Mon.–Sat. Good American deli food, with many sandwiches and a few seafood and meat entrées. Worth a stop for straightforward food and atmosphere. $4.95–15.95.

Schmankerl Stube (301-797-3354; www.schmankerlstube.com), 58 S. Potomac St. Open for lunch and dinner; closed Mon. From the dark sculpted wooden fixtures and beams to the portrait of King Ludwig II, music on the sound system, and original Bavarian wait staff outfits, everything in the restaurant says *Let's go to Bavaria!* Owner Charlie Sekula makes sure that the restaurant reflects his homeland, and the Kassler ripperl ($15.95), Wiener schnitzel ($19.95), and zwiebelrostbraten ($19.95) do a good job. Daily specials and an extensive selection of German brews.

The Plum (301-791-1717), 6 Rochester Place. Open for breakfast and lunch Mon.–Fri. 7:30–3. A gourmet deli serving hot and cold sandwiches ($4.50–5.50). Hartwick's Heap ($5.25) has enough meat to satisfy any carnivore, while Jen's Veggie Pita ($4.10) is for the artery conscious.

Hancock

☆ **Weaver's Restaurant and Bakery** (301-678-6346), 77 W. Main St. A Hancock institution for more than 50 years, this is the kind of place that, if you were to come here often enough, you would eventually meet the town's entire population. The home-cooking menu features hot and cold sandwiches, country-cured ham, pork chops, and seafood. The peanut butter or red raspberry pies are hard to resist, as are the doughnuts, cakes, and other goodies you can take home. The most expensive entrée are around $14.95.

Williamsport

Home Town Diner (301-223-4500), 2 E. Potomac St. Open daily. This is just a diner serving home-cooked food, but the local folks come here often for breakfast, lunch, and dinner. It is also frequented by C&O Canal bikers and hikers, who seem to favor the hamburger casserole. A full

---

Roccoco (301-790-3331; www.roccoco.com), 20 W. Washington St., Hagerstown. Open for lunch Mon.–Fri. 11–3; dinner, Mon.–Sat. 5–10. Cheryl Kenney, Francis Cichy, and Dick McCleary opened their brasserie on the ground floor of an office building in 1998 and have built up a loyal and varied clientele. During lunch, I overheard conversations about a pending business deal, what it takes to be a good Christian, how New Age music improves a massage, and tourists' discussions about where to go next.

All items on the menu, which changes frequently to make use of seasonally available items, are made from scratch. I never thought I would so thoroughly enjoy grilled romaine lettuce served with a warm Caesar dressing ($9). Entrées are equally imaginative and have included shellfish stew ($29), potato-crusted crabcakes with saffron butter ($25), and shrimp scampi pizza ($14). Other entrées $13–33. Pastries are made fresh daily—the chocolate oblivion ($5) is aptly named.

Without a doubt, my current favorite Hagerstown restaurant. I never know what new wonder the chef will be serving.

evening meal will cost you no more than $15, usually much less.

COFFEE BARS Secret's (301-678-6868), 42 W. Main St., Hancock. Open daily. Sip a cup of coffee (many varieties from around the world) while browsing among baskets, sculptures, paintings, leather masks, and other artwork. Deli sandwiches also available.

SNACKS AND GOODIES

Hagerstown

Olympia Candy Kitchen (301-739-0221), 13154 Pennsylvania Ave. The outlet for handmade chocolates produced in nearby Pennsylvania.

Big Dipper (301-797-5422), 1033 Virginia Ave. Soft-serve and Hershey's ice cream available on cones or in shakes of 60 different flavors.

Sharpsburg

Nutter's Ice Cream (301-432-5809), 100 E. Main St. A pleasant place to stop after a hot afternoon's worth of exploring nearby Antietam National Battlefield.

Also see **Weaver's Restaurant and Bakery** under *Eating Out*.

✴ Entertainment

FILM The two first-run movie theaters in the area are located in Hagerstown: **Valley Mall Movie** (301-582-1000), 17301 Valley Mall Rd., and **Hagerstown Cinema** (301-797-4747), Leitersburg Pike.

MUSIC Maryland Symphony Orchestra (301-797-4000; www.mdsymphony.org), 21 S. Potomac St., Hagerstown. There are at least 10 full concerts in the orchestra's year-round schedule, and many smaller venues and outreach programs.

THEATERS

Hagerstown

Maryland Theater (301-790-2000), 21 S. Potomac St. The theater has been a place for the performing arts since 1915. Home to the **Maryland Symphony Orchestra**, it also brings in national and international plays and musicals, events, and performers.

Potomac Players (301-797-8182), 31 S. Potomac St. The local community theater usually stages at least four productions each year, and has been doing so for decades.

Washington County Playhouse (301-739-7469), 44 N. Potomac St. Open Fri. and Sat. evening, and Sun. afternoon. Year-round dinner theater with a huge buffet.

SPORTS ✐ Hagerstown Suns (301-791-6266; www.hagerstownsuns.com), Municipal Stadium, 274 E. Memorial Blvd., Hagerstown. The Suns, affiliates of the San Francisco Giants, play in the Class A South Atlantic League and have some of the most loyal and colorful fans I have seen for a minor-league baseball team. Almost more entertaining than the action on the field are the comments and antics of the spectators in the stands. A low-cost (tickets prices are a bargain) and enjoyable way to spend an evening watching America's favorite pastime. Who knows? You might even see a future star, like the fans who attended Willie Mays's first professional ball game here in 1950.

✴ Selective Shopping
ANTIQUES

Hagerstown

Country Village (301-790-0006), 20136 National Pike. Half a dozen small buildings clustered together and packed with interesting items.

Antique Crossroads (301-739-0858), 20150 National Pike. Closed Wed. More than 200 dealers display wares in separate booths and showcases.

Hancock

Hancock Antique Mall (301-678-5959), 266 N. Pennsylvania Ave. With more than 48,000 square feet of climate-controlled space and close to 400 dealers, just about anything imaginable might be found here. There are antiques of every shape and kind, handcrafted items, memorabilia, and lots of other stuff/junk/pieces.

ART GALLERIES Washington County Arts Council (301-791-3132; www .washcoartscouncil.org), 41 S. Potomac St., Hagerstown. Open daily. A renovated downtown storefront has been turned into a bright and airy place to showcase the best of local and regional people working in all manner of arts and crafts. Definitely worth a stop to look around.

Also see **Washington County Museum of Fine Arts** under *To See.*

BOOKSTORES Black Bird Mysteries (301-432-8781; www.blackbird -mysteries.com), Keedysville. The name describes it well.

Turn the Page (301-432-4588), 18 N. Main St., Boonsboro. Women's fiction author Nora Roberts has written more than 100 novels and sold more than 145 million books. Since this is her store, you should be able to find just about everything she has ever written—in addition to other best sellers and local-interest titles.

USED BOOKS

Hagerstown
Wonder Book and Video (301-733-1888; www.wonderbk.com), 1701

Massey Blvd. (at Valley Plaza). Open daily. They claim to have more than a million used, new, and rare books.

Barnwood Books (301-790-0606), 103 S. Potomac St. Closed Sun. Buys, sells, and trades used books, and specializes in estate and library purchases.

SPECIAL SHOPS

Clear Spring
Wilson's General Store (301-582-4718), 14921 Rufus Wilson Rd. A throwback to another era, the store sells everything from livestock feed to denim jeans. It is like a museum, preserving the decades from when Rufus Wilson first opened it in 1847. Curved wood and glass display cases are filled with lye soap, ointments, elixirs, and spools of sewing thread. The ornately carved wood-and-glass refrigerator still works, keeping meats and cheeses cold. After buying a stick of hard candy, you could sit by the old pot-bellied stove and play a game of checkers with the rough, hand-carved pieces. **Wilson's School**, Washington County's only remaining one-room schoolhouse, is adjacent to the store and will be opened by appointment.

Hagerstown
Homeplace (301-791-2756), 20519 Beaver Creek Rd. The business, on a quiet country road east of town, started as a place to grow and sell herbs and everlasting plants. They still do this, but the shop, decorated and arranged in a very eye-pleasing manner, now contains books, baskets, linens, crafts, and some great folk art and pottery from local and national artisans. Worth a short drive into the country just to browse.

✿ **The Train Room** (301-745-6681; www.the-train-room.com), 360 S.

Burhans Blvd. Besides being a model-train store, the shop contains a **Lionel museum** (adults $2.50, children under 12 free) that is the remarkable collection of owner Charles Mozingo. More than 5,000 items include old transformers, a four-track layout, Lionel chemistry sets and microscopes, and many items made by Lionel for the World War II war effort.

Sharpsburg
Sharpsburg Arsenal (301-432-7700; www.sharpsburg-arsenal.com), 101 W. Main St. It looks like a museum, but every item of Civil War militaria is for sale, from bullets to weapons to clothing to medical items. Be aware that some of the pieces have been transferred from historic sites.

Smithsburg
Heart and Home (301-416-0091), 11622 Crystal Falls Dr. Specializing in log-cabin birdhouses, primitive dolls, and small garden items.

OUTLETS & **Prime Outlet** (1-888-883-6288), I-70 Exit 29, Hagerstown. The local complex of this national developer of outlet malls contains places to purchase Adidas, Bose, Izod, Jockey, Maidenform, Corning Revere, and at least 80 other companies' merchandise at so-called reduced prices.

FARMER'S MARKETS

Hagerstown
City Farmer's Market (301-739-8577), 25 W. Church St. Open Sat. year-round, 5–noon. This has been the area's gathering and gossiping spot since 1791. There are vegetables and fruits for sale, but the real draw is the opportunity to watch local residents meet, greet, and eat. There is no way you can leave here hungry, as there are baked goods, homemade chocolates, hot pretzels, fresh coffee, and a great breakfast stand to tempt you. Arts and crafts are available and become more dominant in the colder months.

Washington County Farmer's Market (301-733-4551), Prime Outlets parking lot. May–Oct., you can stop here on Wed. 4–7 PM. Additionally, produce and other products are available Sat. 10 AM–1 PM, June–Sep.

PICK-YOUR-OWN PRODUCE FARMS
Lewis Orchards (301-824-2811), 22550 Jefferson Blvd., Cavetown. Head to the fields in mid-May to gather strawberries and return in mid-June to pick cherries.

✴ Special Events
March: **Flower and Garden Show** (301-790-2800), Hagerstown Community College. An annual event with more than 100 vendors and the chance to learn about plant care from personnel of the U.S. Botanical Garden and National Arboretum.

May: **Annual Sharpsburg Memorial Day Commemoration** (301-432-8410), Sharpsburg. The oldest continuous Memorial Day parade and celebration in the United States. It started after the Civil War to honor returning veterans.

Late May or early June: **Western Maryland Blues Fest** (301-791-3246), Hagerstown. Annual 3-day celebration of music, a street festival, and workshops with national and international blues luminaries.

June: **Cumberland Valley Artists' Exhibit** (301-739-5727), Hagerstown. Annual juried competition in all media.

July: **Maryland Symphony Orchestra's Annual Salute to Independence** (301-797-4000), Antietam National Battlefield. Celebrate the nation's birthday with patriotic and light classical music accompanied by cannon fire and fireworks.

August: **60s Under the Stars** (301-791-3246), Hagerstown. An annual salute to 1960s rock 'n' roll with performances by many stars of those days. **Augustoberfest** (301-791-3246), Hagerstown. An annual celebration of the city's German heritage. **Washington County Agricultural Expo** (301-791-3246; 1-888-257-2600), Sharpsburg.

September: **Annual Sharpsburg Heritage Festival** (1-800-228-STAY), Sharpsburg. Guided walking tours, living-history demonstrations, period-music concerts, arts and crafts, and historical-topics workshops. **Annual Steam and Craft Show** (301-791-3246), Smithsburg. A lineup of old steam engines, gas-powered tractors, and arts and crafts vendors.

November: **Alsatia Mummers Parade** (301-739-2044), Hagerstown. An annual event with decades of history and tradition.

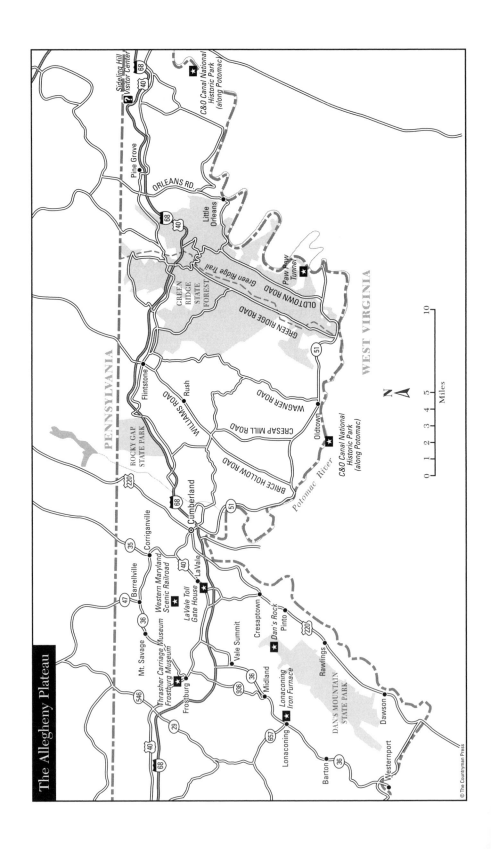

The Allegheny Plateau

PENNSYLVANIA

WEST VIRGINIA

Sideling Hill Visitor Center

C&O Canal National Historic Park (along Potomac)

Pine Grove

ORLEANS RD.

Little Orleans

Paw Paw Tunnel

GREEN RIDGE STATE FOREST

Green Ridge Trail

OLDTOWN ROAD

GREEN RIDGE ROAD

Flintstone

Rush

WAGNER ROAD

CRESAP MILL ROAD

WILLIAMS ROAD

BRICE HOLLOW ROAD

Oldtown

C&O Canal National Historic Park (along Potomac)

Potomac River

ROCKY GAP STATE PARK

Cumberland

Corriganville

Barrellville

Western Maryland Scenic Railroad

LaVale

LaVale Toll Gate House

Cresaptown

Dan's Rock

Pinto

Mt. Savage

Thrasher Carriage Museum

Frostburg Museum

Vale Summit

Midland

Lonaconing Iron Furnace

Rawlings

Dawson

DAN'S MOUNTAIN STATE PARK

Frostburg

Lonaconing

Barton

Westernport

N

0 1 2 3 4 5   10

Miles

THE ALLEGHENY PLATEAU—
Rocky Gap, Cumberland, and Frostburg

West of Hancock, I-68 works its way over Sideling Hill to rise onto the Allegheny Plateau. Once the floor of an ancient ocean, the land was raised to new heights when Africa collided with North America 250 million years ago. Through time, water and wind have cut valleys and eroded softer rock to leave behind higher ridgelines, yet the plateau has remained essentially a mountain tableland with only minor variations in elevation. The mountain streams and ridgelines beckon those in pursuit of outdoor adventure, while the slightly rolling landscape lends itself to agricultural purposes. Some of Maryland's most extensive farms line both sides of the interstate.

Like the more famous Cumberland Gap along the Virginia–Kentucky–Tennessee border, Rocky Gap has been used for centuries by humans as an access route through the mountains. Following the tracks made by game animals, Native Americans were the first to pass through. As settlers from the Old World began pushing into western Maryland, the course was enlarged into the Old Hancock Road, a wagon route connecting Hancock in the east with Fort Cumberland to the west.

The only thing many travelers know about Cumberland is that it is the small city in which winding I-68 takes you past one church steeple after another—all of which are at eye level because of the interstate's elevated route. To get off the four-lane and do a little exploring is to find a place rich in the history of America's westward expansion, yet with a forward-looking population ready to celebrate the life it enjoys today.

The settlement began in 1787, when General Edward Braddock (and a young George Washington) established Fort Cumberland (the Emmanuel Episcopal Church is built on its foundations) during the French and Indian War. Cumberland developed into a transportation center as all of the early-1800s modes of transportation converged upon it. People poured through town on the National Road on their way to the western frontier, the B&O railroad arrived in 1842, and the town became the western terminus of the Chesapeake & Ohio (C&O) Canal in 1850.

Industrialization and coal mining brought unprecedented prosperity after the Civil War, and a walk along the opulent houses of Washington Street, now a National Historic District, lets you see just how successful business leaders were. Railroading became a major employer around the turn of the 20th century, enabling more industries to establish themselves and bringing new wealth and refinement into the area. The Cumberland Academy of Music was so prestigious that it attracted luminaries such as George Gershwin. Many of the downtown's buildings date from this era, and a walking-tour brochure from the Allegany County Convention and Visitors Bureau describes some of them.

When manufacturing jobs began to disappear and city shops began to lose business to malls and outlying areas, Cumberland was one of the first places in America to establish a pedestrian mall in 1980. It has taken awhile, but downtown is once again filled with restaurants, businesses, antiques stores, and eclectic shops. The mall has become the spot for the annual Summer in the City events, a farmer's market, and a pleasant place to stroll and people-watch. It is just a few blocks from the C&O Canal Visitor Center and the Western Maryland Scenic Railroad Depot.

Like Cumberland, Frostburg owes much of its existence to the National Road. When stagecoach service began in 1818, an assemblage of taverns, houses, and businesses grew up around the stagecoach stop. The arrival of the railroad in the 1840s allowed the coal industry to develop, soon followed by the manufacture of bricks from the high-grade clays found in the area. The biggest employer today is Frostburg State University, established as a normal school in 1898. Frostburg may not be the railroading center it once was, but rail enthusiasts still arrive by the thousands each year on their round-trip journey from Cumberland along the Western Maryland Scenic Railroad. Baseball pitching great Lefty Grove, voted the American League's Most Valuable Player in 1931, is buried in the Frostburg cemetery.

CANAL PLACE IN CUMBERLAND

COMMUNITIES LaVale was a sleepy village along US 40 until the expansion of malls and fast-food restaurants overtook many small towns in America. Two interstate exits can deliver you to the Country Club Mall and just about any national restaurant chain you can think of.

Mount Savage, like many of the small towns in the western part of this area, first developed as a coal-mining community. Around the turn of the 20th century, Andrew Ramsey came upon a way to produce a special colored, glazed brick. It soon received worldwide acclaim and was bought for its smooth, bright, and easily cleaned surface. Unfortunately, Ramsey never told anyone exactly what his process was, so his factory closed when he died.

The bituminous coal underlying the mountain lands along MD 36 gave rise to so many coal-mining communities that it is almost hard to tell where one community ends and another begins. These settlements, the largest of which is **Lonaconing**, were once so isolated from the outside world that the local speech still contains slight traces of an English accent.

GUIDANCE The Allegany County Convention and Visitors Bureau (301-777-5132; 1-800-425-2067; www.mdmountainside.com), 13 Canal St., Suite 406, Cumberland, 21502, can be found on the ground floor of Canal Place, conveniently located next to the ticket office for the Western Maryland Scenic Railroad. If the volunteer staff, which is well trained and knowledgeable, can't answer one of your questions, ask them to contact one of the bureau's employees who work upstairs.

The early-1900s **Palace Theater** at 33 E. Main St. in Frostburg now functions as a community auditorium and **tourism center**.

THE NARROWS WEST OF CUMBERLAND

GETTING THERE *By car:* **I-68** is the major highway that will bring you into the area from the east or the west. **US 220** connects with the **Pennsylvania Turnpike** as it comes into the area from the north.

By bus: **Greyhound** (1-800-231-2222) makes a stop at its local terminal (301-722-6226), at 37 Henderson Ave., Cumberland, during an east–west run along I-68.

By rail: Cumberland is lucky enough to be one of the dwindling number of small cities in America that can still be reached by passenger-rail service. The **Amtrak** (1-800-872-7245) station on Harrison St. receives passengers arriving from the west in the morning and those coming from the east in the evening.

GETTING AROUND *By car:* **I-68** is, of course, the fastest way to get around, but consider using **US 40**, which parallels it and will take you through rural areas and some of the smaller towns. It also is along the historic route of the **National Road**. **US 220** and **MD 26** are two-lane roadways that will take you into the more isolated southern regions of this area.

By bus: **Allegany County Transit Division** (301-772-6360) operates 10 routes that can transport you to most of the cities and towns in the area.

By rail: See the **Western Maryland Scenic Railroad** sidebar on page 422.

By taxi: **Morgan Taxi** (301-722-2800) and **Yellow Cab** (301-722-4050) are both based in Cumberland.

MEDICAL EMERGENCY

Cumberland
Cumberland Memorial Hospital (301-723-4000), 600 Memorial Ave.

Sacred Heart Hospital (301-723-4200), 900 Seton Dr.

✳ To See
MUSEUMS

Frostburg
♿ **Thrasher Carriage Museum** (301-689-3380; www.thrashercarriage.com), 19 Depot St. (adjacent to the Western Maryland Scenic Railroad Depot). Open Wed.–Sun., Mar.–Dec. Small admission fee. Contains horse-drawn vehicles from almost every part of American life, including Theodore Roosevelt's inaugural parade carriage. Seek out the buckboard—the work the carpenter did with the wood is remarkable. Guides and interpretive signs provide detailed background.

Frostburg Museum (301-689-5903; www.frostmuseum.org), 69 Hill St. Open Tue. 1–4. Donations accepted. The volunteer-maintained museum is housed in the 1899 Hill Street School, and its exhibits preserve and portray the industrial and social past of the area.

HISTORIC HOMES Gordon-Roberts House (301-777-8678; www.historyhouse .allconet.org), 218 Washington St., Cumberland. Open Tue.–Sat. Guided tours given on the hour; small admission fee. The Second Empire home was built in 1867 for Judge Josiah Hance Gordon, president of the C&O Canal (and a Southern sympathizer arrested during the Civil War). It was later purchased by the West Milner Roberts Sr. family, who lived there until the 1950s. It is furnished with pieces reflecting their time of occupation. A few rooms contain items of local historical interest.

After visiting the house, take a walk along the six blocks of Washington St. listed on the National Register and you will glean a bit of information about Cumberland's earlier days. The Gordon-Roberts House reflects the obvious wealth of the

Gordon and Roberts families, but their former home is quite simple and plain compared with the other, more extravagant houses along the street.

HISTORIC SITES & **George Washington's Headquarters** (301-777-5132), Riverside Park on Greene St., Cumberland. Most easily accessed by a 2-minute walk from Canal Place: Simply cross the railroad tracks and use the Esplanade over Wills Creek. Most places that are open by appointment only have been excluded from this guidebook, but you can get a feel for history just by walking around this small cabin and reading the interpretive signs. Local lore (which some historians question) states that Washington used the structure when he was aide-de-camp to General Braddock in the mid-1700s, and when he returned as president in 1794. The Cresap Chapter of the Daughters of the American Revolution has furnished the cabin with period replicas.

LaVale Toll Gate House (301-777-5132), Old US 40 in Upper LaVale. Open 1:30–4:30 Sat. and Sun., May–Oct. The tollgate house was built in the early 1800s and is now the only surviving such structure in the state. Its seven-sided construction has windows facing all directions so that the gatekeeper could clearly see any approaching traffic. The antique furnishings reflect its earliest days; ask for the story behind the courting candle.

Just a few buildings and a small cemetery remain in **Oldtown** beside the C&O Canal to mark the site where the first settlement in Allegany County once stood. Thomas Cresap established a trading post in the 1740s next to the Potomac River and along the route of the Native American Warrior's Path. His son, Michael, was born in 1741, and his home—now a museum open on an irregular basis—is the only building from the early days that is still standing. (Michael was later engaged in battles with Native Americans along the Ohio

GEORGE WASHINGTON'S HEADQUARTERS IN CUMBERLAND

River. Although Cresap was considered a hero by some, Chief Logan claimed he was the man who sparked the war by murdering, unprovoked, the chief's wife and all of his children.) Also on the site, and open on an irregular basis, is the **Lock House 70**, constructed when the C&O Canal was built in the mid-1800s.

HISTORIC CHURCHES **Emmanuel Episcopal Church** (301-777-3364), 16 Washington St., Cumberland. Constructed in the mid-1800s with a commanding view of the town, the church is one of the earliest uses of the Greek Revival style in America. Louis Tiffany extensively remodeled its interior in the early 1900s. Among other things, he carved the High Altar, and three of the stained-glass windows are his. His original design sketches are on display in the church community room.

All of these things, however, are not the only reasons to visit. The church was built upon the foundations of the mid-1700s **Fort Cumberland**. Some of the earthworks, ammunition magazines, and fort tunnels still exist and are open for public visitation. To walk these narrow passageways is to perceive the ghosts of the soldiers who helped prepare the way for western Maryland's early settlers.

OTHER SITES ⅙ **C&O Canal National Historical Park Cumberland Visitors Center** (301-722-8226), 13 Canal St. (in the Western Maryland Railroad Station), Cumberland. Open daily 9–5. Free. Much more than just a visitors center, it has many exhibits pertaining to the history of the canal and the local area. Interactive displays with audiotapes let you become familiar with canal workers, such as lockkeeper Harvey Brant, who received $22.50 a week and was on call 24 hours a day. I found the exhibit in which Mr. Sandblount describes growing up and working on a canal boat to be both enlightening and entertaining. This is

LaVALE TOLL GATE HOUSE

a great place, especially since it is free. Don't forget to take the short walk to the
Cumberland, a full-scale canal-boat replica. (Also see C&O National Historical
Park under *To Do* for information on the canal in this area.)

The visitors center is located in **Canal Place**, which is being developed as a performing arts/historic site incorporating several buildings and locations around the
canal's western terminus.

Lonaconing Iron Furnace, in the town of Lonaconing. Built in 1837, it was
America's first successful coal- and coke-fired furnace to produce pig iron. Most
furnaces from these days are crumbling shells, but this one is nearly intact and
worth a visit.

Dan's Rock, located on Dan's Rock Rd., off MD 36 near Vale Summit. It is a
twisting mountain road you must negotiate to reach Dan's Rock, but the view is
definitely worth it. Just a few steps from the parking area is an Olympian view of
Savage Mountain rising out of the depths of George's Creek Valley. The Allegheny Mountains of West Virginia recede far to the south, while farmlands
stretch eastward along the Potomac River.

GUIDED TOURS See *Walking Tours* under *To Do*.

✳ To Do

BICYCLING C&O Canal National Historical Park. More than 40 miles of the
canal pass through this area of Maryland. The section is more isolated than any
other portion, which enables you to ride and explore without the crowds often
found elsewhere. Some of the highlights include access to **Oldtown**, the **Green
Ridge Hiking Trail**, and the **Paw Paw Tunnel**. About a dozen designated
campsites (some free, some with a fee) are spaced along the route. Each has
vault toilets and water (in-season) and is available on a first-come, first-served
basis. There are also numerous ramps from which you could launch a boat into
the Potomac River and paddle for
several days while making use of the
riverside campsites. The **C&O Canal
Visitors Center** in Cumberland can
provide detailed information.

LONACONING IRON FURNACE

Cycles and Things (301-722-5496),
165 N. Centre St., Cumberland.
Cycles and Things sells bikes, but
they can also repair yours if you have
a problem while in the area.

Green Ridge State Forest (301-
478-3124), 28700 Headquarters Dr.,
NE, Flintstone. Multiple miles of
trails and dirt roads are open to
mountain biking. An exceptional ride,
which has a variety of terrain (and
may not be suited to beginners), is

SOMETHING TO LOOK FORWARD TO—OR DO RIGHT NOW

The **Allegheny Highlands Trail** is a planned 214-mile bicycle route that will begin near Pittsburgh, Pennsylvania, and connect with the C&O Canal at Cumberland. When the trail is finished, you will be able to ride nearly 400 miles on a pathway devoid of road traffic or other similar hazards.

Actually, most of the trail is built, with only short sections still under construction. Many people have already ridden from Pittsburgh to Washington, DC, by following back roads along the uncompleted portions.

Information on the route in Maryland is available from the Allegheny Highlands Trail of Maryland (301-777-2161; www.ahtmtrail.org), P.O. Box 28, Cumberland, 21501. Pennsylvania trail information can be obtained from the **Allegheny Trail Alliance** (www.atatrail.org), 419 College Ave., Greensburg, PA 15601.

the 12-mile self-guided loop trail. The state forest headquarters can provide you with a map of all the routes.

BIRDING ✏ ♿ **Dan's Mountain State Park**, (301-777-2139), Water Station Run Rd. (off MD 36), Lonaconing. The park's heavily wooded acres are habitat for those species that nest only in forests. Expect to find scarlet tanagers, ovenbirds, and yellow-throated vireos.

BOAT RENTALS See *Outdoor Adventure*, and **Rocky Gap State Park** under *Green Space*.

CARRIAGE RIDES See *Walking Tours*.

FISHING See **Rocky Gap State Park** under *Green Space*.

GOLF **Rocky Gap State Park** (301-784-8400; 1-800-724-0828; www.rockygap resort.com), 16701 Lakeview Rd. (accessed from I-68 Exit 50), Flintstone. The only Jack Nicklaus Signature Golf Course in Maryland. The front nine, carved out of the mountainous terrain and lined by trees, have quite dramatic elevation changes. The back nine course their way over an open, rolling meadow.
Also see **Manhattan Centre Golf and Gallery** under *Selective Shopping*.

HIKING ♣ **Green Ridge Hiking Trail**, Green Ridge State Forest (301-478-3124), 28700 Headquarters Dr., NE, Flintstone. This 18-mile trail is one of the best backpacking outings in Maryland at any time of year, but to get the most fun out of it, wait for a hot summer weekend. The majority of the hike is along one creek or another, each with miles of small ripples and cascades—and a profusion of swimming holes. Even if you don't want to take a plunge, you still need to ford them well over 60 times; wait until warm weather has raised the water temperature a few degrees.

Backcountry camping is permitted; obtain a permit (and pay the fee) at the forest headquarters just off I-68 Exit 64. A pamphlet for the **Pine Lick Hollow Segment** has information describing the natural and human history of the area. (The state forest is the habitat of the rarely seen large blazing star and Kate's mountain clover.) Pets must be on a leash and hunting is permitted during the season, so take proper precautions. Headquarters personnel can also provide information on the more than 20 miles of other pathways in the forest.

KAYAKING AND CANOEING See **C&O Canal National Historical Park** under *Bicycling*, and *Outdoor Adventure*.

OUTDOOR ADVENTURE **Allegany Expeditions Inc.** (301-722-5170; 1-800-819-5170; www.alleganyexpeditions.com), 10310 Columbus Ave., NE, Cumberland. AEI can take care of you for just about any activity in the natural world that you can engage in during a visit to western Maryland. They can provide instructions or set up guided trips for climbing, caving and rappelling, paddling excursions,

Paw Paw Tunnel, off MD 51 (at the Potomac River Bridge and the C&O Canal). Like so many other things associated with the canal, construction of the 3,118-foot tunnel faced difficulties and miscalculations from the outset. Intense friction among camps of Irish, English, and German laborers—in conjunction with a cholera epidemic—compounded the problems. Originally estimated to be built within 2 years at a cost of $33,500, it took 14 years and more than $600,000 to complete. Once finished, though, the tunnel—lined with close to 6 million bricks in layers of 7 to 11 deep—was used from 1850 to the canal's demise in 1924.

Break out the flashlights when you enter the tunnel, which is a little more than half a mile long. Even after its completion, the tunnel proved to be a source of contention. Although upstream boats were supposed to have the right-of-way in the narrow channel, some boat captains would refuse to yield. Local lore tells of an occasion where two barges stayed in place for several days because neither captain would give way. Canal workers finally built a fire to smoke them out.

The pathway is usually wet and slippery, so use the provided handrail. Some of the boards are the original lumber, and your hand can feel the grooves worn into it from years of towropes sliding across. Once through, you can take a break at a small picnic area. You have the choice of going back the way you came or taking the **Tunnel Hill Trail** over the ridgeline the tunnel goes through. The round-trip journey is about 3 miles.

TRAIN EXCURSION

Western Maryland Scenic Railroad (301-759-4400; 1-800-TRAIN-50; www
.wmsr.com), 13 Canal St. Railway Station, Cumberland–Frostburg. May–Sep.,
the diesel engine leaves Cumberland Mon.–Thu. at 11:30 AM; the steam
engine departs Fri.–Sun. at 11:30 AM. In Oct., the diesel operates Mon.–
Wed., the steam Thu.–Sun. In Nov. and Dec., there is only one departure
(the steam engine) at 11:30 AM. Standard fare: adults $22, senior $20, children $11. First class (includes lunch in the dining car): adults $42, senior $40,
children $25.

The 3-hour round-trip excursions (with a 90-minute layover in Frostburg)
travel through some of western Maryland's prettiest scenery by negotiating
the **Narrows,** climbing over 1,900-foot Piney Mountain, and passing through
914-foot **Brush Tunnel. Helmstedder's Curve** is such a long, tight horseshoe
bend that even those sitting in the very rear passenger car can look across
the way and see the engine. There is some taped narration along the way,
but it would be nicer if it would describe more of what you are experiencing.

WESTERN MARYLAND SCENIC RAILROAD

skiing, fishing, and backpacking. All of the required equipment can be rented or purchased.

Adventure Sports (301-689-0345), 113 Main St., Frostburg. Adventure Sports provides all of the services available through Allegany Expeditions (see above) but also offers instructions and guided trips for ice climbing, mountain biking, and even scuba diving.

SCUBA DIVING See **Adventure Sports** under *Outdoor Adventure.*

SKATING YMCA (301-777-YMCA), 601 Kelly Rd., Cumberland. There may be others, but this is the only YMCA I know of that has an ice-skating rink as part of its facilities. Call for the days and times it is open to the public.

SWIMMING See **Rocky Gap State Park** under *Green Space.*

WALKING TOURS Westmar Tours (301-777-0293; www.wstme.com), 13 Canal St., Cumberland. Costumed guides lead walking and riding tours (some in horse-drawn carriages) in historic Cumberland and surrounding areas. A great way to gain intimate knowledge of the region.

✳ Green Space

PARKS ✍ ᾱ **Rocky Gap State Park** (301-784-8400; 1-800-724-0828; www .rockygapresort.com), 16701 Lakeview Rd. (accessed from I-68 Exit 50), Flint-stone. As you descend westward on Martin Mountain on I-68, the first thing to catch your eye will be the dramatic setting of the park's massive 220-room resort lodge, built along the southern shore of Lake Habeeb. Below Evitt's Mountain's lush hillside, the manicured greens of a golf course stretch between the lodge and the four-lane highway.

(There is no doubt that this type of development adds another aspect and attraction to the state park, but there was much debate and protest in the local community, and throughout Maryland, about changing the natural character of the state park. Many people also questioned the propriety of the state's turning such a large amount of public land over to a private, profit-making corporation.)

Within the park are a campground, a camp store, laundry facilities, beaches with modern bathhouses, an outdoor pool, tennis courts, a snack bar, and boat rentals. The 243-acre Lake Habeeb attracts anglers with largemouth bass, panfish, and trout. A trail network brings hikers by the lake, up Evitt's Mountain to an old homesite, and down into scenic Rocky Gap Gorge. Thousands of visitors attend the park's annual music festivals in August. Personnel at the park can arrange for you to participate in many of the state's **Nature Tourism** activities.

✍ ᾱ **Dan's Mountain State Park** (301-777-2139), Water Station Run Rd. (off MD 36), Lonaconing. Open daily during daylight hours. The 485 acres have the feel of a community park, as the local population comes here in significant numbers to enjoy the Olympic-sized swimming pool with waterslide, and beautiful mountain scenery. There is a designated overlook, but the view from the children's playground is equally awe inspiring.

❋ Lodging

RESORTS 🐾 ♿ **Rocky Gap State Park** (301-784-8400; 1-800-724-0828; www.rockygapresort.com), 16701 Lakeview Rd. (accessed from I-68 Exit 50), Flintstone, 21530. The accommodations within the park's lodge are pretty much standard upscale hotel/motel-type rooms—but, oh, those views. I prefer a deluxe room (with a balcony and kitchenette) overlooking the lake and Evitt's Mountain, although there is certainly nothing wrong with the view of the emerald fairways of the golf course. Staying in any room gives you access to all of the park's facilities. Pets are permitted in some rooms, but there is quite a substantial cleaning fee tacked onto your bill. $145–275.

Many package deals—golf, outdoor adventure, and honeymoon—are available. Also see *Camping*.

MOTELS AND HOTELS

Cumberland, 21502

🐾 ♿ **Holiday Inn** (301-724-8800; 1-800-HOLIDAY; www.cumberland-dtn.holiday-inn.com), 100 S. George St. The hotel overlooks the noise and activity of a busy CSX rail-freight yard—which, admittedly, is not the most scenic of places. At one time, the manager had mounted a video cam on the roof, pointed it toward the rail yard, and made the 24-hour action available on the hotel's Web site. It had been receiving more than a million hits a year. Sadly, that is no longer available. Railroading fans still make reservations for one of the rooms with a rail-yard view, though. The hotel also has an outdoor pool, a fitness room, and an on-site restaurant. $80–120.

Frostburg, 21532

Fallingers Hotel Gunter (301-689-6511), 11 W. Main St. Like many

DAN'S MOUNTAIN STATE PARK

older, grand hotels, Fallingers now rents some rooms as residential apartments. However, the 14 remaining hotel rooms have been thoroughly renovated and reflect the property's glory days. Each is furnished differently with antiques and reproductions. The rooms are enjoyable enough, but wander around to appreciate the massive oak stairway in the lobby, the swing on the balcony where you can watch the rest of the world go by, and the stained-glass windows found on each stairway landing. The basement is a small museum with items found during the renovation, plus the town's original jail and a replica of a coal mine. Rates range $65–99.

&. **Hampton Inn** (301-689-1998), 11200 New George's Creek Rd. A whirlpool, heated pool, and exercise room are available to work off the calories you consume during the free continental breakfast. All rooms have an iron and small refrigerator. $89–129.

LaVale, 21502

&. **Best Western** (301-729-3300; 1-800-296-6006; www.bestwestern braddock.com), 1268 National Highway. One of the most meticulously maintained mainstream motels in the state. Rooms are continually being renovated and updated, tanning beds and a sauna are in the exercise room, and the large inside pool adjoins an outside sundeck. Although the motel sits next to a crossroads area, the landscaping and natural brook add an unexpected gentle quality. $69–109.

🐾 &. **Oak Tree Inn** (301-729-6700), 12310 Winchester Rd. A well-maintained facility with a kitchenette in many rooms. Exercise center and coin laundry on the premises. Pets permitted. $75–85.

FALLINGERS HOTEL GUNTER IN FROSTBURG

BED & BREAKFASTS &. **Shaw Mansion Inn** (301-463-3131), 18311 Laurel Run Rd., Barton, 21521. Close to Dan's Mountain State Park and the Big Savage Hiking Trail. I am partial to B&Bs in out-of-the-way rural settings, and this one is really to my liking. I enjoyed strolling across the 7-acre property to watch red-winged blackbirds fly by the pond and around the massive evergreen and maple trees growing in the front yard.

Ruth and Craig Marsh have restored the 1870 Victorian home, built of walnut trees grown on the property and brick made from the plantation's clay. The house is furnished with period antiques, and breakfast is served next to the large bay windows, which almost reach from the floor to the 13-foot ceilings. $95–125.

Inn at Walnut Bottom (301-777-0003; www.iwbinfo.com), 120 Greene St., Cumberland, 21502. The inn's location in the heart of Cumberland made my explorations much easier, and host Grant Irvin's and Kirsten Hanson's knowledge of the area pointed me to many places I would have overlooked. The B&B is actually two adjacent town houses (circa 1820 and 1890) that have been joined together to provide 12 guest rooms and suites. Some share a bath, others have a private bath, and each is uniquely furnished with antiques and period reproductions. The accommodations are attractive and breakfasts are legendary. Do not fail to schedule a massage during your stay. Kirsten is trained in afspaending, a type of massage developed in Denmark (her homeland) that is more relaxing than many other methods. $93–147.

The Castle B&B (301-264-4645; www.noomoon.com/castle), 15925 Mt. Savage Rd., Mount Savage, 21545. The Castle started life in 1840 as a modest stone house, but near the beginning of the 20th century, nouveau riche owner Andrew Ramsey turned it into a replica of Scotland's Craig Castle. You get to enjoy large verandas and terraces of glazed tile, formal gardens, and a 16-foot stone wall (built by Italian masons) surrounding the property. Six guest rooms (some with a private bath) range $120–195.

CAMPING

Flintstone, 21530

Green Ridge State Forest (301-478-3124), 28700 Headquarters Dr., NE. Primitive campsites are designated along many of the roads that snake their way through the 43,000-acre forest. A permit (and payment of a fee) can be obtained in the state forest headquarters.

☗ **Hidden Springs Campground** (814-767-9676), Pleasant Valley Rd.

SHAW MANSION INN IN BARTON

May–Oct. The campground's 58 acres are close to Rocky Gap State Park and contain a swimming pool, playgrounds, miniature golf, and a stocked fishing pond.

☙ **Rocky Gap State Park** (301-784-8400; 1-800-724-0828; www.rocky gapresort.com), 16701 Lakeview Rd. (accessed from I-68 Exit 50). Nearly 300 sites are situated among the trees along the northern shore of Lake Habeeb. Hookups, bathhouses with hot showers, and access to all of the park's facilities. Pets (on leashes) are permitted in two of the campground's loops.

Little Orleans, 21766

Little Orleans Campground (301-478-2325), 31661 Green Forest Dr., SE. Located less than a 5-minute walk from the C&O Canal and bordered on two sides by Green Ridge State Forest. I would classify this almost as resort, as it contains RV and tent sites, a playground, a fishing pond, swimming pools, a game room, volleyball, basketball, and horseshoes—in addition to usual campground facilities.

✷ Where to Eat

DINING OUT ⅛ **Oxford House** (301-777-7101), 129 Baltimore St. (Downtown Pedestrian Mall), Cumberland. Open for lunch Mon.–Fri. 11–2:30; dinner, Mon.–Sat. 5–9:30. The schwitzerschnitzel, rockfish Chesapeake, scallops Provençale, Delmonico *pizzaiola*, and veal and crab served in a Cajun cream sauce are indications that the menu takes its cues from many parts of Europe and the United States. The furnishings and brick floor made me feel as if I were dining in a piazza. Entrées $17.95–25.95

⅛ **Lakeside Restaurant** (301-784-8444; www.rockygapresort.com), in Rocky Gap State Park, Flintstone. Open 6:30 AM–11 PM daily. I have found restaurants in many state parks to be so-so, but Lakeside is an exception. Dress may be casual, but the food has a touch of class. Sesame-crusted shrimp and scallops and mozzarella Caprese are my favorite appetizers. The pine nut dusted Allegheny trout, and the shrimp,

THE CASTLE B&B IN MOUNT SAVAGE

crayfish, scallops, and andouille sausage served over *paglia e fieno* (spinach and egg noodles), are testaments to the kitchen staff's expertise. Other chicken, steak, and vegetarian entrées range $15–30. The view of Lake Habeeb and Evitt's Mountain adds to the overall experience.

🍷 ♿ **Au Petit Paris** (301-689-8946; 1-800-207-0956; www.aupetitparis .com), 86 E. Main St., Frostburg. Open for dinner Tue.–Sat. 6–9:30. Reservations recommended. Although this is the special-occasion restaurant for people from many miles around, the prices are amazingly low—and about half of what you would pay in a heavily populated area like Baltimore or Washington, DC.

Louis and Jeanne St. Marie, and family, have been serving their delightful French cuisine since the mid-1950s. Seafood dishes are succulent, but do not overlook the veal and beef specialties. One of my favorite western Maryland fine-dining experiences. Most entrées are $11–30; special dishes are, of course, higher.

EATING OUT

Cumberland
City Lights (301-722-9800; www.city lightsamericangrill.com), 59 Baltimore St. Open daily 11 AM to closing. Having relocated from the shopping mall in LaVale, City Lights has become a favorite on the Downtown Pedestrian Mall. After a meal of stuffed mushrooms, Greek spinach salad, and walnut apple pork, customers of the two-story restaurant have a tendency to linger, socialize, and imbibe in selections from the bar. Friday and Saturday nights hop. The highest-priced entrée is $23.95.

🍷 ♪ **Bender's Family Restaurant** (301-724-6628), 204 Baltimore St. Open 7 AM–3 PM daily. Painted plywood booths, vinyl chairs, and a listing counter are indications that people don't come here for the atmosphere. It is definitely not upscale, yet office workers, lawyers, and other professionals walk across the railroad tracks to eat here. The draw is honest home cooking at low prices. Breakfast is served all day, the pies are homemade, and the kids have their own lunch and breakfast menu. Proprietor Shirley Bender offers a light menu for those counting calories—a rarity for places such as this. You would be hard-pressed to spend more than $7 here.

Curtis's Famous Wieners (301-789-9707), 35 N. Liberty St. Open 7 AM–10 PM daily. A Cumberland tradition, it has been serving hot dogs, burgers, and hand-dipped milk shakes since 1918. A favorite of downtown office workers for lunch. Most meals will cost you less than $5.

♿ **When Pigs Fly** (301-722-7447), 18 Valley St. Open for lunch and dinner; closed Sun. Extensive beer selection in a pleasant bar area. Steaks, chicken, and seafood—but the main reason to dine here is the BBQ. It is available as pulled pork and ribs, beef, or chicken. Entrées $9.95–20.95.

The name? When the owners told their families they were going to open a restaurant, the skeptical relatives replied, "Yeah, sure. When pigs fly."

Uncle Tucker's 1819 BrewHouse (301-777-7005; www.edmasons.com), I-68 Exit 46. Under contract to build tollhouses along the National Pike, Jacob Hoblitzell built his own home in 1819. Used for many things, including a Civil War field hospital, the house eventually fell into disrepair. Now on the National Register after being restored—from its Georgia pine floors to the horsehair plaster walls—by proprietor Ed Mason in the 1990s, Uncle Tucker's serves a widely varied menu. The Main Helper's Wood-Cooked Pizza, with basil, spinach, tomato, and artichoke hearts, proves a meal doesn't need meat to be tasty. The sauce used on the bruschetta appetizer is unique and flavorful. Other Italian dishes include homemade lasagna and cornmeal-crusted sea bass. A menu that changes often and a choice of the restaurant's own microbrews, including ales, lagers, and dark beers, keep the locals coming back. The upstairs is the quietest spot; the downstairs bar where the pizzas are made gets a little noisy, and many customers opt for the outside patio overlooking a trout stream. Entrées $4.95–14.95.

Mason's other restaurant, **Mason's Barn Family Restaurant** (301-722-6155), is next door.

Frostburg

🐾 ♂ **Princess Restaurant** (301-689-1968), 12 W. Main St. Open 6 AM–8 PM Mon.–Sat. I always take pleasure in finding places such as this—which are becoming increasingly harder to find. It is clean and well kept, but the atmosphere is nothing fancy; in fact, the place is somewhat reminiscent of a diner. Prices are so low that they have not been seen in other restaurants for years. The well-prepared food ranges from more than 40 different sandwiches to full dinners of meat loaf ($7.95), broiled haddock ($8.75), grilled pork chops ($9.50), and T-bone steaks ($14.50). The children's menu even includes an ice cream dessert in the cost of the meal.

Like his grandfather who started the business in this location in 1939 (a portion of the original tin ceiling is still in place), George W. Pappas ensures quality by doing things the old way, such as hand-forming hamburger patties, making gravies from scratch, and fresh-cutting potatoes for the home fries. Entrées $4.95–14.50.

Gandalf's (301-689-2010; www.gandalfs.org), 24 E. Main St. Open 5–10 PM; closed Sun. Within a pub atmosphere, Gandalf's serves a surprisingly universal menu. The expected sandwiches are there, but you will also find dim sum ($6), a seafood sandwich ($5), and hummus ($6) and tofu vegetable ($6) subs. Entrées $6–16. **Gandalf's Pub**, with microbrews and live entertainment, is located at 20 E. Main St. and is open 5 PM–2 AM.

♿ **Giuseppe's Italian Restaurant** (301-689-2220; www.giuseppes.net), 11 Bowery St. Open daily for dinner. Good, traditional Italian fare, such as pizza, chicken cacciatore, shrimp scampi, lasagna, and baked ziti. Very reasonable prices—the most expensive entrée is about $20; most are less than $16.

LaVale

♿ **Gehauf's** (301-729-1746), 1268 National Highway (inside the Best Western hotel). Open daily for breakfast, lunch, and dinner. With lush plants adding a feeling of being outdoors, Gehauf's makes all of its soups, sauces, dressings, and baked goods from scratch. Seafood entrées are prominent, joined by traditional western Maryland dishes of turkey, ham, pork chops, and steak. A few vegetarian items are a pleasant surprise. Entrées $4.95–15.95.

Penny's Diner (301-729-6700), 12310 Winchester Rd., SW. Open 24 hours. People who can actually remember the 1950s are getting to be fewer in number, so if you want to sample a slice of their life, head to Penny's. Shiny aluminum highlights the interior, the jukebox is filled with songs of the decade, and the black-and-white photos show a LaVale that no longer exists. Burgers, fries, and other sandwiches (hot and cold) are joined on the menu by meat loaf, liver and onions, and pot roast. Don't pass up the old-fashioned hand-dipped milk shakes topped by whipped cream and a cherry. Entrées $5–20.

SNACKS AND GOODIES

Cumberland

Queen City Creamery and Deli (301-697-4810), 108 Harrison St. Open daily for breakfast, lunch, and dinner. They have breakfast items, deli sandwiches, and gourmet coffee, but the premium homemade ice cream is what entices me to stop in nearly every time I pass by.

The Fruit Bowl (301-777-2780), US 40 in the Narrows at the western end of town. Yeah, they sell fresh fruits and vegetables, but what you really want to stop for are the 800 bins filled with just about every kind of snack-bar-sized candy you can think of. Snickers, Milky Way, Reeses, 3 Musketeers, and dozens of others are available in bulk.

Flintstone

Alpine Pantry (301-478-3696), 21511 Flintstone Dr., NE, I-68 Exit 56. Open Mon.–Fri. 7:30 AM–5:30 PM, Sat. 7 AM–4 PM. A fun place in which to browse for fresh-baked pies, breads, cakes, and pastries in addition to meats, cheeses, and a vast assortment of bagged candies. The small sign on the door, THANK YOU FOR SHOPPING HERE MODESTLY DRESSED AND WELL COVERED, lets you know this is a Mennonite establishment.

Frostburg

McFarland Candies (301-689-6670; www.mcfarlandcandies.com), 22 Broadway. What a treat. The McFarland family has been making assorted chocolate candies in Frostburg since 1944. Enjoy a taste of the premium nut clusters, chewies, barks, cremes, jellies, and fudges. Ask, and they will take you on a tour of the kitchen to witness the art of homemade candy production.

❋ Entertainment

FILM AMC Country Club (301-729-6633), 1262 Vocke Rd., LaVale. Shows first-run films.

Frostburg Cinema (301-689-1100), Frostburg Plaza, Frostburg. Also presents movies when they are first released.

See **Embassy Theatre** under *Theaters* for information on classic films.

THEATERS

Cumberland

Cumberland Theatre (301-759-4990), 101–103 Johnson St. Western Maryland's only professional theater presents at least six musical, drama, or other theatrical productions during its season, which usually runs Apr.–Dec. The small auditorium provides an intimate setting.

Embassy Theatre (301-722-4692; 1-877-722-4692), 49 Baltimore St. Citizens' efforts saved this 1931 art deco movie house. Classic films, live music, dance, and theatrical productions are presented in the lovingly, and accurately, restored edifice.

✳ Selective Shopping
ANTIQUES

Cumberland
Historic Cumberland Antique Mall (301-777-2979), 113 Baltimore St. Open daily. Antiques of various shapes and forms offered by a number of different vendors.

Yesteryear Antiques and Collectibles (301-722-7531), 60 Baltimore St. There is the usual glassware, china, linens, and pottery found in shops such as this, but also stop by for vintage clothing, lingerie, and jewelry.

ART GALLERIES Allegany Arts Council (301-777-ARTS; www .alleganyartscouncil.org), 52 Baltimore St., Cumberland. The gallery features works by local and regional artisans, and traveling exhibits. The council sponsors performing arts events throughout the year.

C. William Gilchrist Gallery (301-72405800), 104 Washington St., Cumberland. An early-19th-century Federal style mansion houses an art library and galleries that exhibit various media and theme-oriented presentations. Local and state history and culture are also featured, as well as art lectures and classes.

BOOKSTORES Book Center (301-722-2284; 1-800-497-0633; www .thebookcenteronline.com), 15–17 N. Centre St., Cumberland. The only nonchain bookshop for many miles around, it stocks a large selection of local history, railroad, and travel titles,

along with children's books and games, newspapers, and magazines.

CRAFTS

Cumberland
The Country Angel (301-722-5151), 444 N. Centre St. Open Tue.–Fri. 10–6, Sat. 10–3. In addition to her own handmade crafts, Betty Harvey offers a number of items from local and regional craftspeople. The surprising sculptures created from cardboard deserve special attention.

Snyder's Cut Crystal (301-777-8155), 422 N. Centre St. Associated with the once thriving glass industry in western Maryland, the Snyder family hand-etches many of the items available in their store.

SPECIAL SHOPS

Cumberland
&. **Fort Cumberland Emporium** (301-722-4500), 55 Baltimore St. Open daily. A multivendor shop with handmade arts and crafts, antiques, jewelry, furniture, and more.

&. **Manhattan Centre Golf and Gallery** (301-777-0021), 69 Baltimore St. Do you think someone has combined their two passions into one business? The golf part offers complete sales, service, and lessons. The gallery has limited-edition prints and some nice original artwork.

Frostburg
Frostburg Shops by the Depot (301-689-3676), 20 Depot St. Five of the 12 small shops are located in the 1840 Tunnel Hotel that once housed railroad workers and local coal miners. There is no doubt the shops exist to appeal to riders on the Western Maryland Scenic Railroad, but you can find

a few treasures, such as train memorabilia and some not-so-tacky souvenirs.

OUTLETS & **Biederlack of America** (301-759-3633; www.biederlack.com), 11501 Bedford Rd., NE, Cumberland. This is the manufacturing site of one of the world's premier producers of blankets and throws. The large showroom offers the products at outlet prices.

FARMER'S MARKETS **Cumberland Downtown Farmer's Market** (301-724-3320). The Downtown Pedestrian Mall becomes a beehive of activity 9:45–2 on Thu. and Sat., June–Oct.

LaVale Country Club Mall Farmer's Market (301-724-3320). Part of the mall's parking lot becomes a farmer's market 9:30–2 on Tue., June–Oct.

Frostburg Farmer's Market (301-724-3320). Main Street is transformed into an open-air emporium 9:45–1 on Fri., June–Oct.

✳ Special Events

May: **Canalfest** (301-724-3655), Canal Place, Cumberland. A celebration of the C&O Canal's history, with period artisans, music, canal-boat-replica tours, and living-history demonstrations.

Late May–early September: **Summer in the City** (301-777-2787), Cumberland. A concert each Fri., Sat., and Sun. featuring local and regional musicians.

June: **Heritage Days** (301-777-2878), Cumberland. The area's biggest street festival features entertainment, children's activities, a carnival, scenic railroad excursions, arts and crafts, and food demonstrations. **Schoolhouse Quilters Guild Quilt Show** (301-729-5464), Frostburg State University. Western Maryland's largest quilt show. Vendors, demonstrations, and raffles.

July: **Oldtown Celebration** (301-478-5548), Oldtown. Slide shows and

---

EXTRA-SPECIAL SHOPS

There are two shops on the Downtown Pedestrian Mall that I certainly did not expect to find in a city as small as Cumberland. The quality and uniqueness of their products almost make them like small museums, so be sure to stop by, even if you have no intention of purchasing anything.

Bohemia Value (301-722-7300; www.bohemiavalue.com), 64 Baltimore St. Open daily. Fania Knizhnik imports Czech Republic–style art glass, crystals, porcelain, chandeliers, and other items produced by the Bohemia process that dates from the 13th and 14th centuries. Among many other items are Russian religious icons, porcelain from St. Petersburg, and ceramics from Greece.

Jackie's II Gallery (301-724-5700), 105 Baltimore St. Works of art from around the world. The items from Cuba, Belgium, and Africa are especially beguiling. I was taken by the metallic embossed cards, which depict everyday African life, and by the hand-spun, hand-dyed, woolen tapestries with African scenes handwoven into them.

reenactments along the C&O Canal. **Maryland Mountain Cruise** (301-724-3734), fairgrounds, Cumberland. A mixture of several activities: custom-car show, jousting demonstrations, games for all ages, and crafts. **Allegany County Fair** (301-729-1200), fairgrounds, Cumberland.

August: **Rocky Gap Music Festival** (1-888-ROCKY-GAP), Rocky Gap State Park, Flintstone. A major event that draws thousands of people to listen to some of the biggest names in contemporary country music. **Freedom Blues Fest/State Chili Cookoff/Micro-Brewers Beer** (301-722-3621), Ali-Ghan Shrine Picnic Grounds, I-68 Exit 46. If the presentations by nationally known blues acts do not appeal to you, try some samples of the many types of chilis being prepared for judging and wash them down with several swigs of Maryland-produced ales and lagers.

September: **St. Rod Roundup** (301-777-7774), fairgrounds, Cumberland.

More than 1,000 pre-1949 streetcars show up for exhibition and street jousting. **Cumberland Wine and Music Festival** (301-722-1760), Rocky Gap State Park, Flintstone. An annual event of wine tastings, fine food, and music that includes styles from jazz to reggae. **Cumberland Celtic Fest** (301-777-2800), Cumberland. The clans gather for live entertainment, dances, ethnic foods, and children's games.

October: **Railfest** (301-759-4400; 1-800-TRAIN-50), Cumberland. The annual event focuses on western Maryland's railroad legacy with steam-train excursions (short and long ones), displays, entertainment, and activities designed to bring the children in on the fun. **Iron Rail Days** (301-264-3229), Mount Savage. Attended and participated in by much of the residential population. Look for a reenacted bank robbery and jail break, along with guided tours of local sites.

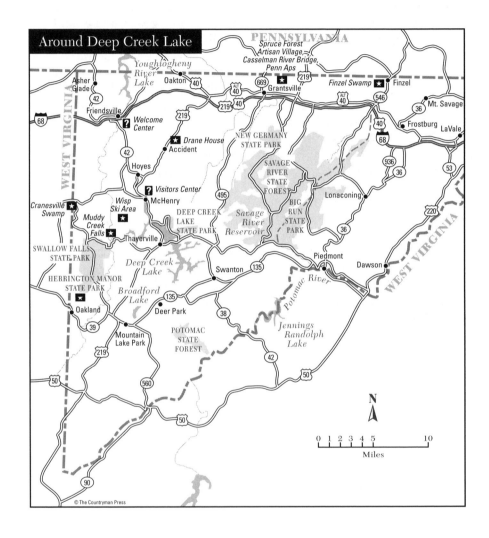

Around Deep Creek Lake

PENNSYLVANIA

Spruce Forest
Artisan Village,
Casselman River Bridge,
Penn Aps

Youghiogheny
River
Lake

Asher
Glade
42
Oakton 40
ALT 40
669
Grantsville
219
Finzel Swamp ★ Finzel
ALT 40
546

68
WEST VIRGINIA
Friendsville
219
Welcome
Center
42
Drane House ★
Accident
Hoyes

40
68
Mt. Savage
36
Frostburg LaVale
936
36
53

NEW GERMANY
STATE PARK

SAVAGE
RIVER
STATE
FOREST

Cranesville ★
Swamp
Muddy
Creek
Falls
Wisp
Ski Area
★
Visitors Center
McHenry
495
DEEP CREEK
LAKE
STATE PARK
Savage
River
Reservoir
BIG
RUN
STATE
PARK
Lonaconing
220

36

SWALLOW FALLS
STATE PARK
Thayerville

HERRINGTON MANOR
STATE PARK
★
Deep Creek
Lake
Swanton 135
Piedmont
Dawson

WEST VIRGINIA

Potomac River

Broadford
Lake
135
Oakland
39
Deer Park
38

Mountain
Lake Park
219
POTOMAC
STATE
FOREST
Jennings
Randolph
Lake
42
50

50
560
50

90

N

0 1 2 3 4 5   10
Miles

© The Countryman Press

AROUND DEEP CREEK LAKE—
Grantsville, McHenry, Thayerville, and Oakland

Outdoor types have been coming here for centuries. Three Native American trails converged at a spot near Grantsville, enabling members of several tribes to use the area for hunting. In the early 1700s, Meshach Browning was one of the area's earliest settlers and known far and wide for his hunting skills. In his book *Forty-Four Years of the Life of a Hunter*, he not only describes life on America's frontier but also estimates he killed "1,800 to 2,000 deer, 300 to 400 bears, about 50 panthers and catamounts, with scores of wolves and wildcats." Self-styled vagabonds Henry Ford, Harvey Firestone, Thomas Edison, and John Burroughs came to the area for some backcountry camping in 1918 and again in 1921.

Situated upon the elevated terrain of the Allegheny Plateau, Deep Creek Lake, Maryland's largest inland body of water, was formed in the 1920s when Deep Creek was dammed as part of a hydroelectric project to provide power to the residents of Pennsylvania. It covers 3,900 acres with approximately 65 miles of shoreline, and has become a destination for those who enjoy motorboating, waterskiing, sailing, and fishing, as well as those who just appreciate its scenic beauty. Six other lakes attract boaters of all kinds, while sport anglers come in search of abundant game fish. The streams that feed these lakes—the Youghiogheny, Savage, Casselman, and North Branch Potomac Rivers; Deep, Muddy, and Herrington Creeks; Buffalo, Laurel, and Hoyes Runs; and others—are considered to be some of the country's best fly-fishing destinations, brimming with brook, rainbow, and brown trout. All of the state's record trout were caught in this area. These same waterways, especially the Youghiogheny, Savage, and North Branch Potomac Rivers, are legendary to kayakers and whitewater rafters.

Nearly 100,000 acres of state parks, state forests, wildlife management areas, and Wild and Scenic River lands are laced with scores of trails, ranging from easy to difficult. Most of the pathways are open to hiking, mountain biking, and cross-country skiing, with multiple miles also available to snowmobiles. There are hundreds of campsites, some in commercially developed campgrounds, others rustically situated in the state parks. Backcountry camping is permitted on thousands of acres of state forest lands.

Maryland's only downhill skiing resort is located here, but it also takes advantage of every season by having a golf course, mountain biking and mountain boarding routes, and other outdoor activities available throughout the year.

COMMUNITIES Only two to three blocks wide and surrounded by farmland, **Grantsville** began as a small settlement clustered around Stanton's Mill, built in 1797. The 1818 Penn Alps and 1824 Casselman Inn were constructed to service travelers along the National Road, and are both still in use. The town developed into a destination center soon after Dr. Alta Shrock established a nonprofit organization in 1957 to study and promote the way of life in the Allegheny Highlands. The Penn Alps Restaurant and Spruce Forest Artisan Village are visible symbols of her efforts.

McHenry grew up after the establishment of Deep Creek Lake and is the commercial strip that greets people as they come into the lake area from the north. **Thayerville** is the business center at the center of the lake.

Oakland, with several (now defunct) grand hotels, was the area's vacation spot before the development of Deep Creek Lake. It is a modern town of 2,000 people, but its brick sidewalks, 1884 Queen Anne–style train station, Victorian homes, and farmer's market in a parklike setting festooned with native plants hark to a time past. The spring next to where George Washington camped is now along a 2.5-mile hiking/biking trail, and a paved route leads to a grandstand view of the town's many architecturally outstanding buildings.

Like Oakland, the stately hotels of **Deer Park** made it a Victorian vacation destination. Before it closed in 1929, the Deer Park Hotel's guests included Presidents Cleveland, Grant, and Harrison. The town is still somewhat famous for its commercially bottled Deer Park Spring Water.

Mountain Lake Park was established in 1881 as a Chautauqua-style summer resort with religious, educational, and recreational activities. A pamphlet available from the Garrett County Chamber of Commerce will take you on a self-guided tour of its historic district.

Local legend says that **Accident** received its name in 1774 when two speculators, wanting to take advantage of Lord Baltimore's offer of land to settlers, surveyed the same acreage "by accident." To this day, it remains a small settlement of just a few hundred spread out on agricultural land.

Friendsville was the first settlement to be established in Garrett County. Although many travelers along I-68 see it as just an interstate exit, the small town sits next to the Youghiogheny River and is well known to whitewater rafters and kayakers.

GUIDANCE The **Garrett County Chamber of Commerce** (301-387-4386; www.garrettchamber.com), 15 Visitors Center Dr., McHenry, 21541, is located off US 219 just as you come into the commercial strip at the north end of Deep

Creek Lake. In addition to the usual information, ask them for the pamphlets and brochures that have discount coupons in them. Another visitors center is located inside the **Oakland Train Station** (301-334-1243) in Oakland.

The *Lake Front* is a free monthly magazine with news, events, and features on places around the lake. You can pick up one in many business establishments.

With a grand view of Youghiogheny Lake, a **Maryland welcome center** (301-746-5979) is at mile marker 6 on I-68, east of Friendsville.

GETTING THERE *By car:* **I-68** will bring you into the area from the east or west, while **US 219** is the way to arrive from the north and south.

By air: There are scheduled flights to the airport in Morgantown, West Virginia, about 40 miles away, and the one in Cumberland, Maryland, about 50 miles away. Of course, you will save quite a few dollars by taking the numerous national and international airline companies that fly into **Pittsburgh, Pennsylvania, International Airport** (412-472-3525), just about a 2-hour drive from Deep Creek Lake.

By bus: **Greyhound** (1-800-229-9424) buses stop in Grantsville as they travel along I-68.

GETTING AROUND *By car:* If coming from the east, take **US 219** to Deep Creek Lake. If from the west, take **MD 42**, which will soon intersect with US 219.

MEDICAL EMERGENCY Garrett County Hospital (301-533-4000), 251 N. 4th St. (on the corner of 4th St. and Memorial Dr.), Oakland.

✳ To See

MUSEUMS Drane House (301-746-6346), Cemetery Rd. (off US 219), Accident. Open by appointment and on special days. Built around 1800 and believed to be the oldest structure in Garrett County, the log-and-frame home still has some of its original mud chinking. Items inside chronicle the town's history.

Garrett County Historical Society (301-334-3226), 2nd St., Oakland. Among the many items pertaining to the human history of the area are a period newspaper containing articles on Lincoln's assassination, glassware from the Glades and Oakland Hotels, and, what interested me the most, Meshach Browning's bear trap.

HISTORIC SITES The Oakland Train Station (301-334-2691), Oakland. A Queen Anne–style structure, it was built in 1884 to service the B&O Railroad's own resort. Be sure to walk by to appreciate the turret and other unique features.

OTHER SITES Spruce Forest Artisan Village (301-895-3332), 177 Casselman Rd. (US Alternate 40), Grantsville. Demonstrations of colonial and contemporary arts and crafts. Some of the best bird carvings, pottery, stained glass, and weaving you will find anywhere. Well worth a visit, especially since it is free.

LAKES **Deep Creek Lake** is the big draw to the area, but several other lakes have their own scenic and recreational attractions.

Youghiogheny River Lake (814-395-3166) spans the Mason-Dixon Line on the Maryland–Pennsylvania border. Powerboating and waterskiing are popular on the 16-mile body of water, and anglers come here for the variety of game and panfish, especially walleye and smallmouth bass. Picnic areas and three campgrounds (one in Maryland; see Mill Run Recreation Area under *Lodging*) are spaced around the lake. The access in Maryland is Mill Run Rd., off MD 53 north of Friendsville.

Savage River Reservoir (301-895-5759), accessed on Savage River Rd. from MD 135 at Bloomington, or

SPRUCE FOREST ARTISAN VILLAGE IN GRANTVILLE

from Big Run Road off New Germany Rd. One of the most spectacular settings of any of the area's lakes. Big Savage Mountain, Mount Nebo, and other ridgelines rise dramatically and quickly from the water. Trout, bass, crappie, walleye, perch, and catfish are in abundance, while a fly-fishing catch-and-release site at the dam's tailwater often yields 6- and 7-pound trout. The tailwaters are a popular kayaking spot and have even been used by those training for the Olympics.

Broadford Lake (301-334-9222), in the town of Mountain Lake Park. Non-gasoline-powered watercraft are welcome, which means the 140-acre body of water is a great place to canoe, kayak, sailboard, and fish for the stocked trout, crappie, bass, and catfish. Boat rentals during the season.

Jennings Randolph Lake (304-355-2346) is more than 5 miles long and is located on the North Branch of the Potomac River, which separates Maryland from West Virginia. Scenically sandwiched in by high ridges, the lake is one of the area's least used for powerboating, waterskiing, and fishing. The fly-fishing tailwater area regularly yields brown, rainbow, cutthroat, and brook trout. Mount Zion Rd., off MD 135, provides the only Maryland access to the lake (call 301-334-9180 for information). There is an inspiring view of the lake on Chestnut Grove Rd., which is also off MD 135.

DRANE HOUSE IN ACCIDENT

Also see **New Germany State Park** and **Herrington Manor State Park** under *Green Space*.

STONE BRIDGES **Casselman River Bridge**, on US Alternate 40 east of Penn Alps Restaurant, Grantsville. An impressive example of the stonemason's art, the 80-foot Casselman River Bridge was the largest stone-arch bridge in the world when it was built in 1813. While standing on it, be sure to look across the road to its two modern successors, the US 40 and I-68 bridges.

✳ To Do

BICYCLING See **Swallow Falls/Herrington Manor Trail** and the text note under *Hiking*, and **New Germany State Park** and **Deep Creek Lake State Park** under *Green Space*.

BIRDING See *Green Space—Nature Preserves*.

BOAT RENTALS

Thayerville/Deep Creek Lake

Aquatic Personal Watercraft Center (301-387-8233; www.Aquatic-Center .com), 634 Deep Creek Dr. Open daily 9–8. I get annoyed when personal watercraft show up at quiet lakes, inlets, or rivers. At Deep Creek Lake, however, it seems that almost all the boaters, whether in a small or huge boat, are trying to see how fast their craft can go, so you might as well join in. I'll admit I did, and I enjoyed it. Rentals by the hour or day.

Bill's Marine Service (301-387-5536), 20721 Garrett Hwy. (US 219). Little boats with less than 10 horsepower to monsters with 190 horsepower.

Silver Tree Marine (301-387-5855; www.silvertreecenter.com), 455 Glendale Rd. (on the way to Deep Creek Lake State Park). Rentals of inboard/outboard

CASSELMAN RIVER BRIDGE IN GRANTSVILLE

DEEP CREEK LAKE

powerboats, pontoon boats, and personal watercraft by the hour, half day, day, and week.

McHenry/Deep Creek Lake
Deep Creek Marina (301-387-6977), 1899 Deep Creek Dr. (off US 219). Hourly, daily, and weekly rentals of canoes as well as fishing, pontoon, and ski boats. Stop by in winter for cross-country ski equipment rentals.

Also see *Outdoor Outfitters*.

DOGSLEDDING

Yellow Snow Dog Sled Adventure (301-616-4996). Owner Kim Trickett, a native of Garrett County, has extensive experience and education in dogsledding in America's North Woods and shares her experience with customers by taking them on a variety of sledding tours (1-hour to half-day to longer trips) into a number of areas in western Maryland.

Huskey Power Dogsledding (301-746-7200), 2800 Bumble Bee Rd., Accident, 21520. Huskey Power offers much the same service as Yellow Dog, but since they have wheeled carts, they can take you on an outing even if there is no snow.

I have to admit that I have never gone on a trip with either of these companies, but having done some dogsledding in the Pacific Northwest, I can say what a grand sensation it is to feel the power and joy of the dogs as they pull you over snow-covered mountainous terrain. Expect to spend $50—100 (or slightly more) for a trip for two people.

McHenry/Deep Creek Lake

𝒮 **Smiley's FunZone** (301-387-5121; www.smileysfunzone.com), on US 219 across from the fairgrounds. There is enough here to keep the kids busy all day. There are batting cages (with slow-pitch softball or fast-pitch baseball), an old-time photo studio, arcade games, indoor laser tag, ice cream, pizza and other foods, and two go-cart tracks (one with a graded incline and the other with carts designed for kids as young as 4 years old). The bumper boats are a great way to get rid of some aggression, while the Smiley-designed miniature-golf course is different from any other you may have played on.

𝒮 **Funland** (301-387-6168), US 219 across from McHenry Plaza. Go-carts, a video arcade, miniature golf, bumper cars, and a "carousel for all ages." There is a free volleyball court and picnic tables to use while eating the burgers, pizza, or ice cream the kids insist on getting.

Swanton

𝒮 **Discovery Center at Deep Creek Lake State Park** (301-387-7067), 898 State Park Rd. Interactive displays about the geology, ecology, and human history of the area.

FISHING I have had the opportunity to go out with just two of many fly-fishing guides in the area:

A. J.'s Streamside Services (301-387-5465), 1951 N. Glade Rd., Swanton. A. J. Fleming is one of the very few professional guides to be certified by the Adventure Sports Institute—and one of the youngest. I had not been fishing since I was a preteen, yet within 10 minutes under A. J.'s tutelage on Big Run, I had a trout in my hands. Half-day, all-day, and overnight trips offered.

BIG RUN

Streams and Dreams (301-387-6881; www.streams-and-dreams.net), 8214 Oakland–Sang Run Rd., Oakland. Don Hershfeld, an aquatic ecologist, is also owner of a B&B on which a trout stream runs through the property. The Youghiogheny is a just a 2-minute walk away, and Don educated me quickly during that short stroll.

Other guides recommended by the Garrett County Chamber of Commerce include:

Spring Creek Outfitters (301-334-4023; www.springcreekoutfitter.com), 208 N. 2nd St., Oakland. A fly shop and guide service that offers float, wading, and overnight horseback fishing trips.

Fishing Deep Creek Lake (304-735-3426), P.O. Box 2125, Mountain Lake Park, 21550. Half-day and full-day lake and fly-fishing trips.

Also see *To See*, and **New Germany State Park** and **Herrington Manor State Park** under *Green Space*.

ICE FISHING Ice fishing on **Deep Creek Lake** and **Savage River Reservoir** has become increasingly popular. Most anglers come in Jan. and Feb. in hopes of hooking yellow perch, walleye, northern pike, and a few other species.

GOLF **Golf Club at Wisp** (301-387-4911; www.golfwisp), 296 Marsh Hill Rd., McHenry/Deep Creek Lake. The course has both open holes and tree-lined fairways, and shares some of the same land used by skiers in winter.

Oakland Golf Club (301-334-3883), 433 N. Bradley Lane, Oakland. Apr.–Oct. Established in 1937, the par-72 course has a maturity that is lacking in newer courses.

MINIATURE GOLF ✍ **A & D Dairy Delite** (301-387-9293), US 219 and Glendale Rd., Thayerville/Deep Creek Lake. An 18-hole course and goodies all in one spot.

Also see **Smiley's FunZone** and **Funland** under *Family Activities*.

HIKING The **Big Savage Hiking Trail** must be one of the best-kept outdoor secrets in Maryland. It offers a fine sense of isolation, relatively minor changes in elevation, several viewpoints (the one from **High Rock** is one of western Maryland's best), and an abundance of deer and other wildlife. The route traverses the crest of Big Savage Mountain for 17 miles. In addition, visitors may set up a back-

THE POTOMAC IN MIDSUMMER

country camp wherever they wish—yet the trail shows very few signs of use. There are no worn-out areas from too many people camping in the same spot, fire rings are almost nonexistent, and the trail's treadway is narrow and shallow.

The required backcountry camping permit (and payment of a fee) can be obtained at the forest headquarters, accessible from I-68 Exit 22 or from the New Germany State Park office (see *Green Space*).

Try the **Swallow Falls/Herrington Manor Trail** for an easier trek. The 5.5-mile pathway follows the bed of a former logging railroad on its way from one state park to the other. It is also popular with mountain bikers and cross-country skiers.

Without a doubt, 4.5-mile **Lost-land Run Trail**, west of Mountain Lake Park, is the showpiece of the **Potomac State Forest** (301-334-2038). Volunteers, members of the Maryland Conservation Corps, and personnel of the forest service have lavished much attention on the route, keeping it well maintained and building a number of bridges—both simple and complex.

The attention is well deserved, as the Lostland Run area is one of the most attractive in western Maryland. The hike begins in a hemlock grove, and soon comes into contact with three lively and gurgling mountain streams before it drops to the calmer waters of the Potomac River. Along the way are an abundance of wildflowers, numerous cascades, ripples, and waterfalls, and the possibility of seeing bobcats, opossums, deer, groundhogs, weasels, minks, and black bears. An additional draw is backcountry camping in this beautiful setting. Because of the proximity of the forest service road, you also have the option of shuttling a car to make it a one-way hike.

Note: The **Garrett County Chamber of Commerce** can provide you with information on the many other trails in this area that open up scores of miles for hiking, mountain biking, cross-country skiing, and snowmobiling.

Also see *Green Space.*

HORSEBACK RIDING Both **Sunny Slope Riding Stables** (310-334-4834), 3153 Bethlehem Rd., Oakland, 21550, and **Circle R Ranch** (301-387-6890), 4151 Sand Flat Rd., Oakland, 21550, offer hour-long trail rides.

KAYAKING AND CANOEING See **Savage River Reservoir** and **Broadford Lake** under *To See*, as well as *Outdoor Outfitters* and *Whitewater Rafting*.

OUTDOOR OUTFITTERS **High Mountain Sports** (301-387-4199; www.high mountainsports.com), 21349 Garrett Hwy. (US 219 at Trader's Landing), Thayerville. A full-service store; if it has to do with the outdoors, they can rent or sell you the equipment and teach you how to use it. This includes mountain biking, hiking, kayaking, snow skiing, waterskiing, and guided mountain bike and kayaking tours.

SAILING **Deep Creek Sailing School** (301-387-4497; www.saildeepcreek .com), located in Deep Creek Yacht Club at Turkey Neck, Swanton. Low-cost group sailing lessons on small sailboats taught by U.S. Sailing–certified instructors.

SCUBA DIVING **Breathe Deep Scuba** (301-387-8035), Route 5, Box 4721, Mountain Lake Park. Provides air fills, equipment rentals, and diving instructions.

SKIING, CROSS-COUNTRY This area receives as much as 220 inches of snow, which can fall from November into April. **New Germany** and **Herrington Manor State Parks** (see *Green Space*) offer miles of wide, well-marked, and groomed trails. Ski rentals and warming lodges are available in both parks.

Many other miles of trails are located in the state forests; information is available from the **Garrett County Chamber of Commerce**.

Also see *Skiing, Downhill*; and *Hiking*.

SKIING, DOWNHILL ♦ **Wisp Ski and Golf Resort** (301-387-4911; www .gcnet.net/wisp), 290 Marsh Hill Rd., McHenry/Deep Creek Lake. Maryland's only downhill skiing area has 22 trails totaling 14 miles. With an elevation over 3,000 feet and a 610-foot vertical drop, the resort also has facilities for ski boarding, cross-country skiing, and tubing. Night skiing is available. Like most such places, you can take lessons and buy or rent equipment; children's lessons and programs also available.

Wisp's snowmaking system is considered to be one of the most efficient in the world, so even if Mother Nature does not supply the white powder, Wisp is capable of making plenty of its own.

SNOWMOBILING There are miles and miles of marked snowmobile trails throughout the state parks and forests. One of the most popular is the route along the crest of Meadow Mountain that runs from **Deep Creek Lake State Park** to **New Germany State Park** and beyond. Another good choice is the 9.5-mile **Garrett State Forest Snowmobile System**.

Permits are required to ride some of the trails; information available from the **Garrett County Chamber of Commerce**.

SWIMMING Lifeguard-patrolled beaches are located at **Deep Creek Lake**, **Herrington Manor**, and **New Germany State Parks**. Many people swim in the Youghiogheny River at **Swallow Falls State Park**; be aware there are no lifeguards and the river can have a strong current.

WHITEWATER RAFTING **Precision Rafting** (301-746-5290; 1-800-477-3723; www.precisionrafting.com), Maple and Morris Sts., Friendsville. The premier company based in Maryland that runs the Upper Youghiogheny River's Class IV and V rapids. Kayaking lessons, family float trips, and runs in West Virginia and Kentucky, too.

✳ Green Space

NATURE PRESERVES Two tracts of land owned by The Nature Conservancy are situated in what are known as "frost pockets." The lower-lying swamplands are surrounded by high ridges, which trap cold air and create an environment more like Canada than Maryland. They are the location of some of America's southernmost occurrences of tamarack, wild calla, Canadian burnet, and insectivorous round-leaved sundew. Each has developed trails and is open daily during daylight hours. More background information can be obtained by contacting the Maryland Chapter of **The Nature Conservancy** (301-897-8570). The **Garrett County Chamber of Commerce** can supply you with directions (which are quite lengthy) to both places.

State-rare breeding birds that have been seen in the 326-acre **Finzel Swamp** are the Virginia rail, sedge wren, alder flycatcher, and saw-whet owl. Others species spotted in the swamp have included the rose-breasted grosbeak, cedar waxwing, and whippoorwill.

Partially in West Virginia and partially in Maryland, 1,600-acre **Cranesville Swamp** has a boardwalk that will take you by bogs, cranberries, and sphagnum moss. State-rare breeding birds found here include the golden-crowned kinglet, alder flycatcher, and Nashville warbler.

PARKS

Grantsville

New Germany State Park (301-895-5453), 349 Headquarters Lane. The park is located off New Germany Rd. In contrast to 3,900-acre Deep Creek Lake, New Germany's lake is all of 13 acres in size. It was formed in the early 1800s when John Swauger dammed Poplar Lick Run to obtain waterpower for a saw- and gristmill. The lake is stocked with sportfish, and rowboat and canoe rentals are available during the summer season. Other attractions include rental cabins (open year-round) with modern amenities, a campground, and a sandy beach for swimming.

The park's trail system was designed with cross-country skiers (who come to the park in large numbers) in mind, so the routes are generally wide, and for the most part rise and fall at a moderate grade. A hike or mountain bike ride will not deliver you to any spectacular waterfalls or open up any grand vistas but does provide the opportunity to meander through a quiet woodland, surveying the different small parts of the forest that come together to make up the whole.

Oakland

Herrington Manor State Park (301-334-9180), 222 Herrington Lane—follow signs from US 219 in Thayerville on a convoluted route to the park. Like New Germany State Park, Herrington Manor's moderately easy trails are popular cross-country ski routes, and are groomed and tracked by park personnel. Ski rentals are available.

The park's blend of recreational opportunities makes use of many of the still-standing 1930s Civilian Conservation Corps constructions, such as rental cabins 1–10. (An exhibit in the park office profiles the corps.) **Herrington Lake**, at 53 acres, is stocked with trout, bass, crappie, bluegills, and catfish. Non-gasoline-powered watercraft only; canoes and paddleboats are rented during summer.

Swallow Falls State Park (see Herrington Manor State Park, above, for contact information). Follow signs from US 219 at Thayerville. A walk of less than

1.5 miles provides you with not just one, but four distinctly different waterfalls. **Muddy Creek Falls** is considered the highest in the state (although some claim Cunningham Falls near Frederick is). The area between **Lower Falls** and **Swallow Falls** on the Youghiogheny River is a popular swimming spot, while the sandy beach at **Toliver Falls** is another inviting place. An added attraction of the hike is a shaded 37-acre, 300-year-old hemlock and white pine forest. The park also has a campground and picnic facilities.

Swanton/Deep Creek Lake

Deep Creek Lake State Park (301-387-5563), 898 State Park Rd. Although you are permitted to walk the shoreline around Deep Creek Lake, much of the land beyond has been turned into housing developments, private-home lots, or commercially operated enterprises. The Maryland General Assembly recognized the need for at least a bit of public land here, and after purchasing a mile of shoreline opened the park in 1959. Its 1,800 acres provide protected terrain for resident black bears, bobcats, wild turkeys, white-tailed deer, skunks, chipmunks, squirrels, raccoons, and numerous small mammals.

In addition to a swimming beach, amenities in the park include a campground, rowboat rentals, and a boat-launch facility. Stocked trout, walleye, bass, and yellow perch keep anglers busy. Ranger-naturalists lead interpretive programs—sometimes throughout the year, but most often during summer months. The **Discovery Center** is part visitors center, part museum.

Approximately 10 miles of trails along the slopes and crest of Meadow Mountain provide an opportunity to get away from the crowds of the lake and campground, visit an old mining site, enjoy a couple of vistas, and study a mountaintop wetland. Be aware that hunting is permitted in the park's backcountry area during regular hunting seasons, and that some of the trails are popular snowmobile routes in the winter and open to mountain bikes year-round.

✷ Lodging

RESORTS ✿ **Wisp Mountain Resort/ Hotel** (1-800-462-9477; www.wisp resort.com), 290 Marsh Hill Rd., McHenry, 21541 (Deep Creek Lake). The 168-room/suite hotel for the **Wisp Ski and Golf Resort** offers a heated pool, tennis courts, an exercise room, and special golf, skiing, and other package deals. Pets permitted with a substantial deposit. $89–329.

MOTELS AND HOTELS

Grantsville, 21536
✿ **The Casselman Inn** (301-895-5055; www.thecasselman.com), Main St. (US Alternate 40). The Casselman was built in 1824 as a stop to serve the stagecoaches, covered wagons, and other travelers along the National Road. The decor and fixtures (Room 5 has an old-fashioned water closet) in the four inn rooms reflect the early days and rent for $58–85. Newer motel rooms have been built next door and have some of the lowest rates in the state, $45–85. The adjacent restaurant (see *Eating Out*) serves Amish/country fare.

McHenry/Deep Creek Lake, 21541
✿ **The Inn at Point View** (301-387-5555; www.pointviewinn.com), MD

☎ ✍ **Savage River Lodge** (301-689-3200; www.savageriverlodge.com), P.O. Box 655, 1600 Mt. Aetna Rd. (within Savage River State Forest), Grantsville, 21536. Call for directions.

The lodge, and its 45 acres surrounded by thousands of Savage River State Forest acreage, is the pet project of Jan Russell and Mike Dreisbach. I like that the facility's construction disturbed the environment as little as possible. The sites for the 18 guest cabins (which can accommodate up to four people) were carved out of the forest but left most of the trees standing. Even at the main lodge, which overlooks the land, Jan and Mike did not cut down trees just to enhance the view. The septic system uses an environmentally friendly method, and even the roadway is designed with water conservation in mind. Although the natural world would be best served by no further development, if we must disturb the land, architects and planners would do well to emulate Savage River Lodge's example.

In addition to self-explorations of the 13 miles of trail (which connect with additional pathways in the state forest), the lodge can arrange all manner of guided outdoor activities: hiking, bicycling, canoeing, kayaking, fly-fishing, and more. This is, by far, one of my favorite outdoor-oriented Maryland places. It is also very pet-friendly. $210; $80 each additional person; $60 for children 2–12 years old. Many packages available.

219 on Deep Creek Lake. The Inn at Point View, family run for more than 30 years, looks like a typical motel from the outside. Yet most rooms have a great view of the lake and are furnished with unique and different types of antiques. There are some suites, but even the standard rooms are larger than you will find in many motels. The restaurant (see *Eating Out*) is known for its crabcakes. $100–140.

Panorama Motel (301-387-5230; 1-800-700-9257; www.deepcreektimes .com/panorama), 921 Mosser Rd. It is not on the lake, so its rooms and efficiencies have some of the lowest rates in the area. $55–99.

Deep Creek Lake/Oakland, 21550
Lake Side Motor Court (301-387-5503, ext. 2205; www.deepcreeklake side.com), 19956 Garrett Hwy. (US 219 near Thayerville). Low-rate, clean lake-view rooms. $74–83.

INNS

Deer Park, 21550
Deer Park Inn (301-334-2308; www .deerparkinn.com), 65 Hotel Rd. The inn was constructed as a 17-room family cottage in 1889 by Baltimore architect Josiah Pennington. Many of the family's furnishings are still here, such as a tiger maple dresser and table, a ruby-colored chandelier, and one of the first Sears & Roebuck mail-order sleigh beds. The plumbing is original (the sinks were made in nearby Mount Savage), the tile work in the bathrooms and fireplaces is quite interesting, and I always get a kick out of pulling the chain on the

toilet's suspended water box. Mattresses have that distinctive French sag in the middle. French country meals are served by candlelight in the downstairs dining rooms (see *Dining Out*). $125–145.

Deep Creek Lake/Oakland, 21550

Carmel Cove (301-387-0067; www .carmelcoveinn.com), P.O. Box 644, Glendale Rd. (off US 219 near Thayerville). The inn, built in 1945 as a monastery for Carmelite Fathers, provides many complimentary items and amenities: billiards, fishing poles for use on the dock, swimming in the lake, canoes and paddleboats, mountain bikes, tennis courts and equipment, beverages and snacks (always available), cross-country skis, and snowshoes.

Some rooms have a private deck, fireplace, and whirlpool bath; all have a private bath. Wood furniture and ceilings, along with a stacked stone fireplace, add an overall warmth to the inn. $155–195.

✐ **Red Run Lodge** (301-387-2626; 1-800-898-7786), 175 Red Run Rd. (on Deep Creek Lake off Mayhew Inn Rd. near Thayerville). The 1937 lakefront lodge's seven guest rooms are furnished with antiques and

THE LAKE POINTE INN

quilts, and each has a private bath. The three rooms on the top floor can interconnect for large groups. The included breakfast is served in an impressive curved-ceiling room overlooking the lake. Other meals are available in the restaurant (see *Eating Out*). $89–145.

BED & BREAKFASTS

Accident, 21520

✐ **Bear Creek Crossing Bed and Breakfast** (301-746-8623; www.bear creekcrossingbedandbreakfast.com), 29380 Garret Hwy. Each guest room in the large country house has an antique Irish bed. If the weather is nice, breakfast (crème brûlée French toast, omelets, quiches, pancakes, French toast sticks, homemade bread and muffins and Amish sausage or bacon) is served on the covered porch. Homemade cookies and "Maggie's Fudge" are available for snacking. $150.

Grantsville, 21536

⌂ **Elliott House Victorian Inn** (301-895-4250; 1-800-272-4090; www .elliotthouse.com), 146 Casselman Rd. Situated next to the Casselman River and across the street from Penn Alps/Spruce Forest. The outdoors members of the family can fly-fish in the stream while others stroll through the artisans' village. The 1870 home is furnished in a mix of contemporary and period pieces. All four guest rooms and three cottages have private bath. The living room, the brightest in the house, is where you can spend hours with the crystal chess set. Mountain bikes available for free guest use. $110–165.

✐ **Casselman Valley Farm Bed & Breakfast** (301-895-3419;

www.bbonline.com/md/casselman),
215 Maple Grove Rd. Located on
a 97-acre farm, the house dates
from the late 1800s and has three
guest rooms, each with a four-poster
bed, country farmhouse decor,
private bath, and air-conditioning.
Nature trails wind around the
property (streams, old barn, open
meadows, and forests), permitting you
to walk off the calories you consume
during the large breakfast served buf-
fet-style. $70.

Deep Creek Lake/McHenry, 21541

Lake Pointe Inn (301-387-0111;
1-800-523-5253; www.deepcreekinns
.com), 174 Lake Pointe Dr. The inn is
the oldest house on Deep Creek
Lake, actually predating the lake by
several decades. It now sits just 13
feet from the water's edge, and the
wraparound porch, with rocking
chairs, is perfect for lazy hours of
lake-watching. The 9-foot stone fireplace, rich woodwork, and handcrafted furniture, fixtures, and pottery
give the feel of a rustic lodge, but
one with modern amenities. All 10
guest rooms have a private bath, air-
conditioning, TV with VCR (an extensive collection of videos is available),
and telephone. There are also bikes,
canoes, kayaks, and a hot tub for
guest use. It is one of my favorite
Deep Creek Lake places because of
the location, laid-back atmosphere,
and attentive staff.

Orange juice, muffins, and snacks are
available throughout the day; hors
d'oeuvres are served in the early
evening. Breakfast may include
scrambled eggs on a puff pastry
and/or a fresh strawberry-mango tart.
$173–259.

Streams and Dreams (301-387-
6881; www.streams-and-dreams.net),
8214 Oakland–Sang Run Rd. Hosted
by Don Hershfeld, an aquatic ecologist, and Karen Hershfeld, a fisheries-
science graduate and physician
assistant, this little retreat sits upon 15
acres bisected by Hoyes Run, a wild
trout stream. An extensive deck overlooks the parklike grounds. Guests of
the three private rooms have access to
refreshments in the parlor, a cedar
sunroom, and a gazebo planted upon
a small island in the stream. Don
offers fly-fishing lessons for individuals and small groups by making use of
any one of the four major trout rivers
within a few minutes' drive (see *To
Do*). Be sure to have him tell you the
story of the fireflies as the two of you
take an evening stroll along the
Youghiogheny River. $110–170.

Thayersville/Oakland, 21550

Haley Farm B&B (301-387-9050;
1-888-231-3276; www.haleyfarm
.com), 16766 Garrett Hwy. (between

HALEY FARM B&B

Thayerville and Oakland on US 219). The wraparound porch looks upon the farm's 65 acres and the surrounding mountains. All of the suites and rooms have a private bath, and everybody has access to a Jacuzzi either in the room or on the deck. Wander the property, sit by the fireplace, fish or row the pond, or borrow a bike for an exploratory ride. $150–205.

SUITES Will O' the Wisp Prestige Condominiums (301-387-5503; www.willothewisp.com), 20160 Garrett Hwy. (US 219 near Thayerville), Oakland, 21550. The one- to three-bedroom condominiums overlook the lake. Indoor pool, sauna, exercise room, and its own sand beach. $123–374.

CABINS Herrington Manor, **New Germany**, and **Deep Creek Lake State Parks** have cabins that can be rented by the week Memorial Day–Labor Day, and for 2-night minimum stays at other times of the year. Reservations can be made by calling 1-888-432-2267.

VACATION RENTALS There are so many rental homes and condos in the area—well over 600—that descriptions of them fill several large advertisement books. Everything from small, rustic cabins to nine-bedroom luxury homes are available. Many are on the Deep Creek Lake shoreline, but others are nestled in quiet, out-of-the-way places. In a sign of the times, some include free computer and Internet access. Most of the individually rented places are listed in the *Vacation Guide* available from the **Garrett County Chamber of Commerce**. However, three companies manage the bulk of the rentals:

McHenry/Deep Creek Lake, 21541
Coldwell Banker Deep Creek Realty Rentals (301-387-6187; 1-800-769-5300; www.DeepCreek Realty.com), 24439 Garrett Hwy. (US 219).

Railey Mountain Lake Vacations (301-387-2124; 1-800-846-7368; www .deepcreek.com), 22491 Garrett Hwy. (US 219).

Long and Foster Resort Rentals (301-387-5832; 1-800-336-7303; www .deepcreekresort.com), 23789 Garrett Hwy. (US 219).

CAMPING

Friendsville, 21531
🐾 **Mill Run Recreation Area** (814-395-3242), Mill Run Rd. (off MD 53, 4 miles north of Friendsville). Mailing address is RD 1, Box 17, Confluence, PA 15424. Usually open May–Sep. The only Youghiogheny Lake campground in Maryland, it has a swimming beach, boat ramp, and flush toilets, but no showers. Pets permitted.

Grantsville, 21536
🐾 **Little Meadows** (301-895-5675), Chestnut Ridge Rd. Offers improved and unimproved sites, along with rowboat rentals, a playground, and a dump station.

🐾 **New Germany State Park** (301-895-5453), 349 Headquarters Lane. The park is located off New Germany Rd. Close to the park's small lake are 39 sites with a playground for the kids.

🐾 **Big Run State Park** (see New Germany State Park, above, for contact information). Near Savage River Reservoir 16 miles south of I-68 Exit 24 on Savage River Rd. Basic sites with few amenities, but open year-round.

McHenry/Deep Creek Lake, 21541

☘ **Double G RV Park** (301-387-5481), Moser Road. Bathhouse, playground, and dump stations.

Oakland, 21550

☘ **Swallow Falls State Park** (301-334-9180), 9 miles northwest of Oakland on Herrington Manor–Swallow Falls Rd. Showers, modern bathhouse, sanitary facilities.

Swanton, 21561

☘ **Deep Creek Lake State Park** (301-387-5563), 898 State Park Rd. The more than 100 campsites, with hot showers and modern sanitary facilities, are just a short walk from the lake. Rental cabins also available.

Note: Thousands of acres of state forest lands are open to backcountry camping (after payment of a fee). Contact the **Potomac and Garret State Forests** (301-334-2038), 1431 Potomac Camp Rd., Oakland, 21550, and **Savage River State Forest** (301-895-5759), 349 Headquarters Lane, Grantsville, 21536, for details.

✳ Where to Eat

DINING OUT Deer Park Inn (301-334-2308; www.deerparkinn.com), 65 Hotel Rd., Deer Park. Open for dinner. Reservations required. Pascal Fontaine moved his family to Deer Park so that he could concentrate on preparing meals influenced by methods he learned growing up in France. The menu changes often, as he makes use of seasonally available items grown locally. I dined on the succulent confit of duck ($19.25), while my companion praised the beef fillet with Cabernet Sauvignon sauce ($24.75). One of Pascal's signature appetizers, corn chowder with applewood-smoked bacon

and crabmeat ($6), is an example of how Maryland cuisine is blended into the offerings. $16–24.95.

🦞 ♂ **Cornish Manor** (301-334-6499), Memorial Dr., Oakland. Open for lunch 11–2, dinner 5 to closing, Tue.–Sat. Reservations required. Who would expect two French restaurants in this far western corner of Maryland, and both located in Victorian homes?

From the wall of masks, to the gold-tinted chairs, to the tassels hanging from the ceiling, Christiane Bergheim has put her mark on the decor, while she and her husband, Fred, share the chef's duties. The names of the dishes are as inventive as the meals themselves: Ménage à Trois (scallops, shrimp, and mussels in cream wine sauce—$22.50); Are You Game? (duck in honey chutney sauce—$15.95); Flirtation Filet Mignon in Say Yes Sauce (market price). The fresh French breads that come with each meal are reason enough to dine here. The almost decadent decor, Christiane's lilting personality, and the great food have turned this into my favorite Deep Creek Lake–area restaurant. $15.50–25.95.

🦞 ♂ **Silver Tree Inn** (301-387-4040; www.silvertreecenter.com), 567 Glendale Rd., Thayerville/Deep Creek Lake. Open for dinner 5–10 Mon.–Thu., 5–11 Fri. and Sat., and 4–9 Sun. Silver Tree is housed in what is believed to be the first place built to cater to tourists after completion of Deep Creek Lake in the early 1900s. The large stone fireplace and log walls may recall a bygone era, but the decidedly fresh menu makes this the most popular Italian restaurant around the lake.

Several items are distinct to Silver Tree. For an appetizer, try the oysters à la Romano—oysters in a mixture of mushrooms, cheese, and water chestnuts that is baked in a cream sauce ($7.95). My favorite dish is the crab soufflé—baked in a crock, well puffed and lightly browned ($16.95). The children's menu is reasonably priced. Arrive very early (or very late) to be seated at one of the lake-view tables. Entrées $14.95–32.95.

EATING OUT

Grantsville

♂ ♿ **Penn Alps Restaurant** (301-895-5985; www.pennalps.com), US 40. Open daily for breakfast, lunch, and dinner. Part of the Penn Alps/Spruce Forest complex, the restaurant serves what I would call an upscale country/Amish/German fare. Hickory-smoked ham ($9.99), pork with sauerkraut ($9.99), and cabbage rolls ($11.99) are representative dishes on the menu. Seemingly out of place, but I thought delicious, is the chickpea burger ($3.50). Three of the dining rooms were once part of a log stagecoach inn, and the front of the restaurant showcases arts and crafts items. The restaurant is part of a non-profit organization, so some of the money you spend goes toward good works. Entrées $8.99–15.99.

♂ **The Casselman Inn** (301-895-5055; www.thecasselman.com), Main St. (US Alternate 40). Open for breakfast, lunch, and dinner; closed Sun. Straightforward, low-cost Amish/country cooking that is popular with locals. Look for fried chicken, breaded fish, grilled ham, and other entrées served with two vegetables for $7–12. The shoofly pie is different from what you will find in Pennsylvania Dutch country.

McHenry/Deep Creek Lake

♂ **The Inn at Point View** (301-387-5555; www.pointviewinn.com), MD 219 on Deep Creek Lake. Open daily. Overlooking the lake, the Inn at Point View is best known for its rainbow trout and crabcakes. (While I and a companion were trying to decide what to order, the ladies at the next table told us they were thoroughly enjoying their crabcakes.) Lunch can be casual with sandwiches, while dinner choices can include steamed crabs or wild game. The adjacent Board-walk Lounge (see *Entertainment*) is a very popular watering hole. Entrées range $16.95–26.95 to market price.

♂ **Deep Creek Brewing Company** (301-387-2182; www.deepcreek brewing.com), located behind the visitors center on US 219. Open daily for lunch and dinner. The lake area's first brewpub has a menu that goes on for page after page. The black bean salsa with chips ($4.50) complements any of the eight handcrafted brews. Sandwiches and panini are available ($5.95–12.95) if you are in a hurry. Entrées range from seafood bake ($18.95) to a filet mignon (market price). Other entrées $15.95–21.95

♂ **Canoe on the Run** (301-387-5933), 2622 Deep Creek Dr. Open for breakfast, lunch, and dinner. A cross between a coffeehouse where you can grab a quick breakfast of baked goodies and a café serving soups, sandwiches, and other finger foods, such as quesadillas and focaccia. $4.75–6.50.

Thayerville/Deep Creek Lake

Red Run Lodge (301-387-2626; 1-800-898-7786; www.deepcreektimes .com/redrun), 175 Red Run Rd. (on Deep Creek Lake off Mayhew Inn Rd. near Thayerville). The lakefront is the prime reason to dine here. House specialties include Maryland crab soup, chicken sandwich topped with crabmeat, bacon, and cheeses, and cod fixed a variety of ways. Seafood, steak, and vegetarian entrées $8.95–25.95.

Oakland

Dottie's Fountain and Grill (301-533-0000), 205 E. Alder St. Open for breakfast, lunch, and "afternoon" dinner, Mon.–Fri. 8:30 AM–3:30 PM, Sat. 8:30 AM–2 PM. Come to Dottie's to experience a time warp. Dottie, the vinyl booths, U-shaped counters, and the menu have been here for more than 30 years. Everything retains the look and feel of when it served as the fountain for a long-gone pharmacy. (The front of the store is now Englander's Antique Mall; see *Selective Shopping*.)

Breakfast is served all day, and the most expensive item you can order is less than $5. Hot dogs, cheeseburgers, grilled cheese, and good ol' PB&J are some of the standard lunch items. Try the deep-fried cauliflower instead of french fries. Dinner is a choice of fried chicken, shrimp, or fish. The hand-dipped milk shakes are not to be missed. Sandwiches and entrées $.70–4.65.

Mountain Lake Park

Long Branch Saloon (301-334-4533), 1501 Maryland Hwy. Open daily for dinner 5–9:30. One half of this large building is a bar; the other half serves as the restaurant (and dance hall on Fri. and Sat. nights—see *Entertainment*). Beef in all shapes—filet mignon, T bone, Delmonico, and others—is the definite house specialty and is served with salad and potato. Chicken, fish, and sandwiches also available. $8.95–23.95.

COFFEE BARS Trader's Coffee House (301-387-9246), US 219 about half a mile south of the Deep Creek Lake bridge, Thayerville/Deep Creek Lake. Open daily at 7:30 AM. Gourmet coffees, breakfast and lunch sandwiches, and fresh-baked goodies. A few sugar-free items, too.

RED RUN LODGE

SNACKS AND GOODIES Sugar and Spice Bakery and Cheese (301-334-1559), 2 miles south of Oakland on US 219. Closed Sun. It looks like someone's private home, but go on in for fresh-baked Amish breads, doughnuts, cookies, pies, and some scrumptious pumpkin rolls.

☙ **Lakeside Creamery** (301-387-2580; www.lakesidecreamery.com), 20282 Garrett Hwy., Thayerville/Deep Creek Lake. This is homemade ice cream at its best. There is a rotating menu of about 80 flavors and no way to choose a bad one. Bill Meagher, who oversees the operation, is so particular that he buys different vanilla extracts from around the world. He has found that Tahitian vanilla complements fruit-flavored ice creams, while an extract with a slight alcoholic taste is suited for heavier flavors. Bill is such a recognized authority that people come from other continents for his college courses about the homemade ice cream business. Enjoy your cones or sundaes on the picnic tables overlooking the lake.

✳ Entertainment

FILM Garrett Eight Cinemas (301-387-2000), 19736 Garrett Hwy. (US 219), Thayerville/Deep Creek Lake. First-run films.

NIGHTLIFE

McHenry/Deep Creek Lake
Boardwalk Lounge (301-387-5555), MD 219 on Deep Creek Lake. In the Inn at Point View. Also known as "the Round Bar," this is one of the most happening places around the lake, especially during live-entertainment weekends.

Black Bear Tavern (301-387-6800), US 219, at "The Fort." Live regional bands every Fri. and Sat. night. No cover charge 10 PM–2 AM.

Thayerville/Deep Creek Lake
Honi Honi (301-387-9172), US 219, across from Garrett Eight Cinemas. This place hops both night and day, as they often have live outdoor entertainment from early afternoon on.

Mountain Lake Park
Long Branch Saloon (301-334-4533), 1501 Maryland Hwy. The restaurant (see *Eating Out*) tables are rolled away on Fri. and Sat. nights to create the largest dance floor in the area. Energetic crowds dance the night away to music supplied by regional musicians.

THEATERS Our Town Theatre (301-334-5640; www.ourtowntheatre.com), 121 Center St., Oakland. The volunteer community theater, housed in a building that has served as a church, armory, and museum, provides space for teen coffeehouses, recitals, meetings, dances, classes, and theatrical performances.

✳ Selective Shopping
ANTIQUES

Grantsville
Spinning Wheel Antiques and Dream Weavers Antiques (301-895-5938), 161-A Main St. Mother and daughter Elizabeth Brant and Debbie Klotz have been in the antiques business for well over a decade.

McHenry/Deep Creek Lake
Reminisce Antique Mall (301-387-8275), US 219. Open daily; closed Wed., Labor Day–Memorial Day. Furniture, glassware, books, toys, prints, and more from 15 dealers.

Oakland

Mt. Panax Antiques (301-334-9249), 27 Norris Welch Rd. About 3 miles south of Oakland. Closed Sun. Glassware, clocks, and some excellent furniture finds.

Englander's Antique Mall (301-533-0000), Alder and 2nd Sts. Four thousand square feet of antiques and collectibles.

Also see **Book Market and Antique Mezzanine** under *Bookstores.*

Note: A pamphlet available from the **Garrett County Chamber of Commerce** describes a couple of antiques driving tours in the area that will take you by scores of dealers.

ART GALLERIES **Garrett County Arts Council** (301-334-6580), 206 E. Alder St., Oakland. Closed Sun. The only fine-arts gallery in the region. Arts and crafts by more than 80 local and regional council members.

BOOKSTORES **Expanding Horizons** (301-387-5700), 19895 Garrett Hwy., Thayerville/Deep Creek Lake. It is a small store, but many volumes and music CDs are displayed in the limited space.

Book Market and Antique Mezzanine (301-387-8778), Oakland. Open Mon.–Sat.; sometimes Sun. A full-service bookstore with best sellers, classics, and an excellent selection of local-interest books. One of the friendliest bookstores I have visited. Antiques on the second floor.

CRAFTS

Mountain Lake Park

Simon Pearce Glassblowing (301-334-5277; www.simonpearce.com), 265 Glass Dr. (off MD 135). Open daily 9–5. A catwalk permits visitors to watch the craftspeople at work on the factory floor. It is amazing to watch as a blob of red-hot, molten silica is turned into a crystal-clear work of glass art.

SPECIAL SHOPS **Yoder Country Market** (301-895-5148; 1-800-321-5148), MD 669, Grantsville. This market had its beginnings when the patriarch started a butchering business on his farm to supplement his meager income during the Great Depression. Today Yoder's is known for its sausages, scrapple, bologna, smoked hams, and other meats. The country market is next door to the packinghouse, so the meats are fresh. Many locals also shop here for the breads and cookies made on premises, or other Amish items such as apple butter, maple syrup, and maple candies produced locally.

Cobblestone Alley (301-387-4644), 2778 Deep Creek Dr., McHenry/Deep Creek Lake. Open 10–6 Sun.–Thu., 10–7 Fri. and Sat. Besides the usual items found in gift shops, Cobblestone Alley has some locally made items such as Bag Lady Totes, Grandma's Jam House, and Laurel Ridge Pottery (whose deep blue glazes are sumptuous).

FARMER'S MARKETS **Oakland Mountain Fresh Farmer's Market** (301-334-6960). In the city parking lot off 2nd St., 10–1 on Sat. and Wed., July–Oct.

WINERY **Deep Creek Cellars** (301-746-4349), 177 Frazee Rd., Friendsville. Tours, tastings, and sales Wed.–Sat. 11–6. Deep Creek Cellars is the farthest west of the state's wineries and, even with its reputation for fine wines, offers its varieties at some of the lowest prices. It's situated on a hillside, so visitors are encouraged to linger, picnic, enjoy the scenic vineyard, and maybe shop in the farm market.

✳ Special Events

January: **Annual Kick and Glide Cross-Country Ski Race and Winter Fest** (301-334-3114), Herrington Manor State Park. Sledding, snowshoeing, snow-people making, horse-drawn sleigh rides.

June: **McHenry Highland Festival** (301-387-9300), fairgrounds, McHenry. Scottish dancing and solo piping contests. The annual daylong event celebrates the heritage of Scotland, Ireland, Wales, and England and includes sheepdog demonstrations, ethnic food and music, and a military encampment. **Loggers/Forestry Day and Equipment Sale**, fairgrounds. A biennial event that showcases the latest in forestry equipment and techniques. Arts and crafts, and presentations for kids and adults. Smokey Bear always shows up. **Grantsville Days** (301-895-5177), town park, Grantsville. Parade and fireworks, tractor and horse pulls, lots of food, and continuous entertainment.

June–September: **Garrett Lakes Arts Festival** (301-387-3082; www.arts andentertainment.org), various sites. A summerlong celebration of visual and performing arts. Classes, workshops, and concerts with classical and contemporary music. **Music at Penn Alps** (301-895-5985; www.musicat pennalps.com), Grantsville. The annual series features classic to contemporary classical music.

July: **Independence Day Exhibition of Art** (301-746-6115), Accident. Annual juried art competition in a variety of media that has categories open to adults and children of various ages. **Summer Festival and Quilt Show** (301-895-3332), Spruce Forest Artisan Village, Grantsville. The annual event includes visiting and resident artisans, children's activities, and hundreds of hand-stitched quilts made in the region and submitted for the juried exhibition.

August: **Annual Western Maryland Tennis Championships** (301-334-3249), Mountain Lake Park. The clay-court competitions have been held for more than 80 years. **Garrett County Fair** (301-533-2321), fairgrounds, McHenry. **Country Fest and Auction** (301-245-4564), fairgrounds, McHenry. Arts and crafts, all-day gospel music, old-time milking, weaving, and apple cider demonstrations. Hay wagon and pony rides. Petting zoo and pedal-tractor pull for the kids. Auction proceeds from homemade items support the local Mennonite school and church.

October: **Autumn Glory Festival** (301-387-4386), various sites throughout the area. An annual 5-day celebration of fall foliage. Parades, live music, arts and crafts, dances, and lots of food.

INDEX

A

A. J.'s Streamside Services, 441
A. M. Thomas Trail, 374
Abercrombie Badger B&B, 219
Aberdeen, 165, 166; eating, 178; entertainment, 178; information, 167; sights/activities, 169, 171; transportation, 167
Aberdeen Cab, 167
Aberdeen Proving Grounds, 166, 169
Abner's Crab House, 328–29
Above All Else @ Windsong, 379
Academy Art Museum, 18, 103, 117, 119
Accident, 436; events, 456; lodging, 448; sights/activities, 437, 440
Accokeek, 280–81
Ace Taxi, 43
Action Taxi, 294
Action Watersports, Ltd., 52
Adkins Arboretum, 126–27
Admiral Fell Inn, 218, 220–21
admission fees: about, 16
Adrenaline High, 19, 70
Adventure Sports (Frostburg), 423
Aesop's Table, 88
African American Community Bicycle Tour (Sandy Spring), 298
African American Cultural Tours (Baltimore), 213
African American Culture, Howard County Center of, 233
African American Family Community Day (St. Leonard), 331
African American Heritage Festival (Baltimore), 229
African American Wax Museum, 209
African Art Museum of Maryland, 17, 233
African Methodist Episcopal Church, 249
Ain't That a Frame, 196
air rides, in Ocean City, 46
airports (air travel): about, 16. See also specific airports
Alfred Memorial Park, 52
ALICE, 63
All American Road, 29
All Books Considered, 308
All Hallows Church (Snow Hill), 46

All Manor of Things, 88
All Saints Episcopal Church, 319
All-County Cab, 294
Allegany Arts Council, 431
Allegany County, 413–33
Allegany County Convention and Visitors Bureau, 415
Allegany County Fair, 433
Allegany County Transit Division, 416
Allegany Expeditions Inc., 421, 423
Allegheny Highlands Trail, 420
Allegheny Plateau, 389, 413–33; map, 412; Deep Creek Lake, 435–56; map, 434
Allegheny Trail Alliance, 420
Allegro Coffee and Tea Salon, 74
Alpine Pantry, 430
Alsatia Mummers Parade, 411
Alternative Gift Gallery, 101
AMC Academy (Greenbelt), 288
AMC Carrollton, 288
AMC City Place 10 (Silver Spring), 306
AMC Country Club (LaVale), 430
AMC Lanes (Waldorf), 353
AMC Rivertown (Oxon Hill), 288
American Chestnut Land Trust, 323
American Craft Council Craft Show, 229
American Heritage Museum (McMahon's Mill), 405
American Indians. See Native Americans; Piscataway Indians
American Music and Arts Festival, 195
American Revolution, 75, 94, 103, 104, 136, 201, 237–38, 253, 341, 355, 395
American Soft Shell Crab Company, 345
American Visionary Art Museum, 17, 209
American Youth Hostel (Knoxville), 379
Amish Quilt Auction, 348
Amphibious Horizons, 255
Amtrak, 167, 204, 232, 276, 293, 316, 415–16
amusement parks: Ocean City, 46–47, 48–49; Six Flags America Theme and Water Parks, 282
Anacostia River, 282
Anacostia Trails, 282
Anchor Inn Seafood Restaurant, 306

A & D Dairy Delite, 442
Andrews Manor, 288
Andy's, 145
Angler Restaurant, 60
Ann Street B&B, 219
Annapolis, 245–69; campgrounds, 261; eating, 261–65; emergencies, 123, 249; entertainment, 265–66; events, 268–69; information, 247–48; lodging, 257–61; maps, 244, 246; parking, 248–49; public restrooms, 249; shopping, 266–68; sights/activities, 249–57; transportation, 248–49
Annapolis Accommodations, Inc., 257
Annapolis and Anne Arundel County Conference and Visitors Bureau, 247, 249, 252, 256
Annapolis by Candlelight, 269
Annapolis Cab, 248
Annapolis Cinema Grill, 265
Annapolis City Dock, 246, 247; boat excursions, 254; events, 268, 269; public restrooms, 249
Annapolis Gourmet, 263
Annapolis Harbour Center, 267
Annapolis Inn, 259
Annapolis Mall, 265, 267
Annapolis Marine Art Gallery, 17, 266
Annapolis Maritime Museum, 28–29
Annapolis Marriott Waterfront Hotel, 258
Annapolis Minibus Tours, 252
Annapolis Opera, 265
Annapolis Pottery, 267
Annapolis Powerboat School, 255–56
Annapolis Sailing School, 31, 255
Annapolis Summer Garden Theatre, 266
Annapolis Symphony Orchestra, 265
Annapolis Tours, 253
Annapolis Transit, 123, 248
Annapolis Treasure Company, 267
Anne Arundel County, 245–69
Anne Arundel County Conference and Visitors Bureau, 247, 249, 252, 256
Anne Arundel County Fair, 268
Anne Arundel County Farmer's Market, 268
Anne Arundel County Recreation and Parks Department, 254, 256
Anne Arundel Medical Center, 123, 249
Anne Arundel Scottish Highland Games, 269
Annie's, 130
Annmarie Garden, 323–24, 331

Antietam Cab, 393
Antietam Creek, 397, 400
Antietam Creek Canoe, 400
Antietam Hagerstown KOA, 405
Antietam National Battlefield, 23, 368, 391, 396–97; campgrounds near, 405; events, 411
Antietam National Cemetery, 397
Antietam Transportation, 393
Antique Aircraft Fly-In, 101
Antique and Classic Boat Festival, 119
Antique Center at Federal Hill, 226–27
Antique Scientific Instruments, 307
antiques: about, 16–17; Annapolis, 266; Baltimore, 226–27; Berlin, 63; Brookeville, 306–7; Cambridge, 100; Chestertown, 145; Columbia, 241; Crumpton, 131; Cumberland, 430; Deep Creek Lake, 454; Easton, 117; Ellicott City, 241; Frederick, 383–84; Gaithersburg, 307; Galena, 145; Grantsville, 454; Hagerstown, 408–9; Hancock, 409; Havre de Grace, 179; Hughesville, 358; Indian Head, 358; Kensington, 307; La Plata, 358; Laurel, 290; Leonardtown, 346; Middletown, 384; Mount Airy, 196; New Market, 16, 384; North Beach, 329–30; North Bethesda, 307; North East, 161; Oakland, 455; Queenstown, 131; St. Michaels, 117; Salisbury, 88; Solomons, 329–30; Stevensville, 131; Westminster, 196
Antiques Dealers Association of Maryland, 17
Antrim 1844, 191–92, 193
Apex Aspen Hill Cinemas, 306
Apex Theatres (Prince Frederick), 329
Appalachian Trail, 20, 32, 171–72, 398, 399, 400; about, 17, 400
Appalachian Trail Club, 21, 374
Appalachian Trail Conservancy, 17
apples (orchards), 74, 162, 197–98, 382
Applewood Farm, 179
April Inn, 141
aquariums: about, 17. See also specific aquariums
Aquatic Personal Watercraft Center, 439
area codes, 16
Ark, 333, 352
Army Ordnance Museum, U.S., 169
Arnold, 247, 255
Arrow Cab, 205

art galleries: about, 17–18; Annapolis, 266–67; Baltimore, 227; Berlin, 63; Cambridge, 100–101; Chesapeake City, 161; Chestertown, 145; College Park, 289; Columbia, 241; Crisfield, 74; Cumberland, 431; Easton, 117–18; Elkton, 161; Ellicott City, 241–42; Frederick, 384; Garrett County, 455; Hagerstown, 18, 409; Havre de Grace, 179; Kensington, 307; Kent Island, 131; Leonardtown, 346; Marbury, 17, 358; North East, 161; Ocean City, 63; Prince Frederick, 330; Rock Hall, 145; Salisbury, 88–89; Silver Spring, 307; Thurmont, 384; Westminster, 196

Art Gallery of Fell's Point, 227

Art in the Park (Rock Hall), 146

Art in the Park (Westminster), 199

Art Institute and Gallery (Salisbury), 88–89

Art League of Ocean City, 63

art museums: about, 17. See also specific art museums

Artfest (Indian Head), 359

ArtFX (Annapolis), 267

ArtQuest (Bel Air), 180

arts councils: about, 18. See also specific arts councils

Arts Marketplace (Easton), 119

Artscape (Baltimore), 229

Artsfest (Solomons), 331

Arundel Mills, 267

Asahi Japanese Steak and Seafood House, 344

Asbury Methodist Church (Annapolis), 252

Asbury United Methodist Church (Crisfield), 69

Ashton: golf, 299

Assateague Adventure, 48

Assateague Crab House, 62

Assateague Island, 39–41, 48, 53; beaches, 18, 52; campgrounds, 22, 57–58; information, 42; map, 38

Assateague Island Explorer, 48

Assateague Island National Seashore, 30, 52, 53; campground, 57–58

Assateague State Park, 30, 53; campground, 57

Atlantic Bike Company, 47

Atlantic Flyway, 19–20, 22, 98, 119, 139, 147, 257, 339

Atlantic General Hospital, 43

Atlantic Hotel (Berlin), 41, 55; eating, 59

Atlantic Hotel (Ocean City), 39, 54

Atlantic House B&B (Ocean City), 56

Atlantic Stand Diner, 60

Attman's, 222

Au Petit Paris, 428

Audubon Society, 20, 108, 110, 302, 308, 309

Augustoberfest, 411

Aunt Betty's General Store, 307

Aunt Rebecca's B&B, 219

Aurora Gallery, 266

auto shows. See car shows

auto racing, 153, 338, 347

Autumn Glory Festival, 456

Avalon Theater, 103, 117

AYS Charters and Sailing School, 31, 255

B

B & B Yacht Charters, 124

Back Creek General Store, 161

Back Creek Inn B&B, 324–25

Bahama Mamas (Ocean City), 61

Bahia Marina, 48, 50

Baker Park, 375, 386

Bald Cypress Nature Trail, 53

bald eagles, 70, 96, 283, 339, 354, 399

Ballet Theatre of Maryland, 265

Ballindullagh Barn Antiques, 241

ballooning, 18, 229, 234, 296

Baltimore, 165, 201–30; activities, 213–16; eating, 219–25; emergencies, 205, 207; entertainment, 225–26; events, 229; information, 204; lodging, 216–19; maps, 200, 202, 206; northern suburbs, 181–99; public restrooms, 205; shopping, 226–29; sightseeing, 207–13; sports, 226; transportation, 204–5; western suburbs, 231–43

Baltimore, Lord, 245, 278, 279, 436

Baltimore and Annapolis Trail, 19, 254, 282

Baltimore & Ohio (B&O) Railroad, 31, 183, 208–9, 233, 293, 295, 437

Baltimore Area Convention and Visitors Association, 204

Baltimore Arena, 226

Baltimore Bayhawks, 226

Baltimore Beltway, 183–84, 204

Baltimore Blast, 226

Baltimore Burn, 226

Baltimore City Paper, 204

Baltimore Civil War Museum, 23, 207

460   Baltimore County Conference and Visitors Bureau, 183

Baltimore Farmer's Market, 229

Baltimore Maritime Museum, 29, 211

Baltimore Marriott Waterfront, 217

Baltimore Museum of Art, 17, 209; eating, 223–24

Baltimore Museum of Industry, 209

Baltimore Museum of Public Works, 207

Baltimore Opera Company, 225

Baltimore Oriole, 289

Baltimore Orioles, 88, 208, 211, 226, 383

Baltimore Ravens, 226

Baltimore Symphony Orchestra, 225

Baltimore Visitor Center, 204

Baltimore Zoo, 213, 229

Baltimore/Washington International Airport, 16, 104, 122, 135, 149, 167, 183, 204, 232, 248, 276, 293, 316, 334, 351, 365; lodging near, 218, 258

Baltimore-Washington Parkway, 204, 276

Bandaloops, 223

B&B Cab, 317

B&J Charters, 97

B&J Community Cabs, 351

B&O Railroad Museum (Baltimore), 31, 208–9

B&O Railroad Station (Gaithersburg), 295

B&O Railroad Station (Oakland), 436, 437

B&O Railroad Station Museum (Ellicott City), 31, 233

Bankhead, Tallulah, gravesite of, 136

Banneker-Douglass Museum, 249, 268

Barbara Fritchie House and Museum, 368–69

Barbara Fritchie Restaurant, 382

Bard's Field B&B, 342

Barn on Howard's Cove, 260

Barnes & Noble (Baltimore), 228

Barnwood Books, 409

Barrier Island Visitor Center, 42

Barton: lodging, 425

Barton, Clara, 393; National Historic Site, 296

Bart's Place, 194

baseball: Baltimore, 226; Babe Ruth Museum, 208; books about, 21; Bowie, 289; Frederick, 383; Hagerstown, 408; Salisbury, 88

Basignani Winery, 198

Basilica of the National Shrine of the Assumption, 212

Battle Creek Cypress Swamp Sanctuary, 320, 324, 331

Baugher's, 27, 194, 195, 197

Bay Bee, 50

Bay Books (California), 346

Bay Books (Prince Frederick), 330

Bay Bridge, 104, 121, 122–23; map, 120

Bay Bridge Walk, 132, 268

Bay Club (Berlin), 50

Bay Cottage (St. Michaels), 113

Bay Country Festival (Cambridge), 101

Bay Country Shop (Cambridge), 101

Bay Country Taxi (Easton), 104

Bay Front Park (Chesapeake Beach), 321

Bay Hundred (Tilghman Island), 116

Bay Sports Unlimited (Ocean City), 46

Bay Views B&B (North Beach), 324

Bay Wolf (Rock Hall), 144

Bayard House, 158–59

Bayou Restaurant (Havre de Grace), 177–78

BaySail (Havre de Grace), 31, 173

Bayside Antiques (Havre de Grace), 179

Bayside Bagels (Chestertown), 143

Bayside Boat Rentals (Ocean City), 48

Bayside Inn (Ewell), 77, 78

Bayside Skillet (Ocean City), 60

Bayview Beach House (Rock Hall), 142

Bazzel Church, 94

Beach Club Golf Links (Ocean City), 50

Beach House Restaurant (Ocean City), 63

beaches: about, 18; sea nettles, 31–32; Assateague Island, 18, 52; Betterton, 18, 138; California, 341; Chesapeake Beach, 18, 321, 323; Dameron, 341; Hollywood, 341; Kent Island, 127; North Beach, 18, 323; Ocean City, 18, 52; Public Landing, 18, 52; Purse State Park, 355; Rock Hall, 138; Salisbury, 85. See also specific beaches

Beacraft's Farm, 309

Beall-Dawson House, 296

Bean Hollow, 240

Beans, Leaves, Etc., 161

Bear Branch Nature Center, 190, 199

Bear Creek Crossing Bed and Breakfast, 448

Beards Hill Movies 7, 178

Bea's B&B, 72

Beautiful Swimmers (Warner), 24, 66

Beaver Creek Christian Church, 396

Beaver Creek Country School, 396

bed & breakfasts (B&Bs): about, 18–19.
  See also specific B&Bs and destinations
Beechtree, 171
Bel Air, 165, 167; emergencies, 168; enter-
  tainment, 178; events, 180; shopping,
  179; sights/activities, 168, 169, 174; trans-
  portation, 167
Bel Air Farmer's Market, 179
Belair Mansion and Stable Museum, 278–79
Bell Island, 83, 85
Beltsville: eating, 287; entertainment, 288;
  lodging, 285; shopping, 289
Bender's Family Restaurant, 428
Bending Water Park Living Village, 75
Benedict, 350; eating, 357
Benson-Hammond House, 251
Berlin, 39, 41; campgrounds, 57–58; eating,
  59, 62; emergencies, 43; information, 42;
  lodging, 55, 56; map, 38; shopping, 63,
  64; sights/activities, 44–45, 50–51, 52;
  transportation, 42–43
Berrywine Plantations Linganore Wine-
  cellars, 198
Bert's 50's Diner, 345
Best Western (Edgewood), 174
Best Western (Elkridge), 237
Best Western (La Plata), 356
Best Western (LaVale), 425
Best Western (Salisbury), 86
Best Western Potomac View (Oxon Hill), 286
Bethesda, 291–309; campgrounds, 303; eat-
  ing, 303–6; emergencies, 294; entertainment, 306; events, 309; information, 293;
  lodging, 302–3; map, 292; shopping,
  306–9; sights/activities, 294–302; trans-
  portation, 293–94
Bethesda Academy of Performing Arts, 306
Bethesda Court Hotel, 302
Bethesda Trolley, 294
Betterton, 134; events, 146; lodging, 140
Betterton Beach, 18, 138; Day and Parade,
  146
bicycling: about, 19; Annapolis, 254; Baltimore, 213; Baltimore and Annapolis
  Trail, 19, 254, 282; Baltimore north, 19,
  187, 189; Bethesda, 296, 298; Brunswick,
  372–73; Calvert County, 320; Cambridge,
  96; C&O Canal, 19, 296, 372–73, 398,
  419; Carroll County, 19, 187, 189;
  Charles County, 353; Chestertown, 137;
  College Park, 282; Columbia, 235; Cum-
  berland, 419–20; Deep Creek Lake, 19,
  439; Dorchester County, 96; Eldersburg,
  187; Frederick, 372–73; Hancock, 398;
  Ocean City, 47; Rockville, 19, 296, 298;
  St. Mary's County, 339; St. Michaels, 106;
  Salisbury, 84; Silver Spring, 19, 296, 298;
  Smith Island, 77; Somerset County, 19,
  70; Tilghman Island, 106; Waldorf, 353;
  Western Maryland Rail Trail, 19, 398
Biederlack of America, 25, 432
Big Dipper, 408
Big Elk Creek Covered Bridge, 23, 150
Big Hunting Creek, 376, 377
Big Mario's Sport Center, 107
Big Pool, 395–96, 398; campgrounds, 405
Big Run, 441
Big Run State Park, 450
Big Savage Hiking Trail, 442–43
Bike Doctor, 353
biking. *See* bicycling
Bill's Marine Service, 439
Billy Goat Trail, 299
birdwatching: about, 19–20, 22, 399; books,
  21; Baltimore, 215–16; Blackwater, 19,
  96, 98; Buckeystown, 371; Cambridge,
  19, 96, 98; Chevy Chase, 20, 302; Col-
  lege Park, 19, 283, 284, 285; Cranesville
  Swamp, 20, 445; Deal Island, 19, 70;
  Eastern Neck, 19, 139; Eastern Neck
  National Wildlife Refuge, 19, 139; Easton, 108, 110; Finzel Swamp, 20, 445;
  Kennedyville, 138; Kent Island, 30, 126;
  Lonaconing, 420; Merkle Wildlife Sanc-
  tuary, 19, 284; Pickering Creek, 20, 108,
  110; Salisbury, 84; Sandy Point State
  Park, 19, 257; Thurmont, 377; Woodend,
  20, 302
Bishop's House (Easton), 112
Bishopville, 51
Bistro St. Michaels, 114
Black Bear Tavern, 454
Black Bird Mysteries, 409
Black Box Theatre, 241–42
Black Olive, 221
Black Rock, 399
Black Walnut Point Inn, 113
Black-eyed Susan, 143
Blackwater National Wildlife Refuge,
  19, 96, 98
Blake, Eubie: National Museum and
  Cultural Center, 210
Blessing of the Fleet, 347
Blue Agave, 222–23

Blue and Gray Days, 347
Blue Crab Coffee Co., 117
blue crabs. *See* crabs
Blue Heron Bed and Breakfast (Solomons), 325
Blue Heron Café (Chestertown), 142
Blue Heron Golf Course (Stevensville), 125
Blue Max Inn, 156
Blue Ridge Mountains, 391–411; activities, 398–403; campgrounds, 405; information, 392; map, 390
Blue Ridge Summit Overlook, 377
blues festivals, 410, 433
Bo Brooks, 224
Boardwalk Lounge (Deep Creek Lake), 454
Boat Bumm's International Cardboard Boat Races, 119
boat excursions: Annapolis, 253, 254; Baltimore, 214; Cambridge, 96–97; Havre de Grace, 171; Hurlock, 97; Kent Island, 124; Ocean City, 48; St. Clement's Island, 335–36; St. Michaels, 106; Solomons, 318, 320; Tilghman Island, 106. *See also* skipjacks
Boat Parades, 132, 146, 269
boat ramps: about, 20
boatbuilding school, in Havre de Grace, 20, 169, 171
boating: about, 20; Annapolis, 254; Baltimore, 214; Chestertown, 137; Clarksburg, 301; Columbia, 235; Deep Creek Lake, 438, 439–40; Elkton, 153; Kent Island, 125; La Plata, 353; Marbury, 355; Ocean City, 48; Rock Hall, 137; Rockville, 301–2; Solomons, 320; Thayerville, 439–40; Tilghman Island, 107. *See also* canoeing; ferries; kayaking; sailing
Boatyard Bar and Grill (Eastport), 262
Bohemia Value, 432
Bohrer Park, 299, 300–301
Bollman Truss Railroad Bridge, 234, 242
Bolton Hill: lodging, 219
Bomboy's Homemade Ice Cream, 27, 178
Bon Vivant, 266
Bonifant Books, Records & CDs, 308
Book Center (Cumberland), 431
Book Center (Frederick), 384
Book Festival (Mount Vernon), 229
Book Market and Antique Mezzanine (Oakland), 455
Bookoo Books for Kids, 308
books, recommended, 20–21

Bookseller's Antiques (North East), 161
bookstores: Annapolis, 267; Baltimore, 228; Bethesda, 307–8; Boonsboro, 409; California, 346; Chestertown, 146; Columbia, 242; Cumberland, 431; Deep Creek Lake, 455; Easton, 118; Ellicott City, 242; Frederick, 384; Hagerstown, 409; Havre de Grace, 179; Kensington, 307–8; Lexington Park, 346; North East, 161; Oakland, 455; Prince Frederick, 330; St. Charles, 358–59; St. Michaels, 118; Salisbury, 89; Snow Hill, 63; Waldorf, 358–59; Westminster, 196–97
Boonsboro, 392; campgrounds, 405; eating, 406; shopping, 409; sights/activities, 393, 398, 400, 402
Boonsborough Museum of History, 393
Boordy Vineyards, 198
Booth, John Wilkes, 242, 277, 350, 351–52, 437
Bounty Hunter, 254
Bowes Books, 346
Bowie, 275, 278–79; eating, 288; entertainment, 288, 289; lodging, 286; map, 275; shopping, 289
Bowie Baysox, 289
Bowie Taxi, 366
Bowles Farm Corn, 335–36
bowling: Aberdeen, 171; Easton, 107; Huntingtown, 320; Waldorf, 353
Boxwood Garden, 71
Boyds, 300, 301
Braddock, Edward, 29, 391, 413, 417
Brandywine, 283, 290; campgrounds, 286
Brannock Maritime Museum, 28, 93–94
Brantwood, 154
Breathe Deep Scuba, 444
Breezy Point, 320, 321, 323
Breezy Point Beach and Campground, 321, 323
Breton Bay Golf and County Club, 340
Brew River Restaurant and Bar, 87
Brewer's Alley, 381
Briars Antiques, 307
Brick Ridge, 194
bridges, covered, 23, 150–51, 170, 367
Broadford Lake, 438, 443
Brome-Howard Inn, 342, 344
Brookeville: lodging, 303; shopping, 306–7
Brooks Barrel Co., 95
Brooks Hill, 370
Brookside Gardens, 301

Broomes Island: eating, 327
Browning, Meshach, 435, 437
Brunswick: campgrounds, 379; events, 386; sights/activities, 367, 372–73; transportation, 365–66
Brunswick Family Campground, 379
Brunswick Railroad Museum, 31, 367, 372, 386
Brush Tunnel, 422
Bryantown, 350; lodging, 356; sights/activities, 352
Buckeystown, 365; eating, 380; lodging, 378; shopping, 385; sights/activities, 371
Budds Creek, 338, 347
Buddy's Crabs and Ribs, 262–63
Bulle Rock, 171
Bunky's Charter Boats, 321
Burley House, 41, 52
Burton Ave. Gallery, 74
bus service: about, 21–22. *See also* specific destinations
Butler's Orchards, 308
Buzzard Rocks, 236

C

C. William Gilchrist Gallery, 431
Cabin Fever Festival, 385–86
Cabin John Regional Park, 300, 303
Cactus Taverna, 87
Caddy Shack, 73–74
Cadwalader, John, gravesite of, 136
Café de Paris, 287
Café des Artistes, 345
Café Tattoo, 225
Calico Gallery, 119
California, 334; beach, 341; eating, 343, 344, 345–46; shopping, 346, 347
California Farmer's Market, 347
Calloway, Cab, 210
Calvary United Methodist Church, 170
Calvert, George: Riversdale Mansion, 278
Calvert Artists Showcase, 331
Calvert Cliffs State Park, 18, 320, 322; lodging, 324
Calvert Country Market, 330–31
Calvert County, 315–31
Calvert County Cultural Arts Council, 330
Calvert County Department of Economic Development, 316, 320, 321
Calvert County Fair, 331
Calvert County Jousting Tournament, 331

Calvert County Public Transportation, 316, 317
Calvert Marine Museum, 17, 28, 318, 320
Calvert Memorial Hospital, 317
Calvert Taxi, 317
Cambridge, 91–101; eating, 99–100; emergencies, 93; entertainment, 100; events, 101; information, 92–93; lodging, 98–99; map, 92; public restrooms, 93; shopping, 100–101; sights/activities, 93–98; transportation, 93
Cambridge Diner, 100
Cambridge Dorchester Airport, 93
Cambridge House, 98
Cambridge Lady, 96–97
Cambridge Scenic Drive, 96
Camden Yards, 226, 229; Sports Legends at, 208
Camp Merryelande, 343
campgrounds: about, 22; Annapolis, 261; Assateague Island, 22, 57–58; Bethesda, 303; Big Pool, 405; Boonsboro, 405; Brunswick, 379; Callaway, 343; Carroll County, 192; Catoctin Mountain Park, 22, 379; Deep Creek Lake, 451; Drayden, 343; Elkton, 158; Ellicott City, 238; Flintstone, 426–27; Frederick, 379; Friendsville, 450; Gapland, 405; Grantsville, 450; Greenbelt Park, 22, 286; Hancock, 405; Havre de Grace, 172; Kent Island, 127; Leonardtown, 343; Little Orleans, 427; Ocean City, 57; Perryville, 158; Port Tobacco, 356; Rockville, 303; St. George Island, 343; St. Leonard, 325; Salisbury, 86–87; Snow Hill, 58; Somerset County, 72–73; Thurmont, 379–80; Whaleyville, 57; Williamsport, 405; Woodbine, 192, 238
Campus Hills Cinema 7, 178
Canal Clipper, 20, 298
Canal Creamery, 27, 161
Canal Place (Cumberland), 415, 417, 419, 432
Canalfest (Cumberland), 432
C&D Canal. *See* Chesapeake & Delaware Canal
candlelight tours: Annapolis, 269; Chestertown, 146; Frederick, 386; Havre de Grace, 180
C&O Bicycle, 398
C&O Canal. *See* Chesapeake & Ohio Canal
Candy Kitchen (Frederick), 382

Candy Kitchens (Ocean City), 62
Cannon Hill Place, 384
Canoe on the Run (McHenry), 452
canoeing: about, 28; Annapolis, 255; Boonsboro, 400; Cambridge, 97, 101; College Park, 284; Crisfield, 70–71; Deep Creek Lake, 438, 443; Elkton, 153; Kent Island, 125; Knoxville, 33, 374–75; Nanjemoy Creek, 354; Ocean City, 48, 51; Rock Hall, 137; Rockville, 300; Solomons, 320, 321; Tilghman Island, 107, 109; White's Ferry, 300
Cantler's Riverside Inn, 264
Canton, 205, 216; shopping, 224
Canton Row (St. Michaels), 117
Canvasback Restaurant and Irish Pub, 99
Cape May (New Jersey)–Lewes (Delaware) Ferry, 25, 42
Capital Beltway, 276, 294
Capital City Brewing Company, 224
Capital Crescent Trail, 19, 296
Capital KOA, 261
Capital Region, 271–309; map, 272
Captain Bob Ritchie, 137
Captain Bruce Wooten, 50
Captain Clyde's Charters, 255
Captain Don Marani, 215
Captain Gary Sacks, 340
Captain Greg Jetton, 137
Captain Jason, 77, 78
Captain Jerry's, 288
Captain John's Crab House, 357
Captain Larry Simns, 137
Captain Marc Van Pelt, 137
Captain Mike Gerek, 340
Captain Mike Shaw, 321
Captain Randy Powers, 340
Captain Smith's Seafood Market, 329
Captain Tyler, 77
Captain's Galley (West Ocean City), 62
Captain's Galley Restaurant (Crisfield), 73
Captains Joe and John Asanovich, 70
Captain's Ketch Seafood, 116
Captain's Wheel, 118
Captiva, 124
car shows, 199, 269, 309, 347, 433
car travel: highway travel, 26; National Road: about, 29; scenic byways: about, 31. See also specific destinations
Cardboard Boat Races, 119
Caribbean Bar and Grill, 62
Carmel Cove, 448

Carolina Trailways, 21, 42, 68, 81, 93, 122–23
Carousel Stained Glass, 197
Carriage House Inn (Emmitsburg), 381
Carroll Arts Center, 196, 198–99
Carroll Community College, 199
Carroll County, 181–99
Carroll County 4-H and FFA Fair, 199
Carroll County Arts Council Gallery, 18
Carroll County Department of Enterprise and Recreation Services, 189
Carroll County Farm Museum, 186, 187, 199
Carroll County Farmer's Market, 197
Carroll County Historical Society, 184
Carroll County Office of Tourism, 183
Carroll County Visitor Center, 183, 186–87
Carroll Hospital Center, 184
Carroll (Charles) House, 250–51
Carroll Kennel Club All-Breed Dog Show, 199
Carrolltown Movies 6, 195
Carrol's Creek, 262
Cascade Falls, 236
Cascade Lake, 187
Casselman Inn, 436, 446, 452
Casselman River Bridge, 439
Casselman Valley Farm Bed & Breakfast, 448–49
Castle B&B, The (Mount Savage), 426
Catalpa Grove Farms, 89
Catoctin Inn and Conference Center, 378
Catoctin Iron Furnace, 370
Catoctin Mountain Orchard, 385
Catoctin Mountain Park, 30, 32, 374, 377; campground, 22, 379
Catoctin Mountains, 363–86; map, 362
Catoctin Pottery, 385
Catoctin Trail, 374, 377
Catoctin Wildlife Preserve and Zoo, 372
Cavetown, 410
CD Café, 327–28
C&D Canal. See Chesapeake & Delaware Canal
Cecil Community College Cultural Center, 161
Cecil County, 147–62
Cecil County Dragway, 153
Cecil County Fair, 162
Cecil County Historical Society, 151
Cecil County Tourism, 148, 149

Cecil's Country Store, 347
Cecil's Old Mill, 346
Cedarville State Forest, 283, 286
Celie's, 219
Celtic Festival of Southern Maryland, 331
Centennial Park, 235
CenterStage, 226
Central Light Rail Line, 184
central Maryland, 163–269; map, 164
Central Maryland Heritage League, 368
Centre at Salisbury, 89
Centreville, 122; eating, 129; events, 132; shopping, 131; sights/activities, 123; transportation, 122–23, 123
Chanceford Hall, 56–57
Chaptico, 336, 340
Charles Carroll House, 250–51
Charles County, 349–59
Charles County Department of Community Services, 351
Charles County Fair, 359
Charles County Visitors Bureau, 350, 351, 353
Charles Theater, 225
Charleston, 220
Charlotte Hall, 334, 336; events, 348; shopping, 347
charter boats. *See* fishing
Charter Day Celebration, 359
Chase-Lloyd House, 250
Checker Cab, 205, 248
Cheesecake Factory, 224
Cherry Beach, 85
Cherry Hill Orchard, 289
Cherry Hill Park, 286
Chesapeake, 211
Chesapeake & Delaware (C&D) Canal, 147–49, 162, 167; Museum, 149, 151
Chesapeake & Ohio (C&O) Canal, 23, 295, 364, 392, 413, 417–18; bicycling, 19, 296, 372–73, 398, 419; boat excursions, 20, 298; books about, 21; campgrounds, 22, 405; Canalfest, 432; cross-country skiing, 32; hiking, 299, 420; kayaking and canoeing, 300
Chesapeake & Ohio (C&O) Canal National Historical Park, 23, 295; bicycling, 19, 372–73, 398, 419; Cumberland Visitors Center, 418–19
Chesapeake & Ohio (C&O) Canal Visitor Centers, 295, 373, 398, 418–19
Chesapeake Antique Center, 131

Chesapeake Art Auction, 132
Chesapeake Bay, 22–23, 37, 76, 147, 313, 315, 333; along the shore, 315–31; head of the, 147–62; maps, 148, 314
Chesapeake Bay: Nature of an Estuary (White), 21
Chesapeake Bay, Susquehanna River and Tidal Tributaries Public Access Guide, 20
Chesapeake Bay Critical Area Driving Tour, 282
Chesapeake Bay Environmental Center, 20, 126, 132
Chesapeake Bay Gateways Network, 23
Chesapeake Bay Golf Club North East, 154
Chesapeake Bay Golf Club Rising Sun, 154
Chesapeake Bay Maritime Museum, 28, 103, 105, 118
Chesapeake Bay Program, 20
Chesapeake Beach, 315–16; beaches, 18, 321, 323; eating, 328–29; events, 331; information, 316; map, 314; public restrooms, 317; sights/activities, 317, 319, 320, 321; transportation, 316–17
Chesapeake Beach Railway Museum, 317
Chesapeake Beach Water Park, 320
Chesapeake Biological Laboratory Visitor Center, 319
Chesapeake Carousel, 282
Chesapeake City, 147–49; eating, 158–61; emergencies, 150; events, 162; information, 149; lodging, 156–58; public restrooms, 150; shopping, 161; sights/activities, 151, 152–53; transportation, 149–50
Chesapeake College, 132
Chesapeake East Handmade Ceramics, 89
Chesapeake Exploration Center, 122
Chesapeake Farms, 136
Chesapeake Gallery and Frame Shop, 161
Chesapeake Hills, 321
Chesapeake Horse Country Tours, 152–53
Chesapeake Inn, 159
Chesapeake Marketplace, 330
Chesapeake Trading Co., 118
Chesapeake Wildlife Showcase, 90
Chesapeake Wood Duck Inn, 113
Chesapeake Wooden Boat Builders School, 20, 169, 171
Chester, 122, 125
Chester River, 133, 135, 137, 138, 146
Chester River Artworks, 145
Chester River Boat Rental, 137

Chester River Kayak Adventures, 137
Chester River Wildlife Exhibition and Sale, 146
Chester Theatres, 145
Chestertown, 133–46; eating, 142–45; emergencies, 123, 135; entertainment, 145; events, 146; information, 134; lodging, 140–42; map, 134; public restrooms, 135; shopping, 145–46; sights/activities, 135–39; transportation, 135
Chestertown Antique and Furniture Center, 145
Chestertown Arts League, 145
Chestertown Farmer's Market, 146
Chestertown Natural Foods, 144
Chestertown Tea Party, 146
Chestertown Used Bookstore, 146
Cheverly, 289; emergencies, 276
Chevy Chase, 302, 309; eating, 303, 305
Chez Amis, 259
Chiapparelli's, 222
Chick and Ruth's Deli, 263
children, especially for, 23. See also specific sights and destinations
Children's Imagination Garden, 110
Children's Museum, Discovery Center, 297
Children's Museum of Rose Hill Manor Park, 373
Children's Spring Party and Easter Egg Hunt, 359
Chimney Rock Trail, 377
China Chef, 73
Chincoteague National Wildlife Refuge, 30, 40, 41, 65
Chincoteague Volunteer Fire Department, 41
Chocolate Festival, 229
Choptank and Tuckahoe Rivers Water Trail, 125
Choptank River, 91, 93, 96–97, 127; fishing, 50, 125; kayaking, 125
Choptank River Queen, 97
Choreographers' Showcase, 290
Christ Church (Cambridge), 94
Christ Church (Chaptico), 336
Christ Church (Columbia), 241
Christ Church (Easton), 106
Christ Church (La Plata), 352
Christ Church (Nanjemoy), 359
Christ Church (Port Republic), 319
Christ Church (Stevensville), 123

Christmas Garden of Trains (Cambridge), 101
Christmas in St. Michaels, 119
Christmas trees, 242, 308, 385
Christmas Walk in Solomons, 331
Church Creek, 91, 94, 97
Church Hill, 122, 123–24; entertainment, 131
Church Hill Theatre, 131
Church Home Hospital, 207
Churchville: sights/activities, 170, 171
Churchville Golf and Baseball, 171
Churchville Recreation Complex, 173–74
Cineplex Odeon (Bethesda), 306
Circle Inn Restaurant, 73
Circle R Ranch, 443
City Lights, 222, 428
Civil War, 21, 186–87, 341, 368–69, 372, 391, 393, 394, 399, 404, 405; about, 23; Antietam National Battlefield, 23, 368, 396–97, 411; Baltimore Civil War Museum, 23, 207; Frederick County driving tour, 368; Monocacy National Battlefield, 23, 368, 369–70; National Museum of Civil War Medicine, 23, 368; reenactments, 132, 347, 386
Civil War Driving Trail, 23
Civil War Medical Seminar, 309
Civil War Military Museum (McMahon's Mill), 405
Civilian Conservation Corps Museum, 395–96
Civista Medical Hospital, 351
Claddaugh Farm, 141
Clarice Smith Performing Arts Center, 275, 277, 288, 290
Clarke's Landing, 344
Clarksburg, 293; campgrounds, 303; sights/activities, 299, 301
Clarksville Inn, 237
Classic Car Show, 309
Claude M. Potterfield Municipal Pool, 401
Clayton Fine Books, 228
Clear Spring, 394; shopping, 409
Clements, 335–36
Cliff House (Calvert Cliffs), 324
climate: about, 33
Clinton: eating, 287; emergencies, 276; lodging, 286; shopping, 289; sights/activities, 277, 279
Clipper City, 214
Clopper Lake, 299

Cloud Dancer, 46
Club 24/Embers Nightclub, 62
Clustered Spires, 373
Clyburn Arboretum, 19, 215–16
Clyde's, 239
C&O Canal. *See* Chesapeake & Ohio Canal
Cobb Island: eating, 357
Cobb Island Day, 359
Cobblestone Alley, 455
Cochran, William M., 371–72
Cockeysville, 181, 190–91
Coffee, Tea and Whimsey, 330
Coffee East (Easton), 116
Cohill Manor, 403–4
Coldwell Banker (Ocean City), 57
Coldwell Banker Deep Creek Realty
  Rentals, 450
College of Southern Maryland, 351
College Park, 275–90; campgrounds, 286;
  eating, 287–88; entertainment, 288–89;
  events, 290; lodging, 285–86; map, 274;
  shopping, 289–90; sights/activities,
  276–85; transportation, 276
College Park Airport, 277
College Park Aviation Museum, 277
College Park Farmer's Market, 289
Colonial Courthouse (Queenstown), 123
Colonial Players (Annapolis), 266
Colony South Hotel and Conference
  Center, 286, 287
Columbia, 231–32; eating, 239; emergen-
  cies, 233; entertainment, 240–41; events,
  243; lodging, 237, 238; shopping, 241,
  242; sights/activities, 233, 235; transpor-
  tation, 232–33
Columbia Association Welcome Center, 235
Columbia Festival of the Arts, 243
Columbia Orchestra, 240–41
Combsberry, 112
Comfort Inn (Baltimore), 218
Comfort Inn (Edgewood), 174
Comfort Inn (Grasonville), 128
Comfort Inn (Salisbury), 86
Comfort Suites (Laurel), 285
Comfort Suites (Linthicum), 258
Comfort Suites (Waldorf), 356
Commodore Joshua Barney House, 237–38
Commodore's Cottage (Cambridge), 99
Common Ground on the Hill, 184, 195
Community Bridge Mural, 371–72
Compleat Bookseller, 146

Compton, 336
Concord Point Lighthouse, 28, 170, 174
Conococheague Creek, 397, 405
Conrad-Miller Studios and Gallery, 227
Constellation, USS, 203, 211
Contemporary Museum (Mount Vernon),
  210
Corks, 221
corn mazes, 162, 309, 339–40
Cornish Manor, 451
Cosca Regional Park, 286
Costen House, 45
Cottages of Governors Run, 325
Country Angel, The, 431
Country House and Country Village (Salis-
  bury), 89
Country Peddler Show (Frederick), 386
County Comfort Farm, 109
Court House Cafe (Snow Hill), 61
Courtney's, 345
Courtyard Book Shop (Havre de Grace),
  179
Courtyard by Marriott (Annapolis), 258
Courtyard by Marriott (Baltimore), 218
Courtyard by Marriott (Frederick), 377
Courtyard by Marriott (Silver Spring), 303
Cove Point Lighthouse, 28, 318
Covered Bridge Theatre Company, 161
covered bridges, 23, 150–51, 170, 367
Cox's Cab, 150
Cozy Country Inn and Restaurant (Thur-
  mont), 377–78, 382
Cozy Village (Thurmont), 385
Crab Alley (Ocean City), 61–62
Crab Claw, The (St. Michaels), 116
Crab Days (St. Michaels), 119
Crab Feast (Annapolis), 268
Crab Festival (Hollywood), 347
Crab Shanty (Ellicott City), 239–40
crabbing, 24, 136; Edgewater, 268; Grason-
  ville, 124; Kent Island, 125; North Beach,
  323; Ocean City, 48; St. Michaels, 119;
  Stevensville, 155; Wye Mills, 125
crabcakes, 24; recipe for, 329
Crabknockers Seafood Market, 345
crabs: about, 22, 23–24; recipe for steamed,
  346; Annapolis, 264; Baltimore, 224;
  Berlin, 62; Cambridge, 100; Chesapeake
  Beach, 328–29; Cobb Island, 357; College Park, 288; Crisfield, 74–75; Drayden,
  345; Eldersburg, 194; Kent Island, 130;

Continued

Continued from previous page

Laurel, 288; North East, 160; Ocean City, 61–62; Port of Crisfield walking tour, 70; Rock Hall, 144; St. Michaels, 116, 119; Salisbury, 87–88; Smith Island, 76, 78; Westminster, 194
Cracker Jacks, 118
Craig's Drug Store, 101
Crain Memorial Welcome Center, 350–51
Cranesville Swamp, 20, 445
Crazy Swede, 176, 177
Crimson Stables, 137
Crisfield, 66; campgrounds, 72; eating, 73; emergencies, 68; events, 74–75; lodging, 72; shopping, 74; sights/activities, 68–71; transportation, 68, 77
Crisfield Seafood Restaurant, 305–6
Crisfield Trolley, 68, 70
Cross Island Trail (Kent Island), 128
cross-country skiing, 32, 190, 374, 377, 400, 444, 445, 456
Crossing at Casey Jones, 356–57
Crown Theaters of Annapolis, 265
Crownsville, 255; events, 268, 269
Crow's Nest Campground, 379–80
cruises. See boat excursions
Crumpton: shopping, 131
Crystal Beach (Earleville), 155
Crystal Beach Hotel (Ocean City), 54
Crystal Grottoes Caverns, 398
Crystal Inn (North East), 156
Cumberland, 389, 413–14; eating, 427, 428, 430; emergencies, 416; entertainment, 430–31; events, 432–33; information, 415; lodging, 424, 425–26; map, 412; shopping, 431, 432; sights/activities, 416–23; transportation, 415–16
Cumberland Antique Mall, 431
Cumberland Celtic Fest, 433
Cumberland Downtown Farmer's Market, 432
Cumberland Memorial Hospital, 416
Cumberland Theatre, 430
Cumberland Valley Artists' Exhibit, 410
Cumberland Visitors Center, 418–19
Cumberland Wine and Music Festival, 433
Cunningham Falls State Park, 32, 374, 376; campgrounds, 380
curling, 107
Currier House, 176
Curtis's Famous Wieners, 428

Cycles and Things (Cumberland), 419
cycling. See bicycling
Cygnet House, 113
Cygnus Wine Cellars, 198

D

Da Mimmo Ristorante, 220
Daedalus Books, 242
Daffodil Show, 74
Dahlgren Hall Ice Rink, 256
Daily Grind, The, 224
Dalesio's, 220
Dameron, 341, 345
dance, 265, 288, 290
Dancing Bear, 385
Daniels Dam, 236
Dan's Mountain State Park, 420, 423
Dan's Rock, 419
Dart Cab, 123
Dave and Buster's, 305
Davis Planetarium, 207–8
Davis Warner Inn, 303
Dawson Gallery, 266
Day Basket Factory, 161–62
Days Inn (Annapolis), 258
Days Inn (Baltimore), 218
Days Inn (Waldorf), 356
Dayton's, 87
Deal Island, 66
Deal Island Harbor, 75
Deal Island Wildlife Management Area, 19, 70
Deale, 247; eating, 264–65; events, 269; shopping, 268
Deale Bluegrass Festival and Car Show, 269
Deale Farmer's Market, 268
Declaration of Independence, 201, 234, 245, 250, 352
decoy carving, 24, 65, 69, 83, 84, 90, 147, 151, 166, 168, 180
Deep Creek Brewing Company, 452
Deep Creek Cellars, 455–56
Deep Creek Lake, 435–56; activities, 19, 32, 437–46; information, 436–37; map, 434; transportation, 437
Deep Creek Lake State Park, 444, 446; cabin rentals, 450; campgrounds, 451; Discovery Center at, 441
Deep Creek Marina, 440
Deep Creek Sailing School, 31, 443
Deer Creek, 172, 173, 174

Deer Park, 436; eating, 451; lodging, 447–48
Deer Park Inn, 447–48, 451
Delaplaine Visual Arts Education Center, 384
Delaware: ferry, 25, 42
Delmar: campgrounds, 87; information, 79; sights/activities, 85
Delmarva: use of term, 24
Delmarva Shorebirds, 88
Dennis and Philip Ratner Museum, 294–95
Dennis Point Marina and Campground, 343, 345
Dennisons Trackside Hobbies, 64
Dent Chapel, 336
Denton, 125, 127
Derwood, 303, 309
Diamond Cab, 205
Dickerson, 374; shopping, 384
DiGiovanni's Dock of the Bay, 326
Discover Dorchester, 94
Discovery Center Children's Museum, 297
Dixon's Furniture, 131
Dr. Samuel A. Mudd House, 351–52
Doctor's Community Hospital (Lanham), 276
Dodson's on Mill Creek, 329
dog-paw symbol: about, 30
dogsledding, 440
Doll Shop (Kensington), 307
Doll Show and Sale (Savage Mill), 242
Dollar Cab, 167
Donald's Duck Shoppe and Gallery, 63
Doncaster State Forest, 354
Donna's Café and Coffee Bar, 223
Dorchester Art Center, 100–101
Dorchester Arts Showcase, 101
Dorchester County, 91–101
Dorchester County Department of Tourism, 92–93, 96
Dorchester County Historical Society, 94
Dorchester County Public Pool, 97
Dorchester General Hospital, 93
Dorchester Heritage Museum, 94, 101
Dorothy & Megan, 97
Dorsey Chapel, 281
Dottie's Fountain and Grill, 453
Double G RV Park, 451
Doubletree Club Hotel (Largo), 286
Dough Roller, 60–61
Douglass, Frederick, 215, 247; Museum and Cultural Center, 251

Dove, 333, 337, 352
Downs Memorial Park, 257
Downtown Deli (Salisbury), 88
DP Cab, 167
Drane House, 437
Drayden, 343, 345
Dream Weavers Antiques, 454
Druid Hill Park, 213, 216
Drum Point Lighthouse, 28, 318
Drummer's Café, 59
Drusilla's Books, 228
Dry Dock Restaurant, 326
Duck Fair, 180
Duck Soup Books and Gifts, 64
Dudley's Chapel, 124
Dulles International Airport, 16, 293, 365
Dumser's Dairyland Drive-In, 27, 62
Duncan's Family Campground, 261
Dunes Manor Hotel, 54, 59
Dunes Motel, 54
Dunkirk, 321; eating, 329; emergencies, 317
Dunkirk Medical Center, 317
Dunkirk Seafood Market, 329
Durding's Store, 145
Durham Parish Festival, 359
Dutch Family Deli, 144
Duvall Tool Museum, 277
Dwight D. Eisenhower Golf Course, 255

E

Eagle's Landing, 50
Earleville, 152; beach, 155
Earthworks Festival, 199
East Coast Jazz Festival, 309
East New Market, 92
Easter Arts and Crafts and Kids Fair, 65
Easter Egg Hunts, 132, 242, 359
Eastern Neck National Wildlife Refuge, 19, 139
Eastern Shore, 35–162; map, 36. See also specific destinations
Eastern Shore Chamber Music Festival, 119
Eastern Shore Life Museum, 123
Easton, 103–19; eating, 114, 116, 117; emergencies, 105; entertainment, 117; events, 119; information, 104; lodging, 110–11, 112; map, 102; shopping, 117–18, 119; sights/activities, 105–10; transportation, 104
Easton Airport, 110

470

INDEX

Easton Aviation, 110
Easton Bowling Center, 107
Easton Business Management Authority, 117
Easton Club, 108
Easton Farmer's Market, 119
Easton Historical Society Museum, 105
Easton Point Marina, 109
Eastport, 247, 256; eating, 262–63; events, 269; lodging, 261
Eastport Yacht Club Lights Parade, 269
Ed Kane's Water Taxi, 205, 211
Eden Mill Park and Nature Center, 174
Edge at the Lighthouse, 55
Edgewater: eating, 264; events, 268; sights/activities, 251–52, 254–55, 257
Edgewood: eating, 178; lodging, 174; shopping, 179; transportation, 167
Edgewood Farmer's Market, 179
Edison, Thomas, 209, 435
1800s Festival (Fairmont), 74
1876 House (Oxford), 112
Eldersburg, 187; eating, 194; entertainment, 195
Elizabeth S, 321
Elk Forge B&B Inn and Retreat, 157
Elk Landing, 154
Elk Mills: lodging, 157
Elk Neck State Park, 28, 156, 158; hiking, 154–55
Elk River, 154–55, 158
Elk River Outfitters, 153
Elk Run Vineyards, 198
Elkridge, 232, 235; eating, 238–39; lodging, 237; shopping, 241
Elkridge Furnace Inn, 238–39
Elkton, 147, 149; campgrounds, 158; eating, 158–59; emergencies, 150; events, 162; lodging, 156, 157, 158; shopping, 161, 162; sights/activities, 151, 153–56; transportation, 149
Elkton Arts Center, 18, 161, 162
Elkton Club at Patriot's Glen, 154
Ella Fitzgerald Performing Arts Center, 68
Ellen's, 143–44
Ellicott, William, 234
Ellicott City, 231; eating, 238–40; entertainment, 240–41; events, 242–43; information, 232; lodging, 237–38; parking, 233; shopping, 241–42; sights/activities, 233–36; transportation, 232–33

Ellicott City B&O Railroad Station Museum, 31, 233
Ellicott City's Country Store, 241
Ellie's Paperback Shack, 359
Elliott House Victorian Inn, 448
Elm's Beach, 341
Embassy Theatre, 430–31
emergencies, 24–25. See also specific destinations
Emmanuel Episcopal Church (Chestertown), 136
Emmanuel Episcopal Church (Cumberland), 418
Emmitsburg, 364; eating, 381; information, 365; sights/activities, 371; transportation, 365–66
Emporium Antiques (Frederick), 384
Englander's Antique Mall, 455
England's Colony on the Bay, 161
Enterprise Golf Course, 283
Equiery, The, 27
Erickson's Farm, 131
ESPN Zone, 221–22
Esther Prangley Rice Gallery, 184, 196
Evangelical Lutheran Church (Frederick), 370
Evangelical Reformed Church (Frederick), 370
Evans Seafood, 345
Evening of Wine and Jazz (Havre de Grace), 180
events: about, 25. See also specific events and destinations
Everedy Square, 385
Evergreen House, 211
Ewell, 76; eating, 78; information, 76; lodging, 77–78; shopping, 78; sights/activities, 77; transportation, 77
Ewell Tide Inn, 77–78
Expanding Horizons, 455
Exploring the Chesapeake in Small Boats (Williams and Portlock), 28
Express Royale, 106

F

factory outlets, 25; Cumberland, 432; Hagerstown, 410; Kent Island, 131; Ocean City, 64; Perryville, 162; Salisbury, 89
Fager's Island Restaurant, 58
Fair Hill Fairgrounds, 162

Fair Hill Inn, 159
Fair Hill Natural Resources Management Area, 150, 155–56, 162
Fair Hill Race Track, 162
Fair Hill Stables, 155
Fairfield Inn (Beltsville), 285
Fairmont Academy, 74
Fairview Information Center, 316
Fall Crafts Festival (Crownsville), 269
Fall Festival (Sykesville), 199
Fall Harvest Days (Sykesville), 199
Falling Branch, 32, 173
Fallingers Hotel Gunter, 424–25
Falls Road Golf Course, 299
families, especially for, 23. *See also* specific sights and destinations
Family Recreation Park (Boonsboro), 398
Family Skating Center (Hagerstown), 401
Family Wildlife Art Festival (Fort Washington), 290
Fantasy Flights, 18, 296
Farm Heritage Days (Woodstock), 243
Farm Museum Spring Festival (Frederick), 386
farmer's markets, 25; Annapolis, 268; Baltimore, 229; Bel Air, 179; Berlin, 64; California, 347; Carroll County, 197; Charlotte Hall, 347; Chestertown, 146; College Park, 289; Cumberland, 432; Easton, 119; Edgewood, 179; Frederick, 385; Frostburg, 432; Gaithersburg, 308; Hagerstown, 410; Havre de Grace, 179; Indian Head, 359; La Plata, 359; LaVale, 432; Oakland, 455; Pocomoke City, 64; Rockville, 308; Salisbury, 89; Silver Spring, 308
farms (pick-your-own), 30–31; Annapolis, 268; Buckeystown, 385; Cavetown, 410; Clinton, 289–90; Elkton, 162; Ellicott City, 242; Germantown, 308; Kent Island, 131; La Plata, 359; New Midway, 385; Newark, 64; Poolesville, 308; Rehobeth, 74; Salisbury, 89; Silver Spring, 309; Thurmont, 385; Westminster, 197–98; Whiteford, 179; Woodbine, 242
Farquhar Gallery, 295
Federal Hill, 203, 209; activities, 213, 216; eating, 221, 222–23; events, 229; lodging, 219; shopping, 226–27, 228; transportation, 204, 205
FedEx Field, 289

Fell's Point, 203, 209–10; activities, 215; eating, 220–21, 224; entertainment, 225–26; events, 229; information, 204; lodging, 218–19; shopping, 226, 227, 228
Fell's Point Antique Dealers' Association, 226
Fell's Point Maritime Museum, 209–10
Fell's Point Visitor Center, 204
Fell's Point Walking Tour, 215
ferries, 25; Ocean City, 25, 42; Oxford-Bellevue, 25, 104, 106–7; Poolesville, 25, 293–94; Salisbury, 84–85; Smith Island, 77
Festival in the Country (Fair Hill), 162
Festival of the Arts (Frederick), 386
Festival of Wreaths (Westminster), 199
festivals: about, 25. *See also* specific festivals and destinations
Fiddlers' Convention, 199
50 Hikes in Maryland (Adkins), 13, 21, 26, 53, 58, 188, 374, 400
film festivals, 229, 309
Findings, 64
Finksburg, 188; eating, 193
Finzel Swamp, 20, 445
Fiore Winery, 179
Fire Museum of Maryland (Luthervill), 181, 185
Firefighters Memorial Park (Emmitsburg), 371
Firehouse Antique Center (Galena), 145
Firehouse Museum (Ellicott Cit), 234
Fireman's Carnival (Kent Island), 132
Fisheries Service, 20, 25
Fisherman's Crab Deck (Grasonville), 130
Fisherman's Seafood (Grasonville), 130
fishing: boat ramps: about, 20; about, 25–26; Annapolis, 254–55; Baltimore, 215; Cambridge, 97; Charles County, 353; Chesapeake Beach, 321; Crisfield, 70; Deep Creek Lake, 435, 438, 441–42, 445; Easton, 108; Elkton, 153; Frederick, 375; Kent Island, 125; tournaments, 132; North East, 162; Ocean City, 49–50; tournaments, 65; Park Hall, 340; Ridge, 340; Rock Hall, 137; St. Mary's County, 340; Solomons, 321, 331; Thurmont, 376; Tilghman Island, 107–8
Fishing Deep Creek Lake, 442
Fitzgerald, F. Scott: Burial Place, 296; Literary Conference, 309
Fitzgerald (Ella) Performing Arts Center, 68

Five Gables Inn and Spa, 111
55 East (Annapolis), 260
5 and 10 Antique Market (North East), 161
Flag House and Star-Spangled Banner
    Museum (Baltimore), 211
Flag House Inn (Baltimore), 258–59
Flag Ponds Nature Park, 18, 320, 321
Flamingo Flats, 118
Flannery's Cajun Café, 87
Flea Market World (Elkridge), 241
Flintstone, 419–21; campgrounds, 426; eat-
    ing, 427–28, 430; events, 433; lodging,
    424
Flower and Garden Show (Hagerstown),
    410
Flower and Jazz Festival (Westminster), 199
Flower and Plant Market (Westminster),
    199
Flower Fair (Cambridge), 101
Flyin' Fred's, 119
football, 226, 289
Fordham Brewing Company, 266
Ford's Seafood Restaurant, 144
Forest Hill Farm Crazy Corn Maze, 340
Forest Hill Recreation Complex, 174
Forest Hills Motel (Upper Marlboro), 286
Forest Motel (Ellicott City), 237
Forest Plaza Shopping Center, 264, 265
Forget-Me-Not Factory, 242
Fort Cumberland, 413, 418
Fort Cumberland Emporium, 431
Fort Foote Park, 280
Fort Frederick State Park, 395–96, 398, 405
Fort Lincoln, 341, 347
Fort McHenry, 201, 212, 216
Fort Washington, 280; events, 290; shop-
    ping, 289; sights/activities, 282, 284
Fort Washington Park, 280
Fort Whaley Campground, 57
49 West Coffeehouse, 263
Four Points by Sheraton, 403
Four Seasons Sports Complex, 188
4 X-Treem Sports, 320
Foxx, Jimmy, 122
France-Merrick Performing Arts Center,
    226
Francis Scott Key Golf Club, 188
Francis Silver Park, 173
Frank, Lake, 302
Frank's 24-Hour Diner, 240
Frederick, 363–86; campgrounds, 379; eat-
    ing, 380–83; emergencies, 367; entertain-

ment, 383; events, 385–86; information,
    365; lodging, 377–79; maps, 362, 366;
    parking, 367; shopping, 383–85; sights/
    activities, 367–77; transportation, 365–67
Frederick Brewing Company, 373
Frederick City Cab, 366
Frederick Coffee Company, 382
Frederick County, 363–86
Frederick County Fairgrounds Market, 385
Frederick County Historical Society, 363,
    367
Frederick County Tourism Council, 365
Frederick Keys Baseball, 383
Frederick Memorial Hospital, 367
Frederick Municipal Forest, 374
Frederick Visitor Center, 365, 367, 368,
    375, 384
Fredericktowne Players, 383
Freedom Blues Fest, 433
Freeland: campgrounds, 192; sights/
    activities, 185, 189
French and Indian War, 29, 391, 395, 413
Fresco's, 58
Friendly Cab, 335
Friendship Farm Park, 354, 355
Friendship Hot Air Balloon Company, 18,
    234
Friendsville, 436; activities, 33, 444; camp-
    grounds, 450; winery, 455
Fritchie, Barbara, 363, 367, 370, 372, 378;
    House and Museum, 368–69
Frontier Town Western Theme Park, 49;
    campground, 57
Frostburg, 413–14; eating, 428–30; enter-
    tainment, 430; events, 432; information,
    415; lodging, 424–25; map, 412; shop-
    ping, 431, 432; sights/activities, 416, 422,
    423; transportation, 415–16
Frostburg Cinema, 430
Frostburg Farmer's Market, 432
Frostburg Museum, 416
Frostburg Shops by the Depot, 431–32
Frostburg State University, 414, 432
Fruit Bowl, The (Cumberland), 430
Fudge Kitchen, 265
Fun Festival, 229
Funk's Democratic Coffee Spot, 224
Funland (McHenry), 441
Furnace Town, 45, 65

G

G. H. Godfrey Farms, 131
G Street Fabrics, 308
Gabriel's Inn, 381
Gaithersburg, 291, 293; eating, 305; emer-
    gencies, 294; entertainment, 306; events,
    309; information, 293; lodging, 302; map,
    292; shopping, 307–8; transportation,
    293–94
Gaithersburg Community Museum, 295
Gaithersburg Farmer's Market, 308
Galaxy Bar and Grill, 58–59
Galena, 134; shopping, 145
Galerie Française, 118
Galesville, 247, 249
Gallery 447, 101
Gallery Wear (Frederick), 384
Galway Bay, 263
Gambrill State Park, 374, 375–76; camp-
    ground, 379
Gandalf's, 429
Gapland: campgrounds, 405
Garden in Lights (Annmarie Garden), 331
Garden of Eden Orchards, 89
Garden Restaurant (College Park), 287
Garrett Country Fest and Auction, 456
Garrett County, 435–56
Garrett County Arts Council, 18, 455
Garrett County Chamber of Commerce,
    32, 436–37, 443, 444, 445, 450, 455
Garrett County Fair, 456
Garrett County Historical Society, 437
Garrett County Hospital, 437
Garrett Eight Cinemas, 454
Garrett Lakes Arts Festival, 456
Garrett State Forest, 32, 444, 451
Gary and Dell's Crab House, 194
Gate House Museum of History, 185
Gatehouse B&B, 260
Gathland State Park, 401–2
Geddes-Piper House, 135–36
Gehauf's, 429
Gem and Mineral Show, 309
genealogy bookstore, 196–97
General Cinema (Owings Mills), 195
General Tanuki's Restaurant, 114
George Washington's Headquarters, 417
Georgetown: eating, 143; events, 146; lodg-
    ing, 140
Georgetown Harbor, 146
Georgian House (Annapolis), 260

Germantown: events, 309; information,
    293; shopping, 308
Germantown Octoberfest, 309
Gertrude's, 223–24
ghost tours (walks), 162, 186, 242–43, 373,
    375
Giant Luxury Taxi Service, 104
Gibson Performing Arts Center, 135, 145
Gibson's Lodgings, 258
Gilpin Falls Covered Bridge, 23, 150–51
Giulianova Groceria, 195
Giuseppe's Italian Restaurant, 429
Glade Valley, 374
Glade-Link Farms, 385
Glasgow Inn B&B, 98–99
Glassburg, The, 131
Glen Burnie, 247, 249
Glen Dale, 281, 282
Glen Echo Park, 296, 297
Global Village Market, 228
Globe Café, 64
Globe Theater, 62, 64
Goddard Space Flight Visitor Center, 281
Goin' Nuts Café, 87
Golden Hill: events, 101
Goldsborough Stable, 94
golf: Aberdeen, 171; about, 26; Annapolis,
    255; Baltimore, 215; Berlin, 50–51;
    Bethesda, 299; Bishopville, 51; Chaptico,
    340; Chesapeake Beach, 321; College
    Park, 282–83; Cumberland, 420; Deep
    Creek Lake, 442; Dunkirk, 321; Easton,
    108; Elkridge, 235; Elkton, 154; Finks-
    burg, 188; Fort Washington, 282; Freder-
    ick, 373; Hagerstown, 399; Havre de
    Grace, 171; Kent Island, 125; Leonard-
    town, 340; Marriottsville, 235; Myersville,
    373; North East, 154; Oakland, 442;
    Ocean City, 50; Queenstown, 125; Rising
    Sun, 154; St. Michaels, 108; Salisbury, 85;
    Stevensville, 125; Thurmont, 373; Urbana,
    373; Walkersville, 374; West Friendship,
    235; Westminster, 188; Westover, 70;
    White Hall, 188; White Plains, 353
Good Samaritan Hospital, 207
Goose Bay Marina and Campground, 356
Gordon-Roberts House, 416–17
Gordon's Confectionery, 73
Gourmet by the Bay, 27, 116
Governor Calvert House, 258
Governor Thomas Johnson Memorial
    Bridge, 316, 334

Grabacrab Charters, 124
Gramercy Mansion B&B, 216
Gramp's Attic Books, 242
Grand Militia Muster, 347
Grandmother's Store Antique Center, 330
Grantsville, 435–36; campgrounds, 450, 451; eating, 452; events, 456; lodging, 446–47, 448–49; map, 434; shopping, 454, 455; sights/activities, 437–39, 445; transportation, 437
Grantsville Days, 456
Grasonville: eating, 130; events, 132; lodging, 128, 132; nightlife, 130; sights/activities, 124, 125, 126; transportation, 123
Grasonville Park, 125
Gratitude Yachting Center, 137
Grayton, 354
Great Atlantic Flyway, 19–20, 22, 98, 119, 139, 147, 257, 339
Great Blacks in Wax Museum, 209
Great Falls, 20, 32, 295, 298, 299, 300
Great Falls Visitor Center, 295, 298
Great Frederick (County) Fair, 386
Great Harvest Bread Co., 265
Great Hope Golf Course, 70, 73–74
Great Kite Fly, 268
Great Marsh Park, 98, 101
Great Mills, 339, 346, 347
Great North American Turtle Races, 90
Great Oak Landing Marina, 137
Great Oak Manor, 141
Great Valley, 391–411; map, 390
Greater Gift, A, 196
Greater Laurel Beltsville Hospital, 276
Greek Festival, 65
Green Ridge Hiking Trail, 419, 420–21
Green Ridge State Forest, 419–21; campgrounds, 426, 427
Greenbelt: campgrounds, 286; entertainment, 288; sights/activities, 277, 281, 284
Greenbelt Museum, 277
Greenbelt Park, 30, 284; campgrounds, 22, 286
Greenbrier State Park, 402, 405
Greenwell State Park, 19, 339, 340–41
Greystone, 188
Grille at Park Circle, 406
Grotto of Lourdes, 371
Gudelsky Gallery, 17, 307
Gunpowder Falls State Park, 181, 188
Gunston Day School, 132

Gwynns Falls, 216
Gypsy's Tea Room, 197

H

Habeeb Lake, 423, 427–28
Hager House and Museum, 395
Hagerstown, 389, 391–411; campgrounds, 405; eating, 406–7, 408; emergencies, 393; entertainment, 408; events, 410–11; information, 392; lodging, 403; map, 390; shopping, 408–10; sights/activities, 394–97, 399, 401–3; transportation, 392–93
Hagerstown Cinema, 408
Hagerstown City Farmer's Market, 410
Hagerstown City Park, 394, 395, 402–3
Hagerstown Ice and Sports Complex, 401
Hagerstown Municipal Golf Course, 399
Hagerstown Municipal Stadium, 408
Hagerstown Regional Airport, 392
Hagerstown Suns, 408
Hagerstown/Washington County Convention and Visitors Bureau, 392, 397
Hale House B&B, 342–43
Haley Farm B&B, 449–50
Hammond-Harwood House, 250
Hampshire Greens, 299
Hampstead: sights/activities, 187, 188
Hampton Inn (Bowie), 286
Hampton Inn (Columbia), 237
Hampton Inn (Frostburg), 425
Hampton National Historic Site, 181, 186
Hancock, 391–92; campgrounds, 405; eating, 407, 408; lodging, 403–4; map, 390; shopping, 409; sights/activities, 394, 397, 398; transportation, 393
Hancock Antique Mall, 409
Hancock Town Museum, 394
handicapped access: about, 26
Happy Hills Campground, 405
Harbor Court Hotel (Baltimore), 217
Harbor Cruises (Baltimore), 214
Harbor House Restaurant (Worton), 142–43
Harborplace (Baltimore), 201, 217–18
Harbourtowne Golf Resort and Conference Center (St. Michaels), 108, 110
Hard Rock Café, 222
Harford Community College, 168
Harford County, 165–80; map, 166
Harford County Department of Parks and Recreation, 173–74

Harford County Farm Fair, 180
Harford County Historical Society, 169
Harford County Tourism Council, 167
Harford County Transportation Services, 167
Harford Lanes, 171
Harford Memorial Hospital, 168
Harlem Renaissance Festival, 290
Harmony Hall Regional Center, 289
harness racing, 284
Harriet Tubman Day, 101
Harriet Tubman Memorial Garden, 98
Harriet Tubman Museum, 23, 95
Harris Cove Cottages, 113
Harris Crab House, 130
Harris Creek, 113
Harrison House, 107
Harrison's Harbor Watch, 59
Harrison's Restaurant, 107
Harry's Main Street Grille, 193–94
Hartage Nautical Museum, 249
Hashawha Environmental Center, 190, 199
Have a Nice Day Café, 225
Havre de Grace, 165–66; eating, 176–78; emergencies, 168; entertainment, 178; events, 180; information, 167; lodging, 174, 176; public restrooms, 168; shopping, 179; sights/activities, 168–74; transportation, 167–68
Havre de Grace Decoy Museum, 24, 166, 168
Havre de Grace Farmer's Market, 179
Havre de Grace Maritime Museum, 28, 168–69
Havre de Grace Tourism Commission, 167
Hayman House, 72
Hays House Museum, 169
Heart and Home, 410
Heather B's, 406
Hebron Diner, 87
Heck with the Malls!, 132
Heinz Bakery, 195
Heirloom Antiques Gallery, 100
Helen Avalynne Tawes Garden, 256
Helmstedder's Curve, 422
Hemingway's, 129–30
Henry, Marguerite, 40
Henson Creek, 282
Her Studio Gallery, 384
Herb and Wildflower Show, 331
Heritage Days, 243, 432
Herring Creek Nature Trail, 53
Herring Run Park, 213, 216

Herrington Lake, 445
Herrington Manor State Park, 32, 443–45, 456; cabin rentals, 450; campgrounds, 451
Hidden Springs Campground, 426–27
Hidden Valley Natural Area, 173
High Mountain Sports, 19, 443
Highland Beach, 247, 251
Highland Gathering, 162
highway travel: about, 26
Hiking, Cycling, and Canoeing in Maryland (MacKay), 109
hiking (walks): about, 26; books, 21, 26; Annapolis, 256–57; Baltimore, 215; Baltimore area, 188–89, 190; Bel Air, 174; Big Savage Hiking Trail, 442–43; Carroll County, 188–89, 190; Catoctin Trail, 374, 377; Chevy Chase, 20, 302; College Park, 283–84; Deep Creek Lake, 442–43; Easton, 108, 110; Ellicott City, 236; Flag Ponds Nature Park, 18, 321; Green Ridge, 419, 420–21; Hagerstown, 399–400; Havre de Grace, 171–73, 174; Hollywood, 340–41; Kent Island, 126–27, 128; La Plata, 353–54; Mason-Dixon Trail System, 171–72; North East, 154–55; Ocean City, 53; Port Republic, 321, 323; Prince Frederick, 324; Rocks State Park, 172; Rockville, 301–2; Salisbury, 85, 86; Sugarloaf Mountain, 374. See also specific trails
Hill House (Frederick), 378–79
Hippodrome Theatre, 226
His Lordship's Kindness (Poplar Hill), 279
Hispanic Festival, 229
Historic Annapolis Foundation Museum Store, 267
Historic Inns of Annapolis, 258
Historic London Town and Gardens, 251–52
Historic Port Tobacco, 352, 353
Historic St. Mary's City, 333, 337, 339, 347
Historic Savage Mill, 242, 243
Hobbit Restaurant, 59
Hobson's Choice Antiques, 266
Hoffman's Home Made Ice Cream, 27, 187, 195
Hog Neck, 108
Holiday, Billie, 210
Holiday Cinemas, 383
Holiday Festival and Craft Fair (Indian Head), 359

476

INDEX

Holiday Inn (Cumberland), 424
Holiday Inn (Gaithersburg), 302
Holiday Inn (Jessup), 237
Holiday Inn (Ocean City), 54–55, 55
Holiday Inn (Waldorf), 356
Holiday Inn Select (Solomons), 324
Holland House B&B, 56
Hollerstown Hill Bed & Breakfast, 379
Holly Ridge, 88
Holly's, 130
Hollywood: beach, 341; eating, 344; events, 347, 348; shopping, 346; sights/activities, 336, 339, 340
Hollywood Ballroom, 306
Hollywood Swing and Swat, 340
Holy Cross Hospital, 294
Home Town Diner (Williamsport), 407–8
Homeplace (Hagerstown), 409
Homestead Farm (Poolesville), 308
Homestead Village Guest Studios (Baltimore), 218
Homewood House, 211–12
Honi Honi, 454
Hooper Island, 92
Hooper Straight Lighthouse, 28, 105
Horse Bridge Golf Course, 85
horse farms, 147, 152–53, 181
horse racing, 215, 229. See also harness racing
horse shows, 90, 243, 290
Horse You Came In On Saloon, 225
horseback riding: about, 27; Carroll County, 189; Chestertown, 137; Fair Hill, 155; Gaithersburg, 299–300; Oakland, 443; Rockville, 299–300; St. Michaels, 109
Horton, Tom, 21, 76
Hospice Festival of Trees, 331
hospitals, 24–25. See also specific hospitals and destinations
hot-air ballooning, 18, 229, 234, 296
hotels: about, 29. See also specific hotels and destinations
House and Garden Pilgrimage, 359
Howard Community College, 241
Howard County, 231–43
Howard County Arts Council, 241–42
Howard County Center of African American Culture, 233
Howard County Fair, 243
Howard County General Hospital, 233
Howard County Tourism, 232

Howard County Yellow Cab, 233
Howard Transit Service, 232
Howl at the Moon, 225
Hoyts Cinema Centre (Salisbury), 88
Hoyts Frederick Towne Mall Cinema, 383
Hoyts Hunt Valley Cinema, 195
Hughesville, 350; eating, 357; shopping, 358; sights/activities, 352
Hughesville Bargain Barn, 358
Hunt Valley, 181; entertainment, 195; information, 183; transportation, 184
Hunter's Seafood, 130
hunting: about, 27
Hunting and Fishing Show (Frederick), 386
Hunting and Trapping in Maryland, 27
Hunting Creek Lake, 376
Hunting Creek Outfitters, 385
Huntingtown, 319, 320; shopping, 329
Hurlock, 91; eating, 99; lodging, 99; sights/activities, 97
Huskey Power Dogsledding, 440
Hyatt Regency (Baltimore), 217
Hyatt Regency (Cambridge), 91, 98
Hyattsville, 289
Hydes: wineries, 198
Hydromont Berry Farm, 359

I

I Made This!, 385
ice cream: about, 27. See also specific places and destinations
Ice Cream Gallery (Crisfield), 74
Ice Cream Sundae Social (Westminster), 199
ice fishing, 442
ice skating. See skating
Ijamsville, 373; eating, 381
Imagination Stage, 306
IMAX Movie Theater, 207–8
Imperial Hotel, 140, 142
Improv Comedy Club, 225
Incandescent Lighting Museum, 209
Indian Head: events, 359; lodging, 356; shopping, 358, 359
Indian Head Farmer's Market, 359
Indian Springs Campground, 405
information sources, 27. See also specific sources and destinations
Inlet Sea-Doos, 52
Inn at Antietam, 404
Inn at Buckeystown, 378, 380
Inn at Easton, 114

Inn at Henderson's Point, 218
Inn at Osprey Point, 140
Inn at Perry Cabin, 111
Inn at Point View, 446–47, 452, 454
Inn at Spa Creek, 261
Inn at the Canal, 156
Inn at Walnut Bottom, 425–26
Inn of Silent Music, 78
Inn on Potomac (Hagerstown), 403
Inn on the Ocean (Ocean City), 56
Inner Harbor, 201, 203, 205; boat excursions, 214; eating, 219–20, 221–22; emergencies, 207; lodging, 216–18; nightlife, 225; public restrooms, 205; shopping, 229; sights/activities, 207–9, 211, 215; Waterfront Promenade, 216
Inn-to-Inn Canoe Trail, 51, 56
insects: about, 27–28
International Hot Rod Association (IHRA), 338, 347
Irish Moon Coffee House, 194–95
Iron Rail Days, 433
Isaac (Thomas) Log Cabin, 234
Isabella's Tavern & Tapas Bar, 380
Island Belle II, 77
Island Creek Outfitters (Owings), 321
Island Jet Ski (Ocean City), 52
Island Parasail (Ocean City), 46
Island Queen, 125
Island Trader Antiques (Solomons), 330

J

J. Millard Tawes Crab and Clam Bake, 74–75
J. Millard Tawes Museum, 68–69, 70
Jackie's II Gallery, 432
Jackson, Stonewall, 368–69, 392
Jacob Rohrbach Inn, 404–5
Jalapeños, 264
James Busick Tennis Courts, 98
J & J Seafood, 144
Janes Island State Park, 18, 71, 72
Janet Fanto, 118
Japan House, 178
Jarretsville, 172, 173
Java by the Bay, 178
jazz festivals, 180, 199, 309
Jefferson, Thomas, 152, 303, 399–400
Jefferson Patterson Park and Museum, 319, 320, 331
Jennings Randolph Lake, 438

Jericho Covered Bridge, 23, 170
Jerusalem Mill, 170
Jessup: eating, 240; lodging, 237
jet skiing, in Ocean City, 52
Jewelry, Mineral and Fossil Show and Sale, 290
Jiffy Water Taxi, 248
Jimmy's Taxi, 184
Joe's Taxi, 150
Johanssons, 193, 195
John L. Stam House, 141
Johns Hopkins Hospital, 207
Johns Hopkins University: Merrick Barn at, 226
Johnson, Thomas, 372, 373
Johnson (Robert) House, 258
Joie de Vivre, 101
Jolly Roger Amusement Park, 46
Jo's Bikes, 47
Joseph C. Lore & Sons Oyster House, 319
Judith M, 50
Jug Bay Natural Area, 282
Jug Bridge Seafood, 381–82
Julia's (Centreville), 129
Julia's Room (Gaithersburg), 307
July 4th Sassafras Boat Parade, 146
Justine's, 117

K

Kali's Court, 221
Kathryn, 138
kayaking: about, 28; Annapolis, 255; Boonsboro, 400; Cambridge, 97, 101; College Park, 284; Crisfield, 70–71; Deep Creek Lake, 438, 443; Easton, 109; Elkton, 153; Kent Island, 125; Knoxville, 33, 374–75; Nanjemoy Creek, 354; Ocean City, 48, 51; Rock Hall, 137; Rockville, 300; Solomons, 320, 321; Tilghman Island, 107, 109; White's Ferry, 300
Kay's Diner, 287
Keedysville, 393, 409
Kemp House Inn, 112
Kennedyville, 136, 138
Kensington: shopping, 307–8
Kensington Antique Center, 307
Kent and Queen Anne's Hospital, 123, 135
Kent County, 133–46
Kent County Fair, 146
Kent County Office of Tourism Development, 134, 137

Kent County Visitor Center, 134, 135, 137
Kent Fort Farm, 27, 131, 132
Kent Island, 121–32; eating, 129–30; emergencies, 123; entertainment, 130–31; events, 132; information, 122; lodging, 128–29; map, 120; public restrooms, 123; shopping, 131; sights/activities, 123–28; transportation, 122–23
Kent Island Days, 132
Kent Island Federation of Art, 131
Kent Manor Inn and Restaurant, 128, 129
Kent Narrows, 121, 124, 125, 128, 132
Kentmorr Restaurant, 130
Key, Francis Scott, 32, 201, 210, 212, 336, 372; Star-Spangled Banner Museum, 211
Kick and Glide Cross-Country Ski Race and Winter Fest, 456
King and Queen's Seat, 172
King of France Tavern, 266
Kingsville: sights/activities, 23, 170, 188
Kirinyaga Coffee and Specialties, 240
Kite Festival, 65
Kite Loft (Ocean City), 51, 63–64
kiteboarding, in Ocean City, 51–52
Kittamaqundi, Lake, 235, 237
Kitty Knight House, 140, 143
Knoxville: activities, 33, 374–75; lodging, 379
Kunta Kinte Celebration, 268

L

La Clé D'or, 176
La Ferme, 303, 305
La Madeleine French Bakery and Café, 239
La Palapa, 240
La Paz Mexican Restaurant, 382
La Petite Galerie, 266
La Plata, 349–50; eating, 356–58; emergencies, 351; entertainment, 358; events, 359; information, 350; lodging, 356; shopping, 358–59; sights/activities, 351–55; transportation, 351
La Plata Farmer's Market, 359
La Plata Summer Concert Series, 359
La Ruota, 143
La Scala, 220
lacrosse, 226, 289
Ladew Topiary Gardens, 175
Lady Patty, 20, 109
Lake Pointe Inn (Deep Creek Lake), 449

Lake Side Motor Court (Deep Creek Lake), 447
Lake Somerset Family Campground, 72
Lakeside Creamery (Thayerville), 27, 454
Lakeside Restaurant (Habeeb Lake), 427–28
Land's End Manor on the Bay, 128
Lantern Inn, 140
Largo: entertainment, 289; events, 290; information, 275–76; lodging, 286; sights/activities, 282
Larriland Farm, 242
Latin Place, 225
Latitude 38, 113–14
Laurel, 275; eating, 287, 288; emergencies, 276; entertainment, 288; events, 290; lodging, 285; map, 274; sights/activities, 277, 278, 281; transportation, 276
Laurel Lakes Cinema, 288
Laurel Museum, 275, 277
Lauretum Inn, 141
LaVale, 415; eating, 428, 429–30; entertainment, 430; lodging, 425; shopping, 432; sights/activities, 417
LaVale Country Club Mall Farmer's Market, 432
LaVale Toll Gate House, 417–18
Lazyjack Inn, 113
Le Grande RV Sales & Camping Resort, 343
League of Maryland Craftsmen, 267
Leakin Park, 216
LeCompte Wildlife Management Area, 96
Lee, Robert E., 187, 391, 396
Leisure Management, LLC, 261
Leonard's Mill Park, 79
Leonardtown, 333–34; campgrounds, 343; eating, 343–44, 345; emergencies, 335; events, 347; information, 334; map, 332; shopping, 346; sights/activities, 336, 340; transportation, 334–35
Leonardtown Cab, 335
Les Folies, 262
Lessig's Pleasant Valley, 306–7
Lewis Orchards, 410
Lewrene Farm, 403
Lexington Park, 334; shopping, 346; sights/activities, 336, 338, 339; transpor-tation, 335
Liberty Bike Shop, 187
Life Saving Museum (Ocean City), 17, 43
Light St. Cycles, 213

Lighted Boat Parades, 132, 269
Lighthouse Club Hotel (Ocean City), 55
Lighthouse Inn (Solomons), 326
lighthouses: about, 28. *See also* specific
  lighthouses
Lilyfield Gallery, 17, 101
Lilypons Water Gardens, 371
Linden Farm B&B, 356
Links at Lighthouse Sound, 51
Linthicum, 247; lodging, 258; sights/
  activities, 251
Linwood: lodging, 192
Liquid Fun, 158
Literary Festival (Bethesda), 309
Little Bennett Golf Course, 299
Little Bennett Regional Park, 301, 303
Little Hunting Creek, 376
Little Italy, 203, 211, 216; eating, 220, 222,
  224; events, 229
Little Italy Open-Air Film Festival, 229
Little Meadows Campground, 450
Little Orleans Campground, 427
Little Seneca Lake, 301
Locust Books, 196
Locust Point Marina, 153
Loew Vineyards, 198
Loews Annapolis Hotel, 257–58
Loews Cineplex (Gaithersburg), 306
Loews Columbia Palace, 240
Loews Theatre Valley Center 9 (Owings
  Mills), 195
Log Cabin (Jessup), 240
Log House Museum (Clear Spring), 394
Loggers/Forestry Day and Equipment Sale,
  456
Lola's, 130
Lombardi's, 87
Lonaconing, 415; sights/activities, 419, 420,
  423
Lonaconing Iron Furnace, 419
London Town and Gardens, 251–52
Long and Foster Resort Rentals, 450
Long Branch Saloon, 453, 454
Long Creek View, 157
Longview Golf Course, 188
Longwood Manor, 303
Lord Calvert Bowl, 320
Lore & Sons Oyster House, 319
Lost Galaxy Golf, 51
Lost Treasure Golf, 51
Lostland Run Trail, 443
Love Point Café, 129

Love Point Park, 125
Lower Falls, 32, 446
Lower Susquehanna Heritage Greenway,
  156, 172
Loy's Station Covered Bridge, 23, 367
Lusby: events, 331; shopping, 329; sights/
  activities, 319, 321, 322
Lutherville, 181; sights/activities, 185; trans-
  portation, 183, 184
Lyric Opera House, 225

M

Ma and Pa Trail, 174
McBride Gallery, 267
McCleery's Flat, 378
McCormick and Schmick's, 219–20
McCready Health Services, 68
McCrillis Gardens and Gallery, 301
McCutcheon's Apple Products, 382
McDaniel College, 184, 195, 196; golf
  course, 188
McFarland Candies, 430
McGarvey's Saloon and Oyster Bar, 262
MacGregor's, 176–77
McHenry, 435–36; activities, 440–42, 444;
  campgrounds, 451; eating, 452; events,
  456; information, 436–37; lodging,
  446–47, 449, 450; nightlife, 454; shop-
  ping, 454–55
McHenry Highland Festival, 456
McMahon's Mill, 405
Madison, James, 152, 333, 338
Maggie Moo's Ice Cream, 27, 224–25
Main Ingredient Café, 263–65
Main St. Contemporary Art (Prince Fred-
  erick), 330
Main St. Farmer's Market (College Park),
  289
Makemie United Presbyterian Church, 46
Mallard Charters, 255
Manchester: wineries, 198
M&T Bank Stadium, 226
Mango Grove, 239
Manhattan Centre Golf and Gallery, 431
Mansion House (Public Landing), 57
Maple Run, 373
Maple Sugarin' Festival, 199
Maple Tree Campground, 405
maps: highway, 26; Maryland, 6; Maryland
  Regions, 8; Allegheny Plateau, 412; Anna-
  polis, 244, 246; Baltimore, 200, 202, 206;

Continued from previous page

Baltimore north, 182; Baltimore west, 230; Bay Bridge, 120; Bethesda, 292; Bowie, 274; Capital Region, 272; Catoctin Mountains, 362; central Maryland, 164; Chesapeake Bay, 148; Chesapeake Bay shore, 314; Chestertown, 134; College Park, 274; Deep Creek Lake, 434; Eastern Shore, 36; Easton, 102; Frederick, 362, 366; Harford County, 166; Kent Island, 120; Laurel, 274; Oxford, 102; Potomac River mouth, 332; Potomac River shore, 350; Rock Hall, 134; St. Michaels, 102; Salisbury, 80, 82; Seaboard, 38; southern Maryland, 312; Tangier Sound area, 67; Upper Marlboro, 274; western Maryland Mountains, 388

Marbury: shopping, 17, 358; sights/activities, 355

MARC: Aberdeen, 167; Baltimore, 204; Bowie, 276; College Park, 276; Dorsey, 233; Edgewood, 167; Frederick, 366; Harpers Ferry, 393; Hunt Valley, 184; Jessup, 233; Laurel, 276; Owings Mills, 184; Perryville, 149; Point of Rocks, 366; Savage, 233; St. Denis, 233

Marconi's, 222

Mardela Springs, 89

Margaret Smith Gallery, 242

Maria's Picture Place, 266

Marion, 70–71, 75

Mario's, 59

Maritime Heritage Festival (Annapolis), 268

maritime museums: about, 28–29. *See also* specific museums

markets. *See* farmer's markets

Market Street Antiques and Collectibles Center (Salisbury), 88

Market Street Books (Frederick), 384

Market Street Books (Salisbury), 89

Marlboro Day and Parade, 290

Marlton Golf Club, 283

Marriott Inn and Conference Center (College Park), 285, 287

Martinak State Park, 127

Marvelous Movies and More, 240

Maryland and Delaware Canoe Trails (Gertler), 28

Maryland Antiques Center, 346

Maryland Cab, 150

Maryland Charter Boat Association, 26

Maryland College of Art and Design, 307

Maryland Colony, 245, 313, 333, 352, 391, 395

Maryland Craft Beer Festival, 229

Maryland Day, 347

Maryland Department of Natural Resources, 25, 27, 29, 30

Maryland Direct Farm Market Association, 30–31

Maryland Ensemble Theatre, 383

Maryland Federation of Art Gallery on the Circle, 267

Maryland General Hospital, 207

Maryland Golf Guide, 26

Maryland Heights, 398, 399–400

Maryland Historical Society, 207, 210

Maryland Horse Center, 299–300

Maryland House Travel Center, 167

Maryland Inn, 258, 261, 266

Maryland International Raceway, 338, 347

Maryland Mass Transit Administration, 205, 248

Maryland Mountain Cruise, 433

Maryland Mountain Festival, 386

Maryland Office of Tourism Development, 23, 25, 26, 27, 31, 32

Maryland Presents, 288

Maryland Renaissance Festival, 269

Maryland Scenic Byways, Office of Environmental Design, 31

Maryland School of Sailing and Seamanship, 31, 138

Maryland Science Center, 207–8, 211

Maryland Seafood Festival, 268–69

Maryland Sheep and Wool Festival, 243

Maryland State Arts Council, 18

Maryland State Fair, 199

Maryland State Highway Administration: Construction Hotline, 26

Maryland State House, 252

Maryland State Quarter Horse Show, 243

Maryland Steamed Crabs: recipe for, 346

Maryland Symphony Orchestra, 408, 411

Maryland Theater, 408

Maryland Wine Festival, 199

Maryland Zoo in Baltimore, 213, 229

Mason-Dixon Trail System, 171–72

Mass Transit Authority, 205, 248

Matapeake Trail and Pier, 123, 125, 127

Mattawoman Creek, 355

Mattawoman Creek Art Center, 17, 358, 359
Maynes Tree Farm, 385
Meadow Gardens, 260–61
Meadowlark Inn, 305
Mealey's, 381
Mears, Otto, 315
Mechanicsville, 340; eating, 345
medical emergencies, 24–25. *See also* specific destinations
Mellomar Golf Park, 321
Memorial Hospital (Easton), 105
Memory Makers, 179
Mercy Hospital, 207
Meredith House, 94
Merkle Wildlife Sanctuary, 19, 284
Metompkin Bay Oyster Company, 70
Metro, 276, 294
Metrobus, 286, 294
Metropolitan United Methodist Church (Princess Anne), 69
Michener, James, 21, 91, 110
Microtel (Annapolis), 258
Microtel (Baltimore), 218
Mid-Atlantic Chevelle Show, 162
Middleham Episcopal Chapel, 319
Middleton Tavern, 263
Middletown, 365; eating, 382–83; shopping, 384; sights/activities, 368, 373
Mike's Bar and Crab House, 264
Mike's Bikes, 47, 353
Milburn Landing Campground, 58
Milburn Orchards, 162
Miles River, 103, 106, 109
Mill Run Recreation Area, 450
Mill Stone Park, 235
Millard E. Tydings Memorial Park, 168, 174, 180
Miller Farms, 289–90
Miller House and Garden, 394
Millington, 138; eating, 144
Milton's Produce, 64
Mimi's Antiques, 241
Mind's Eye, The, 118
miniature golf: Annapolis, 255; Boonsboro, 398; Churchville, 171; College Park, 282; Deep Creek Lake, 441, 442; Easton, 107; Elkridge, 235; Gaithersburg, 299; Hagerstown, 399; Hampstead, 188; Hollywood, 340; Ocean City, 51
Mr. Mole B&B, 219
Mitchell Art Gallery, 249, 266

Mitchellville: sights/activities, 283
Mom and Pop's Ice Cream Shop, 383
Monkton, 175
Monocacy National Battlefield, 23, 368, 369–70, 386
Monocacy River, 367, 370
Monocacy River Aqueduct, 372
Montage Gallery, 227
Montgomery County, 291–309
Montgomery County Bus System, 294
Montgomery County Conference and Visitors Bureau, 293
Montgomery County Department of Parks, 300
Montgomery County Fair, 309
Montgomery General Hospital, 294
Montgomery Taxicab, 294
Montgomery Village Theatres, 306
Montpelier Cultural Arts Center, 278
Montpelier Mansion, 278
Montpelier Spring Festival, 290
Montville Taxi, 167
Moonlight Bay and Marina, 142
Morgan Taxi, 416
Morris Meadows Campground, 192
Morris Meadows Historic Preservation Museum, 185
motels: about, 29. *See also* specific motels and destinations
Mother's Federal Hill Grille, 27, 222
Mount Airy, 183; eating, 194; lodging, 379; shopping, 196; sights/activities, 198, 299
Mt. Airy U-Pick, 268
Mount Harmon Plantation, 152
Mt. Ida, 234
Mount Moriah African Methodist Episcopal Church, 249
Mount Olivet Cemetery, 372
Mt. Panax Antiques, 455
Mt. Pleasant Farm, 243
Mount Savage, 415; events, 433; lodging, 426
Mount Vernon, 203, 215; eating, 221, 223, 224; emergencies, 207; entertainment, 225, 226; events, 229; lodging, 218, 219; map, 206; shopping, 227, 228; sights/activities, 210, 212, 215
Mount Vernon Cultural District, 204, 215, 227
Mount Vernon Place United Methodist Church, 212

Mount Washington, 215–16
Mt. Zion One Room School Museum, 44
Mountain Bike America: Washington-Baltimore (Fernandez and Adams), 19
mountain biking. *See* bicycling
Mountain Gate (Thurmont), 382
Mountain Lake Park, 436; eating, 453; entertainment, 454; events, 456; shopping, 455; sights/activities, 438, 442, 443, 444
mountains of western Maryland, 387–456; map, 388
Mowbray Park, 125
Moxey's Taxi, 93
Mudd (Dr. Samuel A.) House, 351–52
Mudd Puddle Coffee Café, 382
Muddy Creek Falls, 32, 376, 446
Municipal Basin, 96
Museum Shop, LTD (Frederick), 384
museums. *See* specific museums
Music at Penn Alps, 456
Musket Ridge, 373
My Fair Lady B&B, 72
Myersville: activities, 373; information, 365
Myrtle Grove Wildlife Management Area, 353–54
Myrtle Point Park, 341
Mystery Bookshop (Bethesda), 308
Mystery Loves Company (Fell's Point), 228

N

Nanjemoy, 355, 359; events, 359
Nanjemoy Creek, 354, 355
Nanticoke River, 50, 85
Nanticoke River Shad Festival, 101
NASA/Goddard Space Flight Visitor Center, 281
Nassawango Creek, 71
Nassawango Cypress Swamp, 45
Nathan of Dorchester, 20, 96
National 5 and 10 (Havre de Grace), 179
National Aquarium of Baltimore, 17, 201, 203, 208, 211
National Bar-b-que Cook-off, 89
National Capital Trolley Museum, 296
National Colonial Farm (Accokeek), 280–81
National Fallen Firefighters Memorial Park, 371
National Hard Crab Derby and Fair, 75
National Museum of Civil War Medicine, 23, 368

National Outdoor Show (Golden Hill), 101
national parks: about, 30. *See also* specific parks
National Road, 29, 391, 392, 413, 414, 416, 436
National Scenic Byway, 31, 136, 139
National Shrine Grotto of Lourdes, 371
National Shrine of Saint Elizabeth Ann Seton, 371
National Shrine of the Assumption, 212
Native Americans, 44, 69, 75, 83, 94, 139, 257, 337, 353–54, 392, 395, 413, 417–18, 435; events, 75, 101, 162, 331
Nature Conservancy, 323, 444–45
nature tourism: about, 29
nature trails. *See* hiking
Nause-Waiwah Band of Indians Native American Festival, 101
Nautical and Wildlife Art Festival (Ocean City), 64
Naval Academy, U.S., 245–46, 252–53; bookstore, 267; events, 269; ice skating, 256
Naval Air Museum (Patuxent), 336
Naval Air Station (Lexington Park), 338
Navy-Marine Corps Memorial Stadium, 249, 268
Needwood Lake, 296, 301–2
Neet-N-Kleen, 248
Neild Museum and Herb Garden, 94
Neil's Artwork, 161
New Germany State Park, 32, 444, 445; cabin rentals, 450; campgrounds, 450
New Ideal Diner, 178
New Jersey: ferry, 25, 42
New Market, 365; eating, 381; public restrooms, 367; shopping, 16, 384
New Windsor: lodging, 192; shopping, 196, 197–98
Newark: sights/activities, 44, 64
Newburg: eating, 357; information, 350–51
News Center (Easton), 118
Newtown Festival, 86, 90
Newtown Historic District, 79, 83, 86
Nice and Fleazy Antique Center, 330
1908 William Page Inn, 260
94th Aero Squadron, 287
Nook and Monk's, 343–44
Norrisville Recreation Complex, 174
North American Craft Show, 64

North Arundel Hospital, 249
North Bay (North East), 157
North Beach, 315–16, 320; beaches, 18, 323; eating, 327, 329; events, 331; information, 316; lodging, 324; map, 314; public restrooms, 317; shopping, 329, 330; transportation, 317
North Beach Bayfest, 331
North Beach Public Beach, 323
North Beach Welcome Center, 315, 316
North Bethesda: eating, 305; shopping, 307
North Chesapeake Antique Mall, 161
North East, 147, 149; eating, 159–60, 161; entertainment, 161; events, 162; information, 149; lodging, 156, 157, 158; public restrooms, 150; shopping, 161–62; sights/ activities, 150–52, 154, 155, 156; transportation, 149, 150
North East Community Park, 150, 151
North End Gallery (Leonardtown), 346
North End Taxi (Salisbury), 81
North Fork B&B, 99
North St. Mary's Farmer's Market, 347
Northeast River, 149
Northern Central Railroad Trail, 19, 189
Northern Peak Trail, 374
Northside Park, 53, 65
Northwest Hospital Center, 184
Northwood's, 262
Nostalgia Nook, 358
Nutter's Ice Cream, 408

O

Oak Tree Inn, 425
Oakland, 435–36; campgrounds, 451; eating, 451, 453, 454; emergencies, 437; entertainment, 454; lodging, 447, 448, 449–50; map, 434; shopping, 455; sights/activities, 437, 441–43, 445–46; transportation, 437
Oakland Golf Club, 442
Oakland Mountain Fresh Farmer's Market, 455
Oakland Train Station, 436, 437
Oaks, The (Royal Oak), 111
Obrycki's, 224
O.C. Parasail, 46
OC Jamboree, 62–63
OC Rocket, 48
O'Callaghan Hotel Annapolis, 258

Ocean Bowl Skate Park, 52
Ocean City, 39–40; beaches, 18, 52; campgrounds, 57; eating, 58–62; emergencies, 43; entertainment, 62–63; events, 64–65; information, 42; lodging, 54–57; map, 38; public restrooms, 43; shopping, 63–64; sights/activities, 43–44, 46–53; transportation, 42–43
Ocean City Airport, 42, 46
Ocean City Boardwalk, 39–40, 43, 47, 52; eating, 59, 60–61
Ocean City Boardwalk Train, 43
Ocean City Campground, 57
Ocean City Chamber of Commerce, 42
Ocean City Convention and Visitors Bureau, 42
Ocean City Factory Outlets, 64
Ocean City Fishing Center, 50
Ocean City Golf Club, 50
Ocean City Golf Getaway, 50
Ocean City Life Saving Museum, 17, 43
Ocean City Sky Tours, 46
Ocean City Tuna Tournament, 65
Ocean City Weekly Rentals, 57
Ocean Gallery World Center (Ocean City), 17, 63
O'Conor, Piper and Flyn, 57
O'Donnell's, 305
Odyssea Watersports, 52
Oktoberfests, 309, 386, 411
Old Angler's Inn, 304
Old Field Inn, 325–26
Old Glory Antique Marketplace, 384
Old Greenbelt Theater, 288
Old Jail Museum (Leonardtown), 336
Old Line State, 30
Old Maryland Farm, 282
Old Mill Bakery Café, 240
Old Pro Golf (Ocean City), 51
Old South Mountain Inn, 406
Old Town Candy (North Beach), 329
Old Towne Creamery (Easton), 117
Old Trinity Church (Church Creek), 91, 94
Old Wharf Cottage, 157–58
Olde Town Crafters (Leonardtown), 346–47
Oldfields Chapel, 352
Oldies Music Legends, 383
Oldtown, 417–18, 419
Oldtown Celebration, 432–33

Ole Mink Farm Recreation Resort, 380
Olive Tree, 178
Olney: emergencies, 294; entertainment, 306; shopping, 307; sights/activities, 299
Olney 9 Cinemas, 306
Olney Theatre Center, 306
Olsson's Books and Records, 308
Olympia Candy Kitchen, 408
One of a Kind Gallery and Espresso Bar, 329
One World Café, 223
126th Street Medical Center (Ocean City), 43
Open House for Nature (Edgewater), 268
Open-Judged Art Show (Stevensville), 132
opera, 225, 265
Oregon Ridge, 181, 190–91
Orrell's Maryland Beaten Biscuits, 124
Orvis, 385
Osprey Point Restaurant, 143
Our Town Theatre, 454
Out of the Fire, 114
Outdoor Excursions (Boonsboro), 33, 400
outlets. See factory outlets
Overlea Cab, 184
Owen's Creek, 367
Owens Creek Campground, 379
Owings: activities, 321; events, 331; information, 316
Owings Mills, 181, 188–89; entertainment, 195; transportation, 184
Oxford, 103–19; eating, 113–14; events, 119; lodging, 110, 112; map, 102; public restrooms, 104; shopping, 118; sights/activities, 105; transportation, 104
Oxford House, 427
Oxford Inn, 110
Oxford Mews Emporium, 118
Oxford Museum, 105
Oxford-Bellevue Ferry, 25, 104, 106–7
Oxon Cove Park, 279–80
Oxon Hill, 279–80; entertainment, 288; lodging, 286
Oxon Hill Farm, 279–80
Oyster Fest (St. Michaels), 119
Oyster Festival (Leonardtown), 347–48
oysters, 22, 66, 70, 136

P

P. E. Pruitts, 145
P. F. Chang's China Bistro, 239
Paca (William) House and Garden, 250
Packing House Antiques, 100
Paint Branch, 283
P&G Laurel Towne Center, 288
Panorama Motel, 447
Paradiso Ristorante, 193
parasailing, in Ocean City, 46
Park Crest House, 303
Park Hall, 340
Parker House (Chestertown), 141
Parker Place (Salisbury), 88
Parkers Creek, 323
Parkton: wineries, 198
Parsonage Inn, 112–13
Parsonsburg, 89
Part of Plenty Bed & Breakfast, 356
Pasadena, 247, 257
Pasta Plus, 287
Patapsco Female Institute Historic Park, 234, 242, 243
Patapsco River, 231, 232
Patapsco Valley State Park, 232, 236, 238
Patricia Keener, 196
Patriot, 106
Patuxent Camp Sites, 325
Patuxent Naval Air Station, 334, 336
Patuxent Research Refuge, 19, 268, 275, 281, 285
Patuxent River, 28, 313, 315, 320, 339, 349, 350; boat excursions, 318, 320
Patuxent River Naval Air Museum, 336
Patuxent River Park, 282, 284
Patuxent United Methodist Church, 319
Paul Reed Smith Guitars, 131
Paw Paw Museum, 152
Paw Paw Tunnel, 419, 421
Peabody Conservatory of Music, 225
Peach Blossom Farm, 89
Peach Festivals, 27, 131, 132
Peaky's, 73
Pell Gardens, 162
Pemberton Colonial Fair, 90
Pemberton Historical Park, 83, 84, 85, 90
Peninsula Regional Medical Center, 81
Pen-Mar Park, 402
Penn Alps Restaurant, 452
Penning of the Ponies, 41, 65
Pennsylvania Turnpike, 415

Penny's Diner, 430

Pennywhistle, 117

Peralynna Manor at Rose Hill, 238

Perdue Stadium, 88

Perryville, 149; campgrounds, 158; events, 162; shopping, 162; sights/activities, 152, 154; transportation, 149

pet symbol: about, 30

Philadelphia International Airport, 16, 149, 167

Phillips Crab House and Seafood Festival Buffet, 61

Phillips Farm, 308

Pickering Creek Audubon Center, 20, 108, 110

Picture Show Art Gallery, 179

Piedmont Plateau, 165, 172

Pier 5 Hotel, 216–17

Pier One, 160

Pierpoint, 221

Pimlico Race Course, 215

Pine Lick Hollow, 421

Piney Orchard Farmer's Market, 268

Piney Point Lighthouse and Museum, 28, 338, 339, 347

Piney Run Park, 32, 190

Pirate Adventures on the Sea Gypsy, 48–49

Piscataway Indians, 257, 353–54

Piscataway Park, 280–81

Pittsburgh International Airport, 16, 392, 437

Pittsville Dinette, 87

Place on Race Café, 100

Plat du Jour, 268

Play Festival (Largo), 290

Play It Again Sam, 144–45

Plum, The, 407

Plumpton Park Zoo, 153

Pocomoke City, 42; sights/activities, 44, 45, 64

Pocomoke Pier, 125

Pocomoke River, 42; fishing, 50; kayaking, 48, 51, 71

Pocomoke River Canoe Co., 51

Pocomoke River State Park, 53, 58

Point Lookout Lighthouse, 28, 342, 348

Point Lookout State Park, 341–42; bird-watching, 19, 339; events, 347, 348

Point of Rocks, 365, 366, 372

Pony Espresso, 265

Poole's Taxi, 167

Poolesville, 293; eating, 305; ferry, 25, 293–94; shopping, 308

Poplar Hill Mansion (Salisbury), 83

Poplar Hill on His Lordship's Kindness (Clinton), 279

Pop's Seafood and Carry Out, 288

population, 31

Pork In The Park, 89

Port Deposit, 149; eating, 160; sights/activities, 152, 156; transportation, 150

Port Discovery, 211, 215

Port Republic, 317, 319, 323; events, 331; lodging, 325

Port Republic School Number 7, 317, 319

Port Tobacco, 349–50; lodging, 356; sights/activities, 352, 353

Port Tobacco One-Room School House, 352

Port Tobacco Players, 358

Port Tobacco River, 349, 352, 356

Portside (Cambridge), 100

Potomac: eating, 304

Potomac Appalachian Trail Club, 21, 374

Potomac Outdoor Expeditions, 398

Potomac Players, 408

Potomac River, 279, 299, 313, 339, 353, 438; along the shore, 349–59; map, 350; ferry, 25, 293–94; fishing, 353, 355; kayaking and canoeing, 300, 400; mouth of the, 333–48; map, 332; rafting, 33, 374–75, 400

Potomac River Clean Up, 359

Potomac State Forest, 32, 443, 451

Power Boat Regatta (Cambridge), 101

Pratt-Perry House, 141

Preakness Celebration, 229

Precision Rafting, 33, 444

Prevention of Blindness Society Antique Shop, 307

Prime Outlets (Hagerstown), 410

Prime Outlets (Perryville), 162

Prime Outlets (Queenstown), 131

Prince Frederick, 315–16; eating, 325–26; emergencies, 317; entertainment, 329; events, 331; information, 316; lodging, 324–25; map, 314; shopping, 330–31; sights/activities, 324; transportation, 316–17

Prince George County, 275–90

Prince George's County Bus System, 276

Prince George's County Conference and Visitor's Bureau, 275–76

Prince George's Hospital Center, 276

Prince George's Plaza Farmer's Market, 289
Princess Anne, 66; campgrounds, 72–73; eating, 73, 74; events, 74, 75; information, 68; lodging, 72; sights/activities, 68–71
Princess Anne Campground, 72–73
Princess Restaurant, 429
Princess Royale Oceanfront Hotel, 55
Principio Iron Works, 154
Pritchard's, 307
produce. *See* farms
Public Landing: beach, 18, 52; lodging, 57
Publick Playhouse, 289
pumpkins (patches), 74, 131, 179, 197, 289, 290, 308, 309, 385
Purnell (Julia A.) Museum, 44
Purple Orchid, 220
Purse State Park, 18, 355
Pusey's Country Store, 64
Pylesville, 174, 179

Q

Quakers, 105, 170, 275, 293
Queen Anne's County, 121–32
Queen Anne's County Arts Council, 131
Queen Anne's County Fair, 132
Queen Anne's County Office of Tourism, 122, 123, 125
Queen Anne's County Parks and Recreation, 125, 127
Queen City Creamery and Deli, 27, 430
Queenstown, 122; lodging, 128–29; shopping, 131; sights/activities, 123, 125, 126; transportation, 123
Queenstown Harbor Links, 125
Queenstown Inn, 128–29
Queponco Railway Station, 44
Quiet Waters Park, 256–57
Quill and Brush, 384
quilt shows, 347, 348, 432, 456

R

R. J. Bentley's Filling Station, 287–88
Rafael's, 194
rafting, 33; Potomac River, 33, 374–75, 400; Youghiogheny River, 33, 444
Railey Mountain Lake Vacations, 450
Railfest (Cumberland), 433
railroad rides and museums: about, 31. *See also* specific railroads and museums

Railroad-Transportation Artifacts Show and Sale (Gaithersburg), 309
Rails-to-Trails Conservancy, 189
Railway Market (Easton), 116
Ramada Inn (Salisbury), 86
Ramblin' Pines Campground, 192, 238
Rams Head Tavern, 266
Randall House, 259
Randallstown: emergencies, 184
Random House Book Fair, 199
Randy's Ribs and BBQ, 357
Ratner Museum, 294–95
Rattlewood Golf Course, 299
Rebecca T. Ruark, 109
Red Heart American Indian Festival, 162
Red Roof Inn (Baltimore), 218
Red Roost, 88
Red Run Lodge, 448, 452–53
Reflections, 59
Regency Cab, 294
Reistertown: transportation, 184
Reliable Cab, 248
Reminisce Antique Mall, 454
Renaissance Festivals, 269, 290
Renaissance Harborplace, 217–18
Renaissance Productions and Tours, 213
Rep Stage, 241
Residence Inn by Marriott (Ellicott City), 237
Revolutionary War, 75, 94, 104, 136, 201, 237–38, 253, 341, 355, 395
Reynolds of Derwood B&, 303
Rhodes Point, 76
Rhubarb House, The, 406
Richardson Maritime Museum, 28, 94
Ride On, 294
Ride the Ducks Baltimore, 214
Ridge, 340; campgrounds, 343; eating, 345; lodging, 342
Right of Way Hike, 331
Rising Sun: sights/activities, 153, 154
Ristorante Piccola Roma, 261
Ritz, 178
River and Trail Outfitters, 33, 374–75
River House Inn (Snow Hill), 51, 55–56
River Run Golf Course, 51
Riversdale Mansion, 278
Riverside Ponderosa Pines Campground, 158
Riverview Campground (Perryville), 158
Roaring Point Campground, 86
Robert Johnson House, 258
Robert Morris Inn, 110

Roberts, Nora, 21, 409
Robertson's Crab House, 357
Robin Hill Farm Nursery, 290
Roccoco, 407
Rocco's, 406
Rock Bottom Brewery, 306
Rock Creek Regional Park, 299–300, 301–2
Rock Creek Trail, 19, 296, 298
Rock Hall, 133–46; eating, 142–45; entertainment, 145; events, 146; lodging, 140–42; map, 134; shopping, 145–46; sights/activities, 135–39; transportation, 135
Rock Hall Fall Fest, 146
Rock Hall Harbor, 133, 136, 137, 138
Rock Hall Trolley, 135
Rock Hill Regional Park, 301
Rock Run Grist Mill, 169–70
Rockfish Tournaments, 132, 146, 162
Rocks State Park, 32, 165, 172–73
Rockville, 291, 293; campgrounds, 303; eating, 305; emergencies, 294; entertainment, 306; events, 309; lodging, 302; map, 292; shopping, 307, 308; sights/activities, 296–97, 299–302; transportation, 293, 294
Rockville Farmer's Market, 308
Rocky Gap Music Festival, 433
Rocky Gap State Park, 413, 423; campgrounds, 427; eating, 427–28; events, 433; golf, 420; lodging, 424
Rod and Classic Spring Fling, 347
Rod 'N Reel, 321
Roddy Road Covered Bridge, 23, 367
Rodgers Tavern, 152, 162
roller skating. See skating
Ronald Reagan Washington National Airport, 16, 276, 293, 316, 334, 351, 365
Ron's Deli, 406
Rosanini's Gourmet Ice Cream, 74
Rose Hill (Columbia), 238
Rose Hill Cemetery (Hagerstown), 396
Rose Hill Manor Park (Frederick), 373, 386
Rosecroft, 284
Rotary Crab Feast (Annapolis), 268
Roundhouse Museum (Hagerstown), 31, 394
Rounding 3rd Family Entertainment Center, 235
Roundtop Park, 125
Royal Cab, 205
Royal Oak: lodging, 111

Rubini Athletic Complex-Ice Skating Rink, 300
Rudy's 2900, 193
Rueben Rodney Gallery, 145
Ruke's Seafood Deck, 78
Rum Point Seaside Golf Links, 51
Rustic Rentals (Sharpsburg), 405
Ruth, Babe, 208, 234; Museum and Birthplace, 208

S

Sacred Heart Hospital, 416
sailing: lessons, 31; about, 20; Annapolis, 255–56; Chestertown, 146; Deep Creek Lake, 31, 443; Havre de Grace, 31, 173; Ocean City, 48; Rock Hall, 31, 137, 138; St. Michaels, 109; Solomons, 320; Tilghman Island, 109
Sailing Etc. (Ocean City), 48
Sailwinds Park, 100, 101; visitor center, 91, 92–93
St. Anne's Episcopal Church, 252
St. Anthony Shrine, 234
St. Charles Town Center, 358–59
St. Charles Town Cinema, 358
St. Clement's Bay, 339
St. Clement's Island, 333, 335–36
St. Clement's Island Potomac River Museum, 335–36, 347
St. Edmonds United Methodist Church, 319
St. Francis Xavier Church, 336
St. George Island, 334, 339; campgrounds, 343; eating, 345
St. Ignatius Church (Port Tobacco), 352
St. Ignatius Church (St. Inigoes), 337
Saint John the Evangelist Catholic Church, 371
St. John's Chapel, 106
St. John's College, 249, 266, 268
St. Joseph Medical Center, 184
St. Leonard, 319, 320; campgrounds, 325; events, 331; shopping, 330
St. Luke's Episcopal Church, 123–24
St. Mary, Star of the Sea, 94
St. Mary's Catholic Church (Bryantown), 352
St. Mary's Church (Annapolis), 252
St. Mary's City, 313, 333–34, 337, 339; events, 347; information, 334; lodging, 342, 344, 347; map, 332; transportation, 334–35
St. Mary's County, 333–48

St. Mary's County Chamber of Commerce, 334

St. Mary's County Division of Tourism, 334, 339, 340

St. Mary's County Fair, 347

St. Mary's Hospital (Leonardtown), 335

St. Mary's River, 333, 334

St. Mary's Square Museum (St. Michaels), 105

St. Mary's Transit System, 335

St. Michaels, 103–19; eating, 114–17; events, 119; information, 104; lodging, 110, 111, 112–13; map, 102; shopping, 118–19; sights/activities, 105–9; transportation, 104

St. Michaels Candy Co., 117

St. Michaels Christmas, 119

St. Michaels Crab and Steak House, 116

St. Michaels Harbor Shuttle, 106

St. Michaels Harbour Inn, Marina and Spa, 106, 109, 110

St. Michael's Manor, 343

St. Michaels Marina, 106, 109

St. Patrick's Day Parade, 64–65

St. Paul's Catholic Church (Ellicott City), 234

St. Paul's Episcopal Church (near Chestertown), 136

St. Peter's Church, 69

St. Rod Roundup, 433

sales tax, 32

Salisbury, 79–90; campgrounds, 86–87; eating, 87–88; emergencies, 81; entertainment, 88; events, 89–90; information, 79; lodging, 86–87; maps, 80, 82; shopping, 88–89; sights/activities, 81–86; transportation, 79, 81

Salisbury Art and Framing, 89

Salisbury Bicycle Club, 84

Salisbury Festival, 90

Salisbury Kennel Club Dog Show, 90

Salisbury Pewter, 25, 89

Salisbury Symphony Orchestra, 88

Salisbury Taxi, 81

Salisbury University, 81, 88

Salisbury University Bicycle Club, 84

Salisbury Zoological Park, 83–84

Salisbury/Ocean City Airport, 42, 79, 93, 104

San Francisco Giants, 408

Sandy Hill Camp, 155

Sandy Point State Park, 18, 19, 257, 268

Sandy Spring, 293; events, 309; sights/activities, 295, 298

Sandy Spring Museum, 295, 309

Sarah and Desmond's, 240

Sascha's 527, 223

Sassafras River, 135

Sassafras River Natural Resource Management Area, 138

Sassafras Station, 64

Sassy Lady Charter, 97

Savage, 232; events, 242, 243; lodging, 237–38; shopping, 242; sights/activities, 234

Savage Mill, 242, 243

Savage River Lodge, 447

Savage River Reservoir, 438, 442, 443, 447; campgrounds, 450, 451

Savage River State Forest, 32, 447

Sawyer Charters, 97

Scarborough Fair, 219

scenic byways: about, 31

Schifferstadt, 369, 386

Schmankerl Stube, 407

Schnaitman's Boat Rental, 125

Schoolhouse Quilters Guild Quilt Show, 432

Scotland, 339, 341; events, 348; lodging, 342–43

Scotlaur Inn, 258

Scottish Festival, 180

Scotty's Taxi, 104

scuba diving, 341, 423, 444

Sea Gull Cove Gifts, 331

Sea Gypsy, 48–49

sea nettles: about, 31–32

Sea Rocket, 48

Seaboard, 39–65; map, 38. See also specific destinations

Seacrets Bar and Restaurant, 61

Seaside Memorial Horse Show (Salisbury), 90

Seaside View Recreation Park & Campground (Ridge), 343

seasons, 30

Seattle Coffee Company, 265

Second Story Books, 308

Secretary Park, 98

Secret's, 408

Sedwick House, 325

Senator, The, 225

Seneca Creek State Park, 298, 299, 309

Seton, Elizabeth Ann, 364, 371

Sevenfoot Knoll Lighthouse, 28, 211
75th Street Medical Center (Ocean City), 43
Severn River, 245
Severna Park, 247, 255; shopping, 268
Severna Park Farmer's Market, 268
Severna Park Golf Center, 255
Shab Row Farmer's Market, 385
Shad Landing Campground, 58
Shady Grove Adventist Hospital, 294
Shady Hill Farm and Orchard, 197–98
Shady Oaks of Serenity, 356
Shady Side, 247
Shaker Forest Festival, 309
Shark, The, 61, 62
Sharpsburg, 23, 396–97; eating, 408; events, 410, 411; lodging, 404–5; shopping, 410
Sharpsburg Arsenal, 410
Sharpsburg Heritage Festival, 411
Sharpsburg Memorial Day Commemoration, 410
Sharptown, 85
Shaw Mansion Inn, 425
Shenanigan's Irish Pub, 62
Sheraton (Columbia), 237
Sheraton Inner Harbor (Baltimore), 218
Sherwood Park, 215
Ship Watch Inn, 156–57
Shops at Heritage Design, 358
Shops of Yesteryear, 196
Shore Transit, 43, 81, 93
Showcase Market Place Cinema, 288
Shrewsbury Episcopal Church, 136
Shrine of St. Anthony, 234
Shriver-Weybright Exhibition Gallery, 184
Side Street Seafood Market and Restaurant, 74
Sideling Hill, 397
Sidetracked Antiques and Design, 196
Silver Screen Under the Stars, 309
Silver Spring, 291; eating, 305–6; emergencies, 294; entertainment, 306; events, 309; lodging, 303; map, 292; shopping, 307, 308, 309; sights/activities, 296, 299, 300; transportation, 294
Silver Spring Farmer's Market, 308
Silver Tree Inn, 451–52
Silver Tree Marine, 439–40
Simon Pearce Glassblowing, 455
Simple Pleasures Ice Café, 27, 288
Sinai Hospital, 207
Sinking Springs Herb Farm, 158

Sirius, 109
Six Flags America Theme and Water Parks, 282
60s Under the Stars (Hagerstown), 411
65th St. Slide and Ride (Ocean City), 46
skating: Annapolis, 256; Cumberland, 423; Easton, 107; Gaithersburg, 300; Hagerstown, 401; Ocean City, 52; Rockville, 300; White Plains, 354
skiing. See cross-country skiing; Wisp Ski and Golf Resort
skipjacks, 75, 91, 96–97, 104, 109, 171
Skipper's Pier, 264–65
Slayton House Gallery, 240, 241
Sleep Inn (Grasonville), 128
Sleep Inn (Rockville), 302
Sleep Inn (Salisbury), 86
Smallwood Retreat House, 355
Smallwood State Park, 355, 358
Smiley's FunZone, 441
Smith, John, 76
Smith Island, 71, 76–78; map, 67
Smith Island Visitor's Center, 76, 77; Cultural Museum, 77, 78
Smith (Clarice) Performing Arts Center, 275, 277, 288, 290
Smithsburg, 410, 411
Smithsonian Environmental Research Center, 257, 268
Snappers Waterfront Cafe, 100
Sno Biz/Shave Ice, 74
Snow Hill, 41–42; campgrounds, 58; eating, 59–61; information, 42; lodging, 55–57; shopping, 63, 64; sights/activities, 44–46, 50, 52, 53
Snowden Square Stadium, 240
snowmobiling, 32, 443, 444, 446
Snyder's Cut Crystal, 431
So Neat Café, 116
soccer, 226, 289
Soft Shell Spring Fair, 74
Soldier's Delight National Environmental Area, 181, 188–89
Solomons, 315–16; eating, 326–29; emergencies, 317; events, 331; information, 316; lodging, 324–25; map, 314; public restrooms, 317; shopping, 329–31; sights/activities, 318–21, 323; transportation, 316–17
Solomons Boat Rental, 320
Solomons Christmas Walk, 331

Solomons Information Center, 316
Solomons Medical Center, 317
Solomons Pier, 328
Solomons Victorian Inn B&B, 325
Solomons Walkabout, 319
Somers Cove Marina, 68–69, 70, 74–75, 77
Somerset, Lake, 72
Somerset County, 66–78
Somerset County Fair, 75
Somerset County Tourism, 68, 70, 76
Sony Theatres, 288
Sotterley Plantation, 336, 339, 347
South Branch Rapids, 236
South Mountain, Battle of, 368, 391, 396
South Mountain Creamery, 382–83
South Mountain State Park, 20, 400, 401
South River Boat Rentals, 254
South River Golf Links, 255
South Street Art Gallery, 118
Southern Connection Seafood, 70, 74
Southern Cross Charters, 137
southern Maryland, 311–59; map, 312
Southern Maryland Antiques Center, 329
Southern Maryland Hospital Center, 276
Spa Creek, 247
Sparks: wineries, 198
special events: about, 25. See also specific
    events and destinations
Speed World, 47
Spenceola Antique Center, 179
Spencer Silver Mansion, 176
Spicers, 100
Spike's Pub and Subs, 73
Spinning Wheel Antiques, 454
Splash Mountain, 46
Spocott Windmill, 95
Sport Crabber, 48
Sport Fishing Charters (Cambridge), 97
Sportfishing Show and Seminar
    (Solomons), 331
Sports Legends at Camden Yards, 208
Spring Creek Outfitters, 441
Spring Festivals, 65, 132, 290, 347
Spring Fling (Perryville), 162
Springhill Suites by Marriott (Gaithersburg),
    302
Spruce Forest Artisan Village, 437, 456
Spurs, 358
Starland Roller Rink, 401
Star-Spangled Banner Museum, 211
Star-Spangled Banner Trail, 32
State Chili Cookoff, 433

state forests: about, 30. See also specific
    state forests
state parks: about, 30. See also specific state
    parks
State Theater of Maryland, 226
Staybridge Suites (Columbia), 237
Steam and Craft Show (Smithsburg), 411
Steam and Gas Show (Derwood), 309
Steamed Crabs: recipe for, 346
Steppingstone Museum, 169, 173, 180
Stevensville, 121–22; eating, 129–30; events,
    132; lodging, 128; nightlife, 130; shop-
    ping, 131; sights/activities, 123–25, 127
Stevensville Antiques, 131
Still Anchors, 345
Stillridge Herb Farm, 242
Stone, Thomas: National Historic Site, 352
Stonestreet Museum of 19th-Century
    Medicine, 296
Stoney's Seafood House, 327
Storm Brothers Ice Cream Factory, 265
Strathmore Hall, 17, 307
strawberries, 89, 131, 197, 268, 289–90,
    309, 359, 385, 410; festivals (days), 65,
    199, 309
Strawberry Fields Forever (Parsonsburg), 89
Streams and Dreams, 441, 449
Streeter's Taxi, 93
Stronghold, Incorporated, 374
Stuart's Antiques, 63
Sturgis One Room School Museum, 44
Suburban Hospital (Bethesda), 294
Sudlersville, 122; shopping, 131;
    sights/activities, 124
Sugar and Spice Bakery and Cheese, 454
Sugarloaf Crafts Festival, 309
Sugarloaf Mountain, 374
Suicide Bridge Restaurant, 99
Sultana, 146
Summer Concert Series (La Plata), 359
Summer Festival and Quilt Show (Grants-
    ville), 456
Summer in the City (Cumberland), 432
Summer Lakefront Festival (Columbia),
    243
Summer Music in the Park (Chesapeake
    City), 162
Summit Station Restaurant and Brewery,
    305
Sundays at Three, 241
Sunfest (Ocean City), 65
Sunny Slope Riding Stables, 443

Sunsail Sailing Vacations, 255
Sunshine Cab, 43
Super 8 (Indian Head), 356
Super 8 (Jessup), 237
Super 8 (Thurmont), 378
Super 8 (Waldorf), 356
Surratt House Museum, 277
Susquehanna & Tidewater Canal, 165, 166, 168
Susquehanna Flats, 147, 165
Susquehanna Museum of Havre de Grace, 168, 180
Susquehanna River, 147, 149, 156, 169, 172
Susquehanna State Park, 171–72
Swallow Falls State Park, 32, 443, 444, 445–46; campground, 451
Swan Haven Rentals, 137
Swan Point Country and Yacht Club (Issue), 353
Swan Point Inn (Rock Hall), 144
Swanton, 441, 446; campgrounds, 451
Sweet Nina's, 117
Switchback Trail, 236
Sykesville, 183; events, 199; sights/activities, 185

T

Ta-Da, 64
Tailwinds Farm, 157
Take It Easy Campground, 343
Takoma Park: lodging, 303
Takoma Park Folk Festival, 309
Talbot County, 103–19
Talbot County Community Center, 107
Talbot County Fair, 119
Talbot County Office of Tourism, 104, 106, 108, 109
Taney, 211
Taneytown, 181, 183, 187; eating, 193, 194–95; events, 199; lodging, 191–92
Tangier Crab House, 194
Tangier Sound, 66–78; map, 67
Tangier Sound Outfitters, 70–71
Tasting Room, The (Frederick), 380
Tavern At The Village (California), 343
Tavern House B&B (Vienna), 99
Tavern on Green Street (Snow Hill), 59–60
Tavern on Main (North East), 159–60
Tawes Gallery, 145
Tawes (J. Millard) Museum, 68–69, 70
taxes, 32

Taylor, Calvin B.: House, 44–45
Taylor's Antique Mall, 241
Taylors Island, 92
Teackle Mansion, 69
Teddy Bear and Doll Show and Sale, 242
Ten Thousand Villages, 228
tennis: Annapolis, 256; Baltimore, 216; Cambridge, 98; Carroll County, 190; Harford County, 173–74; Kent Island, 125; Mountain Lake Park, 456; Ocean City, 52; Salisbury, 85; Worton, 138
10th Street Medical Center (Ocean City), 43
Terrapin Nature Area, 127, 128
Tersiguel's, 238
Thackery Swamp, 155
Tharpe Antiques, 117
Thayerville, 435–36; activities, 439, 442, 443, 445–46; eating, 452–53, 454; entertainment, 454; lodging, 447–52; map, 434; shopping, 455
theater: Annapolis, 266; Baltimore, 225; Church Hill, 131; College Park, 289; Columbia, 241; Cumberland, 430; Easton, 103, 117; Frederick, 383; Hagerstown, 408; La Plata, 358; Largo, 290; North East, 161; Oakland, 454; Ocean City, 63; Olney, 306; Rockville, 306; Salisbury, 88; Westminster, 195
Theater Hopkins, 226
Theatre on the Hill, 184, 195
Third Haven Meeting House, 103, 105
Thrasher Carriage Museum, 416
Thurmont, 364–65; campgrounds, 379–80; eating, 382, 383; lodging, 377–78; shopping, 384–85; sights/activities, 370, 372, 373, 376, 377; transportation, 365–66
Thursday's, 327
Tidewater Grill, 177
Tidewater Inn, 110–11, 114, 119
Tidewater Marina, 31, 173
Tilghman Island, 104; eating, 115–16; events, 119; lodging, 111–13; sights/activities, 20, 106–10
Tilghman Island Day, 119
Tilghman Island Inn, 111–12, 115
Tilghman Island Marina, 106, 107, 109
Tilghman Island Water Trail, 109
Timbers at Troy, 235
Timonium, 184, 188, 199
Tio Pepe, 221
Toby's, 241

Toddy Hall Pottery, 346
Tolchester Beach Revisited, 136
Toliver Falls, 32, 446
Tollgate Movies 7, 178
Tony's River House, 357
Top of the World Observation Level, 211, 213
Torsk, 211
Town Center Antiques (Berlin), 63
Town Dock Restaurant (St. Michaels), 115
Towson, 181; emergencies, 184; information, 183; sights/activities, 186; transportation, 184
Toy Show and Sale (Taneytown), 199
Trader's Coffee House, 453
Tradestone Gallery, 227
Trail House (Frederick), 374
Train Room (Hagerstown), 409–10
Treat Shop, 195
Treaty of Paris, 261
Tred Avon Movies, 117
Tred Avon River, 25, 104, 106–7
Tremont Plaza Hotel, 218
Triadelphia Lake View Farm, 242
Trident Electric Boat Rentals, 214
Trimper's Rides, 47
Trinity Chapel (Frederick), 370
Trinity Episcopal Church (St. Mary's City), 337
Troika Gallery, 17, 117
Trolley Stop, The, 239
Tropical Chesapeake, 73
Trotter's Glen, 299
True, 220–21
Truxton Park, 257
Tubman, Harriet, 101; Memorial Garden, 98; Museum, 23, 95
Tuck Everlasting (movie), 41, 44
Tuckahoe Creek, 109, 127
Tuckahoe Easter Egg Hunt, 132
Tuckahoe River, 125
Tuckahoe State Park, 126–27, 132
Tuckahoe Triathlon, 132
Tudor Hall (Leonardtown), 336
Tunnel Hill Trail, 421
Turf Valley Resort and Conference Center, 237
Turkey Point Lighthouse, 28, 155
Turn the Page, 409
Turner Van Service, 393
25 Bicycle Tours in Maryland (Oman), 19

Twin Shields Golf Club, 321
Two Swan Inn, 112
208 Talbot (St. Michaels), 114–15
Two-O-One, 260
Tydings Memorial Park, 168, 174, 180
Tyler Spite House, 378
Tylerton, 76; lodging, 78

U

U-1105 Black Panther Historic Ship Preserve, 341
Ukrainian Festival and Carnival, 229
Uncle Tucker's 1819 BrewHouse, 428–29
Underground Railroad, 23, 95, 98, 207
Unicorn Book Shop, 118
Union Bridge: sights/activities, 185
Union Hospital of Cecil County, 150
Union Hotel, 160
Union Mills Homestead, 184–85, 199
Uniontown, 183; sights/activities, 186–87
Unique Boutique, 348
United States Powerboat Show, 269
United States Sailboat Show, 269
University of Maryland Medical Center, 207
University of Maryland Terrapins, 289
University of Maryland-College Park, 275, 276–77; dance, 288; music, 288; sports, 289; theater, 289
University of Maryland-Eastern Shore, 68
Upper Bay Museum, 24, 147, 151
Upper Bay Rockfish Tournament, 162
Upper Chesapeake Medical Center, 168
Upper Ferry, 25, 85
Upper Marlboro, 275; campgrounds, 286; events, 290; lodging, 286; map, 274; sights/activities, 277, 282, 283, 284; transportation, 276
USDA Farmer's Market, 289
USNA Artists Authors Fair, 269
Utica Covered Bridge, 23, 367

V

Vaccaro's, 224
Vagabond Players, 225–26
Vale Summit, 419
Valley Cab, 393
Valley Mall Movie (Hagerstown), 408
Vandiver Inn, 174
Vassey's Orchards, 74

Venuti's Ristorante, 381
Vera's White Sands Restaurant, 326–27
Verna's Island Inn, 130
Viccino, 224
Victorian Room (Ocean City), 59
Victoriana Inn (St. Michaels), 112
Victory Cabs, 167
Vienna, 91; events, 101; lodging, 99; sights/activities, 97
ViewTrail 100 Bike Trail (Ocean City), 19, 47
Vintage Chic, 118
Virginia Gent Decker Arboretum, 135, 138
Vitali's, 178

W

Wades Point Inn, 111
Wagon Wheel Antiques, 241
Wakefield Valley, 188
Waldenbooks (St. Charles), 358–59
Waldorf, 313, 349–50; eating, 357–58; entertainment, 358; lodging, 356; shopping, 358–59; sights/activities, 351–53; transportation, 351
Waldorf Cab, 351
Waldorf North, 358
Walkersville, 374, 375
Walkersville Southern Railroad, 31, 375
walks. See hiking
Walls Bakery, 357–58
Walnut Springs Farm, 162
Walters Art Museum, 17, 210
War of 1812, 201, 211, 238, 280, 331, 336, 341, 350, 352
Ward, Steve and Lem, 24, 65, 69, 83, 84, 90
Ward Brothers' Workshop, 69, 83
Ward Museum of Wildlife Art, 24, 83, 84, 90
Ward World Championship Wildfowl Carving Competition, 24, 65
Warner, William, 24, 66
Washington, D.C., 273, 276; maps, 272, 274
Washington, George, 29, 30, 152, 183, 238, 365, 392, 400, 436; Headquarters (Cumberland), 417
Washington College, 133, 135, 138, 145
Washington County, 391–411
Washington County Agricultural Expo, 411
Washington County Arts Council, 409

Washington County Convention and Visitors Bureau, 392, 397
Washington County Farmer's Market, 410
Washington County Hospital, 393
Washington County Museum of Fine Arts, 17, 394, 402–3
Washington County Playhouse, 408
Washington County Rural Heritage Museum, 393
Washington International Airport. See Baltimore/Washington International Airport
Washington Monument (Baltimore), 203
Washington Monument State Park (Boonsboro), 402
Washington Power Lacrosse, 289
Washington Redskins, 289
Washington Street Books, 179
Washington-McKinney Ford, 370
water taxis, 201, 205, 248, 293–94
waterfalls: about, 32–33. See also specific waterfalls
Waterfowl Festival (Easton), 119
Waterfowl Weekend (Grasonville), 132
Waterfront Warehouse (Annapolis), 249
Waterline Gallery, 63
Waterloo Country Inn, 72
Waterman's Cove (Salisbury), 87–88
Waterman's Crab House (Rock Hall), 144
Waterman's Festival (Grasonville), 132
Waterman's Museum (Rock Hall), 136
Waterman's Rest (Ewell), 77
Watermark Cruises, 253, 254
Watermen's Inn (Crisfield), 73
Watkins Regional Park, 282, 286, 290
Watts Creek, 127
Waverly Street Farmer's Market, 229
Waverly Woods, 235
Way Off Broadway Dinner Theater, 383
Wayfarer, 287
Wayside Inn, 238
weather: about, 33
Weaver's Restaurant and Bakery, 407
Weinberg Center for the Arts, 383
Weitzel's Restaurant, 61
Wenona, 66
West Frederick Farmer's Market, 385
West Friendship: events, 243; sights/activities, 18, 234, 235
West Ridge Cinema, 383
Western Maryland Blues Fest, 410

western Maryland Mountains, 387–456; map, 388

Western Maryland Rail Trail, 19, 398

Western Maryland Railway Historical Society, 185

Western Maryland Scenic Railroad, 31, 422, 431–32

Western Maryland Tennis Championships, 456

Westfield Shoppingtown Annapolis, 267

Westmar Tours, 423

Westminster, 181, 183; eating, 193–95; emergencies, 184; entertainment, 195; events, 198–99; information, 183; lodging, 191; parking, 184; shopping, 196–97; sights/activities, 184–90; transportation, 183–84

Westminster Flower and Jazz Festival, 199

Westminster High School, 199

Westminster Inn, 191

Westover: campgrounds, 72; eating, 73–74; sights/activities, 70

Wetlands Fest, 132

Whaleyville: campgrounds, 57

Wharf, The (Solomons), 328

Wharf Restaurant (Ocean City), 61

Wheat Harvest Fair, 132

Wheaton: eating, 306; shopping, 308; sights/activities, 299–301

Wheaton Regional Park, 299–300

Wheel Doctor Cycle and Sport, Inc., 106

Wheels of Yesterday, 43–44

When Pigs Fly, 428

Whiskey Creek, 373

White Marlin Open, 65

White Oak Golf Course, 299

White Plains Golf Course, 353

White Plains Regional Park, 353, 354

White Sands: eating, 326–27

Whiteford, 179

Whitehaven B&B, 86

Whitehaven Ferry, 25, 84–85

Whites Cab, 43

White's Ferry, 25, 293–94, 300

whitewater rafting. See rafting

Whittier, John Greenleaf, 363, 369, 370

Wicomico County, 79–90

Wicomico County Convention and Visitors Bureau, 79, 84, 86, 89

Wicomico County Department of Recreation and Parks, 85

Wicomico River, 79, 85, 283, 339; ferries, 25, 84–85; fishing, 50

Wicomico Shores, 340

Widow's Walk, 140–41

Wildewood Pastry Shop, 345–46

Wildfowl Trust of North America, 20, 126

wildlife art, 24, 64, 83, 84, 90, 268. See also decoy carving

Will O' the Wisp Prestige Condominiums, 450

William Paca House and Garden, 250

Williamsport, 392; activities, 398; campgrounds, 405; eating, 407

Willow Bend Books, 196–97

Willow Springs, 235

Wilmer Park, 133, 138

Wilson's General Store, 409

Windows on Main, 159–60

windsurfing, 48, 137

wine festivals, 119, 199, 243, 433

wineries, 21, 179, 198, 455–56

Wingrove Manor, 403

Winter Festival of Lights (Upper Marlboro), 290

Winter Lights Festival (Gaithersburg), 309

Winterfest of Lights (Ocean City), 65

Winterplace Park, 89, 90

Wisp Ski and Golf Resort, 32, 444; golf, 442; lodging, 446

Wm. B. Tennison, 318, 320

Woman's Industrial Exchange, 223, 228

Womanship, Inc., 31, 255

Wonder Book and Video (Frederick), 384

Wonder Book and Video (Hagerstown), 409

Woodbine: campground, 192, 238

Woodcreek Golf Links, 85

Woodend Nature Trail, 20, 302

Woodhall Wine Cellars, 198

Woodlands Campground, 158

Woodlawn Family Camping, 87

Wood's Gain, 192

Woodwind, 254

Woody's Crab House, 160

Worcester County, 39–65

Worcester County Arts Council, 63

Worcester County Fair, 65

Worcester County Tourism Office, 42

Worthington Farm Trail, 369–70

Worthington Manor, 373

Worton Harbor: eating, 142–43
Worton Park, 138
Wurzburg-Haus Restaurant, 305
Wye Grist Mill, 124
Wye Island Natural Resource Management
   Area, 126
Wye Mills, 122, 124, 125; events, 132

Y/Z

Yacht Club Restaurant (Chesapeake City),
   160
Ye Olde Church House (Stevensville), 131
Year of the Rabbit Coffee Pub, 288
Yellow Cab, 205, 317, 351, 416

Yellow Snow Dog Sled Adventure, 440
Yellow Turtle Inn, 192
Yesterdays, 162
Yesteryear Antiques and Collectibles, 431
Yin Yankee Café, 262
Yingling's Golf Center, 399
YMCA (Cumberland), 423
Yoder Country Market, 455
Yogi Bear's Jellystone Park, 405
Youghiogheny Lake, 437, 438; camp-
   grounds, 450
Youghiogheny River, 32, 436, 441, 444, 446;
   rafting, 33, 444

Zekiah Swamp, 283, 353

Follow The Countryman Press to your favorite destinations!

Discover more when you travel with our EXPLORER'S GUIDES:

NORTHEAST
Berkshire Hills & Pioneer Valley of Western
  Massachusetts
Cape Cod, Martha's Vineyard & Nantucket
Connecticut
Hudson Valley & Catskill Mountains
Maine
New Hampshire
New York City
Rhode Island
Vermont
Western New York
MID-ATLANTIC
The Blue Ridge & Smoky Mountains
Maryland
New Jersey
The Shenandoah Valley & Mountains of
  the Virginias
SOUTHEAST
Orlando, Central & North Florida
WEST
Montana & Wyoming
Oregon

Savor the best these regions have to offer with our GREAT DESTINATIONS series:

NORTHEAST
The Adirondack Book
The Berkshire Book
The Coast of Maine Book
The Finger Lakes Book
The Hamptons Book
The Hudson Valley Book
The Nantucket Book
MID-ATLANTIC
The Chesapeake Bay Book
SOUTHEAST
The Charleston, Savannah, & Coastal Islands
  Book
The Sarasota, Sanibel Island & Naples Book
Palm Beach, Miami & the Florida Keys
WEST & SOUTHWEST
Big Sur, Monterey Bay & Gold Coast
  Wine Country
The Napa & Sonoma Book
The Santa Fe & Taos Book
The Seattle & Vancouver Book
The Texas Hill Country Book

General Travel
American Rock
Bouldering USA
The 100 Best Art Towns in America
NORTHEAST
Adirondack Odysseys
Chow Maine
The Colors of Fall
Covered Bridges of Vermont
Dog-Friendly New England
Dog-Friendly New York
Eating New England
A Guide to Natural Places in the Berkshire Hills
In-Line Skate New England
Hudson River Journey
Hudson Valley Harvest
Maine Sporting Camps
New England Seacoast Adventures
New England Waterfalls
The Other Islands of New York City
The Photographer's Guide to the Maine Coast
The Photographer's Guide to Vermont
Shawangunks Trail Companion
Touring East Coast Wine Country
Weekending in New England
Weekend Walks Along the New England Coast
Weekend Walks in Historic New England
MID-ATLANTIC
Dog-Friendly Washington D.C. and the
  Mid-Atlantic States
52 Weekends in New Jersey
New Jersey's Great Gardens
New Jersey's Special Places
Waterfalls of the Mid-Atlantic States
SOUTHEAST
Eating New Orleans
Fly Fishing the Louisiana Coast
WEST
The California Coast
The Photographer's Guide to the Grand Canyon
The Photographer's Guide to the Oregon Coast
Wild Weekends in Utah
INTERNATIONAL
Bicycling Cuba
Switzerland's Mountain Inns

We offer many more books on hiking, fly-fishing, travel, nature, and other subjects. Our books are available at bookstores and outdoor stores everywhere. For more information or a free catalog, please call 1-800-245-4151 or write to us at The Countryman Press, P.O. Box 748, Woodstock, Vermont 05091. You can find us on the Internet at www.countrymanpress.com.